Karen Rottink 503.636.9755

When should I travel to get the best airfare?
Where do I go for answers to my travel questions?
What's the best and easiest way to plan and book my trip?

frommers.travelocity.com

Frommer's, the travel guide leader, has teamed up with **Travelocity.com**, the leader in online travel, to bring you an in-depth, easy-to-use resource designed to help you plan and book your trip online.

At **frommers.travelocity.com**, you'll find free online updates about your destination from the experts at Frommer's plus the outstanding travel planning and purchasing features of Travelocity.com. Travelocity.com provides reservations capabilities for 95 percent of all airline seats sold, more than 47,000 hotels, and over 50 car rental companies. In addition, Travelocity.com offers more than 2,000 exciting vacation and cruise packages. Travelocity.com puts you in complete control of your travel planning with these and other great features:

Expert travel guidance from Frommer's - over 150 writers reporting from around the world!

Best Fare Finder - an interactive calendar tells you when to travel to get the best airfare

Fare Watcher - we'll track airfare changes to your favorite destinations

Dream Maps - a mapping feature that suggests travel opportunities based on your budget

Shop Safe Guarantee - 24 hours a day / 7 days a week live customer service, and more!

Whether traveling on a tight budget, looking for a quick weekend getaway, or planning the trip of a lifetime, Frommer's guides and Travelocity.com will make your travel dreams a reality. You've bought the book, now book the trip!

Travelocity.com
A Sabre Company

A New Star-Rating System & Other Exciting News from Frommer's!

In our continuing effort to publish the savviest, most up-to-date, and most appealing travel guides available, we've added some great new features.

Frommer's guides now include a new **star-rating system.** Every hotel, restaurant, and attraction is rated from 0 to 3 stars to help you set priorities and organize your time.

We've also added **seven brand-new features** that point you to the great deals, in-the-know advice, and unique experiences that separate travelers from tourists. Throughout the guide look for:

Finds	Special finds—those places only insiders know about
Fun Fact	Fun facts—details that make travelers more informed and their trips more fun
Kids	Best bets for kids—advice for the whole family
Moments	Special moments—those experiences that memories are made of
Overrated	Places or experiences not worth your time or money
Tips	Insider tips—some great ways to save time and money
Value	Great values—where to get the best deals

We've also added a **"What's New"** section in every guide—a timely crash course in what's hot and what's not in every destination we cover.

Other Great Guides for Your Trip:

Frommer's Great Outdoor Guide to Washington & Oregon

Frommer's Seattle & Portland

Frommer's Vancouver & Victoria

The Unofficial Guide to Bed & Breakfasts in the Northwest

2002 *3/13/20*

Frommer's®
TM

Washington State

3rd Edition

by Karl Samson & Jane Aukshunas

Here's what the critics say about Frommer's:

"Amazingly easy to use. Very portable, very complete."
—*Booklist*

"The only mainstream guide to list specific prices. The Walter Cronkite of guidebooks—with all that implies."
—*Travel & Leisure*

"Complete, concise, and filled with useful information."
—*New York Daily News*

"Hotel information is close to encyclopedic."
—*Des Moines Sunday Register*

"Detailed, accurate, and easy-to-read information for all price ranges."
—*Glamour Magazine*

Hungry Minds™

Best-Selling Books • Digital Downloads • e-Books • Answer Networks
e-Newsletters • Branded Web Sites • e-Learning
New York, NY • Cleveland, OH • Indianapolis, IN

About the Author

Husband-and-wife travel-writing team **Karl Samson** and **Jane Aukshunas** live in the Northwest where they spend their time juggling their obsessions with traveling, outdoor sports, and gardening. Each winter after they've had their fill of skiing, they flee the soggy Northwest to dry out their webbed feet and update the *Frommer's Arizona* guide. However, they always look forward to their return to the land of good coffee. Karl is also author of *Frommer's Guide to Washington & Oregon* and *Frommer's Nepal*.

Published by:

Hungry Minds, Inc.

909 Third Ave.
New York, NY 10022

ISBN 0-7645-6553-2
ISSN 1093-7447

Editor: John Vorwald
Production Editor: Heather Wilcox
Cartographer: John Decamillis
Photo Editor: Richard Fox
Production by Hungry Minds Indianapolis Production Services

Front cover photo: Alpine Meadow of wildflowers in mist
Back cover photo: Seattle: Tugboat races in harbor

Special Sales

For general information on Hungry Minds' products and services please contact our Customer Care department; within the U.S. at 800-762-2974, outside the U.S. at 317-572-3993 or fax 317-572-4002. For sales inquiries and reseller information, including discounts, bulk sales, customized editions, and premium sales, please contact our Customer Care department at 800-434-3422.

Manufactured in the United States of America

5 4 3 2 1

Contents

9 The Cascades 266

10 Eastern Washington 321

Appendix: Washington in Depth 354

Index 365

List of Maps

An Invitation to the Reader

In researching this book, we discovered many wonderful places—hotels, restaurants, shops, and more. We're sure you'll find others. Please tell us about them, so we can share the information with your fellow travelers in upcoming editions. If you were disappointed with a recommendation, we'd love to know that, too. Please write to:

Frommer's Washington State, 3rd Edition
Hungry Minds, Inc. • 909 Third Avenue • New York, NY 10022

An Additional Note

Please be advised that travel information is subject to change at any time—and this is especially true of prices. We therefore suggest that you write or call ahead for confirmation when making your travel plans. The authors, editors, and publisher cannot be held responsible for the experiences of readers while traveling. Your safety is important to us, however, so we encourage you to stay alert and be aware of your surroundings. Keep a close eye on cameras, purses, and wallets, all favorite targets of thieves and pickpockets.

New! Frommer's Star Ratings & Icons

Every hotel, restaurant, and attraction listing in this guide has been ranked for quality, value, service, amenities, and special features using a star-rating scale. In country, state, and regional guides, we also rate towns and regions to help you narrow down your choices and budget your time accordingly. Hotels and restaurants in the Very Expensive and Expensive categories are rated on a scale of one (highly recommended) to three stars (exceptional). Those in the Moderate and Inexpensive categories rate from zero (recommended) to two stars (very highly recommended). Attractions, towns, and regions are rated according to the following scale: zero stars (recommended), one star (highly recommended), two stars (very highly recommended), and three stars (must-see).

In addition to the rating system, we also use seven icons to highlight insider information, useful tips, special bargains, hidden gems, memorable experiences, kid-friendly venues, places to avoid, and other useful information.

| Finds | Fun Fact | Kids | Moments | Overrated | Tips | Value |

The following abbreviations are used for credit cards:

AE	American Express	DISC	Discover	V	Visa
DC	Diners Club	MC	MasterCard		

FROMMERS.COM

Now that you have the guidebook to a great trip, visit our website at **www.frommers.com** for travel information on nearly 2,500 destinations. With features updated regularly, we give you instant access to the most current trip-planning information available. At Frommers.com, you'll also find the best prices on airfares, accommodations, and car rentals—and you can even book travel online through our travel booking partners. At Frommers.com, you'll also find the following:

- Online updates to our most popular guidebooks
- Vacation sweepstakes and contest giveaways
- Newsletter highlighting the hottest travel trends
- Online travel message boards with featured travel discussions

What's New in Washington

The only thing constant in the world of travel is change (and we aren't just talking about fluctuating exchange rates), and Washington is no exception. Highlighted below are some of the most significant changes that have taken place in the state this past year. We've also included mention of some of the great restaurants we've discovered over the past year.

SEATTLE Orientation Prepare for sticker shock when riding the **Washington State Ferries** (© 800/84-FERRY or 888/808-7977 within Washington, or 206/464-6400; www.wsdot.wa.gov/ferries/). Due to reduced funding, which was brought on by a voter tax-reduction initiative, ferry fares have been climbing. At press time, it cost $10 each way for a car and driver to ride the Bainbridge Island or Bremerton ferry during the summer months. Luckily, walk-on and passenger fares haven't jumped quite as much, and these ferry passengers still get a free ride back to Seattle from either Bainbridge Island or Bremerton.

WHERE TO STAY The **Elliott Grand Hyatt Seattle,** 721 Pine St. (© 800/233-1234; www.elliotthotel.com), which opened in summer 2001, immediately became Seattle's most prestigious business hotel. With its emphasis on luxury and high-tech amenities, and with room rates to prove it, this is one of Seattle's first truly world-class hotels.

The dot.com dollars may have dried up, but the **W Seattle,** 1112 Fourth Ave. (© 877/W-HOTELS; www.whotels.com), is still the hippest hotel in Seattle and is totally wired for 21st-century business travelers. The location in the heart of the downtown business district also happens to be convenient if you are here on vacation.

Equally luxurious and with even more high-tech features, the **Willows Lodge,** 14580 NE 145th St., Woodinville (© 877/424-3930; www.willowslodge.com), boasts much more of a Northwest feel than the Elliott. Located in the wine country 30 minutes north of downtown Seattle, this lodge, surrounded by beautiful gardens, shares a parking lot with the Herbfarm restaurant (see below) and even has two guest rooms decorated in Herbfarm's country French style. However, most of the guest rooms at the Willows Lodge feature bold contemporary styling that incorporates lots of wood and stone.

WHERE TO DINE The single biggest piece of news on the Seattle restaurant scene this year has been the opening, after years of planning, of the new Herbfarm restaurant. **The Herbfarm,** 14590 NE 145th St., Woodinville (© 206/784-2222; www.theherbfarm.com), is the Northwest's most expensive and most celebrated restaurant, the ultimate expression of the Northwest's bounty, with an emphasis on fresh, herb-driven preparations, all of which are matched with regional wines. In keeping with its country-inn heritage, the Herbfarm is located out on the edge of Seattle's suburban sprawl.

SEEING THE SIGHTS Paul Allen's **Experience Music Project (EMP),** 325 Fifth Ave. N. (℃ **877/ EMPLIVE;** www.emplive.com), a museum dedicated primarily to Northwest rock 'n' roll, opened to much fanfare in the year 2000. Although the bizarre design by avant-garde architect Frank Gehry has dominated most people's experience with this museum, the Jimi Hendrix collection is a highlight.

To add further authenticity to its African savanna exhibit and to provide visitors (especially children) with insight into what life is like for Africa's human inhabitants, the **Woodland Park Zoo,** 5500 Phinney Ave. N. (℃ **206/684-4800;** www.zoo.org), has added an authentic-feeling African Village. The village is not a Hollywood-ized village, but rather a well-researched rendition of a contemporary African village.

THE SAN JUAN ISLANDS, WHIDBEY ISLAND & THE EMERALD COAST Anacortes At press time, the **Majestic Inn,** which for several years had been the best hotel in Anacortes, was closed due to a fire. It was uncertain when the hotel would reopen.

The San Juan Islands On San Juan Island, **Lakedale Resort,** 2627 Roche Harbor Rd. (℃ **800/617-2267;** www. lakedale.com), has added a new 10-room lodge that is a luxurious rendition of a class log mountain lodge. Up at the north end of San Juan Island, you'll find the new **Westcott Bay Reserve** (℃ **360/370-5050),** a sculpture park that includes more than 50 works of art. The sculptures are set in grassy fields and along the shores of a small pond. In Friday Harbor, be sure to check out **Vinny's,** 165 West St. (℃ **360/378-1934),** a great new Italian restaurant with a good view. Southwest of Friday Harbor, the new **Pelindaba Lavender Farm,**

Wold Road (℃ **360-378-4248;** www. pelindaba.com) offers guided tours and a surprising variety of organic lavender products.

On Orcas Island, **The Sunflower Café,** A Street and Prune Alley, East-sound (℃ **360/376-2335),** is a new restaurant serving imaginative Northwest cuisines. In the tiny community of Olga, **The Olga Store,** Olga Road (℃ **360/376-5862),** which until recently was a little general store, is now a great little cafe and eclectic gift shop that should not be missed.

Bellingham The **Bellingham Antique Radio Museum,** 1316 Bay St. (℃ **360/671-4663;** www.antique-radio.org), has moved to a much larger space and can now show off its hundreds of old radios and recording devices. Bellingham now has two new waterfront hotels.

The **Hotel Bellwether on Bellingham Bay,** One Bellwether Way (℃ **877/411-1200;** www.hotel bellwether.com), is the centerpiece of the new Squalicum Harbor waterfront development and has a very traditional feel. **The Chrysalis Inn & Spa at the Pier,** 804 10th St. (℃ **888/808-0005;** www.thechrysalisinn.com), on the other hand, boasts an impressive contemporary lodge styling that has helped make it the most luxurious hotel in Bellingham.

Keeping the focus on the waterfront, the Anthony's chain of seafood restaurants has opened a waterfront restaurant in Bellingham. **Anthony's,** 25 Bellwether Way (℃ **360/647-5588),** is in the same complex that houses the Hotel Bellwether.

SOUTH PUGET SOUND & WEST SOUND Tacoma Although not yet open at press time, the new **Museum of Glass,** 1801 Dock St. (℃ **253/396-1768;** www.museumof glass.org), was scheduled to open in July 2002. World-renowned glass artist Dale Chihuly a native of Tacoma, so this city is a natural place for a museum dedicated exclusively to art glass.

Olympia Located in downtown Olympia within two blocks of the Percival Landing boardwalk, several restaurants, and the Olympia Farmers Market, the **Phoenix Inn Suites,** 415 Capitol Way N. (© 877/570-0555; www.phoenixinnsuites.com), is a corporate business hotel with a great location. Although Olympia isn't much of a tourist destination, the economical rates here make this a good choice for a south sound base of operations.

OLYMPIC PENINSULA Port Townsend Wineries have been popping up all over the state in recent years. Even Port Townsend, though it grows no wine grapes, now has a couple of wineries. **Sorensen Cellars,** 274 S. Otto St. (© 360/379-6416; www.sorensencellars.com), and **Fair Winds Winery,** 1984 Hastings Ave. W. (© 360/385-6899; www.fairwindswinery.com), are both located south of town.

Sequim The past few years has seen a proliferation of lavender farms in the Sequim area. The mild temperatures and low rainfall make this an ideal climate for growing the fragrant flowers. Between Sequim and Dungeness, you'll find half a dozen lavender farms that are open to the public.

Port Angeles Art lovers should be sure to stop by the **Port Angeles Fine Art Center,** 1203 E. Lauridsen Blvd. (© 360/457-3532; www.olympus.net/community/pafac/), which has an unusual sculpture park in the woods surrounding the center. Sculptures within the park are often barely discernible from natural objects.

Olympic National Park West If you're headed out to the far western shores and rain forest valleys of the Olympic Peninsula, you'll find newly remodeled suites in the town of Forks at **Olympic Suites Inn,** 800 Olympic Dr. (© 800/262-3433; www.olympicgetaways.com/olympicsuites). This modern motel is set back in the woods near the banks of the Calawah River.

Although the Lake Quinault Lodge is still the most popular hotel on Lake Quinault, you'll find more modern and luxurious accommodations on the opposite side of the lake at the **Lake Quinault Resort,** 314 North Shore Rd., Amanda Park (© 800/650-2362; www.lakequinault.com). This small inn also benefits from being on the sunny side of the lake.

SOUTHWEST WASHINGTON Grays Harbor & the Central Coast Although the sandy beaches of the southwest Washington coast are not nearly as dramatic as the shores of the Olympic Peninsula, this stretch of coast has seen the construction of new beach hotels in recent years. The biggest and best of these is the new **Quinault Beach Resort and Casino,** 78 Wash. 115, Ocean Shores (© 888/461-2214; www.quinaultbchresort.com). With its modern beach lodge styling, miles of wide, sandy beaches, casino, and indoor pool, this is the finest beach resort on the Washington coast.

THE CASCADES Mount Baker & the North Cascades Scenic Highway Outside the town of Glacier, on the Mt. Baker Highway, **The Inn at Mt. Baker,** 8174 Mt. Baker Hwy., Glacier (© 877/567-5526; www.theinnatmtbaker.com), provides a superb perch from which to contemplate the majesty of nearby Mount Baker. Located high on a hill facing the mountain, the inn provides knockout views from every room.

Mount St. Helens You can now add another dimension to a visit to Mount St. Helens by signing up for one of the many seminars offered by the **Mount**

St. Helens Institute (© 360/891-5095; www.mountsthelensinstitute.org). This educational institute offers a wide range of seminars ranging in length from 1 to 2 days.

The Columbia Gorge & the Mount Adams Area Out at the eastern end of the Columbia Gorge, there are a couple of new wineries, both of which are noteworthy, although for very different reasons. **Maryhill Winery,** 9774 Hwy. 14, Maryhill (© 877/627-9445; www.maryhillwinery.com), which is perched on the edge of a cliff high above the Columbia River, has the best view of any winery in the Northwest and also produces some very good wines. On the other hand, nearby **Marshal's Winery,** 150 Oak Creek Rd., Dallesport (© 509/767-4633), which is located 2 miles up a gravel road, has absolutely no view, is housed in what feels like a garage, and produces some of Washington's smoothest Cabernet Sauvignons and Merlots.

EASTERN WASHINGTON Yakima & the Wine Country Down at the eastern end of the Yakima Valley, in the Tri-Cities area, it is now possible to take a jet-boat tour of the new Hanford Reach National Monument. **Columbia River Journeys** (© 888/486-9119; www.columbiariverjourneys.com) operates 4-hour tours that travel up the last free-flowing stretch of the Columbia River.

Long overlooked by people touring the central Washington wine country, the Tri-Cities area (Richland, Pasco, and Kennewick) is slowly becoming something of a decent base for a weekend of wine touring. **Aioli's,** 94 Lee Blvd., Richland (© 509/942-1914), is a great little restaurant with a tiny wine bar and a long menu of tapas. The restaurant is located close to riverfront hotels and a large riverside park

and has lots of interesting wines available by the glass.

Walla Walla The Walla Walla area is in the midst of a winery boom that has made this the state's premier wine-touring region. Among the new wineries or wineries with new tasting rooms are **Glen Fiona,** 416 N. Second Ave. (© 509/522-2566; www.glenfiona.com), which has its tasting room in the Walla Walla's old railway depot; **Seven Hills Winery,** 212 N. Third Ave. (© 877/777-7870 or 509/529-7198; www.sevenhillswinery.com), in a renovated former woodworking-mill; **Three Rivers Winery,** 5641 W. Hwy. 12 (© 509/526-9463; www.threeriverswinery.com), which is located east of Walla Walla and has a large, impressive winery and tasting room; and **Trey Marie Winery,** 150 E. Boeing Rd. (© 509/529-1371; www.treymarie.com), which is affiliated with Dunham Cellars.

Not only are there new wineries in Walla Walla, but there is also a recently restored historic hotel. The **Marcus Whitman Hotel,** 6 W. Rose St. (© 866/826-9422; www.marcuswhitmanhotel.com), originally opened in 1928, makes an excellent base for a Walla Walla wine tour. A classic elegance reigns in the wood-paneled lobby, and though only some of the hotel's suites are located in the historic tower building, all the rooms have the same luxurious styling. There's also a good formal restaurant here.

Of course, wine country isn't complete without great restaurants, and Walla Walla now has two other new restaurants that emphasize fine wines and the sort of foods that pair well with wine. **Grapefields,** 4 E. Main St. (© 509/522-3993), is a casual wine bar that serves primarily French-inspired light meals. **Whitehouse-Crawford,** 55 W. Cherry St. © 509/525-2222), housed in the same renovated woodworking mill building that also houses Seven Hills Winery, is the more formal of these two restaurants, yet has a decidedly urban-loft feel.

Spokane Formerly known as the Cheney Cowles Museum, the **Northwest Museum of Arts & Culture,** 2316 W. First Ave. (© **509/456-3931**), reopened in December 2001, after an extensive remodeling that added a beautiful new glass-walled building and lots more exhibit halls. The new museum showcases art, Plateau Indian culture, and the history of the inland Northwest.

1

The Best of Washington

Despite what you may have heard to the contrary, there is more to Washington state than lattes, rain, and Microsoft. Washington is actually such a diverse state that it could have served as a model for the song "America the Beautiful." Out in the eastern high desert country, there are beautiful spacious skies as big as Montana's (part of the Rocky Mountains even reaches into Washington). In the Cascades, there are mountains that turn majestically purple at sunset. In the Palouse country of the southeastern corner of the state, amber waves of grain stripe the steep hillsides. In the Yakima, Wenatchee, and Chelan valleys, the fruited plains produce the world's most familiar apples (and some pretty good wine, too). Out on the Pacific Coast, there are beaches white with foam, and with an inland sea across the Olympic Peninsula from the Pacific, the sun in Washington shines from sea to shining sea. From its mountains to its valleys, Washington is indeed beautiful country.

But the diversity of this state goes far beyond mere song lyrics. There's an island archipelago as beautiful as the coast of Maine (though without the harsh winters). There are beaches as long and sandy as those of North Carolina's Outer Banks (though the waters are too cold for swimming). There are granite mountains as rugged as the Sierra Nevada (though not as crowded with hikers). There are desert canyons like those of the Southwest (though not nearly as hot). There are vineyard-covered hillsides like those of the Napa Valley (though without the crowds). There's even a bay-front city with dauntingly steep streets (no cable cars, though).

With such a complex and diverse landscape to be explored, planning a trip can become a daunting task. Where should we go? Where should we stay? Where should we eat? Planning a trip to Washington involves making a lot of these sorts of decisions, and, especially if you only have a week for your entire trip, you probably want to be sure you get the most from your trip. To help you get a better a grip on the state's highlights, its not-to-be-missed attractions and activities, we've put together this list of some of the best the state has to offer. Keep in mind that most are written up in more detail elsewhere in this book, but this chapter will give you an overview and get you started.

1 The Best Natural Attractions

- **The San Juan Islands:** Forested mountains rise up from the cold waters north of Puget Sound to form the archipelago known as the San Juan Islands. Here, bald eagles wheel overhead while orca whales dive for salmon below. All this natural beauty is a powerful magnet and, despite the hordes of tourists in the summer, the San Juans remain the state's best summer vacation spot. See "The San Juan Islands," in chapter 5.

- **Olympic National Park:** This park contains the only rain forests

Site Seeing: The Best of Washington on the Web

If you're surfing the Web in search of information on Washington, the following websites will provide you with lots of useful information.

- **Washington State Tourism Office (www.experiencewashington. com):** Organized by region and crammed full of links to other travel-related websites, this should be your on-line starting point for planning a trip to Oregon.

- **Seattle Convention and Visitors Bureau (www.seeseattle.org):** Here at the official Seattle–King County Convention and Visitors Bureau website, you can take a virtual tour of the Emerald City. Recently redesigned, the website is not nearly as fun as it once was, but it is still packed with lots of information and includes a photo album of the city's major attractions.

- ***Seattle Times*** **(www.seattletimes.com):** A solid virtual version of Seattle's print stalwart, the *Seattle Times,* offers many of the paper's stories online. There's also an entertainment section with information on movies, theater, and concerts around town.

- **Washington State Parks (www.parks.wa.gov):** Washington State Parks offers an amazingly diverse array of activities and accommodations. Not only are there the expected campgrounds, beaches, and forest trails, but there are also former military installations where you can rent what were once officers' quarters. There are lighthouses to tour and lighthouse keepers' homes to rent. There are parks that are trails and a park that is exclusively for rock climbers. You can learn all about these parks on this website.

- **Nature of the Northwest (www.naturenw.org):** This is sort of a clearing house for information on reservations and rentals on public lands in the Northwest. The website also has information on passes that you'll need in order to park at trailheads and in sno-parks. Plenty of links, too.

- **Forest Service (www.fs.fed.us/r6/):** This website will give you links to all the national forests in Washington (and Oregon), and although the individual national forest websites vary in their usefulness and ease of use, all have lots of information on campgrounds and current trail conditions.

- **www.northolympic.com:** Very dense and very thorough, this website is packed with loads of good information and links to hotels, restaurants, attractions, tour companies, and almost everything travel related on the Olympic Peninsula.

- **Washington State Ferries (www.wsdot.wa.gov/ferries):** This is the official website for Washington State Ferries, which are an essential part of any visit to the Seattle, the Puget Sound, or the San Juan Islands. This site offers route destinations, schedule and fare information, a calendar of events, and an online ferry reservation service for ferries to Sidney, British Columbia (near Victoria).

Washington

in the contiguous United States, and they comprise a fascinating ecosystem—living plants stake out almost every square inch of space, from towering Sitka spruce trees to mosses and lush ferns. The park also preserves miles of pristine, fog-shrouded beaches and beautiful alpine and subalpine scenery dotted with lush meadows. See chapter 7.

• **The North Cascades National Park Complex:** Actually comprised of one national park and two national recreation areas, this remote and rugged region is among the least explored in the state. Most visitors view the park from the North Cascades Scenic Highway, from which there are stupendous views on clear days, but which is closed by snow for nearly half the year. See "Mount Baker & the North Cascades Scenic Highway," in chapter 9.

• **Mount Rainier National Park:** With its glaciers and easily accessible alpine meadows, Mount Rainier is Washington's favorite mountain. Sunrise and Paradise are the two best vantage points for viewing the massive bulk of Mount Rainier, and in these two areas of the park, you'll also find some of the best hiking trails. See "Mount Rainier National Park & Environs," in chapter 9.

• **Mount St. Helens National Volcanic Monument:** Mount St. Helens is slowly recovering from the 1980 volcanic blast that turned one of the Cascades' most beautiful peaks into a scarred landscape of fallen trees and fields of ash. Several visitor centers relate the events of the eruption and what has been happening on the mountain since. See "Mount St. Helens National Volcanic Monument," in chapter 9.

• **Columbia Gorge National Scenic Area:** Carved by ice-age floods that were as much as 1,200 feet deep, the Columbia Gorge is a unique feature of the Northwest landscape. Waterfalls by the dozen cascade from the basalt cliffs on the Oregon side of the Gorge, but the best wide-angle views are from the Washington side, where you'll also find one of the largest monoliths in the world. See "The Columbia Gorge & the Mount Adams Area," in chapter 9.

2 The Best Outdoor Activities

• **Sea Kayaking in the San Juan Islands:** Emerald islands, clear water, orca whales, bald eagles, and remote campsites that can only be reached by boat lure sea kayakers to the San Juan Islands. You can paddle the islands on your own (if you're experienced) or go out with a guide for a few hours or a few days. See "The San Juan Islands," in chapter 5.

• **Hiking the Olympic Coast:** Within the contiguous United States, there are very few miles of wilderness coastline left. Among the longest, and most spectacular, are those of Olympic National Park along the west side of the Olympic Peninsula. Whether you just want to do a good long day hike, or spend several days backpacking along the beach, you've got several options along this coast. See chapter 7.

• **Cross-Country Skiing in the Methow Valley:** This valley on the east side of Washington's North Cascades has more than 105 miles of immaculately groomed trails, making it one of the premier cross-country ski destinations in the country. Skiers can ski from one lodge to the next down the valley, or use one of the luxurious lodges as a base for doing day skis. See "Winthrop & the Methow Valley," in chapter 9.

- **Hiking on Mount Rainier:** Fed by huge amounts of melting snow each summer, the wildflowers of the alpine meadows on the flanks of Mount Rainier burst into bloom each year in July. Through these hillsides of color meander miles of hiking trails that are among the most memorable in the state. Sure you'll encounter crowds, but the wildflower displays, with Mount Rainier for a backdrop, far outweigh the inconvenience of dealing with hordes of other hikers. See "Mount Rainier National Park & Environs," in chapter 9.
- **Climbing Mount St. Helens:** Though it isn't the highest peak in the Washington Cascades, Mount St. Helens is certainly the most interesting mountain to climb (you'll need a permit, and numbers of climbers are limited). You don't need any technical climbing skills for this one, just plenty of stamina and a tolerance for hiking in dusty conditions (you'll likely be hiking in volcanic ash). See "Mount St. Helens National Volcanic Monument," in chapter 9.
- **Boardsailing at Hood River:** Winds that rage through the Columbia Gorge whip up white-capped standing waves and have turned this area into the boardsailing capital of the United States, attracting boardsailors from around the world. See "The Columbia Gorge & the Mount Adams Area," in chapter 9.

3 The Best Beaches

- **Alki Beach (Seattle):** Located in West Seattle, this is the closest Washington comes to a Southern California–style beach scene. There's a sandy beach and a paved path crowded with in-line skaters, walkers, and cyclists. Across the street from the sand, you'll find lots of cheap restaurants and places to buy sunglasses. See chapter 4.
- **Obstruction Pass State Park (Orcas Island):** Set at the end of a half-mile-long trail through the woods, this tiny cove is barely big enough for a dozen sea kayakers to beach their boats on, but therein lies this beach's charm. This is the quintessential little San Juan Islands cove beach, and you don't have to have a boat to get to it. See "The San Juan Islands," in chapter 5.
- **Deception Pass State Park Beaches (Whidbey Island):** There's a reason this is the most popular state park in Washington—the many miles of beach, spread out on two sides of Deception Pass, are among the prettiest in the Puget Sound area. See "Whidbey Island," in chapter 5.
- **Dungeness Spit (Dungeness):** With 6 miles (9.5km) of wind-swept sand stretching out to a lighthouse in the Strait of Juan de Fuca, Dungeness is a hikers' beach, and the reward for hiking several miles out this narrow strip of sand is the chance to see some of the area's resident harbor seals. See "Sequim & Dungeness Valley," in chapter 7.
- **Rialto Beach (Olympic National Park outside Forks):** Located on the north side of the Quillayute River, this beach is the southern terminus of a 29-mile-long (47km) stretch of wilderness beach. However, most visitors

simply walk a mile up the beach to Hole in the Wall, a huge monolith through which the ocean's waves have bored a tunnel. See "Olympic National Park West," in chapter 7.

- **Second Beach & Third Beach (Olympic National Park outside Forks):** It's difficult to pick the best beach in the national park, since they are almost all so ruggedly beautiful, but this pair of beaches just outside the community of La Push are our personal favorites. Here you can listen to the calls of the eagles and gulls and contemplate the sheer vastness of the Pacific. See "Olympic National Park West," in chapter 7.

4 The Best Hikes

- **Trails Out of Hurricane Ridge:** Hurricane Ridge is the most easily accessible alpine region of Olympic National Park, and from here, and nearby Obstruction Peak, there are several possible hikes of varying durations that will give you a glimpse of a superb part of the Olympic wilderness. See "Olympic National Park North & the Northern Olympic Peninsula," in chapter 7.
- **Hall of Mosses Trail/Hoh River Trail (Hoh River Valley):** Whether you're only up for a short walk in the woods or want to do a multiday backpacking trip, this is the best place to experience the Olympic Peninsula's famed rain forest. Just don't forget your rain gear. See "Olympic National Park West," in chapter 7.
- **The Maple Pass Loop Trail:** You simply won't find a more rewarding hike anywhere along the North Cascades Scenic Highway than this one. The trail climbs nearly 2,000 feet from Rainy Pass to a ridge with an astounding view of seemingly all the mountains in Washington. See "Mount Baker & the North Cascades Scenic Highway," in chapter 9.
- **Trails Out of Sunrise:** The Sunrise area, on the northeast flanks of Washington's Mount Rainier, offers fabulous unobstructed views of both the mountain and Emmons Glacier, the largest glacier in the contiguous 48 states. From Sunrise more than a dozen trails of different lengths head off to viewpoints and lakes. Take your pick. See "Mount Rainier National Park & Environs," in chapter 9.
- **The Beacon Rock Trail (Columbia Gorge West of Stevenson):** Although this hike is less than 2 miles (3km) long, it makes up for its short length with its steep pitch. In fact, much of the trail is on metal stairs bolted to the sheer cliff face of Beacon Rock, a massive monolith that rivals the Rock of Gibraltar in size. The view from the top is superb. See "The Columbia Gorge & the Mount Adams Area," in chapter 9.

5 The Best Scenic Drives

- **Chuckanut Drive:** This road winds south from Bellingham through the Chuckanut Mountains, which rise straight up from the waters of Chuckanut and Samish bays. Across the water lie the San Juan Islands, and the sunsets are spectacular. Larrabee State Park provides an opportunity to get out of your car and walk down to a pretty little beach. See "Bellingham & Environs," in chapter 5.

- **The North Cascades Scenic Highway:** Passing through the most rugged and spectacular mountains in the Northwest, this highway was not opened until 1972 because of the difficulty of building any sort of road through Washington's glacier-carved North Cascades. Even now it is closed for half of every year due to heavy snows and avalanches. See "Mount Baker & the North Cascades Scenic Highway," in chapter 9.
- **The Columbia River Scenic Highway:** Wash. 14 parallels the Columbia River from Vancouver, Washington, eastward through the Columbia Gorge, and along its length provides some of the most awe-inspiring vistas in the Northwest. Visible across the river in Oregon are not only the basalt cliffs of the Gorge but also the snow-clad summit of Mount Hood. See "The Columbia Gorge & the Mount Adams Area," in chapter 9.

- **The Palouse:** This wheat-farming region in southeastern Washington is a convoluted landscape of steep hills and narrow valleys, and a meandering drive through the region is a trip into another time. Small towns and boldly striped hillsides make this the most fascinating farm country in the state. See "The Palouse: A Slice of Small-Town Rural Washington," in chapter 10.
- **Soap Lake to the Grand Coulee Dam:** Although today the landscape of central Washington is that of a desert, vast floodwaters once poured across this landscape. Today a drive up the Grand Coulee provides a glimpse into one of the most fascinating events in Northwest geologic history. Canyons, mineral lakes, caves, and a huge dry waterfall provide the roadside distractions. See "The Grand Coulee Dam Area," in chapter 10.

6 The Best Bed-and-Breakfast Inns

- **Gaslight Inn** (Seattle; ✆ **206/325-3654**): Beautifully decorated with lots of original Stickley furniture, this inn consists of two houses in the Capitol Hill neighborhood. One house is done in a more contemporary style if you don't happen to be a fan of Arts-and-Crafts style. There's also a swimming pool. See p. 83.
- **Spring Bay Inn** (Orcas Island; ✆ **360/376-5531**): This secluded waterfront inn is a luxurious island retreat, but a stay here includes not only bed-and-breakfast, but brunch and a daily sea-kayak excursion as well. In-room fireplaces and a hot tub right on the beach add a touch of romance. See p. 171.

- **Willcox House** (The Kitsap Peninsula; ✆ **800/725-9477** or 360/830-4492): This 1930s Art Deco mansion, set on the shore of Hood Canal, is straight out of an old Hollywood movie (and indeed many movie stars did stay here back in the '30s and '40s). Because it is located in such a secluded spot, the inn also serves dinner. See p. 198.
- **Chinaberry Hill** (Tacoma; ✆ **253/272-1282**): Located in Tacoma's Stadium Historic District, this imposing Victorian is as impressive as any of the historic B&Bs in Port Townsend. The inn is steeped in classic Northwest elegance and abounds in beautiful woodwork. See p. 207.

- **The Villa Bed & Breakfast** (Tacoma; ✆ **888/572-1157** or 253/572-1157): Regardless of the fact that this inn would be more appropriate to Santa Barbara, the Italianate villa in Tacoma's Stadium Historic District is a real gem. Large rooms have whirlpool or soaking tubs and most have gas fireplaces. See p. 207.
- **Thornewood Castle Inn** (Lakewood; ✆ **253/584-4393**): Few B&Bs in America can truly claim to be castles, but Thornewood, built in 1909, certainly can. With 28 bedrooms and 22 bathrooms, this sprawling mansion is as close as you'll come in this country to a European manor home. See p. 207.
- **Ann Starrett Mansion** (Port Townsend; ✆ **800/321-0644** or 360/385-3205): This is the premier Victorian B&B in the Northwest. The outrageously ornate Queen Anne–style mansion is packed to the rafters with antiques, and staying here is a bit like spending the night in a museum. See p. 222.
- **Hoquiam's Castle** (Hoquiam; **877/542-2785** or 360/533-2005):

Built in 1897 by a local timber baron, this stately Victorian inn is an amazing assemblage of turrets and gables, balconies and bay windows. Although the town of Hoquiam isn't exactly a major tourist destination, this inn is reason enough to spend a weekend in the area. See p. 252.
- **Abendblume Inn** (Leavenworth; ✆ **800/669-7634** or 509/548-4059): Of all the many alpine chalet accommodations in Leavenworth, this is the most luxurious. The attention to detail shown in the construction of this chalet makes the inn an especially enjoyable place to spend a romantic weekend. See p. 293.
- **Run of the River Bed & Breakfast** (Leavenworth; ✆ **800/288-6491** or 509/548-7171): Set amid beautiful rock gardens on a side channel of the Wenatchee River, this rustic yet contemporary log inn is as tranquil a place to stay as you'll find in the region. The innkeepers are extremely helpful and eager to share their love of the area with guests. See p. 294.

7 The Best Mountain Lodges/Resorts/Retreats

- **Lake Crescent Lodge** (Olympic National Park west of Port Angeles; ✆ **360/928-3211**): Set on the shore of Lake Crescent, a landlocked fjord, in Olympic National Park, is the best base for exploring the north side of the park. The lodge has simple rooms in the old main lodge building and larger though less memorable rooms in various newer buildings around the property. See p. 238.
- **Lake Quinault Lodge** (Lake Quinault; ✆ **800/562-6672** or 360/288-2900): This gracefully aging lodge on the shore of Lake Quinault has the most character

of any of the lodges scattered around the perimeter of Olympic National Park. It's something of a cross between mountain lodge and classic lake resort. See p. 245.
- **The Heathman Lodge** (Vancouver; ✆ **888/475-3100** or 360/254-3100): The only thing wrong with this modern mountain lodge is that it's located in suburban Vancouver, Washington, rather than in the mountains. Nevertheless, with its log, stone, and cedar-shingle construction, it manages to conjure up the Northwest's historic mountain lodges. See p. 264.

- **Sun Mountain Lodge** (Winthrop; ☎ **800/572-0493** or 509/996-2211): Perched atop a mountain and overlooking the remote Methow Valley, this is Washington's premier mountain resort. Luxurious and rustic at the same time, the lodge is a base for cross-country skiing in winter and hiking and mountain biking in summer. See p. 277.
- **Freestone Inn** (Mazama; ☎ **800/639-3809** or 509/996-3906): This impressive log lodge beside a small trout lake at the west end of the Winthrop Valley is not as extensive a place as nearby Sun Mountain Lodge, but the guest rooms here are among the most luxurious in the state. See p. 278.
- **Mountain Home Lodge** (Leavenworth; ☎ **800/414-2378** or 509/548-7077): Set in the middle of a large pasture high on the slopes above the town of Leavenworth, this lodge enjoys a breathtaking view of the Stuart Range, and in winter is only accessible by Sno-Cat snowmobiles (complimentary transport provided by the lodge). See p. 292.
- **Sleeping Lady** (Leavenworth; ☎ **800/574-2123** or 509/548-6344): Although primarily a conference resort, this place on the outskirts of Bavarian Leavenworth is far too pleasant to be reserved for those in town for business.

With the feel of an upscale summer camp, the lodge is tucked amid granite boulders and ponderosa pines. See p. 292.

- **Salish Lodge & Spa** (Snoqualmie Falls; ☎ **800/826-6124,** 800/2SALISH, or 425/888-2556): Perched on the brink of Snoqualmie Falls near the town of North Bend, this elegant country lodge is a favorite weekend getaway for Seattleites who come to be pampered at the spa and to enjoy the nearby farm country, mountain trails, and ski slopes. See p. 298.
- **Paradise Inn** (Mount Rainier National Park; ☎ **360/569-2275**): Perched high on the slopes of Washington's Mount Rainier, this classic mountain lodge was built in 1917, and was completely renovated a few years ago. Because the lodge is only open May through October, it books up early in the year and stays packed throughout the summer. You just can't beat the location. See p. 306.
- **Dolce Skamania Lodge** (Stevenson; ☎ **800/221-7117** or 509/427-7700): Set amid the grandeur of the Columbia Gorge, this modern mountain resort makes the ideal base for exploring the Gorge. The resort's golf course has a very distracting view of the Oregon side of the Columbia Gorge. See p. 319.

8 The Best Island & Beach Resorts & Lodges

- **The Woodmark Hotel on Lake Washington** (Kirkland; ☎ **800/822-3700** or 425/822-3700): Set on spacious grounds on the eastern shore of Lake Washington, this luxurious hotel is the Seattle area's finest waterfront hotel and has a very resortlike feel. See p. 86.
- **Friday Harbor House** (Friday Harbor; ☎ **360/378-8455**): OK, so this one isn't right on the water. Still, it's the most luxurious accommodation on San Juan Island, and the guest rooms have views of the water and distant island peaks. See p. 164.
- **Rosario Resort & Spa** (Orcas Island; ☎ **800/562-8820** or 360/376-2222): With an elegant historic mansion as its focal point

and enough activities and amenities to keep you busy for a week's vacation, this is the premier resort in the San Juan Islands. See p. 171.

• **La Conner Channel Lodge** (La Conner; ℂ **888/466-4113** or 360/466-1500): Set on the shore of the Swinomish Channel, this inn is steeped in Northwest styling. River rocks and weathered wood siding lend an air of age to the exterior, which is brightened by lovely perennial gardens. In the guest rooms, balconies, fireplaces, fir accents, and slate floors yield an unexpected sophistication. See p. 182.

• **The Inn at Langley** (Whidbey Island; ℂ **360/221-3033**): The setting alone, overlooking the Saratoga Passage, would be enough to rank this place firmly among the best small inns in the region. However, Japanese-influenced styling, soaking tubs with water views, and fireplaces all add up to uncommon luxuries at this romantic retreat. See p. 150.

• **Resort Semiahmoo** (Blaine; ℂ **800/770-7992** or 360/371-2000): Located on a spit of land looking across the water to Canada, this is one of Washington's top golf resorts. It also happens to be on a long stretch of beach, which makes this a great place to get away from it all whether you want to play golf or tennis or just walk on the beach. See p. 189.

• **The Captain Whidbey Inn** (Whidbey Island; ℂ **800/366-4097** or 360/678-4097): This unusual inn was built in 1907 of local madrona-tree logs, which give it a thoroughly unique appearance. The island's seafaring history is evoked throughout the inn, and the seat in front of the lobby's beach-stone fireplace is a wonderful spot to while away a gray afternoon. See p. 151.

• **Heron Beach Inn on Ludlow Bay** (Port Ludlow; ℂ **360/437-0411**): Located a few miles south of Port Townsend, this small, luxury inn offers all the best aspects of the San Juan Islands without the hassles of the ferries. A superb restaurant and an adjacent golf course keep guests contented. See p. 224.

• **Kalaloch Lodge** (Forks; ℂ **360/962-2271**): Comprised primarily of bluff-top cabins overlooking a wild and windswept beach, this is Olympic National Park's only oceanfront lodge. As such it is extremely popular. See p. 244.

• **Ocean Crest Resort** (Moclips; ℂ **800/684-8439** or 360/276-4465): Perched high on a forested bluff above the crashing waves of the Pacific Ocean, this casual resort enjoys the most spectacular setting of any lodging on the Washington coast. There's also a good restaurant on the premises. See p. 252.

9 The Best Dining Experiences

• **The Herbfarm** (Woodinville; ℂ **206/784-2222**): This restaurant, located northeast of Seattle adjacent to several wineries, was once little more than a roadside farm stand specializing in herbs, but over the years has become the most highly acclaimed (and most expensive) restaurant in the state. See p. 101.

• **Rover's** (Seattle; ℂ **206/325-7442**): This little cottage restaurant in an unassuming neighborhood east of downtown Seattle is a stage for the French-Northwest culinary fusion of chef Thierry Rautureau. Every course here surprises with flavors both subtle and bold. See p. 99.

- **Salumi** (Seattle; ☎ 206/621-8772): Tucked into a tiny space on the edge of Seattle's Pioneer Square neighborhood, this restaurant specializes in house-cured salamis. The owner, a retired Boeing employee, went to Italy to learn traditional methods for making salami. See p. 91.
- **Country Kitchen at the Inn at Langley** (Langley; ☎ 360/221-3033): This quintessentially Northwestern inn on Whidbey Island is one of the state's most luxurious accommodations. On weekends (only), it serves some of the best multicourse gourmet dinners in Washington. Make reservations early. See p. 152.
- **Molly Ward Gardens** (Poulsbo; ☎ 360/779-4471): Housed in an old barn in a small rural valley outside the Scandinavian theme town of Poulsbo, this restaurant sums up Northwest lifestyles with its country gardens, eclectic decor, and creative cuisine. See p. 199.
- **The Ajax Cafe** (Port Hadlock; ☎ 360/385-3450): With live old-time music on the weekends, silly hats hanging from the ceiling (and frequently worn by dinner guests), and excellent food, the Ajax Café is a hidden gem of a restaurant south of Port Townsend. Housed

in an old wooden waterfront building, the restaurant is a favorite of people with something to celebrate. See p. 226.

- **The Ark Restaurant & Bakery** (Nahcotta; ☎ 360/665-4133): Oyster lovers take note, this restaurant on the Long Beach Peninsula is just down the road from Oysterville and is adjacent to oyster farms and an oyster packing plant, so you know the shellfish here is as fresh as it gets. See p. 260.
- **Sun Mountain Lodge** (Winthrop; ☎ 800/572-0493 or 509/996-2211): If you get vertigo easily, you may want to forego meals at this precipitously perched dining room overlooking the Methow Valley. However, if you relish creative cooking accompanied by dizzying mountain views, this restaurant should not be missed. See p. 277.
- **Patit Creek Restaurant** (Dayton; ☎ 509/382-2625): The small town of Dayton seems an unlikely place for one of the state's best restaurants, but the reliable French-inspired fare served at this unpretentious place draws diners from miles around. See p. 343.
- **Patsy Clark's Mansion** (Spokane; ☎ 509/838-8300): Housed in one of the most magnificent Victorian mansions in Spokane, this elegant restaurant has long been the favored dining establishment of the city's wealthiest residents. Classic Continental fare dominates the menu. See p. 350.

10 The Best Brewpubs

- **Big Time Brewery and Alehouse** (Seattle; ☎ 206/545-4509): Located in the University District and popular with university students, the Big Time serves as many as 12 of its own brews at any given time, and some of these can be pretty unusual. See p. 141.
- **Elysian Brewing Company** (Seattle; ☎ 206/860-1920): Located on Capitol Hill, this locals' brewpub is a big space with an industrial warehouse feel. Elysian has one of the smallest outputs of any brewpub in town, and does exceptional strong ales and stouts. See p. 142.

- **La Conner Brewing Company** (La Conner; ℂ 360/466-1415): Though this pub lacks water views, it more than makes up for this shortcoming with its excellent beers and creative pub fare. Throughout the year there are lots of unusual (and tasty) seasonal brews. See p. 183.
- **Winthrop Brewing Company** (Winthrop; ℂ 509/996-3183): Winthrop, which sports false-fronted cow town facades, just wouldn't be complete without a classic Western saloon. In this case, it's the Winthrop Brewing Company that fits the bill. Wedged into a triangular space on the town's main street, this brew pub is the valley's après-cross-country ski spot of choice. See p. 280.
- **Grant's Pub** (Yakima; ℂ 509/575-2922): Located in a restored railroad depot in downtown Yakima (which is in the middle of hops country as well as wine country), Grant's claims to be the first brewpub in the country and specializes in Scottish-style ales. See p. 334.

11 The Best Museums

- **Seattle Art Museum:** Although the temporary exhibits are usually fascinating, an outstanding collection of Northwest Coast Native American art and artifacts is the highlight of this museum. The African art exhibit is equally impressive, and the 20th-century art collection includes a respectable exhibition of works by regional artists. See p. 109.
- **Museum of Flight** (Seattle): Long the home of Boeing, Seattle has played a historic role in the history of flight, and this museum reflects this heritage with its diverse collection of planes. The location, adjacent to Boeing Field, allows visitors to watch planes take off and land as they study the museum displays. See p. 114.
- **Museum of Northwest Art** (La Conner): The historic Skagit Valley fishing town of La Conner began attracting artists in the middle part of this century and so is a fitting location for a museum dedicated to the work of Northwest artists. See p. 181.
- **Bellingham Antique Radio Museum** (Bellingham): One man's obsession with old radios has blossomed into this unusual museum in downtown Bellingham. Hundreds of old radios and other early electrical and recording devices are on display. See p. 185.
- **Washington State History Museum** (Tacoma): It's big. It's high tech. It's fun. As the archive of state history, this museum works hard to entertain visitors while exploring the state's past. There are lots of interactive exhibits as well as displays on little known and often controversial aspects of Washington history. See p. 205.
- **Makah Cultural and Research Center** (Neah Bay): This museum is located on the extreme northwest tip of the Olympic Peninsula and contains artifacts recovered from a nearby archaeological site. In the museum are totem poles, dugout canoes, and even a mockup of a native longhouse complete with smoked salmon hanging from the rafters. See p. 233.
- **Columbia Gorge Interpretive Center** (Stevenson): With historical photos, quotations from pioneers, and exhibits on various aspects of historic and prehistoric life in the Columbia Gorge, this museum serves as a valuable introduction to one of the Northwest's scenic wonders. See p. 316.

12 The Best Family Attractions

- **Seattle Center** (Seattle): As the site of the Space Needle, Seattle Center is one of the city's required stops. However, families will also find here a children's museum, a children's theater, amusement park rides, and an arcade area. See p. 118.
- **Whale-Watching Tours in the San Juan Islands:** Sure you can see orca whales perform at marine parks, but in the San Juan Islands during the summer, you can see genuinely free Willies, lots of them during whale-watching tours that usually also include sightings of minke whales, harbor seals, and bald eagles. See "The San Juan Islands," in chapter 5.
- **Point Defiance Park** (Tacoma): This gigantic city park at the north end of Tacoma packs in more fun stuff for kids to see and do than a family could ever hope to do in 1 day. There's a zoo, a replica of a historic trading fort, and an old-time logging camp. See p. 203.
- **Long Beach:** With minigolf, horseback riding, miles of wide beaches, and perfect winds for kite flying, this beach community on the southern Washington coast is the state's best family beach. See "The Long Beach Peninsula," in chapter 8.

13 The Best Small Towns

- **La Conner:** Surrounded by tulip fields and filled with art galleries and interesting shops, this former fishing and farming town gets jammed on weekends, but if you stop by on a weekday or in the off-season, you can easily be seduced by its vintage charm. See "La Conner & the Skagit Valley," in chapter 5.
- **Langley:** Located near the south end of Whidbey Island, this former fishing village is now something of an upscale arts community. There are art galleries, upscale antiques and fashion shops, and several good restaurants. All this right on the shore of Saratoga Passage. Some buildings even rise straight out of the water. See "Whidbey Island," in chapter 5.
- **Port Townsend:** Late in the 19th century, this town on the Olympic Peninsula was poised to become the region's most important city, but when the railroad passed it by, it slipped into obscurity. Today,

Port Townsend is obscure no more. With block after block of Victorian homes and a waterfront setting, it has become a favorite weekend destination for Seattleites. See "Port Townsend: A Restored Victorian Seaport," in chapter 7.
- **Leavenworth:** Lederhosen? Dirndls? Polka parties? Sounds like someplace to steer clear of, but actually, the Bavarian theme town of Leavenworth works. Maybe there are too many cuckoo clocks and nutcrackers for sale, but those mountains on the edge of town are the genuine article. See "Leavenworth: Washington's Own Bavarian Village," in chapter 9.
- **Winthrop:** If you saw an 1890s photo of Winthrop and then visited this remote community in north central Washington, you might think the town had been caught in a time warp. It just doesn't look much different than it did back then. See "Winthrop & the Methow Valley," in chapter 9.

2

Planning Your Trip to Washington

Planning your trip before you leave home can make all the difference between enjoying your vacation and wishing you'd stayed home. In fact, for many people, planning a trip is half the fun of going. If you're one of those people, then this chapter should prove useful. When should I go? What is this trip going to cost me? Can I catch a festival during my visit? Where should I head to pursue my favorite sport? These are just some of the questions we'll answer for you in this chapter. Additionally, you can contact information sources listed below to find out more about Washington and to take a look at photos (whether in brochures or on the Web) that are certain to get you excited about your upcoming trip.

1 The Regions in Brief

The state of Washington covers 68,139 square miles (109,704km^2)—roughly the same area as all of New England. Within this large area can be found surprising geographical diversity, including an inland sea dotted with hundreds of islands, temperate rain forests where rainfall is measured in feet, an arid land of sagebrush and junipers, several distinct mountain ranges, volcanoes both dormant and extinct, the West's most important river, and, of course, hundreds of thousands of acres of coniferous forests (hence the state's nickname—the Evergreen State).

Puget Sound Puget Sound, a convoluted maze of waterways, is a vast inland sea that stretches for more than 80 miles (129km), from north of Seattle south to Olympia. Created when glaciers receded at the end of the last ice age, Puget Sound is characterized by deep waterways surrounded by hilly forested terrain. Because the Sound's protected waters make such good harbors and are so full of fish and shellfish, this area has been the most densely populated region of the

state since long before the first Europeans sailed into these waters. Today, the eastern shore of the Sound has become the largest metropolitan area in the state—one huge Pugetopolis that includes Seattle, Tacoma, Olympia, and dozens of smaller cities and bedroom communities. The western and southernmost reaches of the Sound are much less developed. These rural areas are popular weekend escapes for Seattleites and Tacomans but are much less familiar to visitors from out of state, who, though they might appreciate the Sound and Rainier vistas, tend to overlook this region because of its lack of major attractions.

The San Juan Islands Lying just to the north of Puget Sound, the San Juan Islands are a lush, mountainous archipelago, home to orca whales, harbor seals, and bald eagles. Of the 175 or so named San Juan Islands, only four are accessible by public ferry, and of these only three—San Juan, Orcas, and Lopez—have accommodations (however, the fourth, Shaw, does have a campground). The mild climate, watery vistas, and quiet, rural character of these islands have made the San Juans Washington's favorite summer vacation destination. As such the islands are packed to overflowing throughout the summer and it can be impossible to get a hotel reservation at the last minute. A summer trip to the San Juans definitely requires plenty of advance planning. It also requires a great deal of patience, as waits for ferries can stretch into hours. To avoid the crowds, consider visiting in spring or fall, when the weather is often just as good as in the summer. Because the San Juans lie within the rain shadow of the Olympic Mountains, they get far less rain than Seattle (and therein lies much of their appeal for Seattleites).

The Olympic Peninsula Aside from a thin necklace of private land around its perimeter, this huge peninsula, wedged between Puget Sound and the Pacific Ocean, is almost entirely public land. At the heart of the peninsula is Olympic National Park, which encompasses almost the entirety of the Olympic Mountains, and surrounding the park is Olympic National Forest (distinguishable by its many clear-cuts). Due primarily to the immensity of the forests and the size of the trees here, the forests of the Olympic Peninsula have, over the past 100 years, seen some of the most intensive logging in the nation. The gigantic size of the trees here is due to the astounding amount of rain that falls on parts of the peninsula. The western slopes of the Olympic Mountains contain some of the only temperate rain forests in the contiguous United States. In these forests, the annual rainfall often exceeds 150 inches. Rugged remote beaches separated by rocky headlands characterize the Pacific shore of the peninsula, while along the north coast, there are several large towns, including the historic Victorian seaport of Port Townsend. Just remember when planning a vacation out here that you're likely to get rained on even in the summer; be prepared to get wet.

Southwest Washington The southwest corner of the state is, for the most part, a sparsely populated region of huge tree farms. However, along the southern coast, there are long sandy beaches and numerous beach resorts and towns, which, though popular with Portlanders and the residents of Puget Sound, lack a distinctly Northwest character. Inland, up the Columbia River, lies the city of Vancouver (not to be confused with Vancouver, B.C.), which though rich in regional history, has been overshadowed by Portland, Oregon, directly across the Columbia River.

The Cascade Range Dividing the state roughly into eastern and western regions, the Washington Cascades are actually two very distinct mountain ranges. The North Cascades are jagged, glaciated granite peaks, while the central and southern Washington Cascades are primarily volcanic in origin. Mount St. Helens, which erupted with awe-inspiring force in 1980, is the only one of these volcanoes to be active in recent years, but even Mount Rainier, the highest mountain in the state, is merely dormant and is expected to erupt again sometime in the next few hundred years (probably with devastating effect considering the large population that now resides at the foot of the mountain). Within this mountain range are North Cascades National Park, Mount Rainier National Park, Mount St. Helens National Volcanic Monument, the third deepest lake in the country (Lake Chelan), half a dozen ski areas, and a couple of interesting little theme towns. If you're thinking about a summer vacation in these mountains, keep in mind that the snow at higher elevations (where you'll find the beautiful wildflower meadows) often doesn't melt off until well into July.

Eastern Washington While to the west of the Cascade Range is all gray skies and green forests, to the east the sun shines 300 days a year, and less than 10 inches of rain falls in an average year. Consequently, the shrub steppe (also called high desert) of eastern Washington is a sparsely populated region of little interest to out-of-state visitors but highly valued by waterlogged residents of western Washington. Irrigation waters from the Columbia River have allowed the region to become an agricultural powerhouse, and in the Yakima, Wenatchee, and Chelan valleys, apple orchards produce the bulk of the nation's apple crop. Out in the southeast corner of the state lie the rolling Palouse Hills, where rich soils sustain the most productive wheat fields in the nation. Spokane, close to the Idaho state line, is the region's largest metropolitan area.

2 Visitor Information & Money

VISITOR INFORMATION

For information on Washington, contact the **Washington State Tourism Office,** P.O. Box 42500, Olympia, WA 98504-2500 (© **800/544-1800** or 360/725-5051; www.experience washington.com). For information on Seattle and vicinity, contact the **Seattle–King County Convention and Visitors Bureau,** 520 Pike St., Suite 1300, Seattle, WA 98101 (© **206/ 461-5840;** www.seeseattle.org), which operates a Visitor Information Center inside the Washington State Convention and Trade Center, 800 Convention Place, Galleria Level.

Also keep in mind that most cities and towns in Washington have either a tourist office or a chamber of commerce that can provide you with information. When approaching cities and towns, watch for signs along the highway directing you to these information centers. See the individual chapters for specific addresses. For informative websites, visit **www. travel-in-wa.com** or **www.excite. com/travel/countries/united_states/ washington**, which has links to city sites in Washington. For another list of Washington resources, check out **Washington State Department of Tourism**'s site at **www.tourism.wa. gov.** If you're surfing the Net searching for information on the Seattle area, check out **www.seeseattle.org,** the website for Seattle–King County Convention and Visitors Bureau; or **www.ci.seattle.wa.us/html/visitor**, the city of Seattle's visitor information site.

You can also get travel information covering Washington from the **American Automobile Association (AAA)** if you're a member.

To get information on outdoor recreation in national parks and national forests of Washington, write or call the **National Park Service,** Outdoor Recreation Information Center, which is located at REI's main store in Seattle at 222 Yale Ave. N., Seattle, WA 98109 (© **206/470- 4060;** www.fs.fed.us/r6/mbs). To make reservations to camp at a national forest, call © **877/444-6777.**

For information on Washington state parks, contact **Washington State Parks and Recreation,** 7150 Cleanwater Lane (P.O. Box 42650), Olympia, WA 98504-2650 (© **360/ 902-8844;** www.parks.wa.gov). For state campsite reservations, call **Washington State Parks Reservations** (© **888/CAMPOUT** [888/ 226-7688] or www.parks.wa.gov).

For information on ferries, contact **Washington State Ferries,** 2911 Second Ave., Seattle, WA 98121-1081 (© **800/84-FERRY** or 888/808-7977 within Washington state, or 206/ 464-6400; www.wsdot.wa.gov/ferries).

What Things Cost in Seattle	U.S. $
Taxi from the airport to the city center	32.00
Bus ride between any two downtown points	Free
Local telephone call	.35
Double at the Inn at the Market (expensive)	180.00–310.00
Double at University Inn (moderate)	95.00–139.00
Double at Moore Hotel (inexpensive)	59.00–85.00
Lunch for one at Salty's on Alki (expensive)	25.00
Lunch for one at Elliott's (moderate)	15.00
Lunch for one at Belltown Pub (inexpensive)	8.00–11.00
Dinner for one, without wine, at Campagne (expensive)	45.00
Dinner for one, without wine, at Flying Fish (moderate)	33.00
Dinner for one, without wine, at Noodle Ranch (inexpensive)	11.00
Pint of beer	3.75
Coca-Cola	1.50
Cup of coffee (latte)	2.25
Roll of ASA 100 Kodacolor film, 36 exposures	5.50
Movie ticket	8.75
Theater ticket to Seattle Repertory Theater	15.00–44.00

MONEY

Automated-teller machines (ATMs) are linked to a national network that most likely includes your bank at home. **Cirrus** (© **800/424-7787;** www.mastercard.com) and **PLUS** (© **800/843-7587;** www.visa.com) are the two most popular networks; check the back of your ATM card to see which network your bank belongs to. Use the 800 numbers to locate ATMs in your destination. Expect to pay a $1.50 service charge if you use an ATM that is not affiliated with your own bank. At most banks, you can get a cash advance with your credit card at the ATM if you know your PIN number. Other ATM networks found in Seattle and Washington are Accel, The Exchange, and Interlink. Traveler's checks, although generally accepted at most restaurants, hotels, and shops in neighborhoods frequented by tourists, are not nearly as widely accepted as cash and credit cards. For more information on money matters, see chapter 3, "For International Visitors."

3 When to Go

If you're reading this section, there's probably one question on your mind: When can I visit and not get rained on? The answer, of course, is never. Although the Northwest's infamous rains fall primarily between October and early July, it can rain any month of the year, so be sure to bring rain gear of some sort with you. This is especially important if you plan on visiting the Olympic Peninsula, parts of which receive more than 150 inches of rain each year. In fact, if you visit any part of the coast, expect grayer, wetter weather than in the Seattle area. From the coast to the Cascade Range, moist winds off the Pacific Ocean keep temperatures mild year-round, so you're also likely to need a sweater or light jacket at night even in August.

July and August are the most reliably rainless months of the year, and consequently, are the most popular time of the year to visit Washington. It is during these 2 months that the sun is seen most often and rain is almost unheard of (though not unknown). During these dry summer months Washington families flock to the San Juan Islands to, among other things, watch the region's famous orca whales feeding in the waters off San Juan Island. July and August are also the state's main festival months, and several of the big festivals in the Seattle area can make finding a hotel room on a festival weekend difficult. Seafair is the biggest of these festivals, with Labor Day weekend's Bumbershoot festival packing the city as well.

However, Labor Day weekend aside, September is really one of the best months to visit. Skies are often still cloudless, and the kids are back in school (so the crowds at popular destinations such as the San Juan Islands and Mount Rainier are really bad only on weekends). In the mountains, wildflowers are often still in bloom (though peak bloom in the Cascade Range and Olympic Mountains is July–Aug).

With the coming of the rains, Washingtonians begin spending far more time indoors and consequently, the performing arts in Seattle and other major cities begin their annual seasons. So, if you're keen on catching the Seattle Opera or some of Seattle's fringe theater, you'll need to plan a rainy season visit. This may not be as bad as it sounds considering the fact that hotels in Seattle offer substantial discounts during the dreary winter months. Keep in mind, though, that winters usually include one or two blasts of Arctic air that bring snow and freezing weather to the Seattle area.

Winter also brings the ski season and sometimes record-setting snowfalls such as that of the 1998 and 1999 winter, which dumped 1,140 inches of snow on Mount Baker. While the snow in Washington can be heavy and rains often fall in the mountains in the middle of winter, there are several very popular ski areas in the Cascades, as well as some smaller ski areas in eastern Washington.

Note that the preceding discussion applies to the west side of the Cascades. East of the Cascades, the climate is very different and some regions, sometimes referred to as the high desert, are characterized by temperature extremes and a lack of rain. These areas can be very cold in the winter and can get moderate amounts of snow in the foothill regions. In summer the weather can be blazing hot, though nights are often cool enough to require a sweater or light jacket. The dry lands of eastern Washington are primarily agricultural regions, and it is here that most of the state's wine grapes are grown. In winter, most wineries open to the public cut their hours or close down completely.

Seattle's Average Temperature & Days of Rain

	Jan	Feb	Mar	Apr	May	June	July	Aug	Sept	Oct	Nov	Dec
Temp. (°F)	46	50	53	58	65	69	75	74	69	60	52	47
Temp. (°C)	8	10	11	15	18	21	24	23	21	16	11	8
Rain (days)	19	16	17	14	10	9	5	7	9	14	18	20

WASHINGTON CALENDAR OF EVENTS

For additional information on events in Washington State, check the "Festivals and Events" section on the Washington State Tourism Office website at **www.experiencewashington.com**.

February

Northwest Flower & Garden Show (© **800/229-6311** or 206/789-5333; www.gardenshow.com), Washington State Convention and Trade Center. Massive show for avid gardeners. Early to mid-February.

Red Wine and Chocolate, Yakima Valley. Sample Yakima Valley reds, accompanied by tastings of decadent chocolate desserts. For details, call © **800/258-7270;** www.yakimavalleywine.com. Presidents' Weekend.

April

Skagit Valley Tulip Festival, Skagit Valley. View a rainbow of blooming tulip fields. Call © **877/875-2448** or 360/428-5959, or visit www.tulipfestival.org. Second and third week of April.

Spring Barrel Tasting, Yakima Valley. Straight-from-the-barrel wine tasting of spring-release wines at Yakima Valley wineries. Call © **800/258-7270,** or visit www.yakimavalleywine.com. Last full weekend in April.

Washington State Apple Blossom Festival, Wenatchee. Many different events, including a parade and activities for families. For details, call © **509/662-3616.** End of April to early May.

May

Opening Day of Boating Season, Lake Union and Lake Washington. A parade of boats and much fanfare as Seattle boaters bring out everything from kayaks to yachts. For information, call © **206/325-1000.** First Saturday in May.

Irrigation Festival, Sequim. The oldest continuous festival in Washington, with a grand parade, logging show, dancing, and arts and crafts. Call © **360/683-6197.** Early May.

Viking Fest, Poulsbo. Norwegian heritage on display in picturesque Poulsbo, with a parade and entertainment. For details, call © **360/779-4848.** Mid-May.

Spokane Lilac Festival, Spokane. A 60-year tradition celebrating the blooming of the lilacs. Don't miss the lilac gardens at Manito Park. Call © **509/326-3339.** Mid-May.

Northwest Folklife Festival (© 206/684-7300; www.nwfolklife.org). This is the largest folk festival in the country, with dozens of national and regional folk musicians performing on numerous stages. In addition, there are crafts vendors from all over the Northwest, lots of good food, and dancing too. The festival takes place at the Seattle Center, and admission is by donation. Memorial Day weekend.

June

Mural-in-a-Day, Toppenish. The small town of Toppenish has covered its blank walls with murals, and each June one more is added in a day of intense painting. For details, call © **800/569-3982.** Early June.

International Accordion Celebration, Leavenworth. Accordion competitions and a parade are held against the backdrop of this town, which is reminiscent of a Bavarian village. Call © **509/548-5807.** Mid-June.

July

Fourth of July Fireworks, Vancouver, Washington. Vancouver, which is part of the Portland metropolitan area, hosts the biggest fireworks display west of the Mississippi. Call © **360/693-5481.** July 4.

Sweet Onion Festival, Walla Walla. Onion-themed entertainment and food booths featuring the delicious local onion. For information, call ✆ **509/525-0850.** Mid-July.

Bellevue Art Museum Fair (✆ **425/454-3322**), Bellevue Square shopping mall, Bellevue. This is the largest arts and crafts fair in the Northwest. Late July.

Seafair Indian Days Pow Wow, Seattle. Salmon bake, dancing, singing, and drumming are some of the activities held at the Daybreak Star Cultural Center. Call ✆ **206/285-4425.** Third or fourth weekend in July.

Seafair (✆ **206/728-0123;** www.seafair.com). This is the biggest Seattle event of the year, with daily festivities—parades, hydroplane boat races, an air show with the navy's Blue Angels, a Torchlight Parade, ethnic festivals, sporting events, and open house on naval ships. Events take place all over Seattle. Early July to early August.

Pilchuck Open House, Stanwood. The Pilchuck Glass School, founded by internationally renowned glass artist Dale Chihuly, is located in the foothills of the Cascade Mountains 50 miles (81km) north of Seattle. The school opens its doors once a year for visitors and reservations are necessary (✆ **206/621-8422,** ext. 44). Late July.

August

Omak Stampede/World Famous Suicide Race, Omak. Rodeo and horse race down a cliff face. Call ✆ **800/933-6625.** Mid-August.

Chief Seattle Days (✆ **360/598-3311**), at Suquamish tribal headquarters. Celebration of Northwest Native American culture across Puget Sound from Seattle. Third weekend in August.

Washington State International Kite Festival, Long Beach. World-class kite flying competition. For details, call ✆ **800/451-2542.** Third week in August.

Makah Days, Neah Bay. Canoe races, Native American arts, and salmon bake presented by the Makah tribe in the Northwest corner of the Olympic Peninsula. Call ✆ **360/645-2201.** End of August.

September

Bumbershoot, the Seattle Arts Festival (✆ **206/281-8111;** www.bumbershoot.org). Seattle's second most popular festival derives its peculiar name from a British term for umbrella—an obvious reference to the rainy weather. Lots of rock music and other events pack Seattle's youthful set into Seattle Center and other venues. You'll find plenty of art and crafts on display too. Labor Day weekend.

Ellensburg Rodeo, Ellensburg. The state's biggest rodeo, with a carnival and country and rock bands. Call ✆ **800/637-2444** or 509/962-7831, or visit www.ellensburgsrodeo. com. Labor Day weekend.

Wooden Boat Festival, Port Townsend. Historic boats on display, demonstrations. For details, call ✆ **360/385-3628,** or visit www.woodenboat.org. Early September.

Western Washington Fair, Puyallup. One of the 10 largest fairs in the nation. For more info, call ✆ **253/841-5045,** or visit www.thefair.com. Third week in September.

October

Salmon Days Festival (✆ **425/392-0661**). This festival in Issaquah, 15 miles (24km) east of Seattle, celebrates the annual return of salmon that spawn within the city limits. First full weekend in October.

Kinetic Sculpture Race, Port Townsend. The two rules of this race are (1) the vehicle must be people-powered; and (2) the wackier the contraption the better. Call ℂ **888/365-6978,** or visit www. ptguide.com. First Sunday in October.

Oktoberfest, Leavenworth. A traditional Oktoberfest in this Bavarian town comes complete with kegs of beer shipped in from Munich and German stomp dancing. For details, call ℂ **509/548-5807,** or visit www.leavenworth.org. Second weekend in October.

Cranberrian Fair, Ilwaco, Long Beach Peninsula. Cranberry bog tours, cranberry products, arts and crafts. Call ℂ **800/451-2542.** Mid-October.

November

Thanksgiving in the Wine Country, Yakima Valley. Foods and the wines that complement them are offered for tasting by Yakima-area wineries. Call ℂ **800/258-7270,** or visit www.yakimavalleywine.com. Thanksgiving weekend.

Zoolights, Tacoma. The Point Defiance Zoo is decorated with thousands of sparkling lights, creating colorful fantasy scenes. For more info, call ℂ **253/591-5337.** Due to energy conservation measures, call ahead to be sure the lights will be on when you want to visit. Day after Thanksgiving to December 31.

December

Christmas Lighting, Leavenworth. This Bavarian village was practically made for Christmas, and looks most photogenic when surrounded by snow and decorated with twinkling lights. Sleigh rides, roasted chestnuts, and all the traditional Bavarian trimmings. For details, call ℂ **509/548-5807,** or visit www.leavenworth.org. Early December.

Yule Fest, Poulsbo. Traditional Norwegian customs including the arrival of the Lucia Bride in a boat rowed by Vikings, lighting of the yule log, and the arrival of Father Christmas. Call ℂ **360/779-4848.** Early December.

Tree Lighting and Santa's Visit, Port Townsend. Santa arrives in this historic Victorian town in an unusual conveyance: the state ferry from Whidbey Island. Call ℂ **888/365-6978,** or visit www.ptguide. com. First Saturday night in December.

Seattle Christmas Ships (ℂ **206/623-1445**), various locations. Boats decked out with imaginative Christmas lights parade past various waterfront locations. **Argosy Cruises** (ℂ **800/642-7816** or 206/623-1445; www.argosycruises.com) offers tours; see chapter 4, "Seattle," for more details. Throughout December.

AT&T New Year's at the Needle, Seattle Center. The Space Needle ushers in the new year by bursting into light when midnight strikes. Call ℂ **206/443-2100** for information. December 31.

4 The Active Vacation Planner

The abundance of outdoor recreational activities is one of the reasons people choose to live in Washington. With both mountains and beaches within an hour's drive of the major metropolitan areas, there are numerous choices for the active vacationer.

ACTIVITIES A TO Z

BICYCLING/MOUNTAIN BIKING The San Juan Islands, with

their winding country roads and Puget Sound vistas, are the most popular bicycling locale in the state. Of the four main San Juan Islands (San Juan, Orcas, Lopez, and Shaw), Lopez has the easiest and Orcas the most challenging terrain for bikers. Here you can pedal for as many or as few days as you like, stopping at parks, inns, and quaint villages.

Other popular road biking spots include Bainbridge and Vashon islands, with their easy access to Seattle; the Olympic Peninsula, with its scenic vistas and campgrounds; and the Long Beach Peninsula, with its miles of flat roads. Seattle, Tacoma, Spokane, and Yakima also all have many miles of easy bicycle trails that are either in parks or connect parks. The longest of these are in Seattle and Spokane.

The region's national forests provide miles of logging roads and single-track trails for mountain biking. However, the state's premier mountain-biking destination is the Methow Valley, where miles of cross-country ski trails are opened to bicycles in the summer.

To get a bicycling map of Washington, contact the **Bicycle Hot Line,** Washington State Department of Transportation, at © **360/705-7277.**

If you're interested in participating in an organized bicycle tour, there are a couple of companies you might want to contact. **Backroads,** 801 Cedar St., Berkeley, CA 94710-1800 (© **800/ 462-2848** or 510/527-1555; www. backroads.com), offers road bike trips in the San Juan Islands. Tour prices range from $1,098 to $1,998. **Bicycle Adventures,** P.O. Box 11219, Olympia, WA 98508 (© **800/ 443-6060** or 360/786-0989; www. bicycleadventures.com) offers biking trips in the San Juan Islands and Victoria, B.C., on the Olympic Peninsula, and to the volcanoes of Washington.

Tour prices range from $1,300 to $2,300.

BIRD-WATCHING   With a wide variety of habitats, Washington offers many excellent bird-watching spots. Each winter in January, bald eagles flock to the Skagit River, north of Seattle, to feast on salmon. Birders can observe from shore or on a guided raft trip. Migratory shorebirds make annual stops at Bowerman Basin in the Gray's Harbor Wildlife Refuge outside the town of Hoquiam. One of Washington's best birding excursions is a ride through the San Juan Islands on one of the Washington State Ferries. From these floating observation platforms, birders can spot bald eagles and numerous pelagic birds.

BOARDSAILING   The Columbia River Gorge is one of the most renowned boardsailing spots in the world. Here, high winds and a strong current come together to produce radical sailing conditions. As the winds whip up the waves, skilled sailors rocket across the water and launch themselves skyward to perform aerial acrobatics. On calmer days and in spots where the wind isn't blowing so hard, there are also opportunities for novices to learn the basics. Summer is the best sailing season, and the town of Hood River, Oregon, is the center of the boarding scene with plenty of windsurfing schools and rental companies. Boardsailing is also popular on Lake Union in Seattle and Vancouver Lake in Vancouver, Washington.

CAMPING   Public and private campgrounds abound all across Washington, with those in Mount Rainier National Park and Olympic National Park being the most popular. North Cascades National Park has campgrounds as well. At Olympic and North Cascades national parks, camping is on a first-come, first-served basis, while at two campgrounds within Mount Rainier National Park, reservations are taken. To get information on outdoor recreation in Washington's national parks and forests, contact the **National Park Service,** Outdoor Recreation Information Center, which is located at REI's main store in Seattle at 222 Yale Ave. N., Seattle, WA 98109 (© **206/470-4060;** www.nps.gov/ccso/oric.htm). The Forest Service's regional Web page (**www.fs.fed.us/r6**) is another good source of information.

Washington also has more than 80 state parks with campgrounds. Moran State Park on Orcas Island and Deception Pass State Park have two of the most enjoyable campgrounds. For information on Washington state parks, contact **Washington State Parks and Recreation,** 7150 Cleanwater Lane (P.O. Box 42650), Olympia, WA 98504-2650 (© **360/902-8844;** www.parks.wa.gov).

For state campsite reservations, call **Washington State Parks Reservations** (© **888/CAMPOUT** [888/226-7688]; www.parks.wa.gov). To make campsite reservations at national forest campgrounds, call the **National Recreation Reservation Service/Reserve America** (© **877/444-6777**). For reservations at Mount Rainier, the only national park in Washington that offers campsite reservations, contact the National Park Reservation Service (© **800/365-CAMP** or 301/722-1257; http://reservations.nps.gov).

If you're interested in renting an RV for your trip around the state, contact **Western Motorcoach Rentals,** 19303 Hwy. 99, Lynnwood, WA 98036 (© **800/800-1181** or 425/775-1181; www.westernrv.com).

CANOEING/KAYAKING Whitewater kayakers in Washington head for such rivers as the Wenatchee around Leavenworth, the Methow near Winthrop, the Skagit and Skykomish rivers north of Seattle, and the White Salmon River near Trout Lake. On the Olympic Peninsula, the Queets, Hoh, and Elwha rivers are the main kayaking rivers. One of the most popular canoeing lakes in Washington is Lake Ozette in Olympic National Park.

FISHING For information on freshwater fishing in Washington, contact the **Department of Wildlife,** Natural Resources Building, 1111 Washington St. SE, Olympia, WA 98501 (© **360/902-2200;** www.wa.gov/wdfw/); mailing address: 600 Capitol Way N., Olympia, WA 98501-1091.

GOLFING Although the rainy weather in western Washington puts a bit of a damper on golfing, the mild temperatures mean that it's possible to play year-round. The state has only a handful of resorts with golf courses, but most larger cities have public courses.

HIKING & BACKPACKING Washington has an abundance of hiking trails, including the Pacific Crest Trail, which runs along the spine of the Cascades from Canada to the California line (and onward all the way to Mexico). Elsewhere in Washington, you'll find hikes along the beach, up rain-forest valleys, and through alpine meadows in Olympic National Park; through forests and the state's most beautiful meadows in Mount Rainier National Park (hikes from Sunrise and Paradise are the most spectacular); and through the state's most rugged scenery in North Cascades National Park. The Alpine Lakes region outside Leavenworth is breathtakingly beautiful, but so popular that advance-reservation permits are required. Another popular hike is to the top of Mount St. Helens. Lesser known are the hiking trails on Mount Adams in southern Washington. In the Columbia Gorge, the hike up Dog Mountain is strenuous but rewarding. For general information on hiking in the Northwest and for information on the Northwest Forest Pass, which is required at most national forest trailheads in Washington, contact **Nature of the Northwest,** 800 NE Oregon St., Suite 177, Portland, OR 97232 (© **503/872-2750;** www.naturenw.org).

If you'd like to hike the wild country of Washington state with a knowledgeable guide, you've got a couple of good options. The **Olympic Park Institute,** 111 Barnes Point Rd., Port Angeles, WA 98363 (© **360/928-3720;** www.yni.org/opi), offers a variety of hiking and backpacking trips, as does the **North Cascades Institute,** 810 State Rte. 20, Sedro-Woolley, WA 98284 (© **360/856-5700,** ext. 209; www.ncascades.org).

MOUNTAINEERING While Mount Rainier, Mount Adams, Mount Baker, Glacier Peak, Mount St. Helens, and Mount Olympus are the most popular mountaineering peaks in the state, there are countless other peaks throughout the Cascades, North Cascades, and Olympic Mountains that attract climbers. The state's peaks offer challenging mountain climbing and rock climbing for both novices and experts.

If you're interested in learning some mountain-climbing skills or want to hone your existing skills, you can do so on Mount Rainier and other Cascade peaks. **Rainier Mountaineering Inc.,** P.O. Box Q, Ashford, WA 98308 (© **360/569-2227;** www.rmiguides.com), which operates out of Paradise inside Mount Rainier National Park, offers 1-day classes for $154, 3-day summit climbs for $728, and a 5-day mountaineering seminar for $1,094.

SEA KAYAKING Sea kayaks differ from river kayaks in that they are much longer, more stable, and able to carry gear as well as a paddler or two. There are few places in the country that offer better sea kayaking than the waters of Puget Sound and around the San Juan Islands, and therefore this sport is especially popular in the Seattle area. The protected waters of Puget Sound offer numerous spots for a paddle of anywhere from a few hours to a few days. There's even a water trail that links camping spots throughout the Sound called the **Cascadia Marine Trail.** For more information about this trail, contact the Washington Water Trails Association (© **206/545-9161;** www.wwta.org).

The San Juan Islands are by far the most popular sea-kayaking spot in the region, and several tiny islands, accessible only by boat, are designated state campsites. In the Seattle area, Lake Union and Lake Washington are both popular kayaking spots. Willapa Bay, on the Washington coast, is another popular paddling spot.

If you'd like to explore Puget Sound or Seattle's Lake Union in a sea kayak, contact the **Northwest Outdoor Center,** 2100 Westlake Ave. N., Seattle, WA 98109 (© **800/683-0637** or 206/281-9694; www.nwoc.com). This center rents kayaks and also offers various classes and guided trips. Day trips are $70 to $75, 3-day trips are about $295, and 5-day classes are $625.

On San Juan Island, **San Juan Safaris** (© **800/450-6858** or 360/378-1323; www.sanjuansafaris.com) specializes in two- to four-hour kayak treks, which cost from $39 to $49. **San Juan Kayak Expeditions** (© **360/378-4436;** www.sanjuankayak.com), and **Shearwater Adventures,** on Orcas Island (© **360/376-4699;** www.shearwaterkayaks.com)offer multiday kayak trips. **Sea Quest Expeditions/Zoetic Research,** P.O. Box 2424F, Friday Harbor, WA 98250 (© **360/378-5767;** www.sea-quest-kayak.com), is a nonprofit organization that sponsors educational sea-kayaking trips through the San

Juans. Three- to four-day trips range in price from around $329 to $425.

SKIING & SNOWBOARDING

Washington has about half a dozen major ski areas and about the same number of lesser ski areas. The major ski areas are all located in the Cascade Range. These include Mount Baker, a snowboarding mecca near Bellingham and the Canadian border; Mission Ridge, which is located near Wenatchee and is known for its powder snow; Stevens Pass, which is near the Bavarian-theme town of Leavenworth and is the best Seattle area ski area; the Summit at Snoqualmie, which is located less than an hour from Seattle; Crystal Mountain near the northeast corner of Mount Rainier National Park; and White Pass, which is southeast of Mount Rainier National Park. For information on all of these ski areas, see chapter 9, "The Cascades." Smaller and more remote ski areas include Mount Spokane and 49 Degrees North, both north of Spokane; and Ski Bluewood, near Walla Walla (see chapter 10, "Eastern Washington," for information on these three ski areas). Tiny locals-only ski areas with only a handful of runs include Hurricane Ridge, in Olympic National Park (see chapter 7, "The Olympic Peninsula"); Loup Loup, near Winthrop (see chapter 9, "The Cascades"); Echo Valley, near Lake Chelan (see chapter 9, "The Cascades"); and Sitzmark, in central Washington near the Canadian border. Heli-skiing is also available in the Methow Valley (see chapter 9, "The Cascades").

Many downhill ski areas also offer groomed cross-country ski trails. The most popular cross-country areas in Washington include the Methow Valley (one of the largest trail systems in the country), Leavenworth, the Summit at Snoqualmie, White Pass, Stevens Pass, and near Mount St. Helens and Mount Adams.

WHALE-WATCHING

Orca whales, commonly called killer whales, are a symbol of the Northwest and are often seen in Puget Sound and around the San Juan Islands, especially during the summer. Dozens of companies offer whale-watching trips from the San Juans. You can also spot orcas from San Juan Island's Lime Kiln State Park. For information on orca-watching opportunities, see chapter 5, "The San Juan Islands, Whidbey Island & the Emerald Coast." Out on the Washington coast, migrating gray whales can be seen March through May. In the town of Westport, there are both viewing areas and companies operating whale-watching excursions. For more information, see chapter 8, "Southwest Washington."

WHITE-WATER RAFTING

Plenty of rain and lots of mountains combine to produce dozens of good white-water rafting rivers, depending on the time of year and water levels. In the Washington Cascades, some of the popular rafting rivers include the Wenatchee outside Leavenworth, the Methow near Winthrop, the Skagit and Skykomish rivers north of Seattle, and the White Salmon River near Trout Lake. On the Olympic Peninsula, the Queets, Hoh, and Elwha rivers are the main rafting rivers. See the respective chapters for information on rafting companies operating on these rivers. Rates generally range from about $50 for a half day to $140 for a full day of rafting.

Throughout the state there are dozens of rafting companies operating on as many rivers. Many of these companies offer trips on several different rivers throughout most of the year. Among these companies are Alpine Adventures Wild & Scenic River Tours (© **800/RAFT-FUN;** www.alpineadventures.com), DownStream River Runners (© **800/ 234-4644** or 360/805-9899; www. riverpeople.com), North Cascades

River Expeditions (© 800/634-8433; www.riverexpeditions.com), Osprey Rafting Company (© 800/743-6269; www.shoottherapids.com), River Riders (© 800/448-RAFT; www.riverrider.com), and Wildwater River Tours (© 800/522-WILD; www.wildwater-river.com).

5 Educational & Volunteer Vacations

On the Olympic Peninsula, the **Olympic Park Institute,** 111 Barnes Point Rd., Port Angeles, WA 98363 (© **360/928-3720;** www.yni.org/opi), offers a wide array of summer field seminars ranging from painting classes to bird-watching trips to multiday backpacking trips.

The North Cascades Institute, 810 State Rte. 20, Sedro-Woolley, WA 98284 (© **360/856-5700,** ext. 209; www.ncascades.org), is a nonprofit organization that offers field seminars focusing on natural and cultural history in the North Cascades.

Sound Experience, 2310 Washington St., Port Townsend, WA 98368 (© **360/379-0438;** www.soundexp. org), offers day-long and multiday sailing trips on the *Adventuress,* a two-masted schooner. Although programs are geared primarily toward youths (12–18 yr. old), there are also sailings for adults and families. Excursions emphasize hands-on learning and environmental education.

The Nature Conservancy is a nonprofit organization dedicated to the global preservation of natural diversity, and to this end it operates educational field trips and work parties to its own nature preserves and those of other agencies. For information about field trips in Washington, contact **The Nature Conservancy,** 217 Pine St., Suite 1100, Seattle, WA 98101 (© **206/343-4344;** www.tnc.org).

If you enjoy the wilderness and want to get more involved in preserving it, consider a Sierra Club Service Trip. These trips are for the purpose of building, restoring, and maintaining hiking trails in wilderness areas. It's a lot of work, but it's also a lot of fun. For more information on Service Trips, contact **Sierra Club Outing Department,** 85 Second St., Second Floor, San Francisco, CA 94105 (© **415/977-5500;** www.sierraclub.org). Alternatively, you can call your local chapter of the Sierra Club or Washington's Cascade Chapter (© **206/523-2147;** www.cascade chapter.org).

Earth Watch Institute, 3 Clock Tower Place, Suite 100 (Box 75) Maynard, MA 01754 (© **800/776-0188** or 978/461-0081; www.earthwatch. org), sends volunteers on scientific research projects. Contact them for a catalog listing trips and costs. Projects have included studies of orca whales and chimpanzee communication.

Seniors who want to learn something from their trip to Washington or who simply prefer the company of like-minded seniors should look into programs by **Elderhostel,** 11 Avenue de Lafayette, Boston, MA 02110-1746 (© **877/426-8056;** www. elderhostel.org). To participate in an Elderhostel program, either you or your spouse must be 55 years old or older. In addition to 1-week educational programs, Elderhostel offers short getaways with interesting themes.

6 Insurance

Most travelers' needs are met by their existing insurance policies (your homeowners' insurance should cover lost or stolen luggage, for example), but if you have any concerns, contact your insurance company before you leave home and ask them to detail what they'll cover. Some credit- and charge-card companies may insure you against travel accidents if you buy plane, train, or bus tickets with their cards. If you do decide you need additional specific travel coverage, most travel agents can sell you any number of insurance packages tailored to fit your specific needs. But check your existing policies first, and don't buy more than you need.

Among the companies offering specialized travel insurance policies are **Access America** (© 800/284-8300; www.accessamerica.com), **Travel Guard** (© 877/216-4885; www.travel-guard.com), and **Travelex Insurance Services** (© 888/457-4602; www.travelex-insurance.com).

Trip-cancellation insurance may be a good idea if you've paid a large portion of your vacation expenses up front, say, by purchasing a package tour. (But don't buy it from your tour operator—talk about putting all of your eggs in one basket! Buy it from an outside vendor instead.) Coverage should cost approximately 6% to 8% of the total value of your vacation, so a $3,000 trip could be insured for around $210.

Your homeowner's or renter's insurance should cover stolen luggage. The airlines are responsible for losses up to $2,500 on domestic flights if they lose your luggage; if you plan to carry anything more valuable than that, keep it in your carry-on bag.

7 Tips for Travelers with Special Needs

FOR TRAVELERS WITH DISABILITIES When making airline reservations, always mention your disability. Airline policies differ regarding wheelchairs and Seeing Eye dogs. Almost all hotels and motels in the Northwest, aside from bed-and-breakfast inns and older or historic lodges, offer accommodations accessible for travelers with disabilities. However, when making reservations be sure to ask.

The public transit systems found in most Northwest cities either have regular vehicles that are accessible for riders with disabilities or offer special transportation services for people with disabilities.

If you plan to visit any of Washington's national parks, you can avail yourself of the **Golden Access Passport.** This lifetime pass is issued free to any U.S. citizen or permanent resident who has been medically certified as disabled or blind. The pass permits free entry into national parks and monuments.

To get a copy of the booklet titled *Washington Accessible Outdoor Recreation Guide* call the Washington Department of Natural Resources (© 360/902-1234).

A World of Options, a book of resources for travelers with disabilities, covers everything from biking trips to scuba outfitters. It costs $35 ($31.50 for members) and is available from **Mobility International USA,** P.O. Box 10767, Eugene, OR, 97440 (© 541/343-1284 voice and TDD; www.miusa.org). Annual membership for Mobility International is $35, which includes its biannual newsletter, *Over the Rainbow.*

Many of the major car-rental companies now offer hand-controlled cars for drivers with disabilities. Avis can provide such a vehicle at any of its airport locations in the United States with 72-hour advance notice; Hertz requires between 24 and 48 hours of advance reservation at most of its locations. **Wheelchair Getaways** (© 800/642-2042; www.wheelchair-getaways.com) rents specialized vans with wheelchair lifts and other features for travelers with disabilities in about 40 cities across the United States. In the Pacific Northwest Wheelchair Getaways is located near Seattle in the suburb of Woodinville (© **888/376-1500** or 425/788-3718).

In addition, both **Amtrak** (© **800/USA-RAIL;** www.amtrak.com) and **Greyhound** (© **800/752-4841;** www.greyhound.com) offer special services for travelers with disabilities. Amtrak also offers special fares. Call at least a week in advance of your trip for details.

Travelers with disabilities might also want to consider joining a tour that caters specifically to them. **Accessible Journeys** (© **800/TINGLES** or 610/521-0339; www.accessible journeys.com), for slow walkers and wheelchair travelers, offers excursions to the Northwest. **Wilderness Inquiry** (© **800/728-0719** or 612/676-9400; www.wildernessinquiry. org) offers a kayaking trip to the San Juan Islands for persons of all abilities.

FOR GAY & LESBIAN TRAVELERS   Seattle is one of the most gay-friendly cities in the country, with a large gay and lesbian community that's centered around the Capitol Hill neighborhood. In Capitol Hill you'll find numerous bars, nightclubs, stores, and bed-and-breakfast inns catering to the gay community. Broadway Avenue, Capitol Hill's main drag, is also the site of the annual Gay Pride March, held each year in late June.

The *Seattle Gay News* (© **206/324-4297;** www.sgn.org) is the community's newspaper, available at bookstores and gay bars and nightclubs. **Beyond the Closet,** 518 E. Pike St. (© **206/322-4609**), and **Bailey Coy Books,** 414 Broadway Ave. E. (© **206/323-8842**), are the gay community's two main bookstores and are good sources of information on what's going on within the community. The **Lesbian Resource Center,** 2214 S. Jackson St. (© **206/322-3965**), is a community resource center providing housing and job information, therapy, and business referrals.

If you want help planning your trip, the **International Gay & Lesbian Travel Association (IGLTA;** © **800/448-8550** or 954/776-2626; www. iglta.org) can link you up with the appropriate gay-friendly service organization or tour specialist. With around 1,200 members, it offers quarterly newsletters, marketing mailings, and a membership directory that's updated quarterly. Members are kept informed of gay and gay-friendly hoteliers, tour operators, and airline and cruise-line representatives. **GayWired Travel Services (www.gaywired.com)** is another great trip-planning resource; click on "Travel Services."

Out and About (© **800/929-2268** or 415/486-2591; www.outandabout. com) offers a monthly newsletter packed with good information on the global gay and lesbian scene. Its website features links to gay and lesbian tour operators and other gay-themed travel links, plus extensive online travel information to subscribers only. *Out and About's* guidebooks are available at most major bookstores and through www.adlbooks.com.

FOR SENIORS   Don't be shy about asking for discounts, but always carry some kind of identification, such as a driver's license, that shows your date of birth, especially if you've kept your youthful glow. In Seattle, most attractions, some theaters and concert halls, tour companies, and the Washington State Ferries all offer senior discounts. These can add up to substantial savings, but you have to remember to ask.

Discounts abound for seniors, beginning with the 10%-off-your-airfare deal that most airlines offer to anyone age 62 or older. In addition, a number of airlines have clubs you can join and coupon books you can buy that may or may not increase your savings beyond that base 10% discount, depending on how often you travel, where you're going, and how long you're going to stay. Always ask an airline whether it has a club for seniors or sells coupon books, either of which often qualifies "mature" travelers for discounted tickets.

Both **Amtrak** (© **800/USA-RAIL;** www.amtrak.com) and **Greyhound** (© **800/752-4841;** www.greyhound. com) offer discounts to persons over 62.

Many hotels offer senior discounts. **Choice Hotels** (Clarion Hotels, Quality Inns, Comfort Inns, and Sleep Inns), for example, give 20% off their published rates to anyone over 60 depending on availability, provided you book your room through their nationwide toll-free reservations numbers (not directly with the hotels or through a travel agent).

If you plan on visiting either Mount Rainier National Park or Olympic National Park while in the Seattle area, you can save on park admissions by getting a **Golden Age Passport,** which is available for $10 to U.S. citizens and permanent residents age 62 and older. This federal government pass allows lifetime entrance privileges. You can apply in person for this passport at a national park, national forest, or other location where it's honored, as long as you can show reasonable proof of age.

If you aren't a member of **AARP,** 601 E St. NW, Washington, DC 20049 (© **800/424-3410;** www.aarp. org), do yourself a favor and join. This association provides discounts for many lodgings, car rentals, airfares, and attractions throughout Seattle, although you can sometimes get a similar discount simply by showing your ID.

Grand Circle Travel is another of the literally hundreds of travel agencies specializing in vacations for seniors (347 Congress St., Suite 3A, Boston, MA 02210; © **800/221-2610** or 617/350-7500; www.gct. com). *But beware:* Many of them are of the tour-bus variety, with free trips thrown in for those who organize groups of 20 or more. Seniors seeking more independent travel should probably consult a regular travel agent. **SAGA International Holidays,** 222 Berkeley St., Boston, MA 02116 (© **800/343-0273;** www.sagaholidays. com), offers inclusive tours and cruises for those 50 and older. SAGA also sponsors the more substantial "Road Scholar Tours," which are fun-loving but with an educational bent, and is an agent for Smithsonian Institution tours.

If you'd like to do a bit of studying on vacation in the company of like-minded seniors, consider looking into **Elderhostel,** 11 Avenue de Lafayette, Boston, MA 02110-1746 (© **877/426-8056;** www.elderhostel.org).

The Mature Traveler, a monthly newsletter on senior travel, is a valuable resource. It is available by subscription ($32 a year) from GEM Publishing Group by calling © **800/460-6676.** GEM also publishes *The Book of Deals,* a collection of more than 1,000 senior discounts on airlines, lodging, tours, and attractions around the country; it comes free with the newsletter subscription, but is available by itself for $9.95.

Specialty books on the market for seniors include *Unbelievably Good Deals and Great Adventures That You Absolutely Can't Get Unless You're Over 50* (Contemporary Books). Also check out your newsstand for the quarterly magazine *Travel 50 & Beyond,* or subscribe online at www.travel50andbeyond. com for $9.95.

FOR FAMILIES Families traveling in Washington should be sure to take note of family admission fees at many museums and other attractions. These admission prices are often less than what it would cost for individual tickets for the whole family. At hotels and

Fly for Less: Tips for Getting the Best Airfares

If you happen to be flying from another city on the West Coast or some-where else in the West, check first with **Frontier Airlines**, **Shuttle by United**, **Alaska Airlines**, **Horizon Airlines**, or **Southwest**. These airlines often have the best fares between western cities.

Check your newspaper for advertised **sales** or call the airlines directly and ask if any promotional rates or special fares are available. You'll almost never see a sale during the peak summer vacation months of July and August, or during the Thanksgiving or Christmas seasons; but in periods of low-volume travel, you should pay no more than $400 for a cross-country flight.

Note, however, that the lowest-priced fares are often nonrefundable, require advance purchase of 1 to 3 weeks and a certain length of stay, and carry penalties for changing dates of travel. So, when you're quoted a fare, make sure you know exactly what the restrictions are before you commit. If you already hold a ticket when a sale breaks, it may even pay to exchange your ticket, which usually incurs a $50 to $75 charge.

If your schedule is flexible, ask if you can secure a cheaper fare by staying an extra day, staying over Saturday night, or flying midweek. (Many airlines won't volunteer this information, so be aggressive and ask the reservations agent lots of questions.)

Consolidators, also known as bucket shops, are a good place to find low fares. Consolidators buy seats in bulk from the airlines and then sell them back to the public at prices below even the airlines' discounted rates. Their small boxed ads usually run in the Sunday travel section of newspapers at the bottom of the page. Before you pay, however, ask for a confirmation number from the consolidator and then call the air-line itself to confirm your seat. Be prepared to book your ticket with a different consolidator—there are many to choose from—if the airline

motels, children usually stay free if they share their parents' room and no extra bed is required, and sometimes they also get to eat for free in the hotel dining room. Be sure to ask.

An excellent resource for family travel, including information about hotel deals for families, is *Family Travel Times,* a bimonthly newsletter published by FTT Marketing. To sub-scribe or get information, contact *Family Travel Times* (© 888/ 822-4388 or 212/477-5524; www. familytraveltimes.com). For $39 per year, you get six issues of the news-letter and discounts on other publica-tions and back issues.

Family Travel Forum (© 888/ 383-6786; www.familytravelforum. com) is another helpful source of information and travel discounts for families planning trips. You can receive a newsletter in the mail and/or access information online to read tips on traveling with children, staff-writ-ten travel articles, and members' first-hand accounts of experiences in various destinations. Each issue of the newsletter focuses on a specific theme, from traveling with teens to intergen-erational travel. A comprehensive annual membership is $48, or you can subscribe simply to the online service for $28 annually or $3.95 monthly.

can't confirm your reservation. Also be aware that bucket shop tickets are usually nonrefundable or rigged with stiff cancellation penalties, often as high as 50% to 75% of the ticket price. And when an airline runs a special deal, you won't always do better with a consolidator.

Council Travel (℗ **800/226-8624;** www.counciltravel.com) and **STA Travel** (℗ **800/781-4040;** www.statravel.com) cater especially to young travelers, but their bargain basement prices are available to people of all ages. **Travel Bargains** (℗ **800/AIR-FARE;** www.1800airfare.com) was formerly owned by TWA but now offers the deepest discounts on many other airlines, with last-minute purchases available. For discount and last-minute bookings, contact **McCord Consumer Direct** (Air for Less; ℗ **800/FLY-FACTS** or 800/FLY-ASAP; www.better1.com), which can often get you tickets at significantly less than full fare. Other reliable consolidators include **1/800-FLY-CHEAP** (www.flycheap.com); **Cheap Tickets** (℗ **800/377-1000;** www.cheaptickets.com); and **TFI Tours International** (℗ **800/745-8000** or 212/736-1140), which serves as a clearinghouse for unused seats. There are also "rebators," such as **Travel Avenue** (℗ **800/ 333-3335** or 312/876-1116; www.travelavenue.com), which rebate part of their commissions to you.

It's also easy to search the **Internet** for cheap fares—though it's still best to compare your findings with the research of a dedicated travel agent, if you're lucky enough to have one, especially when you're booking more than just a flight. Among the better-respected virtual travel agents are **Travelocity (www.travelocity.com), Expedia (www.expedia. com), Yahoo! Travel (http://travel.yahoo.com),** and **Orbitz (www.orbitz. com). Smarter Living (www.smarterliving.com)** is a great source for discount Internet deals. And don't forget to check the airlines' own websites for special Internet bargains.

8 Getting There

BY PLANE
THE MAJOR AIRLINES

The **Seattle-Tacoma International Airport** (℗ **800/544-1965** or 206/ 431-4444; www.seatac.org/seatac) is served by about 30 airlines. The major carriers include:

Air Canada (℗ 800/247-2262; www.aircanada.ca)

Alaska Airlines (℗ 800/426- 0333; www.alaskaair.com)

American (℗ 800/433-7300; www.im.aa.com)

America West (℗ 800/235-9292; www.americawest.com)

Continental (℗ 800/525-0280; www.continental.com)

Delta (℗ 800/221-1212; www. delta.com)

Frontier (℗ 800/432-1359; www.frontierairlines.com)

Horizon Air (℗ 800/547-9308; www.horizonair.com)

Northwest/KLM (℗ 800/225- 2525; www.nwa.com)

Southwest (℗ 800/435-9792; www.southwest.com)

> ### ⌐Tips What You Can Carry On—And What You Can't
>
> The Federal Aviation Administration (FAA) has devised new restrictions on carry-on baggage, not only to expedite the screening process, but to prevent potential weapons from passing through airport security. Passengers are now limited to bringing just one carry-on bag and one personal item onto the aircraft (previous regulations allowed two carry-on bags and one personal item, like a briefcase or a purse). For more information, go to the FAA's website, www.faa.gov.apa/pr/index.cfm. The agency has released a new list of items passengers are not allowed to carry onto an aircraft:
>
> **Not permitted:** Knives and box cutters, corkscrews, straight razors, metal scissors, metal nail files, golf clubs, baseball bats, pool cues, hockey sticks, ski poles, ice picks, knitting needles.
>
> **Permitted:** Nail clippers, tweezers, eyelash curlers, safety razors (including disposable razors), syringes (with documented proof of medical need), walking canes and umbrellas (must be inspected first).
>
> The airline you fly may have **additional restrictions** on items you can and cannot carry on board. Call ahead to avoid problems.

United and Shuttle by United (© 800/241-6522; www.united.com)

US Airways (© 800/428-4322; www.usairways.com)

For information on flights to the United States from other countries see "Getting to the United States," in chapter 3.

Seaplane service between Seattle and the San Juan Islands and Victoria, British Columbia, is offered by **Kenmore Air** (© **800/543-9595** or 425/486-1257; www.kenmoreair.com), which has its Seattle terminals at the south end of Lake Union and at the north end of Lake Washington.

There is also helicopter service to Seattle's Boeing Field from Victoria and Vancouver, British Columbia, on **Helijet Airways** (© **800/665-4354;** www.helijet.com). The flights take about 35 minutes from Victoria and about 90 minutes from Vancouver (depending on the connection, as you must connect in Victoria for the flight to Seattle). Ballpark round-trip

airfares are about C$369 (Canadian dollars; US$232) between Victoria and Seattle and about C$687 (US$433) between Vancouver and Seattle.

NEW AIR TRAVEL SECURITY MEASURES

In the wake of the terrorist attacks of September 11, 2001, the airline industry began implementing sweeping security measures in airports. Expect a lengthy check-in process and extensive delays. Although regulations vary from airline to airline, you can expedite the process by taking the following steps:

- **Arrive early.** Arrive at the airport at least 2 hours before your scheduled flight.
- **Try not to drive your car to the airport.** Parking and curbside access to the terminal may be limited. Call ahead and check.
- **Don't count on curbside check-in.** Some airlines and airports have stopped curbside check-in altogether, whereas others offer it on a limited basis. For up-to-date

information on specific regulations and implementations, check with the individual airline.

- **Bring plenty of documentation.** A government-issued photo ID (federal, state, or local) is now required. You may need to show this at various checkpoints. With an E-ticket, you may be required to have with you printed confirmation of purchase, and perhaps even the credit card with which you bought your ticket. This varies from airline to airline, so call ahead to make sure you have the proper documentation. And be sure that your ID is **up-to-date:** An expired driver's license, for example, may keep you from boarding the plane altogether.

- **Know what you can carry on— and what you can't.** Travelers in the United States are now limited to one carry-on bag, plus one personal bag (such as a purse or a briefcase). The FAA has also issued a list of newly restricted carry-on items; see the box "What You Can Carry On—And What You Can't," above.

- **Prepare to be searched.** Expect spot-checks. Electronic items, such as a laptop or cellphone, should be readied for additional screening. Limit the metal items you wear on your person.

- **It's no joke.** When a check-in agent asks if someone other than you packed your bag, don't decide that this is the time to be funny. The agents will not hesitate to call an alarm.

- **No ticket, no gate access.** Only ticketed passengers will be allowed beyond the screener checkpoints, except for those people with specific medical or parental needs.

BY CAR

The distance from Los Angeles to Seattle is 1,190 miles (1,916km); from Salt Lake City, 835 miles (1,344km); from Spokane, in the eastern part of Washington, 285 miles (459km); and from Vancouver, British Columbia, 110 miles (177km).

If you're driving up from California, I-5 runs up through the length of the state and continues to the Canadian border; it will take you through both Portland, Oregon, and Seattle. If you're coming from the east, I-90 runs from Montana and Idaho into Washington, eventually hitting Seattle.

One of the most important benefits of belonging to the **American Automobile Association** (② **800/AAA-HELP**) is that they supply members with emergency road service. In Seattle, AAA is located at 330 Sixth Ave. N. (② **206/448-5353**).

BY TRAIN

There is **Amtrak** (② **800/872-7245;** www.amtrak.com) service from Vancouver, B.C., to Seattle and from Portland and as far south as Eugene, Oregon, on the *Cascades* (a high-speed, European-style Talgo train). The train takes about 4 hours from Vancouver to Seattle and 3½ to 4 hours from Portland to Seattle. One-way fares from Vancouver to Seattle are usually between $23 and $34, and fares between Portland and Seattle are usually between $23 and $36. Booking earlier will get you a less expensive ticket. There is also Amtrak service to Seattle from San Diego, Los Angeles, San Francisco, and Portland on the *Coast Starlight,* and from Spokane and points east on the *Empire Builder.* Amtrak also operates a bus between Vancouver and Seattle.

Like the airlines, Amtrak offers several discounted fares; although they're not all based on advance purchase, you have more discount options by reserving early. The discount fares can be used only on certain days and hours of the day; be sure to find out exactly what restrictions apply. Tickets for children ages 2 to 15 cost half the

Washington Driving Distances

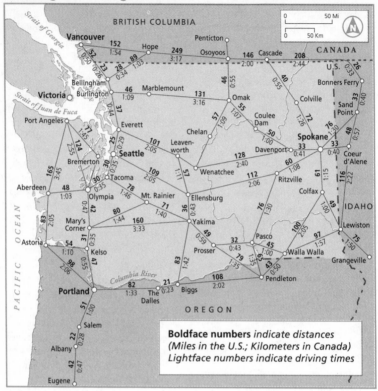

Boldface numbers *indicate distances (Miles in the U.S.; Kilometers in Canada)* Lightface numbers *indicate driving times*

price of a regular coach fare when the children are accompanied by a fare-paying adult. Amtrak's website features a bargain fares service, Rail SALE, which allows you to purchase tickets for one-way designated coach seats at great discounts. This program is only available on **www.amtrak.com** when you charge your tickets by credit card.

Also inquire about money-saving packages that include hotel accommodations, car rentals, tours, and so on with your train fare. Call ✆ **800/321-8684** for details.

BY FERRY

If you are traveling between Victoria, British Columbia, and Seattle, there are several options available from

Victoria Clipper, Pier 69, 2701 Alaskan Way (✆ **800/888-2535** from outside Seattle and Victoria, 206/448-5000 or 250/382-8100 in Victoria; www.victoriaclipper.com). Throughout the year, a ferry taking either 2 or 3 hours makes the trip ($79–$125 round-trip for adults). The lower fare is for advance-purchase tickets. Some scheduled trips also stop in the San Juan Islands.

Bellingham, north of Seattle, is the port for Alaska ferries and cruise ships.

PACKAGE TOURS

Gray Line of Seattle (✆ **800/426-7532** or 206/624-5077; www.graylineofseattle.com) offers 3- to 7-day bus and cruise tours that include Seattle, Mount Rainier, Vancouver, and Victoria. Prices range from about $250 for a 3-day trip to $785 for a 7-day trip.

If you prefer traveling on your own, but would like to have a custom itinerary planned for your trip to Washington or the Northwest, consider consulting **Pacific Northwest Journeys** (© 800/935-9730 or 206/935-9730; www.pnwjourneys.com). They can tailor a trip that suits your personal traveling style.

9 Getting Around

BY CAR

A car is by far the best way to see the state of Washington. There just isn't any other way to get to the more remote natural spectacles or to fully appreciate such regions as the Olympic Peninsula.

All the major car-rental agencies have offices in Seattle at or near Seattle-Tacoma International Airport. Companies with a desk and cars inside the terminal include **Alamo** (© 800/327-9633 or 206/433-0182; www.go alamo.com), **Avis** (© 800/831-2847 or 206/448-1700; www.avis.com), **Budget** (© 800/527-0700 or 206/682-2277; https://www.rent.drive budget. com), **Hertz** (© 800/654-3131 or 206/248-1300; www.hertz. com), and **National** (© 800/227-7368 or 206/433-5500; www.national car.com). Companies with desks inside the terminal but cars parked off the airport premises include **Dollar** (© 800/800-4000 or 206/433-6768; www.dollar.com), **Enterprise** (© 800/736-8222 or 206/382-1051; www.enterprise.com), and **Thrifty** (© 800/367-2277 or 206/625-1133; www.thrifty.com).

Gasoline   Washington is a big state, so keep your gas tank as full as possible when traveling in the mountains or on the sparsely populated east side of the Cascades.

Maps   Maps are available at most highway tourist information centers, at the tourist information offices listed earlier in this chapter, and at gas stations throughout the region. For a free map of Washington call the **Washington State Tourism Office** (© 800/544-1800). Members of the AAA can get detailed road maps of the Northwest by calling their local AAA office.

Driving Rules   A right turn on red is permitted after first coming to a complete stop. You may also turn left on a red light if you're in the far-left lane of a one-way street and are turning into another one-way street. Seat belts are required, as are car seats for children.

Breakdowns/Assistance   In the event of a breakdown, stay with your car, lift the hood, turn on your emergency flashers, and wait for a police patrol car. If you're a member of the American Automobile Association and your car breaks down, call © **800/AAA-HELP** (800/222-4357) for 24-hour emergency road service.

BY PLANE

Washington is a large state, and if you're trying to see every corner of it in a short time, you may want to consider flying. There are airports with regularly scheduled commercial flights at Bellingham, Whidbey Island, Port Angeles, Yakima, and Spokane. Fares vary but at press time, a flight between Bellingham and Spokane (with a stop in Seattle) was quoted at $182 with a 7-day advance purchase, and $227 with no advance purchase. Airlines operating short hops between many of these towns and cities include **Alaska Airlines** (© 800/426-0333; www.alaskaair.com), **Horizon Air** (© 800/547-9308; www.horizonair.com), **Southwest** (© 800/435-9792; www.southwest.com), and **Shuttle by United** (© 800/SHUTTLE; www.united.com).

Seaplane service between Seattle and the San Juan Islands and Victoria, British Columbia, is offered by **Kenmore Air** (© 800/543-9595 or 425/486-1257; www.kenmoreair.com), which has its Seattle terminals at Lake Union and at the north end of Lake Washington. **West Isle Air** (© 800/874-4434; www.westisleair.com) flies to the San Juans from Bellingham and Anacortes, and also to Seattle's Boeing Field.

BY TRAIN

There is **Amtrak** service from Seattle to Spokane and points east, and service between Vancouver, B.C., Seattle, Portland, and points south, but otherwise the train isn't a viable way of getting around Washington state. If you do decide to take the train, booking early will save you money.

BY FERRY

Washington State Ferries (© 800/84-FERRY or 888/808-7977 within Washington state, or 206/464-6400; www.wsdot.wa.gov/ferries) is the most extensive ferry system in the United States. Car ferries travel between downtown Seattle and both Bainbridge Island and Bremerton (on the Kitsap Peninsula) from Pier 52, Colman dock. A passenger-only ferry sails for Bremerton from this dock as well. A passenger-only ferry to Vashon Island uses the adjacent Pier 50. Car ferries also sail between Fauntleroy (in West Seattle) and both Vashon Island and the Kitsap Peninsula at Southworth; between Tahlequah at the south end of Vashon Island and Point Defiance in Tacoma; between Edmonds and Kingston (on the Kitsap Peninsula); between Mukilteo and Whidbey Island; between Whidbey Island at Keystone and Port Townsend; and between Anacortes and the San Juan Islands and Sidney, British Columbia (on Vancouver Island near Victoria).

See specific destinations in chapters 4, 5, 6, and 7 for fare information.

There are also a number of smaller county or private ferries. The most important of these are the **Black Ball Transport** (© 360/457-4491, or 250/386-2202 in Victoria; www.northolympic.com/coho) and **Victoria Express** (© 800/633-1589 in Washington, 360/452-8088 or 250/361-9144 in Victoria; www.victoriaexpress.com) ferries that operate between Port Angeles and Victoria, British Columbia. Victoria Express runs only from Memorial Day weekend to the end of September—three times daily in the peak of summer, with trips dropping to twice daily in the shoulder seasons of spring and fall. The Victoria Clipper runs four times daily in the peak of summer, tapering off to once a day October through March. There's also passenger-ferry service between Seattle and San Juan Island and Orcas Island (summer only), and between Seattle and Victoria, British Columbia, on the **Victoria Clipper ferries** (© 800/888-2535 from outside Seattle and Victoria, 206/448-5000 or 250/382-8100 in Victoria; www.victoriaclipper.com).

BY RV

An economical way to tour the Northwest is with a recreational vehicle. If you're considering renting an RV, look under "Recreational Vehicles—Rent and Lease" in the Yellow Pages of the local phone book. They can be rented for a weekend, a week, or longer. One company, relatively convenient to Sea-Tac Airport, is **Western Motorcoach Rentals,** 19303 Hwy. 99, Lynnwood, WA 98036 (© 800/800-1181 or 425/775-1181; www.westernrv.com). If you're going to be traveling in the peak season of summer, it's important to make reservations for your RV at least 3 months ahead of time.

10 Cruises

While Washington is not a big cruise-ship destination per se, there are several companies offering Alaska cruises that start in Washington and spend a little time cruising through the waters of Puget Sound and the San Juan Islands. There are also several smaller cruise lines that offer specialty cruises on small ships. Note that rates listed below are per person based on double occupancy.

In the big-ship category, there are the 7-day, 6-night Alaska cruises offered by **Norwegian Cruise Lines** (② 800/327-7030; www.ncl.com). These cruises leave from Seattle and cost about $1,818 to $2,778. Cruises on smaller ships are offered by several other companies. **Lindblad Expeditions** (② 800/397-3348; www.expeditions.com) offers a 7-day cruise from Seattle through the San Juan Islands to Victoria, with a bus trip connecting to another leg of the tour that goes up the Columbia River from Portland, Oregon. Rates range from $2,330 to $3,690. **Cruise West** (② 800/888-9378 or 206/441-8687; www.cruisewest.com) offers an 8-day cruise from Seattle to British Columbia and the San Juan Islands. Fares range from about $1,745 to $3,145 per person. **Catalyst Cruises** (② 800/670-7678; www.cruise-nw.com) offers 8-day San Juan Island cruises on a 62-foot yacht. The fare is $2,000 per person based on double occupancy. **Smithsonian Study Tours** (② 202/357-4700; www.smithsonianstudytours.org) includes the San Juan Islands in their exploratory cruise along the Northwest coast between Seattle and Glacier Bay, Alaska. Rates range from $4,260 to $7,900.

There are also a number of cruises up the Columbia River. Most of these play up the Lewis and Clark history and offer plenty of land excursions. If you prefer cruising aboard a small vessel, consider a trip with **Cruise West,** Fourth and Battery Building, Suite 700, Seattle (② 800/426-7702 or 206/441-8687; www.cruisewest.com), which offers an 8-day cruise from Portland on the Columbia and Snake rivers. Fares range from $795 to $3,895 per person. Similar trips, though with naturalists and historians on board, are offered by **Lindblad Expeditions** (② 800/762-0003 or 212/765-7740; www.expeditions.com), which charges from $2,390 to $3,750 per person based on double occupancy.

Paddle-wheel steamboats played a crucial role in the settling of the Northwest, shuttling people and goods down the Columbia River before railroads came to the region. Today, the *Queen of the West,* a paddle-wheel cruise ship operated by the **American West Steamboat Company,** 2101 Fourth Ave., Suite 1150, Seattle, WA 98121 (② 800/434-1232; www.columbiarivercruise.com), is cruising the Columbia offering a luxury never before known in Columbia River paddle wheelers. Fares for the 7-night cruise range from $1,155 to $4,636 per person. Shorter cruises are also available.

 ## *FAST FACTS:* **Washington**

AAA If you're a member of the American Automobile Association and your car breaks down, call ② **800/AAA-HELP** for 24-hour emergency road service.

American Express In Seattle, the Amex office is in the Plaza 600 building at 600 Stewart St. (② **206/441-8622**). The office is open Monday through

Friday from 9am to 5pm. Call this office for information on American Express services in other outlying towns. For card member services, phone ⓒ **800/528-4800.**

ATM Networks The most commonly used ATM networks in Washington are PLUS, Cirrus, The Exchange, Visa, and MasterCard networks.

Car Rentals See "Getting Around," earlier in this chapter.

Climate See "When to Go," earlier in this chapter.

Driving Rules See "Getting Around," earlier in this chapter.

Drugstores Rite-Aid and Walgreens (ⓒ **800/WALGREENS** for locations) are two large pharmacy chains found in the Northwest.

Embassies & Consulates See "Fast Facts: For the International Traveler," in chapter 3.

Emergencies Call ⓒ **911** for fire, police, and ambulance.

Information See "Visitor Information," earlier in this chapter, and individual city chapters for local information offices.

Liquor Laws The legal minimum drinking age in Washington state is 21. Aside from on-premise sales of cocktails in bars and restaurants, hard liquor can only be purchased in liquor stores. Beer and wine are available in convenience stores and grocery stores. Brewpubs tend to sell only beer and wine, but some also have licenses to sell hard liquor.

Maps See "Getting Around," earlier in this chapter.

Pets Many hotels and motels in the Northwest accept small, well-behaved pets. However, a small fee is often charged to allow them into guest rooms. Many places, in particular bed-and-breakfast inns, don't allow pets at all. On the other hand, many bed-and-breakfasts have their own pets, so if you have a dog or cat allergy, be sure to mention it when making a bed-and-breakfast reservation. Pets are usually restricted in national parks for their own safety, so call each park's ranger station to check before setting out.

Police To reach the police, dial ⓒ **911.**

Taxes The state of Washington makes up for its lack of an income tax with its heavy sales tax, and counties add on their own as well. In Seattle you'll pay 8.8%. Hotel-room tax in the Seattle metro area ranges from 11.6% to 15.8%. On rental cars, you'll pay not only an 18.5% car-rental tax, but also, if you rent at the airport, an additional 10% airport concession fee, for a whopping total of 28.5%! You eliminate 10% of this by renting your car somewhere other than the airport.

Time Zone Washington state is on Pacific Standard Time (PST) and observes daylight saving time from the first Sunday in April to the last Sunday in October, making it consistently 3 hours behind the U.S. East Coast.

Weather Currently, Seattle has no phone number for weather information. Check the *Seattle Times* or *Seattle Post-Intelligencer* newspapers for forecasts. If you want to know how to pack before you arrive, go to **www.cnn.com/weather** or **www.weather.com.**

3

For International Visitors

Although American trends have spread across Europe and other parts of the world to the extent that America may seem like familiar territory before your arrival, there are still many peculiarities and uniquely American situations that any foreign visitor will encounter.

1 Preparing for Your Trip

ENTRY REQUIREMENTS

Check at any U.S. embassy or consulate for current information and requirements. You can also obtain a visa application and other information online at the **U.S. State Department**'s website, at **www.travel.state.gov**.

VISAS   The U.S. State Department has a **Visa Waiver Program** that allows citizens of certain countries to enter the United States without a visa for stays of up to 90 days. At press time, this visa waiver program applied to citizens of Andorra, Argentina, Australia, Austria, Belgium, Brunei, Denmark, Finland, France, Germany, Iceland, Ireland, Italy, Japan, Liechtenstein, Luxembourg, Monaco, the Netherlands, New Zealand, Norway, Portugal, San Marino, Singapore, Slovenia, Spain, Sweden, Switzerland, the United Kingdom, and Uruguay. Citizens of these countries need only a valid passport and a round-trip air or cruise ticket in their possession upon arrival. Further information is available from any U.S. embassy or consulate.

Canadian citizens may enter the United States without visas; they need only proof of residence.

Citizens of all other countries must have: (1) a valid passport that expires at least 6 months later than the scheduled end of their visit to the United States, and (2) a tourist visa, which may be obtained from any U.S. consulate.

To obtain a visa, you must submit a completed application form (either in person or by mail) with two 1½-inch-square photos and a US$45 fee, and must demonstrate binding ties to a residence abroad. Usually you can obtain a visa at once or within 24 hours, but it may take longer during the summer rush June through August. If you cannot go in person, contact the nearest U.S. embassy or consulate for directions on applying by mail. Your travel agent or airline office may also be able to provide you with visa applications and instructions. The U.S. consulate or embassy that issues your visa will determine if you will be issued a multiple- or single-entry visa and any restrictions regarding the length of your stay.

British subjects can obtain up-to-date passport and visa information by calling the **U.S. Embassy Visa Information Line** (© 09061/500-590) or the **London Passport Office** (© 0870/521-0410 for recorded information), or by checking the website www.usembassy.org.uk.

Inquiries about visa cases and the application process can be made by calling © 202/663-1225.

MEDICAL REQUIREMENTS   Unless you're arriving from an area known to be suffering from an epidemic (particularly cholera or yellow fever), inoculations or vaccinations are not required for entry into the United States. If you have a disease that requires treatment with narcotics or syringe-administered medications, carry a valid, signed prescription from your physician to allay any suspicions that you may be smuggling narcotics.

Upon entering the United States, foreign nationals are required to declare any dangerous contagious diseases they carry, which includes infection with HIV, the AIDS virus. Anyone who has such a disease is excluded from entry as a tourist. However, you may be able to apply for a waiver if you are attending a conference or have another compelling nontourism reason for your visit; call the **Immigration and Naturalization Service (INS)** at ℂ **800/375-5283** to inquire. Doubtless many HIV-positive visitors come in without declaring their condition, their way of dealing with an archaic law that was originally intended to halt the spread of tuberculosis and the like. The U.S. Immigration and Naturalization Service receives so many questions about the confusing and frequently changing policy regarding HIV-positive visitors that the public affairs office has issued a fact sheet on the subject: **"HIV Infection: Inadmissibility and Waiver Policies."** (Call the number above and ask for it.) Or for even more up-to-the-minute information, contact the Centers for Disease Control's **National Center for HIV** (ℂ **800/HIV-0440;** www.hivatis.org) or the **Gay Men's Health Crisis** (ℂ **800/AIDS-NYC;** www.gmhc.org).

DRIVER'S LICENSES   Foreign driver's licenses are mostly recognized in the United States, although you may want to get an international driver's license if your home license is not written in English.

CUSTOMS

WHAT YOU CAN BRING IN   Every visitor over 21 years of age may bring in, free of duty, the following: (1) 1 liter of wine or hard liquor; (2) 200 cigarettes, 150 cigars (but not from Cuba), or 3 pounds of smoking tobacco; and (3) $100 worth of gifts. These exemptions are offered to travelers who spend at least 72 hours in the United States and who have not claimed them within the preceding 6 months.

Foreign tourists may bring in or take out up to $10,000 in U.S. or foreign currency with no formalities; larger sums must be declared to U.S. Customs upon entering or leaving, which includes filing form CM 4790.

Declare any medicines you are carrying and be prepared to present a letter or prescription from your doctor demonstrating you need the drugs; you may bring in no more than you would normally use in the duration of your visit.

For many more details on what you can and cannot bring, check the informative U.S. Customs website at **www.customs.ustreas.gov** and click "Traveler Information." You can also call the **U.S. Customs** office at ℂ **202/354-1000.** Ask for a copy of "Visiting the United States," which offers travelers more information about what U.S. Customs allows you to bring in. You can also call the **U.S. Department of Agriculture's Animal and Plant Health Inspection Service** (ℂ **301/734-8645**) and ask for a copy of "Traveler's Tips," which provides detailed information on bringing food, plant, and animal products into the United States. You can also find this information on the USDA's website at **www.aphis.usda.gov/travel.html**.

WHAT YOU CAN BRING HOME   Rules governing what you can bring back duty-free vary from country to country, and are subject to change, but they're generally posted on the Web. **Canadians** should check the booklet *I Declare,* which you can download or order from Revenue Canada (℡ **800/461-9999** in Canada, or 613/993-0534; www.ccra-adrc.gc.ca). An even clearer explanation is found in the publication *Bon Voyage, But . . . ,* found at **www.dfait-maeci.gc.ca** (click on "Travel" and then click on "Bon Voyage"), or by ordering the publication from the 800-number listed above. Both booklets are free. **British** citizens should contact HM Customs & Excise (℡ **020/7202-4227;** www.hmce.gov.uk). **Australians** can contact the Australian Customs Service (℡ **300/363-263** within Australia, or 61-2/6275-6666 from outside Australia; www.customs.gov.au). **New Zealand** citizens should contact New Zealand Customs (℡ **09/359-6655;** www.customs.govt.nz/).

INSURANCE

Although it's not required of travelers, health insurance is highly recommended. Unlike many European countries, the United States does not usually offer free or low-cost medical care to its citizens or visitors. Doctors and hospitals are expensive, and in most cases will require advance payment or proof of coverage before they render their services. Travel insurance policies can cover everything from the loss or theft of your baggage and trip cancellation to the costs of an accident, repatriation, or death. See "Insurance" on p. 32 (in chapter 2, "Planning Your Trip to Washington") for more information. Packages such as **Europ Assistance** in Europe are sold by automobile clubs and travel agencies at attractive rates. **Worldwide Assistance Services, Inc.** (℡ **800/821-2828** or 703/204-1897; www.worldwideassistance.com) is the agent for Europ Assistance in the United States. **Specialty Risk International** (℡ **800/335-0611;** www.specialtyrisk.com) is another insurance company that offers packages to travelers from countries around the world.

Though lack of health insurance may prevent you from being admitted to a hospital in nonemergencies, don't worry about being left on a street corner to die: The American way is to fix you now and bill the living daylights out of you later.

MONEY

CURRENCY   The U.S. monetary system has a decimal base: one American **dollar** ($1) = 100 **cents** (100¢).

The most common **bills** (all ugly, all green) are the $1 (colloquially, a "buck"), $5, $10, and $20 denominations. There are also $2 bills (seldom encountered), $50 bills, and $100 bills (the last two are usually not welcome as payment for small purchases). Note that redesigned bills were introduced in the last few years, but the old-style bills are still legal tender.

There are six denominations of **coins:** 1¢ (1 cent, or a penny); 5¢ (5 cents, or a nickel); 10¢ (10 cents, or a dime); 25¢ (25 cents, or a quarter); 50¢ (50 cents, or a half dollar); and the rare $1 piece (the older, large silver dollar and the newer, small Susan B. Anthony coin). In 2000, a new gold-toned $1 piece was introduced.

Note that U.S. coins are not stamped with their numeric value.

CURRENCY EXCHANGE   You'll find currency exchange services in major airports with international service. Seattle-Tacoma International Airport provides Thomas Cook services (℡ **206/248-0401**). Elsewhere, such services are quite difficult to locate.

To exchange money in Seattle, go to **American Express,** 600 Stewart St. (℡ **206/441-8622**), or **Thomas Cook,** at Westlake Center (℡ **206/682-4525**).

TRAVELER'S CHECKS   Though traveler's checks are widely accepted, *make sure that they're denominated in U.S. dollars,* as foreign-currency checks are often difficult to exchange. The three traveler's checks that are most widely recognized—and least likely to be denied—are **Visa, American Express,** and **Thomas Cook/MasterCard.** Be sure to record the numbers of the checks, and keep that information separately in case they get lost or stolen. Most businesses are pretty good about taking traveler's checks, but you're better off cashing them in at a bank (in small amounts, of course) and paying in cash. *Remember:* You'll need identification, such as a driver's license or passport, to change a traveler's check.

CREDIT CARDS   Credit cards are the most widely used form of payment in the United States: **Visa** (BarclayCard in Britain), **MasterCard** (Eurocard in Europe, Access in Britain, and Chargex in Canada), **American Express, Diners Club, Discover,** and **Carte Blanche;** you'll also find that some vendors may accept international cards like **enRoute, Eurocard,** and **JCB,** but not as universally as Amex, MasterCard, or Visa. There are, however, a handful of stores and restaurants that do not take credit cards, so be sure to ask in advance. And be aware that often businesses require a minimum purchase price, usually around $10 or $15, to use a credit card.

ATMs   You'll find automated-teller machines (ATMs) throughout Washington, but the majority are concentrated in urban areas. Most ATMs will allow you to draw U.S. currency against your bank account back home. Check with your bank before leaving home, and ask if you'll need to reprogram your PIN number in the United States. Expect to be charged up to $3 per transaction, however, if you're not using your own bank's ATM.

SAFETY
GENERAL SAFETY SUGGESTIONS   While tourist areas are generally safe, U.S. urban areas tend to be less safe than those in Europe or Japan. You should always stay alert. This is particularly true of large U.S. cities. Ask your hotel front desk staff or the city's or area's tourist office if you're in doubt about which neighborhoods are safe.

Avoid deserted areas, especially at night, and don't go into public parks at night unless there's a concert or similar occasion that will attract a crowd.

Avoid carrying valuables with you on the street, and don't display expensive cameras or electronic equipment. If you are using a map, consult it inconspicuously—or better yet, try to study it before you leave your room. Hold onto your pocketbook, and place your billfold in an inside pocket. In theaters, restaurants, and other public places, keep your possessions in sight.

Remember also that hotels are open to the public, and in a large hotel, security may not be able to screen everyone entering. Always lock your room door—don't assume that once inside your hotel you are automatically safe and no longer need to be aware of your surroundings.

DRIVING   Ask your rental agency about personal safety or request a brochure of traveler safety tips when you pick up your car. Get written directions or a map with the route marked in red from the agency to show you how to get to your destination. If possible, arrive and depart during daylight hours.

Recently, more and more crime has involved cars and drivers. If you drive off a highway into a doubtful-looking neighborhood, leave the area as quickly as possible. If you have an accident, even on the highway, stay in your car with the doors locked until you assess the situation or until the police arrive. If you are bumped from behind on the street or are involved in a minor accident with no injuries, and the situation appears to be suspicious, motion to the other driver to follow you to the nearest police precinct, gas station, or open store. *Never* get out of your car in such situations.

Park in well-lit, well-traveled areas if possible. Always keep your car doors locked, whether the vehicle is attended or unattended. Look around you before you get out of your car and never leave any packages or valuables in sight.

If someone attempts to rob you or steal your car, do *not* try to resist the thief/carjacker—report the incident to the police department immediately by calling © **911.**

Also, make sure that you have enough gasoline in your tank to reach your intended destination, so that you're not forced to look for a service station in an unfamiliar and possibly unsafe neighborhood, especially at night.

2 Getting to the United States
BY PLANE

For an extensive listing of airlines that fly into Seattle, see "Getting There," in chapter 2.

A number of U.S. airlines offer service from Europe to the United States. If they do not have direct flights from Europe to Seattle, they can book you straight through on a connecting flight. You can make reservations by calling the following numbers in Great Britain: **American Airlines** (© 0345/789-789; www.im.aa.com), **Continental** (© 0800/776-464; www.continental.com), **Delta** (© 0800/414-767; www.delta.com), **Northwest/KLM** (© 08705/074-074; www.nwa.com), or **United** (© 0800/888-555; www.united.com).

International carriers that fly from Europe to Los Angeles and San Francisco include **Aer Lingus** (© 01/886-8888 in Ireland; www.aerlingus.com) and **British Airways** (© 0845/773-3377; www.britishairways.com), which also flies direct to Seattle from London.

From New Zealand and Australia, there are flights to Los Angeles on **Qantas** (© 13 13 13; www.qantas.com.au) and **Air New Zealand** (© 0800/737-000 in Auckland; www.airnewzealand.co.nz). From there, you can continue on to Seattle on a regional airline such as **Alaska Airlines** (© 800/426-0333; www.alaskaair.com) or **Southwest** (© 800/435-9792; www.iflyswa.com).

From Toronto, there are flights to Seattle on **Air Canada** (© 888/247-2262; www.aircanada.ca), **American Airlines** (© 800/433-7300; www.aa.com), **Northwest** (© 800/225-2525; www.nwa.com), and **United** (© 800/241-6522; www.united.com).

From Vancouver, B.C., there are flights to Seattle on **Air Canada, United,** and **Alaska Airlines** (© 800/426-0333; www.alaskaair.com).

Operated by the European Travel Network, **www.discount-tickets.com** is a great online source for regular and discounted airfares. ETN operates another useful site at **www.etn.nl.** Students should also try **Campus Travel** (© 0870/240-1010 in England, or 0131/668-3303 in Scotland; www.usitcampus.co.uk).

For more money-saving airline advice, see the "Getting There" section of chapter 2.

BY TRAIN

There is **Amtrak** (© **800/872-7245;** www.amtrak.com) service from Vancouver, B.C., to Seattle, a trip that takes about 4 hours. One-way fares from Vancouver to Seattle are usually between $23 and $34, and fares between Portland

and Seattle are usually between $23 and $36. Booking earlier will get you a less expensive ticket.

Like the airlines, Amtrak offers several discounted fares; although they're not all based on advance purchase, you have more discount options by reserving early.

BY FERRY

If you are traveling between Victoria, British Columbia, and Seattle, there are several options available from **Victoria Clipper,** Pier 69, 2701 Alaskan Way (℡ **800/888-2535** from outside Seattle and Victoria, 206/448-5000, or 250/382-8100 in Victoria; www.victoriaclipper.com). Throughout the year, a ferry taking either 2 or 3 hours makes the trip ($79–$125 round-trip for adults).

3 Getting Around the United States

For specific information on traveling to and around Seattle and Washington, see "Getting There" and "Getting Around," in chapter 2, and "Getting Around," in chapter 4, "Seattle."

BY PLANE

Some large U.S. airlines (including American, Continental, Northwest, United, and Delta) offer travelers on their transatlantic or transpacific flights special discount tickets allowing travel between U.S. destinations at minimum rates. (Two such programs are American's **Visit USA** and Delta's **Discover America.**) These tickets are not on sale in the United States and must be purchased before you leave home. This is the best, easiest, and fastest way to see the United States at low cost. Obtain information well in advance from your travel agent or airline, since the conditions attached to these discount tickets can be changed without advance notice.

If you are arriving by air, allow lots of time to make connections between international and domestic flights—an average of 2 to 3 hours at least.

BY TRAIN

International visitors, except Canadians, can buy a **USA Railpass,** good for 15 or 30 days of unlimited travel on **Amtrak** (℡ **800/USA-RAIL;** www.amtrak.com). The pass is available through many foreign travel agents. Prices in 2001 for a nationwide 15-day pass were $295 off-peak, $440 peak; a nationwide 30-day pass cost $385 off-peak, $550 peak. (With a foreign passport, you can also buy passes at some Amtrak offices in the United States, including locations in San Francisco, Los Angeles, Chicago, New York, Boston, and Washington, D.C.) Reservations should be made for each part of your trip as early as possible.

If your travel plans include visiting both the United States and Canada, you need to purchase a **North American Railpass.** Also available through Amtrak is an **Airail** pass, a joint venture of United Airlines and Amtrak that's available as part of **Amtrak Vacations packages** (℡ **800/321-8684**).

BY BUS

Although bus travel is often the most economical form of public transit for short hops between U.S. cities, it can also be slow and uncomfortable—certainly not an option for everyone (particularly when Amtrak, which is far more luxurious, offers similar rates). **Greyhound/Trailways** (℡ **800/231-2222**), the sole nationwide bus line, offers an **International Ameripass** for unlimited travel for specified amounts of time, from 4 days for $135, to 60 days at $449. You can buy International Ameripasses online, at **www.greyhound.com**, or at participating international travel agents in your country. In this country, you can purchase the domestic versions, simply the **Ameripass,** but they cost a little more; for example, the 60-day pass is $509 (prices good in 2001). You can buy the regular Ameripass online or at Greyhound terminals.

 FAST FACTS: **For the International Traveler**

Automobile Organizations Auto clubs will supply maps, suggested routes, guidebooks, accident and bail-bond insurance, and emergency road service. The **American Automobile Association (AAA)** is the major auto club in the United States. If you belong to an auto club in your home country, inquire about AAA reciprocity before you leave. You may be able to join AAA even if you're not a member of a reciprocal club; to inquire, call AAA (© **800/222-4357;** www.aaa.com). AAA has a nationwide emergency road service telephone number (© **800/AAA-HELP**).

Business Hours The following are general open hours; specific establishments may vary. **Banks:** Monday through Friday from 9am to 5pm (some are also open on Sat mornings); there's usually 24-hour access to ATMs at most banks and other outlets. **Offices:** generally open weekdays from 9am to 5pm. **Stores:** typically open Monday through Saturday between 9 and 10am and close between 5 and 6pm. Some department stores have later hours and are open on Sunday from 11am to 5 or 6pm, and stores in malls are usually open until 9pm. **Bars:** stay open until 1 or 2am; dance clubs often stay open much later.

Climate See "When to Go," in chapter 2.

Currency & Currency Exchange See section 1 of this chapter.

Drinking Laws The legal age for purchase and consumption of alcoholic beverages is 21; proof of age is required and often requested at bars, nightclubs, and restaurants, so it's always a good idea to bring ID when you go out.

Do not carry open containers of alcohol in your car or any public area that isn't zoned for alcohol consumption. The police can fine you on the spot. And nothing will ruin your trip faster than getting a citation for DUI ("driving under the influence"), so don't even think about driving while intoxicated.

See also the "Liquor Laws" entry in "Fast Facts," at the end of chapter 2.

Electricity Like Canada, the United States uses 110 to 120 volts AC (60 cycles), compared to 220 to 240 volts AC (50 cycles) in most of Europe, Australia, and New Zealand. If your small appliances use 220 to 240 volts, you'll need a 110-volt transformer and a plug adapter with two flat parallel pins to operate them here. Downward converters that change 220 to 240 volts to 110 to 120 volts are difficult to find in the United States, so bring one with you.

Embassies & Consulates All embassies are located in Washington, D.C. If your country isn't listed below, call for directory information in Washington, D.C. (© **202/555-1212**) for the number of your embassy.

The embassy of **Australia** is at 1601 Massachusetts Ave. NW, Washington, DC 20036 (© **202/797-3000;** www.austemb.org). The nearest consulate is in **San Francisco** at 625 Market St., Suite 200, San Francisco, CA 94105-3304 (© **415/536-1970**). There are also consulates in Atlanta, New York, Honolulu, and Los Angeles.

The embassy of **Canada** is at 501 Pennsylvania Ave. NW, Washington, DC 20001 (© **202/682-1740;** www.canadianembassy.org). The regional consulate is at Plaza 600 Building, Sixth Avenue and Stewart Street, Seattle, WA 98101-1286 (© **206/443-1777**). Other Canadian consulates are in Buffalo (New York), Detroit, New York, and Los Angeles.

The embassy of **Ireland** is at 2234 Massachusetts Ave. NW, Washington, DC 20008 (© **202/462-3939;** www.irelandemb.org). The nearest consulate is at 44 Montgomery St., Suite 3830, San Francisco, CA 94104 (© **415/392-4214**). Other Irish consulates are in Boston, Chicago, and New York.

The embassy of **New Zealand** is at 37 Observatory Circle NW, Washington, DC 20008 (© **202/328-4800;** www.nzemb.org). There is a consulate in Los Angeles at 12400 Wilshire Blvd., Suite 1150, Los Angeles, CA 90025 (© **310/207-1605**). Other New Zealand consulates are in Atlanta, Boston, Chicago, Hawaii, Houston, New York, Salt Lake City, San Diego, and San Francisco. There is also an honorary consulate in Seattle.

The embassy of the **United Kingdom** is at 3100 Massachusetts Ave. NW, Washington, DC 20008 (© **202/462-1340;** www.britain-info.org). There is a consulate in Seattle at 900 Fourth Ave., Suite 3001, Seattle, WA 98164 (© **206/622-9255**). Other British consulates are in Atlanta, Boston, Chicago, Dallas, Denver, Houston, Los Angeles, Miami, New York, and San Francisco.

Emergencies Call © **911** to report a fire, call the police, or get an ambulance. This is a toll-free call (no coins are required at a public telephone).

Gasoline (Petrol) Petrol is known as gasoline (or simply "gas") in the United States, and petrol stations are known as both gas stations and service stations. Gasoline costs much less here than it does in Europe (about $1.65 per gal. at press time); and taxes are already included in the printed price. One U.S. gallon equals 3.8 liters or .85 Imperial gallons.

Holidays Banks, government offices, post offices, and many stores, restaurants, and museums are closed on the following legal national holidays: January 1 (New Year's Day), the third Monday in January (Martin Luther King Day), the third Monday in February (Presidents' Day, Washington's Birthday), the last Monday in May (Memorial Day), July 4 (Independence Day), the first Monday in September (Labor Day), the second Monday in October (Columbus Day), November 11 (Veterans' Day/Armistice Day), the fourth Thursday in November (Thanksgiving Day), and December 25 (Christmas).

Legal Aid If you are pulled over for a minor infraction (for example, of the highway code, such as speeding), never attempt to pay the fine directly to a police officer; this could be construed as attempted bribery, a much more serious crime. Pay fines by mail, or directly into the hands of the clerk of the court. If accused of a more serious offense, say and do nothing before consulting a lawyer. Here the burden is on the state to prove a person's guilt beyond a reasonable doubt, and everyone has the right to remain silent, whether he or she is suspected of a crime or actually arrested. Once arrested, a person can make one telephone call to a party of his or her choice. Call your embassy or consulate.

Mail Generally found at intersections, mailboxes are blue with a red-and-white stripe and carry the inscription U.S. MAIL. If your mail is addressed to a U.S. destination, don't forget to add the five-digit postal code (or ZIP code) after the two-letter abbreviation of the state to which the mail is addressed.

At press time, domestic postage rates were 22¢ for a postcard and 34¢ for a letter. For international mail, a first-class letter of up to 1 ounce costs 80¢ (60¢ to Canada and Mexico); a first-class postcard costs 70¢ (50¢ to Canada and Mexico); and a preprinted postal aerogramme costs 70¢.

Safety See section 1 of this chapter.

Taxes The United States does not have a value-added tax (VAT) or other indirect tax at a national level. Every state, and each county and city in it, is allowed to levy its own local tax on purchases and services (including hotel and restaurant bills, airline tickets, and so on). Taxes are already included in the price of certain services, such as public transportation, cab fares, telephone calls, and gasoline.

In Seattle, the sales tax rate is 8.8%; throughout the rest of the state, expect to pay a similar amount. Also, you'll pay 28.5% in taxes and concession fees when you rent a car at Seattle-Tacoma Airport. You'll save 11% to 23% by renting somewhere other than the airport. Hotel room taxes range from around 11.5% to 15.8%. Travelers on a budget should keep both car-rental and hotel-room taxes in mind when planning a trip.

Telephone & Fax The telephone system in the United States is run by private corporations, so rates can vary widely. Generally, hotel surcharges on long-distance and local calls are astronomical, so you're usually better off using a **public pay telephone,** which you'll find clearly marked in most public buildings and private establishments as well as on the street. Convenience grocery stores and gas stations always have them. Many convenience groceries and packaging services sell **prepaid calling cards** in denominations up to $50, though these aren't always the least expensive way to call home. Many public phones at airports now accept American Express, MasterCard, and Visa credit cards. **Local calls** made from public pay phones in most locales cost either 25¢ or 35¢. Pay phones do not accept pennies, and few will take anything larger than a quarter.

Most long-distance and international calls can be dialed directly from any phone. **For calls within the United States and to Canada,** dial 1 followed by the area code and the seven-digit number. **For other international calls,** dial 011 followed by the country code, city code, and the telephone number of the person you are calling. Some country and city codes are as follows: **Australia** 61, Melbourne 3, Sydney 2; **Ireland** 353, Dublin 1; **New Zealand** 64, Auckland 9, Wellington 4; **United Kingdom** 44, Belfast 232, Birmingham 21, Glasgow 41, London 71 or 81.

If you're **calling the United States from another country,** the country code is 01.

Calls to area codes **800, 888,** and **877** are toll-free. However, calls to numbers in area codes **700** and **900** (chat lines, bulletin boards, "dating" services, and so on) can be very expensive—usually 95¢ to $3 or more per minute, and they sometimes have minimum charges that can run as high as $15 or more.

For **reversed-charge or collect calls,** and for person-to-person calls, dial 0 (zero, not the letter O) followed by the area code and number you want; an operator will then come on the line, and you should specify that you are calling collect, or person-to-person, or both. If your operator-assisted call is international, ask for the overseas operator.

For **local directory assistance** (information), dial ⓒ **411;** for **long-distance information,** dial 1, then the appropriate area code and ⓒ **555-1212.**

Most hotels have **fax machines** available for guest use (be sure to ask about the charge to use it). A less expensive way to send and receive faxes may be at stores such as **Kinko's** (see "Internet Access," in "Fast Facts" section of chapter 4) or **Mail Boxes Etc.,** a national chain of packing service shops (look in the Yellow Pages directory under "Packing Services").

There are two kinds of telephone directories in the United States. The so-called **White Pages** list private households and business subscribers in alphabetical order. The inside front cover lists emergency numbers. The first few pages will tell you how to make long-distance and international calls, complete with country codes and area codes. Government numbers are usually printed on blue paper within the White Pages. Printed on yellow paper, the so-called **Yellow Pages** list all local services, businesses, industries, and houses of worship according to activity with an index at the front or back.

Time The United States is divided into six time zones. From east to west, they are Eastern Standard Time (EST), Central Standard Time (CST), Mountain Standard Time (MST), Pacific Standard Time (PST), Alaska Standard Time (AST), and Hawaii Standard Time (HST). Washington is on Pacific Standard Time.

Tipping Tipping is so ingrained in the American way of life that the annual income tax of tip-earning service personnel is based on how much they *should* have received in light of their employers' gross revenues.

In hotels, tip **bellhops** about $1 per bag, and tip the **maid** at least $1 to $2 per day (more if you've left a disaster area to clean up, or if you're traveling with kids and/or pets). Tip the **doorman** or **concierge** only if he or she has provided you with some specific service (for example, calling a cab for you or obtaining difficult-to-get theater tickets). Tip the **valet parking attendant** $1 every time you get your car.

In restaurants, bars, and nightclubs, tip your waitperson at least 15% of the check (up to 20% if service was very good), tip **bartenders** about $1 per drink ordered, tip **checkroom attendants** $1 per garment, and tip **valet-parking attendants** $1 per vehicle. Tipping is not expected in cafeterias and fast-food restaurants.

Tip **cab drivers** 15% of the fare.

Tip **skycaps** at airports at least $1 per bag ($2–$3 if you have a lot of luggage) and tip **hairdressers** and **barbers** 15% to 20%. Tipping gas-station attendants and ushers at movies and theaters is not expected.

Toilets You won't find public toilets or "restrooms" on the streets in most U.S. cities, but they can be found in hotel lobbies, bars, coffee bars, restaurants, museums, department stores, and gas stations. Note, however, that restaurants and bars may reserve their restrooms for the use of their patrons. You can ignore this sign or, better yet, avoid arguments by paying for a cup of coffee or a soft drink, which will qualify you as a patron. Large hotels and fast-food restaurants are probably your best bet for good, clean facilities.

4

Seattle

Imagine yourself seated at a table on the Seattle waterfront, a double tall latte and an almond croissant close at hand. The snowy peaks of the Olympic Mountains shimmer on the far side of Puget Sound, and the ferryboats come and go across Elliott Bay. It's a summer day, and the sun is shining. (Hey, as long as we're dreaming, why not dream big?) It just doesn't get much better than this, unless of course you swap the latte for a microbrew and catch a 9:30 summer sunset. No wonder people love this town so much.

OK, so the waterfront is almost as touristy as San Francisco's Fisherman's Wharf, but what a view! Seattle is a city of views, and the must-see vista is, of course, the panorama from the top of the Space Needle. With the 21st century in full swing, this image of the future looks decidedly mid-century modern, but still, it's hard to resist an expensive elevator ride in any city. You can even take a monorail straight out of *The Jetsons* to get to the Space Needle and pass through the Experience Music Project (EMP), Seattle's latest architectural oddity, en route. EMP is the brainchild of Microsoft cofounder Paul Allen, who built this rock 'n' roll cathedral to house his vast collection of Northwest rock memorabilia. Allen's money is also hard at work changing the architectural face of the south end of downtown Seattle, where, on March 26, 2000, the Kingdome stadium came down, imploded to make way for a new football stadium home for Allen's Seattle Seahawks. Over the past decade, an influx of urban residents has brought a new vibrancy to Seattle's downtown, and as the city has grown wealthier and more sophisticated, it has built itself chic urban condominiums, a new symphony hall, a gorgeous new baseball stadium (Safeco Field), new hotels, and countless upscale restaurants and shops. By the end of 2002, the new football stadium should be up and running. Still in the works are a light-rail system and a new aquarium—though these latter two projects are still a couple of years away.

It's clear that Seattle has not grown complacent. Sure, it's become a very congested city, with traffic problems rivaling those of L.A. And yes, the weather really is lousy for most of the year. But Seattleites manage to overcome these minor inconveniences—in large part by spilling out into the streets and parks whenever the sun shines. To visit Seattle in the summer is to witness an exodus; follow the lead of the locals and head for the great outdoors. Should you be brave enough to visit in the rainy season, don't despair: There are compensations for such misfortune, including a roof on Pike Place Market and an espresso bar on every block.

1 Orientation

ARRIVING

BY PLANE

Seattle-Tacoma International Airport (© 800/544-1965 or 206/431-4444; www.seatac.org/seatac), most commonly referred to simply as Sea-Tac, is located about 14 miles (23km) south of Seattle.

Inside the arrivals terminal, you'll find a **Visitor Information Desk** (© 206/ 433-5218) in the baggage-claim area across from carousel no. 8. It's open daily from 9am to 6pm. However, this desk cannot make hotel reservations for you.

Also at the airport, you'll find a Thomas Cook currency exchange desk (© 206/248-0401) and branches of all the major car-rental companies (for further details see "Getting Around," later in this chapter).

GETTING INTO THE CITY BY CAR   There are two main exits from the airport: From the loading/unloading area, take the first exit if you're staying near the airport. Take the second exit (Wash. 518) if you're headed to downtown Seattle. Driving east on Wash. 518 will connect you to I-5, where you'll then follow the signs for Seattle. Generally, allow 30 minutes for the drive between the airport and downtown—45 minutes to an hour during rush hour.

During rush hour, it's sometimes quicker to take Wash. 518 west to Wash. 509 north to Wash. 99 to Wash. 519 (which becomes the Alaskan Way Viaduct along the Seattle waterfront).

GETTING INTO THE CITY BY TAXI, SHUTTLE, OR BUS   A **taxi** into downtown Seattle will cost you about $32. There are usually plenty of taxis around, but if not, call **Yellow Cab/Graytop** (© 206/622-6500) or **Farwest Taxi** (© 206/622-1717). The flag-drop charge is $1.80; after that, it's $1.80 per mile.

Gray Line Airport Express (© 800/426-7505 or 206/626-6088; www.gray lineofseattle.com) provides service between the airport and downtown Seattle daily from about 5am to 11pm and is your best bet for getting to downtown. These shuttle vans pick up from two booths outside the baggage claim area— one outside Door 24 and one outside Door 8. Shuttles operate every 20 minutes and stop at the following hotels: Madison Renaissance, Crowne Plaza, Four Seasons Olympic, Seattle Hilton, Sheraton Seattle, Westin, and Warwick. Fares are $8.50 one-way and $14 round-trip. Connector service to the above hotels is also provided from numerous other downtown hotels, as well as from the Amtrak station, the Washington State Ferries ferry terminal (Pier 52), and the Greyhound station. Connector service is free from some downtown hotels, but from other locations, it costs $2.50 one-way or $5 round-trip; call for details.

Shuttle Express (© 800/487-7433 in Washington, or 425/981-7000; www. shuttleexpress.com) provides 24-hour service between Sea-Tac and the Seattle and Bellevue areas. The rate to downtown Seattle is about $21 plus $3 for an additional person. You need to make a reservation to get to the airport, but to leave the airport, simply call when you arrive. Push 48 on one of the Traveler's Information Center courtesy phones outside the baggage-claim area. If you arrive at a time when the Gray Line shuttle is not operating or are heading to one of the Eastside communities such as Bellevue or Kirkland, this is going to be your best bet for getting into town.

Metro Transit (© 800/542-7876 in Washington, or 206/553-3000; http://transit.metrokc.gov) operates two buses between the airport and downtown. These buses leave from near Door 6 (close to baggage carousel 1) of the baggage claim area. Bus 194 operates to downtown every 30 minutes weekdays from 4:55am to 8:33pm, weekends from about 6:20am to 7:20pm. Bus 174 operates to downtown every 30 minutes from 4:47am to 2:43am (from 5:45am on Sat and from 6:49am on Sun). Bus trips take 30 to 40 minutes. The fare is $1.25 during off-peak hours and $2 during peak hours.

BY TRAIN

Amtrak (© 206/382-4125) trains stop at King Street Station, which is located at Third Avenue South and Jackson Street, within a few blocks of the historic Pioneer Square neighborhood and adjacent to the south entrance of the downtown bus tunnel. Any bus running north through the tunnel will take you to within a few blocks of most downtown hotels. The Waterfront Streetcar also stops within a block of King Street Station and can take you to the Hotel Edgewater.

BY CAR

See "Getting There," in chapter 2, "Planning Your Trip to Washington," and "Getting Around," later in this chapter.

VISITOR INFORMATION

Visitor information on Seattle and the surrounding area is available by contacting the **Seattle–King County Convention & Visitors Bureau Visitor Information Center,** Washington State Convention & Trade Center, 800 Convention Place, Galleria Level, at the corner of Eighth Avenue and Pike Street (© 206/461-5840; www.seeseattle.org). To find it, walk uphill on Union Street until it goes into a tunnel under the Convention Center. You'll see the information center on your left.

CITY LAYOUT

Although downtown Seattle is fairly compact and can easily be navigated on foot, finding your way by car can be frustrating. The Seattle area has been experiencing phenomenal growth for more than a decade, and this has created traffic-congestion problems. Here are some guidelines to help you find your way around.

MAIN ARTERIES & STREETS There are three interstate highways serving Seattle. Seattle's main artery is I-5, which runs through the middle of the city. Take the James Street exit west if you're heading for the Pioneer Square area, take the Seneca Street exit for Pike Place Market, or the Olive Way exit for Capitol Hill. I-405 is the city's north-south bypass and travels up the east shore of Lake Washington through Bellevue and Kirkland (Seattle's high-tech corridor). I-90 comes in from the east, crossing one of the city's two floating bridges, and ends at the south end of downtown.

Downtown is roughly defined as extending from the stadium district just south of the Pioneer Square neighborhood on the south, to Denny Way on the north, and from Elliott Bay on the west to I-5 on the east. Within this area, most avenues are numbered, whereas streets have names. Exceptions to this rule are the first two roads parallel to the waterfront (Alaskan Way and Western Ave.) and avenues east of Ninth Avenue.

Remembering Seattle's Streets

There is an irreverent little mnemonic device locals use for remembering the names of Seattle's downtown streets, and since most visitors spend much of their time downtown, this little phrase could be useful to you as well. It goes like this: "Jesus Christ made Seattle under protest." This stands for all the downtown east-west streets between Yesler Way and Olive Way/Stewart Street—Jefferson, James, Cherry, Columbia, Marion, Madison, Spring, Seneca, University, Union, Pike, Pine.

To get from downtown to Capitol Hill, take Pike Street or Olive Way. Madison Street, Yesler Way, or South Jackson Street will get you over to Lake Washington on the east side of Seattle. If you are heading north across town, Westlake Avenue will take you to the Fremont neighborhood, and Eastlake Avenue will take you to the University District. To get to the arboretum from downtown, take Madison Street.

FINDING AN ADDRESS   After you become familiar with the streets and neighborhoods of Seattle, there is really only one important thing to remember: Pay attention to the compass point of an address. Most downtown streets have no directional designation attached to them, but when you cross I-5 going east, most streets and avenues are designated "East." South of Yesler Way, which runs through Pioneer Square, streets are designated "South." West of Queen Anne Avenue, streets are designated "West." The University District is designated "NE" (Northeast), and the Ballard neighborhood, "NW" (Northwest). So if you're looking for an address on First Avenue South, head south of Yesler Way.

Another helpful hint is that odd-numbered addresses are likely to be on the west and south sides of streets, whereas even-numbered addresses will be on the east and north. Also, in the downtown area, address numbers increase by 100 with each block as you move away from Yesler Way going north or south and as you go east from the waterfront.

STREET MAPS   If the streets of Seattle seem totally unfathomable to you, rest assured that even longtime residents sometimes have a hard time finding their way around. Don't be afraid to ask directions. You can obtain a free map of the city from one of the two Seattle–King County Convention & Visitors Bureau Visitor Information Centers. See "Visitor Information" above.

You can buy a decent map of Seattle in most convenience stores and gas stations around the area, or for a greater selection, stop in at **Metsker Maps,** 702 First Ave. (© **206/623-8747;** www.metskers.com).

If you're a member of AAA, you can get free maps of Seattle and Washington state, either at an AAA office near you or at the Seattle office, 330 Sixth Ave. N. (© **206/448-5353**).

NEIGHBORHOODS IN BRIEF

DOWNTOWN This is Seattle's main business district and can roughly be defined as the area from Pioneer Square in the south, to around Pike Place Market in the north, and from First Avenue to Eighth Avenue. It's characterized by steep streets, high-rise office buildings, luxury hotels, and a high density of retail shops. This is also where you'll find the Seattle Art Museum and Benaroya Hall, which is home to the Seattle Symphony. Because hotels in this area are convenient to both Pioneer Square and Pike Place Market, this is a good neighborhood in which to stay. Unfortunately, the hotels here are the most expensive in the city.

FIRST HILL Known as Pill Hill by Seattleites, this hilly neighborhood, just east of downtown across I-5, is home to several hospitals as well as the Frye Art Museum and a couple of good hotels.

THE WATERFRONT The Seattle waterfront, which stretches along Alaskan Way from roughly Washington Street in the south to Broad Street and Myrtle Edwards Park in the north, is the most touristy neighborhood in Seattle. However, in recent years, Seattleites have been reclaiming the waterfront as a new residential area, and the north end of Alaskan Way is now lined with water-view condos. In addition to the many tacky gift shops, greasy fish-and-chips windows, and tour-boat docks, the waterfront also has the city's only waterfront hotel (The Edgewater), the Seattle Aquarium, and a few excellent seafood restaurants.

PIONEER SQUARE The Pioneer Square Historic District, known for its restored 1890s buildings, is centered on the corner of First Avenue and Yesler Way. The tree-lined streets and cobblestone plazas make this one of the prettiest downtown neighborhoods. Pioneer Square (which refers to the neighborhood, not a specific square) is full of antiques shops, art galleries, restaurants, bars, and nightclubs. Because of the number of bars in this neighborhood, late nights are not a good time to be wandering here. Also, the number of street people in this area can be off-putting to many visitors.

THE INTERNATIONAL DISTRICT The most distinctive of Seattle's neighborhoods, the International District (known to locals as the I.D.) is home to a large Asian population. Here you'll find the Wing Luke Asian Museum, Hing Hay Park (with an ornate pagoda), Uwajimaya (an Asian supermarket), and many other small shops and restaurants. The International District begins around Fifth Avenue South and South Jackson Street. While this neighborhood is interesting for a stroll, there really isn't a lot to do here.

BELLTOWN Located in the blocks north of **Pike Place Market** between Western and Fourth avenues, this area once held mostly warehouses, but over the past decade has become gentrified. Today Belltown is home to upscale Seattle restaurants and numerous nightclubs. Keeping all the restaurants in business are the residents of the neighborhood's many new high-rise condominiums. The area is popular with a young, hip crowd.

QUEEN ANNE HILL Queen Anne is located just northwest of **Seattle Center** and affords impressive views of the city. This affluent neighborhood, one of the most prestigious in Seattle proper, is where you'll find some of Seattle's oldest homes. Today the neighborhood is divided into the Upper Queen Anne and Lower Queen Anne neighborhoods. Upper Queen Anne has a peaceful feel and abounds in inexpensive restaurants. Lower Queen Anne, adjacent to the theaters and Opera House at Seattle Center, is something of a theater district and offers a more urban vibe.

CAPITOL HILL To the northeast of downtown, centered along

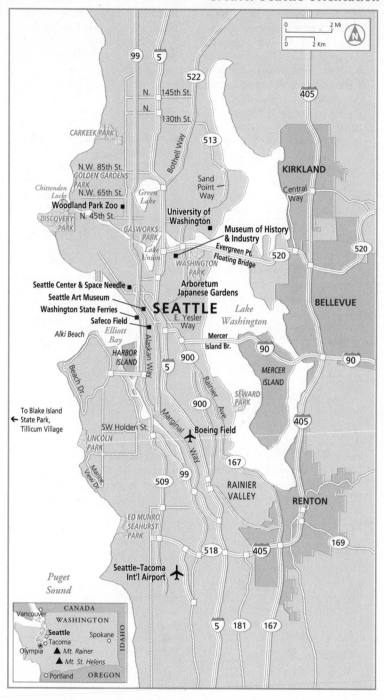

0 | 2 Mi
0 | 2 Km

99
5
522
405
N. 145th St.
N. 130th St.
513
CARKEEK PARK
KIRKLAND
N.W. 85th St.
GOLDEN GARDENS PARK
Sand Point Way
Central Way
Chittenden Locks
N.W. 65th St.
Green Lake
Woodland Park Zoo
N. 45th St.
University of Washington
DISCOVERY PARK
GASWORKS PARK
Museum of History & Industry
Lake Union
Evergreen Pt.
Floating Bridge
520
520
WASHINGTON PARK
Seattle Center & Space Needle
Arboretum Japanese Gardens
BELLEVUE
Seattle Art Museum
SEATTLE
Lake Washington
Washington State Ferries
Safeco Field
E. Yesler Way
Alki Beach
Elliott Bay
HARBOR ISLAND
Alaskan Way
Mercer Island Br.
Mercer
90
90
Beach Dr.
5
900
Rainier Ave.
MERCER ISLAND
SEWARD PARK
To Blake Island State Park, Tillicum Village
900
405
SW Holden St.
Boeing Field
LINCOLN PARK
Marginal Way
167
Marine View Dr.
509
99
RAINIER VALLEY
RENTON
ED MUNRO SEAHURST PARK
518
405
169
Puget Sound
Seattle–Tacoma Int'l Airport

CANADA
Vancouver
WASHINGTON
Seattle
Tacoma
Spokane
Olympia
▲ *Mt. Rainer*
▲ *Mt. St. Helens*
IDAHO
○ Portland
OREGON
5
181
167

Broadway near Volunteer Park, Capitol Hill is Seattle's main gay community and is also a popular shopping district. Broadway sidewalks are always crowded, and it is nearly impossible to find a parking place in the neighborhood. While there are lots of inexpensive restaurants in the area, few are really worth recommending. This is also the city's main hangout for runaways and street kids, many of whom have become involved in the city's infamous heroin scene. There are many old homes and mansions on Capitol Hill, and you'll find many of the city's bed-and-breakfast inns.

UNIVERSITY DISTRICT As the name implies, this neighborhood in the northeast section of the city surrounds the University of Washington. The U District, as it's known to locals, provides all the amenities of a college neighborhood: cheap ethnic restaurants, bars, pubs, espresso bars, and music stores. There are several good hotels in the neighborhood that offer substantial savings over comparable downtown Seattle hotels.

FREMONT Located north of the Lake Washington Ship Canal between Wallingford and Ballard, Fremont is home to Seattle's best-loved piece of public art—*Waiting for the Interurban*—as well as the famous Fremont Troll sculpture. Seattle's wackiest neighborhood, it's filled with eclectic shops and ethnic restaurants. During the summer, there are outdoor movies on Saturday nights and a Sunday flea market. If you have time to visit only one neighborhood outside of downtown, make it Fremont.

BALLARD In northwest Seattle, bordering the Lake Washington Ship Canal and Puget Sound, you'll find Ballard, a former Scandinavian community now known for its busy nightlife but with remnants of its past still visible. Ballard is one of Seattle's up-and-coming neighborhoods and is undergoing a pronounced change in character. There are now art galleries and a few interesting boutiques and shops along the tree-shaded streets of the neighborhood's old commercial center. It's definitely worth a stroll here to see what's happening.

THE EASTSIDE Home to Bill Gates, Microsoft, countless high-tech spinoff companies, and seemingly endless suburbs, the Eastside lies across Lake Washington from Seattle proper and is comprised of the fast-growing cities of **Kirkland, Bellevue, Redmond, Bothell,** and a few other smaller communities. As the presence of Bill Gates's media-hyped mansion attests, there are some pretty wealthy neighborhoods here; but wealth doesn't necessarily equal respect, and the Eastside is still much derided by Seattle citizens, who perceive the Eastside as an uncultured bedroom community.

WEST SEATTLE West Seattle, across the wasteland of the port facility from downtown Seattle, is not just the site of the ferry terminal for ferries to Vashon Island and the Kitsap Peninsula. It's also the site of Seattle's favorite beach (Alki), which is as close to a Southern California beach experience as you can get in the Northwest. This is also the site of the waterfront restaurant with the best view of Seattle: Salty's on Alki.

2 Getting Around

BY PUBLIC TRANSPORTATION

BY BUS   The best thing about Seattle's **Metro** bus system (© 800/542-7876 in Washington, or 206/553-3000; http://transit.metrokc.gov) is that as long as you stay within the downtown area, you can ride for free between 6am and 7pm. The Ride Free Area is between Alaskan Way (the waterfront) in the west, Sixth Avenue and I-5 in the east, Battery Street in the north, and S. Jackson Street in the south. Within this area are Pioneer Square, the waterfront attractions, Pike Place Market, the Seattle Art Museum, and almost all of the city's major hotels. Three blocks from S. Jackson Street is Safeco Field (where the Mariners play), and 6 blocks from Battery Street is Seattle Center. Keeping this in mind, you can see a lot of Seattle without having to spend a dime on transportation.

The Ride Free Area also encompasses the Metro Tunnel, which extends from the International District in the south to the Convention Center in the north and allows buses to drive underneath downtown Seattle. It's open Monday through Friday from 5am to 7pm and Saturday from 10am to 6pm (closed Sun and holidays). When the Bus Tunnel is closed, buses operate on surface streets. Because the tunnel is within the Ride Free Area, there is no charge for riding through it, unless you are traveling to or from outside of the Ride Free Area.

If you travel outside the Ride Free Area, fares range from $1.25 to $2, depending on the distance and time of day. (The higher fares are incurred during commuter hr.) Keep in mind when traveling out of the Ride Free Area that you pay when you get off the bus. When traveling into the Ride Free Area, you pay when you get on the bus. Exact change is required; dollar bills are accepted.

BY WATERFRONT STREETCAR   In addition to the bus system, **Metro** (© 800/542-7876 in Washington, or 206/553-3000; http://transit.metrokc. gov) also operates old-fashioned streetcars that follow a route along the waterfront from Pier 70 to Pioneer Square and then east to the corner of Fifth Avenue S. and S. Jackson Street, which is on the edge of the International District. These streetcars are more tourist attraction than commuter transportation and actually are much more useful to visitors than are most buses. Tourist attractions along the streetcar route include Pioneer Square, the Seattle Aquarium, IMAXDome Film Experience, and Pike Place Market. In summer, streetcars operate Monday through Friday from 6:46am to 11:28pm, departing every 20 to 30 minutes; on Saturday, Sunday, and holidays from 8:46am to 11:58pm (shorter hr. in other months). One-way fare is $1 in off-peak hours and $1.25 in peak hours (75¢ for children ages 5–17); exact change is required. If you plan to transfer to a Metro bus, you can get a transfer good for 90 minutes. Streetcars are wheelchair accessible.

BY MONORAIL   If you are planning a visit to Seattle Center, there is no better way to get there from downtown than on the **Seattle Monorail** (© 206/ 905-2600; www.seattlemonorail.com), which leaves from Westlake Center

---

Value **Discount Passes**

On Saturday, Sunday, and holidays, you can purchase an All Day Pass for $2; it's available on any Metro bus or the Waterfront Streetcar, and it's good for anywhere outside the Ride Free Area.

shopping mall (Fifth Ave. and Pine St.). The elevated trains cover the 1.2 miles in 2 minutes and pass right through the middle of the Experience Music Project. The monorail operates Monday through Friday from 7:30am to 11pm, Saturday and Sunday from 9am to 11pm. Departures are every 10 minutes. The one-way fare is $1.25 for adults and 50¢ for seniors and children ages 5 to 11.

BY WATER TAXI During the past few summers a water taxi has operated between the downtown Seattle waterfront (Pier 54) and West Seattle, providing access to West Seattle's popular Alki Beach and adjacent paved path. For a schedule of service, check with Metro (② 206/553-3000; www.metrokc.gov/kcdot/tp). The one-way fare is $2 (free for children under age 5). Also free with a valid bus transfer or all-day pass.

BY FERRY **Washington State Ferries** (② 800/84-FERRY or 888/808-7977 within Washington, or 206/464-6400; www.wsdot.wa.gov/ferries/) is the most extensive ferry system in the United States, and while these ferries won't help you get around Seattle itself, they do offer scenic options for getting out of town (and cheap cruises, too). From downtown Seattle, car ferries sail to Bremerton (60-min. crossing) and Bainbridge Island (35-min. crossing), and passenger-only ferries sail for Bremerton (30-min. crossing) and Vashon Island (25-min. crossing). From West Seattle, car ferries go to Vashon Island (15-min. crossing) and Southworth (35-min. crossing), which is on the Kitsap Peninsula. One-way fares between Seattle and Bainbridge Island or Bremerton via car ferry are $8 ($10 from mid-May to mid-Oct) for a car and driver, $4.50 for adult car passengers or walk-ons, $2.20 for seniors, and $3.20 for children ages 5 to 18. Car passengers and walk-ons only pay fares on westbound car ferries. One-way fares between Fauntleroy (West Seattle) and Vashon Island or between Southworth and Vashon Island are $10.25 ($13 from mid-May to mid-Oct) for a car and driver, $2.90 for car passengers or walk-ons, $1.40 for seniors, and $2.10 for children ages 5 to 18.

BY CAR

Before you venture into downtown Seattle in a car, keep in mind that traffic congestion is bad, parking is limited (and expensive), and streets are almost all one way. You'll avoid a lot of frustration and aggravation by leaving your car outside the downtown area.

If you plan to spend all your time in downtown Seattle, a car is a liability. The city center is well serviced by public transportation, with free public buses in the downtown area, the monorail from downtown to Seattle Center, and the Waterfront Streetcar connecting Pike Place Market and Pioneer Square by way of the waterfront. You can even take the ferries over to Bainbridge Island or Bremerton for an excursion out of the city. Most Seattle neighborhoods are also well served by public buses.

CAR RENTALS Car-rental rates vary as widely and as wildly as airfares, so it pays to do some comparison-shopping. In Seattle, daily rates for a compact car might run anywhere from around $25 to $60, with weekly rates running between $150 and $350. Rates are, of course, highest in the summer and lowest in the winter, but you'll almost always get lower rates the farther ahead you reserve. Be sure to budget for the 18.5% car-rental tax (and, if you rent at the airport, an additional 10% airport concession fee, for a whopping total of 28.5%!).

All the major car-rental agencies have offices in Seattle and at or near Seattle-Tacoma International Airport. Companies with a desk and cars inside the terminal include **Alamo** (℅ 800/327-9633 or 206/433-0182; www.goalamo. com), **Avis** (℅ 800/831-2847 or 206/448-1700; www.avis.com), **Budget** (℅ 800/ 527-0700 or 206/682-2277; www.budgetrentacar.com), **Hertz** (℅ 800/654-3131 or 206/248-1300; www.hertz.com), and **National** (℅ 800/227-7368 or 206/ 433-5500; www.nationalcar.com). Companies with desks inside the terminal but cars parked off the airport premises include **Dollar** (℅ 800/800-4000 or 206/433-6768; www.dollar.com), **Enterprise** (℅ 800/736-8222 or 206/ 382-1051; www.enterprise.com), and **Thrifty** (℅ 800/367-2277 or 206/625-1133; www.thrifty.com).

PARKING   On-street parking in downtown Seattle is expensive, extremely limited, and, worst of all, rarely available near your destination. Most downtown parking lots (either above or below ground) charge from $12 to $20 per day, though many lots offer early-bird specials that allow you to park all day for around $8 if you park before a certain time in the morning (usually around 9am). With a purchase of $20 or more, many downtown merchants offer City-Park tokens that can be used for $1 off parking fees in many downtown lots (mostly in the main shopping district around Sixth and Pine). Look for the CityPark signs.

You'll also save money by parking near the Space Needle, where parking lots charge $4 to $6 per day. The parking lot at Fifth Avenue North and North Republican Street, on the east side of Seattle Center, charges only $4 for all-day parking if you show up with three or more people in your car. The Pike Place Market parking garage, accessed from Western Avenue under the sky bridge, offers free parking if you park for less than an hour (just enough time to run in and grab a quick bite). If you don't mind a bit of a walk, try the parking lot off Jackson Street between Eighth and Ninth avenues in the International District. This lot charges only $5 to park all day on weekdays. Also in the International District, the Lower Queen Anne neighborhood, and a few streets south of Seattle Center, you'll find free 2-hour on-street parking.

DRIVING RULES   A right turn at a red light is permitted after coming to a full stop. A left turn at a red light is permissible from a one-way street onto another one-way street.

If you park your car on a sloping street, be sure to turn your wheels to the curb—you may be ticketed if you don't. When parking on the street, be sure to check the time limit on your parking meter. Some allow only as little as 15 minutes of parking, while others are good for up to 4 hours. Also be sure to check whether or not you can park in a parking space during rush hour.

BY TAXI

If you decide not to use the public-transit system, call **Yellow Cab/Graytop** (℅ **206/622-6500**) or **Farwest Taxi** (℅ **206/622-1717**). Taxis can be difficult to hail on the street in Seattle, so it's best to call or wait at the taxi stands at major hotels. The flag-drop charge is $1.80; after that, it's $1.80 per mile. A maximum of four passengers can share a cab; the third and fourth passengers will each incur an extra charge of 50¢.

ON FOOT

Seattle is a surprisingly compact city. You can easily walk from Pioneer Square to Pike Place Market and take in most of downtown. Remember, though, that the city is also very hilly. When you head in from the waterfront, you will be climbing a very steep hill. If you get tired while strolling downtown, remember that between 6am and 7pm, you can always catch a bus for free as long as you plan to stay within the Ride Free Area. Cross the street only at corners and only with the lights in your favor. Jaywalking, especially in the downtown area, is a ticketable offense.

 FAST FACTS: Seattle

AAA The **American Automobile Association** (© 800/222-4357; www.aaa. com) has a local Seattle office at 330 Sixth Ave. N. (© 206/448-5353).

Airport See "Getting There" in chapter 2, and "Arriving," earlier in this chapter.

American Express In Seattle, the Amex office is in the Plaza 600 building at 600 Stewart St. (© 206/441-8622). The office is open Monday through Friday from 8:30am to 5:30pm. For card member services, phone © 800/ 528-4800. Call © 800/AXP-TRIP or go to **www.americanexpress.com** for other locations or general information.

Area Code The area code in Seattle is **206**; it's **425** for the Eastside (including Kirkland and Bellevue), and **253** for south King County (near the airport).

Car Rentals See "Getting Around," earlier in this chapter.

Climate See "When to Go," in chapter 2.

Dentist Contact the **Dentist Referral Service,** the Medical Dental Building, 509 Olive Way, Suite 1052 (© 206/448-CARE).

Doctor To find a physician, check at your hotel for a referral, or call the **Medical Dental Building,** 509 Olive Way, Suite 1052 (© 206/448-CARE). See also "Hospitals" below.

Emergencies For police, fire, or medical emergencies, phone © **911.**

Hospitals Hospitals convenient to downtown include **Harborview Medical Center,** 325 Ninth Ave. (© 206/731-3000), and **Virginia Mason Hospital and Clinic,** 925 Seneca St. (© 206/583-6433 for emergencies, or 206/624-1144 for information).

Information See "Visitor Information," earlier in this chapter.

Internet Access First, ask at your hotel to see if it provides Internet access. If not, **Kinko's,** 1335 Second Ave. (© 206/292-9255) and other locations, is an alternative.

Liquor Laws The legal minimum drinking age in Washington state is 21. Aside from on-premise sales of cocktails in bars and restaurants, hard liquor can only be purchased in liquor stores. Beer and wine are available in convenience stores and grocery stores. Brewpubs tend to sell only beer and wine, but some also have licenses to sell hard liquor.

Newspapers & Magazines The *Seattle Post-Intelligencer* and *Seattle Times* are Seattle's two daily newspapers. *Seattle Weekly* is the city's free arts-and-entertainment weekly.

Pharmacies Conveniently located downtown pharmacies include **Rite-Aid,** 802 Third Ave. (© 206/623-8827), and **Pacific Drugs,** 822 First Ave.

(☎ 206/624-1454). However, these two stores have fairly limited hours. For 24-hour service, try **Bartell Drug Store,** 600 First Ave. N. (☎ 206/284-1353), which is located upstairs from Larry's Market.

Photographic Needs **Cameras West,** 1908 Fourth Ave. (☎ 206/622-0066), is the largest-volume camera and video dealer in the Northwest. Best of all, it's right downtown and also offers 1-hour film processing. It's open Monday through Saturday from 9:30am to 6pm, and on Sunday from noon to 5pm.

Police For police emergencies, phone ☎ **911.**

Restrooms There are public restrooms in Pike Place Market, Westlake Center, Pacific Place, Seattle Center, and the Washington State Convention & Trade Center. You'll also find restrooms in most hotel lobbies and coffee bars in downtown Seattle.

Safety Although Seattle is a relatively safe city, it has its share of crime. The most questionable neighborhood you're likely to visit is the Pioneer Square area, which is home to more than a dozen bars and nightclubs. By day, this area is quite safe (though it has a large contingent of street people), but late at night, when the bars are closing, keep your wits about you. Also take extra precautions with your wallet or purse when you're in the crush of people at Pike Place Market. Whenever possible, try to park your car in a garage, instead of on the street, at night.

Smoking Although many of the restaurants listed in this book are smoke-free establishments, there are also many Seattle restaurants that do allow smoking. At most high-end restaurants, the smoking area is usually in the bar/lounge, and although many restaurants have separate bar menus, most will serve you off the regular menu even if you are eating in the bar. There are very few smoke-free bars in Seattle.

Taxes In Seattle you'll pay an 8.8% sales tax, and in restaurants, you'll also pay an additional 0.5% food-and-beverage tax on top of the sales tax. The hotel-room tax in the Seattle metro area ranges from 11.6% to 15.8%. On rental cars, you'll pay not only an 18.5% car-rental tax, but also, if you rent at the airport, an additional 10% airport concession fee, for a whopping total of 28.5%! You eliminate 10% of this by renting your car somewhere other than the airport.

Taxis See "Getting Around," earlier in this chapter.

Time Seattle is on pacific time (PT) and daylight saving time, depending on the time of year, making it 3 hours behind the East Coast.

Transit Info For 24-hour information on Seattle's Metro bus system, call ☎ **800/542-7876** in Washington, or 206/553-3000. For information on the Washington State Ferries, call ☎ **800/84-FERRY** or 888/808-7977 in Washington, or 206/464-6400.

Weather Currently, Seattle has no phone number for weather information. Check the *Seattle Times* or *Seattle Post-Intelligencer* newspapers for forecasts. If you want to know how to pack before you arrive, go to **www.cnn.com/weather** or **www.weather.com.**

3 Where to Stay in Seattle

Seattle is close on the heels of San Francisco as a West Coast summer-in-the-city destination, so its hotels stay pretty much booked solid for July and August, even with the recent proliferation of high-end hotels downtown. If you aren't on an expense account, you may be faced with sticker shock when you see what these places are charging. But if you're willing to head out a bit from downtown, you'll find prices a little easier to swallow.

Be sure to make reservations as far in advance as possible, especially if you plan a visit during Seafair or another major festival. See the "Washington Calendar of Events" on p. 25 for the dates of major festivals.

In the following listings, price categories are based on rates for a double room in high season. Keep in mind that the rates listed do not include taxes, which add up to 15.8% in Seattle.

For comparison purposes, we list what hotels call "rack rates" or walk-in rates—but you should rarely have to pay these highly inflated prices. Various discounts are often available that will reduce these rates, so always ask if there are any specials or discounted rates available (and check the hotel's website for Internet specials). At inexpensive chain motels, there are almost always discounted rates for AAA members and seniors.

Room rates are almost always considerably lower from October through April (the rainy season), and downtown hotels often offer substantially reduced prices on weekends throughout the year (while budget hotels often charge more on weekends).

A few hotels include breakfast in their rates; others offer complimentary breakfast only on certain deluxe floors. Most Seattle hotels offer no-smoking rooms, while most bed-and-breakfast inns are exclusively no-smoking establishments. Most hotels, but few inns, also offer wheelchair-accessible rooms.

If you're having a hard time finding a room in your price range, consider using the services of **Pacific Northwest Journeys** (*©* **800/935-9730** or 206/935-9730; www.pnwjourneys.com). This company specializes in itinerary planning, but also offers a reservation service. The charge is $45 per reservation; however, you can usually make that up in savings on just a 2-night stay. If you're going to be in town for longer than that, you'll definitely save money. Last-minute reservations are often possible, too. A phone and e-mail consultation service is also available for people who have already done a lot of planning but who want a little more assistance with setting out their itinerary.

Every year from November through March, more than two dozen Seattle hotels offer deep-cut discounts on their rooms through the **Seattle Hotel Hotline**'s (*©* **800/535-7071** or 206/461-5882) Seattle Super Saver Package. Room rates under this plan are generally 50% of what they would be in the summer months. Any time of year, you can call this hot line for help with making hotel reservations.

Seattle is a city of diverse neighborhoods, and in many of those neighborhoods, there are fine B&Bs. Often less expensive than downtown hotels, these B&Bs provide an opportunity to see what life in Seattle is like for the locals. We've listed some of our favorites in the pages that follow, but to find out about other good B&Bs in Seattle, contact the **Seattle Bed and Breakfast Association** (*©* **800/348-5630** or 206/547-1020; www.seattlebandbs.com). Alternatively, you can contact **A Pacific Reservation Service** (*©* **800/684-2932** or 206/439-7677; www.seattlebedandbreakfast.com), which represents dozens of accommodations, mostly bed-and-breakfast homes, in the Seattle area. A wide range of rates is available

DOWNTOWN & FIRST HILL

Downtown Seattle is the heart of the city's business community and is home to numerous business hotels. Although these properties are among the most conveniently located Seattle hotels, they are also the most expensive choices and are designed primarily for business travelers on expense accounts, not vacationers.

VERY EXPENSIVE

Alexis Hotel ★★   Listed in the National Register of Historic Places, this century-old building is a sparkling gem in an enviable location halfway between Pike Place Market and Pioneer Square and only 3 blocks from the waterfront, the Seattle Art Museum, and Benaroya Hall. Throughout the hotel there's a pleasant mix of old and new, contemporary and antique; this combination, together with an extensive art collection and the cheerful and personalized service, give the Alexis a very special atmosphere. Classic styling with a European flavor prevails in the guest rooms, each of which is unique. Almost half of the rooms here are suites, including very comfortable fireplace suites with whirlpool tubs. However, the spa suites are the real winners, offering lots of special amenities, plus whirlpool tubs in exceedingly luxurious bathrooms. The hotel's highly recommended restaurant, **The Painted Table,** serves creative Northwest cuisine. There are also complimentary evening wine tastings.

1007 First Ave. (at Madison St.), Seattle, WA 98104. ✆ **800/426-7033** or 206/624-4844. Fax 206/621-9009. www.alexishotel.com. 109 units. $295 double; $525–$825 suite. AE, DC, DISC, MC, V. Valet parking $23. Pets accepted with $25 fee per stay. **Amenities:** Restaurant (Northwest), lounge; exercise room and access to nearby health club; Aveda day spa; steam room; concierge; tour desk; 24-hr. room service; massage; baby-sitting; laundry/dry cleaning; concierge-level rooms. *In room:* A/C, TV, fax, dataport, minibar, hair dryer, iron.

Elliott Grand Hyatt Seattle ★★★   Luxury and technology merge at this, Seattle's newest downtown luxury hotel, which opened in summer 2000 and immediately raised the bar for all of Seattle's business hotels. A Willem de Kooning sculpture outside the hotel's front door and a spacious lobby full of regionally inspired glass art set the tone the moment you arrive. If you are accustomed to staying in the finest hotels, book your room here. However, unless you spring for something pricier than the basic "deluxe guest room," you're going to be a bit cramped. The least expensive rooms at this hotel are definitely designed for solo business travelers. These rooms, and all the other rooms and suites in the hotel, come with three phone lines (one a cordless phone), complimentary high-speed Internet access, two dataports, and an in-room safe large enough for your laptop. Although the health club is well outfitted and stylishly designed, there is no swimming pool, which means families might want to opt for the Four Seasons instead. The large, multilevel dining room provides a number of different ambiences for different meals.

721 Pine St., Seattle, WA 98101. ✆ **800/233-1234** or 206/262-0700. Fax 206/625-1221. www.elliotthotel. com. 425 units. $370–420 double; $445–$3,000 suite. AE, DC, DISC, MC, V. Valet parking $28. **Amenities:** Restaurant (New American), lounge; health club with Jacuzzi, sauna, and steam room; concierge; business center; 24-hr. room service; massage; laundry/dry cleaning. *In room:* A/C, TV, dataport and high-speed Internet access, fridge, coffeemaker, hair dryer, iron, safe.

Four Seasons Olympic Hotel ★★★   If nothing but classically elegant surroundings will do, then head straight for the Four Seasons Olympic Hotel, an Italian Renaissance palace. Without a doubt, this hotel has the grandest lobby

Seattle Accommodations & Dining—
Downtown Including First Hill

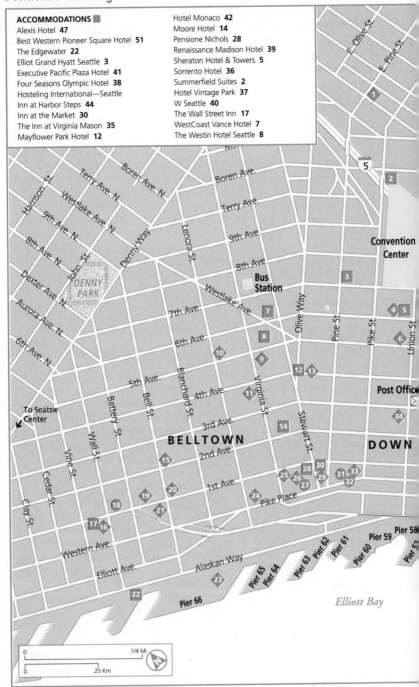

ACCOMMODATIONS ■
Alexis Hotel **47**
Best Western Pioneer Square Hotel **51**
The Edgewater **22**
Elliot Grand Hyatt Seattle **3**
Executive Pacific Plaza Hotel **41**
Four Seasons Olympic Hotel **38**
Hosteling International—Seattle
Inn at Harbor Steps **44**
Inn at the Market **30**
The Inn at Virginia Mason **35**
Mayflower Park Hotel **12**

Hotel Monaco **42**
Moore Hotel **14**
Pensione Nichols **28**
Renaissance Madison Hotel **39**
Sheraton Hotel & Towers **5**
Sorrento Hotel **36**
Summerfield Suites **2**
Hotel Vintage Park **37**
W Seattle **40**
The Wall Street Inn **17**
WestCoast Vance Hotel **7**
The Westin Hotel Seattle **8**

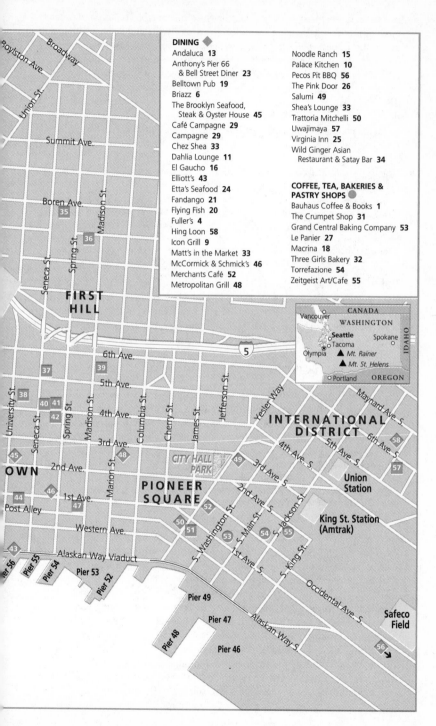

DINING ◆

Andaluca **13**
Anthony's Pier 66 & Bell Street Diner **23**
Belltown Pub **19**
Briazz **6**
The Brooklyn Seafood, Steak & Oyster House **45**
Café Campagne **29**
Campagne **29**
Chez Shea **33**
Dahlia Lounge **11**
El Gaucho **16**
Elliott's **43**
Etta's Seafood **24**
Fandango **21**
Flying Fish **20**
Fuller's **4**
Hing Loon **58**
Icon Grill **9**
Matt's in the Market **33**
McCormick & Schmick's **46**
Merchants Café **52**
Metropolitan Grill **48**

Noodle Ranch **15**
Palace Kitchen **10**
Pecos Pit BBQ **56**
The Pink Door **26**
Salumi **49**
Shea's Lounge **33**
Trattoria Mitchelli **50**
Uwajimaya **57**
Virginia Inn **25**
Wild Ginger Asian Restaurant & Satay Bar **34**

COFFEE, TEA, BAKERIES & PASTRY SHOPS ●

Bauhaus Coffee & Books **1**
The Crumpet Shop **31**
Grand Central Baking Company **53**
Le Panier **27**
Macrina **18**
Three Girls Bakery **32**
Torrefazione **54**
Zeitgeist Art/Cafe **55**

FIRST HILL

INTERNATIONAL DISTRICT

CITY HALL PARK

PIONEER SQUARE

OWN

Post Alley

Union Station

King St. Station (Amtrak)

Safeco Field

CANADA
WASHINGTON
Vancouver
Seattle
Tacoma
Spokane
Olympia
▲ *Mt. Rainer*
▲ *Mt. St. Helens*
Portland   OREGON
IDAHO

Boylston Ave.
Broadway
Union St.
Summit Ave.
Boren Ave.
Spring St.
Seneca St.
Madison St.
6th Ave.
5th Ave.
4th Ave.
3rd Ave.
2nd Ave.
1st Ave.
Western Ave.
University St.
Seneca St.
Spring St.
Madison St.
Marion St.
Columbia St.
Cherry St.
James St.
Jefferson St.
Yesler Way
Maynard Ave. S.
5th Ave. S.
6th Ave. S.
4th Ave. S.
3rd Ave. S.
2nd Ave. S.
S. Washington St.
S. Main St.
S. Jackson St.
1st Ave. S.
S. King St.
Occidental Ave. S.
Alaskan Way Viaduct
Alaskan Way S.
Pier 56
Pier 55
Pier 54
Pier 53
Pier 52
Pier 49
Pier 48
Pier 47
Pier 46

in Seattle. Gilt-and-crystal chandeliers hang from the arched ceiling, and ornate moldings grace the glowing hand-burnished oak walls and pillars. Although many of the guest rooms tend to be rather small (with either two twin beds or one king), all have been recently renovated and are now very elegant. If you crave extra space, opt for one of the suites, of which there are more than 200 (however, be aware that the executive suites aren't much bigger than the hotel's deluxe rooms). For plush surroundings, excellent service, and great amenities, this hotel can't be beat. (Although the Four Seasons doesn't have a full-fledged children's program, it does offer amenities such as kids' menus, kids' robes, baby supplies, and the like.)

In keeping with the overall character of the hotel, **The Georgian** is the most elegant restaurant in Seattle (with prices to match); its menu combines creative Northwest and Continental cuisines.

411 University St., Seattle, WA 98101. © 800/223-8772, 800/821-8106 in Washington, 800/268-6282 in Canada, or 206/621-1700. Fax 206/682-9633. www.fourseasons.com/seattle. 450 units. $315–$385 double; $365–$1,850 suite. AE, DC, MC, V. Valet parking $26. Pets accepted. **Amenities:** 3 restaurants (Continental/Northwest, seafood), 2 lounges; health club with indoor pool, exercise machines, Jacuzzi, and saunas; spa; concierge; downtown courtesy shuttle; business center; shopping arcade; 24-hr. room service; massage; babysitting; laundry/dry cleaning. *In room:* A/C, TV, dataport, minibar, coffeemaker, hair dryer, iron.

Hotel Monaco ✿✿ Housed in a building that was once a telephone company switching center, the Monaco is one of downtown Seattle's hippest business hotels, attracting a young and affluent clientele. If you've got a keen sense of cutting-edge style, you'll likely appreciate the eclectic over-the-top retrocontemporary design here. The lobby features reproductions of ancient Greek murals, while guest rooms are done in wild color schemes, with bold striped wallpaper. All rooms and suites have stereos with CD players. For a view of Mount Rainier, ask for rooms 1019, 1119, or 1219. Missing your pet? Call the front desk, and a staff member will send up a pet goldfish for the night. Sazerac, the hotel's restaurant, is as boldly designed as the rest of the hotel and serves New American cuisine. At the adjacent bar, be sure to order the restaurant's namesake cocktail. There are also complimentary evening wine receptions.

1101 Fourth Ave., Seattle, WA 98101. © 800/945-2240 or 206/621-1770. Fax 206/624-0060. www.monaco seattle.com. 189 units. $275–$295 double; $355–$960 suite. AE, DC, DISC, MC, V. Valet parking $24. Pets accepted. **Amenities:** Restaurant (Southern/New American), lounge; exercise room and access to nearby health club; concierge; business center; 24-hr. room service; massage; babysitting; dry cleaning. *In room:* A/C, TV, fax, dataport, minibar, coffeemaker, hair dryer, iron.

Hotel Vintage Park ✿✿ Small, classically elegant, and exceedingly romantic, the Vintage Park is a must for both lovers and oenophiles. These rooms are perfect for romantic getaways, and every guest room is named for a Washington winery. Each evening in the library-like lobby, there's a complimentary wine tasting featuring Washington vintages (plus late-night port as well). Throughout the hotel, you'll likely also spot numerous references to grapes and wine—even the minibars are stocked with Washington wines. Rooms vary quite a bit here, but when you see the plush draperies framing the beds and the neo-Victorian furnishings in the deluxe rooms, you'll likely want to spend your days luxuriating in the plush surroundings with the one you love. Deluxe rooms have the best views (including some views of Mount Rainier). The bathrooms are small but have attractive granite counters. Standard rooms, though smaller and less luxuriously appointed, are still very comfortable, and surprisingly, their bathrooms are larger than those in the deluxe rooms.

1100 Fifth Ave., Seattle, WA 98101. © 800/624-4433 or 206/624-8000. Fax 206/623-0568. www.hotel vintagepark.com. 126 units. $255–$300 double; $525 suite. AE, DC, DISC, MC, V. Valet parking $24. Pets accepted. **Amenities:** Restaurant (Italian), lounge; access to nearby health club; concierge; 24-hr. room service; massage; laundry/dry cleaning. *In room:* A/C, TV, fax, dataport, minibar, hair dryer, iron.

Renaissance Madison Hotel ☆☆

Despite its large size, the Madison is quieter and less hectic than most convention hotels, and its rooftop restaurant and swimming pool with a view make it is a good choice for leisure travelers as well as the corporate crowd. The biggest drawback is that the hotel is a bit of a walk from the waterfront (and it's all uphill coming back). Most rooms are larger than average and many have views of either Puget Sound or the Cascade Range. For the best views, ask for a room on the west side of the hotel. In the bathroom, you'll find plenty of counter space. Prego, the hotel's Italian restaurant, is up on the 28th floor and has eye-catching views of Seattle. The rooftop indoor pool with a view is by far the best reason to stay here.

515 Madison St., Seattle, WA 98104. © 800/278-4159 or 206/583-0300. Fax 206/624-8125. www. renaissancehotels.com. 553 units. $250–$280 double; $750–$2,000 suite. AE, DC, DISC, MC, V. Valet parking $21; self-parking $20. **Amenities:** 2 restaurants (Italian, Continental), 2 lounges; indoor rooftop pool; exercise room; Jacuzzi; concierge; business center; 24-hr. room service; massage; babysitting; dry cleaning; concierge-level rooms. *In room:* A/C, TV, dataport, minibar, hair dryer, iron.

Sorrento Hotel ☆

With its wrought-iron gates, palm trees in the entrance courtyard, and plush seating in the octagonal lobby, the Sorrento, which first opened its doors in 1909, has a classic elegance and old-world atmosphere. Unfortunately, the guest rooms are not nearly as nice as the lobby would suggest, and considering the rates, they're rather overpriced. No two rooms are alike, and most are set up for business travelers. Although more than half the units are suites, even these can be quite cramped. The hotel does boast commanding views of downtown Seattle from its setting high on First Hill, and yet downtown Seattle is only a few steep blocks away (and there's complimentary downtown limousine service). If you do stay here, be sure to ask for a room on the west side of the hotel; you'll have a view of the city and Puget Sound. The hotel's dining room is a dark, clubby place, and in the lounge, which has live jazz piano, you can get light meals, afternoon tea, and cocktails. In the summer, cafe tables are set up in the hotel's courtyard.

900 Madison St., Seattle, WA 99104-1297. © 800/426-1265 or 206/622-6400. Fax 206/343-6155. www. hotelsorrento.com. 76 units. $235–$250 double; $280–$1,700 suite. AE, DC, DISC, MC, V. Valet parking $21. Pets accepted with $50 deposit. **Amenities:** Restaurant (Northwest/Mediterranean), lounge; exercise room; concierge; business center; salon; room service; massage; laundry/dry cleaning. *In room:* A/C, TV, dataport, minibar, coffeemaker, hair dryer, iron.

W Seattle ☆☆

The W hotel chain has won plenty of national attention and devoted fans for its oh-so-hip accommodations, and here in the land of dot.coms and espresso, the W is a natural. The lobby has the look and feel of a stage set, with dramatic lighting and sleek furniture. Here at the W Seattle, not only are the rooms beautifully designed and filled with lots of plush amenities, but they also tend to be larger than those at other W hotels. If you can spring for an additional $50 per night, the -09 or -02 "Cool Corner" rooms are worth requesting. Guest rooms are full of great perks such as Aveda bath products, goose-down comforters, and CD players (there's a CD library available from which you can borrow some disks).

1112 Fourth Ave., Seattle, WA 98101. © **877/W-HOTELS** or 206/264-6000. Fax 206/264-6100. www.
whotels.com. 419 units. $229–$390 double; from $500 suite. AE, DC, DISC, MC, V. Valet parking $22.
Pets accepted. **Amenities:** Restaurant (New American), lounge; exercise room and access to nearby health
club; concierge; business center; 24-hr. room service; laundry/dry cleaning. *In room:* A/C, TV, dataport,
minibar, coffeemaker, hair dryer, iron, safe.

EXPENSIVE

Inn at Harbor Steps ★★   Located on the lower floors of a modern apartment building across the street from the Seattle Art Museum, this inn offers an
excellent location that's convenient to all of downtown Seattle's major attractions. The guest rooms, which overlook a courtyard garden, are so spacious that
they feel like apartments. Styling leans decidedly toward the Martha Stewart
aesthetic. There are gas fireplaces in every room, and the largest rooms have
whirlpool tubs. The only real drawback here is the lack of views. In the same
building as the hotel, you'll find the Wolfgang Puck Cafe, which features
contemporary food and decor, plus water views. There is also complimentary
afternoon wine and tea.

1221 First Ave., Seattle, WA 98101. © **888/728-8910** or 206/748-0973. Fax 206/748-0533. www.foursisters.
com. 30 units. $175–$230 double. Rates include full breakfast. AE, DC, MC, V. Parking $15. **Amenities:**
Restaurant (New American), lounge; 2 indoor pools; health club with Jacuzzi, sauna, basketball court;
concierge; room service; babysitting; coin-op laundry; dry cleaning. *In room:* A/C, TV, fax, dataport, fridge,
coffeemaker, hair dryer, iron.

Mayflower Park Hotel ★★   If your favorite recreational activities include
shopping or sipping martinis, the Mayflower Park is for you. Built in 1927, this
historic hotel is connected to the upscale Westlake Center shopping plaza and
is within a block of both Nordstrom and The Bon Marché. Most rooms here
are furnished with an eclectic blend of contemporary Italian and traditional
European pieces. Some rooms still have small and old-fashioned bathrooms, but
at press time there were plans to renovate all the bathrooms by early 2002. The
smallest guest rooms here are very cramped, but these standard rooms were also
scheduled to be renovated by early 2002. If you crave space, ask for one of the
larger corner rooms or a suite. Martini drinkers will want to spend time at the
hotel's **Oliver's Lounge,** which serves the best martinis in Seattle and has
free hors d'oeuvres in the evening. The hotel's **Andaluca** restaurant is a plush,
contemporary restaurant serving a highly creative cuisine (see "Dining," later in
this chapter, for a full review).

405 Olive Way, Seattle, WA 98101. © **800/426-5100**, 206/382-6990, or 206/623-8700. Fax 206/382-6997.
www.mayflowerpark.com. 171 units. $150–$210 double; $165–$365 suite. AE, DC, DISC, MC, V. Valet parking $21. **Amenities:** Restaurant (Mediterranean/Northwest), lounge; small state-of-the-art exercise room;
concierge; 24-hr. room service; laundry/dry cleaning. *In room:* A/C, TV, dataport, coffeemaker, hair dryer, iron.

Sheraton Seattle Hotel and Towers ★★★   At 35 stories, this is one of the
two largest hotels in Seattle. Because it's so large, it does a brisk convention business, and you'll almost always find the building buzzing with activity. But don't
let the crowds put you off. There's a reason so many people want to stay here—
the hotel does things right and captures much of the essence of Seattle in its
many features. There's a collection of art glass in the lobby and a 35th-floor exercise room and swimming pool with great views of the city. **Fuller's,** the hotel's
highly recommended main restaurant serves excellent Northwest cuisine (see
"Dining" for a complete review), and, of course, there's an espresso stand in the
lobby. The rooms don't have much character, but they do offer plenty of space
and some decent views from the higher floors. For even more space, book one
of the king rooms, which are designed for business travelers.

1400 Sixth Ave., Seattle, WA 98101. © 800/325-3535 or 206/621-9000. Fax 206/621-8441. www.sheraton. com/seattle. 840 units. $140–$405 double; $220–$750 suite. AE, DC, DISC, MC, V. Valet parking $24; self-parking $22. **Amenities:** 4 restaurants (Northwest, American, oyster bar, pizza), 2 lounges; indoor pool; exercise room; Jacuzzi; sauna; concierge; business center; 24-hr. room service; massage; babysitting; dry cleaning; concierge-level rooms. *In room:* A/C, TV, dataport, minibar, coffeemaker, hair dryer, iron, safe.

The Westin Seattle ★★★   The 47-story Westin caters primarily to conventions and tour groups and consequently can be crowded and impersonal, especially during the busy summer months. This said, it's still one of the better downtown choices. Not only do the hotel's cylindrical twin towers provide interesting vistas from most of the higher floors, but there are also two excellent restaurants and a pool (only a few downtown hotels have them). Primarily because of their unusual curved walls of glass and the fact that the beds face out to the views, guest rooms here are some of the nicest in town. The views are some of the best in the city, so you'll really get to savor the fact that you're in the land of the Space Needle, Puget Sound, and the Olympic Mountains. Of course, some rooms have much better views than others (ask for a western view), and the higher up you get, the better the vistas.

1900 Fifth Ave., Seattle, WA 98101. © 800/WESTIN-1 or 206/728-1000. Fax 206/728-2259. www.westin. com. 891 units. $149–$345 double; $495–$2,500 suite. AE, DC, DISC, MC, V. Valet parking $24; self-parking $22. Small pets accepted ($25 per night). **Amenities:** 3 restaurants (Euro-Asian, Japanese, American), lounge; large indoor pool; 2 exercise rooms; Jacuzzi; concierge; business center; 24-hr. room service; laundry/ dry cleaning. *In room:* A/C, TV, dataport, minibar, coffeemaker, hair dryer, iron.

MODERATE

Executive Pacific Plaza Hotel ★ *Value*   There aren't too many reasonably priced choices left in downtown Seattle, but this hotel, built in 1928, offers recently renovated, moderately priced rooms and a prime location. You're halfway between Pike Place Market and Pioneer Square, and just about the same distance from the waterfront. However, despite the tasteful new decor, the rooms are still small (verging on tiny) and sometimes quite cramped. Also, be aware that there's no air-conditioning here, and west-facing rooms can get warm in the summer. Bathrooms, although very small, were completely upgraded during the recent renovation. Currently, the room rates here are only slightly higher than at motels near the Space Needle, which makes this place a great deal. However, you can bet that it won't be long before the rates take a jump to reflect the new modern furnishings.

400 Spring St., Seattle, WA 98104. © 800/426-1165 or 206/623-3900. Fax 206/623-2059. www.pacific plazahotel.com. 160 units. May–Sept $114–$145 double; Oct–Apr $96–$135 double. Rates include continental breakfast. AE, DC, DISC, MC, V. Parking $14. **Amenities:** Restaurant (American); access to nearby health club; concierge; business center; dry cleaning. *In room:* TV, dataport, coffeemaker, hair dryer, iron.

The Inn at Virginia Mason ★   You may think we've sent you to a hospital rather than a hotel when you first arrive on Pill Hill—but don't have a heart attack. This is definitely a hotel, though it is adjacent to the Virginia Mason Hospital. Regardless of the fact that most guests are here because of the hospital, the hotel is a good choice for vacationers, too, with its economical rates, quiet location, and proximity to downtown. There's a roof sun deck for soaking up rays, and just off the lobby, there's a shady little courtyard. Because this is an old building, room sizes vary, but most have large closets, modern bathrooms, and wingback chairs. Deluxe rooms and suites can be quite large, and some have whirlpool baths and fireplaces. The hotel also keeps good company: The Sorrento Hotel, a great place to stop in for a drink, is only a block away.

1006 Spring St., Seattle, WA 98104. ⓒ 800/283-6453 or 206/583-6453. Fax 206/223-7545. 79 units. $120–$175 double; $165–$245 suite. DC, DISC, MC, V. Parking $7–$8. **Amenities:** Restaurant (American); access to nearby health club; room service; laundry/dry cleaning. *In room:* TV.

Summerfield Suites by Wyndham ⭐ *Value* Located just a block uphill from the Washington State Convention and Trade Center, this hotel caters primarily to business travelers who need a bit of extra room for getting work done while in town. However, the hotel is about equidistant between the waterfront and the hip Capitol Hill shopping and nightlife district, which makes it a good choice if you're just here for fun. Suites are definitely the better choice, though even they are not as big as you would expect. The suites do, however, have two TVs, two phones, and king-size beds. Many rooms have good views that take in the Space Needle, but be aware that a lot of the rooms also get traffic noise from both the freeway and Pike Street. Local restaurants will deliver meals to your room.

1011 Pike St., Seattle, WA 98101. ⓒ 800/833-4353 or 206/682-8282. Fax 206/682-5315. www.wyndham. com. 193 units. $129 double; $189–$360 suite. Rates include continental breakfast. AE, DC, DISC, MC, V. Valet parking $18. **Amenities:** Small outdoor pool; exercise room and access to nearby health club; Jacuzzi; concierge; downtown courtesy shuttle; coin-op laundry; dry cleaning. *In room:* A/C, TV, dataport, coffeemaker, hair dryer, iron.

THE WATERFRONT

The waterfront is Seattle's most touristy neighborhood, yet it also has the city's finest views and is home to several worthwhile attractions and activities. Although there's only one hotel here, it should be the top choice of anyone wanting to spend a Seattle vacation in the thick of things.

EXPENSIVE

The Edgewater ⭐⭐ *Value* Located on a pier at the north end of the waterfront, the Edgewater is Seattle's only waterfront hotel and is designed to resemble a deluxe mountain or fishing lodge. In fact, it's difficult to believe that the crowded streets of downtown Seattle are only steps away. The views out the windows are among the best in the city, and sunsets are memorable. On a clear day you can see the Olympic Mountains rising across Puget Sound. Pull up a seat between the lobby's river-stone fireplace and the wall of glass that looks out on busy Elliott Bay, and you'll see why this is one of our favorite Seattle hotels. The hotel's restaurant and lounge also both serve up those same views. The mountain-lodge theme continues in the rooms, which feature rustic lodgepole pine furniture and fireplaces. While the least expensive rooms here overlook the parking lot (and city), opt for a water-view room if you can afford it. The rooms with balconies, though they're a bit smaller than other rooms, are our top choice. Beatles fans can even stay in the same suite the Fab Four had when they visited (and fished out the window) back in 1964.

Pier 67, 2411 Alaskan Way, Seattle, WA 98121. ⓒ 800/624-0670 or 206/728-7000. Fax 206/441-4119. www.edgewaterhotel.com. 236 units. May–Oct $189–$309 double, $449–$1,250 suite; Nov–Apr $149–$269 double, $399–$850 suite. AE, DC, DISC, MC, V. Valet parking $16. **Amenities:** Restaurant (Pacific Rim/international), lounge; exercise room and access to nearby health club; courtesy bikes; concierge; business center; room service; laundry service; dry cleaning. *In room:* A/C, TV, dataport, coffeemaker, hair dryer, iron.

PIONEER SQUARE & THE INTERNATIONAL DISTRICT

The historic Pioneer Square area is Seattle's main nightlife district and can be a pretty rowdy place on a Saturday night. However, by day, the area's many art galleries and antiques stores attract a very different clientele. While Pioneer

Square can be a very interesting area to explore in the daylight, you'll have to be prepared to encounter a lot of street people. Warnings aside, this is one of the prettiest corners of Seattle and the only downtown neighborhood with historic flavor. The International District lies only a few blocks away from Pioneer Square.

EXPENSIVE

Best Western Pioneer Square Hotel ✦   Located right in the heart of the Pioneer Square historic district, this hotel is only recommended for urban dwellers accustomed to dealing with street people and noise. Pioneer Square is Seattle's nightlife district and gets especially raucous on weekend nights. If you're in town to party (or to attend a baseball game), there's no more convenient location in the city. However, take care on the streets around here late at night. Guest rooms are, for the most part, fairly small (some are positively cramped) and furnished in a classic style.

77 Yesler Way, Seattle, WA 98104. ✆ **800/800-5514** or 206/340-1234. Fax 206/467-0707. www.pioneer square.com. 75 units. July–Sept $149 double, $239 suite; Oct–June $129–$139 double, $219–$229 suite. Rates include continental breakfast. AE, DC, DISC, MC, V. Parking $14. **Amenities:** Concierge; business center; room service; dry cleaning. *In room:* A/C, TV, dataport, hair dryer.

BELLTOWN & PIKE PLACE MARKET

Belltown has for several years now been Seattle's fastest growing urban neighborhood, home to dozens of restaurants and several good hotels. If your Seattle travel plans include lots of eating out at hip restaurants, then Belltown is the place to stay. Belltown begins at the edge of the Pike Place Market neighborhood, which is home to still more great restaurants and a couple of lodging options.

EXPENSIVE

Inn at the Market ✦✦   For romance, convenience, and the chance to immerse yourself in the Seattle aesthetic, it's hard to beat this small, European-style hotel located right in Pike Place Market. A rooftop deck overlooking the harbor provides a tranquil spot to soak up the sun on summer afternoons and further adds to this hotel's distinctive sense of place. Don't look for a grand entrance or large sign here; there's only a small plaque on the wall to indicate that the building in fact houses a tasteful and understated luxury hotel (and two excellent French restaurants).

To make the most of a stay here, make sure to get one of the water-view rooms, 18 of which have wide bay windows that overlook Puget Sound and can be opened to let in refreshing sea breezes. However, even if you don't get a water-view room, you'll still find spacious accommodations and large bathrooms. The decor is tastefully elegant and gives the feel of an upscale European beach resort. If you need more room than a standard hotel room offers, consider the bi-level town house suites.

Campagne, the hotel's formal main dining room, serves excellent southern French fare, while **Café Campagne** offers country-style French food amid casual surroundings. See "Dining," later in this chapter, for full reviews of both restaurants.

86 Pine St., Seattle, WA 98101. ✆ **800/446-4484** or 206/443-3600. www.innatthemarket.com. 70 units. $180–$310 double; $285–$380 suite. AE, DISC, MC, V. Parking $17. **Amenities:** 3 restaurants (southern French, country French, juice cart); access to nearby health club; courtesy downtown shuttle; concierge; room service; dry cleaning. *In room:* A/C, TV, dataport, minibar, coffeemaker, hair dryer, iron, safe.

MODERATE

Pensione Nichols It's never easy finding an economical downtown-area lodging with character, but that's exactly what you'll discover at this European-style B&B, located in the heart of Pike Place Market. It's a popular choice with younger travelers and families. The budget-priced units with shared bathroom are all on the third floor of the building, and though most of the eclectically furnished rooms don't have windows, they do have skylights. However, most guests spend their time in the comfortable dining and lounging area, which has huge windows overlooking Elliott Bay. If you want to splurge, the two suites are quite large and have private bathrooms and windows with water views. Be prepared to climb a lot of stairs.

1923 First Ave., Seattle, WA 98101. ℂ **800/440-7125** or 206/441-7125. www.seattle-bed-breakfast.com. 12 units, 10 with shared bathroom. $110 double with shared bathroom; $195 suite with private bathroom. 2-night minimum on summer weekends. Rates include breakfast. AE, DC, DISC, MC, V. Parking $10. Pets accepted. *In room:* No phone.

The Wall Street Inn ★ *Value* Located in the heart of Belltown, upstairs from El Gaucho (Seattle's most stylish steakhouse), this B&B was once a sailors' union boardinghouse. Today, the rooms are bright and modern, and a few still have kitchenettes. There's a comfortable living room with leather couches and a fireplace, and a small deck with a barbecue. In addition to the morning breakfast, there are always cookies, coffee, and tea set out in the afternoon. Although Belltown is Seattle's most self-consciously hip neighborhood, this is a traditionally styled, comfortable, and conveniently located base from which to explore the city. Best of all, there are loads of terrific restaurants within a few blocks.

2507 First Ave., Seattle, WA 98121. ℂ **800/624-1117** or 206/448-0125. Fax 206/448-2406. www.wallstreet inn.com. 20 units. $100–$179 double. Rates include deluxe continental breakfast. AE, DC, DISC, MC, V. Valet parking $10. **Amenities:** Access to nearby health club; bike rentals; concierge; business center; massage; coin-op laundry. *In room:* TV, dataport, fridge, coffeemaker, hair dryer, iron.

WestCoast Vance Hotel ★ *Value* Built in the 1920s by lumber baron Joseph Vance, this hotel has a very elegant little lobby with wood paneling, marble floors, Oriental carpets, and ornate plasterwork moldings. Accommodations vary in size and style, and some are quite small (bathrooms are uniformly small and have showers only); corner rooms compensate with lots of windows and decent views. Furniture is in keeping with the style of the lobby and for the most part is fairly upscale. If you're here on business or don't care about exercise facilities (there's neither a pool nor an exercise room), this hotel offers good value and a convenient location for a downtown business hotel. With the convention center only a couple of blocks away, this hotel also does put up a lot of convention-goers.

620 Stewart St., Seattle, WA 98101. ℂ **800/325-4000** or 206/441-4200. Fax 206/441-8612. www.westcoast hotels.com/vance. 165 units. Apr–Sept $110–$170 double; Oct–Mar $80–$140 double. AE, DC, DISC, MC, V. Parking $15. **Amenities:** Restaurant (Nuevo Latino); lounge; access to nearby health club; concierge; room service; dry cleaning. *In room:* A/C, TV, dataport, coffeemaker, hair dryer, iron.

INEXPENSIVE

Moore Hotel OK, this place is nothing fancy, and the rooms aren't in the best shape. However, you just won't find too many acceptable downtown-area hotels in this price range, so it's fine for young travelers and other low-maintenance types who don't demand perfection from cheap accommodations. The lobby, with its marble, tiles, and decorative moldings, is in much better shape than the rooms, but if you've ever traveled through Europe on a tight budget, you'll know what to expect from this place. You certainly can't beat the Belltown location.

Trendy restaurants and nightclubs line First and Second avenues starting about a block from the hotel, and Pike Place Market is only 2 blocks away. There's a hip restaurant/lounge on the premises, as well as an adjacent theater that stages rock concerts. Ask for a room with a view of the Sound.

1926 Second Ave., Seattle, WA 98101. (C) 800/421-5508 or 206/448-4851. Fax 206/728-5668. www.moore hotel.com. 140 units, 45 with shared bathroom. $39 double with shared bathroom, $59–$85 double with private bathroom. MC, V. Parking $12. **Amenities:** Restaurant (American), lounge. *In room:* TV.

QUEEN ANNE & SEATTLE CENTER

The Queen Anne neighborhood is divided into both an Upper Queen Anne and a Lower Queen Anne. The upper neighborhood is an upscale residential area with an attractive shopping district. However, most of the hotels listed here are in the lower neighborhood, which conveniently flanks Seattle Center. There are also lots of inexpensive restaurants in the area, which makes this neighborhood a good choice if you're on a budget.

MODERATE

Comfort Suites Downtown/Seattle Center ★ *Kids*   Although it's none too easy to find this place (call and get specific directions for the approach you'll be taking), the bargain rates and spacious new rooms make this chain hotel worth searching out. Since the Comfort Suites is located only 3 blocks from the Seattle Center, you could feasibly leave your car parked at the hotel for most of your stay and walk or use public transit to get around. Be sure to ask for a room away from the busy highway that runs past the hotel. If you've brought the family, the suites are a good deal, and the proximity to Seattle Center will help moms and dads keep the kids entertained.

601 Roy St., Seattle, WA 98109. (C) 800/517-4000 or 206/282-2600. Fax 206/282-1112. www.comfort suites.com. 158 units. $99–$129 double; $129–$149 suite. Rates include continental breakfast. AE, DISC, MC, V. Free parking. **Amenities:** Exercise room; downtown courtesy shuttle; coin-op laundry. *In room:* A/C, TV, dataport, fridge, coffeemaker, hair dryer, iron, free local calls.

Inn at Queen Anne   Located in the Lower Queen Anne neighborhood close to Seattle Center and numerous restaurants and espresso bars, this inn is housed in a converted older apartment building. Though the rooms here aren't as nice as those at the nearby MarQueen, they're comfortable enough, albeit sometimes a bit cramped and not entirely modern. The convenient location and economical rates are the big pluses here. There's also a pleasant garden surrounding the hotel.

505 First Ave. N., Seattle, WA 98109. (C) 800/952-5043 or 206/282-7357. Fax 206/217-9719. www.innat queenanne.com. 68 units. May–Sept $99–$109 double, $119–$159 suite; Oct–Apr $89 double, $109–$139 suite. Rates include continental breakfast. AE, DC, DISC, MC, V. Parking $10. **Amenities:** Coin-op laundry; dry cleaning. *In room:* TV, kitchen or kitchenette, fridge.

MarQueen Hotel ★ *Kids* *Finds*   Located in the up-and-coming neighborhood of Lower Queen Anne, this recently renovated historic hotel is in a 1918 brick building. Seattle Center, with its many performance venues and museums, is only 3 blocks away, and from there you can take the monorail into downtown. Although the hotel is geared toward business travelers (with lots of high-tech amenities), it's a good choice for vacationers as well. Guest rooms are spacious, though a bit oddly laid out due to the hotel's previous incarnation as an apartment building. Many rooms have separate little seating areas and full kitchens, which makes this a good choice for families (especially considering the proximity to Seattle Center's kid-oriented attractions). Lots of dark wood trim and hardwood floors give rooms here a genuinely old-fashioned feel. There's an excellent espresso bar in the hotel building and numerous good restaurants nearby.

Seattle Accommodations & Dining—
Capitol Hill, Lake Union, Queen Anne & North Seattle

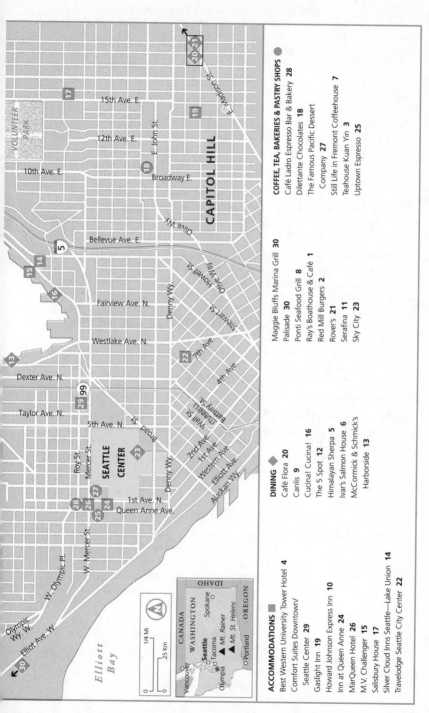

ACCOMMODATIONS ■

Best Western University Tower Hotel **4**
Comfort Suites Downtown/
  Seattle Center **29**
Gaslight Inn **19**
Howard Johnson Express Inn **10**
Inn at Queen Anne **24**
MarQueen Hotel **26**
M.V. Challenger **15**
Salisbury House **17**
Silver Cloud Inns Seattle—Lake Union **14**
Travelodge Seattle City Center **22**

DINING ◆

Café Flora **20**
Canlis **9**
Cucina! Cucina! **16**
The 5 Spot **12**
Himalayan Sherpa **5**
Ivar's Salmon House **6**
McCormick & Schmick's
  Harborside **13**
Maggie Bluffs Marina Grill **30**
Palisade **30**
Ponti Seafood Grill **8**
Ray's Boathouse & Café **1**
Red Mill Burgers **2**
Rover's **21**
Serafina **11**
Sky City **23**

COFFEE, TEA, BAKERIES & PASTRY SHOPS ●

Café Ladro Espresso Bar & Bakery **28**
Dilettante Chocolates **18**
The Famous Pacific Dessert
  Company **27**
Still Life in Fremont Coffeehouse **7**
Teahouse Kuan Yin **3**
Uptown Espresso **25**

81

600 Queen Anne Ave. N., Seattle, WA 98109. © **888/445-3076** or 206/282-7407. Fax 206/283-1499. www. marqueen.com. 53 units. $125–$185 double; $195–$325 suite. AE, DC, DISC, MC, V. Valet parking $12. **Amenities:** Restaurant, espresso bar; access to nearby health club; day spa; concierge; room service; massage; laundry service; dry cleaning. *In room:* A/C, TV, dataport, kitchen, minibar, fridge, coffeemaker, hair dryer, iron.

INEXPENSIVE

Howard Johnson Express Inn ★ *Value*   Located on the eastern slopes of Queen Anne Hill, overlooking Lake Union and the distant Cascade Range, this older motel is just a short drive (or bus ride) from Seattle Center and is just across the Aurora Bridge from Fremont, which has lots of inexpensive restaurants. The best guest rooms, which can usually be had for around $80 to $85 in the summer, have balconies overlooking Lake Union. Right next door to the motel you'll find Canlis, one of Seattle's top restaurants—even if you can't afford to eat here, you can still have a drink at the bar and soak up the atmosphere.

2500 Aurora Ave. N., Seattle, WA 98109. © **877/284-1900** or 206/284-1900. Fax 206/283-5298. www.hojo. com. 94 units. $72–$90 double. Rates include continental breakfast. AE, DC, DISC, MC, V. **Amenities:** Seasonal outdoor pool. *In room:* A/C, TV, coffeemaker.

Travelodge—Seattle City Center   This conveniently located downtown motel can be somewhat overpriced for what you get, but the location, midway between the Westlake Center shopping mall and Seattle Center, makes it a fairly convenient choice if you don't mind doing a bit of walking (alternatively, from here you can ride the bus for free within downtown Seattle). The rooms are up to motel standards (and include free local calls—a nice perk), and some even have balconies and views of the Space Needle.

2213 Eighth Ave., Seattle, WA 98121. © **800/578-7878** or 206/624-6300. Fax 206/233-0185. www. travelodge.com. 73 units. $76–$189 double. Rates include continental breakfast. AE, DC, DISC, MC, V. Free parking. **Amenities:** Tour desk. *In room:* A/C, TV, coffeemaker, safe.

LAKE UNION

Lake Union, located less than a mile from downtown and lined with houseboats, marinas, and waterfront restaurants, has a quintessentially Seattle character. Floatplanes use the lake as a runway, and there are several places around the lake where you can rent a kayak, canoe, or rowboat. If you are happiest when you're close to the water, but want to avoid the crowds of the Seattle waterfront, this area is an excellent alternative.

EXPENSIVE

Silver Cloud Inns Seattle–Lake Union ★★ *Kids* *Value*   Located across the street from Lake Union, this moderately priced hotel offers good views (some of which take in the Space Needle). The rooms are big and filled with lots of amenities, which makes them convenient for long stays and family vacations. The two swimming pools (one indoors and one out) should also appeal to kids. Although the hotel doesn't have a restaurant of its own, there are plenty of waterfront restaurants within walking distance. Floatplane tours also leave from right across the street. This is a good value for such a great location.

1150 Fairview Ave. N., Seattle, WA 98109. © **800/330-5812** or 206/447-9500. Fax 206/812-4900. www. silvercloud.com. 184 units. June–Sept $160–$240 double; Oct–May $140–$215 double. Rates include continental breakfast. AE, DC, DISC, MC, V. Free parking. **Amenities:** Indoor pool and outdoor pool; exercise room and access to nearby health club; 2 Jacuzzis; courtesy local shuttle; business center; laundry service; dry cleaning. *In room:* A/C, TV, dataport, kitchenette, fridge, coffeemaker, hair dryer, iron, free local calls.

MODERATE

The MV Challenger *Finds*   If you love ships and the sea and want a taste of Seattle's water-oriented lifestyle, consider stowing away onboard the MV *Challenger*, a restored and fully operational 1944 tugboat. If, however, you need space, this place is definitely not for you. Guest rooms are as tiny as you would expect berths to be on any small boat. However, for nautical types, a stay here can be a memorable experience—and you just can't beat the marina location and waterside views. The location, at the south end of Lake Union, puts you a hike (or a short bus ride) from downtown, but there are lots of waterfront restaurants within walking distance. This is a great place for a weekend getaway or romantic vacation. There are also two berths on a second, much more modern boat.

Yale Street Landing, 1001 Fairview Ave. N., Suite 1600, Seattle, WA 98109-4416. © **800/288-7521** or 206/ 340-1201. Fax 206/332-0303. www.tugboatchallenger.com. 10 units, 3 with shared bathroom. $85–$185 double. Rates include full breakfast. AE, DC, DISC, MC, V. Free parking.

CAPITOL HILL & EAST SEATTLE

Capitol Hill, located a mile or so uphill and to the east of downtown Seattle, is a neighborhood with a split personality. It's a hangout for the 20-something crowd, and it has a lively gay scene, yet it's also home to numerous large restored homes, several of which have been converted into bed-and-breakfast inns. Although Capitol Hill is a bit of a walk from downtown, the neighborhood has good public bus connections to downtown.

MODERATE

The Gaslight Inn ⭐   Anyone enamored of Craftsman bungalows and the arts-and-crafts movement of the early 20th century should enjoy a stay in this 1906 home. Throughout the inn, there are numerous pieces of Stickley furniture, and everywhere you turn, oak trim frames doors and windows. The common rooms are spacious and attractively decorated with a combination of Western and Northwestern flair, and throughout the inn's two houses, you'll find a number of art-glass pieces. A library filled with interesting books and magazines makes a comfortable spot to spend some free time, or, if it's cold out, take a seat by the fireplace. In summer, guests can swim in the backyard pool or lounge on the deck. Guest rooms continue the design themes of the common areas with lots of oak furnishings and heavy, peeled-log beds in some rooms. An annex next door has a studio and six suites with kitchens, dining areas, and separate bedrooms and living rooms. One of these suites, done in a contemporary style with an art-glass chandelier, has a fireplace and an outstanding view of the city. The innkeepers here can provide a wealth of information about the surrounding Capitol Hill neighborhood, which is the center of Seattle's gay scene.

1727 15th Ave., Seattle, WA 98122. © **206/325-3654.** Fax 206/328-4803. www.gaslight-inn.com. 16 units, 2 with shared bathroom. $88–$148 double; $128 studio; $148–$198 suite. Rates include continental breakfast. AE, MC, V. Off-street parking for suites. **Amenities:** Small outdoor pool; access to nearby health club; concierge; laundry service. *In room:* TV, dataport, hair dryer, iron.

Salisbury House   Located on tree-lined 16th Avenue East, this grand old house has a wide wraparound porch from which you can enjoy one of Seattle's prettiest streetscapes. Inside there's plenty to admire as well. Two living rooms (one with a wood-burning fireplace) and a second-floor sun porch provide plenty of spots for relaxing and meeting other guests. On sunny summer days, breakfast may even be served in the small formal garden in the backyard. Guest rooms all have queen-size beds with down comforters, and one has a fireplace

---

Kids **Family-Friendly Hotels**

MarQueen Hotel (*p. 79*) Located within a few blocks of Seattle Center and its many attractions, this converted apartment building provides a convenient location for families, and spacious suites with kitchenettes.

Seattle Marriott Sea-Tac Airport (*p. 85*) With a huge jungly atrium containing a swimming pool and whirlpool spas, kids can play Tarzan and never leave the hotel. There is also a small game room that will keep the young ones occupied if need be.

Silver Cloud Inns Seattle–Lake Union (*p. 82*) Located right across the street from Lake Union and with a good family restaurant (Cucina!Cucina!) a short walk away, this modern hotel is a good choice for families. There are also two swimming pools and big rooms.

---

and a whirlpool tub. One of the other rooms has an old claw-foot tub in the bathroom. Breakfasts here are deliciously filling and might include fresh fruit, juice, quiche, fresh-baked muffins or bread, and oatmeal pancakes.

750 16th Ave. E., Seattle, WA 98112. (✆) **206/328-8682.** Fax 206/720-1019. www.salisburyhouse.com. 5 units. $105–$165 double. Rates include full breakfast. AE, MC, V. *In room:* Dataport, hair dryer, iron.

NORTH SEATTLE (THE UNIVERSITY DISTRICT)
Located 10 to 15 minutes north of downtown Seattle, the University District (more commonly known as the "U" District) offers less expensive accommodations than downtown, yet is still fairly convenient to Seattle's major attractions. As you would expect in a university neighborhood, there are lots of cheap restaurants, making this an all-round good choice for anyone on a budget.

MODERATE
Best Western University Tower Hotel ★★ (Value) Despite the location away from downtown, this is one of Seattle's handful of hip hotels, and the modern Art Deco decor will surround you in retro style. Best of all, it's considerably cheaper than comparable downtown hotels, and if you need to be near the university, this is definitely the top choice in the neighborhood. You'll even get views of downtown Seattle, distant mountains, and various lakes and waterways. Every room here is a large corner unit, which means plenty of space to spread out and plenty of views from the higher floors. Boldly styled furnishings will appeal to anyone with an appreciation for contemporary furniture design. Bathrooms are small, though.

4507 Brooklyn Ave. NE, Seattle, WA 98105. (✆) **800/WESTERN** or 206/634-2000. Fax 206/547-6029. www. universitytowerhotel.com. 155 units. May–Sept $99–$179 double; Oct–Apr $89–$139 double. Rates include continental breakfast. AE, DC, DISC, MC, V. Free parking. **Amenities:** Restaurant (espresso bar); exercise room. *In room:* TV, fax, dataport, coffeemaker, hair dryer, iron.

NEAR SEA-TAC AIRPORT
The airport is 20 to 30 minutes south of downtown Seattle, and other than convenience, there's nothing to recommend this area as a place to stay.

EXPENSIVE

Seattle Marriott Sea-Tac Airport ★★ *Kids*   With a steamy atrium garden in which you'll find plenty of tropical plants, a swimming pool, and two whirlpool tubs, this resortlike hotel is an excellent choice if you're visiting during the rainy season. There are even waterfalls and totem poles for that Northwest outdoorsy feeling; and best of all, it's always sunny and warm in here (which is more than you can say for the real Northwest outdoors). In the lobby, a huge stone fireplace conjures up images of a remote mountain lodge and helps you forget that this is really an airport hotel. With its stone pillars, rough-hewn beams, and deer-antler chandeliers, the hotel's restaurant perpetuates the lodge feel. Guest rooms don't have the same lodge feel as the public areas, but they're comfortable enough. To get the most out of your stay here, try to get one of the rooms with a view of Mount Rainier.

3201 S. 176th St., Seattle, WA 98188. © 800/228-9290 or 206/241-2000. Fax 206/248-0789. www.marriott. com. 459 units. $129–$189 double ($79–$134 on weekends); $225–$650 suite. AE, DC, DISC, MC, V. Parking $12. Pets accepted. **Amenities:** Restaurant (American), lounge; indoor atrium pool; exercise room; Jacuzzi; sauna; small game room; concierge; car-rental desk; airport shuttle; business center; room service; massage; laundry/dry cleaning; concierge-level rooms. *In room:* A/C, TV, dataport, coffeemaker, hair dryer, iron.

MODERATE

WestCoast Sea-Tac Hotel ★   Located almost directly across from the airport's main entrance, this modern hotel provides comfortable accommodations designed for business travelers. Guest rooms are generally quite large (if you need space, this is the place). In superior king rooms, you also get evening turn-down service, coffee and the morning newspaper, plush terry-cloth robes, and an honor bar. The hotel backs to a small lake, but only a few rooms have lake views.

18220 International Blvd., Seattle, WA 98188. © 800/426-0670 or 206/246-5535. Fax 206/246-9733. www. westcoasthotels.com/seatac. 146 units. $99–$135 double. AE, DC, DISC, MC, V. Free parking. Pets accepted. **Amenities:** Restaurant (American), lounge; outdoor pool; exercise room; Jacuzzi; sauna; courtesy airport shuttle; room service; laundry/dry cleaning. *In room:* A/C, TV, dataport, coffeemaker, hair dryer, iron.

INEXPENSIVE

Among the better and more convenient inexpensive chain motel choices are **Motel 6** (Sea-Tac Airport South), 18900 47th Ave. S. (© **206/241-1648**), charging $56 to $61 for a double; **Super 8 Motel,** 3100 S. 192nd St. (© **206/433-8188**), charging $86 to $93 for a double; and **Travelodge Seattle Airport,** 2900 S. 192nd St. (© **206/241-9292**), charging $66 to $90 for a double.

THE EASTSIDE

The Eastside (a reference to this area's location on the east side of Lake Washington) is Seattle's main high-tech suburb and encompasses the cities of Bellevue, Kirkland, Issaquah, and Redmond. Surprisingly, two of the most luxurious hotels in the entire Seattle area are here on this side of Lake Washington. If it isn't rush hour, you can usually get from the Eastside to downtown in about 20 minutes via the famous floating I-90 and Wash. 520 bridges.

VERY EXPENSIVE

Bellevue Club Hotel ★★★   In its gardens, architecture, and interior design, this hotel epitomizes contemporary Northwest style. Beautifully landscaped gardens surround the entrance, and there are works of contemporary art throughout the public areas. The "club" in this hotel's name refers to a state-of-the-art health club that has everything from an indoor running track and a

50-meter Olympic-sized pool to indoor squash and outdoor tennis courts (there's also a full-service spa), but even if you aren't into aerobic workouts, this hotel has much to offer. You won't find more elegant rooms anywhere in the Seattle area. Accommodations are extremely plush, with the high-ceiling garden rooms among our favorites. These have a floor-to-ceiling wall of glass, massive draperies, and a private patio facing onto a beautiful garden. Luxurious European fabrics are everywhere, giving rooms a romantic feel. Bathrooms are resplendent in granite and glass, and most have whirlpool tubs. The same elegant contemporary design seen in the lobby is found in the hotel's Polaris Restaurant.

11200 SE Sixth St., Bellevue, WA 98004. ⓒ 800/579-1110 or 425/454-4424. Fax 425/688-3101. www. bellevueclub.com. 67 units. $250–$310 double ($125–$230 weekends); $550–$1,450 suite ($325–$895 weekends). AE, DC, MC, V. Parking $5. **Amenities:** 2 restaurants (Northwest); lounge; espresso bar; indoor pool; terrific, expansive health club with Jacuzzi, saunas, steam rooms, tennis courts, racquetball courts, squash courts, aerobics studios; concierge; business center; 24-hr. room service; massage; babysitting; laundry/dry cleaning. *In room:* A/C, TV, dataport, minibar, coffeemaker, hair dryer, iron, safe.

Willows Lodge ★★★ *Finds*   Located on the banks of the Sammamish River (which, unfortunately is little more than a shallow canal) about 30 minutes north of Seattle and adjacent to the much-celebrated Herbfarm restaurant, this lodge is a beautiful blending of rustic and contemporary. From the moment you turn in to the lodge's parking lot, you'll recognize that this is someplace special. A huge fire-darkened tree stump is set like a sculpture right outside the front door, and the landscaping has a distinctly Northwest feel.

Inside, the abundance of polished woods (some of which were salvaged from an old building in Portland) gives the lodge something of a Japanese aesthetic. It's all very soothing and tranquil, an ideal retreat from which you can visit the nearby wineries. In the guest rooms, you'll find beds with lamb's wool mattress pads, European linens, and down duvets; slate tables made from salvaged pool tables; and all kinds of high-tech amenities (including digital shower thermostats).

14580 NE 145th St., Woodinville, WA 98072. ⓒ 877/424-3930 or 425/424-3900. Fax 425/424-2585. www. willowslodge.com. 88 units. $220–$290 double; $350–$750 suite. Rates include continental breakfast. AE, DC, DISC, MC, V. Pets accepted with $200 refundable deposit. **Amenities:** Restaurant (Northwest); lounge; exercise room; full-service spa; Jacuzzi; sauna; bike rentals; room service; massage; laundry service; dry cleaning. *In room:* A/C, TV, dataport, minibar, fridge, coffeemaker, hair dryer, iron, safe.

EXPENSIVE

The Woodmark Hotel on Lake Washington ★★   Despite all the lakes and bays in the area, Seattle has a surprising dearth of waterfront hotels. Although Kirkland's Woodmark Hotel is 20 minutes from downtown Seattle (on a good day), it is the metro area's premier waterfront lodging. Surrounded by a luxury residential community, the Woodmark has the feel of a beach resort and looks out over the very same waters that Bill Gates views from his nearby Xanadu. While there are plenty of lake-view rooms here, you'll pay a premium for them. Creek-view rooms, which are the least expensive, offer a pleasant view of an attractively landscaped little stream. Floor-to-ceiling windows that open are a nice feature on sunny summer days, and high-speed Internet access was being added to the rooms in fall 2001. The hotel's dining room is pricey; for cocktails and afternoon tea, there's the cozy Library Bar, which often has live piano music in the evenings. In addition, complimentary late-night snacks and drinks are available.

1200 Carillon Point, Kirkland, WA 98033. ℂ **800/822-3700** or 425/822-3700. Fax 425/822-3699. www.the woodmark.com. 100 units. $205–$260 double; $320–$1,800 suite. AE, DISC, MC, V. Valet parking $12; self-parking $10. **Amenities:** Restaurant (New American), lounge; exercise room; full-service spa; concierge; room service; massage; babysitting; laundry service; dry cleaning. *In room:* A/C, TV, dataport, minibar, coffeemaker, hair dryer, iron, safe.

INEXPENSIVE

Extended StayAmerica—Bellevue ⭐   Located just off I-405 near down-town Bellevue, this modern off-ramp motel caters primarily to long-term guests. To this end, the rooms are all large, have kitchenettes, and offer free local calls. If you're only staying for a few days, you'll have to pay around $100, but if you stay for a week, rates drop to around $65 per day. This is about the most expensive of the Seattle area's Extended StayAmerica hotels, so if you don't mind staying in a different less upscale suburb, you can find even lower rates.

11400 Main St., Bellevue, WA 98009. ℂ **800/EXT-STAY** or 425/453-8186. Fax 425/453-8178. www.extended stay.com. 148 units. $89–$99 double ($440–$470 weekly). AE, DISC, MC, V. Free parking. **Amenities:** Coin-op laundry. *In room:* A/C, TV, dataport, coffeemaker, kitchenette, fridge.

4 Dining

With its abundant fresh seafood, Northwest berries, rain-fed mushrooms, and other market-fresh produce, Seattle is home to an abundance of excellent restaurants. Although the high-end restaurants in the Belltown neighborhood tend to dominate the city's culinary scene, there are plenty of good restaurants all over the city.

Seattle is a city obsessed with fresh seafood, and a visitor would be remiss if he or she did not take advantage of the great fish and shellfish available here. Salmon, in myriad guises, is almost ubiquitous on Seattle menus, despite what you may have heard about dwindling salmon populations in Northwest rivers (much of the salmon served here is now either farm-raised or caught in Canada or Alaska). There are also dozens of varieties of oysters available throughout the year. Dungeness crabs, another Northwest specialty, may not be as large as king crabs, but they're heftier than the blue crabs of the eastern United States. You may also run across such unfamiliar shellfish as razor clams and geoducks (pronounced "gooey dux"). The former is shaped like a straight razor and can be chewy if not prepared properly, and the latter is a bivalve of prodigious proportions (as heavy as 12 lb.) that now is so highly prized in Asia that it rarely ever shows up on Seattle menus.

You'll find restaurants on the shores of virtually every body of water in the area, so be sure to plan some waterfront dining while you're in town. Views at these restaurants take in not only water, but also everything from marinas to Mount Rainier, the Space Needle to the Olympic Mountains.

DOWNTOWN & FIRST HILL
EXPENSIVE

The Brooklyn Seafood, Steak, and Oyster House ⭐⭐ SEAFOOD Designed to look as if it's been here since the great Seattle fire, the Brooklyn is, in fact, housed in one of the city's oldest buildings. The specialty here is definitely oysters, with about 10 different types piled up at the oyster bar on any given night. If oysters on the half shell don't appeal to you, there are plenty of other tempting appetizers, ranging from cilantro-battered calamari to Dungeness crab cakes and smoked-duck spring rolls. For a classic Northwest dish, try the alder-planked king salmon (roasted on a slab of alder wood). In addition, there are simply prepared aged steaks, and such dishes as seafood pasta in parchment or grilled black tiger prawns in a morel mushroom and brandy cream sauce.

1212 Second Ave. © 206/224-7000. www.thebrooklyn.com. Reservations recommended. Main courses $10–$15 at lunch, $16–$35 at dinner. AE, DC, DISC, MC, V. Mon–Fri 11am–3pm; Mon–Thurs 5–10pm; Fri 5–10:30pm; Sat 4:30–10:30pm; Sun 4–10pm.

Fuller's ★★ NORTHWEST Fuller's, named for the founder of the Seattle Art Museum, is dedicated to both the culinary and the visual arts of the Northwest. Each dish is as beautifully presented as it is superbly prepared, and surrounding you in this very elegant dining room are works of art by some of the Northwest's best artists. Fuller's menu changes seasonally, but Northwest flavors with Asian and Mediterranean accents predominate. A recent spring menu included such appetizers as ahi tuna carpaccio with a coconut emulsion and buttermilk fried quail with a fava-bean purée and a balsamic reduction. Among the main dishes were porcini-dusted striped bass with red-wine risotto and salmon with vanilla bean paste and ginger velouté. For a fuller Fuller's experience, there are four-, six-, and eight-course tasting menus. The wine list reflects the seasonal changes on the menu. Don't miss the displays of glass art in the hotel lobby.

In the Sheraton Seattle Hotel and Towers, 1400 Sixth Ave. © 206/447-5544. Reservations recommended. Main courses $24–$34; tasting menus $55–$95. AE, DISC, MC, V. Tues–Sat 5:30–10pm.

Metropolitan Grill ★★ STEAK Fronted by massive granite columns that make it look more like a bank than a restaurant, the Metropolitan Grill is a very traditional steakhouse that attracts a well-heeled clientele, primarily men in suits (often out to impress business associates and clients). When you walk in the front door, you're immediately confronted by a case full of meat, from filet mignon to triple-cut lamb chops (with the occasional giant lobster tail tossed in). Perfectly cooked 28-day-aged steaks are the primary attraction, and a baked potato and a pile of thick-cut onion rings complete the ultimate carnivorous dinner. Financial matters are a frequent topic of discussion here, and the bar even has a "Guess the Dow" contest. I hope you sold high, since it'll take some capital gains to finance a dinner for two here.

820 Second Ave. © 206/624-3287. Reservations recommended. Main courses $10–$20 at lunch, $18–$42 at dinner. AE, DC, DISC, MC, V. Mon–Fri 11am–3pm and 4:30–11pm; Sat 4–11pm; Sun 4:30–10pm.

MODERATE
Andaluca ★★ NORTHWEST/MEDITERRANEAN Located in the Mayflower Park Hotel, this sumptuous restaurant mixes the traditional and the contemporary like no other place in town. To step through its doors is to enter a world of vibrant artistry, in both decor and cuisine. Specialties include such dishes as traditional Spanish *zarazuela* (shellfish stew) and *cabrales* (crusted beef tenderloin with Spanish blue cheese and grilled pears). The menu is divided into small and large plates, so you'll find something to satisfy your appetite regardless of its size. Don't miss the Dungeness crab tower, made with avocado, palm hearts, and gazpacho salsa—it's a work of art. Keep in mind that you can assemble a meal of small plates here and get away with a smaller bill.

In the Mayflower Park Hotel, 407 Olive Way. © 206/382-6999. www.andaluca.com. Reservations recommended. Main courses $18.50–$30.50; small plates $3–$9.25. AE, DC, DISC, MC, V. Mon–Thurs 6:30–11am, 11:30am–2:30pm, and 5–10pm; Fri–Sat 6:30–11am, 11:30am–2:30pm, and 5–11pm; Sun 7am–noon and 5–9pm.

McCormick and Schmick's ★★ SEAFOOD   Force your way past the crowds of business suits at the bar and you'll find yourself in a classic fish house—complete with cafe curtains, polished brass, leaded glass, and wood paneling. Daily fresh sheets commonly list more than 30 seafood entrees and feature well-prepared seafood dishes such as grilled steelhead with artichokes and spinach, Dungeness crab and shrimp cakes with red-pepper aioli, and cedar-plank–roasted salmon with berry *beurre rouge*. There are also usually a half dozen or more different varieties of oysters available. In late afternoons and late evenings, bar appetizers are only $1.95. If the restaurant is crowded and you can't get a table, consider sitting at the counter and watching the cooks perform amazing feats with fire.

1103 First Ave. ✆ 206/623-5500. Reservations recommended. Main courses $7–$26. AE, DC, DISC, MC, V. Mon–Fri 11:30am–11pm; Sat 4:30–10pm; Sun 4:30–9pm (bar menu served later).

Wild Ginger Asian Restaurant and Satay Bar ★★ PAN-ASIAN   This Pan-Asian restaurant has long been a Seattle favorite and is now located across the street from Benaroya Hall. Pull up a comfortable stool around the large satay grill and watch the cooks grill little skewers of anything from chicken to scallops to pork to prawns to lamb. Each skewer is served with a small cube of sticky rice and pickled cucumber. Order three or four satay sticks and you have a meal. If you prefer to sit at a table and have a more traditional dinner, Wild Ginger can accommodate you. Try the Panang beef curry (rib-eye steak in pungent curry sauce of cardamom, coconut milk, Thai basil, and peanuts). The lunch menu contains many of the dinner entrees, but at lower prices.

1401 Third Ave. ✆ 206/623-4450. Reservations recommended. Satay $2.75–$5.50; main courses $8.75–$22.50. AE, DC, DISC, MC, V. Mon–Thurs 11:30am–3pm and 5–11pm; Fri 11:30am–3pm and 5pm–midnight; Sat 11:30am–3pm and 4:30pm–midnight; Sun 4:30–11pm. Satay bar until 1am nightly.

THE WATERFRONT
MODERATE

Anthony's Pier 66 & Bell Street Diner ★★ SEAFOOD   The Anthony's chain has several outposts around the Seattle area, but this complex is the most

---

Kids Family-Friendly Restaurants

Maggie Bluffs Marina Grill (*p. 97*)   Located at a marina overlooking Elliott Bay and downtown Seattle, this economical place has food the kids will enjoy and provides crayons to keep them occupied while they wait. Before or after a meal, you can take a free boat ride across the marina to an observation deck atop the breakwater.

Ivar's Salmon House (*p. 97*)   This restaurant is built to resemble a Northwest Coast Native American longhouse and is filled with artifacts that kids will find fascinating. If they get restless, they can go out to the floating patio and watch the boats passing by.

Cucina!Cucina! (*p. 98*)   Every day's a party at this lively Italian restaurant on Lake Union, and kids always get special treatment (pictures to color, puzzles to do, pizza dough to shape and then let the kitchen cook). Birthdays are even better!

convenient and versatile. Not only is there an upscale and stylish seafood restaurant with good waterfront views, but Anthony's also includes a moderately priced casual restaurant and a walk-up counter as well. The bold contemporary styling and abundance of art glass set this place apart from most of the waterfront restaurants. The upscale crowd heads upstairs for the likes of Asian-inspired seafood dishes, and the more cost-conscious stay downstairs at the Bell Street Diner where meals are much easier on the wallet (though far less creative). For the higher prices, you get better views, as long as you don't get stuck at the counter that overlooks the exhibition kitchen. In summer, the decks are the place to be.

2201 Alaskan Way. ℭ **206/448-6688.** www.anthonys.com. Reservations recommended. Pier 66 main courses $15–$35. Bell Street Diner main courses $7.50–$30. AE, MC, V. Pier 66 Sun–Thurs 4:30–10:30pm; Fri–Sat 5–11:30pm. Bell Street Diner Sun–Thurs 11:30am–10:30pm; Fri–Sat 11:30am–11:30pm.

Elliott's ★★ SEAFOOD   While most of its neighbors are content to coast along on tourist business, Elliott's actually aims to keep locals happy by serving some of the best seafood in Seattle. Although the restaurant is right on the waterfront, the view really isn't that great. However, if you're looking for superbly prepared fresh seafood, Elliott's is an excellent bet. The oyster bar can have as many as 20 varieties of oysters available, so this is definitely the place to get to know your Northwest oysters. Salmon and Dungeness crabs are always on the menu and are usually prepared any of several different ways. However, with so many oysters in your midst, you might just want to start with oysters on the half shell and then move on to the pan-fried oysters. For lunch, the mesquite-grilled ahi tuna tacos with wasabi lime sauce and mango salsa are terrific.

Pier 56, Alaskan Way. ℭ **206/623-4340.** Reservations recommended. Main courses $9–$17 at lunch, $16–$36 at dinner. AE, DC, DISC, MC, V. Sun–Thurs 11am–10pm; Fri–Sat 11am–11pm. Closes 30 min. to 1 hr. later in summer.

PIONEER SQUARE & THE INTERNATIONAL DISTRICT

In addition to the two International District restaurants listed below, you'll also find a large all-Asian food court at **Uwajimaya,** 600 Fifth Ave. S. (ℭ **206/624-6248**), a huge Asian supermarket. The food court has stalls serving the food of different Asian countries. It all smells great, and everything is good and cheap, which makes this a great place for a quick meal. The bus tunnel entrance is right across the street, which makes Uwajimaya easy to reach even from the north end of downtown.

MODERATE

Trattoria Mitchelli ★ ITALIAN/LATE-NIGHT   Located in the heart of Pioneer Square, Trattoria Mitchelli serves good, basic Italian food in a cozy spot with a friendly old-world atmosphere. An old wooden-topped lunch counter in a room with classic hexagonal tile floors is a popular after-work and late-night gathering spot, and conversation is lively. You can't go wrong here with the fettuccine con pollo, pizza from the wood-fired oven, or the pasta of the week served with your choice of sauce. For a rich dessert, dig into a caramello, a creamy caramel with toasted walnuts and whipped cream. If you're a night owl, keep Mitchelli's in mind—full meals are served until 4am, catering to the starving hordes who pour out of the area's many bars after last call.

84 Yesler Way. ℭ **206/623-3883.** Reservations accepted only for parties of 6 or more people. Main courses $9–$16. AE, MC, V. Mon 7am–11pm; Tues–Fri 7am–4am; Sat 8am–4am; Sun 8am–11pm.

INEXPENSIVE

Hing Loon ⭐ CHINESE/LATE-NIGHT   Bright fluorescent lighting, big Formica-top tables, devoid of atmosphere—this is the sort of place you'd pass by without a thought if you were aimlessly searching for a restaurant in the International District. With so many choices in a few square blocks, it's easy to be distracted by fancy decor. But forget the rest and take a seat in Hing Loon. Seafood is the house specialty, and none is done better than the oysters with ginger and green onion served on a sizzling platter. The restaurant makes all its own noodles, so you can't go wrong ordering chow mein or chow fun—but be prepared for a large helping. Pork dishes tend to be fatty.

628 S. Weller St. ⓒ 206/682-2828. Main courses $4.50–$9.50. DC, MC, V. Sun–Thurs 10am–midnight; Fri–Sat 10am–2am.

Merchants Cafe AMERICAN   Merchants Cafe is Seattle's oldest restaurant and looks every bit of its 100-plus years. A well-scuffed tile floor surrounds the bar, which came around the Horn in the 1800s, and an old safe and gold scales are left over from the days when Seattle was the first, or last, taste of civilization for Yukon prospectors. At one time the restaurant's basement was a card room, and the upper floors were a brothel. In fact, this may be the original Skid Row saloon (Yesler Way was the original Skid Road down which logs were skidded to a sawmill). Straightforward sandwiches, salads, and soups are the mainstays of the menu.

109 Yesler Way. ⓒ 206/624-1515. Main courses and sandwiches $5.50–$8. AE, MC, V. Mon–Thurs 11am–9pm; Fri–Sat 11am–2am; Sun 11am–4am.

Pecos Pit BBQ *Finds* BARBECUE   This barbecue joint, located in an industrial area south of Pioneer Square, looks like an old gas station with picnic tables out front, and the first thing you'll notice is the line of about 30 people standing in front of the walk-up window. The second thing you'll notice is that the bag they give you comes with five napkins and a spoon. Yep, this joint is both popular and a great place to ruin a good shirt, but those sandwiches sure are tasty. Unless you're a confirmed fire-eater, don't go beyond "mild" unless you want to feel your lips burning long after you've finished eating. Pecos Pit BBQ may be out of the way, but it's well worth the drive.

2260 First Ave. S. ⓒ 206/623-0629. Sandwiches $5.50. No credit cards. Mon–Fri 11am–3pm.

Salumi ⭐ *Finds* ITALIAN   For many folks, salami is a guilty pleasure. We all know it's got way too much fat, but it tastes too good to resist. Now, raise the bar on salami, and you have the artisan-cured meats of this closet-size eatery near Pioneer Square. The owner makes all his own salami (as well as traditional Italian-cured beef tongue). Order up a meat plate with a side of cheese and some roasted red bell peppers, pour yourself a glass of wine from the big bottle on the table, and you have a perfect lunchtime repast in the classic Italian style. Did I mention the great breads and tapenades? Wow! If you're down in the Pioneer Square area at lunch, don't miss this place.

309 Third Ave. S. ⓒ 206/621-8772. Reservations not accepted. Main courses $4.50–$9.50. AE, DC, DISC, MC, V. Tues–Fri 11am–4pm.

BELLTOWN & PIKE PLACE MARKET
VERY EXPENSIVE

El Gaucho ⭐⭐ LATE-NIGHT/STEAK   Conjuring up the ghosts of dinner clubs of the 1930s and 1940s, this high-end Belltown steakhouse seems like a

Fred Astaire film set. The pure theatrics make this place a must if you're in the mood to spend big bucks on a thick, juicy steak. Although you might get a better steak at one of the other high-end steakhouses in town, you just can't duplicate the experience of dining at El Gaucho. Stage-set decor aside, the real stars of the show here are the 28-day dry-aged Angus beef steaks, which are among the best in town, but expect to drop a bundle on the perfect steak. All the classics are here, too, including Caesar salad tossed tableside, and chateaubriand carved before your eyes. Not a steak eater? How about venison chops, an ostrich filet, or Australian lobster tail? There's also a classy bar off to one side, a separate cigar lounge, and for after-dinner dancing, the affiliated Pampas Room nightclub.

2505 First Ave. © 206/728-1337. www.elgaucho.com. Reservations recommended. Main courses $16–$90. AE, DC, MC, V. Mon–Sat 5pm–1am; Sun 5–11pm.

EXPENSIVE

Campagne ✦✦ COUNTRY FRENCH   With large windows that look out over the top of Pike Place Market to Elliott Bay, Campagne is an unpretentious, yet elegant, French restaurant. With such a prime location, it shouldn't be surprising that Campagne relies heavily on the wide variety of fresh ingredients that the market provides. The menu leans toward country French, with such dishes as pâté de campagne or lamb loin and lamb sausage with a potato *galette* (potato cake). There are always several interesting salads as well.

Budget tip: One of Seattle's great culinary deals can be had here at Campagne between 5:30 and 6:30pm daily, when three-course dinners are available for only $30.

Inn at the Market, 86 Pine St. © 206/728-2800. www.campagnerestaurant.com. Reservations recommended. Main courses $22–$35; 3-course prix fixe dinner $30. AE, DC, MC, V. Daily 5–10pm; bar menu until midnight.

Chez Shea ✦✦✦ NORTHWEST   Quiet, dark, and intimate, Chez Shea is one of the finest restaurants in Seattle, and with only a dozen candlelit tables and views across Puget Sound to the Olympic Mountains, this is an ideal setting for romance. The menu changes with the season, and ingredients come primarily from the market below. On a recent summer evening, dinner started with savory basil panna cotta and then moved on to potato-leek bisque. There are usually five choices of entree; among these were a pan-roasted salmon filet with a sesame glaze and rhubarb-ginger compote and a shiitake mushroom and spinach lasagna. Though dessert is a la carte, you'll find it impossible to let it pass you by. While there are equally fine restaurants in the city, none has quite the romantic atmosphere as Chez Shea.

Pike Place Market, Corner Market Building, 94 Pike St., Ste. 34. © 206/467-9990. www.chezshea.com. Reservations highly recommended. 4-course prix fixe dinner $43. AE, MC, V. Tues–Sun 5:30–10:30pm.

MODERATE

Cafe Campagne ✦✦ *Finds* FRENCH   This cozy little cafe is an offshoot of the Inn at the Market's popular Campagne, a much more formal French restaurant, and though it's in the heart of the Pike Place Market neighborhood, it's a world away from the market madness. We like to duck in here for lunch and escape the shuffling crowds. What a relief—so civilized, so very French. The dark and cozy place has a hidden feel to it, and most people leave feeling like they've discovered some secret hideaway. The menu changes with the seasons but Monday through Saturday there is always a daily rotisserie special such as stuffed quail or leg of lamb marinated with garlic and anchovy. These are definitely the

Great Brunch Choices

For brunch, there are some great options around the city. Try **Cafe Flora, Ivar's Salmon House, Palisade, Ponti Seafood Grill, Salty's on Alki,** or **SkyCity at the Needle.** All these places have complete reviews in the appropriate neighborhood sections of this chapter.

meals to have here. The cafe also doubles as a wine bar and has a good selection of reasonably priced wines by the glass or by the bottle.

1600 Post Alley. ✆ 206/728-2233. Reservations accepted for dinner only. Main courses $11–$18. AE, DC, MC, V. Mon–Thurs 8–11am, 11:45am–3pm, and 5–10pm; Fri–Sat 8–11am, 11:45am–3pm and 5:30–11pm; Sun 8am–3pm and 5–10pm.

Dahlia Lounge ★★ PAN-ASIAN/NORTHWEST   The neon chef holding a flapping fish may suggest that the Dahlia is little more than a roadside diner, but a glimpse at the stylish interior will likely have you thinking otherwise. One look at the menu, one bite of any dish, will convince you that this is one of Seattle's finest restaurants. Mouthwatering and succulent Dungeness crab cakes, a bow to Chef Tom Douglas's Maryland roots, are the house specialty and should not be missed. The menu, influenced by the far side of the Pacific Rim, changes regularly, with the lunch menu featuring many of the same offerings at slightly lower prices. For dessert, it takes a Herculean effort to resist the crème caramel, and it's way too easy to fill up on the restaurant's breads, which are baked in the adjacent Dahlia Bakery.

2001 Fourth Ave. ✆ 206/682-4142. www.tomdouglas.com. Reservations highly recommended. Main courses $18–$26. AE, DC, DISC, MC, V. Mon–Fri 11:30am–2:30pm; Mon–Thurs 5:30–10pm; Fri–Sat 5:30–11pm; Sun 5–10pm.

Etta's Seafood ★★ SEAFOOD   Seattle chef Tom Douglas's strictly seafood (well, almost) restaurant, Etta's, is located smack in the middle of the Pike Place Market area, and of course, serves Douglas's signature crab cakes (crunchy on the outside, creamy on the inside), which are not to be missed (and if they're not on the menu, just ask). Don't ignore your side dishes, either; they can be exquisite and are usually enough to share among the table. In addition to the great seafood dishes, there are always a few other fine options, including several that date from Douglas's Café Sport days in the early 1980s. Stylish contemporary decor sets the mood and assures that this place is as popular with locals as it is with tourists. ✆ 206/443-6000. www.tomdouglas.com. Reservations recommended. Main courses $10–$28. AE, DC, DISC, MC, V. Mon–Thurs 11:30am–10pm; Fri 11:30am–11pm; Sat 9am–11pm; Sun 9am–10pm.

Fandango ★★ LATIN AMERICAN   Fandango is the latest culinary offering from local celebrity chef Christine Keff, who also operates the ever-popular Flying Fish restaurant diagonally across the street from this establishment. The focus here is on the sunny flavors of Latin America, and Fandango's menu is filled with combinations you aren't likely to have ever encountered this far north before. This just might be the only place in the city where you can a get a *huitlacoche* quesadilla (made with a corn fungus that's considered a delicacy in Mexico). Whether you order the Brazilian seafood stew, suckling pig, or sea scallops with almonds, oranges, and capers, you'll enjoy some real taste treats. If you're lucky, you just might find grilled bananas on the dessert menu, and be sure to try a *mojito* cocktail.

2313 First Ave. © **206/441-1188.** Reservations recommended. Main courses $15–$20. DC, MC, V. Daily 5pm–midnight (until 2am in the bar).

Flying Fish ★★ LATE-NIGHT/NORTHWEST/SEAFOOD   Chef Christine Keff has been on the Seattle restaurant scene for many years now, and with Flying Fish, she hit on something the city really wanted. Not only are there the bold combinations of vibrant flavors demanded by the city's well-traveled palates, but the hip Belltown restaurant serves dinner past midnight every night, keeping late-night partiers from going hungry. Every dish here is a work of art, and with small plates, large plates, and platters for sharing, diners are encouraged to sample a wide variety of the kitchen's creations. To keep the locals coming back, the menu changes almost daily, but keep an eye out for the smoked rock shrimp spring rolls, which are positively sculptural. The festive desserts are often so decorated that they're a miniparty on the plate. There's also a huge wine list.

2234 First Ave. © **206/728-8595.** www.flyingfishseattle.com. Reservations recommended. Main courses $15–$23. DC, MC, V. Daily 5pm–1am.

Icon Grill ★ AMERICAN   With every inch of wall space covered with framed artwork, colorful art glass hanging from chandeliers, and overflowing giant vases, this place goes way overboard with its decor, but that's the exactly what makes it so fun. Basically, it's an over-the-top rendition of a Victorian setting gone 21st century. The food is a mix of basic comfort food (including a molasses-glazed meatloaf that locals swear by) and moderately more inventive dishes such as a grilled pear salad, lemon-rosemary game hen, and rhubarb-and-rosemary-glazed lamb shank. Unfortunately, the food can be unpredictable, so don't come here just for a culinary experience, but rather for a Seattle experience.

1933 Fifth Ave. © **206/441-6330.** Reservations recommended. Main courses $10.50–$33. AE, MC, V. Mon–Fri 11:30am–2pm; Sun–Mon 5:30–9pm; Tues–Thurs 5:30–10pm; Fri–Sat 5:30–11pm.

Matt's in the Market ★★ *Finds* AMERICAN REGIONAL/INTERNA-TIONAL   Quite possibly the smallest gourmet restaurant in Seattle, Matt's is a tiny cubbyhole of a place in the Corner Market Building, which is directly across the street from the market information booth at First and Pike. There are only a handful of tables and a few stools at the counter here, and although the kitchen takes up almost half the restaurant, the cooks still have little more than the space of a walk-in closet in which to work their culinary magic. The menu changes regularly, with an emphasis on fresh ingredients from the market stalls only steps away, and there's a good selection of reasonably priced wines. The menu pulls in whatever influences and styles happen to appeal to the chef at that moment, perhaps Moroccan, perhaps Southern. This is a real Pike Place Market experience.

94 Pike St. © **206/467-7909.** Reservations not accepted. Main courses $8–$9 at lunch, $15–$18 at dinner. MC, V. Tues–Sat 11:30am–2:30pm and 5:30–9:30pm.

Palace Kitchen ★★ AMERICAN REGIONAL/LATE-NIGHT/MEDITER-RANEAN   This is the most casual of chef Tom Douglas's three Seattle establishments, with a bar that attracts nearly as many customers as the restaurant. The atmosphere is urban chic, with cement pillars, simple wood booths, and a few tables in the front window, which overlooks the monorail tracks. The menu is short and features a nightly selection of unusual cheeses and different preparations from the apple-wood grill. To begin a meal, we enjoy the Spanish white anchovies, but wood-grilled chicken wings with cilantro sour cream are also a big hit. Entrees are usually simple and delicious and often draw on Southern influences, as in the pan-seared halibut with grits and orange-rosemary sauce. For dessert, the coconut cream pie is an absolute must, but there's also always a daily cheese selection.

2030 Fifth Ave. ⓒ 206/448-2001. www.tomdouglas.com. Reservations not accepted. Main courses $11–$25. AE, DC, DISC, MC, V. Mon–Fri 11:30am–2:30pm; daily 5pm–1am.

The Pink Door ⭐ ITALIAN/LATE-NIGHT   Pike Place Market's better restaurants tend to be well hidden, and if we didn't tell you about this one, you'd probably never find it. There's no sign out front—only the pink door for which the restaurant is named (look for it between Stewart and Virginia sts.). On the other side of the door, stairs lead to a cellarlike space, which is almost always empty on summer days, when folks forsake it to dine on the deck with a view of Elliott Bay. What makes this place so popular is as much the fun atmosphere as the Italian food. There's a tarot card reader in residence, and sometimes there's a magician. Most nights in the bar you can see some sort of Fellini-esque cabaret performer. Be sure to start your meal with the fragrant roasted garlic and ricotta-Gorgonzola spread or the house-made tapenade. From there, you might move on to an Italian classic such as lasagna or something made with fresh seafood from Pike Place Market.

1919 Post Alley. ⓒ 206/443-3241. Reservations recommended. Main courses $14–$20. AE, MC, V. Tues–Sat 11:30am–2am; Sun 4–11pm.

Shea's Lounge ⭐⭐ NORTHWEST/INTERNATIONAL/LATE-NIGHT Convenient, casual, economical, romantic. What's not to like about this hidden jewel in Pike Place Market? This is the lounge for the ever-popular Chez Shea, and it's one of the most sophisticated little spaces in Seattle. Romantic lighting and a view of the bay make this a popular spot with couples, and whether you just want a cocktail and an appetizer or a full meal, you can get it here. The menu features gourmet pizzas, combination appetizer plates, a few soups and salads, and several nightly specials such as seared rare ahi tuna with chilled Asian noodles tossed in Thai red-curry peanut sauce. You can even order dishes from the main restaurant's menu. The desserts are divinely decadent. This is a great spot for a light or late-night meal.

Pike Place Market, Corner Market Building, 94 Pike St., Ste. 34. ⓒ 206/467-9990. Reservations not accepted. Main courses $13–$26. AE, MC, V. Tues–Thurs and Sun 4:30pm–midnight; Fri–Sat 4:30pm–2am.

INEXPENSIVE

Belltown Pub and Cafe ⭐ *Kids* AMERICAN   Located in Belltown in what was once a sleeping bag factory, this lively pub serves a surprisingly varied menu. Although you'll find everything from spaghetti and meatballs to smoked salmon mousse here, the bacon and cheddar burger is hard to pass up. It's definitely one of the best burgers in Seattle—thick, juicy, well flavored, and set on a large, chewy roll. Accompany your burger with a pint from one of the many micro-brew taps. More sophisticated palates may prefer the likes of chicken Marsala or smoked-salmon ravioli with some wine chosen from a fairly decent wine list. There are tables on the sidewalk in summer, and huge wooden booths for when the weather is inclement. This place is family friendly, which is a rarity in trendy Belltown.

2322 First Ave. ⓒ 206/728-4311. www.belltownpub.com. Reservations accepted. Main courses $8.25–$20. AE, MC, V. Sun–Thurs 11:30am–midnight; Fri–Sat 11:30am–1am.

Noodle Ranch ⭐ *Finds* PAN-ASIAN   This Belltown hole-in-the-wall serves Pan-Asian cuisine for the hip-yet-financially-challenged crowd. It's a lively, boisterous scene, and the food is packed with intense, and often unfamiliar, flavors. Don't miss the fish grilled in grape leaves with its nice presentation and knockout dipping sauce. In fact, all of the dipping sauces here are delicious. The Mekong grill—rice noodles with a rice wine vinegar and herb dressing topped with grilled pork, chicken, catfish, or tofu—is another dish not to be missed. You'll also find the likes of Laotian cucumber salad and Japanese-style eggplant. In fact, there are lots of vegetarian options. Although the place is frequently packed, you can usually get a seat.

2228 Second Ave. ⓒ **206/728-0463.** Main courses $7–$11.25. AE, MC, V. Mon–Thurs 11am–10pm; Fri 11am–11pm; Sat noon–11pm.

Virginia Inn ⭐ AMERICAN/FRENCH   In business since 1903, this restaurant/bar near Pike Place Market is a cozy spot for lunch or a cheap dinner. Big windows let light pour into the small room, but if the sun is shining, most people try to get a seat on the sidewalk patio. This has long been a favorite hangout of Belltown residents and is as popular for its microbrews as it is for its food. The crab cakes are a perennial favorite here.

1937 First Ave. ⓒ **206/728-1937.** Reservations accepted only for parties of 5 or more. Main courses $7.50–$10.50. AE, MC, V. Daily 11:30am–10pm.

QUEEN ANNE & SEATTLE CENTER
VERY EXPENSIVE

SkyCity at the Needle ⭐⭐ NORTHWEST   Both the restaurant and the prices are sky-high at this revolving restaurant, located just below the observation deck at the top of Seattle's famous Space Needle. But because you don't have to pay extra for the elevator ride if you dine here, the high prices start to seem a little bit more in line with those at other Seattle splurge restaurants. OK, so maybe you'd get better food somewhere else, and maybe you can dine with a view at other Seattle restaurants, but you won't get such a spectacular panorama anywhere but here. The menu works hard at offering some distinctly Northwestern flavor combinations but still has plenty of familiar fare for those diners who aren't into culinary adventures. Steak and seafood make up the bulk of the menu, with a couple of vegetarian options as well. We recommend coming here for lunch. The prices are considerably more reasonable and the views, encompassing city skyline, Mount Rainier, and the Olympic Mountains, are unsurpassed.

Space Needle, 400 Broad St. ⓒ **800/937-9582** or 206/905-2100. www.spaceneedle.com. Reservations highly recommended. Main courses $15–$30 at lunch, $26–$42 at dinner; weekend brunch $34.50 adults, $21.50 children 5–12. AE, DC, DISC, MC, V. Mon–Fri 10am–2:45pm and 4:30–10:15pm; Sat–Sun 8am–2:45pm and 4:30–10:15pm.

EXPENSIVE

Canlis ⭐⭐⭐ NORTHWEST   A Seattle institution, Canlis has been in business since 1950. A major remodeling a few years back gave the restaurant a stylish new look that mixes contemporary decor with Asian antiques, and Canlis continues to make improvements aimed at luring in Seattle's new movers and shakers. The Northwest cuisine, with Asian and continental influences, keeps both traditionalists and more adventurous diners content. Steaks from the copper grill are perennial favorites here, as are the spicy Canlis prawns. You'll definitely want to dress up for a meal here. This is the perfect place to close a big deal or celebrate a very special occasion. To finish, why not go all the way and have the Grand Marnier soufflé? Canlis also has one of the best wine lists in Seattle.

2576 Aurora Ave. N. ℂ **206/283-3313.** www.canlis.com. Reservations highly recommended. Main courses $22–$50; chef's tasting menu $95 with wines. AE, DC, DISC, MC, V. Mon–Sat 5:30pm–midnight. Valet parking $5.

Palisade ★★★ NORTHWEST   With a panorama that sweeps from downtown to West Seattle and across the sound to the Olympic Mountains, Palisade has one of the best views of any Seattle waterfront restaurant. It also happens to have fine food and inventive interior design (incorporating a saltwater pond, complete with fish, sea anemones, and starfish, in the middle of the dining room). The extensive menu features dishes prepared on a searing grill, in a wood-fired oven, in a wood-fired rotisserie, and in an applewood broiler—it all adds up to many choices of flavorful seafoods and meats. There's also an excellent and very popular Sunday brunch here. Palisade is not easy to find, but it's more than worth the trouble to search it out. Call for directions.

Elliott Bay Marina, 2601 W. Marina Place. ℂ **206/285-1000.** Reservations recommended. Main courses $17–$48. AE, DC, DISC, MC, V. Mon–Fri 11:30am–2pm and 5–10pm; Sat noon–2pm and 4:30–10pm; Sun 10am–2pm and 4:30–9pm.

INEXPENSIVE

The 5 Spot ★ AMERICAN REGIONAL/LATE-NIGHT   The 5 Spot is one of Seattle's favorite diners. Every 3 months or so, the restaurant changes its menu to reflect a different regional U.S. cuisine. Maybe you'll find Brooklyn comfort food or Cuban-influenced Miami-style meals featured on the menu, but you can bet whatever's featured will be filling and fun. The atmosphere here is pure kitsch—whenever the theme is "Florida," the restaurant is adorned with palm trees and flamingos and looks like the high school gym done up for prom night. This bustling diner is popular with all types, who appreciate the fact that you won't go broke eating here. To find The 5 Spot, look for the neon coffee pouring into the giant coffee cup sign at the top of Queen Anne hill.

1502 Queen Anne Ave. N. ℂ **206/285-SPOT.** www.chowfoods.com. Reservations accepted only for parties of 6–10. Main courses $6.75–$10.25 at lunch, $8.75–$17.75 at dinner. MC, V. Daily 8:30am–midnight.

Maggie Bluffs Marina Grill ★ *(Kids)* AMERICAN   It isn't easy finding affordable waterfront dining in any city, and Seattle is no exception. However, if you're willing to drive a few miles from downtown Seattle, you can save quite a few bucks at this casual marina restaurant located at the foot of Magnolia Bluff (northwest of downtown Seattle). The menu is fairly simple, with burgers and fish and chips, but also includes a few more creative dishes. The restaurant overlooks a marina and, while the view is partially obstructed by a breakwater, you can still see Elliott Bay, West Seattle, downtown, and even the Space Needle. There are crayons to keep the kids entertained, and after a meal, you can walk out Pier G and take a free shuttle boat to an observation deck atop the breakwater. The patio dining area is immensely popular on sunny summer days.

Elliott Bay Marina, 2601 W. Marina Place. ℂ **206/283-8322.** Reservations not accepted. Main courses $7–$11.50. AE, DISC, MC, V. Mon–Thurs 11:30am–9pm; Fri 11:30am–10pm; Sat–Sun 9am–11:30pm.

LAKE UNION
MODERATE

Ivar's Salmon House ★★ *(Kids)* SEAFOOD   With a view of the Space Needle on the far side of Lake Union, flotillas of sea kayaks silently slipping by, sailboats racing across the lake, and powerboaters tying up at the dock out back, this restaurant on the north side of Lake Union is quintessential Seattle. Add to the scene an award-winning building designed to resemble a Northwest Coast Indian longhouse, and you have what just might be the very best place in town for a waterfront meal. OK, so maybe, just maybe, you can find better food at a few other waterfront places, but none has the unequivocally Seattle atmosphere you'll find at Ivar's Salmon House. This place is a magnet for weekend boaters who abandon their own galley fare in favor of Ivar's clam chowder and famous alder-smoked salmon. Lots of artifacts, including long dugout canoes and historic photographic portraits of Native American chiefs, make Ivar's a hit with both kids and adults. Bear in mind that this restaurant's popularity means that service can be slow; just relax and keep enjoying the views.

401 NE Northlake Way. ✆ 206/632-0767. www.ivars.net. Reservations recommended. Main courses $8–$15 at lunch, $13–$27 at dinner. AE, MC, V. Mon–Thurs 11am–10pm; Fri–Sat 11am–11pm; Sun 10am–2pm and 3:30–10pm.

McCormick and Schmick's Harborside ⭐ SEAFOOD   With its waterfront setting and views of the marinas on the west side of Lake Union, this restaurant has the best location of any of Seattle's McCormick and Schmick's restaurants. The menu, which changes daily, includes seemingly endless choices of appetizers, sandwiches, salads, and creative entrees. Just be sure to order something with seafood, such as seared rare ahi with a nori (seaweed) wrap and wasabi; Parmesan-crusted petrale sole; or blackened catfish with tequila and rock shrimp sauce. Sure, there are meat dishes on the menu, but why bother (unless you only came here for the excellent view)? Bar specials for $1.95 are available in the late afternoon and late evening, and there are always plenty of varieties of oysters on the half shell.

1200 Westlake Ave. N. ✆ 206/270-9052. www.mandsharborside.com. Reservations recommended. Main courses $6–$25. AE, DC, DISC, MC, V. Mon–Fri 11:30am–11pm; Sat–Sun 11:30am–3pm (summer only) and 4–11pm.

Serafina ⭐⭐ RUSTIC ITALIAN   Off the beaten tourist track, Serafina is one of our favorite Seattle dining spots. It has a nice touch of sophistication but overall, it's a relaxed, neighborhood sort of place. The rustic, romantic atmosphere underscores the earthy, country-style dishes served here. The antipasti Serafina is always a good choice for a starter and changes daily. It's also hard to resist ordering at least one of the bruschetta appetizers, which come with any of three different toppings. Among the pasta offerings you might find a rabbit ragout served over papperdelle pasta or veal meatballs in a green olive–tomato sauce served over Italian *strangozzi* pasta. If you've brought a big appetite, try the mixed grill. There's live music (mostly jazz and Latin) several nights each week.

2043 Eastlake Ave. E. ✆ 206/323-0807. www.serafinaseattle.com. Reservations recommended. Pastas $8–$16; entrees $14–$22. MC, V. Mon–Fri 11:30am–2pm; Sun–Thurs 5:30–10pm; Fri–Sat 5:30–11pm.

INEXPENSIVE

Cucina!Cucina! ⭐ *Kids* ITALIAN   Although it's part of a local restaurant chain, Cucina!Cucina! is a good bet not only for its waterfront view and reliable pizzas and pasta, but for its lively party atmosphere. Located at the south end of Lake Union, this restaurant is also a favorite of Seattle families because of all the special attention kids are given here. But just because families are welcome doesn't mean this place isn't fun for grown-ups, too. In summer, the deck is the place to be.

Chandler's Cove, 901 Fairview Ave. N. ℭ **206/447-2782.** www.cucinacucina.com. Call ahead to place name on wait list. Main courses $9–$19. AE, DC, DISC, MC, V. Sun–Thurs 11:30am–10pm; Fri–Sat 11:30am–11pm (open 1 hr. later in summer).

CAPITOL HILL & EAST SEATTLE
VERY EXPENSIVE

Rover's ★★★ NORTHWEST   Tucked away in a quaint clapboard house behind a chic little shopping center in the Madison Valley neighborhood east of downtown, this is one of Seattle's most acclaimed restaurants. Thierry Rautureau, Rover's much-celebrated and award-winning chef, received classical French training before falling in love with the Northwest and all the wonderful ingredients it has to offer an imaginative chef. Voilà! Northwest cuisine with a French accent.

The delicacies on the frequently changing menu are enough to send the most jaded of gastronomes into fits of indecision. Luckily, you can simply opt for one of the fixed-price dinners and leave the decision making to a professional—the chef. Culinary creations include such offerings as smoked salmon and cucumber salad, spice-infused pinot noir sorbet, and venison with caramelized turnips and Armagnac sauce. Vegetarians, take note: You won't often find a vegetarian feast that can compare with the ones served here.

2808 E. Madison St. ℭ **206/325-7442.** www.rovers-seattle.com. Reservations required. 5-course menu degustation $70 (vegetarian) and $80; chef's 8-course grand menu $115. AE, DC, MC, V. Tues–Sat 5:30 to about 9:30pm.

INEXPENSIVE

Cafe Flora ★ VEGETARIAN   Big, bright, and airy, this Madison Valley cafe will dispel any ideas you might have about vegetarian food being boring. This is meatless gourmet cooking and draws on influences from around the world—a vegetarian's dream come true. One of the house specialties is a portobello Wellington made with mushroom-pecan pâté and sautéed leeks in a puff pastry. While the menu changes weekly, unusual pizzas (such as roasted fig, Walla Walla onion masala chutney, toasted hazelnuts, and goat cheese) are always on the menu. On weekends, a casual brunch features interesting breakfast fare.

2901 E. Madison St. ℭ **206/325-9100.** www.cafeflora.com. Reservations accepted only for parties of 8 or more. Main courses $9.25–$16. MC, V. Tues–Fri 11:30am–10pm; Sat 9am–2pm and 5–10pm; Sun 9am–2pm and 5–9pm.

NORTH SEATTLE (INCLUDING FREMONT, WALLINGFORD & THE UNIVERSITY DISTRICT)
EXPENSIVE

Ponti Seafood Grill ★★ SEAFOOD   Situated at the south end of the Fremont Bridge overlooking the Lake Washington Ship Canal (not officially in north Seattle), Ponti is one of Seattle's most elegant and sophisticated restaurants. The menu here, which changes weekly, has an international flavor that roams the globe from Thailand to Italy, though it also offers some solidly Northwestern creations. Perennial favorites among the appetizers include Dungeness crab spring rolls with a chili-lime dipping sauce, and Cajun barbecued prawns. The weekly listing of fresh seafoods might include the likes of grilled rare ahi with a coconut-rice cake or a simple penne pasta with grilled prawns. The lunch menu includes some of the same dishes served at dinner (though at sometimes half the price), which makes this restaurant a good bet for a gourmet midday meal on a tight budget. Before or after you dine here, take a walk around Fremont to check out the funky shops and eclectic public art.

3014 Third Ave. N. ℂ 206/284-3000. Reservations recommended. Main courses $8–$14 at lunch, $16–$29 at dinner. AE, DC, DISC, MC, V. Mon–Fri 11:30am–2:30pm; Sun 10am–2:30pm (brunch); Sun–Thurs 5–10pm; Fri–Sat 5–11pm.

MODERATE

Ray's Boathouse and Cafe ★★ SEAFOOD When Seattleites want to impress visiting friends and relatives, this restaurant often ranks right up there with the Space Needle, the ferries, and Pike Place Market. The view across Puget Sound to the Olympic Mountains is superb. You can also watch the boat traffic coming and going from the Lake Washington Ship Canal, and bald eagles can often be seen fishing just offshore. Then there's Ray's dual personality—upstairs there's a lively (and loud) cafe and lounge, while downstairs there's a much more formal and sedate scene. The upstairs menu is more creative and less expensive than the one downstairs, but even upstairs you can order from the downstairs menu. The crab cakes are delicious and are packed full of crab, and the smoked scallops are tender and delicately flavored. The black cod glazed with sake kasu is a typically Northwestern preparation well worth trying. Whatever your mood, Ray's has got you covered. No reservations are taken for dinner upstairs, and waiting times of up to an hour are not unusual (which is why the bar gets so lively).

6049 Seaview Ave. NW. ℂ 206/789-3770. www.rays.com. Reservations recommended (not accepted for dinner in cafe). Main courses $16–$45 (Boathouse), $8.50–$17 (Cafe). AE, DC, DISC, MC, V. Boathouse Mon–Thurs 5–10pm; Fri 5–10:30pm; Sat 4:30–10:30pm; Sun 4:30–10pm. Cafe Sun–Thurs 11:30am–10pm; Fri–Sat 11:30am–10:30pm.

INEXPENSIVE

Himalayan Sherpa Restaurant ★ *Finds* HIMALAYAN If you've ever been to Nepal, you may not remember the food with the fondest of memories. But should you be struck with pangs of nostalgia for that trek you once made, you might be interested to know that you can relive your fonder Himalayan culinary memories in Seattle's University District. The food here is both surprisingly authentic and far superior to most of the Nepali food served in budget restaurants in Nepal. For the full experience, opt for the Nepalese fixed menu or the Himalayan Sherpa combo. With a minimum of four people and an hour's notice, the restaurant can also prepare a traditional Tibetan hot-pot (*gyakok*) dinner for you.

4214 University Way NE. ℂ 206/633-2100. www.himalayansherpa.com. Reservations recommended. Main courses $6.50–$15. AE, MC, V. Daily 10am–10pm.

Red Mill Burgers AMERICAN Located just a little north of the Woodland Park Zoo, this retro burger joint is tiny and always hoppin' because everyone knows they do one of the best burgers in Seattle. Try the verde burger, made with Anaheim peppers for just the right amount of fire. Don't miss the onion rings. Burgers here are definitely multinapkin affairs.

312 N. 67th St. ℂ 206/783-6362. Burgers $3–$5. No credit cards. Tues–Sat 11am–9pm; Sun noon–8pm.

WEST SEATTLE
EXPENSIVE

Salty's on Alki Beach ★ SEAFOOD Although the prices here are almost as out of line as those at the Space Needle, and the service is unpredictable, this restaurant has *the* waterfront view in Seattle, and the food is usually pretty good. Because the restaurant is set on the northeast side of the Alki Peninsula, it faces downtown Seattle on the far side of Elliott Bay. Come at sunset for dinner and watch the setting sun sparkle off skyscraper windows as the lights of the city twinkle on. On sunny summer days, lunch on one of the two decks is a sublimely Seattle experience. Don't be discouraged by the ugly industrial/port area you drive through to get here; Salty's marks the start of Alki Beach, the closest Seattle comes to a Southern California beach scene. Just watch for the giant rusted salmon sculptures swimming amid rebar kelp beds and the remains of an old bridge (hey, Seattle even recycles when it comes to art).

1936 Harbor Ave. SW. ℂ 206/937-1600. www.saltys.com. Reservations recommended. Main courses $20–$40. AE, DC, DISC, MC, V. Daily 11am–11:30pm.

THE EASTSIDE (INCLUDING BELLEVUE & KIRKLAND)
VERY EXPENSIVE

The Herbfarm Restaurant ★★★ NORTHWEST The Herbfarm, the most highly acclaimed restaurant in the Northwest, is known across the nation for its extraordinarily lavish meals. The menu changes throughout the year, with different themes to match the seasons. Wild gathered vegetables, Northwest seafoods and meats, organic vegetables, wild mushrooms, and of course the generous use of fresh herbs from the Herbfarm gardens are the ingredients from which the restaurant's chef, Jerry Traunfeld, creates his culinary extravaganzas. Dinners are paired with complementary Northwest wines (and occasionally something particularly remarkable from Europe).

So what's dinner here like? Well to start with, the restaurant is housed in a reproduction country inn beside a contemporary Northwest-style lodge. Some of the highlights of a recent spring forager's dinner included a paddlefish caviar tart; nettle, green garlic, and lovage soup; fiddlehead ferns and black morel served with an unusual risotto; Douglas fir sorbet; coriander-crusted loin of lamb; cured foie gras; and, for dessert, maple-blossom crème brûlée or sweet cicely-and-currant ice cream. Sure it's expensive, but if you're a foodie, you need to do something like this at least once in your life.

The Herbfarm's dinners are so incredibly popular that reservations are taken only a couple of times each year, so you'll have to plan far in advance if you want to be sure of an Herbfarm experience. However, you can try calling on short notice; cancellations often open up tables.

14590 NE 145th St., Woodinville. ℂ 206/784-2222. www.theherbfarm.com. Reservations required. Fixed-price 9-course dinner $149–$169 per person with 5 or 6 matched wines ($50 per-person deposit required). AE, MC, V. Seatings Thurs–Sat 7pm; Sun 4:30pm.

EXPENSIVE

Yarrow Bay Grill ★★ NORTHWEST The combination of Northwest cuisine and a view across Lake Washington to Seattle has made this restaurant, in the upscale Carillon Point retail, office, and condo development, a favorite of Eastside diners. The setting is decidedly nouveau riche. The menu is not so long that you can't make a decision, yet long enough to provide some serious options. The Thai-style crab cake appetizers with a sweet mustard sauce are favorites of ours, as is the peanut-chili dusted calamari. Entrees are equally divided between seafoods and meats, with at least one vegetarian dish on the menu daily. Keep in mind that the menu changes daily. Nearly every table has a view, and there is a great deck for good weather. By the way, rumor has it that this restaurant is a favorite of Bill Gates.

1270 Carillon Point, Kirkland. ℂ 425/889-9052. www.ybgrill.com. Reservations recommended. Main courses $17–$39. AE, DC, DISC, MC, V. Mon–Fri 11:30am–2:30pm; Sun 10am–2:30pm (brunch); daily 5:30–10pm.

MODERATE

Beach Cafe ★★ INTERNATIONAL   Affiliated with the Yarrow Bay Grill, which is located just upstairs, this casual waterfront cafe is the Eastside's best bet for an economical and creative meal with a view. In summer, the patio dining area just can't be beat. The menu circles the globe bringing a very satisfying mélange of flavors to Bellevue diners. The weekly specials further add to the international flavor. On a recent visit, the Caribbean was the theme of the week and the Haitian *griots* (pork marinated in orange juice, habanero chilies, chives, and onions) was spicy and full of unusual flavor.

1270 Carillon Point, Kirkland. © 425/889-0303. www.ybbeachcafe.com. Reservations recommended. Main courses $13–$24. AE, DC, DISC, MC, V. Mon–Thurs 11am–10:30pm; Fri–Sat 11am–11pm; Sun 11am–10pm.

COFFEE, TEA, BAKERIES & PASTRY SHOPS
CAFES, COFFEE BARS & TEA SHOPS

Unless you've been on Mars for the past decade, you're likely aware that Seattle has become the espresso capital of America. Seattleites are positively rabid about coffee, which isn't just a hot drink or a caffeine fix anymore, but rather a way of life. You'll never be more than about a block from your next cup. There are espresso carts on the sidewalks, drive-through espresso windows, espresso bars, gas station espresso counters, espresso milkshakes, espresso chocolates, even eggnog lattes at Christmas.

Starbucks, the ruling king of coffee, is seemingly everywhere you turn in Seattle. They sell some 36 types and blends of coffee beans. **SBC,** also known as Seattle's Best Coffee, doesn't have as many shops as Starbucks, but it does have a very devoted clientele. Close on the heels of Starbucks and SBC is the **Tully's** chain, which seems to have opened an espresso bar on every corner that doesn't already have a Starbucks or an SBC. However, serious espresso junkies swear by **Torrefazione** and **Caffe Appassionato.** If you see one of either of these chains, check it out and see what you think.

Coffee bars and cafes are as popular as bars and pubs as places to hang out and visit with friends. Among our favorite Seattle cafes are the following (organized by neighborhood):

Pioneer Square & the International District

The Pioneer Square location of **Torrefazione** ★★, 320 Occidental Ave. S. (© 206/624-5847), with its hand-painted Italian crockery, has a very old-world feel. The foam on the lattes here is absolutely perfect. Great pastries, too. Other Torrefaziones can be found at 622 Olive Way (© 206/624-1429), 1310 Fourth Ave. (© 206/583-8970), and in Fremont at 701 N. 34th St. (© 206/545-2721).

Zeitgeist Art/Coffee ★, 171 S. Jackson St. (© 206/583-0497), with its big windows and local artwork, is popular with the Pioneer Square art crowd. Luckily, there's a dictionary on hand so you can look up the word *zeitgeist.*

Belltown & Pike Place Market

The Crumpet Shop ★, 1503 First Ave. (© 206/682-1598), in Pike Place Market, specializes in its British namesake pastries but also does scones. It's almost a requirement that you accompany your crumpet or scone with a pot of tea.

The Seattle Center & Queen Anne Areas

Caffe Ladro Espresso Bar & Bakery ★★, 2205 Queen Anne Ave. N. (© 206/282-5313), in the heart of the pleasant Queen Anne area, has the feel of a cozy neighborhood coffeehouse. There's another Caffe Ladro in the MarQueen

Hotel building in Lower Queen Anne at 600 Queen Anne Ave. N. (© **206/ 282-1549**).

Uptown Espresso, 525 Queen Anne Ave. N. (© **206/285-3757**), with its crystal chandelier, gilt-framed classical painting, and opera music on the stereo, has a very theatrical, European feel. Good baked goodies and Internet access, too. There's another Uptown in Belltown at 2504 Fourth Ave.

Capitol Hill & East Seattle
Bauhaus Coffee & Books ✦, 301 E. Pine St. (© **206/625-1600**), on the downtown edge of Capitol Hill, is a great place to hang out and soak up the neighborhood atmosphere. There are always lots of interesting 30-something types hanging out reading or carrying on heated discussions.

North Seattle
Still Life in Fremont Coffeehouse ✦, 709 N. 35th St. (© **206/547-9850**), in the eclectic Fremont neighborhood, harks back to hippie hangouts of old. It's big and always crowded, offering good vegetarian meals and great weekend breakfasts, too.

Teahouse Kuan Yin, 1911 N. 45th St. (© **206/632-2055**), in the Wallingford neighborhood, is one of Seattle's favorite coffee alternatives. This Asian-inspired tea shop not only serves an amazing variety of teas, but also sells all manner of tea paraphernalia.

BAKERIES & PASTRY SHOPS
Pioneer Square & the International District
Grand Central Baking Company ✦, 214 First Ave. S. (© **206/622-3644**), in Pioneer Square's Grand Central Arcade, is responsible for awakening Seattle to the pleasures of rustic European-style breads. This bakery not only turns out great bread, but also does good pastries and sandwiches.

Belltown & Pike Place Market
Le Panier, 1902 Pike Place (© **206/441-3669**), located in the heart of Pike Place Market, is a great place to get a croissant and a latte and watch the market action.

Macrina ✦✦, 2408 First Ave. (© **206/448-4032**), a neighborhood bakery/ cafe in Belltown, serves some of the best baked goodies in the city and is a cozy place for a quick, cheap breakfast or lunch. In the morning, the smell of baking bread wafts down First Avenue and draws in many a passerby.

With a wall of glass cases full of baked goods and a window facing onto one of the busiest spots in Pike Place Market, **Three Girls Bakery,** 1514 Pike Place, Stall no. 1 (© **206/622-1045**), is a favorite place to grab a few pastries or other goodies to go. There is, however, a counter in back where you can sit down.

The Seattle Center & Queen Anne Areas
Located near the northwest corner of Seattle Center, **The Famous Pacific Dessert Company** ✦✦, 127 Mercer St. (© **206/284-8100**), is an out-of-the-way pastry shop that serves some of the most delicious desserts you'll find in Seattle. A great posttheater spot.

CAPITOL HILL & EAST SEATTLE
Basically, **Dilettante Chocolates** ✦✦, 416 Broadway E. (© **206/329-6463**), is a chocolate restaurant that happens to be Seattle's leading proponent of cocoa as the next drink to take the country by storm. If you don't order something with chocolate here, you're missing the point.

QUICK BITES

If you're just looking for something quick and cheap and don't want to resort to McDonald's or Burger King, consider grabbing a wrap. It can be just about anything in a tortilla and has become the food of choice in Seattle these days. Keep your eyes out for a **World Wraps** (of which there are many all around the city).

For variety of types of foods available, it's hard to beat the food court on the top floor of **Westlake Center** shopping mall, 400 Pine St. If you're downtown at lunch and just want a gourmet sandwich and pasta salad that you can grab out of a case, stop by **Briazz Cafe,** 1400 Fifth Ave. (© **206/343-3099**).

5 What to See & Do in Seattle

I hope you've got a good pair of walking shoes and a lot of stamina (a double latte helps), because Seattle is a walking town. The city's two biggest attractions—the waterfront and Pike Place Market—are the sort of places where you'll spend hours on your feet poking into nooks and crannies. When your feet are beat, you can relax on a tour boat and enjoy the views of the city from out on the waters of the Puget Sound, or you can take a 2-minute rest on the monorail, which links downtown Seattle with Seattle Center, which is home to both the Space Needle and the Experience Music Project. If your energy level sags, don't worry, there's always another espresso bar on the next block.

By the way, that monorail ride will now take you right through the middle of Paul Allen's Experience Music Project, the Frank Gehry–designed rock music museum. Paul Allen, who made his millions as one of the cofounders of Microsoft, is also busily changing the face of the south end of downtown. Here he has renovated Union Station and developed the area adjacent to where the city's new football stadium is being built. (By the way, Allen also owns the Seattle Seahawks football team that will play in the new stadium.) That stadium is scheduled to be ready for the 2002 football season, but the Seattle Mariners have already settled into their impressive $500 million Safeco Field, which debuted in 1999 as one of the few stadiums in the country with a retractable roof.

However, despite Seattle's many downtown diversions, the city's natural surroundings are still its primary attraction. You can easily cover all of Seattle's museums and major sights in 2 or 3 days, and with the help of the itineraries below, you should have a good idea of what not to miss. These itineraries will provide a good overview of the history, natural resources, and cultural diversity that have made Seattle the city it is today.

ON THE WATERFRONT

The Seattle waterfront, which lies along Alaskan Way between Yesler Way in the south and Bay Street and Myrtle Edwards Park in the north, is the city's most popular attraction. Yes, it's very touristy, with tacky gift shops, saltwater taffy, T-shirts galore, and lots of overpriced restaurants, but it's also home to the Seattle Aquarium, the IMAXDome Theater, Odyssey—The Maritime Discovery Center, and Ye Olde Curiosity Shop (king of the tacky gift shops). Ferries to Bainbridge Island and Bremerton, as well as several different boat tours, also operate from the waterfront. This is also the best place to hire a horse-drawn carriage for a spin around downtown.

You'll find the Washington State Ferries terminal at **Pier 52,** which is at the south end of the waterfront near Pioneer Square. (A ferry ride makes for a cheap cruise.) At **Pier 55,** you'll find excursion boats offering harbor cruises and trips to Tillicum Village on Blake Island. At **Pier 56,** cruise boats leave for trips

Seattle Attractions

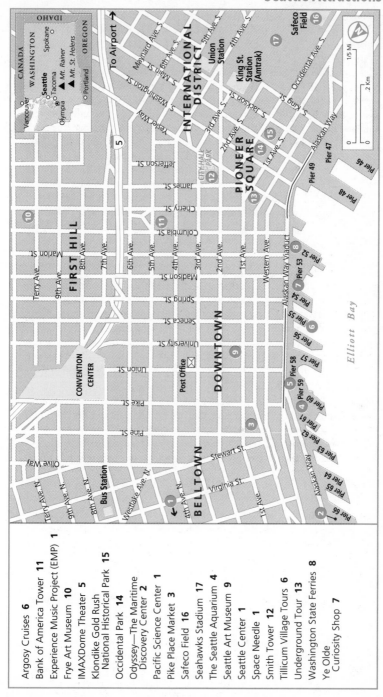

Argosy Cruises **6**
Bank of America Tower **11**
Experience Music Project (EMP) **1**
Frye Art Museum **10**
IMAXDome Theater **5**
Klondike Gold Rush
   National Historical Park **15**
Occidental Park **14**
Odyssey—The Maritime
   Discovery Center **2**
Pacific Science Center **1**
Pike Place Market **3**
Safeco Field **16**
Seahawks Stadium **17**
The Seattle Aquarium **4**
Seattle Art Museum **9**
Seattle Center **1**
Space Needle **1**
Smith Tower **12**
Tillicum Village Tours **6**
Underground Tour **13**
Washington State Ferries **8**
Ye Olde
   Curiosity Shop **7**

through the Chittenden (Ballard) Locks to Lake Union. See section 6, "Organized Tours," later in this chapter, for details. Here you'll also find the Bay Pavilion, which has a vintage carousel and a video arcade to keep the kids busy.

At **Pier 59,** you'll find the Seattle Aquarium (see below), the IMAXDome Theater (see below), and a small waterfront park. Continuing up the waterfront, you'll find **Pier 66,** the Bell Street Pier, which has a rooftop park. This is also the site of Odyssey—The Maritime Discovery Center (see below), which is dedicated to the history of shipping and fishing in Puget Sound, and Anthony's, the hippest restaurant on the waterfront (see section 4, "Dining," for a full review). At **Pier 67,** you'll find the Edgewater hotel, a great place to take in the sunset over a drink or dinner (see section 3, "Accommodations," for details).

Next door, at **Pier 69,** you'll come to the dock for the ferries that ply the waters between Seattle and Victoria, British Columbia, and at **Pier 70,** you'll find the *Spirit of Puget Sound* cruise ship (p. 120). Just north of this pier is grassy Myrtle Edwards Park, a nice finale to a very pleasant waterfront. This park has a popular bicycling and skating trail, and is the northern terminus for the Waterfront Streetcar, which can take you back to your starting point.

IMAXDome Theater ⭐ The IMAXDome is a movie theater with a 180° screen that fills your peripheral vision and puts you right in the middle of the action. This huge wraparound theater is adjacent to the Seattle Aquarium, and for many years now has featured a film about the eruption of Mount St. Helens. Various other special features are screened throughout the year, and in 2002, *Island of the Sharks* and *Dolphins* will both be showing here.

Pier 59, 1483 Alaskan Way. ✆ **206/622-1868.** www.seattleimaxdome.com. Admission $7 adults, $6.50 seniors, $6 youth, free for under 5 (IMAXDome–Aquarium combination tickets available). Screenings daily beginning at 10am. Closed Christmas. Bus: 15 or 18, then walk through Pike Place Market to the waterfront. Waterfront Streetcar: To Pike Place Market stop.

Odyssey—The Maritime Discovery Center Sort of an interactive promotion for modern fishing and shipping, this facility at the north end of the Seattle waterfront is aimed primarily at kids and has more than 40 hands-on exhibits highlighting Seattle's modern working waterfront and its links to the sea. Exhibits include a kid-size fishing boat, a virtual kayak trip through the Puget

---

Value **Saving Money on Sightseeing**

If you're a see-it-all, do-it-all kind of person, you'll definitely want to buy a **CityPass** (✆ **707/256-0490**; www.citypass.com), which gets you into the Space Needle, Pacific Science Center, Seattle Aquarium, Woodland Park Zoo, and Museum of Flight at a savings of 50% if you visit all six attractions. The pass also includes a harbor cruise with Argosy Cruises. The passes, good for 9 days from date of first use, cost $33.50 for adults, $29 for seniors, and $21.50 for children. Purchase your CityPass at any of the participating attractions.

You might also want to drop by the **Seattle–King County Convention and Visitors Bureau Visitor Center,** Washington State Convention & Trade Center, 800 Convention Place, Galleria Level, at the corner of Eighth Avenue and Pike Street (✆ **206/461-5840**; www.seeseattle.org). Here you can grab a copy of the "Seattle's Favorite Attractions" booklet, which includes coupons good for discounts at numerous area attractions.

Sound, and a live radar center that allows you to track the movement of vessels in Elliott Bay. In another exhibit, you get to use a simulated crane to practice loading a scale model of a cargo ship.

Pier 66 (Bell St. Pier), 2205 Alaskan Way. ✆ **206/374-4000.** www.ody.org. Admission $6.75 adults, $4.50 seniors and students, free for children under 5. Tues–Sat 10am–5pm; Sun noon–5pm. Bus: 15 or 18, then walk through Pike Place Market to the waterfront. Waterfront Trolley: Bell St. Station.

The Seattle Aquarium ★★   Although not nearly as large and impressive as either the Monterey Bay Aquarium or the Oregon Coast Aquarium, the Seattle Aquarium is still quite enjoyable and presents well-designed exhibits dealing with the water worlds of the Puget Sound region. The star attractions here are the playful river otters and the sea otters, as well as the giant octopus. There's also an underwater viewing dome, from which you get a fish's-eye view of life beneath the waves, and each September, you can watch salmon return up a fish ladder to spawn. Of course there are also plenty of small tanks that allow you to familiarize yourself with the many fish of the Northwest. There's also a beautiful large coral-reef tank, as well as many smaller tanks that exhibit fish from distant waters.

Pier 59, 1483 Alaskan Way. ✆ **206/386-4300.** www.seattleaquarium.org. Admission $9 adults, $8 seniors, $6.25 children 6–18, $4.25 children 3–5 (joint Aquarium–IMAXDome tickets also available). Labor Day–Memorial Day daily 10am–5pm; Memorial Day–Labor Day daily 9:30am–7pm. Bus: 15 or 18, then walk through Pike Place Market to the waterfront. Waterfront Streetcar: To Pike Place Market stop.

PIKE PLACE MARKET TO PIONEER SQUARE

Pike Place Market and the Pioneer Square historic district lie at opposite ends of First Avenue; midway between the two is the Seattle Art Museum.

The **Pioneer Square** area, with its historic buildings, interesting shops, museum, and **Seattle Underground Tour** (see the box "Good Times in Bad Taste," below), is well worth exploring.

Pike Place Market ★★★   Pike Place Market, originally a farmers' market, was founded in 1907 when housewives complained that middlemen were raising the price of produce. The market allowed shoppers to buy directly from producers, and thus save on grocery bills. By the 1960s, however, the market was no longer the popular spot it had been. World War II had deprived it of nearly half its farmers when Japanese Americans were moved to internment camps. The postwar flight to the suburbs almost spelled the end of the market, and the site was being eyed for a major redevelopment project. However, a grassroots movement to save the 9-acre market culminated in its being declared a National Historic District.

Today it is once again bustling, but the 100 or so farmers and fishmongers who set up shop on the premises are only a small part of the attraction. More than 200 local craftspeople and artists can be found here, selling their creations. There are also excellent restaurants, and hundreds of shops fill the market area. Street performers serenade milling crowds. At the information booth almost directly below the large Pike Place Market sign, you can pick up a free map and guide to the market. Watch for Rachel, the giant piggy bank, and the flying fish at the Pike Place Fish stall.

Victor Steinbrueck Park, which is at the north end of the market at the intersection of Pike Place, Virginia Street, and Western Avenue, is a popular lounging area for both the homeless and people just looking for a grassy place in which to sit in the sun. In the park, you'll find two 50-foot-tall totem poles.

Good Times in Bad Taste

If you love bad jokes and are fascinated by the bizarre (or maybe this describes your children), you won't want to miss the Underground Tour and a visit to Ye Olde Curiosity Shop. Together, these two outings should reassure you that, espresso, traffic jams, and Microsoft aside, Seattle really does have a sense of humor.

If you have an appreciation for off-color humor and are curious about the seamier side of Seattle history, **The Underground Tour,** 608 First Ave. (© **206/682-4646;** www.undergroundtour.com), will likely entertain and enlighten you. The tours lead down below street level in the Pioneer Square area, where you can still find the vestiges of Seattle businesses built before the great fire of 1889. Learn the lowdown dirt on early Seattle, a town where plumbing was problematic and a person could drown in a pothole. (Tours are held daily. The cost is $9 for adults, $7 for seniors and students ages 13–17 or with college ID, $5 for children ages 6–12; not recommended for children under 6.)

Ye Olde Curiosity Shop, 1001 Alaskan Way, Pier 54 (© **206/682-5844),** is a cross between a souvenir store and Ripley's Believe It or Not! The collection of oddities was started in 1899 by Joe Standley, who developed a more-than-passing interest in strange curios. It's weird! It's tacky! It's always packed! See Siamese-twin calves, a natural mummy, the Lord's Prayer on a grain of rice, a narwhal tusk, shrunken heads, a 67-pound snail, fleas in dresses—all the stuff that fascinated you as a kid.

For a glimpse behind the scenes at the market and to learn all about its history, you can take a 1-hour guided **Market Heritage Tour** (© **206/682-7453,** ext. 653, for information and reservations). Tours are offered Wednesday through Saturday at 11am and 2pm and Sunday at noon and 2pm. Tours depart from the market's Heritage Center, 1531 Western Ave. (take the Skybridge to the Market Garage and then take the elevator to the Western Ave. level). The Heritage Center is an open-air building filled with historical exhibits. Tours cost $7 for adults and $5 for seniors and children under age 18.

One-hour tours are also offered by the **Pike Place Market Merchants Association** (© **206/587-0351;** www.seattlepublicmarket.com). The tours, which are offered by reservation and cost $7 for adults and $5 for seniors and children under 12, include a healthy dose of fun and facts plus a bit of fiction. You'll even get to meet some market merchants and learn their stories.

Between Pike and Pine sts. at First Ave. © 206/682-PIKE. www.pikeplacemarket.org. Mon–Sat 10am–6pm; Sun 11am–5pm. Closed New Year's Day, Easter, Thanksgiving, Christmas. Bus: 15 or 18. Waterfront Streetcar: To Pike Place Market stop.

Klondike Gold Rush National Historical Park   It isn't in the Klondike (that's in Canada) and it isn't really a park (it's a single room in an old store), but this is a fascinating little museum. "At 3 o'clock this morning the steamship *Portland,* from St. Michaels for Seattle, passed up [Puget] Sound with more than a ton of gold on board and 68 passengers." When the *Seattle Post-Intelligencer* published that sentence on July 17, 1897, it started a stampede. Would-be miners heading for the Klondike goldfields in the 1890s made Seattle their outfitting center and helped turn it into a prosperous city. When they struck it rich up north, they headed back to Seattle, the first U.S. outpost of civilization, and unloaded their gold, making Seattle doubly rich. It seems only fitting that this museum should be here. Another unit of the park is in Skagway, Alaska.

117 S. Main St. ℂ 206/553-7220. www.nps.gov/klse. Free admission. Daily 9am–5pm. Closed Thanksgiving, Christmas, and New Year's Day. Bus: 15, 16, 18, 21, or 22. Waterfront Streetcar: To Occidental Park stop.

Seattle Art Museum ★★   Two blocks from Pike Place Market, Jonathon Borofsky's *Hammering Man,* an animated three-story steel sculpture, hammers away in front of the Seattle Art Museum. Inside you'll find one of the nation's premier collections of Northwest Coast Indian art and artifacts and an equally large collection of African art. Exhibits cover European and American art ranging from ancient Mediterranean works to pieces from the medieval, Renaissance, and Baroque periods. A large 18th-century collection and a smaller 19th-century exhibition lead up to a large 20th-century collection that includes a room devoted to Northwest contemporary art. (There's also a smattering of Asian art at this museum, but the city's major collection of Asian art is at the Seattle Asian Art Museum in Volunteer Park; see below for details.) Free guided tours of the different collections are offered.

100 University St. ℂ 206/625-8900. www.seattleartmuseum.org. Admission $7 adults, $5 seniors and students, free 12 and under. Free first Thurs of each month (free for seniors on first Fri of each month). Admission ticket also valid at Seattle Asian Art Museum if used within 1 week. Tues–Sun 10am–5pm (Thurs until 9pm). Also open Martin Luther King Day, Presidents' Day, Memorial Day, and Labor Day. Closed Thanksgiving, Christmas, and New Year's Day (open holiday Mon). Bus: 10, 15, 18, or any bus using the bus tunnel.

SEATTLE CENTER & LAKE UNION ATTRACTIONS

Built in 1962 for the World's Fair, Seattle Center is today not only the site of Seattle's famous Space Needle—it's a cultural and entertainment park that doubles as the city's favorite festival grounds as well. Within Seattle Center's boundaries, you'll find the Experience Music Project (EMP), the Pacific Science Center, the Seattle Children's Museum, the Seattle Children's Theatre, Key Arena (home of the NBA's Seattle Supersonics), the Seattle Center Opera House, a children's amusement park, a fountain that is a favorite summertime hangout, the Intiman Theatre, and the Bagley Wright Theatre. See p. 117, "Especially for Kids," for further details on Seattle Center attractions that young travelers will enjoy.

Experience Music Project ★★   The creation of Microsoft cofounder Paul Allen and designed by architect Frank Gehry, who is known for pushing the envelope of architectural design, this rock 'n' roll museum is a massive multicolored blob at the foot of the Space Needle. Originally planned as a memorial to Seattle native Jimi Hendrix, the museum grew to encompass not only Hendrix, but all of the Northwest's rock scene (from "Louie Louie" to grunge) and the general history of American popular music.

One museum exhibit focuses on the history of guitars and includes some of the earliest electric guitars, which date from the early 1930s. The museum even has a sort of rock 'n' roll thrill ride, which has been featuring funk music since the museum's opening. The "ride" consists of a platform of seats that are bounced around giving you the sensation of being on a roller coaster. However, the most popular exhibits here (after the Jimi Hendrix room) are the interactive rooms. In one you can play a guitar, drums, keyboards, or even DJ turntables. In another, you can experience what it's like to be onstage performing in front of adoring fans.

In the museum's main hall, known as the Sky Church, there are regularly scheduled concerts. To help you get the most out of your visit (and at almost $20 for a ticket, you certainly expect plenty), every visitor is issued a Museum Exhibit Guide (MEG), a hand-held electronic player filled with recorded audio clips explaining the various exhibits. Expect long lines in the summer and leave plenty of time to see this unusual museum.

325 Fifth Ave. N. ✆ 877/EMPLIVE or 206/EMPLIVE. www.emplive.com. Admission $19.95 adults, $15.95 seniors, $14.95 children 7–12, free for children 6 and under. Daily 9am–11pm. Bus: 1, 2, 3, 4, 13, 15, 16, 18, 24, or 33. Monorail: From Westlake Center at Pine St. and Fourth Ave.

Pacific Science Center ★★ *Kids*   Although its exhibits are aimed primarily at children, the Pacific Science Center is fun for all ages. The main goal of this sprawling complex at Seattle Center is to teach kids about science and to instill a desire to study it. To that end, there are life-size robotic dinosaurs, a butterfly house and insect village (with giant robotic insects), a Tech Zone where kids can play virtual-reality soccer or play tic-tac-toe with a robot, and dozens of other fun hands-on exhibits addressing the biological sciences, physics, and chemistry. The August Bubble Festival is always a big hit, as is April's Gross Out Week. There's a planetarium for learning about the skies (plus laser shows for the fun of it), and an IMAX theater. There are always special exhibits, so be sure to check the schedule when you're in town.

200 Second Ave. N., Seattle Center. ✆ 206/443-2880. www.pacsci.org. Admission $8 adults, $5.50 seniors and children 3–13, free for children under 2. IMAX $6.75–$7.50 adults, $5.75–$6.50 seniors and children 3–13, free for children under 2. Laser show $5–$7.50. Various discounted combination tickets available. Mid-June to Labor Day daily 10am–6pm; Labor Day to mid-June Mon–Fri 10am–5pm, Sat–Sun and holidays 10am–6pm. Closed Thanksgiving and Christmas. Bus: 1, 2, 3, 4, 13, 15, 16, 18, 24, or 33. Monorail: To Seattle Center.

The Space Needle ★★   From a distance it resembles a flying saucer on top of a tripod, and when it was built for the 1962 World's Fair, the 605-foot-tall Space Needle was meant to suggest future architectural trends. Today the Space Needle is the quintessential symbol of Seattle, and at 520 feet above ground level, the observation deck provides superb views of the city and its surroundings. There are displays identifying more than 60 sites and activities in the Seattle area, and high-powered telescopes let you zoom in on distant sights. You'll also find a pricey restaurant atop the tower (see the review of SkyCity on p. 96). If you don't mind standing in line and paying quite a bit for an elevator ride, make this your first stop in Seattle so you can orient yourself. There are, however, cheaper alternatives if you just want a view of the city (see the box "Space Needle Alternatives," below).

Seattle Center, Fourth Ave. N at Broad St. ✆ 800/937-9582 or 206/905-2100. www.spaceneedle.com. Admission $11 adults, $9 seniors, $5 children 5–12, free for children under 5. Free if dining in either restaurant. Summer daily 8am–midnight; other months Sun–Thurs 9am–11pm, Fri–Sat 9am–midnight. Valet parking $10 for 4 hr. Bus: 1, 2, 3, 4, 13, 15, 16, 18, 24, or 33. Monorail: From Westlake Center at Pine St. and Fourth Ave.

THE NEIGHBORHOODS
THE INTERNATIONAL DISTRICT

While Seattle today boasts of its strategic location on the Pacific Rim, its ties to Asia are nothing new. This is evident in the International District, Seattle's main Asian neighborhood, which is centered between Fifth Avenue South and 12th Avenue South (between S. Washington St. and S. Lane St.). Called the International District rather than Chinatown because so many Asian nationalities have made this area home, this neighborhood has been the center of the city's Asian communities for more than 100 years. You can learn about the district's history at the **Wing Luke Asian Museum,** 407 Seventh Ave. S. (✆ **206/623-5124;** www.wingluke.org), where you can also pick up a walking-tour map of the area.

There are many restaurants, import stores, and food markets, and the huge **Uwajimaya** is all of these rolled up in one (see section 9, "Shopping," for details).

At the corner of Maynard Avenue South and South King Street, you'll find **Hing Hay Park,** the site of an ornate and colorful pavilion given to the city by Taipei, Taiwan.

FIRST HILL (PILL HILL) & CAPITOL HILL

Seattle is justly proud of its parks, and **Volunteer Park,** on Capitol Hill (drive north on Broadway and watch for signs), is one of the most popular. Here you'll find not only acres of lawns, groves of trees, and huge old rhododendrons, but also an old water tower that provides one of the best panoramas in the city. A winding staircase leads to the top of the water tower, from which you get 360° views. On the observatory level there is also an interesting exhibit about the

---

 Space Needle Alternatives

If you don't want to deal with the crowds at the Space Needle but still want an elevated downtown view, you have some alternatives. One is the big, black **Bank of America Tower** (✆ 206/386-5151) at the corner of Fifth Avenue and Columbia Street. At 943 feet, this is the tallest building in Seattle (twice as tall as the Space Needle), more stories (76, to be exact) than any other building west of the Mississippi. Up on the 73rd floor, you'll find an observation deck with views that dwarf those from the Space Needle. Admission is only $5 for adults and $3 for seniors and children. It's open Monday through Friday from 8:30am to 4:30pm.

Not far from the Bank of America Tower, you'll find the **Smith Tower,** 506 Second Ave. (✆ 206/622-4004). Opened in 1914, this was Seattle's first skyscraper and, for 50 years, was the tallest building west of Chicago. Although Smith Tower has only 42 stories, it still offers excellent views from its 35th-floor observation deck, which surrounds the ornate Chinese Room, a banquet hall with an ornate carved ceiling. A lavish lobby and original manual elevators all make this a fun and historic place to take in the Seattle skyline. The observation deck is open from May 15 to October 31, daily from 10am to 4pm; admission is $5 for adults, $3 for seniors, students, and children ages 6 to 12.

If you've ever seen a photo of the Space Needle framed by the high-rises of downtown Seattle, it was probably taken from **Kerry View-point** on Queen Anne Hill. If you want to take your own drop-dead photo of the Seattle skyline from this elevated perspective, head north from Seattle Center on Queen Anne Avenue North and turn left on West Highland Drive. When you reach the park, you'll immediately recognize the view.

Another great panorama is from the water tower in **Volunteer Park** on Capitol Hill at East Prospect Street and 14th Avenue East. See p. 112.

Olmsted Brothers and the system of parks they designed for Seattle. To find the water tower, park near the Seattle Asian Art Museum if you can, and walk back out of the parking lot to where the road splits. The view from directly in front of the museum isn't bad either.

Frye Art Museum ✫   Located on First Hill not far from downtown Seattle, this museum is primarily an exhibit space for the extensive personal art collection of Charles and Emma Frye, Seattle pioneers who began collecting art in the 1890s. The collection focuses on late-19th-century and early-20th-century representational art by European and American painters, and there are works by Andrew Wyeth, Thomas Hart Benton, Edward Hopper, Albert Bierstadt, and Pablo Picasso, as well as a large collection of engravings by Winslow Homer. In addition to galleries filled with works from the permanent collection, there are temporary exhibitions throughout the year.

704 Terry Ave. (at Cherry St.). ✆ **206/622-9250.** www.fryeart.org. Free admission. Tues–Sat 10am–5pm (Thurs until 9pm); Sun noon–5pm. Closed July 4, Thanksgiving, Christmas, and New Year's Day. Bus: 3, 4, or 12.

Seattle Asian Art Museum ✫   Housed in a renovated Art Deco building, the Asian art collection has an emphasis on Chinese and Japanese art but also includes pieces from Korea, Southeast Asia, South Asia, and the Himalayas. Collections of Chinese terra-cotta funerary art, snuff bottles, and Japanese netsukes (belt decorations) are among the museum's most notable. One room is devoted to Japanese ceramics, while three rooms are devoted to Chinese ceramics. The central hall is devoted to the stone religious sculptures of South Asia (primarily India). There are frequent lectures and concerts.

1400 E. Prospect St., Volunteer Park (14th Ave. E. and E. Prospect St.). ✆ **206/654-3100.** www.seattleart museum.org. Admission $3 adults, free for children 12 and under. Free to all on first Thurs and first Sat of each month (free for seniors on first Fri of each month). Admission ticket plus $4 will get you into the Seattle Art Museum if used within 1 week. Tues–Sun 10am–5pm (Thurs until 9pm). Closed Thanksgiving, Christmas, and New Year's Day (open holiday Mon). Bus: 7, 9, or 10.

Volunteer Park Conservatory ✫   This stately old Victorian conservatory, built in 1912, houses a large collection of tropical and desert plants, including palm trees, orchids, and cacti. There are seasonal floral displays also.

1400 E. Galer St. ✆ **206/684-4743.** Free admission. May 1–Sept 15 daily 10am–7pm; Sept 16–Apr 30 daily 10am–4pm. Bus: 7, 9, or 10.

NORTH SEATTLE (INCLUDING THE U DISTRICT, FREMONT & MONTLAKE)

The **Fremont District,** which begins at the north end of the Fremont Bridge near the intersection of Fremont Avenue North and North 36th Street, is Seattle's funkiest and most unusual neighborhood. Even livelier, though not nearly as eclectic or artistic, the **University District** (known locally as the U District) has loads of cheap restaurants and all the types of shops you would associate with a college-age clientele. However, the main attractions for visitors are the two excellent museums on the university campus and the nearby Museum of History and Industry, which is just across the Montlake Bridge from the U District.

Burke Museum ✫   Located in the northwest corner of the University of Washington campus, the Burke Museum features exhibits on the natural and cultural heritage of the Pacific Rim. Permanent exhibits include *Life & Times,* which covers 500 million years of Washington history (and prehistory) with lots of fossils, including a complete mastodon, on display. The second permanent

Insider Tip

University of Washington campus parking is expensive on weekdays and Saturday mornings, so try to visit the Burke Museum or Henry Art Gallery on a Saturday afternoon or a Sunday, when parking is free.

exhibit, *Pacific Voices,* focuses on the many cultures of the Pacific Rim and their connections to Washington state. There is also a smaller temporary exhibit gallery. In front of the museum stand three modern totem poles that were carved in the style of the 1870s and 1880s.

17th Ave. NE and NE 45th St. *C* **206/543-5590.** www.burkemuseum.org. Admission $5.50 adults, $4 seniors, $2.50 students, free for children under 6. Daily 10am–5pm (Thurs until 8pm). Closed July 4, Thanksgiving, Christmas, and New Year's Day. Bus: 7, 43, 70, 71, 72, or 73.

Henry Art Gallery   The focus here is on contemporary art with retrospectives of individual artists, as well as exhibits focusing on specific themes or media. Photography and video are both well represented, and for the most part, the exhibits are the most avant-garde in the Seattle area. Located on the west side of the University of Washington campus, this museum benefits from large well-lit gallery spaces that are illuminated by pyramidal and cubic skylights that can be seen near the main museum entrance. There's also a cafe here and a small sculpture courtyard. Parking is often available at the Central Parking Garage at NE 41st Street and 15th Avenue NE.

University of Washington, 15th Ave. NE and NE 41st St. *C* **206/543-2280.** www.henryart.org. Admission $6 adults, $4.50 seniors, free for students and children under 14. Pay what you wish Thurs 5–8pm. Tues–Sun 11am–5pm (Thurs until 8pm). Closed July 4, Thanksgiving, Christmas, and New Year's Day. Bus: 7, 43, 70, 71, 72, and 73.

Museum of History and Industry (MOHAI) ⭐   If the Seattle Underground Tour's vivid description of life before the 1889 fire has you curious about what the city's more respectable citizens were doing back in those days, you can find out here, where re-created storefronts provide glimpses into their lives. Located at the north end of Washington Park Arboretum, this museum explores Seattle's history, with frequently changing exhibits on more obscure aspects of the city's past. While many of the displays will be of interest only to Seattle residents, anyone wishing to gain a better understanding of the history of the city and the Northwest may also enjoy the exhibits here. There's a Boeing mail plane from the 1920s, plus an exhibit on the 1889 fire that leveled the city. This museum also hosts touring exhibitions that address Northwest history. Although not actually in north Seattle, this museum is just across the Montlake Bridge from the University District.

McCurdy Park, 2700 24th Ave. E. *C* **206/324-1126.** www.seattlehistory.org. Admission $5.50 adults, $3 seniors and children 6–12, $1 children 2–5, free for children under 2. Daily 10am–5pm. Closed Thanksgiving, Christmas, and New Year's Day. From I-5, take Wash. 520 east (exit 168B) to the Montlake exit, go straight through the stoplight to 24th Ave. E and turn left. Bus: 25 or 43.

Woodland Park Zoo ⭐⭐ *Kids*   Located in north Seattle, this sprawling zoo has outstanding exhibits focusing on Alaska, tropical Asia, the African savanna, and the tropical rain forest. The brown bear enclosure, one of the zoo's best exhibits, is a very realistic reproduction of an Alaskan stream and hillside. In the savanna, zebras gambol and antelopes and giraffes graze contentedly near a reproduction of an African village that opened in 2001. An elephant forest provides plenty of space for the zoo's pachyderms. The gorilla and orangutan habitats are also very well done, and there's a large walk-through butterfly house ($1 additional fee) during the summer months. Don't miss the giant Komodo lizards from Indonesia. A farm animal area and petting zoo are big hits with the little ones.

5500 Phinney Ave. N. © **206/684-4800.** www.zoo.org. Admission $9 adults, $8.25 seniors and college students, $6.50 travelers with disabilities and children 6–17, $4.25 children 3–5, free for children 2 and under. Mar 15–Apr 30 daily 9:30am–5pm; May 1–Sept 14 daily 9:30am–6pm; Sept 15–Oct 14 daily 9:30am–5pm; Oct 15–Mar 14 daily 9:30am–4pm. Parking $3.50. Bus: 5.

SOUTH SEATTLE

Museum of Flight (Kids) Located right next door to busy Boeing Field, 15 minutes south of downtown Seattle, this museum will have aviation buffs walking on air. Within the six-story glass-and-steel repository are displayed some of history's most famous planes.

To start things off, there's a replica of the Wright brothers' first glider, and from there the collection of planes brings you to the present state of flight. Suspended in the Great Hall are more than 20 planes, including a 1935 DC-3, the first Air Force F-5 supersonic fighter, and the Gossamer Condor, a human-powered airplane, plus there are some 34 other planes on display. You'll also see one of the famous Blackbird spy planes, which were once the world's fastest jets (and you can even sit in the cockpit of one of these babies). A rare World War II Corsair fighter rescued from Lake Washington and restored to its original glory is also on display. Visitors also get to board the original Air Force One presidential plane, used by Eisenhower, and can sit in the cockpit of an F/A-18 Hornet fighter. An exhibit on the U.S. space program features an Apollo command module. Of course, you'll also see plenty of Boeing planes, including a reproduction of Boeing's first plane, which was built in 1916. The museum also incorporates part of Boeing's old wooden factory building from its early years.

See p. 121 for information on a tour of the Boeing plant.

9404 E. Marginal Way S. © **206/764-5720.** www.museumofflight.org. Admission $9.50 adults, $8.50 seniors, $5 children 5–17, free for children under 5. Free first Thurs 5–9pm. Daily 10am–5pm (until 9pm Thurs). Closed Thanksgiving and Christmas. Take exit 158 off I-5. Bus: 174.

BEACHES, PARKS & PUBLIC GARDENS
BEACHES

Alki (rhymes with *sky*) **Beach** ⊛, across Elliott Bay from downtown Seattle, is the city's most popular beach and is the nearest approximation you'll find in the Northwest to a Southern California beach scene. The paved path that runs along this 2½-mile-long (4km) beach is popular with skaters, walkers, and cyclists; and the road that parallels the beach is lined with shops, restaurants, and beachy houses and apartment buildings. But the views across Puget Sound to the Olympic Mountains confirm that this is indeed the Northwest. Despite the views, this beach lacks the greenery that makes some of the city's other beaches so much more appealing. In the summer, a water taxi operates between the downtown Seattle waterfront and Alki Beach (see section 2, "Getting Around," for details).

For a more Northwestern beach experience (which usually includes a bit of hiking or walking), head to one of the area's many waterfront parks. **Lincoln Park,** 8011 Fauntleroy Ave. SW, south of Alki Beach in West Seattle, has bluffs and forests backing the beach. Northwest of downtown Seattle in the Magnolia area, you'll find **Discovery Park** ⊛⊛, 3801 W. Government Way (© **206/386-4236**), where miles of beaches are the primary destination of most park visitors. To reach Discovery Park, follow the Elliott Avenue north along the water-front from downtown Seattle, then take the Magnolia Bridge west toward the Magnolia neighborhood and follow Grayfield Street to Galer Street to Magnolia Boulevard.

Golden Gardens Park ★★, 8499 Seaview Place NW, which is located north of Ballard and Shilshole Bay, is our favorite Seattle beach park. Although the park isn't very large and is backed by railroad tracks, the views of the Olympic Mountains are magnificent and on summer evenings people build fires on the beach. There are also lawns and shade trees that make this park ideal for a picnic.

PARKS

Seattle's many parks are what make this such a livable city. In the downtown area, **Myrtle Edwards Park** ★, 3130 Alaska Way W. (© **206/684-4075**), at the north end of the waterfront, is an ideal spot for a sunset stroll with views of Puget Sound and the Olympic Mountains. The park includes a 1¼-mile (2km) paved pathway.

Freeway Park, at Sixth Avenue and Seneca Street, is one of Seattle's most unusual parks. Built right on top of busy Interstate 5, this green space is more a series of urban plazas, with lots of terraces, waterfalls, and cement planters creating walls of greenery. You'd never know there's a roaring freeway beneath your feet. Unfortunately, although this park is convenient, it often has a deserted and slightly threatening feel due to the isolated nature of the park's many nooks and crannies.

For serious communing with nature, however, nothing will do but **Discovery Park** ★★, 3801 W. Government Way (© **206/386-4236**). Occupying a high bluff and sandy point jutting into Puget Sound, this is Seattle's largest and wildest park. You can easily spend a day wandering the trails and beaches here. The park's visitor center is open daily from 8:30am to 5pm. Discovery Park is a 15-minute drive from downtown; to reach the park, follow the waterfront north from downtown Seattle toward the Magnolia neighborhood and watch for signs to the park. When you reach the park, follow signed trails down to the beach and out to the lighthouse at the point. Although the lighthouse is not open to the public, the views from the beach make this a good destination for an hour's walk. The beach and park's bluff-top meadows both make good picnic spots.

Up on Capitol Hill, at East Prospect Street and 14th Avenue East, you'll find **Volunteer Park** ★★, 1247 15th Ave. East (© **206/684-4075**), which is surrounded by the elegant mansions of Capitol Hill. It's a popular spot for sunning and playing Frisbee, and it's home to the Seattle Asian Art Museum (p. 112), an amphitheater, a water tower with a superb view of the city, and a conservatory filled with tropical and desert plants (p. 112). With so much variety, you can easily spend a morning or afternoon exploring this park.

On the east side of Seattle, along the shore of Lake Washington, you'll find not only swimming beaches but also **Seward Park** ★, 5898 Lake Washington Blvd. (© **206/684-4075**). While this large park's waterfront areas are its biggest attraction, it also has a dense forest with trails winding through it. Keep an eye out for the bald eagles that nest here. This park is south of the I-90 floating bridge off Lake Washington Boulevard South. From downtown Seattle, follow Madison Street northeast to a right onto Lake Washington Boulevard.

In north Seattle, you'll find several parks worth visiting. These include the unique **Gasworks Park** ★, 2101 N. Northlake Way, at Meridian Avenue North (© **206/684-4075**), at the north end of Lake Union. This park has, in the middle of its green lawns, the rusting hulk of an old industrial plant. Kite Hill is the city's favorite kite-flying spot. North of here, on Green Lake Way North near the Woodland Park Zoo, you'll find **Green Lake Park** ★★, 7201 E. Green Lake Dr. N. (© **206/684-4075**), which is a center for exercise buffs who jog, bike, and skate around the park on a 2¾-mile (4.5km) paved path. It's also possible to swim in the lake (there are changing rooms and a beach with summer lifeguards), and there are plenty of grassy areas. For information on renting in-line skates or a bike for riding the path here, see p. 122.

PUBLIC GARDENS
See also the listing for Volunteer Park Conservatory on p. 112.

Bellevue Botanical Gardens Any avid gardener should be sure to make a trip across one of Seattle's two floating bridges to the city of Bellevue and the Bellevue Botanical Garden. Although this 36-acre garden opened only in 1992, it has matured very quickly and has become one of the Northwest's most talked-about perennial gardens. The summertime displays of flowers, in expansive mixed borders, are absolutely gorgeous. There is also a Japanese garden, a shade border, and a water-wise garden (designed to conserve water).

Wilburton Hill Park, 12001 Main St., Bellevue. © 425/452-2750. www.bellevuebotanical.org. Free admission. Daily 7:30am–dusk; visitor center daily 9am–4pm. Take the NE Fourth St. exit off I-405.

Japanese Garden Situated on 3½ acres of land, the Japanese Garden is a perfect little world unto itself, with babbling brooks, a lake rimmed with Japanese irises and filled with colorful koi (Japanese carp), and a cherry orchard (for

---

⌀ Fish Gotta Swim

While salmon in the Puget Sound region have dwindled to dangerously low numbers in recent years, it is still possible in various places to witness the annual return of salmon.

In the autumn, on the waterfront, you can see returning salmon at the **Seattle Aquarium,** which has its own fish ladder. However, the very best place to see salmon is at **Hiram M. Chittenden Locks,** 3015 NW 54th St. (© **206/783-7059**), which are located a 10-minute drive north of downtown Seattle (drive north from the waterfront on Elliott Ave., which becomes 15th Ave. W.; after crossing the Ballard Bridge, turn left on Market St. and follow this road for about 1 mile/1.5km). Between June and September (July–Aug are the peak months), you can view salmon through underwater observation windows as they leap up the locks' fish ladder. These locks connect Lake Union and Lake Washington with the waters of Puget Sound, and depending on the tides and lake levels, there is a difference of 6 to 26 feet on either side of the locks. The locks and surrounding park are open daily from 7am to 9pm, and the visitor's center is open daily from 10am to 6pm (closed Thanksgiving, Christmas, and New Year's Day). Take bus 17.

East of Seattle, in downtown **Issaquah,** salmon can be seen year-round at the Issaquah Salmon Hatchery, 125 Sunset Way (© **425/391-9094**). However, it is in October that adult salmon can be seen returning to the hatchery. Each year in October, the city of Issaquah holds a Salmon Days Festival to celebrate the return of the natives.

spring color). A special Tea Garden encloses a Tea House, where, between April and October, on the third Saturday of each month at 1:30pm, you can attend a traditional tea ceremony. Unfortunately, noise from a nearby road can be distracting at times.

Washington Park Arboretum, Lake Washington Blvd. E. (north of E. Madison St.). © 206/684-4725. Admission $2.50 adults; $1.50 seniors, persons with disabilities, and children 6–18; free for children under 6. Mar daily 10am–6pm; Apr–May daily 10am–7pm; June–Aug daily 10am–8pm; Sept–Oct daily 10am–6pm; Nov daily 10am–4pm. Closed Dec–Feb. Bus: 11.

Washington Park Arboretum ★ Acres of trees and shrubs stretch from the far side of Capitol Hill all the way to the Montlake Cut, a canal connecting Lake Washington to Lake Union. Within the 230-acre arboretum, there are 5,000 varieties of plants and quiet trails that are pleasant throughout the year but which are most beautiful in spring, when the azaleas, cherry trees, rhododendrons, and dogwoods are all in flower. The north end of the arboretum, a marshland that is home to ducks and herons, is popular with kayakers, canoeists (see p. 123 in "Outdoor Pursuits," below, for places to rent a canoe or kayak), and bird watchers. A boardwalk with views across Lake Washington meanders along the water in this area (though noise from the adjacent freeway detracts considerably from the experience). Free tours are offered Saturday and Sunday at 1pm.

2300 Arboretum Dr. E. © 206/543-8800. Free admission. Daily 7am–dusk; Graham Visitors Center daily 10am–4pm. Enter on Lake Washington Blvd. off E. Madison St.; or take Wash. 520 off I-5 north of downtown, take the Montlake Blvd. exit, and go straight through the first intersection. Bus: 11, 43, or 48.

ESPECIALLY FOR KIDS

In addition to the listings below, kids will also enjoy many of the attractions described earlier in this chapter, including the **Pacific Science Center** (p. 110), the **Seattle Aquarium** (p. 107), the **IMAXDome Theater** (p. 106), **Odyssey** (p. 106), and the **Woodland Park Zoo** (p. 113).

Even the surliest teenagers will think you're pretty cool for taking them to the **Experience Music Project** (p. 109).

Adolescent and preadolescent boys seem to unfailingly love **Ye Olde Curiosity Shop** and the **Seattle Underground Tour** (see the "Good Times in Bad Taste" box, p. 108). Younger boys also seem to love the **Museum of Flight** (p. 114).

When the kids need to burn off some energy, see above for descriptions of Seattle's best recreational areas; section 7, "Outdoor Pursuits," later in this chapter, will give you the lowdown on for beaches, biking, in-line skating, and more. You can also take the kids to a sporting event; Seattle supports professional football, basketball, and baseball teams. See section 8, "Spectator Sports," later in this chapter.

You might also be able to catch a performance at the **Seattle Children's Theatre** (© 206/441-3322; www.sct.org), or the **Northwest Puppet Center,** 9123 15th Ave. NE (© 206/523-2579; www.nwpuppet.org).

Children's Museum _Kids_ Seattle's Children's Museum is located in the basement of the Center House at Seattle Center. The museum includes plenty of hands-on cultural exhibits, a child-size neighborhood, a Discovery Bay for toddlers, a mountain wilderness area, a global village, and other special exhibits to keep the little ones busy learning and playing for hours.

Center House, in Seattle Center. © 206/441-1768. www.thechildrensmuseum.org. Admission $5.50 per person. Daily 10am–5pm. Closed Thanksgiving, Christmas, and New Year's Day. Bus: 1, 2, 3, 4, 13, 15, 16, 18, 24, or 33. Monorail: from Westlake Center at the corner of Pine St. and Fourth Ave.

Seattle Center ★ (Kids) If you want to keep the kids entertained all day long, head to Seattle Center. This 74-acre cultural center and amusement park was built for the Seattle World's Fair in 1962 and stands on the northern edge of downtown at the end of the monorail line. The most visible building at the center is the **Space Needle** (p. 110), which provides an outstanding panorama of the city from its observation deck. However, of much more interest to children is the **Fun Forest** (© 206/728-1586), with its roller coaster, log flume, merry-go-round, Ferris wheel, arcade games, and minigolf. Seattle Center is also the site of the **Children's Museum** (see above) and **Seattle Children's Theatre** (© 206/441-3322; www.sct.org). This is Seattle's main festival site, and in the summer months hardly a weekend goes by without some special event or another filling its grounds. On hot summer days, the **International Fountain** is a great place for kids to keep cool (bring a change of clothes).

305 Harrison St. © 206/684-7200. www.seattlecenter.com. Free admission; pay per ride or game (various multiride tickets available). Fun Forest June–Labor Day Mon–Thurs noon–11pm or midnight; spring and fall Fri 7–11pm, Sat noon–11pm, Sun noon–8pm. Bus: 1, 2, 3, 4, 13, 15, 16, 18, 24, or 33. Monorail: From Westlake Center at the corner of Pine St. and Fourth Ave.

6 Organized Tours

For information on the **Seattle Underground tour,** see the box titled "Good Times in Bad Taste," on p. 108.

WALKING TOURS

In addition to the walking tours mentioned here, there are two different Pike Place Market tours offered by market organizations. See the Pike Place Market listing on p. 107 for details.

If you'd like to explore downtown Seattle with a knowledgeable guide, join one of the informative walking tours offered by **See Seattle Walking Tours** (© 425/226-7641; www.see-seattle.com). The tours visit Pike Place Market, the waterfront, the Pioneer Square district, and the International District. Tours are split into two parts ($15 per person for part one, $10 per person for part two).

You can also learn lots of Seattle history and wander through hidden corners of the city on 2-hour tours run by **Duse McLean** (© 425/885-3173). These tours start with a ride through the Bus Tunnel to the International District and then make their way back north to Pike Place Market, taking in historic buildings, public art, and scenic vistas. Tours are $15 per person and are offered year-round by reservation.

BUS TOURS

If you'd like an overview of Seattle's main tourist attractions, or if you're pressed for time during your visit, you can pack in a lot of sights on a tour with **Gray Line of Seattle** (© 800/426-7532 or 206/626-5208; www.graylineofseattle.com). Half-day tours are $27 for adults, $13.50 for children; full-day tours are $39 for adults, $19.50 for children. Many other tours, including tours to Mount Rainier National Park and to the Boeing plant in Everett, are also available.

From mid-May through mid-October, Gray Line also offers a **Trolley Tour** on a bus made up to look like an old trolley. The tour is really a day pass that allows you to use the trolley, which follows a set route that passes nearly all the major tourist attractions in downtown Seattle. The trolley stops several places along the waterfront and at Seattle Center, Pike Place Market, the Seattle Art Museum, and Pioneer Square. Tickets are $16 for adults and $8 for children.

uggjers, dancers and an assortment of acrobats fill the street.

he shoots you a wide-eyed look as a seven-foot cartoon character approaches.

What brought you here was wanting the kids

o see something magical while they still believed in magic.

merica Online Keyword: Travel

ith 700 airlines, 50,000 hotels and over 5,000 cruise and vaca-

on getaways, you can now go places you've always dreamed of.

ORLD'S LEADING TRAVEL WEB SITE, 5 YEARS IN A ROW" WORLD TRAVEL AWARDS

Travelocity.com
A Sabre Company
Go Virtually Anywhere.

Seattle by Duck

Paul Revere would have had a hard time figuring out what to tell his fellow colonists if the British had arrived by Duck. A Duck, if you didn't know, is a World War II vintage amphibious vehicle that can arrive by land or sea, and these odd-looking things are now being used to provide tours of Seattle on both land and water. Duck tours take in the standard Seattle sights but then plunge right into Lake Union for a tour of the Portage Bay waterfront, with its many houseboats and great views. Ninety-minute tours leave from near the Space Needle and cost $20 for adults and $10 for kids. Contact **Seattle Duck Tours** ★ (© **800/817-1116** or 206/441-DUCK). Tours leave from a parking lot across from the Space Needle. Because these tours encourage Seattle visitors to get a little daffy while they're in town, they are very popular; reservations are recommended.

Because buses in downtown are free and because both the Waterfront Streetcar and the monorail to Seattle Center cost no more than $1.25, the trolley is not a very good deal; but if you don't want to worry about finding the right bus stop, it's worth considering. There's also a $36 family pass that allows two adults and up to four children to use the trolley for 2 days.

BOAT TOURS

In addition to the boat tours and cruises mentioned below, you can do your own low-budget cruise simply by hopping on one of the ferries operated by **Washington State Ferries** (© **800/84-FERRY** or 888/808-7977 in Washington, or 206/464-6400; www.wsdot.wa.gov/ferries/). Try the Bainbridge Island or Bremerton ferries out of Seattle for a 1½- to 2½-hour round-trip. There are both car ferries and foot ferries on the Bremerton run; the passenger-only ferries leave from the dock to the south of the car ferry terminal in Seattle. For more information on these ferries, see section 9, "Getting Around," in chapter 2.

For a boat excursion that also includes a salmon dinner and Northwest Coast Indian masked dances, consider coughing up the cash for the **Tillicum Village Tour** ★★, Pier 55 (© **800/426-1205** or 206/933-8600; www.tillicumvillage. com). Located at Blake Island State Park across Puget Sound from Seattle and only accessible by tour boat or private boat, Tillicum Village was built in conjunction with the 1962 Seattle World's Fair. The "village" is actually just a large restaurant and performance hall fashioned after a traditional Northwest Coast longhouse, but with totem poles standing vigil out front, the forest encircling the longhouse, and the waters of Puget Sound stretching out into the distance, Tillicum Village is a beautiful spot. After the dinner and dances, you can strike out on forest trails to explore the island (you can return on a later boat if you want to spend a couple of extra hr. hiking). There are even beaches on which to relax. Tours cost $65 for adults, $59 for seniors, $25 for children ages 5 to 12, and are free for children under age 5. Tours are offered daily from May through early October; other months on weekends only. If you can opt for only one tour while in Seattle, this should be it—it's unique, truly Northwestern, the salmon dinner is pretty good, and the traditional masked dances are fascinating (although more for the craftsmanship of the masks than for the dancing itself).

Seattle is a city surrounded by water, and if you'd like to see it from various aquatic perspectives, you can head out with **Argosy Cruises** ★ (© **800/642-7816** or 206/623-1445; www.argosycruises.com). Offerings include a 1-hour harbor cruise (departs from Pier 55; $16 adults, $14 seniors, and $10 children ages 4–12), a 2½-hour cruise through the Hiram Chittenden Locks to Lake Union (departs from Pier 56; $30 adults, $28 seniors, $16 children ages 4–12), and two cruises around Lake Washington (a 2-hr. cruise departs from the AGC Marina at the south end of Lake Union and a 1½-hr. cruise departs from downtown Kirkland on the east side of the lake; $26 adults, $24 seniors, $14 children ages 4–12). The latter two cruises will take you past the fabled Xanadu built by Bill Gates on the shore of Lake Washington. However, of all these options, we'd recommend the cruise through the locks; although this is the most expensive outing, you get not only good views but also the chance to navigate the locks.

Want a meal with your cruise? Try one of Argosy Cruises' lunch or dinner cruises (lunch cruises $42–$46 for adults, $38–$42 for seniors , $26–$29 for children ages 4–12; dinner cruises $78–$83 for adults, $74–$79 for seniors, $52–$56 for children ages 4–12). These cruises are aboard a ship that evokes the style of the *Titanic,* albeit on a much smaller and less luxurious scale. Meals are prepared on board the ship by one of our favorite waterfront restaurants, so these cruises get our vote for best dinners afloat. Reservations are recommended for all cruises.

Less expensive dinner cruises are offered on board the very modern **Spirit of Puget Sound,** Pier 70 (© **206/674-3500;** www.spiritofpugetsound.com). This big sleek yacht does lunch, dinner, and moonlight party cruises. Adult fares range from $28 to $35.50 for lunch cruises and from $44 to $65 for dinner cruises.

Looking for a quieter way to see Seattle from the water? From May 1 to October 15, **Emerald City Charters,** Pier 54 (© **800/831-3274** or 206/624-3931; www.sailingseattle.com), offers 1½- and 2½-hour sailboat cruises. The longer excursions are at sunset. Cruises are $23 to $38 for adults, $20 to $35 for seniors, and $18 to $30 for children under age 12.

VICTORIA EXCURSIONS

Among Seattle's most popular boat tours are day-long excursions to Victoria, British Columbia. These trips are offered by **Victoria Clipper** ★★, Pier 69, 2701 Alaskan Way (© **800/888-2535,** 206/448-5000, or 250/382-8100 in Victoria; www.victoriaclipper.com), and operate several times a day during the summer (once or twice a day in other months). The high-speed catamaran passenger ferry takes 2 to 3 hours to reach Victoria. If you leave on the earliest ferry, you can spend the better part of the day exploring Victoria and be back in Seattle for a late dinner. Round-trip fares range from $59 (7-day advance purchase) to $125 for adults, $59 (7-day advance purchase) to $115 for seniors, and $49.50 to $62.50 for children ages 1 to 11 (between mid-Oct and mid-May, one child travels free with each adult paying for a 7-day advance purchase round-trip fare). Some scheduled trips also stop in the San Juan Islands during the summer. Various tour packages are also available, including an add-on tour to Butchart Gardens. Overnight trips can also be arranged.

(Value **Money-Saving Tip**

The **Ticket/Ticket** booth under the big clock at Pike Place Market sometimes has boat tour tickets available at discounted prices. If your schedule is flexible, be sure to check here first.

Seattle Noir

If your tastes run to the macabre, you might be interested in the **Private Eye on Seattle** ✈ tours ((℗ **206/365-3739**; www.privateeyetours.com) offered by Windsor Olson. These somewhat bizarre van tours are led by a retired private investigator who shares stories of the interesting and unusual cases he handled over his 40 years as a private eye in the Emerald City. Tours are $20 per person. To balance things out, Olson also offers a tour of some of Seattle's most distinctive churches ($25 per person).

For more information on Victoria, pick up a copy of *Frommer's Vancouver & Victoria.*

SCENIC FLIGHTS

Seattle is one of the few cities in the United States where floatplanes are a regular sight in the skies and on the lakes. If you'd like to see what it's like to take off and land from the water, you've got a couple of options. **Seattle Seaplanes** ✈, 1325 Fairview Ave. E. ((℗ **800/637-5553** or 206/329-9638), which takes off from the southeast corner of Lake Union, offers 20-minute scenic flights over the city for $57.50.

If you'd rather pretend you're back in the days of *The English Patient,* you can go up in a vintage biplane with **Olde Thyme Aviation** ✈ ((℗ **206/730-1412;** www.oldethymeaviation.com), which operates from the Museum of Flight on Boeing Field. Flights are offered on sunny weekends, and, if you have a gift certificate, weekday flights can also be arranged (weather permitting). A 20-minute flight along the Seattle waterfront to the Space Needle costs $99 for two people; other flights range in price from $149 to $395 for two people.

A RAILWAY EXCURSION

If you're a fan of riding the rails, consider the **Spirit of Washington Dinner Train,** 625 S. Fourth St., Renton ((℗ **800/876-RAIL** or 425/227-RAIL; www. spiritofwashingtondinnertrain.com). Running from Renton, at the south end of Lake Washington, to the Columbia Winery near Woodinville, at the north end of Lake Washington, this train rolls past views of the lake and Mount Rainier. Along the way, you're fed a filling lunch or dinner. At the turnaround point, you get to tour a winery and taste some wines. Dinner tours range from $60 to $70; lunch tours range from $50 to $60. The higher prices are for seatings in the dome car, which definitely offers finer views.

THE BOEING TOUR ✈✈

Until Bill Gates and Microsoft came to town, Boeing was the largest employer (by far) in the Seattle area. Although the company announced in 2001 that it was moving its corporate headquarters out of Seattle, Boeing is still a major presence in the city, and it still has something that Microsoft can never claim: the single largest building, by volume, in the world. This building, the company's Everett assembly plant, could easily hold 911 basketball courts, 74 football fields, 2,142 average-size homes, or all of Disneyland (with room left over for covered parking). Tours of the building let you see just how they put together the huge passenger jets that travelers take for granted.

The tours are quite fascinating and well worth the time it takes to get here from downtown Seattle. Guided 1-hour tours of the facility are held Monday through Friday throughout the year. The schedule varies with the time of year, so be sure to call ahead for details and directions to the plant. Tours cost $5 for adults and $3 for seniors and children under 16 who meet the height requirement (minimum 50 in. tall). Tickets for same-day use are sold on a first-come, first-served basis beginning at 8am (8:30am Oct–May); in summer, tickets for any given day's tours usually sell out by noon. To check availability of same-day tickets, call *Ⓒ* **425/342-8500** between 8:30am and 2pm. It is possible to make reservations 24 hours or more in advance. However, when making reservations, you'll pay $10 per person regardless of age.

For more information or to make reservations, contact the **Boeing Tour Center,** Wash. 526, Everett, WA (*Ⓒ* **800/464-1476** or 206/544-1264; www. boeing.com/companyoffices/aboutus/tours/). Everett is roughly 30 miles north of Seattle (a 30- to 45-min. drive) off I-5.

If you're in town without a car, you can book a tour to the plant through **Customized Tours and Charter Service** (*Ⓒ* **800/770-8769** or 206/878-3965), which charges $40 and will pick you up at your Seattle hotel.

7 Outdoor Pursuits

See "Beaches, Parks & Public Gardens," earlier in this chapter, for a rundown of great places to play.

BIKING

On the waterfront, bike rentals are available from **Blazing Saddles** ✦, 1230 Western Ave. (*Ⓒ* **206/341-9994**). Along with your bike you also get detailed route descriptions for popular and fun rides originating on the waterfront, including a route on Bainbridge Island and mountain bike trails on Vashon Island. Choose to ride one of the island routes and you'll get to have the thoroughly Seattle experience of riding a bike onto a huge ferry. With its lush, green back roads, and variety of eateries at the end of a loop ride, Bainbridge Island is our favorite bike excursion from downtown Seattle. Blazing Saddles also rents bikes at Seattle Center. Rental rates range from $7 to $11 per hour and from $28 to $48 per day.

Gregg's Green Lake Cycle, 7007 Woodlawn Ave. NE (*Ⓒ* **206/523-1822**); and the **Bicycle Center,** 4529 Sand Point Way NE (*Ⓒ* **206/523-8300**), both rent bikes by the hour, day, or week. Rates range from $3 to $7 per hour and $15 to $30 per day. These shops are both convenient to the **Burke-Gilman/ Sammamish River Trail** ✦✦, a 27-mile paved pathway created mostly from an old railway bed. This path is immensely popular and is a great place for a family bike ride or to get in a long, vigorous ride without having to deal with traffic. The Burke-Gilman portion of this trail starts in the Ballard neighborhood of north Seattle, but the most convenient place to start a ride is at **Gasworks Park** on the north shore of Lake Union. From here you can ride north and east, by way of the University of Washington, to **Kenmore Logboom Park** at the north end of Lake Washington. Serious riders can then continue on from Kenmore Logboom Park on the Sammamish River portion of the trail, which leads to the north end of Lake Sammamish and Marymoor Park, which is the site of a velodrome (a bicycle racetrack). This latter half of the trail is actually our favorite portion of a ride along this trail. This section of the path follows the Sammamish River and passes through several pretty parks. Riding the entire trail out and back is a 54-mile round-trip ride popular with riders in training for races. There are lots of great picnicking spots along both trails.

The West Seattle bike path along **Alki Beach** is another good place to ride and offers great views of the sound and the Olympics.

GOLF

While Seattle isn't a name that springs immediately to mind when folks think of golf, the sport is just as much a passion here as it is all across the country these days. Should you wish to get in a round of golf while you're in town, Seattle has three conveniently located municipal golf courses: **Jackson Park Golf Course,** 1000 NE 135th St. (© **206/363-4747**); **Jefferson Park Golf Course,** 4101 Beacon Ave. S. (© **206/762-4513**); and **West Seattle Golf Course,** 4470 35th Ave. SW (© **206/935-5187**). All three charge very reasonable greens fees of $25 to $28. For information on the Web, check out **www.seattlegolf.com**.

HIKING

Within Seattle itself, there are several large natural parks laced with enough trails to allow for a few good long walks. Among these are **Seward Park,** 5898 Lake Washington Blvd., southeast of downtown, and **Lincoln Park,** 8011 Fauntleroy Ave. SW, south of Alki Beach in West Seattle. However, the city's largest natural park and Seattleites' favorite quick dose of nature is **Discovery Park,** 3801 W. Government Way (© **206/386-4236**), northwest of downtown at the western tip of the Magnolia neighborhood. This park covers more than 500 acres and has many miles of trails and beaches to hike. There are gorgeous views, forest paths, and meadows for lazing in after a long walk. To reach Discovery Park, follow Elliott Avenue north along the waterfront from downtown Seattle, then take the Magnolia Bridge west toward the Magnolia neighborhood and follow Grayfield Street to Galer Street to Magnolia Boulevard.

IN-LINE SKATING

Throughout the city, there are dozens of miles of paved paths that are perfect for skating. You can rent in-line skates at **Greg's Green Lake Cycle,** 7007 Woodlawn Ave. NE (© **206/523-1822**), for $20 per day or $7 per hour. The trail around **Green Lake** in north Seattle and the **Burke-Gilman/Sammamish River Trail** (see the description under "Biking," above) are both good places for skating and are convenient to Gregg's. Other favorite skating spots to try include the paved path in **Myrtle Edwards Park** just north of the Seattle waterfront, the paved path along **Lake Washington Boulevard** north of Seward Park, and the **Alki Beach** pathway in West Seattle.

JOGGING

The waterfront, from **Pioneer Square north to Myrtle Edwards Park,** where a paved path parallels the water, is a favorite downtown jogging route. The residential streets of **Capitol Hill,** when combined with roads and sidewalks through **Volunteer Park,** are another good choice. If you happen to be staying in the University District, you can access the 27-mile-long **Burke-Gilman/ Sammamish River Trail** or run the ever-popular trail around **Green Lake.** Out in West Seattle, the **Alki Beach** pathway is also very popular and provides great views of the Olympics.

SEA KAYAKING, CANOEING, ROWING & SAILING

If you'd like to try your hand at **sea kayaking** ✵✵, try the **Northwest Outdoor Center** ✵✵, 2100 Westlake Ave. N. (© **800/683-0637** or 206/281-9694), which is located on the west side of Lake Union. Here you can rent a sea kayak for between $10 and $15 per hour. You can also opt for guided tours lasting from a few hours to several days, and there are plenty of classes available for those who are interested.

Moss Bay Rowing and Kayak Center, 1001 Fairview Ave. N. (© **206/682-2031;** www.mossbay.net), rents sea kayaks (as well as canoes, bicycle boats, and sailboats) at the south end of Lake Union near Chandler's Cove. Rates range from $10 per hour for a single to $15 per hour for a double. Because this rental center is a little closer to downtown Seattle, it makes a better choice if you are here without a car.

You can also rent wooden rowboats and sailboats on Lake Union at the **Center for Wooden Boats,** 1010 Valley St. (© **206/382-2628;** www.cwb.org), which is located on Waterway 4 at the south end of Lake Union. This unusual little museum is basically a collection of wooden boats of all kinds. Dedicated to the preservation of historic wooden boats, the center is unique in that many exhibits can be rented and taken out on Lake Union. There are both rowboats and sailboats. Rates range from $12.50 to $37.50 per hour (call for hr. of availability). Individual sailing instruction is also available.

8 Spectator Sports

With professional football, baseball, basketball, women's basketball, and ice hockey teams, as well as the various University of Washington Huskies teams, Seattle is definitely a city of sports fans. For those many fans, the sports landscape has been changing dramatically in recent years. In 1999, a state-of-the-art baseball stadium was unveiled in the form of the retractable-roof Safeco Field. In 2000, the venerable and much disparaged Kingdome was demolished to make way for a new football stadium that should be ready for the 2002 season.

Ticketmaster (© **206/622-HITS;** www.ticketmaster.com) sells tickets to almost all sporting events in the Seattle area. There are Ticketmaster outlets at area Rite-Aid, Wherehouse, and Tower Record and Video stores. If they're sold out, try **Pacific Northwest Ticket Service** (© **206/232-0150**).

BASEBALL

Of all of Seattle's major league sports teams, none is more popular than the American League's **Seattle Mariners** (© **800/MY-MARINERS** or 206/346-4000; www.mariners.org). Despite the high-profile departures in recent years of superstars Randy Johnson, Ken Griffey Jr., and A-Rod, the Mariners won at an astounding clip in 2001, tying the 1906 Chicago Cubs for the most regular-season wins in baseball history. The team has a devoted following, which only grew more fanatical in 2001 with the addition of Japanese sensation Ichiro Suzuki.

The Mariners' retro style **Safeco Field** ★★★, which hosted the All-Star Game in 2001, is indisputably one of the most gorgeous ballparks in the country. It's also one of only a handful of stadiums with a retractable roof (which can open or close in about 10–20 min.), allowing the Mariners to have a real grass playing field without having to worry about getting rained out.

Ticket prices range from $6 to $36. Though you may be able to get a single ticket on game day at the Safeco Field box office, that's about all (it would be tough to get two seats together). Mariners' tickets are a hot commodity, so if you want to ensure that you get good seats, order in advance at Mariners Team Stores (see below), or through Ticketmaster (© **206/622-HITS;** www.ticketmaster.com), which has outlets at many Rite-Aid pharmacies, as well as Wherehouse and Tower record stores. Parking is next to impossible in the immediate vicinity of Safeco Field, so plan to leave your car behind.

If you'd like a behind-the-scenes look at the stadium, you can take a **1-hour tour** ($7 for adults, $5 for seniors, $3 for kids ages 3–12); tickets can be purchased at the Mariners Team Store at Safeco Field, other Mariners Team Stores around the city (there are locations at Fourth and Stewart sts. downtown and in Bellevue Square), or through Ticketmaster. Tour times vary, and tours are not offered on days when day games are scheduled.

BASKETBALL

The NBA's **Seattle SuperSonics** (✆ 206/281-5800; www.supersonics.com) play in the Key Arena at Seattle Center, and though they always seem to trail behind Portland's Trailblazers, they generally put in a good showing every season. Tickets are $9 to $110 and are available at the arena box office and through Ticketmaster (✆ **206/628-0888**). Tickets can generally be had even on short notice, except for games against the Lakers and Blazers, which are always well attended.

The University of Washington Huskies women's basketball team has been pretty popular for years, and Seattle also has a pro women's basketball team. The Women's National Basketball Association's (WNBA) **Seattle Storm** (✆ **206/ 217-WNBA;** www.storm.wnba.com) brought professional women's basketball to Seattle's Key Arena. Ticket prices range from $8 to $45 and are available at the arena box office and through Ticketmaster (✆ **206/628-0888**).

For information on the women's and men's Huskies basketball games, contact **University of Washington Sports** (✆ **206/543-2200**).

FOOTBALL

Although the NFL's **Seattle Seahawks** (✆ **888/NFL-HAWK** or 206/682-2800; www.seahawks.com) aren't the most highly regarded of Seattle's professional sports teams, the people of Washington state obviously didn't want to see the Seahawks leave town, or they wouldn't have voted to tax themselves in order to build a new stadium. Starting with the 2002 season, the Seahawks will begin playing in their new stadium, which stands on the site of the old Kingdome. Expect the team's popularity to pick up once they're in the new stadium. Tickets run $15 to $68 and are generally available, depending on how well the team is doing. Games against Oakland, Denver, and a couple of other teams usually sell out as soon as tickets first go on sale in August. Traffic and parking in the vicinity of the new stadium will likely be a nightmare on game days, so take the bus if you can.

Not surprisingly, the **University of Washington Huskies** (✆ **206/543-2200**), who play in Husky Stadium on the university campus, have a loyal following. Big games (Nebraska or Washington State) sell out as soon as tickets go on sale in the summer. Other games can sell out in advance, but there are usually obstructed-view tickets available on the day of the game. Ticket prices range from $32 to $36.

9 Shopping

As the largest city in the state, Seattle has always been where Washingtonians shop. Nordstrom, Eddie Bauer, and REI (all of which were founded in Seattle) have become familiar to shoppers all across the country, and these stores remain some of the busiest in the city. However, in the past few years, as Seattle has developed a national reputation as a great place to put down roots, the retail face of the city has changed considerably.

National chains have taken over many of the storefronts of downtown Seattle, opening up flashy new stores and cashing in on the city's newfound popularity. The names and merchandise at these stores are familiar: Banana Republic, Nike, Levi Strauss, Ann Taylor, FAO Schwartz, Barneys New York. These and many others now have stores in Seattle, so if you forgot to pick up that dress in Chicago or those running shoes in New York, have no fear—you can find them here.

Seattle does, however, have one last bastion of local merchandising, **Pike Place Market.** Whether shopping is your passion or an occasional indulgence, you shouldn't miss this historic market, which is actually one of Seattle's top tourist attractions. Once the city's main produce market (and quite a few produce stalls remain), this sprawling collection of buildings is today filled with hundreds of unusual shops, including **Market Magic** (for magicians and aspiring magicians; ✆ **206/624-4271**), **The Spanish Table** (filled with Spanish cooking supplies; ✆ **206/682-2814**), **Tenzing Momo** (selling body oils, incense, herbs, and such; ✆ **206/623-9837**), and **Left Bank Books** (a bookstore for anarchists and their kin; ✆ **206/622-0195**). See also the listing for Pike Place Market (p. 107).

THE SHOPPING SCENE

Although Seattle is a city of neighborhoods, many of which have great little shops, the focal point of the Seattle shopping scene is the corner of **Pine Street and Fifth Avenue.** Within 2 blocks of this intersection are two major department stores (Nordstrom and The Bon Marché) and two upscale urban shopping malls (Westlake Center and Pacific Place). There's even a sky bridge between Nordstrom and Pacific Place to make shopping just that much easier. Fanning out east and south from this intersection are blocks of upscale stores that have begun to take on a very familiar look. Small local shops are rapidly being replaced by national and international boutiques and megastores. Here in this neighborhood you'll now find Ann Taylor, Barneys New York, NIKETOWN, Gap, MaxMara, Banana Republic, and FAO Schwarz. However, you'll still find a few local mom-and-pop stores in the neighborhood.

The city's main tourist shopping district is the **Pike Place Market** neighborhood. Here you'll find dozens of T-shirt and souvenir shops, as well as import shops and stores appealing to teenagers and 20-somethings. Pike Place Market itself is a fascinating warren of cubbyholes that pass for shops. While produce isn't usually something you stock up on while on vacation, there are several market shops that sell ethnic cooking supplies that are less perishable than a dozen oysters or a king salmon. While you may never find anything here you really need, it's still fun to look (at least that's what millions of Seattle visitors each year seem to think).

Just west of Pike Place Market is the Seattle **waterfront,** where you'll find many more gift and souvenir shops.

South of downtown, in the historic **Pioneer Square area,** you'll find the city's greatest concentration of art galleries, some of which specialize in Native American art. This neighborhood also has several antiques stores, but is also home to numerous bars and attracts a large number of homeless people.

As the center of both the gay community and the city's youth culture, **Capitol Hill** has the most eclectic selection of shops in the city. Beads, imports, CDs, vintage clothing, politically correct merchandise, and gay-oriented goods fill the shops along Broadway. Capitol Hill's main shopping plaza is the Broadway Market, which has lots of small shops.

Even funkier than Capitol Hill, the **Fremont** neighborhood just north of Lake Union is filled with retro stores selling vintage clothing, mid-century furniture and collectibles, and curious crafts. However, this neighborhood is undergoing a fairly rapid gentrification that is forcing out many of the smaller and more unusual shops.

A couple of miles east of Fremont there's the **Wallingford** neighborhood, which is anchored by an old schoolhouse that has been converted into a shopping arcade with interesting crafts, fashions, and gifts.

The **University District,** also in north Seattle, has everything necessary to support a student population and also goes upscale at the University Village shopping center.

SHOPPING A TO Z
ANTIQUES & COLLECTIBLES

If antiques are your passion, you won't want to miss the opportunity to spend a day browsing the many antiques stores in the historic farm town of **Snohomish.** Located roughly 30 miles north of Seattle off I-5, Snohomish was established in 1859 on the banks of the Snohomish River and was the county seat until 1897. When the county seat was moved to Everett, Snohomish lost its regional importance and development slowed considerably. Today, an abundance of turn-of-the-20th-century buildings are the legacy of the town's early economic growth. By the 1960s, these old homes had begun attracting people interested in restoring them to their original condition, and soon antiques shops began proliferating in the historic downtown area. Today the town has more than 400 antiques dealers and is without a doubt the antiques capital of the Northwest.

The Crane Gallery   Chinese, Japanese, and Korean antiquities are the focus of this shop in the Queen Anne neighborhood, which prides itself on selling only the best pieces. Imperial Chinese porcelains, bronze statues of Buddhist deities, rosewood furniture, Japanese ceramics, netsukes, snuff bottles, and Chinese archaeological artifacts are just some of the quality antiques you'll find here. Some Southeast Asian and Indian objects are also available. 104 W. Roy St. ✆ 206/298-9425.

Honeychurch Antiques   For high-quality Asian antiques, including Japanese wood-block prints, textiles, furniture, and ivory and woodcarvings, few Seattle antiques stores can approach Honeychurch Antiques. Regular special exhibits give this shop the feel of a tiny museum. The store's annex, called **Glenn Richards,** 964 Denny Way (✆ **206/287-1877**), specializes in "entry-level" antiques. 1008 James St. ✆ 206/622-1225.

Jean Williams Antiques   If your taste in antiques runs to 18th- and 19th-century French and English formal or country furniture, this Pioneer Square antiques dealer may have something to add to your collection. 115 S. Jackson St. ✆ 206/622-1110.

Laguna Vintage Pottery   Twentieth-century art pottery is the specialty of this shop in Pioneer Square. Pieces by such mid-century pottery factories as Fiesta, Roseville, Bauer, Weller, and Franciscan are stacked on the shelves here in this old brick building. This is a great place to look for dinnerware and vintage tiles. 116 S. Washington St. ✆ 206/682-6162.

ANTIQUES MALLS & FLEA MARKETS

Antiques at Pike Place   Located in the Pike Place Market area, this antiques and collectibles mall is one of the finest in Seattle. There are more than 80 dealers, and much of what's available here is fairly small, which means you might be able to fit your find into a suitcase. 92 Stewart St. ℂ **206/441-9643**. www.antiques atpikeplace.com.

Fremont Sunday Market   Crafts, imports, antiques, collectibles, and fresh produce all combine to make this Seattle's second favorite public market (after Pike Place Market). The market is open Sunday from 10am to 5pm year-round. N. 34th St. and Stone Way N. (3 blocks east of the Fremont Bridge). ℂ **206/781-6776**.

Pioneer Square Antique Mall   This underground antiques mall is in the heart of Pioneer Square right beside the ticket booth for the Seattle Underground tour and contains about 60 stalls selling all manner of antiques and collectibles. Look for glass, old jewelry, and small collectibles here. 602 First Ave. ℂ **206/624-1164**.

ART GALLERIES

The **Pioneer Square area** has for many years been Seattle's main art gallery district, and although there are still quite a few galleries there, many have moved to other parts of the metropolitan area, including the two wealthy east-side suburbs of Bellevue and Kirkland, in the past few years. Still, there are enough galleries left around Pioneer Square that anyone interested in art should be sure to wander around south of Yesler Way. Some galleries are closed on Mondays.

General Art Galleries

Carolyn Staley   A wide range of old prints, including a large collection of 19th- and 20th-century Japanese wood-block prints, are on view at this Pioneer Square gallery. Whatever your personal interest, you'll likely find something intriguing in the gallery's large collection. 314 Occidental Ave. S. ℂ **206/621-1888**.

Davidson Galleries   Located in the heart of the Pioneer Square neighborhood, this gallery is divided into three different areas of focus—contemporary paintings and sculptures (often by Northwest artists); contemporary prints by American and European artists; and antique prints, some of which date from the 1500s. 313 Occidental Ave. S. ℂ **206/624-7684**. www.davidsongalleries.com.

Greg Kucera Gallery   Established in 1983, this showroom in the Pioneer Square area serves as one of Seattle's most reliably cutting-edge galleries. The shows here tend to have themes that address political or social issues or movements within the art world. Don't miss the outdoor sculpture deck. 212 Third Ave. S. ℂ **206/624-0770**. www.gregkucera.com.

Lisa Harris Gallery   Landscapes and figurative works, by both expressionist and realist Northwest and West Coast artists, are a specialty of this gallery, which is located on the second floor of a building in Pike Place Market. 1922 Pike Place. ℂ **206/443-3315**. www.lisaharrisgallery.com.

Art Glass

Foster/White Gallery   If you are enamored of art glass, as we are, be sure to stop by one or both of the Foster/White galleries, which represent Dale Chihuly in Seattle and always have a few works by this master glass artist for sale. Some of Chihuly's pieces even sell for less than $10,000! Foster/White also represents top-notch Northwest artists in the disciplines of paintings, ceramics, and sculpture. Also in Kirkland at 126 Central Way (ℂ **425/822-2305**). 123 S. Jackson St. ℂ **206/622-2833**. www.fosterwhite.com.

Glasshouse Studio   Located in the Pioneer Square area and founded in 1972, Glasshouse claims to be the oldest glass-blowing studio in the Northwest.

In the studio, you can watch handblown art glass being made, and then, in the gallery, you can check out the works of numerous local glass artists. 311 Occidental Ave. S. © 206/682-9939. www.glasshouse-studio.com.

Phoenix Rising Gallery   The art glass here is more high-end than what you'll find at the nearby Glass Eye Gallery. Artists from around the country are represented, and there is always some highly imaginative decorative work on display. This gallery also now sells ceramic pieces and wooden crafts. 2030 Western Ave. © 206/728-2332. www.phoenixrisinggallery.com.

Vetri   Vetri, which is affiliated with the prestigious William Traver Gallery, showcases innovative work primarily from emerging glass artists and local area studios, but also works by artists from other countries. It's all high quality and riotously colorful. Prices are relatively affordable. 1404 First Ave. © 206/667-9608. www.vetriglass.com.

William Traver Gallery   In business for more than 25 years, this is one of the nation's top art-glass galleries and showcases the works of 80 glass artists. Works shown here are, so to speak, on the cutting edge of glass art and will give you a good idea of the broad spectrum of work being created by contemporary glass artists. You'll find the gallery on the second floor. 110 Union St. © 206/587-6501. www.travergallery.com.

Native American Art

Flury and Company   This Pioneer Square gallery specializes in prints by famed Seattle photographer Edward S. Curtis, who is known for his portraits of Native Americans. The gallery also has an excellent selection of antique Native American art. 322 First Ave. S. © 206/587-0260. www.fluryco.com.

The Legacy Ltd.   The Legacy Ltd. is Seattle's oldest and finest gallery of contemporary and historic Northwest Coast Indian and Alaskan Eskimo art and artifacts. You'll find a large selection of masks, boxes, bowls, baskets, ivory artifacts, jewelry, prints, and books for the serious collector. 1003 First Ave. © 800/729-1562 or 206/624-6350. www.thelegacyltd.com.

Stonington Gallery   This is one of Seattle's top galleries specializing in contemporary Native American arts and crafts. Here you'll find a good selection of Northwest Coast Indian masks, totem poles, mixed-media pieces, prints, carvings, and Northwest Coast–style jewelry. 119 S. Jackson St. © 206/405-4040.

BOOKS

In addition to the stores listed below, you'll find more than a half dozen locations of **Barnes & Nobles** around the metro area, including one downtown at 600 Pine St. (© 206/264-0156). There's also a **Borders** at 1501 Fourth Ave. (© 206/622-4599).

Elliott Bay Book Company   With battered wooden floors, a maze of rooms full of books, and frequent readings and in-store appearances by authors, this Pioneer Square bookstore feels as if it has been around forever. There's an excellent selection of books on Seattle and the Northwest, so if you want to learn more about the region or are planning further excursions, stop by. There is also a good little cafe down in the basement. 101 S. Main St. © 206/624-6600. www.elliott baybook.com.

Flora & Fauna   Gardeners, bird-watchers, and other nature-philes, take note. Down below street level in what passes for the active Seattle underground of the Pioneer Square area, you'll find a store filled with books that'll have you wishing you were in your garden or out in the woods identifying birds and flowers. 121 First Ave. S. ℂ 206/623-4727.

Seattle Mystery Bookshop If books that keep you wondering whodunit are your passion, don't miss an opportunity to peruse the shelves of this specialty bookstore in the Pioneer Square area. You'll find all your favorite mystery authors, books signings, and lots of signed copies. 117 Cherry St. ℂ 206/587-5737.

COFFEE & TEA

All over the city, on almost every corner, you'll find espresso bars, cafes, and coffeehouses. And while you can get coffee back home, you might want to stock up on whichever local coffee turns out to be your favorite. If you're a latte junkie, you can make a pilgrimage to the shop that started it all, the original Starbucks, listed below.

Starbucks Seattle is well-known as a city of coffeeholics, and Starbucks is the main reason why. This company has coffeehouses all over town (and all over the world), but this is the original. Although you won't find any tables or chairs here, Starbucks fans shouldn't miss an opportunity to get their coffee at the source. 1912 Pike Place, Pike Place Market. ℂ 206/448-8762. www.starbucks.com.

Ten Ren Tea Co., Ltd. Ever wondered what $150-a-pound Chinese tea tastes like? At this International District tea shop, you can find out. Not only do they have dozens of different types of teas here, but they also have a little table in back where you can sample various varieties and observe the traditional Chinese tea ceremony. 506 S. King St. ℂ 206/749-9855.

CRAFTS

The Northwest is a leading center for craftspeople, and one place to see what they are creating and meet the artisans themselves is Pike Place Market.

Fireworks Fine Crafts Gallery Playful, outrageous, bizarre, beautiful— these are just some of the terms that can be used to describe the eclectic collection of Northwest crafts on sale at this Pioneer Square gallery. Cosmic clocks, wildly creative jewelry, and artistic picture frames are some of the fine and unusual items you'll find here. Also at Westlake Center, 400 Pine St. (ℂ 206/682-6462); Bellevue Square, NE Eighth Street and Bellevue Way, Bellevue (ℂ 425/688-0933); and the University Village shopping plaza, 2629 NE University Village Mall (ℂ 206/527-2858). 210 First Ave. S. ℂ 206/682-8707. www.fireworksgallery.net.

Frank and Dunya Located in the middle of funky Fremont, this store epitomizes the Fremont aesthetic. The art, jewelry, and crafts here all tend toward the colorful and the humorous, and just about everything is made by Northwest artists and artisans. 3418 Fremont Ave. N. ℂ 206/547-6760.

Northwest Fine Woodworking This store is a showcase for some of the most amazing woodworking you'll ever see. Be sure to stroll through here while in the Pioneer Square area even if you aren't in the market for a one-of-a-kind piece of furniture. The warm hues of the exotic woods are soothing and the designs are beautiful. Furniture, boxes, sculptures, vases, bowls, and much more are created by more than 35 Northwest artisans. Also in Bellevue at the Bellevue Pedestrian Corridor, 601 108th Ave. NE, Plaza 100 (ℂ 425/462-5382). 101 S. Jackson St. ℂ 206/625-0542. www.nwfinewoodworking.com.

Twist This impressively large store is filled with items such as unusual artist-created jewelry, Adirondack chairs made from recycled water skis, twisted glass vases, candlesticks, and ceramics. All are slightly offbeat yet tasteful objets d'art. 1503 Fifth Ave. ✆ 206/315-8080.

DEPARTMENT STORES

The Bon Marché   Seattle's "other" department store, established in 1890, is every bit as well stocked as the neighboring Nordstrom department store, and with such competition nearby, The Bon, as it's known, tries every bit as hard to keep its customers happy. Third Ave. and Pine St. ✆ 206/506-6000.

Nordstrom   Known for personal service, Nordstrom stores have gained a reputation for being among the premier department stores in the United States. The company originated here in Seattle (opening its first store in 1901), and its customers are devotedly loyal. This is a state-of-the-art store, with all sorts of little boutiques, cafes, and other features to make your shopping excursion an experience.

Best of all, whether it's your first visit or your 50th, the knowledgeable staff will help you in any way they can. Prices may be a bit higher than those at other department stores, but for your money you get the best service available. The store is packed with shoppers during the half-year sale in June and the anniversary sale in July. You'll also find Nordstrom at area shopping malls. 1601 Fifth Ave. ✆ 206/628-2111. www.nordstrom.com.

DISCOUNT SHOPPING

Nordstrom Rack *Value*   This is the Nordstrom overflow shop where you'll find three floors of discontinued lines as well as overstock, and all at greatly reduced prices. Women's fashions make up the bulk of the merchandise here, but there is also a floor full of men's clothes and shoes, plus plenty of kids' clothes. 1601 Second Ave. ✆ 206/448-8522.

FASHION

In addition to the stores listed below, you'll find quite a few familiar names in downtown Seattle, including Ann Taylor, Banana Republic, Barneys New York, Eddie Bauer, Gap, and MaxMara.

Accessories

Byrnie Utz Hats   In the same location since 1934 and boasting the largest selection of hats in the Northwest, this cramped hat-wearer's heaven looks as if it hasn't changed in 50 years. There are Borsalino Panama hats, Kangol caps, and, of course, plenty of Stetsons. 310 Union St. ✆ 206/623-0233.

Men's & Women's Clothing

Eddie Bauer   Eddie Bauer got his start here in Seattle back in 1922, and today the chain is one of the country's foremost purveyors of upscale outdoor fashions—although these days, outdoor fashion is looking quite a bit more urban. 1330 Fifth Ave. ✆ 206/622-2766. www.eddiebauer.com.

NIKETOWN   Around the country, there are currently more than a dozen NIKETOWNs selling all things Nike and only things Nike. If you don't live near one of these high-tech megastores, and you do wear swooshes, then this store should definitely be on your shopping itinerary. 1500 Sixth Ave. ✆ 206/447-6453.

Northwest Pendleton   For Northwesterners, and many other people across the nation, Pendleton is and always will be *the* name in classic wool fashions. This store features tartan plaids and Indian-pattern separates, accessories, shawls, and blankets. 1313 Fourth Ave. ✆ 800/593-6773 or 206/682-4430. www.pendletonblankets.com.

Women's Clothing

Alhambra Alhambra stocks an eclectic collection of women's clothing, jewelry, and home furnishings. Expect to find a fun and quirky selection of dressy hats and accessories as well. 101 Pine St. ℂ 206/621-9571. www.alhambranet.com.

Baby and Co. Claiming stores in Seattle and on Mars, this up-to-the-minute store stocks fashions that can be trendy, outrageous, or out of this world. Whether you're into earth tones or bright colors, you'll likely find something you can't live without. 1936 First Ave. ℂ 206/448-4077.

Passport Clothing Company Soft and easygoing is the current style at this large store near Pike Place Market. Velvet, linen, cotton, rayon, and other natural fibers are the fabrics of choice here. 123 Pine St. ℂ 206/628-9799.

Ragazzi's Flying Shuttle Fashion becomes art and art becomes fashion at this chic boutique-cum-gallery on Pioneer Square. Handwoven fabrics and hand-painted silks are the specialties here, but of course such sophisticated fashions require equally unique body decorations in the form of exquisite jewelry creations. Designers and artists from the Northwest and the rest of the nation find an outlet for their creativity at the Flying Shuttle. 607 First Ave. ℂ 206/343-9762.

GIFTS/SOUVENIRS

Pike Place Market is the Grand Central Station of Seattle souvenirs, with stiff competition from Seattle Center and Pioneer Square.

Made in Washington Whether it's salmon, wine, or Northwest crafts, you'll find a selection of Washington state products in this shop. This is an excellent place to pick up gifts for all those friends and family members who didn't get to come to Seattle with you. Also in Washington store in downtown's Westlake Center mall (ℂ 206/623-9753). Pike Place Market (Post Alley at Pine St.). ℂ 206/467-0788. www.madeinwashington.com.

Portage Bay Goods If you'd like to give a gift with a conscience, drop by this unusual store in the Fremont neighborhood. Almost everything here is made from recycled materials. We like the notebooks with covers made from computer boards, but there are lots of fun decorative home accessories as well. 706 N. 34th St. ℂ 206/547-5221. www.portagebaygoods.com.

Ye Olde Curiosity Shop If you can elbow your way into this waterfront institution, you'll find every inch of space, horizontal and vertical, covered with souvenirs and crafts, both tacky and tasteful (but mostly tacky). Surrounding all this merchandise are the weird artifacts that have made this one of the most visited shops in Seattle. 1001 Alaskan Way, Pier 54. ℂ 206/682-5844. www.yeoldecuriosity shop.com.

JEWELRY

Unique artist-crafted jewelry can be found at **Ragazzi's Flying Shuttle** (p. 132) and **Twist** (p. 130).

Fox's Gem Shop Seattle's premier jeweler, Fox's has been around for 90 years, and always has plenty of a girl's best friend. Colorless or fancy colored diamonds available here are of the finest cut. 1341 Fifth Ave. ℂ 206/623-2528.

MALLS/SHOPPING CENTERS

City Centre This upscale downtown shopping center is the Seattle address of such familiar high-end retailers as Barneys New York, FAO Schwarz, and Ann Taylor. There are works of art by Dale Chihuly and other Northwest glass artists on display throughout City Centre, and also a very comfortable lounge where you can rest your feet and escape from the Seattle weather. Sixth Ave. and Union St. © **206/624-8800.**

Pacific Place   This downtown mall is located adjacent to Nordstrom and contains five levels of upscale shop-o-tainment, including Cartier, Tiffany & Co., J. Crew, MaxMara, five restaurants, and an 11-screen cinema. A huge skylight fills the interior space with much-appreciated natural light, and an adjoining garage ensures that you'll be able to find a place to park (maybe). 600 Pine St. © **206/405-2655.** www.pacificplaceseattle.com.

Westlake Center   Before the opening of Pacific Place, this was Seattle's premier downtown, upscale, urban shopping mall. Located in the heart of Seattle's main shopping district, this mall has more than 80 specialty shops, including Godiva Chocolatier, Crabtree & Evelyn, and Made in Washington. There is an extensive food court, and the mall is also the southern terminus for the monorail to Seattle Center. 400 Pine St. © **206/467-3044.** www.therousecompany.com.

MARKETS

Pike Place Market   Pike Place Market is one of Seattle's most famous landmarks and tourist attractions. It shelters not only produce vendors, fishmongers, and butchers, but also artists, craftspeople, and performers. There are hundreds of shops and dozens of restaurants (including some of Seattle's best) tucked away in hidden nooks and crannies on the numerous levels of the market. With so much to see and do, a trip to Pike Place Market can easily turn into an all-day affair. See listing under "What to See & Do in Seattle," on p. 107. Pike St. and First Ave. © **206/682-7453.** www.pikeplacemarket.org.

Uwajimaya   Typically, your local neighborhood supermarket has a section of Chinese cooking ingredients; it's probably about 10 feet long, with half that space taken up by various brands of soy sauce. Now imagine your local supermarket with nothing but Asian foods, housewares, produce, and toys. That's Uwajimaya, Seattle's Asian supermarket in the heart of the International District. There's also a big food court here serving all kinds of Asian food. 600 Fifth Ave. S. © **206/624-6248.** www.uwajimaya.com.

RECREATIONAL GEAR

Filson   Ever since the Alaskan gold rush at the end of the 1890s, this Seattle company has been outfitting people headed outdoors. You won't find any high-tech fabrics here, just good old-fashioned wool, and plenty of it. Filson's clothes are meant to last a lifetime (and have the prices to prove it), so if you demand only the best, even when it comes to outdoor gear, be sure to check out this Seattle institution. 1555 Fourth Ave. S. © **206/622-3147.** www.filson.com.

REI   Recreational Equipment, Incorporated (REI), was founded here in Seattle back in 1938 and today is the nation's largest co-op selling outdoor gear. A few years ago, REI opened an impressive flagship store just off I-5 not far from Lake Union. The store, a cross between a high-tech warehouse and a mountain lodge, is massive and sells almost anything you could ever need for pursuing your favorite outdoor sport. The store also has a 65-foot climbing pinnacle, a rain room for testing rain gear, a mountain-bike trail for test-driving bikes, a footwear test trail, even a play area for kids. With all this under one roof, who needs to go outside? Up on the top floor, there's also a World Wraps Cafe with an outstanding view of downtown. 222 Yale Ave. N. © **206/223-1944.**

SALMON

If you think the fish at Pike Place Market looks great, but you could never get it home on the plane, think again. Any of the seafood vendors in Pike Place Market will pack your fresh salmon or Dungeness crab in an airline-approved container that will keep it fresh for up to 48 hours. Alternatively, you can buy vacuum-packed smoked salmon that will keep for years without refrigeration.

Pike Place Fish   Located just behind Rachel, Pike Place Market's life-sized bronze pig, this fishmonger is just about the busiest spot in the market most days. What pulls in the crowds are the antics of the workers here. Order a big silvery salmon and you'll have employees shouting out your order and throwing the fish over the counter. Crowds are always gathered around the stall hoping to see some of the famous "flying fish." 86 Pike Place, Pike Place Market. ℭ **800/542-7732** or 206/682-7181.

Totem Smokehouse   Northwest Coast Indians relied heavily on salmon for sustenance, and to preserve the fish they used alder-wood smoke. This tradition is still carried on today to produce smoked salmon, one of the Northwest's most delicious food products. This store, located at street level in Pike Place Market, sells vacuum-packed smoked salmon that will keep without refrigeration until the package is opened. 1906 Pike Place, Pike Place Market. ℭ **800/972-5666** or 206/ 443-1710.

TOYS

Archie McPhee   You may already be familiar with this temple of the absurd through its mail-order catalog. Now imagine wandering through aisles full of goofy gags. Give yourself plenty of time and take a friend. You'll find Archie's place in the Ballard neighborhood. 2428 NW Market St. ℭ **206/297-0240**. www. mcphee.com.

Magic Mouse   Adults and children alike have a hard time pulling themselves away from this, the wackiest toy store in downtown Seattle. It is conveniently located in Pioneer Square and has a good selection of European toys. 603 First Ave. ℭ **206/682-8097**.

10 Seattle After Dark

Though Seattleites spend much of their free time enjoying the city's natural surroundings, they do not overlook the more cultured evening pursuits. In fact, the winter weather that keeps people indoors, combined with a long-time desire to be the cultural mecca of the Northwest, have fueled a surprisingly active and diverse nightlife scene. The Seattle Opera is ranked as one of the top operas in the country, and its stagings of Wagner's *Ring* series have achieved near-legendary status. The Seattle Symphony also receives frequent accolades. Likewise, the Seattle Repertory Theatre has won Tony awards for its productions, and there is also a thriving fringe theater scene. Music lovers will also find a plethora of classical, jazz, and rock offerings.

To find out what's going on when you're in town, pick up a free copy of **Seattle Weekly** (**www.seattleweekly.com**), Seattle's arts-and-entertainment newspaper. You'll find it in bookstores, convenience stores, grocery stores, newsstands, and newspaper boxes around downtown and other neighborhoods. On Friday, the **Seattle Times** includes a section called "Ticket," which is a guide to the week's arts and entertainment offerings.

THE PERFORMING ARTS

While the Seattle Symphony performs in downtown's Benaroya Hall, the main venues for the performing arts in Seattle are primarily clustered in **Seattle Center,** the special events complex that was built for the 1962 Seattle World's Fair. Here, in the shadow of the Space Needle, you'll find the Opera House, Bagley Wright Theater, Intiman Playhouse, Seattle Children's Theatre, Seattle Center Coliseum, Memorial Stadium, and the Experience Music Project's Sky Church performance hall.

OPERA & CLASSICAL MUSIC

The **Seattle Opera** (© 206/389-7676; www.seattleopera.org), which performs at the Seattle Center Opera House, is considered one of the finest opera companies in the country, and *the* Wagnerian opera company. The stagings of Wagner's four-opera *The Ring of the Nibelungen* are breathtaking spectacles that draw crowds from around the country. However, the *Ring* cycle was just staged in 2001, and won't be staged again for several years. In addition to classical operas such as *The Magic Flute* and *The Barber of Seville,* the season usually includes a more contemporary production. Ticket prices range from $31 to $107.

The 90-musician **Seattle Symphony** (© 206/215-4747; www.seattle symphony.org), which performs in the acoustically superb Benaroya Hall, offers an amazingly diverse musical season that runs from September to July. With several different musical series, there is a little something for every type of classical music fan. There are evenings of classical, light classical, and pops, plus afternoon concerts, guest artists, and more. Ticket prices range from $10 to $69.

The **Northwest Chamber Orchestra** (© 206/343-0445; www.nwco.org), a perennial favorite with Seattle classical music fans, is a showcase for Northwest performers. The season runs from September to May, and performances are held primarily in Benaroya Hall in downtown Seattle, although there are also concert series at the Seattle Asian Art Museum. Ticket prices range from $14.50 to $30.

THEATER
Mainstream Theaters

The **Seattle Repertory Theater** (© 877/900-9285 or 206/443-2222; www. seattlerep.org), which performs at the Bagley Wright and Leo K. theaters, Seattle Center, 155 Mercer St., has been around for more than 30 years. As Seattle's top professional theater, it stages the most consistently entertaining productions in the city. The Rep's season runs from September to June, with five plays performed in the main theater and four more in the more intimate Leo K. Theatre. Productions range from classics to world premieres. Ticket prices range from $15 to $44. When available, rush tickets are available half an hour before shows for $20.

With a season that runs from March to December, the **Intiman Theatre Company** (© 206/269-1900; www.intiman.org), which performs at the Intiman Playhouse, Seattle Center, 201 Mercer St., picks up where the Seattle Rep leaves off, filling in the gap left by those months when the Seattle Rep's lights are dark. Ticket prices range from $27 to $43.

Performing in the historic Eagles Building theater adjacent to the Washington State Convention and Trade Center, **A Contemporary Theater (ACT),** 700 Union St. (© 206/292-7676; www.acttheatre.org), offers slightly more adventurous productions than the other major theater companies in Seattle, though it's not nearly as avant-garde as some of the smaller companies. The season runs from the end of May to November (plus *A Christmas Carol* in Dec). Ticket prices usually range from $30 to $42.

Fringe Theater

Not only does Seattle have a healthy mainstream performing-arts community, it also has developed the sort of fringe theater life once only associated with such cities as New York, Los Angeles, London, and Edinburgh. The city's more avant-garde performance companies frequently grab their share of the limelight with daring, outrageous, and thought-provoking productions.

Seattle's interest in fringe theater finds its greatest expression each September, when the **Seattle Fringe Theater Festival** (© 206/342-9172; www.seattle fringe.org), a showcase for small, self-producing theater companies, takes over various venues. There are usually performances by more than 70 theater groups from around the country.

Even if you don't happen to be in town for Seattle's annual fringe binge, check the listings in *Seattle Weekly* or the *Seattle Times*'s Friday "Ticket" entertainment guide to see what's going on during your visit. The following venues are some of Seattle's more reliable places for way-off Broadway productions, performance art, and spoken word performances:

- **Book-It Repertory Theater** (© 206/216-0877 for information, or 206/ 325-6500 for tickets; www.book-it.org). Works by local playwrights, adaptations of literary works in a style that preserves narrative text as written. Performances are held at various venues around the city.
- **Empty Space Theatre,** 3509 Fremont Ave. N. (© **206/547-7500;** www. emptyspace.org). One of Seattle's biggest little theaters, Empty Space stages mostly comedies and is popular with a young crowd.
- **Northwest Asian-American Theater,** Theatre Off Jackson, 409 Seventh Ave. S. (© **206/340-1049**). Works by Asian-American writers, actors, and musicians.
- **Theater Schmeater,** 1500 Summit St. (© **206/324-5801;** www.schmeater. org). Lots of weird and sometimes wonderful comedy, including ever-popular live late-night stagings of episodes from *The Twilight Zone.*

Ticket, Please

Full-price advance-purchase tickets to the Seattle Symphony and to many performing arts events are handled by **Ticketmaster** (© **206/292-ARTS;** www.ticketmaster.com).

For half-price, day-of-show tickets (and 1-day advance tickets for matinees) to a wide variety of performances all over the city, stop by **Ticket/Ticket** (© **206/324-2744**), which has three sales booths in the Seattle area: one in Pike Place Market, one on Capitol Hill, and one in Bellevue. The Pike Place Market location, in the Pike Place Market information booth, First Avenue and Pike Street, is open Tuesday through Sunday from noon to 6pm. The Capitol Hill booth is in the Broadway Market, 401 Broadway E., and is open Tuesday through Saturday from noon to 7pm and Sunday from noon to 6pm. The Bellevue booth is in the Meydenbauer Center, NE Sixth Street and 112th Avenue, and is open Tuesday through Sunday from noon to 6pm. Ticket/Ticket charges a small service fee, the amount of which depends on the ticket price.

DANCE

Although it has a well-regarded ballet company and a theater dedicated to contemporary dance and performance art, Seattle is not nearly as devoted to dance as it is to theater and classical music. This said, hardly a week passes without some sort of dance performance being staged somewhere in the city. Touring companies of all types, the University of Washington Dance Department faculty and student performances, and the UW World Dance Series (see below for details), all bring plenty of creative movement to the stages of Seattle. When you're in town, check *Seattle Weekly* or the *Seattle Times* for a calendar of upcoming performances.

The **Pacific Northwest Ballet,** Seattle Center Opera House, 301 Mercer St. (© **206/441-2424;** www.pnb.org), is Seattle's premier dance company. During the season, which runs from September to June, the company presents a wide range of classics, new works, and (the company's specialty) pieces choreographed by George Balanchine (tickets $15–$115). This company's performance of *The Nutcracker,* with outstanding dancing and sets and costumes by children's book author Maurice Sendak, is the highlight of every season.

Much more adventurous choreography is the domain of **On the Boards,** Behnke Center for Contemporary Performance, 100 W. Roy St. (© **206/217-9888;** www.ontheboards.org), which, although it stages a wide variety of performance art, is best known as Seattle's premier modern-dance venue (tickets $7–$20). In addition to dance performances by Northwest artists, there are a variety of productions each year by internationally known artists.

MAJOR PERFORMANCE HALLS

With ticket prices for shows and concerts so high these days, it pays to be choosy about what you see, but sometimes *where* you see it is just as important. Benaroya Hall, the Seattle Symphony's downtown home, has such excellent acoustics that it's worth attending a performance here just for the sake of hearing how a good symphony hall should sound. Seattle also has two restored historic theaters that are as much a part of a performance as what goes on up on the stage.

Benaroya Hall (© **206/215-4747**), on Third Avenue between Union and University streets in downtown Seattle, is the home of the Seattle Symphony. This state-of-the-art performance hall houses two concert halls—the main hall and a smaller recital hall. The concert hall is also home to the Watjen concert organ, a magnificent pipe organ. There's also a Starbucks, a cafe, and a symphony store. But all the amenities aside, it's the main hall's excellent acoustics that are the main attraction here.

The **5th Avenue Theatre,** 1308 Fifth Ave. (© **206/625-1418** for information, or 206/292-ARTS for tickets; www.5thavenuetheatre.org), which first opened its doors in 1926 as a vaudeville house, is a loose re-creation of the imperial throne room in Beijing's Forbidden City. In 1980, the theater underwent a complete renovation that restored this Seattle jewel to its original splendor, and today the astounding interior is as good a reason as any to see a show here. Don't miss an opportunity to attend a performance. Broadway shows are the theater's mainstay (tickets $15–$65).

The **Paramount Theatre,** 911 Pine St. (© **206/682-1414;** www.the paramount.com), one of Seattle's few historic theaters, has been restored to its original beauty and today shines with all the brilliance it did when it first opened. New lighting and sound systems have brought the theater up to contemporary standards. The theater stages everything from rock concerts to Broadway musicals (tickets $11.50–$65). Tickets are available through Ticketmaster.

PERFORMING ARTS SERIES

When Seattle's own resident performing arts companies aren't taking to the dozens of stages around the city, various touring companies from around the world are. If you're a fan of Broadway shows, check the calendars at the Paramount Theatre and the 5th Avenue Theatre, both of which regularly serve as Seattle stops for touring shows. While winters are a time for enjoying the performing arts indoors, summers bring an array of outdoor festivals. See the "Washington Calendar of Events" in chapter 2 for information on some of the bigger festivals.

The **UW World Series** (© 206/543-4880), held at Meany Hall on the University of Washington campus, is actually several different series including a chamber music series, a classical piano series, a dance series, and a world music and theater series. Together these four series keep the Meany Hall stage busy between October and May. Special events are also scheduled (tickets $28–$55).

Another series worth checking out is the **Seattle Art Museum's "After Hours."** Every Thursday from 5 to 9pm, the museum hosts live music, frequently jazz, and sets up a bar in its main lobby. Shows are free with museum admission.

AT&T Wireless Summer Nights at the Pier (© 206/628-0888; www. summernights.org) presents a summer's worth of big-name acts at Pier 62/63 on the waterfront. Blues, jazz, rock, and folk acts generally pull in a 30-something to 50-something crowd (tickets $15–$45).

At **Woodland Park Zoo** (© 206/615-0076; www.zoo.org), the Zoo Tunes concert series brings in more big-name performers from the world of jazz, easy listening, blues, and rock (tickets $12–$18).

In Woodinville, on the east side of Lake Washington, Chateau Ste. Michele, 14111 NE 145th St., Washington's largest winery, stages the area's most enjoyable outdoor summer concert series. The **Summer Festival on the Green** (© 425/415-3300 for information, or 206/628-0888 for tickets) is held at the winery's amphitheater, which is surrounded by beautiful estatelike grounds. Once again the lineup is calculated to appeal to the 30- to 50-something crowd (A Prairie Home Companion, Diana Krall, Gipsy Kings).

THE CLUB & MUSIC SCENE

If you have the urge to do a bit of clubbing and barhopping, there's no better place to start than in **Pioneer Square.** Good times are guaranteed, whether you want to hear a live band, hang out in a good old-fashioned bar, or dance. However, keep in mind that this neighborhood tends to attract a very rowdy crowd and can be pretty rough late at night.

Belltown, north of Pike Place Market, is another good place to club hop. Clubs here are more trend-conscious, as are the customers.

Seattle's other nightlife district is the former Scandinavian neighborhood of **Ballard,** where you'll find more than half of Seattle's nightlife establishments, including a brewpub, taverns, bars, live-music clubs, and a wine bar.

FOLK, ROCK & REGGAE
Pioneer Square

The Pioneer Square area is Seattle's main live music neighborhood, and the clubs have banded together to make things easy on music fans. The **"Joint Cover"** plan lets you pay one admission to get into nine different clubs. The charge is $5 Sunday through Thursday and $10 on Friday and Saturday ($8 8–9pm Fri–Sat; occasionally $12 for national-act nights). Participating clubs currently include Larry's Greenfront Cafe, Doc Maynard's, the Central Saloon, The Bohemian Café, Old Timer's Cafe, Zasu, and the New Orleans. Most of these clubs are short on style and hit-or-miss when it comes to music (which makes the joint cover a great way to find out where the good music is on any given night).

The Central Saloon   Established in 1892, the Central is the oldest saloon in Seattle. As a Seattle institution, it's a must-stop during a night out in Pioneer Square. You might catch sounds ranging from funk to reggae. 207 First Ave. S. ℂ 206/622-0209. Cover $5–$10 (joint cover).

Belltown & Environs

Crocodile   With its rambunctious decor, this Belltown establishment is a combination nightclub, bar, and restaurant. There's live rock Tuesday through Saturday nights. The music calendar here is always eclectic with everything from rock to folk to jazz, though alternative rock dominates. 2200 Second Ave. ℂ 206/441-5611. www.thecrocodile.com. Cover $5–$20.

EMP   The Experience Music Project, Seattle's humongous lump o' color rock museum, isn't just some morgue for dead rockers. This place is a showcase for real live rockers, too. EMP's main hall, the **Sky Church,** plays host to everything from indie rockers to theater productions with live rock accompaniment. There's also the smaller **Liquid Lounge,** a club with no cover and a wide range of musical sensibilities. One night might be a reggae dance party while another night might feature hip-hop or an acoustic show. 325 Fifth Ave. N. ℂ 206/770-2702. www.emplive.com. Cover Liquid Lounge free; Sky Church $10–$20.

Showbox   Located across the street from Pike Place Market, this club books a wide variety of local and name rock acts. Definitely *the* downtown rock venue for performers with a national following. 1426 First Ave. ℂ 206/628-3151. Cover $10–$30.

Capitol Hill

Baltic Room   This swanky Capitol Hill hangout for the beautiful people provides live lounge music from 6 to 9pm nightly. Later in the night there's live or DJ dance music ranging from Britpop to hip-hop and house. 1207 Pine St. ℂ 206/625-4444. Cover $3–$6.

Century Ballroom   With a beautiful wooden dance floor and a genuine bandstand, this classic ballroom now plays host to some of the best touring acts to come to town. This is also Seattle's top spot for swing and salsa dancing, each of which tops the bill a couple of nights per week. The crowd here is very diverse, with customers of all ages who come to check out a schedule that might include acts like Hot Tuna or evenings of Hawaiian guitar music. 915 E. Pine St. ℂ 206/324-7263. www.centuryballroom.com. Cover $5–$30.

Ballard

Ballard Firehouse   An eclectic assortment of musical styles finds its way onto the bandstand of this converted firehouse in Ballard. Now it's just the music that's hot, and that's the way they want to keep it. The crowd is young and the music generally ranges from techno/trance to hip-hop to the latest local indie rockers. 5429 Russell Ave. NW ℂ 206/784-3516. No cover–$10.

Tractor Tavern   For an ever-eclectic schedule of music for people whose tastes go beyond the latest rap artist, the Tractor Tavern is the place to be. You can catch almost anything form Hawaiian slack-key guitar to rockabilly to singer-songwriters to banjo music to Celtic to folk to alternative. Sound like your kind of place? 5213 Ballard Ave. NW. ℂ 206/789-3599. www.tractortavern.com. No cover–$20.

JAZZ & BLUES

Dimitriou's Jazz Alley   Cool and sophisticated, this Belltown establishment is reminiscent of a New York jazz club and has been around for more than 20 years. Seattle's premier jazz venue, it books only the best performers, including big-name acts. 2033 Sixth Ave. ℂ 206/441-9729. www.jazzalley.org. Cover $13.50–$30.

New Orleans   If you like your food and your jazz hot, check out the New Orleans in Pioneer Square. Throughout the week, there's Cajun, Dixieland, R&B, jazz, and blues. 114 First Ave. S. ℂ 206/622-2563. Cover $5–$10 (joint cover).

Tula's   This is the real thing: a jazz club that's a popular jazz musicians' after-hours hangout and a good place to catch up-and-coming musicians. American and Mediterranean food is served. 2214 Second Ave. ℂ 206/443-4221. www.tulas.com. Cover $5–$10.

COMEDY, CABARET & DINNER THEATER

The Cabaret at Crepe de Paris   Throughout the year, this club stages a wide variety of entertaining programs of music, dance, and humor. Updated torch songs and numbers from classic musicals assure that the shows here will appeal to young and old alike. Rainier Sq., 1333 Fifth Ave. ℂ 206/623-4111. $45 dinner and show; $16 show only. Reservations required.

Comedy Underground   This club is located in Pioneer Square, where the Seattle Underground tour has proven that too much time beneath the city streets can lead even normal people to tell bad jokes. 222 S. Main St. ℂ 206/628-0303. www.comedyunderground.com. Cover $4–$10.

The Pink Door   Better known as Pike Place Market's unmarked restaurant, the Pink Door has a hopping after-work bar scene that tends to attract a 30-something crowd. It also doubles as a cabaret featuring Seattle's most eclectic lineup of performers. Lots of fun and not to be missed. 1919 Post Alley. ℂ 206/443-3241. No cover.

DANCE CLUBS

Downunder   Located in the Belltown neighborhood north of Pike Place Market, the Downunder doesn't necessarily play underground music, but it is down a flight of stairs from street level. Wild decor, light shows, and high-energy music, mostly house mix and techno, attract a young crowd. Open Wednesday through Saturday. 2407 First Ave. ℂ 206/728-4053. No cover (before 10pm) or up to $7.

Polly Esther's/Culture Club   If disco, funk, and '80s new wave music are what get your booty shakin', don't miss this club (part of a national chain) across the street from the Experience Music Project. There are two clubs under one roof. As you can imagine, this place tends to attract a clientele that wasn't even born when disco was all the rage. In other words, this is a 20-something pickup joint. 332 Fifth Ave. ℂ 206/441-1970. www.pollyesthers.com. Cover $10 (free before 9pm).

THE BAR & PUB SCENE
BARS
Belltown & Environs

Alibi Room   If you've been on your feet all day in Pike Place Market and have had it with the crowds of people, duck down the alley under the market clock and slip through the door of this hideaway. The back-alley setting gives this place an atmospheric speakeasy feel. 85 Pike St. ⓒ 206/623-3180.

The Virginia Inn   Although the Virginia Inn is located in oh-so-stylish Belltown, this bar/restaurant has a decidedly old Seattle feel, which is due in large part to the fact that this place has been around since 1903. Best of all, this is a no-smoking bar and it serves French food! 1937 First Ave. ⓒ 206/728-1937.

Downtown

The Bookstore—A Bar   Located just off the lobby of the posh Alexis Hotel, this cozy little bar is—surprise—filled with books. There are plenty of interesting magazines on hand as well, so if you want to sip a single malt and smoke a cigar but don't want to deal with crowds and noise, this is a great option. Very classy. In the Alexis Hotel, 1007 First Ave. ⓒ 206/382-1506.

McCormick and Schmick's   The mahogany paneling and sparkling cut glass lend this restaurant bar a touch of class, but otherwise the place could have been the inspiration for *Cheers*. Very popular as an after-work watering hole of Seattle moneymakers, McCormick and Schmick's is best known for its excellent and inexpensive happy-hour snacks. 1103 First Ave. ⓒ 206/623-5500.

Oliver's   Oliver's is martini central for Seattle, and year after year this bar keeps claiming top honors in the annual Martini Classic Challenge (which also happens to be sponsored by the Mayflower Park Hotel). Only you can decide. In the Mayflower Park Hotel, 405 Olive Way. ⓒ 206/623-8700.

Restaurant 67 Bar   If you got any closer to the water, you'd have wet feet. Located inside downtown Seattle's only waterfront hotel, this bar boasts what just might be the best bar view in the city. Watch the ferries coming and going, or see the sun set over Puget Sound and the Olympics. In the Edgewater Hotel, Pier 67, 2411 Alaskan Way. ⓒ 206/728-7000.

Pioneer Square

FX McRory's   Located across the street from Seattle's new football stadium and not far from Safeco Field, this bar attracts upscale sports fans (with the occasional Mariners and Seahawks players thrown in for good measure). You'll find Seattle's largest selection of bourbon. There's also an oyster bar and good food. 419 Occidental Ave. S. ⓒ 206/623-4800. www.mickmchughs.com.

Marcus's   Seattle's only underground martini and cigar bar, Marcus's is hidden beneath a Taco del Mar just off First Avenue in Pioneer Square. You'll be drinking below street level with the ghosts of Seattle's past and the lounge lizards of today. A variety of DJ music Tuesday through Saturday. This is a much mellower alternative to Pioneer Square's rowdy street-level bars. 88 Yesler Way. ⓒ 206/624-3323.

BREWPUBS

Big Time Brewery and Alehouse   Big Time is located in the University District and is done up to look like a turn-of-the-20th-century tavern, complete with a 100-year-old back bar and a wooden refrigerator. The pub serves as many as 12 of its own brews at any given time, and some of these can be pretty unusual. 4133 University Way NE. ℂ 206/545-4509. www.bigtimebrewing.com.

Elysian Brewing Company Although the brewery at this Capitol Hill brewpub is one of the smallest in the city, the pub itself is quite large and has an industrial feel that says "local brewpub" all over. The stout and strong ales are especially good, and the brewers' creativity here just can't be beat. Hands-down the best brewpub in Seattle. 1221 E. Pike St. ℂ 206/860-1920.

Hales Ales Brewery and Pub Located about a mile west of the Fremont Bridge heading toward Ballard, this is a much bigger and livelier brewpub than Redhook Ales' nearby Trolleyman (see below). 4301 Leary Way NW. ℂ 206/782-0737. www.halesales.com.

The Pike Pub and Brewery Located in an open, central space inside Pike Place Market, this brewpub makes excellent stout and pale ale. There's live instrumental music a couple of nights a week, and, with its comfortable couches, the Pike makes a great place to get off your feet after a day of exploring the market. 1415 First Ave. ℂ 206/622-6044.

Pyramid Ale House Located south of Pioneer Square in a big old warehouse, this pub is part of the brewery that makes Thomas Kemper lagers and Pyramid ales and is a favorite spot for dinner and drinks before or after baseball games at Safeco Field. There's good pub food, too. 1201 First Ave. S. ℂ 206/682-3377.

Trolleyman Pub This is the taproom of the Redhook Ale Brewery, one of the Northwest's most celebrated craft breweries, and is located in a restored trolley barn across the street from the Lake Washington Ship Canal. You can sample the ales brewed here, have a bite to eat, and even tour the brewery if you're interested. Redhook has a second (and much larger) brewery and pub in Woodinville at 14300 NE 145th St. (ℂ 425/483-3232) on the east side of Lake Washington. 3400 Phinney Ave. N. ℂ 206/634-4213.

IRISH PUBS

Kells At one time the space now occupied by this pub was the embalming room of a mortuary. However, these days the scene is much more lively and has the feel of a casual Dublin pub. They pull a good pint of Guinness and feature live traditional Irish music 7 nights a week. Kells also serves traditional Irish meals. 1916 Post Alley, Pike Place Market. ℂ 206/728-1916. www.kellsirish.com. Cover Fri–Sat $4.

Fadó This Irish pub is part of a national pub chain but has the feel of an independent. Lots of antiques, old signs, and a dark, cozy feel make it a very comfortable place for a pint. There's live Irish music several nights a week. 801 First Ave. ℂ 206/264-2700. www.fadoirishpub.com.

THE GAY & LESBIAN SCENE

Capitol Hill is Seattle's main gay neighborhood, where you'll find the greatest concentration of gay and lesbian bars and dance clubs. Look for the readily available *Seattle Gay News* (ℂ 206/324-4297), where you'll find ads for many of the city's gay bars and nightclubs.

BARS

C. C. Attle's Located across the street from Thumpers, this bar is a Seattle landmark on the gay bar scene. This bar is well known for its cheap, strong cocktails, but it can be something of a regulars' scene. There are a couple of patios and three separate bars. 1501 E. Madison St. ℂ **206/726-0565.**

Thumpers   Perched high on Capitol Hill with an excellent view of downtown Seattle, Thumpers is a classy bar/restaurant done up in oak. The seats by the fireplace are perfect on a cold and rainy night, and for sunny days there are two decks with great views. There's live music Thursday through Sunday. 1500 E. Madison St. ℂ **206/328-3800.**

Wildrose   This friendly restaurant/bar is a long-time favorite with the Capitol Hill lesbian community and claims to be the oldest lesbian bar on the West Coast. During the spring and summer, there is an outdoor seating area. 1021 E. Pike St. ℂ **206/324-9210.**

DANCE CLUBS

Neighbours   This has been the favorite dance club of Capitol Hill's gay community for years. As at other clubs, different nights of the week feature different styles of music. You'll find this club's entrance down the alley. 1509 Broadway Ave. ℂ **206/324-5358.** Cover $1–$5.

Re-Bar   Each night there's a different theme, with the DJs spinning everything from world beat to funk and hip-hop. This club isn't exclusively gay, but Thursday nights are currently Queer Disco Night, and Saturday nights are women's night. 1114 Howell St. ℂ **206/233-9873.** Cover $3–$6.

Timberline Spirits   If the boot-scootin' boogie is your favorite dance, the Timberline is the place to be. There's dancing to C&W music several nights a week. This place is also home to Seattle's largest tea dance, and also plays disco and trance. 2015 Boren Ave. ℂ **206/622-6220.** Cover free–$3.

AT THE MOVIES

The **Seattle International Film Festival** (**SIFF;** www.seattlefilm.com) takes place each May and early June, with around 150 films shown at various theaters. For information, check the website or, at festival time, the local papers.

In Fremont, there's the **Fremont Saturday Nite Outdoor Movies** series (ℂ **206/781-4230;** www.outdoorcinema.com), a summer event that shows modern classics, B movies (sometimes with live overdubbing by a local improv comedy company), and indie shorts. Films are screened in the parking lot across from the Trolleyman Pub, North 35th Street and Phinney Avenue North. The parking lot opens at 7:30pm, and there is a $5 suggested donation.

AT&T Outdoor Cinema screens movies at the Seattle Center Mural Stage and in Marymoor Park in Redmond. For information on these movies, contact **Lunar Flicks** (ℂ **206/720-1058;** www.lunarflicks.com). Gates open at 6pm, with music at 7pm and movies at dusk.

11 Easy Excursions: Seattle's Wine Country & an Island Getaway

SEATTLE'S WINE COUNTRY

Although most of Washington's wine grapes are grown far from Seattle in the eastern part of the state, there are several operating wineries within 20 miles of downtown Seattle in the vicinity of the town of Woodinville. To find these wineries, head east from Seattle (crossing Lake Washington on one of the bridges) to I-405 north. Then take Wash. 522 east 1 mile (1.5km) to the Woodinville/Wash. 202 exit and continue south on Wash. 202 (Woodinville-Redmond Rd.).

The first winery you'll come to is the small **Facelli Winery,** 16120 Woodinville-Redmond NE (© **425/488-1020**), which is open Saturday and Sunday from noon to 4pm and produces some of our favorite Washington red wines. Don't miss this hidden gem. Continuing south on Woodinville-Redmond Road (Wash. 202), you'll next come to **Silver Lake Winery,** 15029 Woodinville-Redmond Rd. NE, Woodinville (© **425/486-1900;** www. washingtonwine.com). This winery crafts some good reds but can be hit-and-miss (Apr–Dec daily noon–5pm; Jan–Mar Wed–Sun noon–5pm).

Continuing south, you'll next come to the largest and most famous of the wineries in the area, **Chateau Ste. Michelle** ✦, 14111 NE 145th St., Woodinville (© **425/415-3300;** www.ste-michelle.com). This is by far the most beautiful winery in the Northwest, and is located in a grand mansion on a historic 1912 estate. It's also the largest winery in the state, and is known for its consistent quality (daily 10am–4:30pm). Tours of the winery are available, and an amphitheater on the grounds stages big-name music performances throughout the summer.

Across Wash. 202 from the Chateau Ste. Michelle, you'll find **Columbia Winery,** 14030 NE 145th St., Woodinville (© **800/488-2347** or 425/488-2776; www.columbiawinery.com), which has Washington's largest wine-tasting bar, and produces a wide range of good wines (daily 10am–7pm).

If, at the end of the day, you decide you'd like to have dinner in this area, try the **Forecaster's Public House** at the Redhook Ale Brewery, 14300 NE 145th St. (© **425/483-3232**), which is right next door to the Columbia Winery. On the other hand, if you want to turn a visit to the wineries into a luxurious overnight getaway, consider spending the night at the Willows Lodge (see "Accommodations," earlier in this chapter). Have dinner at either the lodge's restaurant or the highly acclaimed Herbfarm (see "Dining," earlier in this chapter), which is adjacent to the Willows Lodge.

The San Juan Islands, Whidbey Island & the Emerald Coast

Water, water everywhere, and quite a few islands, too. That about sums up the landscape of the north Puget Sound and San Juan Islands region. Here, within a vast inland sea, lie hundreds of islands both large and small, and the lure of these emerald isles is powerful. There may not be any turquoise waters, white-sand beaches, or palm trees swaying in the breeze, but an island is a getaway no matter where it is—and these islands are no exception. The fact that many of the region's islands bear Spanish names seems to further add to the romance of a trip to the San Juans.

When English explorer Capt. George Vancouver first sailed down the Strait of Juan de Fuca in 1792, he discovered a vast inland sea he named Puget Sound. To the north of this sound, within a convolution of twisting channels, narrow straits, and elongated bays, lays an archipelago of islands, and rising to the east in a magnificent backdrop stood a range of snowcapped peaks. Several of the archipelago's islands—San Juan, Lopez, Fidalgo, Guemes, Sucia, and Matia—had already been named by earlier Spanish explorers, but Vancouver's 2 months of exploring and charting the waters of the region left Northwest maps with many new names—Deception Pass, Whidbey Island, Bellingham Bay, Mount Baker.

From the mid–19th century to the mid–20th century, this region was primarily a fishing, farming, and logging region, but as early as the first decade of the 20th century, Washingtonians from the mainland had begun to discover the charms of island life. Today, the northern Puget Sound and San Juan Islands are Washington's favorite summer playgrounds and weekend getaways. Shimmering waters, mountain vistas, and tranquil islands are the ingredients of the tonic that revives the weary souls of vacationers from the densely populated and industrialized southern Puget Sound. Though it's only 30 miles (48km) from Seattle to Whidbey Island and 85 miles (137km) to the San Juans, the distance is multiplied by the serenity that descends as you cross the sound by ferry and leave the mainland behind.

However, this corner of the state isn't all about island life. On the mainland, the historic fishing village of La Conner has become the most charming little town in the state. Surrounding La Conner are the Skagit Valley bulb fields, which burst into bloom each spring with acres and acres of tulips and daffodils.

Farther north, the town of Bellingham serves as a base for exploring the Emerald Coast, one of the least visited stretches of coastline in the state (the San Juans seem to siphon off all the traffic). However, though there are few crowds here, the vistas (and the oysters) are as good as any you'll find in the islands. It is also on this coast that you'll find the state's premier waterfront golf resort.

1 Whidbey Island

30 miles (48km) N of Seattle, 40 miles (64km) S of Bellingham

While the San Juan Islands are beautiful, their beauty has become something of a liability—during the summer, they're just too crowded. If you don't relish the hours-long waits for ferries, you can still have an island experience here on Whidbey Island. At 45 miles (72km) in length, Whidbey is one of the largest islands in the continental United States; and, at only 30 miles (48km) from Seattle, it's also a popular weekend getaway for Seattleites who come here seeking tranquillity and relaxation. However, outside of Washington, Whidbey Island isn't nearly as well known as the San Juans. And that is exactly why it is less crowded in the summer.

Never more than a few miles wide, Whidbey offers views of the water at seemingly every turn of its winding country roads. Farms, forests, bluffs, and beaches provide the foregrounds to the aquatic vistas, and two historic villages, Langley and Coupeville, offer the same sort of quaint settings people expect from the San Juans. Old wooden commercial buildings have been restored and now house excellent restaurants, art galleries, and unique shops. Charming bed-and-breakfast inns (and one of the state's most luxurious small hotels) pamper visitors to the island and provide the romantic surroundings that are so much a part of the Whidbey experience.

But what, you wonder, is there to do on Whidbey Island? Next to nothing. And that is the island's main appeal. This is an island you visit in order to rest and rejuvenate. You don't have to do anything, just sit back and relax. However, there are a few options for burning off excess energy: wine tasting, shopping, garden touring, hiking in state parks and a national historic reserve, sea kayaking. Sounds a lot like the San Juans, doesn't it?

Lest you get the impression that Whidbey Island is heaven on earth, let us make you aware of the Whidbey Island Naval Air Station, which, with its thundering jets, has considerably altered the idyllic atmosphere of the island's northern half. Oak Harbor, the island's largest community, is located just outside the base and is characterized by the sort of strip-mall sprawl that surrounds most military bases. For this reason, the vast majority of the island's B&Bs are located in central and south Whidbey. It's partly because of what has happened to Oak Harbor that Ebey's Landing National Historic Reserve was created. When people who had moved to the island because of its tranquil atmosphere saw the sprawl that was spreading around Oak Harbor, they acted quickly to preserve some of the island's rural beauty, the very essence of Whidbey Island.

ESSENTIALS

GETTING THERE From I-5, take Wash. 20 west at Burlington. The highway turns south before you reach Anacortes and crosses over the Deception Pass Bridge to reach the north end of Whidbey Island.

Washington State Ferries (© 800/84-FERRY or 888/808-7977 in Washington, or 206/464-6400; www.wsdot.wa.gov/ferries/) operates ferries between Mukilteo and Clinton at the south end of the island and from Port Townsend to Keystone near Coupeville. Fares are $5 to $6.25 for a car and driver and $2.70 for passengers between Mukilteo and Clinton and $7 to $8.75 for a car and driver and $2 for passengers between Port Townsend and Keystone. The **Airporter Shuttle** (© 866/235-5247 or 360/380-8800; www.airporter.com)

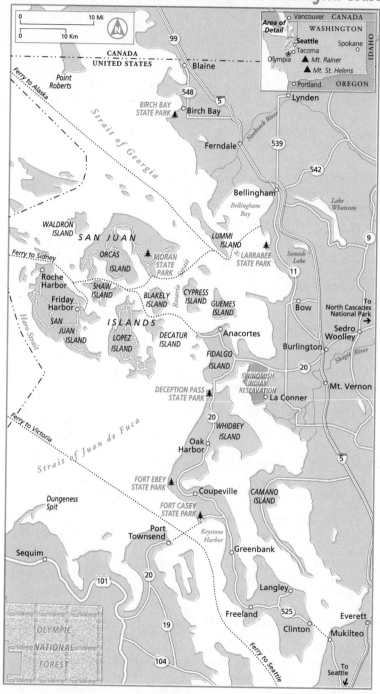

offers daily service from Sea-Tac International Airport to Oak Harbor. The fare is $34 one-way and $60 round-trip.

VISITOR INFORMATION   Contact **Island County Tourism,** P.O. Box 1641, Coupeville, WA 98239 (© **888/747-7777;** www.islandweb.org); **Central Whidbey Chamber of Commerce,** 107 S. Main St., Coupeville, WA 98239 (© **360/678-5434;** www.whidbey.net/coup); or the **Langley South Whidbey Chamber of Commerce,** 208 Anthes St., Langley, WA 98260 (© **360/ 221-6765;** www.whidbey.com/langley).

GETTING AROUND   Car rentals are available from **Budget** and **Enterprise** in Oak Harbor. **Island Transit** (© **360/678-7771**) offers free public bus service on Whidbey Island.

FESTIVALS   Each year in mid-July, Langley celebrates the visual and performing arts with the **Choochokam** street festival. In early August, there's the **Coupeville Arts and Crafts Festival.**

EXPLORING THE ISLAND
If you're coming from the south and take the ferry from Mukilteo, then the best place to start exploring Whidbey Island is in the historic fishing village of Langley, which is reached by taking Langley Road off Wash. 525. Before you ever reach town, you'll pass by the **Whidbey Island Vineyard & Winery,** 5237 S. Langley Rd. (© **360/221-2040;** www.whidbeyislandwinery.com), where you can taste a few wines before heading into town. Their white wines are made from grapes grown here on the island, while their reds are made from grapes grown in eastern Washington. The tasting room is open Wednesday through Sunday from noon to 5pm.

Langley today is a compact little village with a mix of sophisticated shops, interesting art galleries, and good, moderately priced restaurants occupying restored wooden commercial buildings along the waterfront. **First Street Park,** right in downtown, provides access to a narrow, rocky beach and offers views of Saratoga Passage and the distant Cascades. A couple of blocks away, at the corner of Anthes Avenue and Second Street, you'll find the eclectic and artistic little **Langley Park,** which is a great place to sit and sip a latte. Across the street from this park, you'll find the **South Whidbey Historical Museum,** 312 Second St. (© **360/221-2101**), a small museum housing displays on local history. The museum is open Saturday and Sunday from 1 to 4pm; admission is a $2 suggested donation.

There are several art galleries worth checking out here in Langley. These include **Artists' Cooperative Gallery,** 314 First St. (© **360/221-7675**), the island's cooperative art gallery; the **Gaskill/Olson Gallery,** 302 First St. (© **360/221-2978**), featuring works by established and emerging Northwest artists; the **Hellebore Studio & Gallery,** 308 First St. (© **360/221-2067**), an art-glass gallery; and **Museo,** 215 First St. (© **360/221-7737**), which features fine art by top local artists. Another shop not to be missed is **Lowry-James Fine Antiques,** 101 Anthes St. (© **360/221-0477**), which specializes in first edition prints, including lots of Audubon prints. Also here in Langley you'll find the **Whidbey Island Center for the Arts,** 565 Camano Ave. (© **800/638-7631** or 360/221-8268; www.whidbey.com/wica), which stages a wide range of performances throughout the year.

Four miles (6.5km) northwest of Freeland, which is the narrowest point of the island, you'll find **South Whidbey State Park** (© **360/331-4559**), with 2 miles (3km) of shoreline, hiking trails through some old-growth forest, and a campground. Continuing north, you come to **Whidbey Island Greenbank Farm** (*②* 360/678-7700), at Wash. 525 and Wonn Road in Greenbank, a former loganberry farm that is now a park. For many years the farm was known for its loganberry liqueur; however, today, the farm gift shop sells primarily gourmet foods and Washington state wines. With its big red barns and rolling farmlands, Greenbank Farm is as picture perfect a farm as you will find anywhere in western Washington. A network of trails meanders around the farm property, making this a good place to stretch your legs. Also in Greenbank (just off Wash. 525) is **Meerkerk Rhododendron Gardens,** 3531 S. Meerkerk Lane (*②* **360/ 678-1912;** www.meerkerkgardens.org), which was originally a private garden but is now operated by the Seattle Rhododendron Society as a display and test garden. It's open daily from 9am to 4pm (peak bloom is Apr–May). Admission is $3. Gardeners will also want to stop at **Sweetwater Lavender Farm,** Wash. 20 and Jacobs Road (*②* **800/884-9287** or 360/678-1790), which is located 1 mile (1.5km) east of the Coupeville stoplight and is open daily from 10am to 5pm. The farm's 50,000 to 60,000 lavender plants bloom in the summer, but the gift shop, which sells various lavender products, is open year-round.

Coupeville, located in central Whidbey Island just north of the turnoff for the ferry to Port Townsend, is another historic waterfront village. This town was founded in 1852 by Capt. Thomas Coupe, and the captain's 1853 home is among those in town that have been restored. The quiet charm of yesteryear is Coupeville's greatest appeal, and many of its old wooden commercial buildings now house antiques stores. At the north end of downtown, a gravel path leads up a bluff to the Coupeville Town Park, which is a good spot for a picnic. At the end of the Coupeville Wharf, you can see the skeleton of Rosie the gray whale, which hangs from the ceiling of the building at the end of the wharf.

Here in Coupeville, you'll find the **Island County Historical Museum,** 908 NW Alexander St. (*②* **360/678-3310**), which is the best place to learn about the island's seafaring, farming, and military history. Between May and September, the museum is open daily from 10am to 5pm; October through April, it's open Friday through Monday from 10am to 4pm. Admission is $2 for adults, and $1.50 for seniors and children under 18.

Much of the land around Coupeville is now part of the **Ebey's Landing National Historic Reserve.** The reserve, one of the first of its kind in the nation, was created "to preserve and protect a rural community which provides an unbroken historic record from the nineteenth century exploration and settlement of Puget Sound to the present time." There is no visitor center for the reserve, but there is an information kiosk near the dock in Coupeville, and the adjacent museum has copies of an informative brochure about the reserve.

Three miles (5km) south of Coupeville, adjacent to the Keystone ferry landing, is **Fort Casey State Park,** 1280 Engle Rd. (*②* **360/678-4519**), a former military base that was built in the 1890s to guard Puget Sound and still has its gun batteries. In addition to the fort, the park includes beaches, hiking trails, a campground, and the 1897 **Admiralty Head lighthouse** (*②* **360/678-7391**), which is now an interpretive center. Just south of Fort Casey State Park near the Keystone Ferry landing (Port Townsend ferries) is **Keystone State Park,** which is a designated underwater park for scuba divers. A few miles north of Fort Casey is the smaller **Fort Ebey State Park,** Libbey Road (*②* **360/678-4636**), another former military site built to protect the sound. Here there are excellent views of the Strait of Juan de Fuca, as well as a campground, hiking and mountain biking trails, and a lake for swimming and fishing.

Between Coupeville and Oak Harbor, you can make a detour to **Humming-bird Farm Nursery,** 2319 N. Zylstra Rd. in Oak Harbor (© **360/679-5044**), which is an herb and dried-flower farm with a display garden, shop, and fields of herbs and flowers. **Oak Harbor,** at the north end of the island, was settled by Dutch immigrants, and here, at City Beach Park, which has a swimming lagoon, you'll find a large Dutch **windmill.** As the largest town on the island, Oak Harbor lacks the charm of Langley and Coupeville. At **Joseph Whidbey State Park,** west of Oak Harbor, there are great westerly views and a long sandy beach. North of Oak Harbor, **Lavender Heart Botanicals,** 4233 N. DeGraff Rd. (© **360/675-3987**), offers everything from indoor topiary to candles to soaps and lotions.

Deception Pass State Park (© **360/675-2417**), at the northern tip of the island, is the most popular state park in Washington. What draws the crowds are miles of beaches, quiet coves, freshwater lakes, dark forests, hiking trails, camping, and views of Deception Pass, the churning channel between Whidbey Island and Fidalgo Island. A high bridge connects these two large islands by way of a smaller island in the middle of Deception Pass, and overlooks at the bridge allow you to gaze down on the tidal waters that surge and swirl between the islands.

SPORTS & OUTDOOR ACTIVITIES

BICYCLING   The country roads of Whidbey Island are perfect for exploring by bicycle. If you don't have your own bike, you can rent one from **Velocity Bikes,** 1832 Scott Rd., Freeland (© **360/331-2453;** www.velocitybikes.com). Bikes rent for $25 per day.

BOAT CHARTERS   Between May and September, the *Cutty Sark,* which operates out of the Captain Whidbey Inn, 2072 W. Captain Whidbey Inn Rd. (© **800/366-4097**), offers scheduled day-sail cruises for around $40 per person.

SEA KAYAKING   The easiest way to explore the waters off Whidbey Island is to rent a sea kayak at Coupeville's **Harbor Store on the Wharf** (© **260/678-3625**), which rents boats from the Coupeville Wharf. Single kayaks rent for $15 per hour, and double kayaks rent for $20 per hour.

WHERE TO STAY
IN LANGLEY

Boatyard Inn ⋆⋆   Located right on Langley's little marina and designed to look like an old cannery building, this three-story inn is clad in a combination of wood, cedar shingles, and corrugated metal. Guest rooms are all huge and have full kitchens, water views, gas fireplaces, and small balconies. There are also four two-bedroom loft suites. Downtown Langley is a few hundred yards uphill from the inn, and there's a small adjacent beach as well as the marina. This is a good choice if you like to have lots of space or need a kitchen.

200 Wharf St. (P.O. Box 866), Langley, WA 98260. © **360/221-5120.** Fax 360/221-5124. www.boatyard inn.com. 10 units. $165–$210 double (lower midweek rates in winter). AE, DC, DISC, MC, V. **Amenities:** Massage; babysitting. *In room:* TV/VCR, kitchen, fridge, coffeemaker, hair dryer, iron.

The Inn at Langley ⋆⋆   Quite simply, this is one of the most luxurious and romantic inns in the Northwest. With its weathered cedar shingles, exposed beams, works of contemporary art, and colorful garden, the inn evokes all the best of life in the region, and the guest rooms have a Zen-like quality that soothes and relaxes. The inn's four floors jut out from a bluff overlooking Saratoga

Passage, and with 180° views from every room, you'll have plenty of opportunities to spot orca whales and bald eagles. While the bedrooms and balconies are luxurious enough, it's the bathrooms that are the star attractions here. Each comes with an open shower and a double whirlpool tub that looks out over the water. Pull back an opaque sliding window and you also get a view of the room's fireplace. Every Friday and Saturday, the inn's dining room serves a five-course fixed-price dinner focusing on creative Northwest flavors ($75 per person).

400 First St. (P.O. Box 835), Langley, WA 98260. ℂ 360/221-3033. www.innatlangley.com. 26 units. $215–$245 double; $375 suite; $550 cottage. Rates include continental breakfast. 2-night minimum on weekends. AE, MC, V. **Amenities:** Restaurant (Northwest); access to nearby health club; spa; massage. *In room:* TV/VCR, dataport, fridge, coffeemaker, hair dryer.

The Whidbey Inn ⭐   Located right on the waterfront in downtown Langley, this inn is so low key, you'd hardly know it was there (especially since it's in back of a pizza parlor). However, the rooms are attractively decorated with antiques and beds with down comforters, and have unobstructed water views. The inn also has views of Cascade Range in the distance. The three suites all have fireplaces, and the Wicker Suite has its own little atrium. Breakfast is served in your room, and sherry, afternoon snacks, and evening truffles are all part of a stay here.

106 First St. (P.O. Box 156), Langley, WA 98260. ℂ 888/313-2070 or 360/221-7115. www.whidbeyinn.com. 6 units. Apr–Oct $120 double, $150–$175 suite; Nov–Mar $95 double, $120–$175 suite. Rates include full breakfast. AE, MC, V. *In room:* Fridge, hair dryer.

IN COUPEVILLE

The Captain Whidbey Inn ⭐⭐   Three miles (5km) west of Coupeville off Madrona Way stands one of the Northwest's most unusual inns. Shady, quiet grounds offer a tranquil setting that has revived flagging spirits for almost a century. Built in 1907 of small madrona logs, the historic inn is architecturally fascinating, a bit of American folk art. I love the character of this place, though it is not for everyone. The rooms in the main building are small and lack private bathrooms, but they manage to capture the feel of the island's seafaring past. Suites, cottages, and cabins are available for those who need more space (though none of these have as much character as the inn rooms despite the considerably higher room rates). The inn's dining room and adjacent bar both overlook Penn Cove. Dinners here are pricey ($32 for two courses, $38 for three courses, and $42 for five courses). Meals can be uneven, but the mussels, fresh from the bay in front of the inn, are always reliable.

2072 W. Captain Whidbey Inn Rd., Coupeville, WA 98239. ℂ 800/366-4097 or 360/678-4097. Fax 360/678-4110. www.captainwhidbey.com. 32 units, 12 with shared bathroom. $85–$95 double with shared bathroom, $150 double with bathroom; $155 suite; $175 cabin; $275–$285 cottage. Rates include full breakfast. 2-night minimum on weekends, 3-night minimum on holidays. AE, DC, DISC, MC, V. **Amenities:** Restaurant (Northwest) and lounge. *In room:* No phone.

The Colonel Crockett Farm ⭐   Built in 1855, this stately farmhouse is surrounded by rolling meadows and looks out over Crockett Lake to Admiralty Bay. The views are some of the best on the island, and no other inn on Whidbey better captures the island's idyllic rural feel. The guest rooms are furnished with antiques, and there is a beautiful, wood-paneled library where guests can peruse the extensive book collection. The Crockett Room, with its canopied four-poster bed and claw-foot tub, is our favorite. On the edge of the property is the 19th-century Crockett blockhouse, a log structure once used to protect settlers.

1012 S. Fort Casey Rd., Coupeville, WA 98239. ℂ 360/678-3711. Fax 360/678-3707. www.crockettfarm.com. 5 units. $75–$105 double. Rates include full breakfast. MC, V. *In room:* No phone.

The Coupeville Inn ⭐ Located right in the heart of Coupeville's historic district, and designed to fit in with the surrounding historic architecture, this modern motel offers large, comfortable rooms overlooking Coupeville and Penn Cove. All the rooms have small balconies. A good choice if you aren't a B&B person.

200 NW Coveland St. (P.O. box 370), Coupeville, WA 98239. © **800/247-6162** in Washington and British Columbia, or 360/678-6668. Fax 360/678-3059. www.agspub.com/coupevilleinn/. 24 units. $68–$150 double. Rates include continental breakfast. AE, DISC, MC, V. **Amenities:** Bike rentals. *In room:* TV/VCR.

Fort Casey Inn ⭐ Built in 1909 as officers' quarters for Fort Casey, this row of four Georgian Revival houses now serves as a bed-and-breakfast inn operated by Seattle Pacific University, which also uses other nearby buildings that were once part of the fort. Most of the accommodations here are two-level, two-bedroom town houses that offer lots of space for families or two couples. Eagles, military memorabilia, and a red, white, and blue color scheme reflect the houses' history, and Fort Casey State Park and the beach are just a short walk away. The grand old homes are each divided into two apartments that have farm kitchens and spacious living rooms on the first floor and two bedrooms and a bathroom with a claw-foot tub on the second floor. Big front porches overlook Crockett Lake.

1124 S. Engle Rd., Coupeville, WA 98239. © **866/661-6604** or 360/678-8792. www.fortcaseyinn.com. 10 units. $85–$135 double. Rates include full breakfast. MC, V. *In room:* Kitchen, fridge, coffeemaker, no phone.

The Inn at Penn Cove ⭐ Housed in two Victorian homes that stand side by side, this inn offers rooms for those seeking both romantic Victorian luxuries (fireplaces, antiques, antique or whirlpool tubs) and a more casual place to stay. The latter rooms are in the Coupe-Gillespie House, which was moved to this site in 1990. The most expensive room here has a gas fireplace, a double whirlpool tub, a separate seating area, and views of both the water and Mount Baker, while another room has an interesting antique double pedestal sink. Asian antiques throughout the two houses give these two inns an interesting character.

702 N. Main St. (P.O. Box 85), Coupeville, WA 98239. © **800/688-2683** or 360/678-8000. www.whidbey. net/penncove. 6 units, 4 with private bathroom. $60–$65 double with shared bathroom, $75–$125 double with private bathroom. Rates include full breakfast. 2-night minimum on holidays. AE, DISC, MC, V. *In room:* No phone.

WHERE TO DINE

At the far north end of the island, 1 mile (1.5km) south of the Deception Pass Bridge, you can get good smoked salmon at **Seabolt's Smokehouse,** 40928 Wash. 20 (© **800/574-1120;** www.seabolts.com).

IN LANGLEY

The **Country Kitchen** ⭐⭐ at the Inn at Langley serves the finest meals on the island. However, these five-course, fixed-price dinners are only available on Friday and Saturday evenings (and Sun evenings in summer) and cost a whopping $150 per couple (plus tax and tip). See "Where to Stay," above, for details. For baked goods and espresso, drop by the **Langley Village Bakery,** 221 Second St. (© **360/221-3525**), and for decadent pastries, check out **P.S. Suisse,** 221 Second St. (© **360/221-9434**). For breakfasts, sandwiches, and light lunches, try **Sapori,** 197D Second St. (© **360/221-3211**).

Café Langley ⭐⭐ MEDITERRANEAN/NORTHWEST Romantic and intimate, this restaurant seamlessly fuses Northwest and Middle Eastern flavors and aesthetics and has long been one of Langley's most popular restaurants. The

---

⌐ **Finds** Take a Break

When its time for a latte and a muffin, search out **Great Times Waterfront Coffee House** ⚲, 12 Front St. (© **360/678-5358**), which is down a flight of stairs on the waterfront. With its battered wooden floors and great water views, this cozy place is the perfect place to hole up if the weather turns bad.

---

cafe has been around for years and serves up familiar dishes such as spanakopita and shish kebabs, but also is known for its flank steak marinated in sherry and herbs and its crab stuffed scampi Milanese. The prawns à la Greque are another good choice, as are the Penn Cove mussels. The latter are available as either an appetizer or an entree. Weekly specials add yet another dimension to the reliable menu. Much less lively than the nearby Star Bistro, Cafe Langley is a good bet for a romantic dinner.

113 First St. © 360/221-3090. Reservations recommended. Main courses $11–$18. AE, MC, V. Mon–Thurs 11:30am–2:30pm and 5–8:30pm; Fri 11:30am–2:30pm and 5–9pm; Sat 11:30am–3pm and 5–9pm; Sun 11:30am–3pm and 5–8pm.

Star Bistro ⚲⚲ NORTHWEST/MEDITERRANEAN   Boisterous and boldly styled, this lively bistro is down a few doors from Café Langley and up a flight of stairs (on the second floor of one of Langley's old commercial buildings). Big black-and-white floor tiles and bold splashes of color give the bistro something of a party atmosphere. Creamy pasta dishes, flavorful salads, and fresh seafoods are all reliable choices, and in addition there are nightly specials. Keep an eye out for the chicken with wild mushrooms and Whidbey's Port sauce. On sunny days everyone heads out to the rooftop patio.

201½ First St. © 360/221-2627. www.whidbeynet.net/starbistro. Reservations recommended. Main courses $8–$16 at lunch, $9–$22 at dinner. AE, MC, V. Tues–Thurs 11:30am–8pm; Fri–Sat 11:30am–9pm; Sun noon–8pm.

IN COUPEVILLE

Captain's Galley ⚲ *Kids* AMERICAN   While the food here is relatively simple and straightforward fare, the waterfront location provides views that can't be beat. The appetizer menu is long on seafoods (Penn Cove mussels, crab cakes, oysters on the half shell) and there are also plenty of seafood entrees. However, there are also burgers, steaks, chicken, and pasta dishes. The low prices make the Captain's Galley a favorite with families.

10 Front St. © 360/678-0241. Reservations recommended daily in summer, weekends only in other months. Main courses $7–$20. DISC, MC, V. Daily 11am–10pm.

Christopher's ⚲ NORTHWEST   Located in a warehouse-style building in downtown Coupeville, Christopher's may not have any water views, but it does have a cozy cafe atmosphere with lots of books all around for that literary feel. The menu sticks mostly to familiar fare such as shrimp scampi and cioppino, but you'll also find barbecued salmon with raspberry barbecue sauce. However, it would be foolish to pass up the Penn Cove mussels and clams, which are steamed with ale, garlic, and spices.

23 Front St. © 360/678-5480. Reservations recommended. Main courses $7.50–$9 at lunch, $9–$21 at dinner. AE, DISC, MC, V. Mon–Fri 11:30am–2:30pm and 5–9pm; Sat–Sun noon–3pm and 5–9pm (Sun shorter hr. in winter).

2 Anacortes

75 miles (121km) N of Seattle, 39 miles (63km) S of Bellingham, 92 miles (148km) S of Vancouver, B.C.

For most people, Anacortes is little more than that town you drive through on the way to the San Juan Islands ferry terminal. That's only partially true. Actually, Anacortes has much more to offer than a driver late for the ferry could ever know. The route to the ferry sticks to roads that are fine examples of commercial and suburban sprawl—strip malls, gas stations, aging motels, housing developments. However, if you have time to detour off the main road, you'll find a town that, while not nearly as quaint as those on the San Juans, does have some historic character and, perhaps best of all, plenty of good places to eat. The restored downtown business district, residential neighborhoods full of old Victorian homes, a large, forested waterfront park, and a mountain-top viewpoint are all worth a look. So, if you can, slow down and take a look at Anacortes before or after a trip to the San Juans.

Anacortes made its early fortunes on lumbering and fishing, and today commercial fishing, as well as boat building, are still important to the town's economy. This marine orientation has given the town its character, which can be seen in the many restored buildings along Commercial Avenue.

Anacortes also makes a good base for exploring the San Juans if you either can't get or can't afford a room on the islands. Using Anacortes as a base and leaving your car here on the mainland, you can travel as a passenger on the ferries and, by using public transit, mopeds, or bicycles, still manage to see plenty of the San Juan Islands. In any event, Anacortes is also on an island, Fidalgo Island, and has plenty of water views, the best of which are from Washington Park near the ferry terminal, from atop Mount Erie in the middle of the island, and from Deception Pass State Park at the south end of the island.

ESSENTIALS

GETTING THERE   From I-5 at Burlington, take Wash. 20 west to the Wash. 20 Spur. South of Anacortes, Wash. 20 connects to Whidbey Island by way of the Deception Pass Bridge.

See "Getting There," under "The San Juan Islands," below, for details on airport service to Anacortes from Seattle Tacoma International Airport and for information on ferry connections to Anacortes from the islands and Vancouver Island, British Columbia.

VISITOR INFORMATION   For information on Anacortes, contact the **Anacortes Chamber of Commerce,** 819 Commercial Ave., Anacortes, WA 98221 (© **360/293-3832;** www.anacortes-chamber.com). Or, check out www.anacortes.org. online.

 The Name Game

Founded in the 1850s by Amos Bowman, Anacortes was named after Bowman's wife, Annie Curtis, but over the years the spelling and pronunciation were slowly corrupted to its current Spanish-sounding pronunciation (in keeping with such local Spanish names as San Juan, Lopez, and Guemes).

GETTING AROUND Public transit in Skagit County is provided free of charge on **SKAT** (② **360/757-4433;** www.skat.org) buses, which make stops in Anacortes, La Conner, and Mount Vernon among other places.

EXPLORING ANACORTES

If you want to learn more about local history, stop by the **Anacortes History Museum,** 1305 Eighth St. (② **360/293-1915;** www.anacorteshistorymuseum. org), housed in a former Carnegie Library. It's open Thursday through Monday from 1 to 5pm; admission is a suggested $2 donation. Across the street from the museum is **Causland Memorial Park,** the town's most unusual attraction. Built in 1919 to honor servicemen who died in World War I, the park contains rock walls that were constructed as giant mosaics. It's a piece of folk art that reflects a much simpler era. **Murals** are a mainstay of the Northwest's historic towns, and here in Anacortes they take the shape of more than 50 life-size cutouts of the town's forefathers. The murals, based on historic photos, were done by artist Bill Mitchell.

Any walking tour of downtown should be sure to include a visit to the historic **stern-wheeler *W. T. Preston,*** which was built in the 1890s to clear log jams on Puget Sound and now sits on dry land in a little park at the corner of Seventh Street and R Avenue. At press time, the boat was no long open for tours, but there were plans to reopen it sometime in spring 2002. For more information, contact the Anacortes Museum, 1305 Eighth St. (② **360/293-1916**). Next door, at the corner of Seventh Street and R Avenue, is **The Depot Arts Center** (② **360/293-3663**), a restored 1911 railway depot that now serves as an arts center, with a collection of art by regional artists.

For a glimpse of an old-fashioned hardware store, stop by **Marine Supply and Hardware,** 202 Commercial St. (② **360/293-3014**), which is the oldest continuously operating marine supply store on the West Coast.

Nature lovers can head to **Washington Park,** just a short distance past the ferry terminal. The park contains not only a campground and several miles of hiking trails, but tranquil **Sunset Beach,** which looks out across Rosario Strait to the San Juan Islands. For even more spectacular views, head up to **Mount Erie Park** ⚑⚑ on the summit of 1,270-foot Mount Erie. From here, on a clear day you can see Mount Rainier, Mount Baker, and the Olympic Mountains. You'll find this park by heading south out of Anacortes on Commercial Avenue, turning right on 32nd Street and then left on H Avenue (which becomes Heart Lake Rd.), and then taking Erie Mountain Drive to the top of the mountain.

You don't have to go all the way to the San Juans if you want to do some whale-watching. Orca-viewing excursions are offered by **Island Adventures** (② **800/465-4604** or 360/293-2428; www.island-adventures.com), which charges $45 to $65, and also by **Mystic Sea Charters** (② **800/308-9387;** www. mysticseacharters.com), which charges $50 to $70. This latter company also offers sightseeing and dinner cruises. It's also possible to do a little sea kayaking here in the Anacortes area. Sea-kayak rentals are available at **Eddyline**

Watersports Center, 1019 Q Ave. (© **866/445-7506** or 360/299-2300; www.
seakayakshop.com), which charges $30 to $45 for a half-day rental and $45 to
$65 for a full-day rental. Guided kayak tours are also offered throughout the
year.

WHERE TO STAY

At press time, the **Majestic Inn,** which for several years had been the best hotel
in Anacortes, was closed due to a fire. It was uncertain when the hotel would
reopen, but it is worth contacting the Anacortes Chamber of Commerce (see
"Visitor Information," above) to find out if it has reopened by the time you plan
to visit.

Ship Harbor Inn ★   Located immediately adjacent to the ferry terminal for San
Juan Islands ferries and overlooking a wetland that offers good bird-watching, this
inn is a good choice if you weren't able to get a room on the islands or are planning on taking the early ferry all the way to Vancouver Island, Canada. This is also
a good choice if you are planning on exploring the islands by bicycle. Rooms are
large and most have balconies and views of the water. If you plan to spend more
than 1 night here, you might want to opt for one of the "cabin" rooms, which have
full kitchens. There's also a Jacuzzi suite.

5316 Ferry Terminal Rd., Anacortes, WA 98221. © **800/852-8568** or 360/293-5177. Fax 360/299-2412.
www.shipharborinn.com. 26 units. $55–$75 double; $125 suite. Rates include continental breakfast. AE, DC,
DISC, MC, V. **Amenities:** Coin-op laundry. *In room:* TV, fridge, free local calls.

WHERE TO DINE

Gere-a-Deli ★ DELI   Many places claim to be New York–style delis, but this
is the only one in the Northwest that comes close to duplicating the feel of a
genuine New York deli. Big and bustling, Gere-a-Deli is *the* place for lunch in
Anacortes, and while the sandwiches may not be as good as those in the Big
Apple, the urban feel, vintage signs, huge windows, and lively chatter of conversation all add up to a classic deli experience. Note that dinners are only served
on Friday night.

502 Commercial Ave. © **360/293-7383.** Reservations required for Fri dinner. Sandwiches $3–$7.50. AE,
DISC, MC, V. Mon–Sat 7am–4pm; Fri 5–9pm.

La Petite Restaurant ★★ *Finds* DUTCH   Dutch cuisine is not something you
run across all that often in the United States, so should you be the least bit curious, here is a prime opportunity to find out what it's all about. This is sort of nou-
velle Dutch—halibut with dill sauce, grilled breast of duck with Chambord sauce,
beef tenderloin with peppercorn cream sauce. But the menu, which changes daily,
is not entirely Dutch; you'll also find pasta dishes and the likes of oysters with

---

Finds **Smoothies, Sweets & Salmon**

For good pastries and baked goodies, be sure to drop by **La Vie En
Rose** ★, 418 Commercial Ave. (© **360/299-9546**), a great little French pastry shop that also serves interesting light meals. For healthy, light meals,
fresh juices, and smoothies, try the **Star Bar Café**, 416½ Commercial Ave.
(© **360/299-2120**). Before leaving town, you should also be sure to pick up
some smoked salmon at **Seabear Smokehouse and Store** ★, 605 30th St.
(© **800/645-FISH** or 360/293-4661; www.seabear.com), which offers tours
of its smokehouse.

curry sauce. Because Indonesia was once a Dutch colony, you'll also usually find on the menu an Indonesian-inspired dish. The menu is limited to six entrees, which come with both soup and salad. With the freshness of the ingredients and the view of Mount Baker, a dinner here is always a memorable experience.

Islands Inn, 3401 Commercial Ave. ☎ 360/293-4644. Reservations recommended. Main dishes $18–$29. AE, DC, DISC, MC, V. Tues–Sun 5–10pm.

3 The San Juan Islands

On a late afternoon on a clear summer day, the sun slants low, suffusing the scene with a golden light. The fresh salt breeze and the low rumble of the ferry's engine lulls you into a half-waking state. All around you are emerald green islands that rise from a shimmering sea. A bald eagle swoops from its perch on a twisted madrona tree. Off the port bow, the knifelike fins of two orca whales slice the water. As the engine slows, you glide toward a narrow wooden dock with a simple sign above it that reads "Orcas Island." With a sigh of content-ment, you step out onto the San Juan Islands and a slower pace of life.

There's something magical about traveling to the San Juans. Some people say it's the light, some say it's the sea air, some say it's the weather (temperatures are always moderate and rainfall is roughly half what it is in Seattle). Whatever it is that so entrances, the San Juans are indeed magical. They have become the favorite getaway of urban Washingtonians, and if you make time to visit these idyllic islands, we think you, too, will fall under their spell.

There is, however, one caveat. The San Juans have been discovered. In sum-mer, if you're driving a car, there can be waits of several hours to get on the fer-ries. One solution is to leave your car on the mainland and come over either on foot or with a bicycle. If you choose to come over on foot, you can rent a car, moped, or bicycle, take the San Juan Island shuttle bus, or use taxis to get around. Then again, you can just stay in one place and really relax. Along with crowded ferries come hotels, inns, and campgrounds that can get booked up months in advance and restaurants that can't seat you unless you have a reserva-tion. If it's summer, don't expect to find anyplace to stay if you arrive on the islands without a reservation. Other months of the year, it's a different story. During the spring and fall, it is relatively easy to get a reservation and room rates are much lower than they are during the summer. Although it can be pretty dreary out here in the dead of winter, spring and fall are often clear, and in spring, the island's gardens and hedgerows of wild roses burst into bloom, mak-ing this one of the best times of year to visit. Just be aware that many of the islands' best restaurants are closed in the winter.

The San Juan Islands are the tops of glacier-carved mountains that were flooded at the end of the last Ice Age, and depending on whom you listen to there are between 175 and 786 islands in the San Juans. The lower number con-stitutes those islands large enough to have been named, while the larger number represents all the islands, rocks, and reefs that poke above the water on the low-est possible tide. However, of all these islands, only four (San Juan, Orcas, Lopez, and Shaw) are serviced by the Washington State Ferries, and, of these, only three (San Juan, Orcas, and Lopez) have anything in the way of tourist accommodations (Shaw does, however, have a campground).

ESSENTIALS

VISITOR INFORMATION   Contact the **San Juan Island Chamber of Commerce,** P.O. Box 98, Friday Harbor, WA 98250 (☎ **360/378-5240;**

www.sanjuanisland.org); or the **Orcas Island Chamber of Commerce,** P.O. Box 252, Eastsound, WA 98245 (℡ **360/376-2273;** www.orcasisland.org). On the Internet, check out the following:

- www.sanjuanweb.com
- www.orcasisle.com
- www.thesanjuans.com

GETTING THERE Washington State Ferries (℡ **800/84-FERRY** or 888/ 808-7977 in Washington, or 206/464-6400; www.wsdot.wa.gov/ferries/) operates ferries between Anacortes and four of the San Juan Islands (Lopez, Shaw, Orcas, and San Juan) and Sidney, British Columbia (on Vancouver Island near Victoria). The fare for a vehicle and driver from Anacortes to Lopez is $17 to $21.25, to Shaw or Orcas $20 to $25, to San Juan $22.50 to $28.25, and to Sidney $29.75 to $41. The higher fares reflect a summer surcharge.

The fare for passengers from Anacortes to any of the islands is $6.80 (though it's $11 to Sidney). The fare for a vehicle and driver on all westbound interisland ferries is $9 to $11.25, and foot passengers ride free. Except for service from Sidney, fares are not collected on eastbound ferries, nor are walk-on passengers charged for interisland ferry service. If you plan to explore the islands by car, you'll save some money by starting your tour on San Juan Island and making your way back east through the islands.

During the summer you may have to wait several hours to get on a ferry, so arrive early. If you plan to leave your car on the mainland, any time between late May and late September, you'll pay $7 to park it overnight at the Anacortes ferry terminal ($14 for 3 days, $25 for 1 week). There is also a free park-and-ride lot on the east side of Anacortes on South March Point Road (off Wash. 20). A free shuttle operates from this parking lot to the ferry terminal.

There are also passenger-ferry services from several cities around the region. **Victoria Clipper** (℡ **800/888-2535** or 206/448-5000; www.victoriaclipper. com) operates excursion boats between Seattle and both Friday Harbor on San Juan Island and Rosario Resort on Orcas Island and also stops in Victoria. The round-trip fare to Friday Harbor is $59; the fare to Rosario Resort is $69. Advance-purchase discounts are available on round-trip tickets.

Between Port Townsend and Friday Harbor, passenger service is available from late March to early October from **P.S. Express** (℡ **360/385-5288;** www.puget soundexpress.com), which will also carry bicycles and sea kayaks for an additional charge. Fares are $31 to $34.50 one-way and $47 to $52.50 round-trip.

From Bellingham, between April and October, **San Juan Island Shuttle Express,** Bellingham Cruise Terminal, 335 Harris Ave. (℡ **888/373-8522;** www.orcawhales.com), operates passenger ferry service to Friday Harbor on San Juan Island, Lieber Haven Resort on Orcas Island, and Odlin County Park on Lopez Island. The round-trip fare is $33 for adults, $29 for seniors, and $27 for students and children.

From Bellingham, there is passenger service to Rosario Resort on Orcas Island and Friday Harbor on San Juan Island, on the **San Juan Island Commuter,** Bellingham Cruise Terminal, 335 Harris Ave. (℡ **888/734-8180** or 360/ 734-8180; www.islandcommuter.com). The round-trip adult fare to either island is $35. These passenger ferries operate between mid-May and mid-September.

If you're short on time, it's also possible to fly to the San Juans. **Kenmore Air,** 950 Westlake Ave. N. (℡ **800/543-9595** or 425/486-1257; www.kenmoreair. com), offers flights in floatplanes that take off from Lake Union (and also from

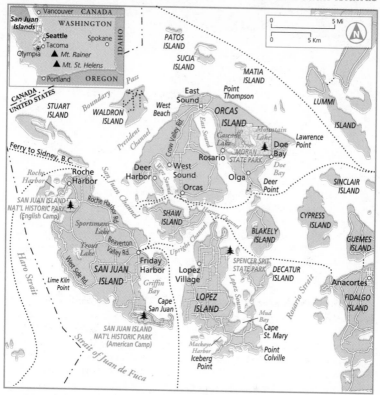

the north end of Lake Washington). Round-trip fares to the San Juans are between $150 and $160 (lower for children). Flights operate to Friday Harbor and Roche Harbor on San Juan Island, Rosario Resort and Westsound on Orcas Island, and the Lopez Islander on Lopez Island.

West Isle Air (© **800/874-4434** or 360/293-4691; www.westisleair.com) flies from Bellingham and Anacortes to San Juan, Orcas, Lopez and several of the outer islands. Fares from Bellingham to Friday Harbor on San Juan Island are $38 one-way and $76 round-trip. Note that these airplanes are not float-planes, but instead use island airports.

You can also get from Sea-Tac Airport to the San Juan Islands ferry terminal in Anacortes on the **Airporter Shuttle** (© **866/235-5247** or 360/380-8800; www.airporter.com), which charges $31 one-way and $56 round-trip.

GETTING AROUND   Car rentals are available on San Juan Island from **Susie's Mopeds** (© **800/532-0087** or 360/378-5244; www.susiesmopeds. com), the **Inn at Friday Harbor** (© **800/752-5752** or 360/378-3031; www. theinns.com), and **M&W Auto Sales** (© **360/378-2886**). On Orcas Island, contact **Rosario Resort** (© **800/562-8820** or 360/376-2222). Expect to pay $45 to $96 per day.

For a taxi on San Juan, call **San Juan Transit** (© **360/378-3550**); on Orcas, call **Orcas Island Taxi** (© **360/376-8294**); on Lopez, call **Lopez Cab** (© **360/ 468-2227**).

Did You Know?

- With 375 miles (604km) of saltwater shoreline, San Juan County, which encompasses the San Juan Islands, has more shoreline than any other county in the United States.
- Orcas Island isn't named for orca whales but rather for an 18th-century Mexican viceroy.
- Channels between the San Juan Islands range between 600 and 1,000 feet deep.
- Water temperatures off the San Juan Islands range between 45°F in winter and 52°F in summer.
- Lt. Henry Martyn Robert, author of the "Robert's Rules of Order," was stationed on San Juan Island during the Pig War.
- All Washington State Ferries have Native American names, except those of the Evergreen class.
- Puget Sound's first ferry went into operation on January 1, 1889, and car ferries were added in 1915. The first ferry cost 5¢.

San Juan Transit (© **800/887-8387,** or 360/378-8887 on San Juan Island; www.sanjuantransit.com) operates a shuttle bus on San Juan during the summer. This shuttle can be boarded at the ferry terminal and operates frequently throughout the day, stopping at all the major attractions on the island, which makes this a great way to get around if you come without a car. Day passes are $10 for adults, $9 for seniors, and $5 for kids ages 5 to 12, with discounted 2-day rates available. One-way ($4 ages 13 and up, $2 kids 12 and under) and round-trip ($7 adults, $3 kids 12 and under) tickets are also available. Children ages 4 and under always ride free.

SAN JUAN ISLAND
San Juan Island is not the largest of these islands, but it is the most populous, and is home to the county seat, Friday Harbor, which is the biggest and most developed town in the islands. As the hub of island activity, San Juan Island is home to more whale-watching and sea-kayaking companies than any of the other islands. It also has charter boats, fishing boats, moped rentals, and lots of souvenir shops. This all adds up to crowds in the summer, so if you're looking for an idyllic island getaway, you might want to try Orcas or Lopez.

However, what San Juan Island has going for it is lots of history, plus great views of the Olympic Mountains across the Strait of Juan de Fuca, and the only place in the islands where you can reliably see orca whales from shore.

EXPLORING FRIDAY HARBOR
Friday Harbor is the only real town on all of the islands, and as such it is home to numerous tourist-oriented shops, restaurants, motels, and B&Bs, as well as such island necessities as grocery and hardware stores. With its well-protected, large marina, it's also one of the most popular places in the islands for boaters to drop anchor.

If you arrived by car, you'll first want to find a parking space, which can be difficult in the summer. Once on foot, stroll around town admiring the simple wood-frame shop buildings built back at the turn of the 20th century. At that time, Friday Harbor was referred to as the southernmost port in Alaska and was a busy harbor. Schooners and steamships hauled the island's fruit, livestock, and lime (for cement) off to more populous markets. Today these pursuits have all died off, but reminders of the island's rural roots linger on, and these memories fuel the island's new breadwinner—tourism.

Whale-watching is one of the most popular summer activities in the San Juans, and before you head out, stop by the **Whale Museum** ✈, 62 First St. N. (ℂ **800/946-7227** or 360/378-4710; www.whale-museum.org). Here you can see whale skeletons and models of whales and learn all about the area's pods of orcas (also known as killer whales). Between Memorial Day and Labor Day, the museum is open daily from 9am to 5pm (10am–5pm other months); admission is $5 for adults, $4 for seniors, and $2 for children 5 to 18 and college students.

Here in Friday Harbor, you'll also find the headquarters of the **San Juan National Historic Park** ✈ (ℂ **360/378-2240**), at the corner of Spring and First streets. It's open daily from 8:30am to 5pm in summer (Mon–Fri 8:30am–4:30pm in winter). This park commemorates the San Juan Island Pig War, one of North America's most unusual and least remembered confrontations. Way back in 1859, San Juan Island nearly became the site of a battle between the British and the Americans. The two countries had not yet agreed upon the border between the United States and Canada when a British pig on San Juan Island decided to have dinner in an American garden. The owner of the garden didn't take too kindly to this and shot the pig. The Brits, rather than welcoming this succulent addition to their evening's repast, threatened redress. In less time than it takes to smoke a ham, both sides were calling in reinforcements. Luckily, this pigheadedness was defused and a more serious confrontation was avoided. While the park's headquarters is here in Friday Harbor, the main historic sites are English Camp, at the north end of the island, and American Camp, at the south end of the island. At both camps, you can visit historic buildings that are much as they might have looked in 1859.

If you're interested in island history, stop by the **San Juan Historical Museum,** 405 Price St. (ℂ **360/378-3949;** www.sjmuseum.org), which is housed in an 1894 farmhouse and also includes several other historic buildings on its grounds. May to September the museum is open Thursday through Sunday from 10am to 4pm and Sunday from 1 to 4pm; October, March, and April the museum is open Saturday from 1 to 4pm. Open by appointment in other months. Admission is $2 for adults, $1 for children ages 6 to 18; free to children under 6.

Friday Harbor is also home to quite a few good art galleries and other interesting shops. At **Waterworks Gallery,** Argyle and Spring streets (ℂ **360/ 378-3060**), you'll find fine art and contemporary crafts by local and regional artists. At **Arctic Raven Gallery,** 1 Front St. (ℂ **360/378-3433**), you'll find contemporary Native American arts and crafts. At **The Garuda & I,** 60 First St. (ℂ **360/378-3733**), you'll find fascinating imported items from throughout the world, with an emphasis on Asian imports.

If you need some wine for your vacation or want to take some home with you, be sure to stop by the tasting room at **Island Wine Company,** Cannery Landing (ℂ **360/378-3229**), which is the only place you can buy San Juan Cellars wines (made with grapes from eastern Washington). You'll find the wine shop on the immediate left as you leave the ferry.

SEEING THE REST OF THE ISLAND

Most of the island's main attractions can be seen on a long loop drive around the perimeter of the island. Start the drive by following Roche Harbor signs north out of Friday Harbor (take Spring St. to Second St. to Tucker Ave.). In about 3 miles (5km), you'll come to **San Juan Vineyards** ✷, 2000 Roche Harbor Rd. (© **360/378-WINE**), which makes wines both from grapes grown off the island and also from its own estate-grown Siegrebbe and Madeline Angevine grapes. The tasting room is housed in an old schoolhouse that was built in 1896 and is open daily 11am to 6pm in summer and on weekends only from mid-October to December and February through May.

A little farther north, you come to **Roche Harbor Village,** which was once the site of large limestone quarries that supplied lime to much of the West Coast. Today many of the quarries' old structures are still visible, giving this area a decaying industrial look, but amidst the abandoned machinery stands the historic Hotel de Haro, a simple whitewashed wooden building with verandas across its two floors. Stop and admire the old-fashioned marina and colorful gardens. The deck of the hotel's lounge is one of the best places on the island to linger over a drink. In an old pasture on the edge of the resort property, you'll see the **Westcott Bay Reserve** ✷ (© **360/370-5050**), a beautiful new sculpture park that includes more than 50 works of art set in grassy fields and along the shores of a small pond. Back in the woods near the resort you'll find an unusual **mausoleum** that was erected by the founder of the quarries and the Hotel de Haro.

South of Roche Harbor, on West Valley Road, you'll find **English Camp.** Set amid shady trees and spacious lawns, the camp is the picture of British civility. There's even a formal garden surrounded by a white picket fence. You can look inside the reconstructed buildings and imagine the days when this was one of the most far-flung corners of the British Empire. If you're full of energy, hike up to the top of 650-foot **Mount Young** for a panorama of the island. An easier hike is out to the end of **Bel Point.** Note that the English Camp visitor center is closed in winter.

South of English Camp, watch for the Bay Road turnoff. This connects to the Westside Road, which leads down the island's west coast. Along this road, you'll find **San Juan County Park,** a great spot for a picnic. A little farther south you'll come to **Lime Kiln State Park** ✷✷, the country's first whale-watching park and a great place to spot these gentle giants in summer. As Westside Road moves inland, a left onto Wold Road will bring you to the new **Pelindaba Lavender Farm** (© **360/378-4248;** www.pelindaba.com). The farm, open 11am to 4pm, currently grows 9,000 plants on about five acres, and a cutting field for visitors was set to open in 2002. Guided tours are offered May through October, but the Gatehouse Store, which sells all manner of lavender products, is open 11 months out of the year (closed January).

Near the south end of the island you'll find the windswept promontory on which stood the **American Camp** during the Pig War. Here you'll find a visitor center, a few reconstructed buildings, a beach, and several miles of trails. Before the American Camp was built here, this was the site of a Hudson's Bay Company farm. The meadows sweeping down to the sea were once grazed by sheep and cattle, but today you'll see only rabbits browsing amid the high grasses and wildflowers. Some of the hiking trails here lead along the grassy bluffs and down to the beach. Our favorite area trails are the **Mt. Finlayson Trail,** which leads to the top of a grassy hill, and the **Lagoon Trail,** which leads through a dark forest of Douglas firs to a small log-choked Jackle's Lagoon, which is a good spot for bird-watching. Keep your eyes peeled for bald eagles. Note that in winter, the American Camp visitor center is only open Thursday through Sunday.

Continuing past American Camp will bring you to Cattle Point, site of a lighthouse and the **Cattle Point Interpretive Area.** This latter locale was, in the 1920s, a Navy Radio Compass Station that helped ships navigate the nearby waters. Today, there are rock outcrops, two tiny beaches, great views of Lopez Island, interpretive signs, and a few picnic tables that make this one of the best picnic spots on the island. Cattle Point is also a good destination for a bike ride from Friday Harbor.

BOAT & BUS TOURS

If you happen to be on a tight schedule but still want to have a look at Victoria, you can arrange a day cruise through Vancouver Island's **Oak Bay Beach Hotel** (© **800/668-7758** or 250/598-4556; www.oakbaybeachhotel.com), which operates its tours out of the marina at Roche Harbor Resort. The tours operate daily from May 15 to October 15 and cost $49 for adults and $35 for children 12 and under. An add-on excursion to famed Butchart Gardens can also be arranged.

If you come over to San Juan Island without a car and want to see as much of the island as possible in a short amount of time, consider taking a narrated bus tour through **San Juan Island Transit & Tours,** Cannery Landing building, Front and East streets (© **800/887-8387** or 360/378-8887; www.sanjuan transit.com), which has its office right at the ferry landing and charges $18 for adults, $16 for seniors, $10 for kids 9 to 17 with adult, free for children 8 and under with adult.

SPORTS & OUTDOOR ACTIVITIES

BICYCLING   Bicycling is another favorite sport of island visitors. Winding country roads are almost ideal for leisurely trips. If you didn't bring your own bike, you can rent one from **Island Bicycles,** 380 Argyle St., in Friday Harbor (© **360/378-4941**), which charges $6 per hour and $25 per day. Here on San Juan Island you can also rent scooters and mopeds. They're available in Friday Harbor by the hour or by the day from **Island Scooter Rental,** 85 Front St. (© **360/378-8811**), or **Susie's Mopeds** (© **800/532-0087** or 360/378-5244; www.susiesmopeds.com), which is located at the top of the ferry lanes. Expect to pay $16 per hour or $48 for the day.

BOAT CHARTERS   If you and a few friends would just like to get out on the water for a leisurely cruise, there are always boats to be chartered in Friday Harbor. Check around the marina for notices. You can also try contacting **Cap'n Howard's Sailing Charters** (© **877/346-7245** or 360/378-3958; www.sanjuan web.com/sanjuan/capnhoward), which charges $70 per hour for two people. If you're looking for a week-long bareboat charter, contact **Charters Northwest** (© **360/378-7196;** www.chartersnw.com).

FISHING   If you want to try catching some salmon, contact **Buffalo Works** (© **360/378-4612;** www.rockisland.com/~captnjer/) or **Trophy Charters** (© **360/378-2110;** www.globaltelesis.com/trophy), both of which also offer salmon and bottom-fishing trips.

SCUBA DIVING   Believe it or not, scuba diving is also extremely popular in the San Juans. Though the water stays frigid year-round, it's also exceedingly clear. If you're a diver and want to rent equipment or go on a guided dive, or if you want to take a diving class while you're here, contact **Emerald Seas Outfitters,**

2A Spring St. Landing, Friday Harbor (© **800/942-2507** or 360/378-2772; www.emeraldseas.com). A two-tank dive will cost you $70.

SEA KAYAKING ★★   Two- to four-hour **sea-kayak tours** ($39–$49) are offered by **San Juan Safaris** (© **800/450-6858** or 360/378-1323; www.sanjuan safaris.com) at Roche Harbor Village and Friday Harbor. **Leisure Kayak Adventures** (© **800/836-1402** or 360/378-5992; www.leisurekayak.com), and **Crystal Seas Kayaking** (© **877/SEAS-877** or 360/378-7899; www.crystalseas. com). Most of these companies also offer full-day and overnight trips. Three- and four-day trips are offered by **San Juan Kayak Expeditions** (© **360/ 378-4436;** www.sanjuankayak.com), which charges $325 and $420, respectively, for its outings.

WHALE-WATCHING ★★   When it's time to spot some whales, you have two choices. You can take a whale-watching cruise or head over to **Lime Kiln State Park** ★★, where a short trail leads down to a rocky coastline from which orca whales, minke whales, Dall's porpoises, and sea lions can sometimes be seen. The best months to see orcas are June to September, but it's possible to see them year-round.

Whale-watching cruises lasting from 4 to 6 hours are offered in the summer by **San Juan Excursions** (© **800/80-WHALE** or 360/378-6636; www.watch whales.com), which operates out of Friday Harbor. Cruises are $49 for adults and $35 for children age 4 to 12. Three-hour whale-watching trips from Roche Harbor Resort, on the north side of the island, are offered by **San Juan Safaris** (© **360/378-1323;** www.sanjuansafaris.com), which charges $49 for adults and $39 for children 4 through 12.

WHERE TO STAY

In addition to the hotels, B&Bs, and inns listed here, there are also lots of vaca- tion rentals available on San Juan Island through **Windermere San Juan Island,** 520 Spring St. (P.O. Box 488), Friday Harbor, WA 98250 (© **800/262-3596** or 360/378-3600; www.windermeresji.com). Rates range from $950 to $3,150 per week.

EXPENSIVE

Friday Harbor House ★★   With its contemporary yet distinctly Northwest architecture, this luxurious little boutique hotel brings urban sophistication to Friday Harbor. The hotel's bluff-top location assures excellent views of the ferry landing, the adjacent marina, and, in the distance, Orcas Island. With their fire- places and double whirlpool tubs, guest rooms are designed for romantic get- aways, and as you relax in your tub, you can gaze out at the view and your own crackling fire. Most rooms also have decks or balconies. If you enjoy contempo- rary styling, these are the best rooms in all the San Juan Islands. The dining room here is one of the best on the island and serves Northwest cuisine.

130 West St. (P.O. Box 1385), Friday Harbor, WA 98250. © **360/378-8455.** Fax 360/378-8453. www.friday harborhouse.com. 20 units. Memorial Day–Sept $200–$265 double, $300 suite; Oct–Memorial Day $140–$195 double, $255 suite. Rates include continental breakfast. AE, MC, V. **Amenities:** Restaurant (North- west); access to nearby health club; Jacuzzi; concierge; massage. *In room:* TV, fax, dataport, minibar, fridge, coffeemaker, hair dryer, iron, safe.

Lakedale Resort ★★ *(Kids)*   Although best known as the island's favorite pri- vate campground, Lakedale Resort also has six very attractive modern cabins and a new 10-room lodge that is a luxurious rendition of a class log mountain lodge. The cabins are attractively and individually decorated and have porches that

The Truth About Killer Whales

Killer whales, once maligned as the wolves of the deep and dreaded as ruthless marauders of the sea, have been going through a change of image over the past decade or so. As more has been learned about these highly intelligent members of the porpoise family, an unofficial public-relations campaign has been waged to convince people that these are not killer whales, but orca whales. The more one learns about these intelligent, family-oriented animals, the more evident it becomes that past images of this whale are misinformed.

Orcas can be found in every ocean, but one of their highest concentrations is in the waters stretching north from Puget Sound along the coast of British Columbia. Consequently, this has become one of the most studied and most publicized populations of orcas in the world.

Orcas, which can grow to 30 feet long and weigh almost 9,000 pounds, are the largest member of the porpoise family. In the wild, they can live for up to 80 years, with female orcas commonly living 20 to 30 years longer than males. Orcas are among the most family-oriented animals on earth, and related whales will often live together for their entire lives, sometimes with three generations present at the same time. These family groups frequently band together with other closely related groups into extended families known as pods. A community of orcas consists of several pods, and in this area these communities number around 100 individuals. There are three populations of orcas living in the waters off Vancouver Island, British Columbia. These are known as the northern and southern resident communities and the transient community. It's the southern resident community that whale-watchers in the San Juan Islands are most likely to encounter.

As predators, orcas do live up to the name "killer," and have been known to attack other whales much larger than themselves. Some orcas off the coast of Argentina even swim up onto the shore, beaching themselves to attack resting sea lions, then thrashing and twisting their way back into the water. However, not all orcas feed on other marine mammals. Of the three communities in this area, only the transients feed on mammals. The two resident communities feed primarily on salmon, which are abundant in these waters, especially off the west side of San Juan Island during the summer.

overlook the forest, and all have two bedrooms, two bathrooms, a full kitchen, and a gas fireplace. There's a hot tub in a gazebo, and guests have access to the resort's 82 acres, which include trails and several lakes that are good for swimming, canoeing (boat rentals are also available), and trout fishing. Think of this as a sort of summer camp for the entire family. Lots of fun and very woodsy. Guests staying in the lodge get a continental breakfast.

2627 Roche Harbor Rd., Friday Harbor, WA 98250. ℰ **800/617-2267** or 360/378-2350. Fax 360/378-0944. www.lakedale.com. 16 units. $80–$180 lodge double; $110–$340 lodge suite; $135–$210 cabin. AE, DC, DISC, MC, V. **Amenities:** Jacuzzi; canoe rentals. *In room:* No phone in cabins.

MODERATE

Duffy House Bed & Breakfast Inn ⭐ Don't despair when you find yourself in a gravel pit as you try to find this B&B. Keep going and you'll come out the other side of the rock quarry to find a secluded point on the slopes of which stands this 1920s Tudor home. Surrounded by a small farm, the inn has a great view over the water. The country-style guest rooms can be a bit cramped but are still comfortable enough. Our favorite is the one with the view of the eagle's nest tree.

4214 Pear Point Rd., Friday Harbor, WA 98250. ⓒ **800/972-2089** or 360/378-5604. Fax 360/378-6535. www.duffyhousebnb.com. 5 units. $115–$135 double. MC, V. *In room:* No phone.

Friday's ⭐ Located right in downtown Friday Harbor only 2 blocks from the ferry landing, this B&B-style inn is conveniently located and offers a few affordable rooms (and even the more expensive rooms are relatively good deals considering the generally high room rates on the island). The less expensive guest rooms are small and simply furnished, with the occasional antique and unusual driftwood headboards in some rooms. A few of the rooms have kitchens and three have double whirlpool tubs. The best rooms are the new ground-floor rooms, including a two-bedroom suite that's a good choice for families. Most rooms have a TV and VCR, and many also have in-room Jacuzzi tubs, kitchenettes, or fireplaces.

35 First St. (P.O. Box 2023), Friday Harbor, WA 98250. ⓒ **800/352-2632** or 360/378-5848. www.friday-harbor.com. 15 units, 4 with shared bathroom. $90–$120 double with shared bathroom, $135–$215 double with private bathroom. Rates include continental breakfast. MC, V. *In room:* No phone.

Hillside House Bed & Breakfast ⭐ Located less than a mile from the ferry landing and walking distance to a couple of good restaurants, this contemporary home sits atop a hill and has good views of both Mount Baker and the water from many of its guest rooms. The inn's best room is the Eagle's Nest, which takes up the entire top floor and has a bird's-eye view of the harbor. This room also has a whirlpool tub and balcony. Other rooms are much smaller and less luxurious but comfortable nonetheless.

365 Carter Ave., Friday Harbor, WA 98250. ⓒ **800/232-4730** or 360/378-4730. Fax 360/378-4715. www.hillsidehouse.com. 7 units. $90–$250 double; lower rates off-season. Rates include full breakfast. AE, DISC, MC, V. **Amenities:** Concierge; business center. *In room:* Hair dryer, iron.

Lonesome Cove Resort ⭐ If you want to be alone, there's no better place on San Juan Island than Lonesome Cove. This is the sort of place your grandparents might have frequented on summer vacation 50 years ago. Forests hide the 6-acre property from the rest of the world, while lawns and orchards surround the waterfront cabins. Each of the rustic cabins has a large deck, stone fireplace, and full kitchen. There's a quarter mile of private beach, a trout pond, friendly ducks, romantic sunsets, and more peace and solitude than you'll find anywhere else on the island.

416 Lonesome Cove Rd., Friday Harbor, WA 98250. ⓒ **360/378-4477**. www.lonesomecove.com. 6 units. $115 cabin (sleeps 2 people). 2-night minimum Sept–May, 5-night minimum June–Aug. MC, V. **Amenities:** Activities desk. *In room:* Kitchen, fridge, coffeemaker.

Olympic Lights Bed and Breakfast ⭐⭐ Located at San Juan's dry southwestern tip, the Olympic Lights is a Victorian farmhouse surrounded by windswept meadows, and if it weren't for the sight of Puget Sound out the window, you could easily mistake the setting for the prairies of the Midwest. There are colorful gardens, an old barn, even some hens to lay the eggs for your breakfast.

The ocean breezes, nearby beach, and friendliness of innkeepers Christian and Lea Andrade lend a special feel to this American classic. Our favorite room here is the Ra Room, which is named for the Egyptian sun god and features a big bay window. The view out the windows is enough to settle the most stressed-out soul.

146 Starlight Way, Friday Harbor, WA 98250. © 888/211-6195 or 360/378-3186. Fax 360/378-2097. www. olympiclightsbnb.com. 4 units. $120–$140 double. Rates include full breakfast. No credit cards. *In room:* Hair dryer, no phone.

Roche Harbor Village ★★ *Kids*   Located at the north end of the island, Roche Harbor Village is steeped in island history, with the historic Hotel de Haro, established in 1886, serving as the resort's centerpiece. A brick driveway and manicured gardens provide the foreground for the white two-story hotel, which overlooks the marina and has porches running the length of both floors. Although the rooms in the Hotel de Haro are quite basic (all but four have shared bathrooms) and have not been updated in years, the building has loads of atmosphere. The best accommodations here, however, are the four new luxury McMillin suites in a restored home adjacent to the historic hotel. The modern condominiums are good bets for families. The resort's dining room has a view of the marina, and the deck makes a great spot for a sunset cocktail. In addition to amenities listed below, there are whale-watching cruises, sea-kayak tours, a marina, and a general store.

P.O. Box 4001, Roche Harbor, WA 98250. © 800/451-8910 or 360/378-2155. Fax 360/378-6809. www. rocheharbor.com. Historic hotel 20 units (16 with shared bathroom). Modern accommodations 25 condos, 9 cottages, 4 suites. May–Sept $79–$99 double with shared bathroom, $139–$319 suite, $179–$299 condo, $159–$239 cottage; lower rates Oct–Apr. AE, MC, V. **Amenities:** 3 restaurants (Continental/Northwest, American); lounge; outdoor pool; 2 tennis courts; Jacuzzi; bike and moped rentals; shopping arcade; coin-op laundry. *In room:* Hair dryer, iron.

CAMPGROUNDS

Lakedale Campground ★★, 2627 Roche Harbor Rd., Friday Harbor, WA 98250 (© 800/617-2267 or 360/378-2350; www.lakedale.com), is 4 miles (6.5km) north of Friday Harbor. With 82 acres, several lakes, and campsites for tents as well as RVs, this private campground makes an ideal spot for a family vacation.

Our favorite campground on the island is **San Juan County Park** ★★, 380 Westside Rd. N., Friday Harbor, WA 98250 (© **360/378-8420** for information, or 360/378-1842 for reservations), which has unbeatable views and is set on the site of an old waterfront farm. Reservations can be made up to 90 days in advance.

WHERE TO DINE

In addition to the restaurants listed below, there are several other places in Friday Harbor where you can get a quick, simple meal. At the top of the ferry lanes, on A Street, you'll find **Madelyn's Bagel Bakery** (© **360/378-4545**), a small bagel and sandwich shop, and not far away is the **Garden Path Café,** 135 Second St. (© **360/378-6255**), which usually has a good selection of deli salads, soups, and baked goods. Just around the corner is the popular **Felicitations,** 120 Nichols St. (© **360/378-1198**), which is the best bakery on the island.

If you're up near the north end of the island and suddenly find yourself hungry for lunch or a light dinner, try the **Lime Kiln Cafe** (© **360/378-2155**) on the dock at Roche Harbor Resort. This lively little cafe serves filling breakfasts and good chowder and fish and chips. Big windows let you gaze out at the boats in the marina.

Duck Soup Inn ★★ NORTHWEST/INTERNATIONAL   North of Friday Harbor 4½ miles (7km) you'll find the Duck Soup Inn, a barnlike restaurant beside a pond frequented by—you guessed it—ducks. Inside this quintessentially Northwestern building you'll find lots of exposed wood and a fieldstone fireplace. The menu changes frequently, depending on the availability of fresh produce, but is always very creative. The chef has a penchant for the flavors of Asia and you might find sesame calamari with Korean dipping sauce or spicy Sri Lankan prawns. Specials always incorporate whatever produce is freshest that week. In spring and fall, you might even find duck soup on the menu!

50 Duck Soup Lane. ⓒ 360/378-4878. www.ducksoupinn.com. Reservations highly recommended. Main courses $19.50–$28. DISC, MC, V. Summer Wed–Sun 5:30–9:30pm; spring and fall Fri–Sat 5:30–9:30pm. Closed Nov–early Apr.

Friday Harbor House Dining Room ★★ NORTHWEST   Located in the luxurious Friday Harbor House boutique hotel, this is the most sophisticated restaurant on San Juan Island. Striking contemporary decor sets the tone, but can't distract diners from the harbor views out the glass walls. The menu is short and relies heavily on local ingredients, including island-grown greens and Westcott Bay oysters (perhaps prepared with chanterelle mushrooms and Parmesan cheese). The chef draws on diverse inspirations for the dishes served here, which are always attractively presented as well as carefully prepared. A recent menu included perfectly cooked salmon with coconut-red curry sauce. Also noteworthy was halibut baked in parchment.

130 West St. ⓒ 360/378-8455. Reservations highly recommended. Main courses $15–$23. AE, DISC, MC, V. Daily 5:30–9:30pm (until 8:30pm Oct to mid-June).

The Place Next to the San Juan Ferry ★★ NORTHWEST/INTERNATIONAL   Located on the waterfront to the right as you get off the ferry and housed in a small wooden building that was once part of a U.S. Coast Guard station, this aptly named establishment is San Juan Island's finest waterfront restaurant. With local art adorning the walls, this place aims to attract the upscale Seattle market, and it's right on target. The menu changes regularly with an emphasis on seafood preparations such as Asian-style crab cakes and Pacific Rim bouillabaisse.

1 Spring St. ⓒ 360/378-8707. Reservations highly recommended. Main courses $17–$32. MC, V. Daily 5:30–9pm (Tues–Sat in winter).

Vinny's ★★ ITALIAN   From the name you might guess that this place is some dark dive serving New York–style pizza. Not exactly. Located across the street from the Friday Harbor House and claiming the same good views of the marina, Vinny's is San Juan Island's premier Italian restaurant. This is the sort of place you discover on the first night of your visit and decide to eat at every night until you leave. Local oysters and mussels dominate the appetizer menu, although the calamari with pine nuts, tomatoes, raisins, lemon, and vinaigrette should not be missed. And while this is seafood country, the charbroiled, dry-aged Delmonico steaks are a big hit (try it with Gorgonzola-Parmesan butter). Of course there are plenty of well-prepared standards such as lasagna, penne alla puttanesca, and shrimp scampi.

165 West St. ⓒ 360/378-1934. Reservations recommended. Main courses $14–$28. AE, DISC, MC, V. Daily 5–10pm.

ORCAS ISLAND

Orcas Island, the largest of the San Juans, is also the most beautiful of the islands. If you have time to visit only one island, make it Orcas. The island, which covers 58 square miles (93.5km²), is a particular favorite of nature lovers who come to enjoy the views of green rolling pastures, the hiking trails of Moran State Park, the forested mountains (at 2,409 ft. tall, Mount Constitution is the highest point in the islands), and fjordlike bays (East Sound, West Sound, and Deer Harbor).

EXPLORING THE ISLAND

Eastsound is the largest town on the island and has several interesting shops and good restaurants. Shops here worth checking out include **Darvill's Rare Print Shop,** Horseshoe Highway (© 360/376-2351), which sells antique prints and maps, and the adjacent **Darvill's Book Store** (© 360/376-2135), which specializes in Northwest fiction, history, and guidebooks. Just outside Eastsound, on Horseshoe Highway, you'll find **Howe Art** (© 360/376-2945; www.howe art.net), a studio and gallery run by sculptor Anthony Howe, who fashions fascinating hanging kinetic sculptures from stainless steel. The studio is open by appointment only. Other smaller villages include Deer Harbor, West Sound, and Olga.

To learn a little about the history of Orcas Island, drop by the **Orcas Island Historical Museum,** 181 North Beach Rd., Eastsound (© 360/376-4849; www.orcasisland.org/~history). Between late May and September, the museum is open Tuesday through Sunday from 1 to 4pm (Fri until 7pm). Admission is $1. A second historical museum, the **Crow Valley School Museum** (© 360/ 376-4260), an old one-room schoolhouse, is located 3 miles (5km) southwest of Eastsound on Crow Valley Road. This museum is open Memorial Day through Labor Day Thursday through Saturday from 1 to 4pm. At the **Lambiel Home Museum** (© 360/376-4544), on Horseshoe Highway southeast of Eastsound, you can view a private collection of artwork by 169 artists from around the San Juan Islands. The museum is open daily by appointment. Admission is $10 and tours take about 2 hours.

Around the island you'll find several interesting pottery shops. A few miles west of Eastsound off Enchanted Forest Road is **Orcas Island Pottery** (© 360/ 376-2813), the oldest pottery studio in the Northwest; and, at the end of this same road, on West Beach across from the West Beach Resort, you'll find **The Right Place Pottery Shop** (© 360/376-4023). Between Eastsound and Orcas on Horseshoe Highway, you'll find **Crow Valley Pottery** (© 360/376-4260), which is in an 1866 log cabin. On the east side of the island in the community of Olga, you'll find **Orcas Island Artworks** (© 360/376-4408), which is full of beautiful work by more than 70 island artists.

If you're looking for something to do after dark, check the calendar at **Orcas Center** (© 360/376-ACT1; www.orcascenter.org), the island's performing arts center. It's located a quarter-mile north of Eastsound near the airport.

SPORTS & OUTDOOR ACTIVITIES

Moran State Park ★★ (© 360/376-2326; www.parks.wa.gov), which covers approximately 5,000 acres of the island, is the largest park in the San Juans and the main destination of most visitors to Orcas Island. If the weather is clear, you'll find great views from the summit of Mount Constitution, which rises 2,409 feet above Puget Sound. There are also five lakes and 32 miles (52km) of hiking trails. Fishing, hiking, boating, mountain biking, and camping are all popular park activities. The park is off Horseshoe Highway, approximately 12½ miles (20km) from the ferry landing.

BICYCLING   Although Orcas is considered the most challenging of the San Juan Islands for bicycling, plenty of cyclists still pedal the island's roads. One of the best places to rent bikes here is from **Dolphin Bay Bicycles** (© 360/376-4157; www.rockisland.com/~dolphin), which is located just to the right as you get off the ferry. From here you can explore Orcas Island or take a free ferry to Lopez Island or Shaw Island. Bikes rent for $25 per day and $55 for 3 days. Guided bike rides are also sometimes available. In Eastsound, you can rent bikes from **Wildlife Cycles,** North Beach Road, Eastsound (© 360/376-4708; www.wildlifecycles.com). Bikes rent for between $10 and $12 per hour or $30 to $35 per day. If you're exploring the island by mountain bike, you may want to take the unpaved Dolphin Bay Road to Eastsound; otherwise, take the Crow Valley Road.

BIPLANE RIDES   For a very fun overview of Orcas Island, try a scenic biplane ride in a restored 1929 Travelair. Thirty-minute flights with **Magic Air Tours** (© 800/376-1929 or 360/376-2733; www.magicair.com) cost $195 for two people.

BOAT CHARTERS   If you're interested in heading out on the water in a 33-foot sailboat, contact Capt. Don Palmer at **Amante Sail Tours** (© 360/376-4231), which charges $35 per person (with a two-person minimum and a maximum of six) for a half-day sail. At the **Rosario Resort Activities Center** (© 360/376-2222), you can arrange a 3-hour sail ($45–$55 per person) aboard the *Morning Star,* a 56-foot, two-masted sailboat. You can also rent small sailboats and powerboats at **Orcas Boat Rentals,** Deer Harbor Marina, Deer Harbor Road (© 360/376-7616; www.orcasboats.com), which charges between $150 and $175 for an 8-hour rental.

GOLF   Golfers can head to the nine-hole **Orcas Island Country Golf Club** (© 360/376-4400) near Eastsound on the Horseshoe Highway.

HIKING   With 32 miles (52km) of hiking trails, Moran State Park offers hikes ranging from short, easy strolls alongside lakes, to strenuous, all-day hikes. South of the community of Olga, on the east arm of the island, you'll also find a half-mile trail through **Obstruction Pass Park** ⚘⚘. This trail leads to a quiet little cove that has a few walk-in/paddle-in campsites. The park is at the end of Obstruction Pass Road.

HORSEBACK RIDING   Guided trail rides ($50 per person) can be arranged through **Walking Horse Country Farm** (© 360/376-5306; www.walkinghorsefarm.com), which also has a rental cabin available.

SCUBA DIVING   Sure the waters are cold, but they're usually quite clear and there's lots to see. If you're interested in diving the waters off Orcas Island, make arrangements through **Island Dive and Water Sports** (© 800/303-8386 or 360/376-7615; www.divesanjuan.com), which operates out of Rosario Resort. A two-tank boat dive is $75.

SEA KAYAKING ⚘⚘   The best way to see the Orcas Island coast is by sea kayak. Located right at the Orcas Island ferry landing, **Orcas Outdoors** (© 360/376-4611; www.orcasoutdoors.com) offers guided sea-kayak tours lasting from 1 hour ($25) to overnight ($220). Three-hour guided tours ($44) are also offered by **Shearwater Adventures** (© 360/376-4699; www.shearwaterkayaks.com). Two-hour paddles ($25) are offered by **Spring Bay Inn** (© 360/376-5531; www.springbayinn.com), which is located on the east side of the island near the village of Olga. These trips are in an area where bald eagles nest in the summer.

WHALE-WATCHING ★★ If you want to see some of the orca whales for which the San Juans are famous, you can take a whale-watching excursion with **Deer Harbor Charters** (✆ **800/544-5758** or 360/376-5989; www.deerharbor charters.com), which operates out of both Deer Harbor and Rosario Resort and charges $45 for adults and $30 for children, or **Orcas Island Eclipse Charters** (✆ **800/376-6566** or 360/376-6566), which operates out of the Orcas Island ferry dock and charges $46.50 for adults and $30 for children.

WHERE TO STAY
Expensive

The Resort at Deer Harbor ★★ Set on an open hillside above the spectac-ular Deer Harbor inlet, this casual resort looks across the water to a forested cliff and offers the best views on the island. Add to this a few small islands at the mouth of the inlet and a marina with sailboats bobbing at anchor, and you have the quintessential island setting. All the cottages here have hot tubs on their porches. However, the 11 large modern cottages, which are the most luxurious accommodations here, also have double whirlpool tubs in the bathrooms, fire-places, and separate seating areas. The restaurant here, a casual and moderately priced bistro, is under the same management as Christina's, one of the best restaurants in the San Juans (see review, below).

31 Jack and Jill Lane (P.O. Box 200), Deer Harbor, WA 98243. ✆ 888/376-4480 or 360/376-4420. Fax 360/376-5523. www.deerharbor.com. 26 units. May 15–Sept 30 $189–$399 suite or cottage; Oct 1–May 14 $149–$299 suite or cottage. Rates include continental breakfast. AE, DISC, MC, V. **Amenities:** Restaurant (International); outdoor pool. *In room:* TV/VCR, fridge, coffeemaker, hair dryer.

Rosario Resort & Spa ★★★ *Kids* Rosario is the most luxurious accommo-dation on Orcas Island and is the only place in the San Juans that can actually claim to be a resort. Its centerpiece remains the 1904 Moran Mansion, an imposing white stucco building on the shore of Cascade Bay. The mansion houses the resort's main dining room, lounge, spa, and library. The larger and more luxurious rooms (with fireplaces, good views, and French country decor) are across the marina and up a steep hill from this main building, so if you aren't keen on walking, request a room in one of the buildings directly adjacent to the Moran Mansion. Sailing charters are available from the marina here.

1 Rosario Way, Eastsound, WA 98245. ✆ 800/562-8820 or 360/376-2222. Fax 360/376-2289. www.rosario resort.com. 127 units. June–Sept $219–$329 double, $319–$629 suite; Oct–May $89–$249 double, $239–$499 suite. AE, DC, DISC, MC, V. **Amenities:** 3 restaurants (seafood); lounge; indoor and 2 outdoor pools; 2 tennis courts; exercise room; spa; Jacuzzi; sauna; watersports equipment rentals; bike rentals; chil-dren's center; concierge; car-rental desk; shopping arcade; room service; massage; babysitting; coin-op laun-dry; laundry service. *In room:* TV, dataport, fridge, coffeemaker, hair dryer, iron.

Spring Bay Inn ★★ Just by virtue of being one of the only waterfront B&Bs in the San Juans, this inn would deserve a recommendation. However, innkeep-ers Sandy Playa and Carl Burger, both retired park rangers, make a stay here both fun and educational, and the setting and inn itself are great for a romantic getaway. You can soak in the hot tub on the beach and watch the sunset, spot bald eagles from just outside the inn's front door, hike on the nature trails, and best of all, go for a guided sea-kayak tour each morning. Four of the five guest rooms have fireplaces, two have views from their tubs, and two have balconies.

P.O. Box 97, Olga, WA 98279. ✆ 360/376-5531. Fax 360/376-2193. www.springbayinn.com. 5 units. $220–$260 double. 2-night minimum. Rates include continental breakfast, brunch, and daily kayak tour. DISC, MC, V. **Amenities:** Access to nearby health club; Jacuzzi; concierge. *In room:* Fridge, hair dryer.

Turtleback Farm Inn ★★ Nowhere on Orcas will you find a more idyllic setting than this bright-green restored farmhouse overlooking 80 acres of farmland at the foot of Turtleback Mountain. Simply furnished with antiques, the guest rooms range from cozy to spacious, and each has its own special view. Our favorite room in the main house is the Meadow View Room, which has a private deck and claw-foot tub. The four rooms in the orchard house are among the biggest and most luxurious on the island (gas fireplaces, claw-foot tubs, balconies, wood floors, kitchenettes). Days here start with a big farm breakfast served at valley-view tables that are set with bone china, silver, and linen. Finish your day with a nip of sherry by the fire.

1981 Crow Valley Rd., Eastsound, WA 98245. ✆ **800/376-4914** or 360/376-4914. Fax 360/376-5329. www. turtlebackinn.com. 11 units. Main house May 1–Oct 15 $80–$160 double. Orchard House June 15–Sept 15 $210 double. Lower rates other months. 2-night minimum stay June 15–Sept 15, weekends, and holidays. Rates include full breakfast. DISC, MC, V. **Amenities:** Access to nearby health club; concierge. *In room:* Hair dryer.

Moderate

Cascade Harbor Inn ★ Formerly a part of Rosario Resort, this hotel enjoys similar Eastsound views and is adjacent to both the Rosario marina and Moran State Park. Guest rooms range from standard motel rooms to studios with Murphy beds to spacious suites with kitchens. All the rooms have water views, though in some cases it is somewhat hidden by trees. The lodge sits on a steep hillside above the water, and a path leads down to the Rosario marina.

1800 Rosario Rd., Eastsound, WA 98245. ✆ **800/201-2120** or 360/376-6350. Fax 360/376-6354. www. cascadeharborinn.com. 48 units. Summer $119–$349 double; winter $89–$239 double. Rates include continental breakfast (summer only). DISC, MC, V. **Amenities:** Concierge; activities desk. *In room:* TV, coffeemaker.

The Kingfish Inn ★ *(Finds)* Housed in the old West Sound general store, this inn is about as quaint as they come. Downstairs, the old general store has been converted into a cozy little cafe, while upstairs, there are three rooms with views over West Sound. These views are among the best on the island. The fourth room is just off the cafe's deck and oddly enough, has a huge antique piano in the room. However, the upstairs rooms are much more attractively furnished despite the old piano and you should try to get one of them. These rooms have rustic armoires and beautiful beds with fluffy duvets. One of the rooms has a woodstove and one has a picture-perfect porch. Bathrooms, however, are very basic and have showers only.

Deer Harbor and Crow Valley rds., Westsound (mailing address 4362 Crow Valley Rd., Eastsound, WA 98245). ✆ **360/376-4440**. www.kingfishinn.com. 4 units. $90–$140 double. Rates include breakfast. MC, V. **Amenities:** Restaurant (American); access to nearby health club; bike rentals; sea-kayak rentals; massage; babysitting. *In room:* TV/VCR, hair dryer, iron.

Orcas Hotel ★ Located right at the Orcas ferry landing, this B&B is a good choice for anyone coming over without a car. On the other hand, the proximity of the ferry precludes the tranquil setting available at other island B&Bs. Nonetheless, the Orcas is an attractive old Victorian hotel and has been welcoming guests since 1904. The guest rooms, done in a simple country style, vary in size, but all are carpeted and furnished with antiques. A couple of the rooms have whirlpool tubs with stained-glass windows above them. On the first floor of this three-story building you'll find a lounge, bakery/cafe, and a good restaurant, which together can meet all your dining needs should you be using this hotel as a base for a car-free vacation here on Orcas.

P.O. Box 155, Orcas, WA 98280. ✆ **888/672-2792** or 360/376-4300. Fax 360/376-4399. www.orcashotel. com. 12 units, 4 with shared bathroom, 3 with half bathroom. $79–$109 double with shared bathroom;

$129–$159 double with half bathroom; $149–$198 double with private bathroom. Rates include continental breakfast. AE, MC, V. **Amenities:** 2 restaurants (Northwest, bakery); lounge; access to nearby health club; concierge; massage. *In room:* No phone.

Inexpensive

Doe Bay Resort & Retreat   Far more retreat than resort, this funky collection of cottages, tiny cabins, and tent cabins 24 miles from the ferry landing is a sort of counterculture resort popular with Deadheads and hostelers from around the world. The cottages are furnished in early Salvation Army style (battered couches, futons), though many have their own kitchens. The Guest House is the best and most expensive accommodation here, with a deck above the water of the resort's tiny cove. However, despite the fact that the cabins here are utterly basic, this place remains quite popular due to its spring-fed hot tubs and sauna. The tubs and sauna are set on a big deck overlooking a picturesque little cove and are clothing optional. There are also campsites and a hostel room. Kayak tours operate from the resort, and massages are available. The tubs and sauna are also open to the public for a small fee.

Horseshoe Highway (P.O. Box 437), Olga, WA 98279. ⓒ 360/376-2291. Fax 260/376-5809. www.doebay. com. 31 units (plus 6 hostel beds and 30 campsites). $45–$90 double; $25 hostel bed; $25 campsite. AE, DISC, MC, V. 2-night minimum in summer and weekends throughout the year. Pets accepted (except between mid-June and mid-Sept) with $20 per night fee. **Amenities:** Restaurant (eclectic); hot tub; sauna; massage. *In room:* No phone.

CAMPGROUNDS

With 151 sites, **Moran State Park** ⭐⭐ (ⓒ 360/376-2326) is the most popular camping spot on the island. Reservations are accepted (and highly recommended) May 15 through September 15 and can be made up to 9 months in advance through **Washington State Parks Reservations** (ⓒ 888/226-7688; www.parks.wa.gov). Additional campsites are available at the **Doe Bay Village Resort** ⭐ (ⓒ 360/376-2291; www.doebay.com), a sort of Deadhead beach resort. If you enjoy roughing it, there are hike-in or paddle-in sites at **Obstruction Pass State Park** ⭐ at the south end of the east arm of the island (near Olga). Keep in mind that there is no water available at this isolated and beautifully situated park.

WHERE TO DINE

For soups, sandwiches, and lattes, you can't beat the **Comet Café,** Eastsound Square, North Beach Road, Eastsound (ⓒ 360/376-4220). For baked goods, imported cheeses, and other gourmet foodstuffs, stop by **Rose's Bread and Specialties** (ⓒ 360/376-5805), which is also in Eastsound Square. For great cookies, don't miss **Teezer's Cookies** (ⓒ 360/376-2913) at the corner of North Beach Road and A Street. In Olga, don't miss **The Olga Store,** Olga Road (ⓒ 360/376-5862), which until recently was a little general store but is now a great little cafe and eclectic gift shop. In West Sound, at the corner of Deer Harbor Road and Crow Valley Road, the **West Sound Cafe** (ⓒ 360/376-4440), housed in a former general store and with a great view of the water, serves good breakfasts, lunches, and light meals.

Bilbo's Festivo ⭐ MEXICAN   Housed in an old bungalow in the heart of Eastsound, Bilbo's melds a Northwest setting with Southwestern food. The garden outside is purely Northwestern but the stucco, tile work, and low wall around the patio dining area all say New Mexico. The menu, though it has plenty of Mexican standards, is most noteworthy for its more unusual regional dishes such as mesquite-grilled chicken in an herb-and-orange juice marinade or mesquite-grilled flank steak marinated in lime juice. Summers see the crowds lining up to get into the restaurant's patio where the barbecue grill stays fired up with mesquite. The margaritas here are the best on the island.

N. Beach Rd., Eastsound. ✆ 360/376-4728. Reservations recommended. Main courses $7–$21. MC, V. Apr–Sept daily 11:30am–3pm and 5–10pm; Oct–Mar shorter dinner hours, closed for lunch.

Café Olga ⭐ *Finds* INTERNATIONAL   Housed in an old strawberry-packing plant that dates from the days when these islands were known for their fruit, Café Olga is the best place on the island for breakfast or lunch. Everything here is homemade, using fresh local produce whenever possible. The blackberry pie is a special treat, especially when accompanied by Lopez Island Creamery ice cream. This building also houses Orcas Island Artworks, a gallery representing more than 70 Orcas Island artists.

Horseshoe Hwy., Olga. ✆ 360/376-5098. Main courses $7–$15. MC, V. Daily 10am–6pm (until 5pm in Nov–Dec). Closed Jan–Feb.

Christina's ⭐⭐ NORTHWEST   Located on the second floor of an old waterfront building in Eastsound, Christina's has a beautiful view down the sound, just right for sunsets. If the weather is pleasant, the deck is *the* place on the island for a sunset dinner. The menu here is short, changes regularly, and features innovative cuisine prepared with an emphasis on local ingredients. For the most part, Christina's showcases its creativity in its appetizers rather than in its entrees, so whether you crave the unusual or the more familiar, you'll likely be satisfied here. If you're a fan of clam chowder, don't miss Christina's chowder. The desserts can be heavenly. The **Starfish Grille** (✆ **360/376-2482**), at the Resort at Deer Harbor (see above), is affiliated with this restaurant and offers simpler fare at lower prices. However, there are still those decadent desserts.

Main St. and North Beach Rd., Eastsound. ✆ 360/376-4904. Reservations highly recommended. Main courses $24–$34. AE, DISC, MC, V. Daily 5:30–9 or 9:30pm. Closed 3 weeks in Nov and all of Jan.

Orcas Wine Company & Oyster Bar ⭐⭐ SEAFOOD   Located right on the water in Eastsound village, the Orcas Wine Company claims one of the better views on the island (which it shares with Christina's restaurant, the upstairs neighbor), so try to get a dinner reservation that will let you enjoy the sunset. The restaurant has the feel of an old dock warehouse, which sort of sets the tone for the menu that focuses on fresh seafood. As far as we're concerned, there's no need to even glance past the appetizers list, which usually includes numerous oyster dishes, including baked oysters with chili paste, cabbage, ginger, and soy sauce; roasted oysters topped with habanero-apricot jelly; and oysters sautéed with pancetta, chanterelles, parsnips, garlic, and white wine. If you absolutely must have something other than oysters, you can count on finding well-prepared salmon and halibut.

Porter Station Building, Main St. and North Beach Rd., Eastsound. ✆ 360/376-6244. Reservations accepted. Main dishes $19–$26. AE, MC, V. Sun–Thurs 5:30–8pm; Fri–Sat 5:30–9pm.

Ship Bay Oyster House ⭐⭐ NORTHWEST   About midway between Eastsound and the turnoff for the Rosario Resort, you'll spot this restaurant, which is part of the Inn at Ship Bay. The buildings that comprise this inn sit on a bluff high above the waters of East Sound. Inside the restaurant, plenty of windows let you gaze out to sea, but it's the food, and not the views, that is the main attraction here. Oysters are a specialty; you can opt for pan-fried oysters, oyster shooters, and of course, fresh local oysters on the half shell. You can make a meal on oysters alone, but the entree menu includes plenty of other tempting dishes.

Horseshoe Hwy. ℭ **360/376-5886.** www.innatshipbay.com. Reservations recommended. Main courses $15–$23. AE, DC, DISC, MC, V. Tues–Sun 5:30–8:30pm (closed Sun fall and spring). Closed Thanksgiving–Feb.

The Sunflower Café ★★ NORTHWEST ⸱ Located in the village of East-sound, this casual and eclectic restaurant serves some of the most creative cuisine on the island, and whether you come for lunch, dinner, or even Sunday brunch, you'll likely leave pleasantly surprised by your meal here. Sure you can start your meal with a good cup of oyster stew, but you might also encounter cannellini bean and butternut squash soup with pesto or steamed clams in cilantro-lime broth. Salmon, ubiquitous throughout the islands, here might get a tropical twist with honey-ancho chili glaze, ginger-red onion salsa, coconut curry yams, and hearts of palm. Likewise, in season, beef tenderloin might be served with chanterelle and lobster mushrooms.

A St. and Prune Alley, Eastsound. ℭ **360/376-2335.** Reservations recommended. Main courses $10–$13 at lunch, $16–$21 at dinner. MC, V. Mon 5:30–9pm; Wed–Fri 11:30am–2:30pm and 5:30–9pm; Sat 8–11am, 11:30am–2:30pm, and 5:30–9pm; Sun 8am–2:30pm and 5:30–9pm.

LOPEZ ISLAND

Of the three islands with accommodations, Lopez is the least developed. Although it is less spectacular than Orcas or San Juan, it is flatter, which makes it popular with bicyclists who often prefer easy grades to stunning panoramas. Lopez maintains more of its agricultural roots than either of the two previously mentioned islands, and likewise has fewer activities for tourists. If you just want to get away from it all and hole up with a good book for a few days, Lopez may be the place for you.

EXPLORING THE ISLAND

Lopez Village is the closest this island has to a town, and here you'll find almost all of the island's restaurants and shops. At **Chimera Gallery,** Lopez Village Plaza (ℭ **360/468-3265**), you can see the work of island artists and artisans. Here in the village, you'll also find the **Lopez Historical Museum** (ℭ **360/468-2049;** www.rockisland.com/~lopezmuseum/), where you can learn about the island's history and pick up a map of historic buildings. In July and August the museum is open Wednesday through Sunday from noon to 4pm; and in May, June, and September, it's open Friday through Sunday from noon to 4pm. Admission is $1.

    Lopez Island Vineyards ★ (ℭ **360/468-3644**), which is located on Fisher-man Bay Road between the ferry landing and Lopez Village, was until recently the only winery that actually made wine from fruit grown here in the San Juans. Both their Siegerrebe and their Madeleine Angevine are from local grapes, as are their organic fruit wines. They also make wines from grapes grown in the Yakima Valley. The winery tasting room is open from April or May to September, Wednesday through Saturday from noon to 5pm.

The Lopez Wave

Want to feel like a Lopez Island native? As you drive the island, give passing cars a quick wave of the hand. Among the friendly residents of this island, the drivers' greeting is so commonplace that it has come to be known as the Lopez Wave.

SPORTS & OUTDOOR ACTIVITIES

Eight county parks and one state park provide plenty of access to the woods and water on Lopez Island. The first park off the ferry is **Odlin County Park** (© **360/468-2496**), which has a long beach, picnic tables, and a campground. Athletic fields make this more of a community sports center than a natural area, so this should be a last resort camping choice. For a more natural setting for a short easy hike, check out **Upright Channel Park,** which is on Military Road (about a mile north of Lopez Village in the northwest corner of the island). A little farther south and over on the east side of the island, you'll find **Spencer Spit State Park** ✯ (© **360/468-2251**), which also has a campground. Here, the forest meets the sea on a rocky beach that looks across a narrow channel to Frost Island. You can hike the trails through the forest or explore the beach. South of Lopez Village on Bay Shore Road, you'll find the small **Otis Perkins Park,** which is between Fisherman Bay and the open water and has one of the longest beaches on the island.

Down at the south end of the island, you'll find the tiny **Shark Reef Sanctuary** ✯✯, where a short trail leads through the forest to a rocky stretch of coast that is among the prettiest on all the ferry-accessible islands. Small islands offshore create strong currents that swirl past the rocks here. Seals and occasionally whales can be seen just offshore. This is a great spot for a picnic.

BIKING ✯✯   Because of its size, lack of traffic, numerous parks, and relatively flat terrain, Lopez is a favorite of cyclists. You can rent bikes for $5 an hour or $25 a day from **Lopez Bicycle Works & Kayaks,** 2847 Fisherman Bay Rd. (© **360/468-2847**), at the marina on Fisherman Bay Road.

SEA KAYAKING ✯✯   If you want to explore the island's coastline by kayak, contact **Lopez Island Sea Kayaks** (© **360/468-2847;** www.lopezkayaks.com), which is located at the marina on Fisherman Bay Road and is open May through October. Tours cost $75 for a full-day trip with lunch included. Single kayaks can also be rented here for $12 to $25 per hour, or $25 to $50 per half-day. Double kayaks rent for $20 to $35 per hour and $40 to $60 per half-day.

WHERE TO STAY

Edenwild Inn ✯✯   Located right in Lopez Village, this modern Victorian B&B is a good choice if you've come to Lopez to go biking or if you just want to use your car as little as possible. Within a block of the inn are all the island's best restaurants. Most of the guest rooms here are quite large, and most also have views of the water. All the rooms have interesting antique furnishings, and several have fireplaces. In summer, colorful gardens surround the inn, and guests can breakfast on a large brick patio. The front veranda, overlooking Fisherman Bay, is a great place to relax in the afternoon.

132 Lopez Rd. (P.O. Box 271), Lopez Island, WA 98261. © **800/606-0662** or 360/468-3238. Fax 360/468-4080. www.edenwildinn.com. 8 units. $110–$170 double. Rates include full breakfast. AE, MC, V. *In room:* No phone.

Lopez Farm Cottages and Tent Camping ✯✯ *Value*   Set on 30 acres of pastures, old orchards, and forest between the ferry landing and Lopez Village, these modern cottages are tucked into a grove of cedar trees on the edge of a large lawn (in the middle of which stand three huge boulders). From the outside, the board-and-batten cottages look like old farm buildings, but inside you'll find a combination of Eddie Bauer and Scandinavian design. There are kitchenettes, plush beds with lots of pillows, and, in the bathrooms, showers with double shower heads. If showering together isn't romantic enough for you, there's a hot tub tucked down a garden path. Also on the property is a deluxe tents-only campground.

555 Fisherman Bay Rd., Lopez Island, WA 98261. © 800/440-3556. www.lopezfarmcottages.com. 4 units. $99–$150 double. Tent sites (available May–Oct) $28 double. Cottage rates include continental breakfast. MC, V. **Amenities:** Jacuzzi. *In room:* Kitchenette, coffeemaker.

Lopez Islander *Kids* Located about a mile south of Lopez Village, the Lopez Islander may not look too impressive from the outside, but it's a very comfortable lodging. All the rooms have great views of Fisherman Bay, and most rooms have balconies. The more expensive rooms also have coffeemakers, wet bars, microwaves, and refrigerators. In addition to amenities listed below, the Islander also has a full-service marina with kayak rentals.

Fisherman Bay Rd. (P.O. Box 459), Lopez Island, WA 98261. © 800/736-3434 or 360/468-2233. Fax 360/468-3382. www.lopezislander.com. 28 units. July–Sept $79.50–$139.50 double, $200–$260 suite; lower rates Oct–June. AE, DISC, MC, V. **Amenities:** Restaurant (American); lounge; outdoor pool; exercise room; Jacuzzi; bike rentals; children's center; coin-op laundry. *In room:* TV, fridge.

MacKaye Harbor Inn This home was originally built in 1904 and was the first home on the island to have electric lights. Since that time this old house has gone through quite a few incarnations, but is today a very comfortable B&B with classic country B&B styling and plenty of modern creature comforts besides electric lights. Located down at the south end of the island, this big white farmhouse is set on a pretty little stretch of flat beach. With kayaks for rent and the calm water of MacKaye Harbor right across the road, this is a good place to give sea kayaking a try. There are also bikes available for guests, which makes this a good choice for an active vacation.

949 MacKaye Harbor Rd., Lopez Island, WA 98261. © 888/314-6140 or 360/468-2253. Fax 360/468-2393. www.mackayeharborinn.com. 5 units. $99–$175 double. 2-night minimum weekends and holidays. Rates include full breakfast. MC, V. **Amenities:** Bikes; sea-kayak rentals/instruction. *In room:* Hair dryer.

CAMPGROUNDS

Spencer Spit State Park (© 360/468-2251) is the island's largest and best campground. This park has 35 campsites set amid tall fir trees. For reservations, contact **Reservations Northwest** (© 800/452-5687). There are also campsites at **Odlin County Park** (© 360/468-2496 for information, or 360/378-1842 for reservations, which are taken noon–4pm Mon–Fri), which is just south of the ferry landing and has 30 campsites along the water. Athletic fields make this more of a community sports center than a natural area. Tent campsites are also available at the privately owned **Lopez Farm Cottages and Tent Camping**, 555 Fisherman Bay Rd. (© 800/440-3556; www.lopezfarmcottages.com), which has 10 walk-in campsites about 2½ miles (4km) south of the ferry landing. These campsites have a very private feel, and both showers and a covered cooking area are provided. This campground is open May through October. Campsites are $28 per night for one or two people, and campers must be 14 or older.

WHERE TO DINE

When it's time for coffee, you'll find the island's best in Lopez Village at **Caffé Verdi,** Lopez Plaza (© 360/468-2257); and right next door, you'll find divinely decadent pastries and other baked goods at **Holly B's Bakery** (© 360/468-2133). Across the street, in Lopez Island Pharmacy, you'll find the old-fashioned **Lopez Island Soda Fountain** (© 360/468-2616).

Bay Café NORTHWEST/INTERNATIONAL Housed in an eclectically decorated old waterfront commercial building with a deck that overlooks

Fisherman Bay, the Bay Café serves some of the best food in the state. This is the sort of place where diners animatedly discuss what that other flavor is in the savory cheesecake with macadamia-cilantro pesto, where the dipping sauces with the pork satay are unlike anything you've ever tasted before, and where people walk through the door and exclaim, "I want whatever it is that smells so good." The menu, though short, spans the globe and changes frequently. Come with a hearty appetite; meals include soup and salad, and the desserts are absolutely to die for (imagine velvety pumpkin crème caramel decorated with a nasturtium flower and candied ginger). Accompany your meal with a bottle of wine from Lopez Island Vineyards for the quintessential Lopez dinner.

Village Center, Lopez Village. ✆ 360/468-3700. Reservations highly recommended. Main courses $8–$15 at lunch, $15–$28 at dinner. AE, DISC, MC, V. Summer daily 3:30–9pm; hr. vary other months.

Bucky's ⭐ AMERICAN   With a laid-back island feeling and an outside water-front deck, this tiny place is where the locals hang out. The food, though simple, is consistently good—nothing fancy, just delicious. The black-and-blue burger with blue cheese and Cajun spices definitely gets our vote for best burger in the islands. If you're feeling more like seafood, there are fish tacos and fish and chips.

Lopez Village Plaza. ✆ 360/468-2595. Reservations taken for parties of 5 or more only. Main courses $5–$15. MC, V. Apr–Sept Sun–Thurs 11:30am–8:30pm; Fri–Sat 11:30am–9pm; usually closed other months.

SHAW ISLAND

Shaw Island is the least developed of the four San Juan Islands served by regular ferries. Most San Juan visitors know Shaw Island only as the island where the nuns run the ferry dock. In addition to having a convent, the island is home to a few hundred tranquillity-loving residents who like the solitude of the island and want to keep it undeveloped. If you enjoy leisurely drives (or bike rides) in the country, Shaw Island makes a good day trip from any of the other three islands. However, there are no hotels, B&Bs, or restaurants, only a general store at the ferry landing and one small county park down at the south end of the island. The park, **Shaw Island County Park** (✆ 360/378-1842), does, how-ever, have a small campground (that takes summer reservations) and is popular with sea kayakers. Reservations can be made up to 90 days in advance.

THE OTHER SAN JUAN ISLANDS: SEA-KAYAK TRIPS & CHARTER BOAT CRUISES

If you want to explore some of the other 168 islands that are not served by the ferries, you'll need a boat. Sailboats, powerboats, and sea kayaks are all popular vessels for exploring these other San Juans, and during the summer months, these waters are full of vessels of all shapes and sizes. Although many of the islands are private property, a few are, or have on them, state parks with campsites. If you want to find out about these marine parks, contact the **Washington State Parks Information Center** (✆ 360/902-8844; www.parks.wa.gov). Those without their own boat can still visit some of these islands either on a multiday kayak tour or on a charter boat cruise.

See "The Active Vacation Planner," in chapter 2, "Planning Your Trip to Washington," for information on companies offering multiday sea-kayak tours in the San Juan Islands.

Charter boats, both motorboats and sailboats, can also be hired for multiday cruises around the San Juan Islands. This is the easiest (though not the cheapest) way to see some of these outer islands. Anchoring in secluded coves, exploring marine parks, scanning the skies for bald eagles, spying on orcas, porpoises, and

Know Before You Go

If you're considering adding Victoria or Vancouver, British Columbia, to your travel plans, be sure you have the necessary documents to make the trip across the border and back. U.S. citizens born in the United States need to carry two pieces of ID, one of which needs to be a picture ID such as a driver's license or passport. The other ID can be a credit card, birth certificate, or voter's registration. If you are not a citizen of the U.S. or Canada, you need to carry your passport and valid visa (if you needed a visa to enter the country). For naturalized U.S. citizens (those not born in the U.S.), a passport or certificate of naturalization is required. Children traveling with both parents must have a birth certificate. Children traveling with only one parent should have both a birth certificate and, from the other parent, a notarized letter of permission to leave the country.

sea lions, these are the activities that make a charter cruise through the San Juans such a memorable experience.

During the summer, **Viking Cruises** (© 360/466-2639; www.vikingcruises.com) operates 3-day/2-night San Juan cruises that overnight at Rosario Resort on Orcas Island. Rates are $465 to $514 per person, and though the trips are usually booked by groups, individuals can often find space on these cruises. Cruises of from 5 to 8 days are offered by **Fantasy Cruises** (© 800/234-3861 or 360/378-1874; www.sanjuanislandcruises.com). These cruises, aboard a small cruise ship that carries only 34 passengers, stop not only in the San Juans, but at other picturesque area ports including La Conner and Port Townsend.

Boats can also be chartered through **Anacortes Yacht Charters** (© 800/233-3004 or 360/293-4555; www.ayc.com), which has more than 100 boats in its fleet (half powerboats and half sailboats).

4 La Conner & the Skagit Valley

70 miles (113km) N of Seattle, 10 miles (16km) E of Anacortes, 32 miles (52km) S of Bellingham

In a competition for quaintest town in Washington, La Conner would leave the other contenders wallowing in the winter mud. This town, a former fishing village, has a waterfront street lined with restored wooden commercial buildings, back streets of Victorian homes, and acres of tulip and daffodil fields stretching out from the town limits. Add to this three museums (including the Museum of Northwest Art and a quilting museum), numerous plant nurseries and gardening related stores, art galleries, luxurious inns, and good restaurants, and you have a town almost too good to be true.

La Conner does, however, have a couple of shortcomings. In the springtime, when the tulips blossom, the town and surrounding country roads are so jammed with cars that it can make a Seattle rush hour commute seem pleasant. The other drawback is that La Conner is so close to the San Juans that it is hard to justify spending more than a day here when the islands are calling. If, however, you have some free time in your schedule, this town should not be missed.

La Conner dates from a time when Puget Sound towns were connected by water and not by road, and consequently, the town clings to the shore of Swinomish Channel. The town reached a commercial peak around 1900 (when steamers made the run to Seattle) and continued as an important grain- and log-shipping port until the Great Depression. La Conner never recovered from the hard times of the 1930s, and when the highways bypassed the town it became a neglected backwater. The wooden false-fronted buildings built during the town's heyday were spared the waves of progress that swept over the Northwest during the latter half of the 20th century, and today these quaint old buildings give the town its charm.

Beginning in the 1940s, La Conner's picturesque setting attracted several artists and writers. By the 1970s, La Conner had become known as an artists' community (Tom Robbins wrote about the area in his novel *Another Roadside Attraction*), and tourism began to revive the economy. The town's artistic legacy eventually led to the building here of the Museum of Northwest Art, dedicated to the region's many contemporary artists.

Adding still more color to this vibrant little town are the commercial flower farms of the surrounding Skagit Valley. In the spring, tulips and daffodils carpet the surrounding farmlands with great swaths of red, yellow, and white. These flowers are grown to supply the fall bulb planting needs of gardeners across the country, and heartbreaking as it sounds, the flowers are cut off in their prime to channel more energy into the bulbs.

One more thing, although the name sounds as if it's a combination of Spanish and Irish, La Conner is actually named for Louisa A. (LA) Conner, who helped found the town in the 1870s.

ESSENTIALS

GETTING THERE   From I-5, take U.S. 20 west toward Anacortes. La Conner is south of U.S. 20 on La Conner–Whitney Road. Alternatively, take exit 221 off I-5 and head west on Fir Island Road to a left onto Chilberg Road, which leads into La Conner.

The **Airporter Shuttle** (✆ **866/235-5247** or 360/380-8800; www.airporter. com) operates between Sea-Tac Airport and the Anacortes ferry terminal, stopping at the Farmhouse Inn, which is at the junction of Wash. 20 and La Conner–Whitney Road, north of La Conner ($30 one-way, $53 round-trip).

VISITOR INFORMATION   Contact the **La Conner Chamber of Commerce,** 413-A Morris St. (P.O. Box 1610), La Conner, WA 98257 (✆ **888/ 642-9284** or 360/466-4778; www.laconnerchamber.com).

GETTING AROUND   Public transit in Skagit County is provided free of charge on **SKAT** (✆ **360/757-4433;** www.skat.org) buses, which make stops in La Conner, Anacortes, and Mount Vernon among other places.

FESTIVALS   In addition to the Skagit Valley Tulip Festival (see below), La Conner celebrates its artistic heritage with the **Art's Alive!** festival on the first weekend in November.

For a few short weeks each year, from late March to mid-April, the countryside around La Conner is awash with color as hundreds of acres of Skagit Valley tulip and daffodil fields burst into bloom in a floral display that rivals that of the Netherlands. These flowers are grown for their bulbs, which each fall are shipped to gardeners all over the world. The **Skagit Valley Tulip Festival** (✆ **360/ 428-5959;** www.tulipfestival.org), held each year during bloom time, is La Conner's biggest annual festival and includes dozens of events. Contact the festival office or stop by the La Conner Chamber of Commerce (see above), for a scenic tour map of the flower fields. On festival weekends area roads are clogged with cars, so you should consider opting to ride the Tulip Transit buses that loop through the flower fields. Contact the festival office to find out about these buses.

Whether you're here in tulip time or not, you might want to stop by some of the area's farms, gardens, and nurseries. **Roozengaarde Flowers & Bulbs,** 15867 Beaver Marsh Rd. (© **800/732-3266** or 360/424-8531; www.tulips. com), is the largest grower of tulips, daffodils, and irises in the country and has a gift shop open. At **Christianson's Nursery & Greenhouse,** 15806 Best Rd. (© **360/466-3821**), you'll find more than 600 varieties of roses and lots of other plants as well. Both of these nurseries are northeast of town off McLean Road (the main road to Mount Vernon). Back in town, there's the **Tillinghast Seed Company,** 623 Morris St. (© **800/466-3329** or 360/466-3329), which is the oldest seed company in the Northwest and now includes a country store, nursery, gardening supply store, and florist.

EXPLORING LA CONNER & ITS ENVIRONS

The Museum of Northwest Art ★★, 121 S. First St. (© **360/466-4446;** www. museumofnwart.org), occupies a large contemporary building in downtown La Conner. The museum, which mounts a variety of exhibits throughout the year, features works by Northwest artists, including Morris Graves, Mark Tobey, and Guy Anderson, all of whom once worked in La Conner. This museum would be right at home in downtown Seattle, so it comes as a very pleasant surprise to find it in this tiny town. It's open Tuesday through Sunday from 10am to 5pm; admission is $3.

High atop a hill in the center of town, you can learn about the history of this area at the **Skagit County Historical Museum,** 501 S. Fourth St. (© **360/ 466-3365;** www.skagitcounty.net/museum.htm). It's open Tuesday through Sunday from 11am to 5pm; admission is $2 for adults, $1 for seniors and children ages 6 to 12, free for children 5 and under. A few blocks away, you'll find the **La Conner Quilt Museum,** 703 S. Second St. (© **360/466-4288;** www. laconnerquilts.com), which is housed in the historic Gaches Mansion. On the first floor of this museum, you'll find rooms furnished with turn-of-the-20th-century antiques, while on the second floor there are quilt displays. The museum is open Wednesday through Saturday from 11am to 4pm and Sunday from noon to 4pm; admission is $4. Two blocks down the street from the Gaches Mansion is the much less pretentious **Magnus Anderson Cabin,** built in 1869 by the area's first white settler. Beside the cabin is the **La Conner Town Hall,** which is housed in a triangular bank building that was built in 1886. Across the street from these two buildings is **Totem Pole Park,** which in addition to having a totem pole, has a dugout canoe carved by local Swinomish artisans, whose reservation is just across the Swinomish Channel.

There is excellent bird-watching around the Skagit Valley, especially during the winter months when migratory waterfowl, including trumpeter swans and snow geese, and various raptors, including peregrine falcons and bald eagles, flock to the area's marshes, bays, and farm fields. Eight miles north of La Conner at the **Padilla Bay National Estuarine Research Reserve and Breazeale Interpretive Center,** 10441 Bayview-Edison Rd. (© **360/428-1558**), you can bird-watch along 3 miles (5km) of trails through fields and along a dike. Interpretive exhibits explain the importance of estuaries and allow visitors to explore life in Padilla Bay and its salt marshes. The reserve is open daily; the interpretive center, Wednesday through Sunday from 10am to 5pm. Admission is free. The Skagit Wildlife Area, south of La Conner and west of Conway, is another good winter birding area.

From May through September, **Viking Cruises,** 109 N. First St. (© **360/ 466-2639;** www.vikingcruises.com), offers 5- to 7-hour whale-watching cruises that usually turn up plenty of orca whales. Tours are $59 for adults and $49 for children ages 6 to 12.

Shopping is the most popular pastime in La Conner, and as you wander up and down First Street, stop in at **The Wood Merchant,** 709 S. First St. (✆ **360/ 466-4741**), which features handcrafted wooden furniture and accent pieces; and **Earthenworks Gallery,** 713 S. First St. (✆ **360/466-4422**), which has fine crafts in ceramic, glass, wood, and other media. Other interesting shops include **Two Moons,** 620 S. First St. (✆ **360/466-1920**), a gallery featuring regional art and fine crafts; and **Caravan Gallery,** 619 S. First St. (✆ **360/466-4808**), which sells fascinating crafts and jewelry from around the world.

If you are heading north to Bellingham, consider driving the scenic Chuckanut Drive, which begins about 15 miles north of La Conner. For details on this beautiful stretch of road, see "Chuckanut Drive," in "Bellingham & Environs," below.

WHERE TO STAY

La Conner Channel Lodge ★★ Luxurious accommodations, Northwest styling, and views of Swinomish Channel from all but seven of the rooms make this a truly memorable lodge. A flagstone entry and woodsy garden, cedar-shake siding, and a river-rock fireplace in the lobby set the tone for the rest of the lodge, and the lobby, with its small library alcove, has a the sort of nautical feel you'd expect to find in a home built 100 years ago by a ship's captain. Most guest rooms are large and all have small balconies and gas fireplaces. Fir accents and a combination of slate flooring and carpeting give the rooms a natural richness. Fireplaces make the rooms cozy and romantic, and there are tiny balconies overlooking the channel.

205 N. First St., La Conner, WA 98257. ✆ **888/466-4113** or 360/466-1500. Fax 360/466-1525. www. laconnerlodging.com. 40 units. Apr–Sept $165–$255 double; Oct–Mar $130–$190 double. Rates include continental breakfast. AE, DC, DISC, MC, V. *In room:* TV, fridge, coffeemaker, hair dryer, iron.

La Conner Country Inn ★★ Under the same management as the La Conner Channel Lodge, the Country Inn is a much more casual, folksy sort of place. Although it's also in downtown La Conner, it's set back a block from the water and lacks much in the way of views. However, if you can do without the water views, you'll save a bundle on your room bill. The exterior of the inn gives the impression that this is a mountain lodge, though the interior is more modern country inn than classic mountain lodge. In the cozy lobby there's a huge stone fireplace, and every guest room also has its own fireplace. The second floor rooms have high, beamed ceilings, for that rustic country inn feel. Although the rooms are fairly large, the furnishings are quite basic. Room 28 has the feel of a separate cottage and is worth requesting.

107 S. Second St., La Conner, WA 98257. ✆ 360/466-3101. Fax 360/466-5902. www.laconnerlodging.com. 28 units. Apr–Sept $99–$130 double; Oct–Mar $92–$112 double. Rates include continental breakfast. AE, DC, DISC, MC, V. Pets accepted with $25 fee. **Amenities:** Restaurant (International), pub. *In room:* TV.

White Swan Guest House ★ If you're here for the tulip blossoms or if you're a gardener, make this your first choice. Located out in the country, this yellow Victorian farmhouse is set beneath ancient poplar trees and is surrounded by stunning perennial gardens. Of the guest rooms in the main house, we like the one with the turret, though all are comfortable enough. For more space and privacy, opt for the rustic little cottage set on the far side of the gardens. Peter Goldfarb, the owner, bakes up some of the best chocolate chip cookies around.

15872 Moore Rd., Mount Vernon, WA 98273-7139. www.thewhiteswan.com. ℂ 360/445-6805. 4 units, 1 (cottage) with private bathroom. $75–$85 double; $135–$160 cottage. Rates include country-continental breakfast. MC, V. *In room:* No phone.

The Wild Iris ★★ The Wild Iris is a modern Victorian inn on the edge of town, and most second floor rooms have views of distant Mount Baker (these rooms are definitely worth asking for). The inn was designed for romantic week-ends, and many of the rooms have double whirlpool tubs. In some the whirlpool tub is in the room, while in others it's on the balcony. Tuesday through Satur-day, dinner is also available ($18–$25 for entrees) in the inn's small dining room, which serves up some of the best meals in town. This is a good bet for a roman-tic getaway.

121 Maple Ave. (P.O. Box 696), La Conner, WA 98257. ℂ 800/477-1400 or 360/466-1400. Fax 360/466-1221. www.wildiris.com. 19 units. $95–$115 double; $120–$180 suite. Rates include full breakfast. AE, MC, V. **Amenities:** Restaurant (Northwest); concierge. *In room:* TV, dataport.

WHERE TO DINE

If it's baked goodies you need, stop by **Georgia's Bakery,** 109 N. First St. (ℂ **360/466-2149**), in the Lime Dock Building.

Kerstin's ★★ NORTHWEST It seems the best restaurants rarely have the best views, and Kerstin's is no exception. Located in a tall, narrow building across the street from the water, this contemporary restaurant and wine bar focuses on good food rather than waterside views. While it looks from the street as though this restaurant only has a couple of tables, you'll find a larger dining room on the second floor. The local Samish Bay oysters, whether pan-fried or baked on the half shell, should not be missed. You'll also find plenty of other well-prepared local seafood, including smoked salmon (perhaps in puff pastry). Lamb shanks, prepared various ways, also show up regularly on the menu.

505 S. First St. ℂ 360/466-9111. Reservations recommended. Main courses $9–$12 at lunch, $17–$29 at dinner. AE, DC, MC, V. Wed–Mon noon–9pm.

La Conner Brewing Company ★ *Finds* PIZZAS/PUB FARE If you eschew tourist haunts when it comes time to dine, then you might want to check out the menu at this stylish modern pub. A favorite of the locals, the pub lacks water views but more than makes up for this with its excellent beers and creative pub fare. While pizzas are the main beer accompaniment here, there are also inter-esting panini (Italian sandwiches), quesadillas (including one with smoked salmon), and good Caesar salads.

117 S. First St. ℂ **360/466-1415.** www.laconnerbrewing.com. Main courses $6–$11. MC, V. Daily 11:30am–10pm.

Palmer's ★★ INTERNATIONAL Some of La Conner's finest meals are to be had at Palmer's, a cozy little restaurant attached to the La Conner Country Inn. In the dining room, elegant furnishings are a contrast to the rustic, mountain-lodge styling. The menu here is essentially traditional gourmet (escargot, French onion soup, beef tenderloin with Bordelaise sauce) with an occasional contem-porary twist thrown in (pan-fried oysters with chipotle aioli). For less expensive meals in a casual atmosphere, you can dine in the pub, which is a good rendition of a cramped 19th-century English pub. Here you'll find a few of the menu items from the main restaurant plus gourmet renditions of traditional pub fare.

La Conner Country Inn, 205 E. Washington Ave. ℂ 360/466-4261. Reservations recommended. Main courses $19–$29; pub entrees $7–$14. AE, MC, V. Mon–Thurs 4–10pm; Fri 4–11pm; Sat 11:30am–11pm; Sun 11:30am–10pm.

5 Bellingham & Environs

90 miles (145km) N of Seattle, 60 miles (97km) S of Vancouver

Perhaps best known outside of Washington state as the southern terminus for ferries and cruise ships heading north to Alaska, Bellingham is a vibrant little city due in large part to the presence of Western Washington University. Still an active shipping port, Bellingham enjoys excellent views across Puget Sound to the San Juan Islands, and at Squalicum Harbor there's a large commercial and private boat marina, a hotel and commercial complex, and a park that together provide residents and visitors with a chance to enjoy the bay. South of downtown Bellingham, near the Alaska ferry terminal, is the historic community of Fairhaven, which was once a separate town but which has now been incorporated into the greater Bellingham metro area. Fairhaven's old brick commercial buildings and interesting shops are a highlight of a visit to Bellingham.

Whatcom County, which extends from the coast to the top of 10,778-foot Mount Baker and beyond, is still, however, primarily a rural area. Near the coast, farming predominates, and several nearby farm towns are worth visiting for a glimpse of local history and a chance to explore the countryside. Mount Baker itself is a popular downhill skiing and snowboarding area in winter, while in summer hiking trails lead through meadows and forest. South of the city the mountains rise up from the waters of the sound along one of Washington's most scenic stretches of coastline. Winding along this coastline is Chuckanut Drive, which provides glimpses of spectacular coastline and the San Juan Islands.

ESSENTIALS

GETTING THERE   I-5 connects Bellingham with Seattle to the south and Vancouver to the north. Wash. 542, the North Cascades Scenic Highway, connects Bellingham with eastern Washington by way of Winthrop.

Bellingham International Airport, 5 miles (8km) northwest of downtown Bellingham, is served by Horizon Airlines and United Express. The **Airporter Shuttle** (✆ **866/235-5247** or 360/380-8800; www.airporter.com) runs between Sea-Tac Airport, Bellingham ($32 one-way, $55 round-trip). Between April and October, **San Juan Island Shuttle Express,** Bellingham Cruise Terminal, 335 Harris Ave. (✆ **888/373-8522;** www.orcawhales.com), operates passenger ferry service to Friday Harbor on San Juan Island, Lieber Haven Resort on Orcas Island, and Odlin County Park on Lopez Island. The round-trip fare is $33 for adults, $29 for seniors, and $27 for students and children.

Both **Amtrak** trains and **Greyhound** buses stop in Bellingham at the Fairhaven Station, which is adjacent to the Bellingham Cruise Terminal on Harris Avenue in the Fairhaven district.

VISITOR INFORMATION   Contact the **Bellingham/Whatcom County Convention & Visitors Bureau,** 904 Potter St., Bellingham, WA 98226 (✆ **800/487-2032** or 360/671-3990; www.bellingham.org), which is located just east of I-5 at exit 253. On the Internet, check out http://whatcom.kulshan.com, which is filled with great information on the area.

GETTING AROUND   Rental cars are available at Bellingham International Airport from Avis, Budget, Hertz, and National. If you need a taxi, contact **Yellow Cab** (✆ **360/734-8294**). Public bus service around the Bellingham area is provided by the **Whatcom Transportation Authority** (✆ **360/676-7433;** www.ridewta.com).

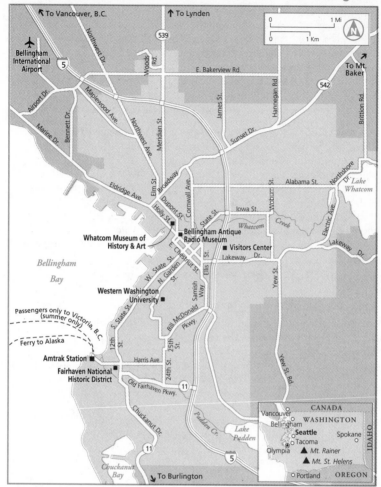

WHAT TO SEE & DO
MUSEUMS

If your interest is art, you shouldn't miss the **Western Washington University Outdoor Sculpture Collection,** off the Bill McDonald Parkway south of downtown. With more than 20 large sculptures, including one by Isamu Noguchi, this is the largest collection of monumental sculptures on the West Coast. You can pick up a map and guide to the collection at Bellingham/Watcom County Convention & Visitors Bureau or at the university's visitor center or the **Western Gallery** (© 360/650-3900), which is also on the campus and features exhibits of contemporary art. When the university is in session, the gallery is open Monday, Tuesday, Thursday, and Friday from 10am to 4pm, Wednesday from 10am to 8pm, and Saturday from noon to 4pm.

Bellingham Antique Radio Museum ★★ These days MP3s, CDs, and DVDs are so much a part of everyday life that it is easy to forget that sound recording is barely 100 years old. At this not-to-be-missed museum in downtown Bellingham, you can examine more than 800 antique radios (mostly pre-1930s wooden table-top models) and lots of other unusual instruments of early electrical technology. Among the displays is a mock-up of the radio room from the *Titanic,* and if you're lucky, curator Jonathon Winter might demonstrate the Tesla coil, which can generate enough electricity to light up a fluorescent light several feet away.

1316 Bay St. ⓒ 360/671-4663. www.antique-radio.org. Free admission. Wed–Sat noon–4pm.

Whatcom Museum of History and Art ★★ This museum is housed in the former city hall building, which was built in 1892 and is one of Washington's finest examples of Victorian municipal architecture. Inside you'll find reconstructions of old stores from early-20th-century Bellingham, and a variety of exhibits on area history. You'll also find a large collection of Native American baskets, and exhibits focusing on Northwest artists. Up on the museum's third floor you'll find old toys, tools, and fashions. A building across the street houses the gift shop and a gallery that often is used for unusual art installations. A block away, in the city's old fire hall, you'll find a photo archive and more historical exhibits.

121 Prospect St. ⓒ 360/676-6981. www.whatcommuseum.org. Admission by donation. Tues–Sun noon–5pm.

FAIRHAVEN HISTORIC DISTRICT

Though downtown Bellingham has a fair number of restaurants and a few galleries, the **Fairhaven Historic District** is the most interesting neighborhood in town (and is also the site of the Bellingham Cruise Terminal, the southern terminus for ferries to Alaska). Fairhaven was once a separate town, and many of its brick buildings, built between 1880 and 1900, have now been restored and house interesting shops, art galleries, and several good restaurants. Around the neighborhood, you'll find more than two dozen historical markers, many of which commemorate the seamier side of life in Fairhaven in the 1890s.

Today, **Village Books,** 1210 11th St. (ⓒ **360/671-2626**), serves as the cultural anchor for the neighborhood and has frequent readings and book signings. **Artwood,** 1000 Harris Ave. (ⓒ **360/647-1628**), a cooperative gallery filled with beautiful woodcraft, is one of the most interesting shops in the neighborhood. Right next door is **Good Earth Pottery,** 1000 Harris Ave. (ⓒ **360/671-3998**), which is full of unusual and unique pottery pieces. Across the street, you'll find **Mud in Your Eye,** 911 Harris Ave. (ⓒ **360/650-9007**), another big pottery store. Also worth visiting is **Gallery West,** 1300 12th St. (ⓒ **360/734-8414**), which carries fine crafts and art by regional artists. Here in Fairhaven, you'll also find several cafes and bakeries and even an old double-decker British bus that serves fish and chips.

CHUCKANUT DRIVE

Chuckanut Drive (Wash. 11), which begins on the southern edge of the Fairhaven Historic District and heads south for almost a dozen miles to the Samish farmlands, is one of the most scenic stretches of road in northwestern Washington. The road clings to the shoreline of Chuckanut and Samish bays as it winds south through the Chuckanut Mountains, which rise straight out of the water. Though most of the way is through dense woods, there are several pull-offs where you can gaze out to the San Juan Islands or up and down this rugged section of coastline. There are also numerous trail heads that allow you head

Factoid

Although it is part of Washington state, the community of Point Roberts can only be reached by first driving into Canada (unless, of course, you have your own boat). This odd situation came about when the boundary between Canada and the United States was established. A peninsula in Canada extended so far south that it extended south of the border, making Point Roberts U.S. territory.

down to the shore or up into the Chuckanut Mountains, which are home to an extensive network of hiking and mountain biking trails. Chuckanut Drive is particularly popular at sunset, and there are several good restaurants at the southern end of the drive (see "Where to Dine," below).

At the northern end of the drive, be sure to stop in at the **Chuckanut Bay Gallery and Garden Shop,** 700 Chuckanut Dr. (© **360/734-4885**), which is full of interesting artworks by Northwest artists and craftspeople. Continuing south, watch for the **North Chuckanut Mountain Trail Head,** which provides access to **Teddy Bear Cove** , where you'll find a pair of tiny beaches separated by a small, rocky promontory. It's about a 2-mile (3km) round-trip hike to the cove. Although part of the trail is quite steep, part of the route follows the **Interurban Trail** , a 6-mile-long (10km) hiking and mountain-biking trail that follows the route of an old trolley line and extends from Fairhaven Parkway and 20th Street in Fairhaven to **Larrabee State Park** (© **360/676-2093**). This latter park is the most popular stop along Chuckanut Drive and can be quite crowded in summer. However, the pretty little beach and access to miles of hiking trails make this a required stop along the scenic drive.

OTHER ATTRACTIONS AND ACTIVITIES

If you're a fan of riding the rails, check the schedule of the **Lake Whatcom Railway** (© **360/595-2218**), which operates a historic excursion train from the town of Wickersham southeast of Bellingham. There are Saturday and Tuesday trips from early July to early September, as well as runs in October and December. Along the route, you'll get occasional glimpses of Mount Baker. The trips last 1½ hours and the fare is $10 for adults and $5 for children under age 18.

If you'd like to do some whale-watching in the San Juan Islands, contact **San Juan Island Shuttle Express,** Bellingham Cruise Terminal, 355 Harris Ave. (© **888/373-8522** or 360/671-1137; www.orcawhales.com), which charges $65 for adults, $60 for seniors, and $55 for students and children. To explore Chuckanut Bay from a sea kayak, contact **Moondance Sea Kayak Adventures** (© **360/738-7664;** www.moondancekayak.com), which offers half-day ($40 per person) and full-day ($70 per person) excursions that start at Larrabee State Park.

WHERE TO STAY

Hotel Bellwether on Bellingham Bay   This new hotel is the centerpiece of the new Squalicum Harbor waterfront development, which also includes several restaurants, shops, a marina, and grassy Zuanich Park. The marina setting seems to have served as the design theme for this hotel, which has a distinct yacht club feel. Dark wood paneling abounds, and a traditional styling predominates. Guest rooms are large and have soaking tubs (for one person), fireplaces, and balconies. The hotel's most unusual room is a three-story "lighthouse" suite that was designed to resemble a lighthouse and has a viewing deck on its third floor. This hotel lacks much in the way of Northwest character and seems designed to appeal to an older and more conservative crowd than the nearby Chrysalis.

1 Bellwether Way, Bellingham, WA 98225. © **877/411-1200** or 360/392-3100. Fax 360/392-3101. www. hotelbellwether.com. 68 units. May–Oct 159–$229 double, $189–$699 suite; Nov–Apr $99–$159 double, $129–$499 suite. Rates include continental breakfast. AE, DISC, MC, V. Parking $5. **Amenities:** Restaurant (Northwest); lounge; putting green; exercise room; room service; massage; laundry service; dry cleaning. *In room:* A/C, TV, dataport, minibar, coffeemaker, hair dryer, iron, safe.

The Chrysalis Inn & Spa at the Pier ★★ *Finds*   The Chrysalis is the most luxurious hotel in Bellingham, and, with its contemporary lodge styling, perfectly captures the essence of the Northwest today. In the lobby, big walls of glass focus the attention on the waters of Bellingham Bay, but the slate floors, burnished wood beams, and fireplace all give the views some stiff competition. Guest rooms all have water views and are designed both for romantic getaways and for business travel. Double tubs, gas fireplaces, and window seats (complete with pillow and comforter) make these rooms the ideal place to hide away on a rainy Northwest weekend. To make a getaway even better, there is a full-service spa and a boldly styled wine bar serving good Mediterranean meals. About the only drawback to this inn is the presence of a railroad track between the inn and the water. However, excellent insulation keep the train noises to a minimum and earplugs are provided free of charge.

804 10th St., Bellingham, WA 98225. © **888/808-0005** or 360/756-1005. www.thechrysalisinn.com. 43 units. July–Sept $169–$180 double, $209–$299 suite; Oct–June $149–$169 double, $189–$279 suite. Rates include full breakfast. AE, DISC, MC, V. **Amenities:** Restaurant (Mediterranean); lounge; full service spa; concierge; room service; massage; laundry service; dry cleaning. *In room:* A/C, TV/VCR, dataport, minibar, coffeemaker, hair dryer, iron.

Fairhaven Village Inn ★★   Although this hotel in the heart of Fairhaven was only recently constructed, it was designed to resemble an old hotel and blends in quite well with the adjacent historic buildings. There's even a cashier's cage for a front desk. Guest rooms are, however, quite modern and are tastefully traditional in their decor and furnishings. While the balcony rooms, which also have fireplaces, are the most luxurious rooms, they really aren't worth the additional cost since they only look out on adjacent rooftops (with the bay in the distance). The location amid Fairhaven's shops and restaurants and only a few blocks from the Alaska ferry terminal makes this one of Bellingham's best hotel choices.

1200 Tenth St., Bellingham, WA 98225. © **877/733-1100** or 360/733-1311. Fax 360/756-2797. www.nw countryinns.com. 22 units. Summer $139–$159 double; other months $109–$159 double. Rates include continental breakfast. AE, DC, DISC, MC, V. Pets accepted with $20 fee per night. *In room:* A/C, TV, dataport, coffeemaker, hair dryer, iron.

North Garden Inn ★   Located about midway between downtown Bellingham and Fairhaven, this B&B is in an elaborate Victorian home built in 1897. The inn sits high above the street, up a winding flight of stairs, and from many of the rooms there are excellent views of the bay. The decor here is very simple, not the usual Victorian excess so often found in such B&Bs. All in all, the feeling is more that of a simple homestay in Europe. It's popular with professors visiting nearby Western Washington University.

1014 N. Garden St., Bellingham, WA 98225. © **800/922-6414** or 360/671-7828. http://northgardeninn. com/ngi. 10 units, 8 with private bathroom. $60 double with shared bathroom, $89–$124 double with private bathroom. Rates include full breakfast. AE, DISC, MC, V. *In room:* No phone.

NEARBY ACCOMMODATIONS

Resort Semiahmoo ★★★   Located on 1,100 acres at the end of a long sandy spit that reaches almost to Canada, Resort Semiahmoo is, despite the remote location, Washington's premier golf resort and health spa. Gables and gray shingles give the resort a timeless look, and throughout the classically styled interior of the main lodge are numerous lounges overlooking the water. Artwork abounds, with Native American and nautical themes prevailing. Not all guest rooms have views, but those that do, have beds facing out to sea. The main dining room overlooks the water and offers excellent Northwest-style meals and an extensive wine list. There's also an oyster bar and lounge in an old salmon-packing plant. In addition to amenities listed below, the resort has a marina and paved bike and running paths. Very popular with Canadians.

9565 Semiahmoo Pkwy., Blaine, WA 98230-9326. (€) 800/770-7992 or 360/318-2000. www.semiahmoo. com. 198 units. May–Sept $119–$259 double, $269–$399 suite; Oct–Apr $99–$199 double, $239–$319 suite (all rates plus $3 resort fee). AE, DC, DISC, MC, V. Pets accepted with $50 fee per stay. **Amenities:** 3 restaurants (Northwest, American); lounge; indoor and outdoor pool; 2 18-hole golf courses; 7 tennis courts; health club and exercise room; spa; Jacuzzi; sauna; bike rentals; children's programs; game room; concierge; room service; massage; babysitting; laundry service; dry cleaning. *In room:* A/C, TV, dataport, fridge, coffeemaker, hair dryer, iron.

WHERE TO DINE
IN TOWN

For great coffee, stop in at **Tony's Coffee House,** 1101 Harris Ave. ((€) **360/ 738-4710**), a classic Fairhaven hangout for many years. At downtown's **La Vie en Rose,** 111 W. Holly St. ((€) **360/715-1839**), you can start your day with a French pastry. For regional microbrews, imported beers, and pub fare, try the very atmospheric and traditional **Archer Ale House,** 1212 Tenth St. ((€) **360/ 647-7002**), in a basement in Fairhaven; or, for locally brewed beers, try **Boundary Bay Brewery & Bistro,** 1107 Railroad Ave. ((€) **360/647-5593**), in downtown Bellingham.

Anthony's ★★ SEAFOOD   Just about every waterfront city from Bellingham to Olympia now boasts an outpost of Seattle's popular Anthony's seafood restaurant chain, and for good reason. These places just seem to do things right. This impressive lodgelike waterfront building has big walls of glass overlooking a marina, an open kitchen with an eating bar, a lounge, and a bi-level dining room that assures everyone a water view. Whether you're in the mood for fish and chips or swordfish with orange-tequila glaze, there is always plenty of variety on the menu. However, you can be sure there will be plenty of salmon (the alder-planked preparation is a Northwest classic). Be sure to save room for the delicious blackberry cobbler. Monday through Friday, four-course sunset dinners ($14.95) are served from 4:30 to 6pm.

25 Bellwether Way. (€) 360/647-5588. Reservations recommended. Main courses $8–$13 at lunch, $14–$30 at dinner. AE, DISC, MC, V. Sun–Thurs 11:30am–9:30pm; Fri–Sat 11:30am–10:30pm.

Colophon Café & Deli ★ SOUPS/SANDWICHES   Northwesterners spend a lot of time in bookstores hiding from the rain, so, of necessity, bookstores often provide sustenance. Here at the Colophon, you can chill out with some ice cream in summer, warm up with an espresso in winter, or make a filling meal of the star attractions here—homemade soups. You'll always find African peanut soup on the menu, as well as big sandwiches, quiches, salads, and great homemade desserts. The cafe also has an affiliated adjacent diner for dogs (and people, too).

In Village Books, 1208 11th St. 🄯 360/647-0092. www.colophoncafe.com. Main courses $5–$11. AE, DC, DISC, MC, V. Mon–Sat 9am–10pm; Sun 10am–8pm (summer 10am–10pm).

Pacific Café ★★ NORTHWEST   Located in the Mount Baker Theater building, this romantic little cafe is, of course, the perfect spot for dinner before the show, but it's also a good choice for a flavorful lunch or dinner even if you aren't on your way to a performance. The menu is always eclectic and usually reflects current trends in flavor combinations, but you can be sure you'll find plenty of Asian and Mediterranean influences. The Punjabi chicken curry is always a good bet if you like Indian food, and keep an eye out for the passion-fruit sorbet. Lunches are among the most creative in the city, and many of the same dishes served at dinner are also served at lunch. There's also an excellent wine list.

100 N. Commercial St. 🄯 360/647-0800. Reservations recommended. Main courses $9–$11 at lunch, $15–$23 at dinner. AE, DC, MC, V. Mon–Thurs 11:30am–2pm and 5:30–9pm; Fri 11:30am–2pm and from 5:30pm; Sat from 5:30pm.

ON CHUCKANUT DRIVE

The Oyster Bar ★★ NORTHWEST   Located near the southern end of Chuckanut Drive, this restaurant is the most upscale and formal of the handful of restaurants along the scenic drive. Of course, as the name implies, fresh local oysters are one of the specialties here, but the restaurant also serves up a wide range of imaginative dishes, the likes of which you aren't likely to find on any other area menus (wild boar with wild mushroom gravy, salmon with lemon-garlic caramel sauce, abalone with hazelnuts and lime butter). Of course, there are also great views of Samish Bay and the distant San Juan Islands. If they're on the menu, the house-smoked salmon and oysters shouldn't be missed. Desserts here often feature local fruits and berries, and there is an excellent wine cellar.

2578 Chuckanut Dr. 🄯 360/766-6185. Reservations highly recommended. Main courses $19–$29.50. AE, DISC, MC, V. Daily 5–8:30 or 9pm.

Rhododendron Café ★★ *Finds* NORTHWEST/INTERNATIONAL   Located at the southern end of Chuckanut Drive amid the Samish farmlands, this place looks from the outside like any other farm-country roadside diner. However, take one look at the menu, and you'll find that the farmers in this area are a lucky group. The menu melds creative Northwest cookery with influences from around the world, and each month there are specials from a different part of the world. You might find Vietnamese, Guatemalan, Turkish, or Caribbean food on the menu when you stop by, and these adventurous specials are always worth trying. The regular menu includes lots of local produce, fresh herbs from the restaurant's garden, and oysters from nearby Samish Bay. The casual atmosphere and creative meals are a surprising and very welcome mix.

5521 Chuckanut Dr., Bow. 🄯 360/766-6667. www.rhodycafe.com. Main courses $8–$11 at lunch, $12–$17 at dinner. MC, V. Wed–Fri 11:30am–9pm; Sat–Sun 9am–9pm. Closed Thanksgiving–Jan 1.

BELLINGHAM NIGHTLIFE

The **Mount Baker Theatre,** 104 N. Commercial St. (🄯 **360/733-5793;** www.mtbakertheatre.com), is downtown Bellingham's other major landmark and is the city's premier performing arts venue. The theater's 110-foot-tall light-house tower is visible from all over the city, and though the exterior decor is quite subdued, inside you'll find an extravagant lobby designed to resemble a Spanish galleon.

6

South Puget Sound & West Sound

With more arms than an octopus, the southern reaches of Puget Sound are a region of convoluted waterways, inlets, bays, and harbors. Tucked among the coves, peninsulas, and islands that separate all this salt water are some of Washington's quaintest little towns. Past glacial activity gave this region the look of Scandinavian fjords, and it was that very similarity that more than a century ago attracted Scandinavian fishermen who founded what are today two of the region's most picturesque towns: Poulsbo and Gig Harbor. However, this region is also home to a couple of the state's largest cities—Tacoma and Olympia. While there aren't many major attractions in the area, there is an abundance of natural beauty (with plenty of parks to explore) and, in Tacoma, several interesting museums and attractions as well.

The people who choose to live in this region, as well as those who visit, tend to do so for the water. Forest-ringed waterways, old fishing villages turned yacht havens, idyllic rural settings, the romance of living on an island—these are the aspects of life that attract people to this area. However, down in the southern reaches of the Sound a very different aesthetic

rules. Here are found Tacoma and Olympia. The former, once derided as an industrial wasteland, is in the middle of a renaissance that is turning it into a very livable city. The latter, as the capital of the state and home of a particularly liberal, liberal-arts university, has a mellow, laid-back air and, when the state legislature and the university shut down, becomes one of the quietest cities in the Northwest.

While green forests and blue waters are this region's dominant characteristics, life here is ruled by ferries and bridges, and visitors are advised to keep this in mind as they explore the region. While distances here are not great, missed ferries and traffic backups at the Tacoma Narrows bridge can add significantly to travel time. Leave plenty of room in your travel schedule for unforeseen delays.

However, it is these transportation problems that provide much of the region with its slower pace of life, and that slower pace in turn presents opportunities for Seattleites and others to make quick escapes to the country by simply crossing to the west side of Puget Sound, where island time prevails and the views of the Olympic Mountains are just that much better.

1 Bainbridge Island

10 miles (16km) W of Seattle (by ferry), 35 miles (56km) NE of Bremerton, 46 miles (74km) SE of Port Townsend

Bainbridge Island, popular for its miles of waterfront, sound-and-mountain views, and rural feel, is for the most part an affluent bedroom community for

Seattle. However, with its bustling little downtown area (somewhat reminiscent of tony towns in the San Francisco Bay area), excellent restaurants and B&Bs, many parks, and good bicycling and sea kayaking, it is also a great spot for a quick getaway.

Roughly 10 miles (16km) long and 3½ miles (5.5km) wide, Bainbridge Island had long been the home of the Suquamish Indians when the island was first charted by Capt. George Vancouver in 1792. Within less than a century after Vancouver's visit, the island had become the site of the world's largest lumber mill (though this is now long gone). The island's early settlement centered around the ferry docks of what was known as the mosquito fleet, though eventually, when car ferries began using the community of Winslow (now known as downtown Bainbridge Island), that community became the island's business center. The island was not linked to the mainland by bridge until the Agate Pass Bridge was opened in 1950.

ESSENTIALS

GETTING THERE   **Washington State Ferries** (© **800/84-FERRY** or 888/ 808-7977 within Washington state, or 206/464-6400; www.wsdot.wa.gov/ ferries/) operates a ferry service between Seattle's Pier 52 Colman Dock ferry terminal and Bainbridge Island. The trip takes 35 minutes and costs $8 ($10 mid-May to mid-Oct) for a car and driver one way, $4.50 for adult car passengers or walk-ons, $2.20 for seniors, and $3.20 for children ages 5 to 18; free for children 4 and under. Car passengers and walk-ons only pay fares on westbound ferries.

VISITOR INFORMATION   For more information on Bainbridge Island, contact the **Bainbridge Island Chamber of Commerce,** 590 Winslow Way E., Bainbridge Island, WA 98110 (© **206/842-3700;** www.bainbridge chamber.com).

EXPLORING BAINBRIDGE ISLAND

Just up the hill from the Bainbridge Island ferry terminal is the island's main shopping district, where you'll find some interesting shops and restaurants. If you'd like to sample some local wines, drop in at the **Bainbridge Island Vineyards and Winery,** 682 Wash. 305 (© **206/842-9463**), which is located a half mile up the hill from the ferry landing and specializes in estate-grown European-style wines. These wines are quite good and are only available here and at a few select restaurants. The winery is open Wednesday through Sunday from noon to 5pm.

There are two state parks on Bainbridge Island. Down at the south end of the island, you'll find **Fort Ward State Park** (© **206/842-4041**) on the quiet shore of Rich Passage. The park offers picnicking and good bird watching. Up at the northern tip of the island, you'll find **Fay Bainbridge State Park** (© **206/ 842-3931**), which offers camping and great views across the sound to the Seattle skyline. This park will give you a good idea of why people are willing to pay a premium to live on this island.

Garden enthusiasts will want to call ahead and make a reservation to visit the **Bloedel Reserve** ✦✦, 7571 NE Dolphin Dr. (© **206/842-7631**), which is 6 miles (10km) north of the ferry terminal off Wash. 305 (turn right on Agate Point Rd.). Expansive and elegant grounds are the ideal place for a quiet stroll amid plants from around the world. Admission is $6 for adults and $4 for seniors; children 5 to 12 are $4, and children under 5 are free. Also well worth a visit is **Bainbridge Gardens,** 9415 Miller Rd. NE (© **206/842-5888**), which is on the west side of the island. These gardens, which today are primarily a plant nursery for garden-crazed Bainbridge Islanders, are also the site of gardens started in 1908 by Zenhichi Harui when he emigrated from Japan. The gardens were abandoned in the 1940s when Harui and his family were forced to leave the island. Today little remains of the original gardens, but the grounds are still quite beautiful. Gardeners should also be sure to visit the award-winning gardens surrounding the **Bainbridge Island Public Library** at the corner of High School Road and Madison Avenue on the edge of Winslow (downtown Bainbridge Island).

If you'd like to get closer to the water and do a little paddling in a sea kayak, turn left as you get off the ferry and head to Waterfront Park, where you'll find **Bainbridge Island Boat Rentals** (© 206/842-9229), which rents single sea kayaks ($12 per hr.) and double kayaks ($18 per hr.). They also rent rowboats, sailboats, motorboats, and swan boats.

With its water views and winding country roads, Bainbridge is a favorite of bicyclists. If you'd like to explore the island by bike, you can rent a bike from **B. I. Cycle Rentals,** 162 Bjune Ave. (© 206/842-6413), which charges $5 per hour or $25 a day for mountain bikes. They can also give you a map of the island and outline a good ride for you. This shop also rents bikes right at the ferry landing.

WHERE TO STAY

Island Country Inn ✿ Located right in downtown Bainbridge Island, this is the only motel-style lodging on the island, and with its convenient location and its outdoor swimming pool and Jacuzzi, it makes a good choice for anyone coming to the island in summer. Guest rooms are just a cut above your usual motel room. If you're planning a longer stay, the suites, which have kitchens, might be what you need.

920 Hildebrand Way NE, Bainbridge Island, WA 98110. ✆ **800/842-8429** or 206/842-6861. www.NW CountryInns.com/Island. 46 units. $99–$109 double; $129–$149 suite. Rates include continental breakfast. AE, DISC, MC, V. **Amenities:** Small outdoor pool; Jacuzzi. *In room:* A/C, TV, dataport, coffeemaker, hair dryer, iron, free local calls.

Waterfall Gardens ✿ This unusual B&B is located in the middle of the island on 5 acres of gardens and natural landscaping. A salmon and trout stream flows through the property and has been slowly brought back to a natural state by the inn's owners. Accommodations are in two buildings, one of which is an old farmhouse with 15-foot ceilings and a full kitchen. However, for most people, the smaller Waterfall and Weeping Cedars rooms should be more than adequate. Both of these rooms are quite large and the Waterfall Room has a double whirlpool tub. Be sure to ask about the inn's "Bobo golf" course (it's played with a tennis ball).

7269 Bergman Rd., Bainbridge Island, WA 98110. ✆ **206/842-1434**. www.waterfall-gardens.com. 4 units. $95–$165 double. Rates include continental breakfast. No credit cards.

WHERE TO DINE

When you need a steaming cup of espresso to warm you and wake you, head to the **Pegasus Coffee House & Gallery,** 131 Parfitt Way SW (✆ **206/842-6725**), which is located near the marina in Winslow. Soups, salads, sandwiches, and pastries are also available. If you'd prefer a pint of ale in a cozy waterfront pub, drop in at the **Harbour Public House,** 231 Parfitt Way SW (✆ **206/842-0969**), which overlooks a marina about a block away from Pegasus Coffee. This place also serves good pub food including burgers, fish and chips, and other seafood. To find either of these, follow Winslow Way east through "downtown" Bainbridge Island and turn left onto Madison Avenue.

The Four Swallows ✿✿ ITALIAN/NORTHWEST   Located less than a block off Winslow Way in downtown Bainbridge Island, this casual and unpretentious restaurant is housed in a restored farmhouse that was built in 1889. Out front, under the shade trees, is a big deck for summer alfresco dining, and inside, rustic "primitive" antiques and old, high-backed wooden booths set the tone. The menu changes daily, but any month of the year the antipasti for two, which showcases a wide range of seasonal specialties, makes a good starter. If you like seafood, keep an eye out for the delicious *brodetto,* a fish stew similar to bouillabaisse. Pizzas and pastas make up a good portion of the menu, and there are always plenty of fresh seafood dishes.

481 Madison Ave. ✆ **206/842-3397**. Reservations recommended. Main dishes $10–$27. AE, MC, V. Tues–Sat 5:30–9pm (longer hours in summer).

Winslow Way Cafe ✿✿ MEDITERRANEAN/NORTHWEST   Although pasta and pizzas dominate the menu here and prices are reasonable, this contemporary place oozes Seattle attitude. Sure, the restaurant is housed in the funkiest building in downtown Bainbridge Island (it looks as though it could be on a beach in the Caribbean), but inside all is indirect lighting and contemporary styling. The big bar to one side fairly screams "Have a martini!" The pizzas are just the sort of designer pies you would expect in such a setting and are generally excellent, but it is often hard to ignore the creative seafood dishes on the daily fresh sheet.

122 Winslow Way E. ✆ 206/842-0517. Reservations recommended. Main dishes $6.75–$14 at lunch, $8.50–$25 at dinner. MC, V. Mon–Sat 11am–9pm; Sun 10am–2:30pm.

2 Poulsbo & the Kitsap Peninsula

Poulsbo: 15 miles (24km) NW of Bainbridge Island ferry dock, 35 miles (56km) S of Port Townsend, 45 miles (73km) N of Tacoma

Roughly 45 miles (73km) long and confusingly convoluted, this peninsula looks something like an arrowhead wedged between Seattle and the Olympic Peninsula. Tucked amid the folds of its many glacial hills and its fjordlike waterways is an eclectic assortment of small towns, each with a very different character.

For thousands of years this region was home to several tribes of Native Americans, including the Suquamish tribe, which once had a 900-foot-long longhouse on the shores of Agate Pass between the Kitsap Peninsula and Bainbridge Island. Chief Sealth (pronounced *see*-alth), for whom Seattle is named, was a member of the Suquamish tribe and today his grave can be visited near the town of Suquamish.

The region's earliest pioneer history is linked to the logging industry. It was at Port Gamble, on the north end of the peninsula, that Andrew Pope and William Talbot chose to build their sawmill, which went on to become the longest operating mill in the Northwest. Although the mill is now closed, Port Gamble remains a company town and looks as if it hasn't changed in 100 years.

The state of Washington seems obsessed with theme towns; there's a Dutch town, a Wild West town, a Bavarian town, and here on the Kitsap Peninsula, a Scandinavian town. Though at first the town of Poulsbo seems merely a contrivance to sell tacky Scandinavian souvenirs, on closer inspection it proves to have much more character than that. The town's waterfront park, marinas, and picturesque setting on Liberty Bay leave no doubt that this town has great appeal for the boating crowd.

The deep, protected harbors of the Kitsap Peninsula have for more than a century seen the comings and goings of the U.S. Navy, which has naval yards here in the town of Bremerton. Today the Bremerton Naval Yards are also home to a large fleet of mothballed navy ships, and these have become the town's greatest tourist asset in recent years, with two museums and a Vietnam-era destroyer open to the public. Not far away there is also a Trident nuclear submarine base, which, however, is not open to the public.

Across Sinclair Inlet from Bremerton, and accessible via the last privately owned passenger ferry still operating on the Puget Sound, lies the small town of Port Orchard, which is filled with antiques malls.

ESSENTIALS

GETTING THERE   The Kitsap Peninsula lies between Puget Sound and the east side of the Olympic Peninsula and is bounded on its west side by Hood Canal (which is not a canal but rather a long fjordlike extension of Puget Sound). Wash. 16 connects the peninsula with I-5 at Tacoma, while Wash. 3 connects the peninsula with U.S. 101 west of Olympia and continues north to the Hood Canal Bridge, a floating bridge that serves as the Kitsap Peninsula's northern link to the Olympic Peninsula. Bainbridge Island is connected to the Kitsap Peninsula by the Agate Pass Bridge on Wash. 305.

Washington State Ferries (© 800/84-FERRY or 888/808-7977 in Washington, or 206/464-6400; www.wsdot.wa.gov/ferries/) operates three ferries between the Kitsap Peninsula and the east side of Puget Sound: the Fauntleroy-Southworth ferry (a 35-min. crossing) from West Seattle, the Seattle-Bremerton ferry (a 60-min. crossing) from downtown Seattle, and the Edmonds-Kingston ferry (a 30-min. crossing) from north of Seattle. Fares range between $7 and $8.75 for a car and driver on the Fauntleroy-Southworth ferry and between $8 and $10 for a car and driver on the other two ferries. Passenger fares range from $4 to $4.50. Car passengers and walk-ons only pay fares on westbound ferries.

VISITOR INFORMATION   For information on the Kitsap Peninsula, contact the **Kitsap Peninsula Visitor and Convention Bureau,** 2 Rainier St. (P.O. Box 270), Port Gamble, WA 98364 (© **800/416-5615** or 360/297-8200; www. visitkitsap.com). For more information on Poulsbo, contact the **Greater Poulsbo Chamber of Commerce,** 19168 Jensen Way NE (P.O. Box 1063), Poulsbo, WA 98370 (© **877/768-5726** or 360/779-4848; www.poulsbo.net).

FESTIVALS   In Poulsbo each May the **Viking Fest** celebrates traditional Scandinavian culture, as do the October **First Lutheran Church Annual Lutefisk Dinner** and the December **Yul Fest.**

EXPLORING THE KITSAP PENINSULA

Just across the Agate Pass Bridge from Bainbridge Island lies the Kitsap Peninsula and the Suquamish Indian Reservation. Take your first right after crossing the bridge from Bainbridge Island, and in the village of **Suquamish,** you'll see signs for the grave of Chief Sealth, for whom Seattle was named. Nearby (turn at the Texaco station on the edge of town) you'll also find **Old Man House State Park,** which preserves the site of a large Native American longhouse. The Old Man House itself is long gone, but you'll find an informative sign and a small park with picnic tables. From Suquamish, head back to Wash. 305, continue a little farther west and watch for signs to the **Suquamish Museum,** 15838 Sandy Hook Rd. (© **360/394-5275**), on the Port Madison Indian Reservation. The museum houses a compelling history of Puget Sound's native people, with lots of historic photos and quotes from tribal elders about growing up in the area. May through September, the museum is open daily from 10am to 5pm; October through April, it's open Friday through Sunday from 11am to 4pm. Admission is $4 for adults and $3 for seniors, and $2 for children 12 and under. In this same general area, right on Wash. 305 at the west end of the Agate Pass Bridge, you'll also find the **Clearwater Casino** (© **800/375-6073** or 360/598-6889).

Continuing north on Wash. 305, you next come to the small town of **Poulsbo,** which overlooks fjordlike Liberty Bay. Settled in the late 1880s by Scandinavians, Poulsbo was primarily a fishing, logging, and farming town until the town decided to play up its Scandinavian heritage. Shops in the Scandinavian-inspired downtown sell all manner of Viking and Scandinavian souvenirs. Between downtown and the waterfront, you'll find Liberty Bay Park, and at the south end of Front Street, you'll find the **Marine Science Center,** 18743 Front St. NE (© **360/779-5549;** www.poulsbomsc.org), which houses interpretive displays on Puget Sound. The center is open daily 11am to 5pm. Admission is $4 for adults, $3 for seniors and teenagers, and $2 for children ages 2 through 12.

If you're interested in seeing Poulsbo from the water, you can rent a sea kayak from **Olympic Outdoor Center,** 18971 Front St. (© **360/697-6095; www.kayakproshop.com**), which charges $12 to $17 per hour or $30 to $50 by the day.

If you have time and enjoy visiting historic towns, continue north from Poulsbo on Wash. 3 to **Port Gamble,** which looks like a New England village dropped down in the middle of the Northwest woods. This community was established in 1853 as a company town for the Pope and Talbot lumber mill. Along the town's shady streets are many Victorian homes that were restored by Pope and Talbot. Stop by the Port Gamble Country Store, which now houses the **Port Gamble Historical Museum** (© **360/297-8074**), a collection of local memorabilia. Admission is $2.50 for adults and $1.50 for seniors and students (free for children 5 and under). From May 1 to October 31, the museum is open daily from 10:30am to 5pm; the rest of the year, it's open by appointment. The same location is home to the **Of Sea and Shore Museum** (© **360/297-2426**), which houses an exhibit of seashells from around the world. This museum is open daily from 9am to 5pm, and admission is free.

South of Port Gamble on Wash. 3, you can explore the Kitsap Peninsula's naval history. Between Poulsbo and Silverdale, you will be passing just east of the Bangor Navy Base, which is home port for a fleet of Trident nuclear submarines. The base is on Hood Canal, a long narrow arm of Puget Sound. Near the town of Keyport, you can visit the **Naval Undersea Museum,** Garnett Way (© **360/ 396-4148**), which is located 3 miles (5km) east of Wash. 3 on Wash. 308. The museum examines all aspects of undersea exploration, with interactive exhibits, models, displays that include a deep-sea exploration and research craft, a Japanese kamikaze torpedo, and a deep-sea rescue vehicle. The museum is open daily from 10am to 4pm (closed Tues Oct–May), and admission is free.

Continuing south, you come to **Bremerton,** which is home to the Puget Sound Naval Shipyard, where mothballed U.S. Navy ships have included the aircraft carriers USS *Nimitz* and USS *Midway* and the battleships USS *Missouri* and USS *New Jersey.* If you'd like to see the shipyards and mothballed fleet from the water, take a tour with **Kitsap Harbor Tours,** 110 Harrison Ave. (© **360/ 876-1260**). June through August, tours are offered daily between 11am and 4pm. Tours are $8.50 for adults, $7.50 for seniors, and $5.50 for children ages 5 to 12 (free for children under 5). This company also offers dinner tours to Tillicum Village (a reproduction Native American long house) on Blake Island, which is a state park. These tours, which are offered May through September, include dinner and performances of traditional Native American dances. Dinner tours are $55 for adults, $50 for seniors, $22 for children ages 5 to 12, and free for children 4 and under.

One mothballed destroyer, the USS *Turner Joy,* is now operated by the **Bremerton Historic Ships Association** (© **360/792-2457**) and is open to the public as a memorial to those who have served in the U.S. Navy and who have helped build the navy's ships. The *Turner Joy* is docked about 150 yards east of the Washington State Ferries terminal. May through September, the ship is open daily from 10am to 5pm; call for hours in other months. Admission is $7 for adults, $6 for seniors and military, and $5 for children ages 5 to 12 (free for children under 5). Combination *Turner Joy*–Harbor Tour tickets are also available.

Nearby is the **Bremerton Naval Museum,** 130 Washington Ave. (© **360/ 479-7447**), which showcases naval history and the historic contributions of the

Puget Sound Naval Shipyard. From Memorial Day to Labor Day, the museum is open Monday through Saturday from 10am to 5pm and Sunday from 1 to 5pm; other months the museum is closed on Monday. Admission is free.

Connecting all of these waterfront attractions is the Bremerton Boardwalk, which provides a pleasant place to stroll along the waters of Sinclair Inlet. Also here in Bremerton, you'll find the **Kitsap County Historical Society Museum,** 280 Fourth St. (© **360/479-6226;** www.waynes.net/kchsm/), which is housed in a 1940s-era streamline moderne bank building. The interesting architecture of the building is reason enough for a visit, but there are also historical photos by Edward S. Curtis and his brother Asahel, who at one time resided here in Kitsap County. The museum is open Tuesday through Saturday from 9am to 5pm (until 8pm first Fri of each month). Admission is by suggested donation ($2 adults, $1 seniors and students).

One of the last remaining private mosquito fleet ferries still operates between Bremerton and **Port Orchard.** If you park your car on the waterfront in Bremerton, you can step aboard the little passenger-only ferry and cross the bay to Port Orchard. In this little waterfront town, you'll find several antiques malls that can provide hours of interesting browsing.

WHERE TO STAY

Manor Farm Inn 🐾🐾   Although it's located only about an hour from Seattle, between Poulsbo and the Hood Canal Bridge, Manor Farm Inn (which is actually a working farm) feels a little like a New England country inn. Whether you want to hide away in the comfort of your room or hang out with the farm animals, you're likely to feel content at this retreat from urban stress. If you crave lots of space, you might want to opt for the Carriage Room, which has the original carriage house doors as a backdrop to the bed. For a large bathroom request The Loft, which is up a flight of stairs and has great views. Scones at your door in the morning are followed by a full breakfast in the dining room. In the afternoon, tea and cookies are available in the common drawing room.

26069 Big Valley Rd. NE, Poulsbo, WA 98370. © **360/779-4628.** Fax 360/779-4876. www.manorfarminn. com. 7 units. $140–$170 double; Jan–Apr Sun–Thurs $125 double. Rates include full breakfast. AE, MC, V. *In room:* No phone.

Willcox House ★★   Set on the shore of Hood Canal and with a superb view of the Olympic Mountains, this 1930s Art Deco mansion is one of the state's finest inns. The inn is surrounded by lush gardens of rhododendrons and azaleas that erupt into bloom each spring and was once a private estate. Today guests get the feeling that they have stepped into a Merchant Ivory drama. There's a library where you can curl up in a leather chair beside the fire, a billiards room (also with a fireplace), a home theater with big-screen TV and an eclectic assortment of videotapes, and, of course, an elegant great room. Guest rooms are similarly elegant. In the Constance Room, the inn's largest, you'll find a fireplace and an Art Deco bathroom. Stay in the Clark Gable Room, and you'll have your own private balcony. Dinners are also served at the inn (reservation only) with fixed-price meals ranging in price from $21.50 on weeknights to $32.50 on Saturday nights. Regional cuisine and an excellent wine list make this one of the finest restaurants on the Kitsap Peninsula.

2390 Tekiu Rd. NW, Seabeck, WA 98380. © **800/725-9477** or 360/830-4492. www.willcoxhouse.com. 5 units. $129–$199 double. Rates include full breakfast. DISC, MC, V. **Amenities:** Dining room (Northwest). *In room:* Hair dryer.

WHERE TO DINE

The most elegant meals on the Kitsap Peninsula are served at the Willcox House, a luxurious inn overlooking the Hood Canal. Although it is mostly guests of the inn who dine here, the fixed-price meals are also open to the public by reservation. See above for details.

IN POULSBO

If you have a sweet tooth, don't miss **Sluys Poulsbo Bakery,** 18924 Front St. NE (ⓒ **360/697-2253**), which bakes mounds of Scandinavian-inspired goodies (very sweet), as well as stick-to-your-ribs breads. When you need a cup of espresso, head to the **Poulsbohemian Coffeehouse,** 19003 Front St. (ⓒ **360/ 779-9199**), which has an excellent view of Liberty Bay from atop the bluff on the edge of downtown.

Molly Ward Gardens ★★ *Finds* NORTHWEST   What a surprise to open the door of this rambling old barn in a picturesque little valley and find that inside is a magical hobbitlike interior trimmed to the rafters with dried flowers and herbs. This is a husband-and wife-operation. Sam, the chef, turns out such dishes as pan-seared halibut filet with mango salsa, herb-rubbed rack of lamb with rosemary infusion, and asparagus strudel. Fresh fish, lamb, and duck are sure to pop up on the menu, and vegetarian dishes are available. She's the artist, and at Christmas the restaurant is decked out with splendiferous garlands and arrangements created with bounty from woods and field. In summer, there's outdoor seating among the flowers. Molly Ward Gardens is located quite near the Manor Farm Inn.

27462 Big Valley Rd. ⓒ **360/779-4471.** www.mollywardgardens.com. Reservations recommended. Main courses $8.50–$11 at lunch, $15–$30 at dinner. Tues 11am–3pm; Wed–Sat 11am–3pm and 6–9:30pm; Sun 10am–3pm and 6–9:30pm; Mon 6–9:30pm.

Sheila's Bay Café ★ *Finds* NORWEGIAN/AMERICAN   Although this place is nothing fancy, just a casual diner where fishermen feel comfortable in their rain gear, it is one of the few places in town that actually serves Scandinavian food. On Saturday nights there is a special "Taste of Norway" menu. Lutefisk is available with 24 hours advance notice and although this and other Scandinavian specialties aren't likely to ever replace Thai food as our ethnic cuisine of choice, such dishes are worth a try if you're here in town to soak up the Scandinavian atmosphere. Breakfast here is great, and is served all day.

On the marina, Poulsbo. ⓒ **360/779-2997.** Main dishes $7.50–$11. MC, V. Mon–Thurs 7am–3pm; Fri 7am–3pm and 4–8pm; Sat 8am–3pm and 4–8pm; Sun 8am–3pm.

3 Gig Harbor

45 miles (73km) S of Seattle, 30 miles (50km) S of Bremerton, 45 miles (73km) N of Olympia

On the far side of the Tacoma Narrows Bridge from Tacoma is the quaint waterfront town of Gig Harbor. With its interesting little shops, art galleries, seafood restaurants, fleet of commercial fishing boats, and marinas full of private pleasure craft, this town is the quintessential Puget Sound fishing village. Framing this picture of Puget Sound's past is the snowcapped bulk of Mount Rainier, which lends this town a near storybook quality.

Long the site of a Native American village, Gig Harbor was not discovered by Euro-Americans until 1841 when sailors from an exploratory expedition who were charting the area from a gig (a small boat that had been launched from the expedition's main ship) rowed into the bay. Settlers arrived here in 1867 and soon Gig Harbor was a thriving fishing village of Scandinavians and Croatians.

ESSENTIALS

GETTING THERE   Gig Harbor lies just across the Tacoma Narrows Bridge from Tacoma off Wash. 16.

VISITOR INFORMATION   For more information on this area, contact the **Gig Harbor Peninsula Chamber of Commerce,** 3302 Harborview Dr., Gig Harbor, WA 98332 (© **253/851-6865;** www.gigharborchamber.com).

EXPLORING GIG HARBOR

Gig Harbor is a boaters' town. Up and down the length of the town's waterfront there are marinas crowded with sailboats and powerboats, and shops along the waterfront cater primarily to the boating crowd. However, all the boats, and the backdrop of Mount Rainier, also make this a very pleasant town for a leisurely stroll. There are also a couple of options for casual visitors to get out on the water.

On the waterfront you'll find **Gig Harbor Rent-a-Boat,** 8829 N. Harborview Dr. (© **253/858-7341;** www.gigharborrentaboat.com), where you can rent a sailboat, powerboat, pedal boat, or kayak. Rates range from $10 for a pedal boat to $60 an hour for an 18-foot powerboat. Guided sea-kayak trips are also available from **Gig Harbor Kayak Center,** 8809 N. Harborview Dr. (© **888/42-YAKIT** or 253/851-7987; www.clearlight.com/kayak), and cost $22 to $38.

Most visitors to Gig Harbor come because of the boating opportunities, but landlubbers can stroll the town's main street, Harborview Drive, enjoying the view of the harbor and stopping to browse in dozens of interesting little shops and art galleries along the waterfront. Toward the south end of the waterfront, you'll find Jerisich Park, which has a public dock and is a good place for a picnic. At the north end, after you make the bend in the bay, you'll come to the Finholm area. Across from the water here stands the Finholm View Climb, a flight of 90 steps that lead up a steep hill. At the top of the hill, you'll find the quintessential Gig Harbor view of the bay and Mount Rainier.

If you're curious about the history of the area, visit the **Gig Harbor Peninsula Historical Society & Museum,** 4218 Harborview Dr. (© **253/858-6722;** www.gigharbormuseum.org), which is located on the bend of the bay just before Finholm. The museum is open Tuesday through Saturday from 10am to 4pm, and admission is free.

Within a short drive of Gig Harbor, you'll also find three waterfront state parks—**Penrose Point, Joemma,** and **Kopachuck**—all of which have beaches and campgrounds. Of these, Penrose Point (© **253/265-3606**) is the prettiest. This park is situated on Mayo Cove and has 2 miles (3km) of shoreline. To reach this park from Gig Harbor, drive north on Wash. 16 to Purdy, take Wash. 302 west and then follow signs to Key Center and the park. From both Joemma (which is about 4 miles/6.5km beyond Penrose Point) and Kopachuck (from Wash. 16 in Gig Harbor, follow signs for the park) there are good sunset spots, and there is a nice sandy beach at Kopachuck.

WHERE TO STAY

The Maritime Inn ★★   Located across from the waterfront in downtown Gig Harbor, this small modern hotel manages to conjure up the image of old beach resort cottages with its classic, simple styling. All the guest rooms have gas fireplaces and are romantic without being frilly. Pine furnishings lend a further air of classicism to the rooms. While most rooms have some sort of view of the water, the views are better from those few rooms that are on the second floor.

3212 Harborview Dr., Gig Harbor, WA 98335. © 253/858-1818. Fax 253/858-1817. www.maritimeinn.com. 15 units. $69–$139 double. Rates include continental breakfast. AE, DC, DISC, MC, V. *In room:* A/C, TV, data-port, coffeemaker, hair dryer.

WHERE TO DINE

When it's time for coffee, head to **Le Bistro Coffee House,** 4120 Harborview Dr. (© **253/851-1033**), at the north end of downtown. If you need some good bread for a picnic or have a passion for pastries, don't miss **Harbor Bread Company,** 8822 N. Harborview Dr. (© **253/851-4181**).

The Green Turtle ★★ PAN-ASIAN/INTERNATIONAL   With the hands-down best view in town (Mount Rainier looming beyond the mouth of the harbor on clear days), this elegant little restaurant is tucked away in an unlikely spot next door to a yacht sales office. Two walls of glass let everyone enjoy the views, and in summer there is a deck under a big old maple tree. The menu is almost entirely seafood, but you will find a few chicken, duck, and steak dishes on the menu. Preparations lean toward the far side of the Pacific, with such dishes as sautéed calamari in spicy black bean sauce, pan-seared ahi with a roasted garlic and ginger glaze, and halibut with artichoke hearts and a creamy basil and curry sauce.

2905 Harborview Dr. © **253/851-3167**. www.greenturtle.com. Reservations recommended. Main courses $18–$27. AE, DC, DISC, MC, V. Sun and Wed–Thurs 4:30–9pm; Fri–Sat 4:30–10pm.

Tides Tavern ★ AMERICAN   This is basically just a tavern with an extensive menu, but because of its great location over the water at the east end of town, it's a good place for lunch or a casual dinner. The building that houses the tavern was originally constructed as a general store back in 1910, but has been the Tides Tavern since 1973. The menu is basic tavern fare—burgers, sandwiches, and pizzas—and if not entirely memorable, can be tasty. On Friday and Saturday nights there's live music. Because this is a tavern, you must be 21 or older to eat here.

2925 Harborview Dr. © **253/858-3982**. Reservations recommended for large parties. Main courses $5–$15. AE, MC, V. Sun–Thurs 11am–10pm; Fri–Sat 11am–midnight.

4 Tacoma

32 miles (52km) S of Seattle, 31 miles (50km) N of Olympia, 93 miles (150km) S of Port Townsend

Tacoma is a city that, in the words of Rodney Dangerfield, just don't get no respect. For years, its industrial image made it the brunt of jokes, many of which centered around the aroma of Tacoma. I'd like to be able to tell you that the skies over Tacoma are always clear and that the air is fresh and clean, but that would be stretching the truth just a bit. However, it is definitely time to forget the old jokes and take a new look at this city in the midst of a profound transformation.

Things have changed quite a bit here since the days when the city's waterfront was lined with smoke-belching lumber and paper mills, and, with a newfound commitment to the arts, Tacoma is slowly beginning to compete with Seattle as a city on the move. Tacoma has been making great strides toward reinventing itself, and the past decade has seen the renovation of Union Station (and the placement there of an impressive Dale Chihuly art-glass installation), the opening of a modern performing arts center (complete with two renovated historic theaters), construction of the huge Washington State History Museum, and the opening of a new University of Washington campus (in renovated historic buildings). At press time, the new International Glass Museum (with an art-glass pedestrian bridge spanning I-705 and connecting the new museum with the rest of the downtown) was approaching completion and construction was underway on the new Tacoma Art Museum building. However, despite all this recent cultural expansion, Tacoma's downtown still becomes something of a ghost town after the office workers head home at the end of the day.

Tacoma is also in the process of reclaiming its shoreline, and today a waterfront park runs the length of Ruston Way just north of downtown. Walkers, joggers, cyclists, and in-line skaters all flock to the paved trail that runs through this park, and along the park's length there are several good waterfront restaurants. Despite Tacoma's ongoing makeover, however, Point Defiance Park remains the city's top attraction. With miles of trails, a world-class zoo and aquarium, numerous other attractions, and great bicycling and in-line skating, this is one of the premier parks in Puget Sound.

In between Point Defiance and downtown Tacoma lies one of the most impressive historic neighborhoods in the state. The streets of the Stadium Historic District are lined with beautiful mansions, most of which have been renovated and some of which are now B&Bs. These homes are a testament to the important role Tacoma played in Washington history. In 1883, Tacoma became the end of the line for the Northern Pacific Railroad, thus sealing the city's fate as the industrial center of the Puget Sound. It was largely due to the railroad that Tacoma became a center of industry in this region, a fate that the city today is trying to overcome.

To see the past and the future of Tacoma, drop by downtown's Fireman's Park. From this small park, you can look down on smoke-belching mills and commercial port facilities, but if you then turn around, you'll be facing a new, revitalized Tacoma where the arts are flourishing and historic buildings are being preserved and renovated.

ESSENTIALS

GETTING THERE   Tacoma is on I-5 south of Seattle at the junction of Wash. 16, which is the main route north through the Kitsap Peninsula to Port Townsend and the Olympic Peninsula. Wash. 7 from the Mount Rainier area leads into downtown Tacoma from the south. Tacoma's city center is accessed by I-705, a short spur that leads from I-5 into the middle of downtown.

Seattle-Tacoma International Airport is located 22 miles (35km) north of Tacoma. **ShuttleExpress** (© 800/487-7433 or 425/981-7000; www.shuttle express.com) operates an airport shuttle service; the fare is $23 one-way to downtown Tacoma.

Amtrak has service to Tacoma. The station is at 1001 Puyallup Ave.

VISITOR INFORMATION   For more information on this area, contact the **Tacoma–Pierce County Visitor & Convention Bureau,** P.O. Box 1754, Tacoma, WA 98401-1754 (© 800/272-2662 or 253/627-2836; www.travel tacoma.com), which has an information desk inside the gift shop at the Washington State History Museum, 1911 Pacific Ave.

GETTING AROUND   See "Getting Around," in chapter 4, "Seattle," for information on renting cars at Sea-Tac International Airport. If you need a taxi, contact **Yellow Cab** (© 253/472-3303). Public bus service is provided by **Pierce Transit** (© 253/581-8000; www.piercetransit.org).

WHAT TO SEE & DO
POINT DEFIANCE PARK

Point Defiance Park, on the north side of town at the end of Pearl Street, is Tacoma's center of activity and one of the largest urban parks in the country. In the park are several of the city's top attractions, including the Point Defiance Zoo & Aquarium, Fort Nisqually Historic Site, and the Camp 6 Logging Museum. Founded in 1888, this park preserved one of the region's most scenic points of land. Winding through the wooded park is **Five Mile Drive,** which connects all the park's main attractions as well as the picnic areas, and hiking and biking trails. Also in the park are a rose garden, a Japanese garden, a rhododendron garden, a dahlia test garden, and a native-plant garden. You can reach the park by following Ruston Way or Pearl Street north.

Point Defiance Zoo & Aquarium ★★ *Kids*   As the name implies, this is both a zoo and an aquarium, and both facilities are outstanding. This focus here is on the wildlife of the Pacific Rim countries, and to that end you'll find animals from such far-flung locations as the Arctic tundra, Southeast Asia, and the Andes Mountains. In the aquarium, the *Rocky Shores* exhibit features marine mammals, including beluga whales, and the *Jewels of the Sea* exhibit sheds a new light on jellyfish. Other exhibits include a northern Pacific aquarium, a tropical coral reef aquarium that's home to more than 40 sharks, and an aquarium of deadly sea creatures. At the farm zoo, kids can pet various animals. The zoo's biggest event of the year is its annual Zoolights program, which each December turns the grounds into a fantasy of Christmas lights.

5400 N. Pearl St. ✆ **253/591-5337.** www.pdza.org. Admission $7.75 adults, $7 seniors, $6 children 4–13, free for children under 4. Memorial Day weekend to Labor Day daily 10am–7pm; day after Labor Day to Fri before Memorial Day daily 10am–4pm. Closed third Fri in July, Thanksgiving, and Dec 25.

Fort Nisqually Living History Museum ⭐ Fort Nisqually was a trading post founded in 1833 by the Hudson's Bay Company for the purpose of acquiring beaver pelts. However, it was established at a time when the fur trade was in decline and was soon moved to a new location and converted to a commercial farming business. This reconstruction, built in the 1930s, is based on the design of that second fort. Inside the stockade walls are two original buildings and several reconstructed buildings. Throughout the summer (and on weekends in other months), costumed interpreters are on hand. Numerous living history events are staged throughout the year.

5400 N. Pearl St. ✆ **253/591-5339.** www.fortnisqually.org. Admission $3 adults, $2 seniors, $1 children 5–12, free for children under 5. Memorial Day weekend to Labor Day daily 11am–6pm; day after Labor Day to Fri before Memorial Day Wed–Sun 11am–4pm (admission charged weekends only).

Camp 6 Logging Museum ⭐ *Kids* This museum focuses on the days of steam power in Washington's logging history. Exhibits include plenty of steam equipment as well as old bunkhouses and a rail-car camp. The latter was a rolling logging camp with bunkhouses built on railroad cars. Although the indoor exhibits are closed November through January, outdoor exhibits can be viewed throughout the year. On weekends in spring and summer and again in December, Camp 6 offers rides on an old logging train.

5400 N. Pearl St. ✆ **253/752-0047.** Free admission to museum; logging train rides $1. Feb–Memorial Day and Oct Wed–Sun (and holidays) 10am–4pm; Memorial Day–Sept 30 Wed–Fri 10am–5pm, Sat–Sun 10am–7pm. Closed Nov–Jan.

MUSEUMS

Museum of Glass ⭐⭐ Although not yet open at press time (scheduled opening is July 2002), this museum will be the Northwest's most talked about new museum when it does open and will become a not-to-be-missed stop. World-renowned glass artist Dale Chihuly hails from Tacoma, which is partly why this world-class museum has been built here, and Chihuly has designed a bridge of glass to span I-705 and connect the waterfront museum with Washington State History Museum and the adjacent Union Station, which has a large Chihuly installation. From the outside, the museum's focal point is a massive glass cone, slightly askew, that conjures up both Mount Rainier and the Tacoma Dome.

1801 Dock St. ✆ **253/396-1768.** www.museumofglass.org. Call or check website for hr. and admission.

Tacoma Art Museum ⭐⭐ A small but far-reaching permanent collection features works by such artists as Degas, Renoir, Corot, Pissarro, Edward Hopper, and Roy Lichtenstein. In addition, contemporary art with modern themes is presented in shows that are changed several times annually. However, the museum's greatest claim to fame is the Dale Chihuly Retrospective Gallery. Chihuly, a Northwest glass artist who grew up in Tacoma, is widely acclaimed as the nation's foremost creator of art glass. This is the only comprehensive permanent public display of his works. In 2003, the museum will be moving into a new facility at 1701 Pacific Ave.

1123 Pacific Ave. ✆ **253/272-4258.** www.tacomartmuseum.org. Admission $5 adults, $4 seniors and students, free for children 6 and under; free 3rd Thurs of every month. Tues–Sat 10am–5pm (until 8pm Thurs); Sun noon–5pm.

Washington State History Museum ★★ *(Kids)* A massive archive of Washington state history, this impressive museum is like no other history museum in the Northwest and is one of the best reasons to pay a visit to downtown Tacoma. The museum uses a full barrage of high-tech displays to make history both fun and interesting. From a covered wagon to a sprawling HO-scale (3.5mm: 1 ft.) model railroad layout, a Coast Salish longhouse to a Hooverville shack, the state's history comes alive through the use of life-size mannequins, recorded narration, and "overheard" conversations. With loads of interactive exhibits and several films screened daily, it's obvious that this museum is trying to appeal to the video-game generation, but older visitors will have fun, too.

1911 Pacific Ave. ℂ 888/238-4373. www.wshs.org. Admission $7 adults, $6.25 seniors, $5 students 6–18, free for children 5 and under, family $20. Free for all Thurs 5–8pm. Late Mar–Labor Day Mon–Sat 10am–5pm (until 8pm Thurs), Sun 11am–5pm; day after Labor Day–late Mar closed Mon.

Karpeles Manuscript Library Museum ★ Housed in an imposing building across the street from Wright Park and one of eight of such manuscript libraries across the country, this museum is dedicated to the preservation of original hand-written documents and letters. The founder of the libraries has amassed an astounding collection of original manuscripts ranging from original musical scores by Beethoven to ancient papyrus texts to the cover letter for the Declaration of Independence. Exhibits change every 2 months and always have some specific theme.

407 South G St. ℂ 253/383-2575. Free admission. Tues–Sun 10am–4pm.

TACOMA AREA PUBLIC GARDENS

Lakewold Gardens ★ Formerly a private estate, this 10-acre garden, designed by noted landscape architect Thomas Church, includes extensive collections of Japanese maples and rhododendrons. There are also rose, fern, and alpine gardens that include numerous rare and unusual plants.

12317 Gravelly Lake Dr. SW. ℂ 253/584-3360. www.lakewold.org. Admission $5 adults, $3 seniors and students, free for children under 12. Apr–Sept Thurs–Mon 10am–4pm; Oct–Mar Fri–Sun 10am–3pm.

Pacific Rim Bonsai Collection ★★ Assembled by the Weyerhaeuser Company in 1989 to honor trade relations with Pacific Rim nations, this bonsai collection includes more than 50 miniature trees from Japan, China, Korea, Taiwan, and Canada. This is the most impressive public bonsai collection in the state.

33663 Weyerhaeuser Way S., Weyerhaeuser Corporate campus, Federal Way. ℂ 253/924-5206. www. weyerhauser.com/bonsai. Free admission. Mar–May Fri–Wed 10am–4pm; June–Feb Sat–Wed 11am–4pm.

Rhododendron Species Botanical Garden ★★ Covering 22 acres, this garden has one of the most extensive collections of species (wild) rhododendrons and azaleas in the world. More than 2,100 different varieties of plants put on an amazing floral display March through May. Also included in these gardens are collections of ferns, maples, heathers, and bamboos. For serious gardeners, this is one of the Northwest's garden musts.

2525 S. 336 St., Weyerhaeuser Corporate campus, Federal Way. ℂ 253/661-9377. www.halcyon.com/rsf/. Admission $3.50 adults, $2.50 seniors and students, free for children under 12. Mar–May Fri–Wed 10am–4pm; June–Feb Sat–Wed 11am–4pm.

W.W. Seymour Botanical Conservatory ★ Constructed in 1908, this elegant Victorian conservatory is one of only three of this kind on the West Coast and is listed on the National Register of Historic Places. More than 200 species of exotic plants (including plenty of orchids) are housed in the huge greenhouse, which is built of more than 4,000 panes of glass. The conservatory stands in Wright Park, which has more than 700 trees of 100 species and is a shady retreat from downtown's pavement.

Wright Park, 316 South G St. ✆ 253/591-5330. Free admission. Daily 10am–4:30pm. Closed Thanksgiving and Dec 25.

OTHER TACOMA PARKS

Although Point Defiance Park is Tacoma's premier park, the **Ruston Way Parks** rank a close second. Once jammed with smoking, decaying industrial buildings and piers, the Tacoma waterfront was an industrial area of national infamy. However, since the city of Tacoma reclaimed the shore of Commencement Bay and turned it into parkland, it has become one of the most attractive waterfront parks on Puget Sound. With grassy areas, a sandy beach, a public fishing pier, and a paved pathway, the waterfront is popular with strollers, cyclists, and in-line skaters.

Downtown at the corner of A Street and South Ninth, you'll find **Fireman's Park,** which has one of the world's tallest totem poles (carved in 1903) as well as a view of the Port of Tacoma below. After gazing down on the port, if you want to have a closer look, stop by the **Port of Tacoma Observation Tower** off East 11th Street. Here you can watch as ships from around the world are loaded and unloaded. To reach the port tower, take the 11th Street bridge from downtown.

HISTORIC DISTRICTS & BUILDINGS

Tacoma has quite a few historic buildings, the most noticeable of which is **Union Station,** 1717 Pacific Ave. Built in the beaux arts style as the terminal for the first transcontinental railroad to reach the Northwest, the imposing building is now home to the federal courts and is adjacent to the Washington State History Museum. In the lobby of this building you'll find a large glass installation by Dale Chihuly.

Stadium High School, 111 North E St., is a French château–style structure that was built as a hotel and later converted to a high school. The school is the centerpiece of the historic **Stadium District,** which is at the north end of Broadway and has more than 100 Victorian homes. This is one of the prettiest residential neighborhoods in the entire state, and many of the old homes verge on being mansions. At the south end of the Stadium District is the **Old City Hall Historic District,** which is the city's main antiques neighborhood. Along Broadway just north of Ninth Street, you'll find a dozen or so large antiques stores and malls. On the east side of town you'll find **Freighthouse Square,** 25th and East D streets (✆ 253/305-0678), which is near the Tacoma Dome at the corner of and is housed in the renovated Milwaukee Railroad freight house. The building is now a public market along the lines of Seattle's Pike Place Market (although most of the stores here sell primarily cheap souvenirs). At the visitor center in the Washington State History Museum, you can pick up brochures on the city's historic districts.

WHERE TO STAY

Despite its size, Tacoma suffers from a pronounced shortage of hotels. Aside from the Sheraton and a few bed-and-breakfast inns, your only options are chain motels along the interstate. If you're interested in staying at a bed-and-breakfast, contact **A Greater Tacoma Bed & Breakfast Reservation Service,** c/o 3312 N. Union Ave., Tacoma, WA 98407 (✆ **800/406-4088** or 253/759-4088; www. gotacoma.com).

Chinaberry Hill ★★ Located amid the stately old homes of the Stadium Historic District, this imposing Victorian features luxurious guest rooms and commanding views of Commencement Bay. Throughout the inn, you'll find beautiful woodwork, including an ornate built-in hutch. For sheer opulence, it's hard to beat the Pantages Suite, which features a beautifully dressed bed, harbor views, and a whirlpool tub tucked into an alcove under the eaves. The Carriage Suite, in the former carriage house, features a bathroom fashioned from a horse stall. Above this suite is a room in what was once the hayloft. Beautiful century-old trees shade the grounds. Classic Northwest elegance makes this one of the finest inns in the state.

302 Tacoma Ave. N., Tacoma, WA 98403. (**253/272-1282.** Fax 253/272-1335. www.telisphere. com/~chinaberry/. 6 units. $120–$295 double. Rates include full breakfast. MC, V. *In room:* TV/VCR, dataport.

Sheraton Tacoma Hotel ★★ This 26-story downtown high-rise is Tacoma's biggest, best, and only downtown business hotel, and because it is attached to the Tacoma Convention Center, it stays busy most of the year. Guest rooms are none too large, but are both comfortable and tastefully decorated. Be sure to ask for a room with a view of Mount Rainier (these are the even-numbered rooms). For more personal services such as evening turndown, morning newspaper, and a continental breakfast, opt for a room on one of the concierge floors. Up on the 26th floor, you'll find an Italian restaurant with one of the best views in town.

1320 Broadway Plaza, Tacoma, WA 98402. (**800/325-3535** or 253/572-3200. Fax 253/591-4105. www. sheratontacoma.com. 319 units. $109–$164 double; $229–$239 suite. AE, DC, DISC, MC, V. Valet parking $15; self-parking $12. Pets accepted with $250 deposit. **Amenities:** 2 restaurants (Italian, American), lounge; exercise room and access to nearby health club; concierge; business center; room service; laundry service; dry cleaning; concierge level. *In room:* A/C, TV, dataport, coffeemaker, hair dryer, iron.

Thornewood Castle Inn ★★★ *Finds* There may not be any real castles in the United States, but this imposing 30,000-square-foot manor house, located a few miles south of Tacoma, sure comes close. Built in 1909, Thornewood has 28 bedrooms and 22 bathrooms, and incorporated into its design are a 15th-century wood-paneled staircase and stained-glass windows dating from the 15th to 17th centuries. Guest rooms are, as you might expect, quite large, and if not quite as sumptuously appointed as the rest of the house, they are certainly grand in design. The mansion sits on the shore of American Lake, and the gardens were designed by the Olmsted Brothers. About the only drawback here is that nearby suburban homes dispel the fantasy that you are lord or lady of all you survey. This is truly a one-of-a-kind inn.

8601 N. Thorne Lane SW, Lakewood, WA 98498. (**253/584-4393.** Fax 253/584-4497. www.thornewood castle.com. 8 units. $175–$250 double. Rates include full breakfast. AE, MC, V. *In room:* TV/VCR, coffeemaker, no phone.

The Villa Bed & Breakfast ★★ From the red roof tiles to the covered portico to the naiad statue in the garden pond, this inn cries out authentic Italianate villa. The only odd thing about this 1920s mansion is that it is in Tacoma and not Santa Barbara. Lovingly restored and filled with antiques as well as unusual pieces of furniture handmade by innkeeper Greg Anglemyer, the inn feels for all the world like a villa in Italy. Designed for romantic getaways, all the rooms have either a whirlpool or antique soaking tub. All but one room also have fireplaces, and three of the rooms have their own private verandas. If you crave lots of space, opt for the Sorrento Suite, which has views of the Olympic Mountains, a gas fireplace, a private veranda, and a four-poster bed.

705 N. Fifth St., Tacoma, WA 98403. ℂ 888/572-1157 or 253/572-1157. Fax 253/572-1805. www.villabb. com. 6 units. $125–$210 double. Rates include full breakfast. AE, MC, V. **Amenities:** Exercise room; Jacuzzi; concierge; business center. *In room:* TV, dataport, hair dryer.

WHERE TO DINE

When you just have to have a cup of espresso, **Tully's,** 764 Broadway (ℂ **253/ 627-5646**), is the place to go. This coffeehouse claims the narrow corner space of a flat-iron style building in downtown Tacoma's antiques neighborhood.

Anthony's at Point Defiance ★★ SEAFOOD Located adjacent to the Vashon Island ferry landing on the edge of Point Defiance Park, this modern seafood restaurant, part of a very popular Seattle restaurant chain, has the best location of any of Tacoma's many waterfront restaurants. When the skies are clear, it's possible to see Mount Rainier rising beyond the adjacent marina (although the best views of the mountain are from the bar area), and then, of course, there are the comings and goings of the ferries. The menu is surprisingly reasonably priced considering both the location and the contemporary decor, and not surprisingly, Anthony's stays pretty busy. You'll find everything from clam chowder and pan-fried oysters to alder-planked salmon and cioppino. For a light meal, try the fish tacos, which are quite good. Monday nights are all-you-can-eat fish-and-chips nights.

5910 N. Waterfront Dr. ℂ 253/752-9700. Reservations not accepted (call-ahead wait list available). Main courses $7–$17. AE, DISC, MC, V. Mon–Thurs 11am–9:30pm; Fri–Sat 11am–10:30pm; Sun 10am–9:30pm.

Harmon Pub and Brewery ★ AMERICAN Located in a renovated old commercial building across from the Washington State History Museum, this large pub is Tacoma's favorite downtown after-work hangout and business lunch spot. The menu is primarily burgers and pizza, but there are also usually more interesting specials, and, of course, plenty of good microbrews. The pub has adopted an outdoors theme, with the winter ski season seeing various skiing-oriented special events.

1938 Pacific Ave. ℂ 253/383-2739. Reservations not accepted. Main courses $6–$17. AE, DC, DISC, MC, V. Mon–Sat 11am–around midnight; Sun 1–8pm.

The Lobster Shop ★★ SEAFOOD This is the most upscale and expensive of the Ruston Way seafood places and has long been the city's top special-occasion seafood restaurant. The view's the thing here, and in summer there is lots of outdoor seating on the deck. Starters include a respectable New England–style clam chowder and a good lobster bisque. But the appetizer not to miss is the hot Dungeness crab dip, made with crab, artichoke hearts, onions, and Parmesan. Dishes on the main menu tend toward simple preparations made with lots of butter, but the daily fresh sheet has more creative dishes. The crab cakes (most recently served with a sweet and spicy Thai sauce) and the cioppino are always good bets, too.

4013 Ruston Way. ℂ 253/756-9040. www.lobstershop.com. Reservations recommended. Main courses $10–$15 at lunch, $17–$25 at dinner; brunch $17.95. AE, DC, DISC, MC, V. Mon–Thurs 11:30am–2pm and 4:30–9pm; Fri 11:30am–2:30pm and 4:30–10:30pm; Sat 4:30–10:30pm; Sun 9:30am–1:30pm (brunch) and 3:30–9pm.

Trattoria Grazie ★ ITALIAN Located only a block from the Ruston Way Parks in the Old Town neighborhood, this upscale Italian restaurant has the look and feel of an old New England tavern. Huge multipaned windows take in views of the water with the preferred seats being those on the second floor. Upstairs is also where you'll find the restaurant's small lounge, which, with its wood floors

Tacoma After Dark

Opened in 1983, the **Tacoma Dome,** 2727 East D St. (© 253/272-3663; www.tacomadome.org), which rises beside I-5 on the east side of the city, is Tacoma's most visible landmark and is the world's largest wood-domed arena. With seating for 28,000 people, it is the site of concerts, sporting events, and other large exhibitions. Smaller productions take to the stages at the **Broadway Center for the Performing Arts,** 901 Broadway (© 253/591-5894; www.broadwaycenter.org). This center consists of three theaters within a block of each other. The **Pantages,** a renovated vaudeville theater with a neoclassical terra-cotta façade, and the **Rialto Theatre,** a classic Italianate movie palace, were both built in 1918, while the **Theatre on the Square** was built in 1993. Together these three theaters present a wide variety of nationally rec-ognized theater, music, and dance, including performances by the **Tacoma Actors Guild,** the **Tacoma Philharmonic,** the **Tacoma Symphony Orchestra,** the **Tacoma Opera,** and the **Tacoma City Ballet.**

Tacoma supports a lively theater scene that includes the **Tacoma Little Theatre,** 210 North I St. (© 253/272-2281; www.tacomalittle theatre.com), which claims to be the oldest continuously performing theater west of the Mississippi and has been staging plays for more than 80 years (tickets $13–$17). The **Tacoma Actors Guild,** 901 Broad-way (© 253/272-2145; www.tacomaactorsguild.org), is Tacoma's pre-mier professional theater company and presents six productions a year (tickets $20–$28), including both well-known and more experimental plays. Performances are held in the Theatre on the Square right next door to the Pantages Theatre. Fans of musicals have the **Tacoma Musi-cal Playhouse,** Narrows Theatre, 7116 Sixth Ave. (© 253/565-6TMP; www.TMP.org), which has been growing ever more popular since its founding in 1994 (tickets $10–$17).

and abundance of polished wood, has a very classic feel to it. A wood-burning oven is the centerpiece in the kitchen and turns out good pizzas.

2301 N. 30th St. © 253/627-0231. Reservations recommended. Main courses $15–$27. AE, DC, MC, V. Sun–Thurs 11am–10pm; Fri–Sat 11am–11pm.

BETWEEN TACOMA & OLYMPIA: HISTORIC STEILACOOM ⭐

Founded in 1854 by a Maine sea captain, Steilacoom is Washington's oldest incorporated town. Once a bustling seaport, the quiet little community is today a National Historic District with 32 preserved historic buildings. To reach Steilacoom, take exit 125 off I-5 south between Tacoma and Olympia, drive to Lakewood and turn left on Steilacoom Boulevard.

The Steilacoom Museum, 112 Main St. (© 253/584-4133), in the old town hall, houses exhibits on Steilacoom's pioneer history. The museum is open March through October, Tuesday through Sunday from 1 to 4pm; in February, November, and December, Friday through Sunday from 1 to 4pm (closed Jan). Suggested donation is $2. This museum is operated by the Steilacoom Histori-cal Museum Association, which also maintains the nearby **Nathaniel Orr**

Pioneer Home and Orchard, 1811 Rainier St., which was built between 1854 and 1857 and contains original furnishings. This house has been recently restored and, between April and October, is open on Sunday from 1 to 4pm. At the **Steilacoom Tribal Museum,** 1515 Lafayette St. (© **253/584-6308**), you'll find an old-fashioned museum with displays on the area's Steilacoom tribe. It's open Tuesday through Saturday from 10am to 4pm; admission is $2 for adults and $1 for seniors and students.

Steilacoom is also the site of the ferry landing for the small ferry that runs to **Anderson Island,** a quiet rural island that is popular with bicyclists. There are several parks on the island and enough scenic Puget Sound vistas to make the island a pleasant place for a leisurely afternoon drive.

WHERE TO DINE

The Bair Restaurant at Bair the Drug & Hardware Store ★ *Finds* SODA FOUNTAIN/INTERNATIONAL   Perhaps the best reason to visit Steilacoom is to have a milkshake or an ice cream soda at this historic 1906 soda fountain. While people no longer drop in for nails or tools, they do line up for ice cream sundaes and the like. The interior of this old wooden building is kept the way it might have looked back when it opened, making the place part museum, part soda fountain. This is the oldest soda fountain we know of in the Northwest and is one of our favorites. Although dinner is served on Friday and Saturday nights, and the real reason to come here is for an old-fashioned soda fountain experience.

1617 Lafayette St. © **253/588-9668.** Reservations recommended for dinner. Main courses $12–$20 at dinner, otherwise $4–$8. MC, V. Mon–Thurs 8am–3pm; Fri 9am–3pm and 5–9pm; Sat 7am–noon and 12:15–3pm; Sun 7am–1pm and 1:15–3pm.

5 Olympia

60 miles (97km) S of Seattle, 100 miles (161km) N of Portland

Located at the southernmost end of Puget Sound, Olympia is the capital of Washington and a pleasant little city, though aside from the state capitol building and a few parks, it has little of interest to attract visitors. However, the city clings to the shores of Budd Inlet's twin bays and boasts a fairly lively downtown and attractive waterfront. The city is further divided by Capitol Lake, above which, on a high bluff, stands the capitol building. Despite the political importance of being the state capital, Olympia still has the air of a small town. The downtown is compact and low-rise, and when the legislature isn't in session the city can be downright ghostly. Keeping things alive, however, are the students of Evergreen State College, a very progressive liberal-arts college.

The Olympia area has a long history, and it was near here, in what is now the city of Tumwater, that the first pioneers settled in 1844. A historic district and historical park along the Deschutes River preserve a bit of this history.

ESSENTIALS

GETTING THERE   Olympia is on I-5 at the junction with U.S. 101, which leads north around the Olympic Peninsula. Connecting the city to the central Washington coast and Aberdeen/Hoquiam is U.S. 12/Wash. 8.

The nearest airport with scheduled service is Seattle-Tacoma International Airport, 54 miles (87km) north. **Capital Aeroporter** (© **800/962-3579** or 360/754-7113; www.capair.com) provides a shuttle between the airport and Olympia. The one-way fare is $24 to $28.

Priest Point Park **1**
Olympia Farmers Market **2**
Percival Landing **3**
Washington State Capitol **4**
Washington State Capital Museum **5**

There is **Amtrak** rail service to Olympia; the station is at 6600 Yelm Hwy. SE.

VISITOR INFORMATION   Contact the **Olympia/Thurston County Visitor & Convention Bureau,** 521 Legion Way (P.O. Box 7338), Olympia, WA 98507 (✆ **877/704-7500** or 360/704-7544; www.visitolympia.com), or the **State Capitol Visitor Information Center,** 14th Avenue and Capitol Way, Olympia, WA 98501 (✆ **360/586-3460**).

GETTING AROUND   If you need a taxi, contact **Capitol City Taxi** (✆ **360/357-4949**). Public bus service is provided by **Intercity Transit** (✆ **360/786-1881**), which operates free downtown shuttle buses.

THE CAPITOL CAMPUS

Located at 14th Avenue and Capitol Way, the neoclassical **Washington State Capitol building,** constructed between 1911 and 1928, is set amid a large and attractively landscaped campus known for its flowering cherry trees and rose gardens. At 267 feet tall, this is the tallest domed masonry state capitol in the country and bears a surprising resemblance to the Capitol in that other Washington. Around its campus you'll see sculptures, the Tivoli fountain, and a conservatory (Mon–Fri 8am–3pm). The capitol is open daily with tours offered hourly between 10am and 3pm. For more information on tours of the grounds, contact the **State Capitol Visitor Center** (✆ **360/586-8687**).

OTHER AREA ATTRACTIONS

In downtown Olympia, you'll find the **Olympia Farmers Market,** 700 N. Capitol Way (© 360/352-9096), on the waterfront adjacent to Percival Landing Park. This is the second largest open-air produce market in the state; it also has numerous prepared-food vendors and features live music on the weekends. Between April and October, the market is open Thursday through Sunday from 10am to 3pm; from November to mid-December it's open Saturday and Sunday only.

If you'd like to learn more about the area's history, especially that of the Native Americans who have called this region home for thousands of years, stop by the small **Washington State Capital Museum,** 211 W. 21st Ave. (© 360/753-2580; www.wshs.org). However, it is the building itself, an Italian Renaissance mansion built in the 1920s for a former mayor of Olympia, that is the most interesting part of a visit to this museum. The museum is open Tuesday through Friday from 10am to 4pm and Saturday from noon to 4pm. Admission is $2 for adults, $1.75 for seniors, and $1 for children 6 to 18; free for children under 6.

PRESERVES, PARKS & GARDENS

Lying at the edge of downtown Olympia, **Capitol Lake** and its surrounding park lands are favorites of area joggers, canoeists, and anglers. There is an excellent view of the Capitol from the west side of the lake. Also in downtown is the 1½-mile-long (2.5km) **Percival Landing** boardwalk, which wanders along the shore of Budd Inlet past marinas, restaurants, public art, and interpretive panels. Between these two parks, you'll find Heritage Park and the Heritage Fountain, which has 47 choreographed water jets that are fun to watch. In summer, the fountain is a popular spot with local children who run through the fountains.

On the north side of Olympia along the East Bay of Budd Inlet, you'll find formal gardens, several miles of hiking trails, nice water views, and a beach at **Priest Point Park,** on East Bay Drive. The 3-mile (5km) round-trip Ellis Cove Trail provides beach access.

Just across I-5 from Olympia, you'll also find **Tumwater Falls Park,** along a rocky stretch of the Deschutes River. Here small waterfalls cascade over rocks and in the autumn, Chinook salmon can be seen as they return to the park's holding ponds. Within the park you'll find a couple of historic homes that are open to the public. The **Crosby House,** 703 Deschutes Way SW (© 360/943-9884), was built by Bing Crosby's grandparents and is open for tours from mid-March to mid-October Thursdays and Sundays from 1 to 3pm; admission is $2. The adjacent **Henderson House,** 602 Deschutes Way SW (© 360/754-4163), is open Thursday, Friday, and Sunday between 1 and 4pm; admission $2 for adults and $1 for children ages 12 to 18. Despite the waterfalls, salmon, and historic homes, the presence of the Miller Brewing Company's huge Tumwater Brewery (formerly the Olympia Brewery) looming overhead and the roaring traffic on I-5 a few feet away detract quite a bit from the aesthetics of the setting. Still, for the riverside trails and the chance to see salmon in the fall, this park is worth a visit. Oh, and by the way, if you're interested, the **Tumwater Brewery** (© 360/754-5177) offers brewery tours Monday through Saturday between 9am and 4:30pm.

Nisqually National Wildlife Refuge (© 360/753-9467), located 10 miles (16km) north of Olympia at exit 114 off I-5, preserves the delta of the Nisqually River, which is a resting and wintering ground for large numbers of migratory birds. There are 7 miles (11km) of trails through the refuge. The visitor center is open Wednesday through Sunday from 9am to 4pm. A $3 vehicle admission fee is charged.

Some 13 miles (21km) south of Olympia, near the town of Littlerock, you'll find the **Mima Mounds Natural Area Preserve,** which is an area of hundreds of small hills, each around 7 feet high. No one is sure how the mounds were formed, but their curious topography has produced much speculation over the years. The preserve is open daily, and in spring the wildflower displays here are quite impressive.

TWO NEARBY WILDLIFE ATTRACTIONS

Northwest Trek Wildlife Park ★★ *Kids*   The animals of North America are the focus of Northwest Trek, a wildlife park that covers more than 600 acres and is near the town of Eatonville. Bison roam, elk bugle, and moose munch contentedly knee-deep in the park's lake. Visitors are driven around the grounds in a naturalist-guided tram, and at certain spots, you're allowed to get out and walk to various enclosures. Among the residents here are a grizzly bear, a wolf, cougars, lynx, and bobcats. There are also more than 5 miles (8km) of nature trails to wander after viewing the animals.

11610 Trek Dr. E., Eatonville. (© 360/832-6117. www.nwtrek.org. Admission $8.75 adults, $8.25 seniors, $6 children 5–17, $4 children 3–4. Mar–Oct daily; Nov–Feb Fri–Sun and selected holidays. Call for hours. To reach the park, take Wash. 510 southeast from I-5 (exit 111) to Yelm and continue west on Wash. 702.

Wolf Haven International ★ *Kids*   Dedicated to the preservation of wolves and the education of the general public on the subject of wolves, Wolf Haven is a sanctuary for more than 30 wolves. During tours of the facility, you'll get to meet many of these canines, including a small pack that allows visitors to observe wolf pack behavior in action. Throughout the summer there are regularly scheduled special programs for both adults and children.

3111 Offut Lake Rd., Tenino. (© 800/448-9653 or 360/264-4695. www.wolfhaven.org. Admission $6 adults, $4 children 3–12. May–Sept Wed–Mon 10am–4pm; call for hours Oct–Apr. Closed Feb.

WHERE TO STAY

Phoenix Inn Suites ★ *Value*   Located within 2 blocks of the water, the Percival Landing boardwalk, several restaurants, and the Olympia Farmers Market, this new downtown hotel is a great choice for vacationers who like to leave their car parked as much as possible. Although the hotel is geared toward business travelers, the great location, large guest rooms, and many amenities make this an especially good value. Although the rooms are more junior suites than the sort of two-room suites you might find at an Embassy Suites hotel, they are quite large and well designed.

415 Capitol Way N., Olympia, WA 98501-1024. (© 877/570-0555 or 360/570-0555. Fax 360/570-1200. www.phoenixinnsuites.com. 102 units. $99–$169 double. Rates include continental breakfast. AE, DC, DISC, MC, V. **Amenities:** Indoor pool; exercise room; Jacuzzi; business center; coin-op laundry. *In room:* A/C, TV, dataport, fridge, coffeemaker, hair dryer, iron, free local calls.

WHERE TO DINE

When it's time for coffee, drop by **Batdorf & Bronson,** 513 S. Capitol Way (© **360/786-6717**), which is located right downtown. Java junkies should also be sure to stop by the **Batdorf & Bronson Tasting Room,** 200 Market St. NE (© **800/955-5282** or 360/753-4057), which is located at the company roastery and usually has five different coffees available to taste (and buy by the cup or by the pound). If tea is your preferred drink, don't miss the **Tea Lady,** 430 Washington St. SE (© **877/330-7521** or 360/786-0350), a shop that celebrates all things tea and always has several different hot teas available. If it's local micro-brews you're after, drop by the **Fishbowl Brewpub,** 515 Jefferson St. SE (℃ **360/943-3650**), which is very popular as an after-work gathering spot.

Budd Bay Café ★★ SEAFOOD   Located right in downtown Olympia, the Budd Bay Café is the city's favorite waterfront restaurant and is a perennial favorite for its lavish Sunday seafood brunch. The views from both the dining room and large deck take in the waters of Budd Bay as well as the state capitol, Just outside, the Percival Landing Waterfront Park boardwalk stretches for 1½ miles (2.5km), ideal for that after-dinner stroll. The menu includes such standards as seafood fettuccine and pan-fried oysters, but you'll also find a Mediterranean-style chicken with rosemary, artichokes, and sun-dried tomatoes. There are several good salads, including a delicious hot seafood salad. Monday through Friday, the sunset dinners ($13.95) are a good deal.

Percival Landing, 525 N. Columbia St. ℃ **360/357-6963.** www.olywa.net/bbaycafe. Reservations recommended. Main courses $7.25–$12 at lunch, $12–$30 at dinner. AE, DC, DISC, MC, V. Mon–Thurs 11am–9pm; Fri–Sat 11am–10pm; Sun 9:30am–9pm.

Capitale Espresso Grill ★ ITALIAN/MEXICAN   This casual little place, which abounds in contemporary Italian styling, is primarily known for its good, inexpensive Italian dishes (chicken and mushroom lasagna with smoked Gouda cheese, risotto, polenta), but it also does more adventurous dishes that draw on influences from Mexico and the Southwest (grilled chipotle shrimp tostadas, black bean ravioli with chipotle-lime cream sauce). This restaurant always seems to be filled with luscious aromas that tantalize the taste buds, and no matter which style of food you're in the mood for, you'll probably end up saying, "I'll take whatever it is that smells so good."

609 Capitol Way S. ℃ **360/352-8007.** Reservations recommended. Main courses $10–$12. MC, V. Mon–Fri 11:30am–9pm; Sat 5–9pm.

The Spar Cafe ★ AMERICAN   In business since 1935, this downtown diner is a Northwest classic. On the walls hang old black-and-white photos of period logging activities (the cafe's name refers to the spar trees that were used for rigging cables and pulleys), and along one wall is the original cigar counter, which is lined with glass-fronted humidor cabinets full of premium cigars. In back, through a swinging door, is a dark bar, but it's the cozy old booths out front that are the main attraction. Breakfasts here are some of the best in town (try the Fourth Avenue Mess). If it's genuine Olympia atmosphere you're looking for, this is the place.

114 E. Fourth Ave. ℃ **360/357-6444.** Main courses $6–$14. AE, DC, DISC, MC, V. Mon–Thurs 6am–10pm; Fri–Sat 6am–11pm; Sun 6am–9pm.

7

The Olympic Peninsula

The Olympic Peninsula, located in the extreme northwestern corner of Washington and home to Olympic National Park, is a rugged and remote region that was one of the last places in the continental United States to be explored. For decades its nearly impenetrable rain-soaked forests and steep, glacier-carved mountains effectively restricted settlement of the peninsula's coastal regions.

Though much of the Olympic Peninsula was designated a National Forest Preserve in 1897, and in 1909 became a national monument, it was not until 1938 that the heart of the peninsula—the jagged, snowcapped Olympic Mountains—became Olympic National Park. This region was originally preserved in order to protect the area's rapidly dwindling herds of Roosevelt elk, which are named for Pres. Theodore Roosevelt (who was responsible for the area becoming a national monument). At the time, these elk herds were being decimated by commercial hunters.

Today, however, Olympic National Park, which is roughly the size of Rhode Island, is far more than an elk reserve. It is recognized as one of the world's most important wild ecosystems. The park is unique in the contiguous United States for its temperate rain forests, which are found in the west-facing valleys of the Hoh, Queets, Bogachiel, Clearwater, and Quinault rivers. In these valleys, rainfall can exceed 150 inches per year, trees (Sitka spruce, western red cedar, Douglas fir, and western hemlock)

grow nearly 300 feet tall, and mosses enshroud the limbs of big-leaf maples.

Within a few short miles of the park's rain forests, the Olympic Mountains rise up to the 7,965-foot peak of Mount Olympus and an alpine zone where no trees grow at all. Together, elevation and heavy snowfall (the rain of lower elevations is replaced by snow at higher elevations) combine to form 60 glaciers within the park. It is these glaciers that have carved the Olympic Mountains into the jagged peaks that mesmerize visitors and beckon to hikers and climbers. Rugged and spectacular sections of the coast have also been preserved as part of the national park, and the offshore waters are designated as the Olympic Coast National Marine Sanctuary.

With fewer than a dozen roads, none of which leads more than a few miles into the park, Olympic National Park is, for the most part, inaccessible to the casual visitor. Only two roads penetrate the high country, and only one of these is paved. Likewise, only two paved roads lead into the park's famed rain forests. Although a long stretch of beach within the national park is paralleled by U.S. 101, the park's most spectacular beaches can only be reached on foot.

While the park is inaccessible to cars, it is a wonderland for hikers and backpackers. Its rugged beaches, rain-forest valleys, alpine meadows, and mountaintop glaciers offer an amazing variety of hiking and backpacking opportunities. For alpine hikes, there are the trail heads at Hurricane Ridge

The Olympic Peninsula

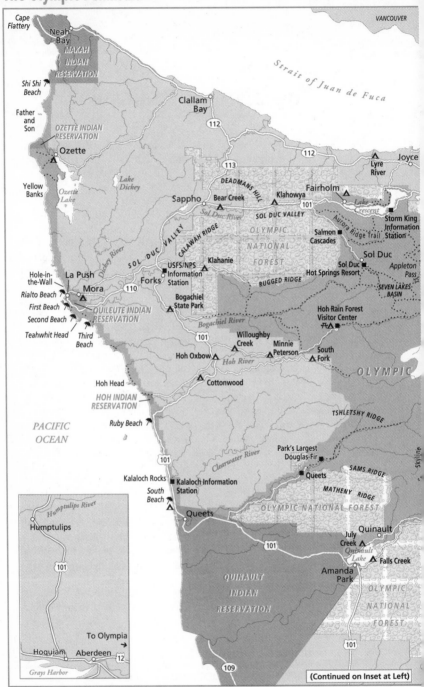

(Continued on Inset at Left)

ISLAND

Vancouver CANADA
WASHINGTON
Area of Detail
Seattle
Spokane
Tacoma
Olympia
IDAHO
Mt. Rainer
Mt. St. Helens
Portland OREGON

0 _____ 10 Mi
0 _____ 10 Km

Dungeness National Wildlife Refuge

Fort Worden S.P.

Dungeness Recreation Area

Port Townsend

Fort Flagler S.P.

Freshwater Bay

Old Fort Townsend S.P.

112

Port Angeles

Port Angeles Harbor

Olympic National Park Visitor Center

101

Port Hadlock

116

THE FOOTHILLS

Heart O' the Hills

Chimacum

101

Elwha Altaire

KLAHHANE RIDGE

Lake Mills

Deer Park

20

101

Whiskey Bend
MOUNT FITZHENRY

Hurricane Ridge

OLYMPIC

19

Port Ludlow

Mt. Carrie

Obstruction Peak

NATIONAL

104

World's Largest Subalpine Fir

Elwha River

Elkhorn

GRAY WOLF RIDGE

FOREST

Quilcene

Mt. Olympus

Cameron Pass

BAILEY RANGE

Hayes River

THE NEEDLES

Mt. Deception

Dabob Bay

NATIONAL PARK

Mt. Queets

DIAMOND MOUNTAIN

Dosewallips

Dosewallips River

Low Divide

West Peak

Mt. Anderson

Brinnon

Trail

World's Largest Western Hemlock

Duckabush River

Mt. Christie

Enchanted Valley

101

Muncaster Mountain

E. Fork Quinault River

O'Neill Peak

North Fork

Lena Creek

Quinault River

SIX RIDGE

Hamma Hamma River

Hood Canal

Graves Creek

Staircase

Lilliwaup Creek

16

Wynoochee Falls

E. Fork Skokomish River

Lake Cushman

Big Creek

Lake Cushman State Park

3

OLYMPIC

Wynoochee River

NATIONAL

Hoodsport

FOREST

106

101

To Shelton: 3 miles
To Olympia: 23 miles

3

and Deer Park. To experience the rain forest in all its drippy glory, there are the trails of the Bogachiel, Hoh, Queets, and Quinault valleys. Of these rain-forest trails, the Hoh Valley has the more accessible (and consequently more popular) trails, including the trail head for the multiday hike to the summit of Mount Olympus. Favorite coastal hikes include the stretch of coast between La Push and Oil City and from Rialto Beach north to Lake Ozette and onward to Shi Shi Beach.

The restored Victorian seaport of Port Townsend in the northeast corner of the peninsula offers a striking contrast to the wildness of Olympic National Park. Here in Port Townsend, a restored historic district filled with shops and restaurants and residential areas filled with dozens of stately Victorian homes (many of which are now bed-and-breakfast inns) have made Port Townsend one of the most popular destinations in Washington.

The rural community of Sequim (pronounced *skwim*) has also been developing quite a reputation in recent years for a very different reason. The Sequim area lies in the rain shadow of the Olympic Mountains and receives fewer than 20 inches of rain per year, less than half the average of Seattle. Sure, the skies here are still cloudy much of the year, but anyone who has lived very long in the Northwest begins to dream of someplace where it doesn't rain quite so much. In Sequim, these dreamers are building retirement homes as fast as they can.

Long before the first white settlers arrived, various Native American tribes called the Olympic Peninsula home. The Makah, Quinault, Hoh, Elwha, and Skokomish tribes all inhabited different regions of the peninsula, but all stayed close to the coast, where they could harvest the plentiful mollusks, fish, and whales. Today, there are numerous Indian reservations, both large and small, on the peninsula. On the Jamestown S'Klallam Reservation you'll find a casino, and on the Makah Reservation, a fascinating museum of culture and history.

While at first it might seem that the entire peninsula is a pristine wilderness, that just isn't the case. When the first white settlers arrived, they took one look at the 300-foot-tall trees that grew on the Olympic Peninsula and started sharpening their axes. The supply of trees seemed endless, but by the 1980s the end was in sight for the trees that had not been preserved within Olympic National Park. Today, U.S. 101, which loops around the east, north, and west side of the peninsula is lined with clear-cuts and second- and third-growth forests for much of its length, a fact that takes many first-time visitors by surprise.

1 Port Townsend: A Restored Victorian Seaport

60 miles (97km) NW of Seattle, 48 miles (77km) E of Port Angeles, 40 miles (64km) S of Anacortes

Named by English explorer Capt. George Vancouver in 1792, Port Townsend did not attract its first settlers until 1851. However, by the 1880s the town had become an important shipping port and was expected to grow into one of the most important cities on the West Coast. Port Townsend felt that it was the logical end of the line for the transcontinental railroad that was pushing westward in the 1880s; and based on the certainty of a railroad connection, real estate speculation and development boomed. Merchants and investors erected mercantile palaces along Water Street and elaborate Victorian homes on the bluff above the wharf district. However, the railroad never arrived. Tacoma got the rails, and Port Townsend got the shaft.

With its importance as a shipping port usurped by Seattle and Tacoma, Port Townsend slipped into quiet obscurity. Progress passed it by and its elegant homes and commercial buildings were left to slowly fade away. However, in 1976 the waterfront district and bluff-top residential neighborhood were declared a National Historic District and the town began a slow revival. Today the streets of Port Townsend are once again crowded with people. The waterfront district is filled with boutiques, galleries, and other interesting shops, and many of the Victorian homes atop the bluff have become bed-and-breakfast inns.

ESSENTIALS

GETTING THERE   Port Townsend is on Wash. 20, off U.S. 101 in the northeast corner of the Olympic Peninsula. The Hood Canal Bridge, which connects the Kitsap Peninsula with the Olympic Peninsula and is on the route from Seattle to Port Townsend, sometimes closes down due to high winds; if you want to be certain that it's open, call ℂ **800/695-7623**.

Washington State Ferries (ℂ **800/84-FERRY** or 888/808-7977 within Washington state, or 206/464-6400; www.wsdot.wa.gov/ferries) operates a ferry between Port Townsend and Keystone on Whidbey Island. The crossing takes 30 minutes and costs $7 to $8.75 for a vehicle and driver and $2 for passengers.

Between Port Townsend and Friday Harbor, passenger service is available from mid-April to early October from **P.S. Express** (ℂ **360/385-5288;** www. pugetsoundexpress.com), which will also carry bicycles and sea kayaks. One-way fares are $31 to $34.50 for adults and $22 to $24.50 for children; round-trip fares are $47 to $52.50 for adults and $32 to $36 for children.

You can also fly to Port Townsend from either Seattle's Boeing Field or Friday Harbor on **West Isle Air** (ℂ **800/874-4434** or 360/293-4691; www.westisleair. com). The round-trip fare from Friday Harbor is $88 and from Seattle is $150.

VISITOR INFORMATION   Contact the **Port Townsend Chamber of Commerce Visitors Information Center,** 2437 E. Sims Way, Port Townsend, WA 98368 (ℂ **888/365-6978** or 360/385-2722; www.ptguide.com).

GETTING AROUND   Because parking spaces are hard to come by in downtown Port Townsend on weekends and anytime in the summer, **Jefferson Transit** (ℂ **360/385-4777;** www.jeffersontransit.com), the local public bus service, provides a free shuttle into downtown Port Townsend from a park-and-ride lot on the south side of town. Jefferson Transit also operates other buses around Port Townsend. Fares are 50¢ to $1. If you need a taxi, call **Peninsula Taxi** (ℂ **360/385-1872).**

FESTIVALS   As a tourist town, Port Townsend schedules quite a few festivals throughout the year. The last week of March, the town celebrates its Victorian heritage with the **Victorian Festival** (ℂ **888/698-1116;** www.victorianfestival. org). The **Jazz Port Townsend** festival is held toward the end of July. The **Wooden Boat Festival,** the largest of its kind in the United States, is on the first weekend after Labor Day. During the **Kinetic Sculpture Race,** held the first Sunday in October, outrageous human-powered vehicles race on land, on water, and through a mud bog. To see inside some of the town's many restored homes, schedule a visit during the **Historic Homes Tour** on the third weekend in September.

The **Olympic Music Festival** (ℂ **206/527-8839;** www.musicfest.net), held nearby in an old barn near the town of Quilcene, is the area's most important music festival. This series of weekend concerts takes place between mid-June and mid-September.

EXPLORING THE TOWN

With its abundance of restored Victorian homes and commercial buildings, Port Townsend's most popular activity is simply walking or driving through the historic districts. The town is divided into the commercial waterfront district and the residential Uptown Port Townsend, which is atop a bluff that rises precipitously only 2 blocks from the water. Uptown Port Townsend developed in part so that proper Victorian ladies would not have to associate with the riffraff that frequented the waterfront. At the Port Townsend Visitor Information Center you can pick up a guide that lists the town's many historic homes and commercial buildings.

Water Street ✶✶ is the town's main commercial district and for several blocks is lined with 100-year-old brick buildings, many of which have ornate facades. Within these restored buildings are dozens of interesting shops and boutiques, several restaurants, and a handful of hotels and inns. To learn a little more about the history of this part of town and to gain a different perspective, walk out on **Union Wharf,** which is located at the foot of Taylor Street. Here you'll find interpretive plaques covering topics ranging from sea grass to waterfront history.

Before starting out on an exploration of the town, stop by the **Jefferson County Historical Museum and Library** ✶, 210 Madison St. (© **360/385-1003;** www. jchsmuseum.org), where you can learn about the history of the area. Among the collections here are regional Native American artifacts and antiques from the Victorian era. It's open Monday through Saturday from 11am to 4pm and Sunday from 1 to 4pm (Jan–Feb Sat–Sun only). Admission is $2 for adults and $1 for children under 12.

The town's noted Victorian homes are to be found in Uptown Port Townsend, atop the bluff that rises behind the waterfront's commercial buildings. Here you'll find stately homes, views, and the city's favorite park. To reach Uptown, either drive up Washington Street (1 block over from Water St.) or walk up the stairs at the end of Taylor Street, which start behind the Haller Fountain.

At the top of the stairs are both an 1890 bell tower that once summoned volunteer firemen and the **Rothschild House** ✶, Taylor and Jefferson streets (© **360/379-8076;** www.jchsmuseum.org), which is a Washington State Parks Heritage Site. Built in 1868, this Greek revival–style house is one of the oldest buildings in town and displays a relatively sober architecture compared to other area homes. The gardens contain a wide variety of roses, peonies, and lilacs. It's open May through September, daily from 10am to 5pm. Admission is $2 for adults and $1 for children.

However, the most fascinating Uptown home open to the public is the **Ann Starrett Mansion** ✶✶, 744 Clay St. (© **360/385-3205**), which is Port Townsend's most astoundingly ornate Queen Anne Victorian home. Currently operated as a bed-and-breakfast inn, this mansion is best known for its imposing turret, ceiling frescoes, and unusual spiral staircase. The house is open for guided tours daily from noon to 3pm. Tours cost $2.

Also here in Uptown, at the corner of Garfield and Jackson streets, you'll find **Chetzemoka Park** ✶, which was established in 1904 and is named for a local S'Klallum Indian chief. The park perches on a bluff overlooking Admiralty Inlet and has access to a pleasant beach. However, it is the rose garden, arbor, and waterfall garden that attract many visitors.

If shopping is your game, several stores stand out from the many shops that line Water Street and environs. **Earthenworks Gallery,** 702 Water St. (© 360/385-0328), showcases colorful ceramics, glass, jewelry, and other American-made crafts; **Ancestral Spirits Gallery,** 701 Water St. (© 360/385-0078), is a large space with a great selection of Northwest Native American prints, masks, and carvings; and **Artisans on Taylor,** a small boutique at 236 Taylor (© 360/379-8098), specializes in blown glass and pottery by local craftspeople. Women enamored of Port Townsend's Victorian styling will want to visit the **Palace Emporium,** 1002 Water St. (© 360/379-1661), a dress shop specializing in modern Victorian fashions. **The Wine Seller,** 940 Water St. (© 360/385-7673), has a great selection of wines chosen by the knowledgeable owner.

FORT WORDEN STATE PARK

Fort Worden State Park, once a military installation that guarded the mouth of Puget Sound, is north of the historic district and can be reached by turning onto Kearney Street at the south end of town, or onto Monroe Street at the north end of town, and following the signs. Built at the turn of the century, the fort is now a 360-acre state park where a wide array of attractions and activities assure that it's busy for much of the year. Many of the fort's old wooden buildings have been restored and put to new uses.

At the **Fort Worden Commanding Officer's House** (© 360/385-4730; www.olympus.net/ftworden), you can see what life was like for a Victorian-era officer and his family. The home has been fully restored and is filled with period antiques. In summer, it's open daily from 10am to 5pm, and in spring and fall, it's open weekends from 1 to 4pm; admission is $1 for adults, free for under 12. More military history is on display at the **Puget Sound Coast Artillery Museum** (© 360/385-0373; www.olympus.net/ftworden). In summer, the museum is open Tuesday through Sunday from 11am to 4pm, and in spring and fall, it's open Friday and Saturday from 11am to 4pm. Admission is $2 for adults and $1 for children.

Here at the park you can also learn about life below the waters of Puget Sound at the **Port Townsend Marine Science Center,** 532 Battery Way (© 360/385-5582; www.olympus.net/ptmsc). In summer, the center is open Tuesday through Sunday from 11am to 5pm, and in spring and fall, it's open weekends from noon to 4pm. Admission is $3 for adults and $2 for students and children.

However, for many people, the main reason to visit the park is to hang out on the beach or at one of the picnic areas. Scuba divers also frequent the park, which has an underwater park just offshore. In spring, the Rhododendron Garden puts on a colorful floral display. Throughout the year, there are also a wide variety of concerts and other performances at the **Centrum** (© 800/733-3608 or 360/385-5320; www.centrum.org). Also within the park are campgrounds, a restaurant, a **youth hostel** (© 360/385-0655; www.washingtonhostels.org), and restored officers' quarters that can be rented as vacation homes.

PORT TOWNSEND FROM THE WATER (& AIR)

If you'd like to explore the town from the water, there are a number of ways to do so. **The Wooden Boat Foundation,** 380 Jefferson St. (© 360/385-3628; www.woodenboat.org), which sponsors the annual Wooden Boat Festival, also offers 2-hour sailboat excursions aboard the *Araminta,* a 33-foot ketch designed in 1948 and built in 1999. Tours leave from Union Wharf at the foot of Taylor Street. Sailboat tours are also offered by **Brisa Charters** (© 360/385-2309;

www.olympus.net/brisa_charters/) and the *Bryony* (© 360/385-7639; www.
sailbryony.com), which operates between April and October and charges $65 for
a 3-hour sail. **Port Townsend Marine Science Center** (© 360/385-5582;
www.olympus.net/ptmsc) operates educational boat tours ($40) to nearby Pro-
tection Island, a wildlife refuge that is home to more than 70% of Puget Sound's
nesting seabirds. April through September, cruises ($47–$52.50 per adult)
through the San Juan Islands are offered by **Puget Sound Express,** 431 Water
St. (© 360/385-5288; www.pugetsoundexpress.com), which also offers passenger ferry service to Friday Harbor. During the summer you're almost certain to
see orca whales on these trips.

If you'd like to try your hand at paddling a sea kayak around the area's waters,
contact **Kayak Port Townsend,** 435 Water St. (© 800/853-2252 or 360/
385-6240; www.kayakpt.com), which offers 2-hour ($32), half-day ($44), and
full-day tours ($76) and also rents sea kayaks. At the nearby **Port Ludlow
Marina** (© 360/437-0513), south of Port Townsend, you can rent sea kayaks
and motorboats.

OTHER AREA ACTIVITIES

While in town, you might want to check out Port Townsend's two wineries, both
of which are located south of town. **Sorensen Cellars,** 274 S. Otto St.
(© 360/379-6416; www.sorensencellars.com), is open March through September, Friday through Sunday from noon to 5pm (or by appointment). Most wines
here are priced at a reasonable $13. To find this winery, turn east off Wash. 20
onto Frederick Street and then south on Otto Street. **Fair Winds Winery,** 1984
Hastings Ave. W. (© 360/385-6899; www.fairwindswinery.com), is open Thursday through Monday from 10am to 6pm. Be sure to try the unusual Aligoté
white wine. This is the only winery in the state producing this French-style wine.
To find this winery, drive south from Port Townsend on Wash. 20 and turn west
on Jacob Miller Road.

MARROWSTONE ISLAND

You'll find another old fort turned state park on nearby Marrowstone Island,
which is reached by driving south 9 miles (14km) to Port Hadlock on Wash. 19
and then turning east on Wash. 116. From Port Hadlock it is another 11 miles
(18km) to the northern tip of Marrowstone Island and **Fort Flagler State Park.**
This large park has a campground, boat ramp, beaches, and hiking trails.

Between Port Hadlock and Marrowstone Island is Indian Island, most of
which is an active military base. However, the waters off the island are popular
with sea kayakers. At the south end of Indian Island is a small park popular with
windsurfers.

WHERE TO STAY
IN PORT TOWNSEND
Moderate

Ann Starrett Mansion ★★   Built in 1889 for $6,000 as a wedding present
for Ann Starrett, this Victorian jewel box is by far the most elegant and ornate
bed-and-breakfast in Port Townsend (and the entire state for that matter). A
three-story turret towers over the front door of this rose and teal-green mansion,
and inside every room is exquisitely furnished with period antiques that makes
this home a museum of the Victorian era. In fact, if you aren't staying here, you
can still have a look during one of the afternoon house tours ($2). Breakfast is
an extravaganza that can last all morning and will certainly make you consider

skipping lunch. Have no doubt: This B&B is all about being pampered amid Victorian elegance.

744 Clay St., Port Townsend, WA 98368. ℰ **800/321-0644** or 360/385-3205. Fax 360/385-2976. www. starrettmansion.com. 11 units. $95–$225 double. Rates include full breakfast. AE, DISC, MC, V. *In room:* No phone.

F.W. Hastings House/Old Consulate Inn ★★
Though not quite as elaborate as the Starrett Mansion, the Old Consulate Inn is another example of the sort of Victorian excess that's so wonderfully appealing today. The attention to detail and quality craftsmanship both in the construction and the restoration of this elegant mansion are evident wherever you look. However, despite its heritage, the Old Consulate avoids being a museum; it's just a comfortable, yet elegant, place to stay. If you're here for a special occasion, consider splurging on one of the turret suites. Of the other rooms, our favorite is the Parkside. For entertainment, you'll find a grand piano, a billiards table, and a VCR, as well as stunning views out most of the windows. A multicourse breakfast is meant to be lingered over, so don't make any early morning appointments. Afternoon tea, evening cordials, and a hot tub add to the experience here.

313 Walker St., Port Townsend, WA 98368. ℰ **800/300-6753** or 360/385-6753. Fax 360/385-2097. www. oldconsulateinn.com. 8 units. $106–$160 double; $160–$210 suite. Rates include full breakfast. MC, V. **Amenities:** Jacuzzi. *In room:* Hair dryer, no phone.

James House ★★
With an eclectic blend of antique and new furnishings, this grand 1889 Victorian sits atop the bluff overlooking Admiralty Inlet. The entry hall features a parquet floor and a big staircase climbing straight up to the second floor. In the two parlors you'll find fireplaces that are the perfect gathering spot on a cool evening. The views from the upper front rooms are some of the best in town (ask for the Chintz Room, which has views and a deck, or the Master Suite). You can even see Mount Rainier on a clear day. If you don't like climbing stairs, opt for one of the ground floor suites or the Gardener's Cottage. An additional private bungalow, done in a contemporary style, is adjacent to the James House, and has a water and mountain view.

1238 Washington St., Port Townsend, WA 98368. ℰ **800/385-1238** or 360/385-1238. Fax 360/379-5551. www.jameshouse.com. 12 units. $125–$225 double. Rates include full breakfast. AE, DISC, MC, V. **Amenities:** Access to nearby health club; massage. *In room:* Dataport, hair dryer.

Manresa Castle ★★ (Value)
Built in 1892 by a wealthy baker, this reproduction of a medieval castle later became a Jesuit retreat and school. Today traditional elegance pervades Manresa Castle, and of all the hotels and B&Bs in Port Townsend, this castle offers the most historic elegance for the money. The guest rooms have a genuine, vintage appeal that manages to avoid the contrived feeling that so often sneaks into the room decor of B&Bs. The best deal in the hotel is the tower suite during the off-season. For about $130 a night you'll get a huge room with sweeping views from its circular seating area. An elegant lounge and dining room further add to the Grand Hotel feel of this unusual accommodation.

Seventh and Sheridan sts., Port Townsend, WA 98368. ℰ **800/732-1281** or 360/385-5750. Fax 360/385-5883. www.manresacastle.com. 40 units. Summer $85–$95 double; $100–$175 suite. Lower rates mid-Oct to Apr. Rates include continental breakfast. DISC, MC, V. **Amenities:** Restaurant (Continental/International) and lounge. *In room:* TV.

Palace Hotel ★
Located in the heart of the historic district, the Palace Hotel occupies a building that once served as a bordello. Today Madame Marie's suite—a big corner room with a kitchenette—is the best room in the house.

Most of the other rooms are named for former working girls. Miss Kitty's room is as nice as the Madame's and includes a cast-iron woodstove and the best views at the Palace. The Crow's Nest room is another interesting space, and features a sleeping loft, nautical theme, and woodstove. *Be forewarned:* The hotel is up a steep flight of stairs from the street, and some rooms are up on the third floor. The bathroom shared by three rooms has a big claw-foot tub, so you aren't doing too badly if you take one of these rooms.

1004 Water St., Port Townsend, WA 98368. ✆ **800/962-0741** or 360/385-0773. Fax 360/385-0780. www. olympus.net/palace. 18 units (3 with shared bathroom). $39–$85 double without bathroom, $49–$149 double with bathroom; $69–$159 suite. Rates include continental breakfast. AE, DISC, MC, V. Pets accepted ($10 per day). **Amenities:** Guest laundry. *In room:* TV, coffeemaker.

Ravenscroft Inn ★★   Built in 1987 but designed in keeping with Port Townsend's historic homes, this inn offers rooms with distinctively different moods. The Mount Rainier Room, with its gorgeous views, fireplace, and whirlpool tub for two, is a perennial favorite; as is the Fireside Room, which has a fireplace, veranda, and four-poster bed. Two other rooms also open onto a veranda, and some rooms on the upper levels have good views of the mountains and water. Pretty gardens surround the house.

533 Quincy St., Port Townsend, WA 98368. ✆ **800/782-2691** or 360/385-2784. www.ravenscroftinn.com. 8 units. $85–$190 double. Rates include full breakfast. AE, DISC, MC, V. *In room:* No phone.

Inexpensive

The Belmont ★   Built in 1885, The Belmont is the oldest waterfront restaurant and saloon in town, and on the second floor, you'll find four very spacious, if not exactly luxurious, rooms. The two in back open right onto the water and offer one of the best views in town. Exposed brick walls provide character, and three of the rooms have loft sleeping areas. Expect some noise from the saloon downstairs. The Belmont also rents out three suites across the street, four cottages in nearby Port Hadlock, and a few vacation homes as well. Although these rooms are definitely not for the finicky, they've got loads of character.

925 Water St., Port Townsend, WA 98368. ✆ **360/385-3007.** Fax 360/344-3213. www.the-belmont.com. 11 units. $59–$99 double. AE, DC, DISC, MC, V. **Amenities:** Restaurant (Regional American); room service. *In room:* Coffeemaker.

IN PORT LUDLOW

Heron Beach Inn on Ludlow Bay ★★   Set on a tiny peninsula jutting into Ludlow Bay, this luxurious inn is one of the finest in the Northwest and has helped the Ludlow Bay resort community realize its dream of becoming one of *the* Puget Sound waterfront destinations. The setting rivals anything in the San Juan Islands, and the inn itself conjures up the image of a New England summer home at the shore. Designed for romantic getaways, the guest rooms are spacious and plush, with whirlpool tubs, fireplaces, and down-filled duvets on the beds. Best of all, every room has a water view and from some you can see Mount Baker or the Olympic Mountains. Breakfasts are served in a bright sunroom with teak furnishings that evoke a nautical feel, and in the evening, the dining room (the finest restaurant in this neck of the Olympic Peninsula) serves superb Northwest cuisine. Additional amenities include paved walking paths through the adjacent resort and a croquet lawn.

One Heron Rd., Port Ludlow, WA 98365. ✆ **360/437-0411.** Fax 360/437-0310. www.heronbeachinn.com. 37 units. $125–$225 double; $250–$450 suite. Rates include continental breakfast. AE, MC, V. **Amenities:** Restaurant (Northwest) and lounge; 27-hole golf course; tennis courts; spa services; bike rentals; watersports rentals; massage. *In room:* TV/VCR, dataport, fridge, coffeemaker, hair dryer, iron.

WHERE TO DINE
IN PORT TOWNSEND

One place on nearly everyone's itinerary during a visit to Port Townsend is **Elevated Ice Cream** ★, 627 Water St. (© **360/385-1156**), which is open daily and scoops up the best ice cream in town. For espresso, drop by **Tyler Street Coffee House**, 215 Tyler St. (© **360/379-4185**). For tea instead of coffee, check out **Wild Sage**, 227 Adams St. (© **360/379-1222**). For pastries, light meals, and good coffee, try **Bread & Roses Bakery**, 230 Quincy St. (© **360/385-1044**).

Moderate

The Belmont ★ NORTHWEST   With so much water all around, the most surprising thing about dining in Port Townsend is that there are so few waterfront restaurants. This, the best of them, is also the oldest waterfront restaurant and hotel in town, dating from 1889. While the interior doesn't really conjure up the 1890s, the view out the back, especially from the small deck, is great. The menu delves into some interesting flavor combinations and draws on a lot of different influences (chicken with a pistachio and raspberry-bacon vinaigrette, grilled prawns with a citrus Grand Marnier sauce and cranberries, baby back pork ribs baked in ale, brown sugar, and barbecue sauce).

925 Water St. © 360/385-3007. www.the-belmont.com. Reservations recommended. Main courses $7–$25. AE, DC, DISC, MC, V. Summer Mon–Thurs 11:30am–3pm and 4:30–9pm, Fri–Sun 11:30am–9pm; winter Mon–Thurs 11:30am–3pm and 4:30–8:30pm, Fri–Sat 11:30am–9pm.

Lonny's Restaurant ★★ ITALIAN/NORTHWEST   Located across the street from the Boat Haven marina south of downtown Port Townsend, this is a romantic, low-key place that's a welcome alternative to the touristy restaurants downtown. The menu is fairly long and there are always plenty of daily specials. Whether you come for lunch or dinner, be sure to start with the oyster stew, which is made with pancetta and fennel. Also at both lunch and dinner, you'll find a wide variety of interesting pasta dishes from which to choose, but the rigatoni Gorgonzola is our favorite. Traditional Spanish paella is another tasty dish. Local oysters, mussels, and clams show up frequently on the fresh sheet and are hard to resist. There are usually some interesting wines available by the glass.

2330 Washington St. © 360/385-0700. Reservations recommended. Main courses, lunch $7.50–$11, dinner $12–$22. AE, DISC, MC, V. Wed–Mon 5–9pm.

Silverwater Café ★★ Value NORTHWEST   Works by local artists, lots of plants, and New Age music on the stereo set the tone for this casually chic restaurant. Though the menu focuses on Northwest dishes, it includes preparations from around the world. You can start your meal with an artichoke-and-Parmesan paté and then move on to ahi tuna with lavender pepper, prawns with cilantro-ginger-lime butter, or smoked chicken with brandy and apples. The oysters in a blue cheese sauce are a favorite of ours. If you're a vegetarian, there are half-a-dozen options available here.

237 Taylor St. © 360/385-6448. www.silverwatercafe.com. Reservations accepted only for 6 or more. Main courses lunch $5–$9, dinner $9–$17. MC, V. Daily, 11:30am–3pm and 5–10pm. In winter, closes at 9pm.

Inexpensive

The Fountain Café ★ Finds ECLECTIC   Housed in a narrow clapboard building, this funky little place is smaller and even more casual than the Silverwater Café, above. Eclectic furnishings decorate the room and there are a few stools at the counter. The menu changes seasonally, but you can rest assured that the simple fare here will be utterly fresh and will provide plenty of shellfish and pasta. The Greek pasta is a menu mainstay that's hard to beat, and a wide range of flavors assures that everyone will find something to his or her liking. This is a local and counterculture favorite.

920 Washington St. ℰ **360/385-1364.** Reservations not accepted. Main courses $6.50–$15. MC, V. Mon–Fri 11:30am–3pm and 5–9pm; Sat–Sun 8am–3pm and 5–9pm.

Khu Larb Thai ⊛ THAI   Located half a block off busy Water Street, Khu Larb seems a world removed from Port Townsend's sometimes-overdone Victorian decor. Thai easy-listening music plays on the stereo and the pungent fragrance of Thai spices wafts through the dining room. One taste of any dish on the menu and you'll be convinced that this is great Thai food. The *tom kha gai*, a sour-and-spicy soup with a coconut-milk base, is particularly memorable. The curry dishes made with mussels are also good bets.

225 Adams St. ℰ **360/385-5023.** Reservations not accepted. Main courses $7.50–$9. MC, V. July–Sept daily 11am–9pm (until 10pm on weekends); other months closed Mon.

IN PORT HADLOCK & PORT LUDLOW

Ajax Cafe ⊛⊛ *Value* INTERNATIONAL   With not a matching glass or two chairs the same in the whole restaurant, this long-time local favorite is as eclectic a place as you'll find—and a lot of fun, too. Located on the old waterfront in Port Hadlock in an old wooden storefront, the restaurant is out of the way and funky, and that's exactly why it's so popular. Silly hats hang from the ceiling and the restroom walls are hung with loud ties, and patrons are encouraged to don silly garb while dining. The menu runs the gamut from a Mediterranean seafood stew to ribs spiked with Jack Daniel's whiskey, and specials incorporate whatever is fresh and seasonal (a delicious appetizer of sautéed wild mushrooms on a recent autumn night). Best of all, there's live music on the weekends. If you like good times and good food, this is a "don't miss." The perpetual party atmosphere makes this is a great place for a celebration.

Lower Hadlock Rd., Port Hadlock. ℰ **360/385-3450.** Reservations recommended. Main courses $12–$17. MC, V. Sun and Tues–Thurs 5–9pm; Fri–Sat 5–9:30pm. Closed Jan.

Waypoints ⊛⊛ NORTHWEST   With its water views, immaculately set tables, and superb cuisine, this is the finest restaurant in the area these days, which is in keeping with the luxurious surroundings of this waterfront lodge south of Port Townsend. The menu, which changes seasonally, is short, with creative flavor combinations as the keynote. Be sure to start with the tangy coconut-lime seafood chowder. Among the entrees were a bacon-wrapped salmon stuffed with wild mushrooms and topped with cilantro pesto. Want to enjoy the inn's atmosphere but can't afford the prices? Although the food isn't the same (with the exception of the seafood chowder), the adjacent Fireside Room lounge does serve simple meals.

Heron Beach Inn on Ludlow Bay, One Heron Rd., Port Ludlow. ℰ **360/437-0411.** Reservations recommended. Main courses $18–$29. AE, DISC, MC, V. July–Sept daily 5:30–9:30pm; Oct–June Wed–Sun 5:30–9:30pm.

PORT TOWNSEND AFTER DARK

On weekend nights, you can catch live music at **Lanza's,** 1020 Lawrence St. (ℰ **360/379-1900**), an Italian restaurant; and the **Public House,** 1038 Water St. (ℰ **360/385-9708**), which books an eclectic range of music and has the feel of a 19th-century tavern. If you're lucky, you might catch a performance by Port Townsend's own **Flying Karamazov Brothers,** though they spend most of their time on the road. Check with the Visitors Information Center for a schedule of area events.

HIKING OLYMPIC PENINSULA EAST

South of Port Townsend, U.S. 101 follows the west shore of Hood Canal. Off this highway are several dead-end roads that lead to trail heads in Olympic National Forest. These trail heads are the starting points for many of the best day hikes on the Olympic Peninsula and lead into several different wilderness areas, as well as into Olympic National Park. Many of these hikes lead to the summits of mountains with astounding views across the Olympic Mountains and Puget Sound.

Two miles (3km) south of Quilcene, you'll find Penny Creek/Big Quilcene River Road, which leads to the trail heads for both **Marmot Pass** and **Mount Townsend**—two of the best day-hike destinations on the peninsula. Both of these trails are between 10- and 11-mile round-trip hikes. Up the Dosewallips River Road west of Brinnon, you'll find the trail head for the very popular 4-mile (6km) round-trip hike to **Lake Constance.** Up the Hamma Hamma River Road, just north of Eldon, you'll find the trail head for the hike to the beautiful **Lena Lakes** area. West of Hoodsport are the popular **Lake Cushman** and the trail heads for the 2-mile (3km) round-trip hike along the scenic **Staircase Trail,** the 4½-mile (7km) round-trip hike to the summit of **Mount Ellinor,** and the 16-mile (26km) round-trip hike to the **Flapjack Lakes,** which are a very popular overnight destination. For information contact **Quilcene Ranger Station,** 295142 U.S. 101 S. (P.O. Box 280), Quilcene, WA 98376 (✆ **360/765-2200**).

2 Sequim & Dungeness Valley

17 miles (27km) E of Port Angeles, 31 miles (50km) W of Port Townsend

Located in the rain shadow of the Olympic Mountains, Sequim (remember, it's pronounced *skwim*) is the driest region of the state west of the Cascade Range and, consequently, sodden, moss-laden Northwesterners have taken to retiring here in droves. While the rains descend on the rest of the region, the fortunate few who call Sequim home bask in their own personal microclimate of sunshine and warmth.

The lack of rainfall and temperate climate here also make this an almost perfect place to grow lavender plants and today, parts of Sequim take on the look of Provence each summer when the lavender plants are in bloom. There are U-pick farms, shops selling all manner of lavender products, and, of course, an annual lavender festival.

Before this area became known for its lavender farms, it was famous for its hefty crustaceans. The nearby town of Dungeness is set at the foot of Dungeness Spit, which, at more than 6 miles (9.5km) in length, is the longest sand spit in the world. However, it is for lending its name to the Northwest's favorite crab that Dungeness is most famous. The Dungeness crab is as much a staple of Washington waters as the blue crab is in the Chesapeake Bay region.

ESSENTIALS

GETTING THERE   The Sequim-Dungeness Valley lies to the north of U.S. 101 between Port Townsend and Port Angeles. **Jefferson Transit** (✆ **360/385-4777;** www.jeffersontransit.com) has service from Port Townsend to Sequim, and **Clallam Transit** (✆ **800/858-3747** or 360/452-4511; www.clallamtransit.com) operates west from Sequim and around the peninsula to Lake Crescent, Neah Bay, La Push, and Forks.

VISITOR INFORMATION   For more information contact the **Sequim-Dungeness Valley Chamber of Commerce,** 1192 E. Washington St. (P.O. Box 907), Sequim, WA 98382-0907 (© **800/737-8462** or 360/683-6197; www.visitsun.com).

FESTIVALS   The **Irrigation Festival** (© **800/737-8563;** www.irrigation festival.com), the oldest continuous festival in Washington, takes place in early May. In mid-July, when the lavender gardens are in full bloom, the town observes the season with its **Celebrate Lavender** Festival (© **800/500-8401;** www.lavenderfestival.com).

EXPLORING THE AREA

Just east of Sequim on U.S. 101, you'll find the **7 Cedars Casino,** 270756 U.S. 101 (© **800/4-LUCKY-7** or 360/683-7777), which is operated by the Jamestown S'Klallam Tribe and is designed to resemble a traditional longhouse, with several large totem poles out front. Nearby, you can visit the tribe's **Native Art Gallery,** 1033 Old Blyn Hwy. (© **360/681-4640**), where both quality and prices are high.

In downtown Sequim, you'll find the **Museum & Arts Center,** 175 W. Cedar St., Sequim (© **360/683-8110;** www.sequimmusuem.org), which houses a pair of mastodon tusks that were found near here in 1977. The mastodon had been killed by human hunters, a discovery that helped establish the presence of humans in this area 12,000 years ago. The museum also has an exhibit on the much more recent culture of the region's Native Americans. Open Monday through Saturday from 9am to 4pm (Sun 1–4pm in summer; closed Mon in winter); admission is free.

If you've got the kids with you, Sequim's **Olympic Game Farm** ⊛, 1423 Ward Rd. (© **800/778-4295** or 360/683-4295; www.olygamefarm.com), is a must. The animals here have appeared in more than 80 movies and TV shows. You'll get up close and personal with bison, Kodiak bears, zebras, wolves, elk, deer, and many other species. There are drive-through and walking tours as well as a petting farm. The farm is open daily from 9am; admission is $9 for adults, $7 for seniors and children ages 6 to 12, and free for children 5 and under.

The biggest attraction is Dungeness Spit, which is protected as the **Dungeness National Wildlife Refuge** ⊛⊛ (© **360/457-8451**). Within the refuge there is a half-mile trail to a bluff-top overlook, but it is the spit, where you can hike for more than 5 miles (8km) to the lighthouse, that is the favorite hiking area (a $3 fee per family is charged to walk the spit). Along the way you're likely to see numerous species of birds as well as harbor seals. Near the base of the spit, you'll find the **Dungeness Recreation Area** (© **360/683-5847**), which has a camp-ground, picnic area, and trail leading out to the spit. Camping and water access are available at **Sequim Bay State Park** (© **360/683-4235**), about 3 miles (5km) southeast of Sequim.

Sequim has also become known for its many lavender farms, which paint the landscape with their colorful blooms each summer. Sequim's climate is ideal for growing lavender, and you'll likely pass numerous large fields of this fragrant Mediterranean plant as you tour the area. If you want to get into a lavender field, you've got plenty of options. **Purple Haze Lavender,** 180 Bell Bottom Rd. (© **360/683-1714;** www.purplehazelavender.com), a U-pick farm that is located east of downtown Sequim off W. Sequim Bay Road, is one of our favorites. The farm is open daily from 9 to 5pm and has a gift shop in a small barn. Up near the Dungeness Spit, you'll find another great farm, **Jardin du Soleil Lavender,** 3932 Sequim Dungeness Way (© **877/527-3461** or

360/582-1185; www.jardindusoleil.com). This organic lavender farm surrounds an old farmhouse that has Victorian gardens. The farm is open daily from 10am to 5pm. In the same area, you can visit the **Olympic Lavender Farm,** 1432 Marine Dr. (© **360/683-4475;** www.olympiclavender.com), which is open daily from noon to 5pm in July and August. Although **Cedarbrook Herb Farm,** 1345 Sequim Ave. S. (© **360/683-7733;** www.lavenderfarms.com), isn't specifically a lavender farm, it is well worth a visit. Here you can buy herb plants as well as herb vinegars, potpourris, dried flowers, lavender wands, garlic braids, and the like. You'll find this farm south of downtown Sequim at the top of a hill overlooking the town. It's open Monday through Saturday from 9am to 5pm and Sunday from 10am to 4pm. Off to the southwest of Sequim, you'll find **Lost Mountain Lavender,** 1541 Taylor Cutoff Rd. (© **360/681-2782;** www.lavenderfarms.com). This farm is open daily from 10am to 5pm in July and August and on weekends in June, September, and October.

If you're interested in tasting some locally produced wine, drive out to the **Lost Mountain Winery,** 3174 Lost Mountain Rd. (© **360/683-5229;** www.lostmountain.com), which produces Italian-style wines with no added sulfites. To find the winery from U.S. 101, go south 3 miles (5km) on Taylor Cut Off Road and turn right on Lost Mountain Road.

The Sequim-Dungeness Valley is one of the best areas in the state for **bicycle touring.** The roads are flat, there are great views, and you don't have to worry as much about getting rained on.

WHERE TO STAY

Juan de Fuca Cottages ★   Located across the street from the water and surrounded by wide green lawns, these well-tended cottages have excellent views. While most face the water, the best views are actually from the one cottage that faces the Olympic Mountains to the south. This cabin has skylights and a long wall of windows. Other cottages also have skylights and all have whirlpool tubs and kitchenettes. The cottages also have their own little private beach. Although prices seem high for what you get, these cottages can all sleep at least four people.

182 Marine Dr., Sequim, WA 98382. © 360/683-4433. www.juandefucacottages.com. 6 units. $100–$200 double. DISC, MC, V. *In room:* TV/VCR, kitchenette, fridge, coffeemaker, hair dryer, iron.

WHERE TO DINE

If you're in need of a light lunch, don't miss **Jean's Deli** ★, 134 S. Second St. (© **360/683-6727**). **Petals Garden Café** ★, Cedarbrook Herb Farm, 1345 S. Sequim Ave. (© **360/683-4541**), at the top of a hill on the south side of the highway bypass around Sequim, is a great place for lunch if you are an avid gardener. This sandwich shop is located in a historic church building a block off Sequim's main street. For coffee, head for **Hurricane Coffee,** 104 W. Washington St. (© **360/681-6008**).

Khu Larb Thai ★ THAI   Located a block off Sequim's main drag, this is our favorite Sequim restaurant. Sure it doesn't exactly conjure up the Northwest with its spicy cuisine, but on a damp dreary day, a plate of spicy Thai food goes a long way toward warming a person. The *tom kha gai,* a sour-and-spicy soup with a coconut-milk base, should not be missed.

120 W. Bell St. © 360/681-8550. Main courses $7.50–$9. MC, V. Tues–Sun 11am–2:30pm and 4:30–9pm.

The Original Oyster House ★ SEAFOOD   Located on the shore of Discovery Bay east of Sequim, this restaurant is hidden from the highway, down a winding driveway through an associated condominium complex. The restaurant has a cozy little dining room with big windows that offer a pristine view of the bay and the hills on the opposite shore. In summer, the deck is the place to dine. Not surprisingly, the menu is heavy on oyster dishes, our favorite is the Discovery Bay oysters dish (baked oysters with brandy, garlic, pine nuts, and Parmesan). If you don't eat oysters, try the coconut-almond prawns, cioppino, and salmon. Monday through Friday, there are $11.95 early-bird dinners between 4 and 6pm.

280417 U.S. 101. © **360/385-1785.** Reservations recommended. Main dishes $12.75–$31.50. AE, DC, DISC, MC, V. Daily 4–8 or 9pm (in summer, Sun noon–8 or 9pm).

3 Olympic National Park North & the Northern Olympic Peninsula

Port Angeles park entrance: 48 miles (77km) W of Port Townsend, 57 miles (92km) E of Forks

The northern portions of Olympic National Park are both the most accessible and most heavily visited. It is here, south of Port Angeles, that the only two roads leading into the high country of the national park are found. Of these the Hurricane Ridge area is the more easily reached. The Deer Park area is at the end of a harrowing gravel road and thus is little visited. West of Port Angeles and within the national park lie two large lakes, Lake Crescent and Lake Ozette, that attract boaters and anglers. Also in this region are two hot springs—the developed Sol Duc Resort and the natural Olympic Hot Springs.

Outside the park boundaries, along the northern coast of the peninsula, are several campgrounds, and a couple of small sportfishing ports, Sekiu and Neah Bay, that are also popular with scuba divers. Neah Bay, which is on the Makah Indian Reservation, is also the site of one of the most interesting culture and history museums in the state. This reservation encompasses Cape Flattery, which is the northwesternmost point in the contiguous United States. Along the coastline between Port Angeles and Neah Bay are several spots popular with sea kayakers.

Port Angeles, primarily a lumber-shipping port, is the largest town on the north Olympic Peninsula and serves both as a base for people exploring the national park and as a port for ferries crossing the Strait of Juan de Fuca to Victoria, British Columbia. It is here that you will find the region's greatest concentration of lodgings and restaurants.

ESSENTIALS

GETTING THERE   U.S. 101 circles Olympic National Park, with main park entrances south of Port Angeles, at Lake Crescent, and at the Hoh River south of Forks.

Horizon Air (© **800/547-9308;** www.horizonair.com) flies between Seattle-Tacoma International Airport and Port Angeles. Rental cars are available in Port Angeles from Budget Rent-A-Car.

There is a **bus shuttle** to Port Angeles from Seattle and Sea-Tac Airport on **Olympic Bus Lines** (© **800/457-4492** or 360/417-0700; www.olympicbus lines.com). Reservations are recommended. **Jefferson Transit** (© **360/ 385-4777;** www.jeffersontransit.com) has service from Port Townsend to Sequim, where you can transfer to service on **Clallam Transit** (© **800/ 858-3747** or 360/452-4511; www.clallamtransit.com), which operates from Sequim around the peninsula to Lake Crescent, Neah Bay, La Push, and Forks.

Two **ferries,** one for foot passengers only and the other for vehicles and foot passengers, connect Port Angeles and Victoria, British Columbia. The ferry terminal for both ferries is at the corner of Laurel Street and Railroad Avenue. **Victoria Express** (✆ **800/633-1589;** www.victoriaexpress.com) is the faster of the two ferries (1 hr. between Victoria and Port Angeles) and carries foot passengers only. This ferry runs only between Memorial Day weekend and the end of September. One-way fares are $12.50 for adults, $11.50 for seniors, $7.50 for children 5 to 11; and free for children under 5. The **Black Ball Transport** (✆ **360/457-4491** or 250/386-2202 in Victoria; www.northolympic.com/coho) ferry operates year-round except for 2 weeks in late January or early February and carries vehicles as well as walk-on passengers. The crossing takes slightly more than 1½ hours. The one-way fares are $7.75 for adults, $3.90 for children 5 to 11; $29.75 for a car, van, camper, or motor home and driver. Note that Black Ball Transport does not accept personal checks or credit/charge cards.

VISITOR INFORMATION   For more information on the national park, contact the **Olympic National Park,** 600 E. Park Ave., Port Angeles, WA 98362 (✆ **360/565-3130;** www.nps.gov/olym). For more information on Port Angeles and the rest of the northern Olympic Peninsula, contact the **North Olympic Peninsula Visitor and Convention Bureau,** 338 W. First St. (P.O. Box 670), Port Angeles, WA 98362 (✆ **800/942-4042** or 360/452-8552; www.olympic peninsula.org); or the **Port Angeles Visitors Center,** 121 E. Railroad Ave., Port Angeles, WA 98362 (✆ **877/456-8372** or 360/452-2363; www.cityofpa.com).

FESTIVALS   Each year in late August, **Makah Days** are celebrated in Neah Bay (on the Makah Indian Reservation) with canoe races, Indian dancing, a salmon bake, and other events.

PARK ADMISSION   Park admission is $10 per vehicle and $5 per pedestrian or cyclist.

EXPLORING THE PARK'S NORTH SIDE

Port Angeles is the headquarters for the park, and it's here that you'll find the **Olympic National Park Visitor Center,** 3002 Mount Angeles Rd. (✆ **360/565-3130**). Mount Angeles Road is on the south edge of town and leads up to **Hurricane Ridge.** In addition to having lots of information, maps, and books about the park, the center has exhibits on the park's flora and fauna, old-growth forests, and whaling by local Native Americans. It's open daily from 9am to 4pm, with longer hours in the summer.

From the visitor center, continue another 17 miles (27km) on this road to Hurricane Ridge, which on clear days offers the most breathtaking views in the park. In summer the surrounding subalpine meadows are carpeted with wildflowers. Several hiking trails lead into the park from here, and several day hikes are possible (the 3-mile/5km **Hurricane Hill Trail** ★★ and the 1-mile/1.5km **Meadow Loop Trail** ★★ are the most scenic). In winter Hurricane Ridge is a popular cross-country skiing area and also has two rope tows and a Poma lift for downhill skiing. For more information, contact **Hurricane Ridge Public Development Authority** (✆ 360/457-4519 or 360/565-3131 for road conditions; www.hurricaneridge.net). The Hurricane Ridge Visitor Center has exhibits on alpine plants and wildlife. In summer, you're likely to see deer grazing in the meadows here and marmots, relatives of squirrels, lounging on rocks or nibbling on flowers.

A few miles east of Port Angeles, another road heads south into the park to an area called **Deer Park.** This narrow, winding gravel road is a real test of nerves and consequently is not nearly as popular a route as the road to Hurricane Ridge. However, the scenery once you reach the end of the road is just as breathtaking as that from Hurricane Ridge. As the name implies, deer are common in this area. To reach this area, turn south at the Deer Park movie theater.

West of Port Angeles a few miles, up the Elwha River, you'll find the short trail (actually an abandoned road) that leads to **Olympic Hot Springs** ✿. These natural hot pools are in a forest setting and are extremely popular and often crowded, especially on weekends. For more developed hot springs soaking, head to Sol Duc Resort, west of Lake Crescent.

West of Port Angeles on U.S. 101 lies **Lake Crescent** ✿✿, a glacier-carved lake surrounded by steep forested mountains that give the lake the feel of a fjord. This is one of the most beautiful lakes in the state and has long been a popular destination. Near the east end of the lake, you'll find the **Storm King Ranger Station** (✆ 360/928-3380), which is usually open in the summer and at other seasons when a ranger is in the station, and the 1-mile (1.5km) trail to 90-foot-tall **Marymere Falls** ✿. From this trail, you can also hike the steep 1¾ miles (3km) up **Mount Storm King** to a viewpoint overlooking Lake Crescent (climbing above the viewpoint is not recommended). On the north side of the lake, you'll find the **Spruce Railroad Trail,** which parallels the shore of the lake, crosses a picturesque little bridge, and is one of the only trails in the park that is open to mountain bikes. As the name implies, this was once the route of the railroad built to haul spruce out of these forests during World War I. Spruce was the ideal wood for building biplanes because of its strength and light weight. However, by the time the railroad was completed, the war was over and the demand for spruce had dwindled.

There are several places on the lake where you can rent various types of small boats during the warmer months. At **Lake Crescent Lodge** ✿✿ you can rent rowboats, and at the **Fairholm General Store** (✆ 360/928-3020), at the lake's west end, rowboats, canoes, and motorboats are available between April and October. The **Log Cabin Resort** on the north side of Lake Crescent rents rowboats, canoes, and pedal boats.

Continuing west from Lake Crescent, watch for the turnoff to **Sol Duc Hot Springs** ✿✿ (✆ 360/327-3583). For 14 miles (23km) the road follows the Soleduck River, passing the Salmon Cascades along the way. Sol Duc Hot Springs were for centuries considered healing waters by local Indians, and after white settlers arrived in the area, the springs became a popular resort. In addition to the hot swimming pool and soaking tubs, you'll find cabins, a campground, a restaurant, and a snack bar. The springs are open daily from mid-April to late October; admission is $10 for adults. A 4½-mile (2.5km) loop trail leads from the hot springs to **Sol Duc Falls,** which are among the most photographed falls in the park. Alternatively, you can drive to the end of the Sol Duc Road and make this an easy 1½-mile (2.5km) hike. Along this same road, you can also hike the half-mile **Ancient Groves Nature Trail.** Note that Sol Duc Road is one of the roads on which you'll have to pay an Olympic National Park admission fee.

EXPLORING THE PENINSULA'S NORTHWEST CORNER

Continuing west on U.S. 101 from the junction with the road to Sol Duc Hot Springs brings you to the crossroads of Sappho. Heading north at Sappho will bring you to Wash. 112, which is an alternative route from Port Angeles. It is about 40 miles (64km) from this road junction to the town of **Neah Bay** on the Makah Indian Reservation.

Between Clallam Bay and Neah Bay, the road runs right alongside the water and there are opportunities to spot seabirds and marine mammals, including gray, orca, humpback, and pilot whales. Between February and April, keep an eye out for the dozens of bald eagles that gather along this stretch of coast. In Clallam Bay, at the county day-use park, you can hunt for agates and explore tide pools. Near Slip Point Lighthouse, there are fossil beds that are exposed at low tides.

Neah Bay is a busy commercial and sportfishing port, and is also home to the impressive **Makah Cultural and Research Center** ✦✦, Bayview Avenue (© **360/645-2711;** www.makah.com/museum.htm), which displays artifacts from a Native American village that was inundated by a mudslide 500 years ago. This is the most perfectly preserved collection of Native American artifacts in the Northwest; part of the exhibit includes reproductions of canoes the Makah once used for hunting whales. There's also a longhouse that shows the traditional lifestyle of the Makah people. Between Memorial Day and September 15, the museum is open daily from 10am to 5pm, and between September 16 and Memorial Day, it's open Wednesday through Sunday from 10am to 5pm; admission is $4 for adults, $3 for students and seniors, free for children 5 and under.

The reservation land includes **Cape Flattery** ✦✦✦, which is the northwest-ernmost point of land in the contiguous United States. Just off the cape lies Tatoosh Island, site of one of the oldest lighthouses in Washington. Cape Flat-tery is one of the most dramatic stretches of Pacific coastline in the Northwest, and is a popular spot for a bit of hiking and ocean viewing. There is an excellent 1½-mile (2.5km) round-trip trail, complete with boardwalks, stairs, and viewing platforms, that leads out to the cliffs overlooking Tatoosh Island. Keep an eye out for whales and sea otters. Bird-watchers will definitely want to visit Cape Flattery, which is on the Pacific Fly Way. More than 250 species of birds have been spotted here, and in the spring, raptors gather here before crossing the Strait of Juan de Fuca. Also be aware that car break-ins are not uncommon here, so take your valuables with you. For directions to the trail head, stop by the Makah Museum. At the museum, you'll also need to purchase a $7 Recreational Use Permit that will allow you to park at the Cape Flattery trail head.

A turnoff 16 miles (26km) east of Neah Bay leads south to **Ozette Lake** ✦✦, where there are boat ramps, a campground, and, stretching north and south, miles of beaches that are only accessible on foot. A 3¼-mile (5.5km) trail on a raised boardwalk leads from the Ozette Lake trail head to **Cape Alava** ✦✦, which is one of two places claiming to be the westernmost point in the contiguous United States (the other is Cape Blanco, on the Oregon coast). The large rocks just offshore here are known as haystack rocks or sea stacks and are common all along the rocky western coast of the Olympic Peninsula, which is characterized by a rugged coastline. Aside from five coastal Indian reservations, almost all this northern coastline is preserved as part of the national park.

GUIDED TOURS, EDUCATIONAL PROGRAMS & OUTDOOR ADVENTURES
GUIDED TOURS
If you'd like to see the park on a guided tour, contact **Olympic Tours and Charters** (© **360/452-3500;** www.tourtheolympics.com), which offers tours to Hurricane Ridge, the Hoh River rain forest, and ocean beaches. Tours range from a few hours to all day and cost $19 to $52.

For an interesting offshore tour to the Olympic Coast National Marine Sanctuary, contact **Puffin Adventures** (© **888/305-2437** or 360/963-2744; www. olypen.com/puffinadventures). These boat tours, which operate between April and September, explore the waters off Cape Flattery and Tatoosh Island, where you can see as many as eight species of pelagic birds, including tufted puffins.

EDUCATIONAL PROGRAMS

The **Olympic Park Institute,** 111 Barnes Point Rd., Port Angeles, WA 98363 (© **360/928-3720;** www.yni.org/opi), which is located in the Rosemary Inn on Lake Crescent, offers a wide array of summer field seminars ranging from painting classes to bird-watching trips to multiday backpacking trips.

OUTDOOR ADVENTURES

BICYCLING If you're interested in exploring the region on a bike, you can rent one at **Sound Bikes & Kayaks,** 120 E. Front St., Port Angeles (© **360/ 457-1240**), which can recommend good rides in the area and also offers bicycle tours. Bikes are $26 per day or $9 per hour.

FISHING The rivers of the Olympic Peninsula are well known for their fighting salmon, steelhead, and trout. In Lakes Crescent and Ozette you can fish for such elusive species as Beardslee and Crescenti trout. No fishing license is necessary to fish for trout on national park rivers and streams or in Lake Crescent or Lake Ozette. However, you will need a state punch card—available wherever fishing licenses are sold—to fish for salmon or steelhead. For more information on freshwater fishing in the park, contact Olympic National Park. Boat rentals are available on Lake Crescent at Fairholm General Store, the Log Cabin Resort, and Lake Crescent Lodge.

If you want to hire a guide to take you out on the rivers to where the big salmon and steelhead are biting, try **Diamond Back Guide Service** (© **360/ 452-9966;** www.northolympic.com/diamondback/), which charges $225 per day for two people, or **Sol Duc River Lodge Guide Service** (© **866/868-0128** or 360/327-3709; www.solducriverfishing.com), which charges $380 per day for two people, but that rate includes your room, breakfast, and lunch.

If you're more interested in heading out on open water to do a bit of salmon or deep-sea fishing, numerous charter boats operate out of Sekiu and Neah Bay. In the Sekiu/Clallam Bay area, contact **Puffin Adventures** (© **888/305-2437** or 360/963-2744; www.olypen.com/puffinadventures), or **Olson's Charters** (© **360/963-2311;** www.olsonsresort.com). In Neah Bay, try **King Fisher Charters** (© **888/622-8216** or 360/645-2150; www.kingfisherenterprises. com). Expect to pay from $85 to $150 per person for a day of fishing.

HIKING & BACKPACKING For several of the most popular backpacking destinations in Olympic National Park (the Ozette Coast Loop, Grand Valley, Royal Basin, Badger Valley, Flapjack Lakes, and Lake Constance), advance-reservation hiking permits are required or highly recommended between May 1 and September 30 and can be made up to 30 days in advance. Reservations can be made by contacting the **Wilderness Information Center** (© **360/ 565-3100**). Both a Wilderness Use Fee ($5 for a group of up to 12 people) and a nightly camping fee ($2 per person per night) are charged. Should you be doing the Ozette Coast Loop, you'll also have to pay a $1 per day trail head parking fee. For most other overnight hikes you can pick up a permit at a ranger station or at the trail head. If in doubt, check with a park ranger before heading out to a trail head for a backpacking trip. Also keep in mind that some trails start at trail heads on national forest land; for these trails, you'll need a Northwest Forest Pass. Also, should you be planning to backpack along the coast, keep in mind that some headlands can only be rounded at low tide, and others cannot be rounded at all. These latter headlands have marked (though often steep, muddy, and difficult) trails over them. In some cases these "trails" consist of cable ladders or handhold ropes. Also be aware that you'll have to ford quite a few creeks and even a river depending on which section of the coast you plan to hike. Always carry a tide table.

Most of the best backpacking trips in Olympic National Park are long and aren't easily turned into loop trips. If you want to do a one-way backpacking trip, you can arrange a shuttle through **Olympic Tours and Charters** (© 360/ 452-3500; www.tourtheolympics.com).

LLAMA TREKKING   If you want to do an overnight trip into the back-country of the national park but don't want to carry all the gear, consider letting a llama carry your stuff. **Kit's Llamas,** P.O. Box 116, Olalla, WA 98359 (© 253/857-5274; www.northolympic.com/llamas), offers llama trekking in the Olympic Mountains. Prices, based on a group of six to eight adults, are $35 to $85 per person for day hikes, $85 to $170 per person per day for overnights and multiday trips, with special rates for children. **Deli Llama,** 17045 Llama Lane, Bow, WA 98232 (© 360/757-4212; www.delillama.com), also does trips of 4 to 7 days in Olympic National Park ($125–$145 per person per day).

MOUNTAINEERING & ROCK CLIMBING   More adventurous tours ranging in length from half a day to 5 days are offered by **Olympic Mountaineering,** 140 W. Front St., Port Angeles 98362 (© 360/452-0240; www. olymtn.com). This company's most popular tour is its climb to the summit of Mount Olympus, the highest peak on the Olympic Peninsula. Prices range from $75 for a half day of rock climbing to $395 for a combination climb to the summit of Mount Olympus and a day of ice climbing.

SCUBA DIVING   The waters off the town of Sekiu are the Olympic Peninsula's favorite dive site. For advice, air, and dive charters, divers will want to stop in at **Curley's Resort & Dive Center** (© 360/963-2281; www.curleysresort. com), on the main road through town.

SEA KAYAKING & CANOEING   Sea-kayaking trips on nearby Lake Aldwell, Freshwater Bay, and at Dungeness National Wildlife Refuge are offered by **Olympic Raft & Kayak** (© 888/452-1443 or 360/452-1443; www. raftandkayak.com), which charges between $42 and $99 per person. Sea-kayak rentals are available at **Sound Bikes & Kayaks,** 120 E. Front St., Port Angeles (© 360/457-1240; www.soundbikekayaks.com), which charges $12 per hour or $40 per day.

SKIING/SNOWBOARDING/SNOWSHOEING   Cross-country skiing, downhill skiing and snowboarding, and snowshoeing are all possible in the winter at **Hurricane Ridge.** Here you'll find a tiny ski area with two rope tows and a Poma lift for downhill skiing and snowboarding. There are also many miles of marked, though ungroomed, cross-country ski trails here. For more information, contact **Hurricane Ridge Public Development Authority** (© 360/ 457-4519 or 360/565-3131 for road conditions; www.hurricaneridge.net).

There are also 90-minute ranger-led **snowshoe walks** here on Fridays, Saturdays, and Sundays from late December through March (conditions permitting). Snowshoes are provided, and a $2 donation is requested. Contact the park visitor center for details.

WHALE-WATCHING Puffin Adventures (© **888/305-2437** or 360/ 963-2744; www.olypen.com/puffinadventures) offers whale-watching and wildlife cruises for $40 per person.

WHITE-WATER RAFTING The steep mountains and plentiful rains of the Olympic Peninsula are the source of some great white-water rafting on the Elwha and Hoh rivers. Contact **Olympic Raft & Kayak** (© **888/452-1443** or 360/452-1443). Rates start at $49 for a 2- to 2½-hour rafting trip.

EXPLORING AROUND PORT ANGELES

If you're curious about the general history of this area, you may want to check out exhibits presented by **Clallam County Historical Society** at the Federal Building at First and Oak streets (© **360/452-2662**). It's open Monday through Friday from 8:30am to 4pm and admission is free.

The **Port Angeles Fine Art Center** ✪, 1203 E. Lauridsen Blvd. (© **360/ 457-3532;** www.olympus.net/community/pafac/), is the town's only other museum and hosts changing exhibits of contemporary art. The museum also maintains an unusual sculpture park in the woods surrounding the center. Sculptures within the park are often barely discernible from natural objects and are fascinating. It's open Tuesday through Sunday from 11am to 5pm; admission is free.

If you'd like to get a close-up look at some of the peninsula's aquatic inhabitants, stop by the **Arthur D. Feiro Marine Life Center,** Port Angeles City Pier, 315 N. Lincoln St. (© **360/417-6254;** www.olypen.com/feirolab). In the center's tanks, you may spot a wolf eel or octopus, and there's a touch tank where you can pick up a starfish or sea cucumber. In summer the center is open Tuesday through Sunday from 10am to 6pm; October through Memorial Day, on Saturday and Sunday from noon to 4pm. Admission is $2.50 for adults, $1 for seniors and children 6 to 12, and free for children 5 and under.

If you'd like to taste some local wine, stop by **Olympic Cellars Winery,** 255410 U.S. 101 (© **360/452-0160;** www.olympiccellars.com), which has its tasting room in a huge old barn between Sequim and Port Angeles. The winery is open daily from 9:30am to 5:30pm. You can also visit **Black Diamond Winery,** 2976 Black Diamond Rd. (© **360/457-0748**), which produces both fruit and grape wines and is open February through December, Thursday through Sunday from 10am to 4pm.

WHERE TO STAY

Beyond Port Angeles, accommodations are few and far between, and those places worth recommending tend to be very popular. Try to have room reservations before heading west from Port Angeles.

IN PORT ANGELES

Domaine Madeleine ✪✪ Located 7 miles (11.5km) east of Port Angeles, this contemporary B&B is set at the back of a small pasture and has a very secluded feel. Big windows take in the views, while inside you'll find lots of Asian antiques and other interesting touches. Combine this with the waterfront setting and you have a fabulous hideaway—you may not even bother exploring the park. All the rooms have fireplaces and views of the Strait of Juan de Fuca and the mountains beyond. Some rooms have whirlpool tubs, and some have kitchens or air-conditioning. For added privacy, there is a separate cottage. The guest rooms are in several different buildings that are surrounded by colorful gardens.

Look Out: Banana Slugs Crossing

If you happen to be a gardener who lives where summers are humid, you probably curse slugs, which can do immense damage to a vegetable patch. Now, imagine that those slimy little slugs chomping on your tomatoes are not an inch long, but a foot in length! Sound like a late-night monster movie? Think again. And if you go into the woods today, be sure to watch your step.

The banana slug (*Ariolimax columbianus*), which can grow to be a foot long and live for up to 5 years, is the only slug native to the Pacific Northwest. Making its yellowish, elongated way through the region's lowland forests, these slugs dine on plants, mushrooms, and decaying vegetable matter. Though slugs may seem to wander aimlessly, they have two eyes on the ends of long stalks and two olfactory organs on short stalks. The eyes detect light and dark and help them find cool dark places to sleep away the day, while the olfactory organs are used to locate food. A slug eats by shredding organic matter with a tonguelike structure called a radula, which is covered with thousands of tiny teeth.

Aside from their repulsive appearance and annoying habit of devouring gardens, slugs get a bad rap for sliming anyone unlucky enough to grab one accidentally. Slug slime, if you take the time to study it instead of just rubbing your fingers furiously to remove it, is amazing stuff. It's at once as slippery as soap and as sticky as glue, an unusual combination of properties that allows slugs to use their slime as a sort of instant highway on which to travel. Secreting the slime from their chin like so much drool, slugs coat the surface of whatever they're crawling on and then just slide along.

Slug slime may also serve as a defense mechanism. Lacking the protective shell of their close relatives the snails, slugs defend themselves by secreting copious amounts of slime, rendering them unpalatable to predators such as shrews, beetles, crows, and garter snakes.

Think slugs are sluggish? Think again. One of these babies can do 0.007 miles per hour (3–4 in. per min.) on the straightaway as the muscles along its foot constrict in waves and move it forward.

It's hard to believe that something as soft and slow moving as a slug could ever be a threat to anything, but slugs are real scrappers. That same serrated tongue that shreds lettuce so efficiently can also be used as a weapon against other slugs. If you start checking slugs closely, you're likely to find a few with old battle scars on their backs.

We know that birds do it and bees do it, but how do slugs do it? With any slug they chance to meet, if the mood strikes. Slugs are hermaphroditic, and they can mate with any other slug of the same species. What this means is that each one of those slugs out in your garden is capable of laying eggs!

And how did banana slugs get their name? No one is quite sure whether it's because they so closely resemble bananas, right down to the brown spots, or because when stepped on, they have an effect similar to that of a banana peel. Either way, it's appropriate.

146 Wildflower Lane, Port Angeles, WA 98362. ℂ **888/811-8376** or 360/457-4174. Fax 360/457-3037. www.domainemadeleine.com. 5 units. $145–$225 double. Rates include full breakfast. 2-night minimum on weekends and holidays. AE, DISC, MC, V. **Amenities:** Access to nearby health club; massage. *In room:* TV/VCR, dataport, hair dryer, iron.

Red Lion Hotel (★   If you're on your way to or from Victoria, there's no more convenient hotel than the Red Lion. This is Port Angeles's only waterfront hotel, and is located only steps from the Victoria ferry terminal. Rooms are large, if without much character, and most have balconies and large bathrooms. However, you'll pay a premium for a room with a view of the Strait of Juan de Fuca.

221 N. Lincoln St., Port Angeles, WA 98362. ℂ **800/RED-LION** or 360/452-9215. Fax 360/452-4734. www. redlion.com. 187 units. June 15–Sept 30 $119–$139 double; $160 suite. Lower rates off-season. AE, DISC, MC, V. Pets accepted ($10). **Amenities:** Restaurant (steak and seafood) and lounge; outdoor pool; exercise room; Jacuzzi; bike rental; business center; room service; coin-op laundry. *In room:* A/C, TV, dataport, coffeemaker, hair dryer, iron.

The Tudor Inn (★   Located in a quiet residential neighborhood 13 blocks from the waterfront, this 1910 Tudor home is surrounded by a large yard and pretty gardens. On the ground floor you'll find a living room and library, both with fireplaces that get a lot of use. Upstairs there are five rooms furnished with European antiques. Several rooms have good views of the Olympic Mountains.

1108 S. Oak St., Port Angeles, WA 98362. ℂ **360/452-3138.** www.tudorinn.com. 5 units. Summer $85–$135 double. Other months $75–$125 double. AE, DISC, MC, V. *In room:* No phone.

WEST OF PORT ANGELES

Elwha Ranch Bed & Breakfast (★   Located adjacent to Olympic National Park, this cedar-log inn, on a 95-acre ranch high above the Elwha River valley, has a superb view up the valley into the park, and deer and elk are regular visitors here. The two suites are in the main house, which has a casual Western ranch feel and plenty of windows to take in the views. If you're traveling with friends or family, opt for the two-bedroom suite. However, the nicest and most comfortable room here is a modern cabin outside the front door of the main house. Fresh pies are a specialty of innkeeper Margaret Mitchell. Be sure to get directions to the inn.

905 Herrick Rd., Port Angeles, WA 98363. ℂ **360/457-6540.** www.elwharanch.com. 3 units. $95–$135 double. Rates include full breakfast. No credit cards. **Amenities:** Guest laundry. *In room:* TV/VCR, fridge, coffeemaker.

Lake Crescent Lodge (★★   This historic lodge is located 20 miles (32km) west of Port Angeles on the south shore of picturesque Lake Crescent and is the lodging of choice for national park visitors wishing to stay on the north side of the park. Wood paneling, hardwood floors, a stone fireplace, and a sunroom make the lobby a popular spot for just sitting and relaxing (especially on rainy days). The guest rooms in this main lodge building are the oldest and have shared bathrooms. If you'd like more modern accommodations, there are a number of standard motel-style rooms, but these lack the character of the lodge rooms. If you have your family or some friends along, we recommend reserving a cottage. Those with fireplaces are the most comfortable, but the others are nice as well. All but the main lodge rooms have views of either the lake or the mountains. The lodge dining room has a good view across the lake. In winter, the lodge is only open on weekends, and only the fireplace and Singer cottages are available. The dining room is not open in winter.

416 Lake Crescent Rd., Port Angeles, WA 98363-8672. ℂ **360/928-3211.** Fax 360/928-3253. www.lake crescentlodge.com. 52 units (4 with shared bathroom). $70.50 double without bathroom, $106–$125 double

with bathroom; $112–$150.50 cottage. AE, DISC, MC, V. Pets accepted ($11.50). **Amenities:** Restaurant (Continental) and lounge; watersports rentals. *In room:* No phone.

Log Cabin Resort ⭐ This log-cabin resort on the north shore of Lake Crescent first opened in 1895 and still has buildings that date from the 1920s. The least expensive accommodations are rustic one-room log cabins in which you provide the bedding and share a bathroom a short walk away (basically this is camping without the tent). More comfortable are the 1928 cabins with private bathrooms, some of which also have kitchenettes (you provide the cooking and eating utensils). The lodge rooms and a chalet offer the greatest comfort and best views. The lodge dining room overlooks the lake and specializes in local seafood. The resort also has a general store and RV sites.

3183 E. Beach Rd., Port Angeles, WA 98363. ☎ 360/928-3325. Fax 360/928-2088. www.logcabinresort.net. 28 units. $49 cabin for 2 without bathroom, $76–$90 cabin for 2 with bathroom; $110 double; $134 chalet. DISC, MC, V. Closed Nov–Mar. Pets accepted ($6.75 per night). **Amenities:** Restaurant (American); coin-op laundry. *In room:* No phone.

Sol Duc Hot Springs Resort ⭐ The Sol Duc Hot Springs have for decades been a popular family vacation spot, with campers, day-trippers, and resort guests all spending their days soaking and playing in the hot-water swimming pool. The grounds of the resort are grassy and open, but the forest is kept just at arm's reach. The cabins are done in modern motel style and are comfortable if not spacious. There's a good restaurant here, as well as a poolside deli and grocery store. Three hot spring–fed swimming pools are the focal point, and the pools are open to the public for a small fee.

Sol Duc Rd., U.S. 101 (P.O. Box 2169), Port Angeles, WA 98362. ☎ 360/327-3583. Fax 360/327-3593. www. northolympic.com/solduc. 32 units. $104–$125 cabin for 2. AE, DISC, MC, V. Closed Nov–Mar. **Amenities:** 2 restaurants (American, deli); outdoor pool; 3 hot springs–fed soaking pools; massage. *In room:* No phone.

CAMPGROUNDS

The six national park campgrounds on the northern edge of the park are some of the busiest in the park due to their proximity to U.S. 101. **Deer Park Campground** ⭐⭐ (14 campsites) is the easternmost of these campgrounds (take Deer Park Rd. from U.S. 101 east of Port Angeles) and the only high-elevation (5,400 ft.) campground in Olympic National Park. Deer Park is reached by a winding one-lane gravel road. The national park's **Heart O' the Hills Campground** (105 campsites), on Hurricane Ridge Road 5 miles (8km) south of the Olympic National Park Visitor Center, is also very popular. On Olympic Hot Springs Road up the Elwha River, you'll find **Elwha Campground** (41 campsites) and **Altaire Campground** (30 campsites).

West of Port Angeles along Wash. 112, there are three public campgrounds on the shore of the Strait of Juan de Fuca. **Salt Creek County Park** ⭐ (90 campsites), 13 miles (21km) west of Port Angeles, is among the most scenic spots on this whole coast. About 20 miles (32km) west of Port Angeles is the Washington Department of Natural Resources' **Lyre River Park** (16 tent sites plus RV hookups, seasonal). Also in this same area is the **Lyre River Park** ⭐⭐, 596 W. Lyre River Rd. (☎ 360/928-3436), a very pleasant private campground.

The only campground on Lake Crescent is at **Fairholm** (87 campsites) at the west end of the lake. The nearby **Sol Duc Campground** ⭐ (80 campsites), set amid impressive stands of old-growth trees, is adjacent to the Sol Duc Hot Springs.

Heading west from Lake Crescent on U.S. 101, there are several campgrounds along the banks of the Sol Duc River.

The national park's remote **Ozette Campground** (14 campsites), on the north shore of Lake Ozette, is a good choice both for sea kayakers/canoeists and people wanting to day hike out to the beaches on either side of Cape Alava.

National park and other campgrounds in this area don't take reservations. However, for general information, contact **Olympic National Park** (© **360/ 565-3130**) or **Olympic National Forest, Forks Ranger Station,** 437 Tillicum Lane, Forks (© **360/374-6522**).

WHERE TO DINE
IN PORT ANGELES

For sandwiches, pastries, and espresso, don't miss **Bonny's Bakery,** 215 S. Lincoln St. (© **360/457-3585**), which is housed in an old fire station. For microbrews and pub fare, there's the **Sirens of Port Angeles,** 134 W. Front St. (© **360/417-9152**).

Bella Italia ⭐ ITALIAN   Located in downtown Port Angeles, this restaurant is only a couple of blocks from the ferry terminal and the Red Lion Hotel, which makes it very convenient for many travelers. Dinners start with a basket of delicious bread accompanied by an olive oil, balsamic vinegar, garlic, and herb dipping sauce. Fresh local seafood makes it onto the menu in a few places, including in smoked salmon ravioli, smoked salmon fettuccine, and steamed mussels and clams. There are also some interesting individual pizzas and a good selection of wines, as well as a wine bar, an espresso bar, and plenty of excellent Italian desserts.

118 E. First St. © 360/457-5442. www.bellaitaliapa.com. Main dishes $7–$18. AE, DC, DISC, MC, V. Summer Sun–Thurs 11am–9pm, Fri–Sat 11am–10pm; winter Sun–Thurs 4–9pm, Fri–Sat 4–10pm.

C'est Si Bon ⭐⭐ FRENCH   Located 4 miles (6.5km) south of town just off U.S. 101, C'est Si Bon is painted a striking combination of turquoise, pink, and purple that gives the restaurant a sort of happy elegance. Inside, the nontraditional paint job gives way to more classic decor—reproductions of European works of art, crystal chandeliers, and old musical instruments used as wall decorations. The restaurant serves deftly prepared Gallic standards such as French onion soup or escargot for starters. Follow that up with *coquille Saint Jacques* or a Dungeness crab soufflé, and finish with a rich, creamy *mousse au chocolat,* and *voilà!,* you have the perfect French meal. Specials feature whatever is fresh.

23 Cedar Park Rd. © 360/452-8888. www.northolympic.com/cestsibon. Reservations recommended. Main courses $20–$25. AE, MC, V. Tues–Sun 5–11pm.

Toga's International Cuisine ⭐ INTERNATIONAL/GERMAN   Located on the west side of Port Angeles, this restaurant is an unexpected treat and serves some very unusual dishes the likes of which are not to be found anywhere else in the state. Chef Toga Hertzog apprenticed in the Black Forest and has brought to his restaurant the traditional *Jagerstein* style of cooking in which diners cook their own meat or prawns on a hot rock. With 24 hours notice you can also have traditional Swiss cheese fondue or a lighter seafood fondue. To start your meal, you might try the crabmeat Rockefeller or the sampler of house-smoked salmon, scallops, oysters, and prawns. For dessert nothing hits the spot like the chocolate mousse.

122 W. Lauridsen Blvd. © 360/452-1952. Reservations recommended. Main dishes $17–$27. DISC, MC, V. Tues–Sat 5–10pm.

WEST OF PORT ANGELES

Outside of Port Angeles, the restaurant choices become exceedingly slim. Your best choices are the dining rooms at **Lake Crescent Lodge** (open Apr to mid-Nov) and the **Log Cabin Resort** (open Apr–Oct), both of which are on the shores of Lake Crescent. One other dining option on this lake is the **Fairholm General Store & Cafe,** 221121 U.S. 101 (© **360/928-3020**), which is at the west end of the lake and is open between April and October. Although all you'll get here are burgers, sandwiches, and breakfasts, the cafe has a deck with a view of the lake.

Continuing west, you'll find food at the dining room of **Sol Duc Hot Springs Resort** (open Apr–Oct). Way out west, near Ozette Lake, you'll find **The Lost Resort,** Hoko-Ozette Road (© **800/950-2899** or 360/963-2899), a general store with a deli, espresso, and a tavern serving lots of microbrews (daily 7am–10pm May–Oct).

4 Olympic National Park West

Forks: 57 miles (92km) W of Port Angeles, 50 miles (81km) S of Neah Bay, 77 miles (124km) N of Lake Quinault

The western regions of Olympic National Park can be roughly divided into two distinct sections—the rugged coastal strip and the famous rain-forest valleys. Of course, these are the rainiest areas within the park, and many a visitor has called short a vacation here due to the rain. Well, what do you expect? It is, after all, a rain forest. Come prepared to get wet.

The coastal strip can be divided into three segments. North of La Push, which is on the Quileute Indian Reservation, the 20 miles (32km) of shoreline from Rialto Beach to Cape Alava are accessible only on foot. The northern end of this stretch of coast is accessed from Lake Ozette off Wash. 112 in the northwest corner of the peninsula. South of La Push, the park's coastline stretches for 17 miles (28km) from Third Beach to the Hoh River mouth and is also accessible only on foot. The third segment of Olympic Park coastline begins at Ruby Beach just south of the Hoh River mouth and the Hoh Indian Reservation and stretches south to South Beach. This stretch of coastline is paralleled by U.S. 101.

Inland of these coastal areas, which are not contiguous with the rest of the park, lie the four rain-forest valleys of the Bogachiel, Hoh, Queets, and Quinault rivers. Of these valleys, only the Hoh and Quinault are penetrated by roads, and it is in the Hoh Valley that the rain forests are the primary attraction.

Located just outside the northwest corner of the park, the timber town of Forks serves as the gateway to Olympic National Park's west side. This town was at the heart of the controversy over protecting the northern spotted owl, and is still struggling to recover from the employment bust after the logging boom of the 1980s.

ESSENTIALS
GETTING THERE   The town of Forks is the largest community in this northwest corner of the Olympic Peninsula and is on U.S. 101, which continues south along the west side of the peninsula to the town of Hoquiam.

Bus service from Sequim to Lake Crescent, Neah Bay, La Push, and Forks is operated by **Clallam Transit** (© **800/858-3747** or 360/452-4511; www. clallamtransit.com). Bus service between Forks and Lake Quinault is provided by **West Jefferson Connection** (© **800/436-3950**). There is service to Quinault Lake from Olympia and Aberdeen on **Grays Harbor Transit** (© **800/ 562-9730** or 360/532-2770; www.ghtransit.com).

VISITOR INFORMATION   For more information on this western section of Olympic National Park, see "Visitor Information," above, in the "Olympic

National Park North" section of this chapter. For more information on the Forks area, contact the **Forks Chamber of Commerce,** 1411 S. Forks Ave. (P.O. Box 1249), Forks, WA 98331 (© **800/44-FORKS** or 360/374-2531; www. forkswa.com).

FESTIVALS Each year in mid-July, **Quileute Days** are celebrated in La Push (on the Quileute Indian Reservation) with canoe races, Indian dancing, a salmon bake, and other events.

EXPLORING THE PARK'S WEST SIDE

If you want to learn more about the area's logging history, stop by the **Forks Timber Museum,** south of town on U.S. 101 (© **360/374-9663**). The museum chronicles the history of logging in this region, but it also has displays on Native American culture and pioneer days. It's open from mid-April to October, daily from 10am to 4pm; admission is by donation.

Also in the Forks area, there are quite a few artists' studios and galleries. You can pick up an **Olympic West Arttrek** guide and map to these studios and galleries at the Forks Chamber of Commerce (see above for address and phone number).

West of Forks lie miles of pristine beaches and a narrow strip of forest (called the Olympic Coastal Strip) that are part of the national park, though not connected to the inland, mountainous section. The first place where you can actually drive right to the Pacific Ocean is just west of Forks. At the end of a spur road you come to the Quileute Indian Reservation and the community of **La Push.** Right in town there's a beach at the mouth of the Quillayute River; however, before you reach La Push, you'll see signs for **Third Beach** ★★ and **Second Beach** ★★, which are two of the prettiest beaches on the peninsula. Third Beach is a 1½-mile (2.5km) walk and Second Beach is just over half a mile from the trail head. **Rialto Beach** ★★, just north of La Push, is another beautiful and rugged beach; it's reached from a turnoff east of La Push. From here you can walk north for 24 miles (39km) to Cape Alava, although this is also a very popular spot for day hikes. One mile (1.5km) up the beach is a spot called Hole in the Wall, where ceaseless wave action has bored a large tunnel through solid rock. On any of these beaches, keep an eye out for bald eagles, seals, and sea lions.

The waters, islands, and rocks offshore from this stretch of coastline are all part of the **Olympic Coast National Marine Sanctuary,** which was designated in 1994 and covers 3,300 square miles (5313km^2). The sanctuary protects habitat for fish, seabirds, and marine mammals. Among these latter are gray, humpback, and orca whales, as well as harbor porpoises, Steller and California sea lions, harbor and elephant seals, and sea otters. For information, contact Olympic Coast National Marine Sanctuary, 138 W. First St., Port Angeles, WA 98362 (© **360/457-6622**).

Roughly 8 miles (13km) south of Forks is the turnoff for the Hoh River valley. It's 17 miles (27km) up this side road to the **Hoh Visitor Center** (© **360/ 374-6925**), campground, and trail heads. This valley receives an average of 140 inches of rain per year (and as much as 190 in.), making it the wettest region in the continental United States. At the visitor center you can learn all about the natural forces that cause this tremendous rainfall. To see the effect of so much rain on the landscape, walk the ¾-mile (1km) **Hall of Mosses Trail** ★★ where the trees, primarily Sitka spruce, western red cedar, and western hemlock, tower 200 feet tall. Here you'll see big-leaf maple trees with limbs draped in thick carpets of mosses. If you're up for a longer walk, try the **Spruce Nature Trail** ★★. If you've come with a backpack, there's no better way to see the park and all its habitats than by hiking the **Hoh River Trail** ⭑⭑, which is 17 miles (27km) long and leads to Glacier Meadows and Blue Glacier on the flanks of Mount Olympus. A herd of elk calls the Hoh Valley home and can sometimes be seen along these trails.

On your way up the Hoh Valley, you might want to stop in at **Peak 6 Adventure Store,** 4883 Upper Hoh Rd. (🕻 **360/374-5254**), an outfitter that sells not only any outdoors gear you might have forgotten, but also Native American baskets and art by local artists.

Continuing south on U.S. 101, but before crossing the Hoh River, you'll come to a secondary road (Oil City Rd.) that heads west from the Hoh Oxbow campground. From the end of the road it's a hike of less than a mile to a rocky beach at the **mouth of the Hoh River.** You're likely to see sea lions or harbor seals feeding just offshore here, and to the north are several haystack rocks that are nesting sites for numerous seabirds. Primitive camping is permitted on this beach, and from here hikers can continue hiking for 17 miles (27km) north along a pristine wilderness of rugged headlands and secluded beaches.

South of the Hoh River off U.S. 101, you can drive to the **world's largest red cedar.** The tree, which stands 178 feet tall and is almost 20 feet in diameter, is about 4 miles (6.5km) off the highway on Nolan Creek Road. Near milepost 170, watch for road N1000 on the east side of U.S. 101 and follow this road to a right fork onto N1100. Then turn right onto road N1112, and right again onto N112.

U.S. 101 finally reaches the coast at **Ruby Beach** ⭑. This beach gets its name from its pink sand, which is comprised of tiny grains of garnet. With its colorful sands, tide pools, sea stacks, and driftwood logs, Ruby Beach is the prettiest of the beaches along this stretch of coast. For another 17 miles (27km) or so south of Ruby Beach, the highway parallels the wave-swept coastline. Along this stretch of highway there are turnoffs for five beaches that have only numbers for names. Beach 6 is a good place to look for whales and sea lions and also to see the effects of erosion on this coast (the trail that used to lead down to the beach here has been washed away). At low tide, the northern beaches offer lots of tide pools to be explored. Near the south end of this stretch of road, you'll find Kalaloch Lodge, which has a gas station, and the **Kalaloch Ranger Station** (🕻 **360/962-2283**), which is usually open in the summer and at other seasons when a ranger is in the station.

Shortly beyond Kalaloch the highway turns inland again and passes through the community of **Queets** on the river of the same name. The Queets River valley is another rainy valley, and if you'd like to do a bit of hiking away from the crowds, head up the gravel road to the Queets campground, from which a hiking trail leads up the valley.

A long stretch of clear-cuts and tree farms, mostly on the Quinault Indian Reservation, will bring you to **Quinault Lake** ⭑. Surrounded by forested mountains, this deep lake is the site of the rustic Lake Quinault Lodge and offers boating and freshwater fishing opportunities, as well as more rain forests to explore on a couple of short trails (there are a total of about 10 miles/16km of trails on the south side of the lake). Also, on the north shore of the lake, you'll find one of the peninsula's largest red cedar trees. This is also a good area in which to spot Roosevelt elk.

For more information on guided tours and other outdoor recreational possibilities throughout the park's west side, see "Guided Tours, Educational Programs & Outdoor Adventures" in the "Olympic National Park North" section above.

WHERE TO STAY
IN THE FORKS AREA

The town of Forks has several inexpensive motels and is a good place to look for cheap lodgings if you happen to be out this way without a reservation. These include the **Forks Motel,** 351 S. Forks Ave. (© **800/544-3416** or 360/374-6243), which has a pool; and the **Pacific Inn Motel,** 352 S. Forks Ave. (© **800/235-7344** or 360/374-9400).

Manitou Lodge ⚸ This secluded B&B is set on 10 private acres and is only minutes from some of the most beautiful and remote beaches in the Northwest. The best room in the house is the Sacagawea, which has a marble fireplace and king-size bed. A separate cabin houses two of the rooms. Guests tend to gravitate to the comfortable living room, where a huge stone fireplace is the center of attention (fires help chase away the chill and damp of this rainy corner of the Olympic Peninsula). Breakfasts are hearty, although in the winter, you can also opt for a light breakfast. There's also a gift gallery here that specializes in Native American crafts and local artwork.

Kilmer Rd. (P.O. Box 600), Forks, WA 98331. © 360/374-6295. Fax 360/374-7495. www.manitoulodge.com. 7 units. $95–$125 double. Rates include full breakfast. AE, DC, MC, V. Take Wash. 110 west from north of Forks; turn right on Mora Rd. and then right on Kilmer Rd. Pets allowed in 2 units with $10 fee per night. **Amenities:** Bikes. *In room:* Coffeemaker, hair dryer.

Miller Tree Inn ⚸ Located just a few blocks east of downtown Forks, this large farmhouse B&B is surrounded by pastures and big old trees. With its classic styling, it feels very civilized compared to the wilds of the Olympic Peninsula and is a welcome sight at the end of the long drive out to Forks. A recent addition has helped to upgrade many of the rooms here, and there are now rooms with jetted tubs, fireplaces, and TVs and VCRs. One room also has a kitchenette (a definite bonus out in this neck of the woods). There's nothing fussy or pretentious about this place—just a comfortable, friendly inn that caters primarily to outdoors enthusiasts. At the end of a long day of hiking, the hot tub on the back deck is very welcome.

654 E. Division St. (P.O. Box 1565), Forks, WA 98331. © 800/943-6563 or 360/374-6806. Fax 360/374-6807. www.millertreeinn.com. 7 units. Summer $90–$175 double. Winter $65–$150 double. In winter rates include full breakfast. DISC, MC, V. **Amenities:** Jacuzzi. *In room:* No phone.

Olympic Suites Inn ⚸ Located just off U.S. 101 at the north end of town and set back in the forest a bit, this modern motel is your best bet in the area if you don't want to stay at a B&B. The motel has the look and feel of an apartment complex, and most of the rooms are suites with full kitchens. The Calawah River and a boat ramp are just downhill from the motel, and some rooms have limited river views. Other rooms look into the forest.

800 Olympic Dr., Forks, WA 98331. © 800/262-3433 or 360/374-5400. Fax 360/374-2528. www. olympicgetaways.com/olympicsuites. 32 units. $49–$69 double. AE, DISC, MC, V. **Amenities:** Coin-op laundry. *In room:* TV, refrigerator, coffeemaker.

ALONG THE PARK'S WEST SIDE, SOUTH OF FORKS

Kalaloch Lodge ⚸⚸ This is the national park's only oceanfront accommodation, and the rustic, cedar-shingled lodge and its cluster of cabins perch on a grassy bluff above the thundering Pacific Ocean. Wide sand beaches stretch north and south from the lodge, and at the base of the bluff huge driftwood logs are scattered like so many twigs. The rooms in the old lodge are the least expensive, and the ocean-view bluff cabins are the most in demand. The log cabins across the street from the bluff cabins don't have the knockout views. For modern comforts there are motel-like rooms in the Sea Crest House. A casual coffee shop serves breakfast and lunch while a slightly more formal dining room serves rather unmemorable meals in the $11 to $21 range. The lodge also has a general store and gas station. Because this lodge is extremely popular throughout the year, you should try to make reservations at least 4 months in advance.

157151 U.S. 101, Forks, WA 98331. (*) 360/962-2271. Fax 360/962-3391. www.visitkalaloch.com. 64 units. Early June to early Oct $126–$134 double; $138–$232 suite; $163–$241 bluff cabin; $143–$165 log cabin. Lower rates Sun–Thurs in other months. AE, MC, V. Pets accepted in cabins ($10 per night). **Amenities:** 2 restaurants (American). *In room:* No phone.

Lake Quinault Lodge ★★   Located on the shore of Lake Quinault in the southwest corner of the park, this imposing grande dame of the Olympic Peninsula wears an ageless tranquillity. Huge old firs and cedars shade the rustic lodge, and Adirondack chairs on the deck command a view of the lawn. The accommodations range from small rooms in the main lodge to modern rooms with wicker furniture and little balconies to rooms with fireplaces. The annex rooms are the least attractive, but they do have huge bathtubs. The dining room here has the most creative menu on this side of the peninsula. The lodge also has lawn games and offers rain-forest tours.

345 South Shore Rd. (P.O. Box 7), Quinault, WA 98575-0007. (*) 800/562-6672 or 360/288-2900. www.visit lakequinault.com. 92 units. June–Sept and winter holidays $110–$170 double; $250 suite. Oct–May $68–$130 double; $195 suite. AE, MC, V. Pets accepted in Boat House building ($10 per night). **Amenities:** Restaurant (Northwest) and lounge; indoor swimming pool; sauna; boat rentals; game room; tour desk; massage. *In room:* No phone.

Lake Quinault Resort ★★ *Finds*   Located on the north shore of Lake Quinault, this recently renovated little resort is more of a luxury motel or casual inn than a resort, but whatever you want to call it, it's exceedingly comfortable. It is also located on the sunny side of the lake (as opposed to the shady side, which is where the ever-popular Lake Quinault Lodge is located). Consequently, at the end of a day hiking in the darkness of the rain forest, you can return here and enjoy the sunset over the lake. There's a long covered veranda and a narrow lawn for enjoying those sunsets. Guest rooms are spacious and modern, with a bit of modern country decor and Northwest style. Several of the rooms have kitchens, and one has the original knotty pine walls.

314 North Shore Rd., Amanda Park, WA 98526. (*) 800/650-2362 or 360/288-2362. www.lakequinault.com. 9 units. Mid-June to early Oct $119–$149 double; early Oct to mid-June $55–$100 double. AE, DISC, MC, V. *In room:* TV, refrigerator, coffeemaker, hair dryer.

Rain Forest Resort Village ★ *Kids*   If you can't get a room at the Lake Quinault Lodge, this should be your second choice in the area. Although the cabins and motel rooms here are for the most part pretty basic, they are comfortable enough (and are actually as nice as some of the lodge rooms). All the cabins have fireplaces and some have either a kitchen or a Jacuzzi tub. Wide lawns slope down to the lake, and most rooms and cabins have water views. In summer, you can rent canoes for exploring the lake.

516 South Shore Rd., Lake Quinault, WA 98575. (*) 800/255-6936 or 360/288-2535. Fax 360/288-2957. www.rainforestresort.com. 26 units. Late June to early Sept $90–$99 double; $130–$190 cabin. Lower rates other months. AE, DISC, MC, V. **Amenities:** Restaurant (American); boat rentals. *In room:* TV.

CAMPGROUNDS

If you want to say you've camped at the wettest campground in the contiguous United States, head for the national park's **Hoh Campground** ★ (89 campsites) in the Hoh River valley. Almost as wet is the national park's **Queets**

Campground (20 campsites). This campground is 14 miles (23km) up the Queets Road from U.S. 101. On Quinault Lake there are three campgrounds. On the north shore is the walk-in **July Creek Campground** (27 campsites). On the south shore are two national forest campgrounds—**Willaby** (34 campsites) and **Falls Creek** (31 campsites). East of Lake Quinault, up the Quinault River valley, are two more national park rain-forest campgrounds—**North Fork** (7 campsites) and **Graves Creek** (30 campsites)—that provide access to a couple of the park's long-distance hiking trails.

Campsites at **Bogachiel State Park** (42 campsites), on the Bogachiel River 6 miles (9.5km) south of Forks on U.S. 101, are set under huge old spruce trees. On the banks of the Hoh River, the Washington Department of Natural Resources operates four primitive campgrounds for tenters. **Hoh Oxbow Campground** (7 campsites) is right on U.S. 101 and is the most convenient. Heading upriver on the Hoh Rain Forest Road are **Willoughby Creek** (19 campsites) and **Minnie Peterson** (7 campsites). Down river on Oil City Road is **Cottonwood Campground** (7 campsites), which is a good place to camp if you want to explore the national park coast north of the Hoh River. An alternative here is to hike ½ mile to the beach and camp there.

Along the peninsula's west side, there are also several beach campgrounds. These include the national park's **Mora Campground** (94 campsites) on the beautiful Rialto Beach at the mouth of the Quillayute River west of Forks. If you're prepared to hike in with your gear, you can also camp on Second Beach (half-mile hike) and Third Beach (1½-mile/2.5km hike). South of the Hoh River, along the only stretch of U.S. 101 that is right on the beach, you'll find **Kalaloch Campground** (177 campsites), which is the national park's largest campground. For general information on national park campgrounds, contact **Olympic National Park** (© **360/565-3130**). For information on nearby national forest campgrounds, contact the **Olympic National Forest, Quinault Ranger Station,** 353 South Shore Rd., Quinault (© **360/288-2525**).

WHERE TO DINE

In the town of Forks, you'll find several basic diners and family restaurants, but nothing really worth recommending, with the exception of the one restaurant listed below. South of Forks, your best bets are the dining rooms at the Kalaloch Lodge and the Lake Quinault Lodge. If you happen to be hungry up the Hoh River, don't miss the juicy burgers at the **Hard Rain Cafe,** 5763 Upper Hoh Rd. (© **360/374-9288**). Feeling sleepy? Drop by **Espresso Elegante,** 71 North Forks Ave., Forks (© **360/374-7580**), which is located inside the Tinker's Tales bookstore.

The Smoke House Restaurant AMERICAN   The name says it all here. This place smokes fish, and their salmon is some of the best we've ever had. It's got a good smoky flavor yet is tender and moist. If you're a fan of smoked salmon, don't miss this place. If you don't feel like sitting down for the smoked salmon dinner, smoked salmon salad, or smoked salmon and cheddar cheese tray appetizer, then consider getting some to go. It's great beach picnic food. If for some reason you don't care for salmon, there's always steaks, salads, and other kinds of seafood offered here.

U.S. 101 and La Push Rd. © **360/374-6258.** Main dishes $6–$19. DISC, MC, V. Mon–Fri 11am–9pm; Sat–Sun 4–9pm.

8

Southwest Washington

Southwest Washington, which for the purposes of this book is defined as the area west of I-5 and south of U.S. 12, is for the most part sparsely populated and heavily dependent on the timber industry for its economic base. This said, however, the region also contains the state's busiest beach resort areas—the Long Beach Peninsula and the Central Coast area—as well as the often-overlooked city of Vancouver, which shares a name with the far more famous Canadian city to the north. And although present-day Vancouver, Washington, is little more than a bedroom community for Portland, it abounds in pioneer history.

Aside from two last rocky headlands at the mouth of the Columbia River, the coastline of southwest Washington is a tame strip of sandy beaches and windswept dunes. Grays Harbor and Willapa Bay divide this stretch of coast into three distinct strips of sand: North Beach, South Beach, and the Long Beach Peninsula. These three strands have far more in common with one another than they do with the wild, rock-strewn beaches to the north. And although these beaches are far less spectacular than those to the north, the abundance of tourist accommodations along this stretch of coast makes these the favored beach vacation destinations of the state.

Summers along the coast tend to be short and often wet or foggy, and the coastal waters are too cold and rough for swimming (although surfing is fairly popular). Consequently, the traditional beach pursuits of swimming and sunning aren't high on vacation priority lists around these parts. Instead, these beaches have come to rely on other activities to attract visitors. All up and down this coast, digging for razor clams is a popular pastime, though open seasons are now short and as closely regulated as the salmon-fishing seasons. The towns of Westport, at the north end of the South Beach area, and Ilwaco, at the south end of the Long Beach Peninsula, have become the region's main charter boat ports, with Westport charter boats also doing double duty as whale-watching excursion boats. South Beach and the Long Beach Peninsula are also among the few regions in the country where cranberries are grown commercially. Long Beach, a beach resort town for more than 100 years, bills itself as the kite-flying capital of America and boasts of having the longest drivable beach in the world. While vacationing families drive the local economy, oysters still reign supreme in Willapa Bay, one of the cleanest estuaries in the country. However, an invasive, nonnative marsh grass called spartina has taken hold in this estuary and is slowly crowding out native salt marsh plants and turning this bay into unproductive mud flats.

While most of this region's development has taken place around fishing and shipping ports both along the coast and up the Columbia River, the heart of the region is the Willapa Hills. These forested hills are almost entirely privately owned, mostly by large lumber companies. Consequently the forests of the Willapa Hills are among the hardest working forests in the region. Much of the region's forests have already been cut twice since the first settlers arrived in the area.

However, despite the lack of publicly held or otherwise protected forests, this coast still has its pockets of wildness. The Willapa National Wildlife Refuge and the Long Beach Peninsula's Leadbetter Point together host a vast number of bird species each year. These areas, when combined with the Grays Harbor National Wildlife Refuge to the north, offer the best bird-watching in the entire Northwest. Sea kayakers also are attracted to Willapa Bay, where the paddle around Long Island is as rewarding as any in the Puget Sound or San Juan Islands.

1 Grays Harbor & the Central Coast

67 miles (108km) W of Olympia, 67 miles (108km) S of Lake Quinault, 92 miles (148km) N of Long Beach

Washington's central coast, consisting of the North and South Beach areas and the Grays Harbor towns of Aberdeen and Hoquiam, is something of an anomaly. Though far from being the most scenic stretch of Washington coast, it contains the state's most popular beach destination, Ocean Shores, a modern beach development that now consists of numerous oceanfront hotels and hundreds of vacation homes. Although not as scenic as the Olympic Peninsula coastline, this area is popular for its easy access to the cities of Puget Sound, and because Ocean Shores is less than an hour east of Olympia, it is a popular weekend vacation spot.

The most scenic stretch of this coastline is the area known as North Beach, which consists of the beach north of the mouth of Grays Harbor. The farther north you go on this stretch of coast the more spectacular is the scenery, even rivaling the beauty of the Olympic Peninsula's shoreline in some places. The South Beach area, so named because it occupies the south side of Grays Harbor, is an 18-mile (29km) stretch of flat beach that is bordered on the south by Willapa Bay. At the north end of South Beach is the town of Westport, Washington's busiest sportfishing and whale-watching port, while at the southern end is Washaway Beach, so named because of the rapid rate at which it has eroded over the years. The old highway past this beach long ago began caving into the ocean, and the current highway has had to be protected with rocks to prevent it from disappearing into the breakers as well. Directly south of Washaway Beach, across the mouth of Willapa Bay, lies the northern tip of the Long Beach Peninsula.

Dividing North Beach and South Beach is the large bay known as Grays Harbor, on whose shores are the two lumber-mill towns of Aberdeen and Hoquiam. These towns were once some of the most prosperous in the state, as attested to by each town's stately Victorian mansions and imposing commercial buildings. Unfortunately, these towns have yet to benefit from the prosperity that has overtaken the Puget Sound region, and historic commercial buildings stand empty and abandoned. Still, there is history to be seen in these towns, though it is for the beaches, the fishing, and the clamming that most people visit this region.

ESSENTIALS

GETTING THERE U.S. 12 and Wash. 8 together connect Aberdeen with Olympia to the east, while U.S. 101 connects Aberdeen with Forks and Port Angeles to the north and Long Beach and Astoria to the south. Ocean Shores and the North Beach area are 20 miles (32km) west of Aberdeen on Wash. 109. The South Beach area is 20 miles (32km) west of Aberdeen on Wash. 105.

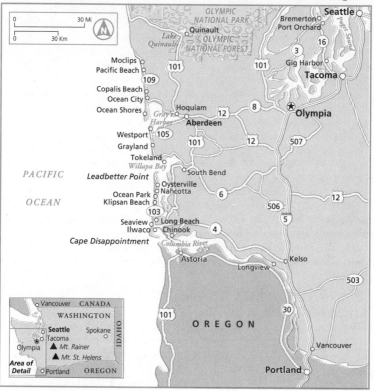

VISITOR INFORMATION For more information on this area, contact **Tourism Grays Harbor,** P.O. Box 225, Aberdeen, WA 98520 (© **800/621-9625** or 360/533-7895; www.graysharbor.com); **Ocean Shores Chamber of Commerce,** 120 W. Chance-A-La-Mer (P.O. Box 382), Ocean Shores, WA 98569 (© **800/76-BEACH** or 360/289-2451; www.oceanshores.org); or the **Westport-Grayland Chamber of Commerce,** 2985 S. Montesano Ave. (P.O. Box 306), Westport, WA 98595 (© **800/345-6223** or 360/268-9422; www.westportgrayland-chamber.org).

LEARNING ABOUT THE REGION'S HISTORY

Aberdeen and Hoquiam together comprise the largest urban area on the Washington coast and have long been dependent on the lumber industry, which once made this a very prosperous part of the state. If you're interested in the history of this region, stop by the **Polson Museum,** 1611 Riverside Ave., Hoquiam (© **360/533-5862**), which contains rooms full of antique furnishings and also houses various collections including dolls, vintage clothing, Native American artifacts, and logging memorabilia. It's open in summer, Wednesday through Sunday from 11am to 4pm; other months, on Saturday and Sunday from noon to 4pm. Admission is $2 for adults and 50¢ for children under age 12. The **Aberdeen Museum of History,** 111 E. Third St., Aberdeen (© **360/533-1976**), has similar displays and is open Tuesday through Saturday from 10am to 5pm and Sunday from 11am to 5pm; admission is by donation.

If maritime history floats your boat, be sure to see if the *Lady Washington* is in town during your visit. The tall ship, a replica of one of the ships Capt. Robert Gray sailed when he first explored the Northwest coast in 1788, berths beside the Wal-Mart in Aberdeen at **Aberdeen Landing,** 320 S. Newell St. (© **800/200-LADY** or 360/532-8611; www.ladywashington.org). The *Lady Washington* isn't always in port, but when it is, tours are available ($3 adults, $2 seniors and students, $1 children ages 12 and under) and sailing excursions are also offered ($40 for adults and $20 for children 12 and under). By the way, this was the boat in the movie *Star Trek Generations.*

If you aren't here during the whale-watching season, you can at least have a look at a couple of whale skeletons at the **Westport Maritime Museum,** 2201 Westhaven Dr., Westport (© **360/268-0078;** http://westportwa.com/museum). Housed in a 1939 Coast Guard station, the museum contains Coast Guard exhibits, displays on early pioneer life in the area, and, in a glass-enclosed building outside, the skeletons of a minke whale, a gray whale, and part of a blue whale. The museum is open daily from 10am to 4pm (fall–spring, Wed–Sun noon–4pm), and admission is $3 for adults and $1 for children 5 to 14, free for children 4 and under. The museum is also the place to arrange tours of the nearby Grays Harbor Lighthouse, which was built in 1898 and is the tallest lighthouse in Washington.

FISHING, CLAMMING, WHALE-WATCHING & OTHER OUTDOOR ACTIVITIES

The stretch of coast known as North Beach begins in the vacation and retirement community of Ocean Shores and stretches north for 30 miles (48km) to Taholah, on the Quinault Indian Reservation. In the southern section of North Beach, in Ocean Shores, low windswept dunes covered with beach grass back the wide, sandy beach. Kite flying and horseback riding are among the favorite activities here. Horses can be rented at the north end of Ocean Shores from **Chenois Creek Horse Rental** (© **360/533-5591**), which is located on the beach at the end of Damon Road (beside the Best Western Lighthouse Suites Inn) and charges $15 for a 1-hour ride. Also in Ocean Shores are 23 miles (37km) of canals and interconnecting lakes that are fun to explore. Canoes and motorboats can be rented at **Summer Sails** (© **360/289-2884**), which is located at Point Brown. The flat roads of Ocean Shores are also good for bicycling, and bikes of various types can be rented from **Mac's Food & Fun Center,** 662 Ocean Shores Blvd. NW (© **360/289-9303**). If you're looking for a game of golf, head to the **Ocean Shores Golf Course,** 500 Canal Dr. NE (© **360/289-3357**).

North of Ocean City, high bluffs, haystack rocks, secluded beaches, and dark forests create a more dramatic coastline. Along this stretch of coast there is **beach access** at Ocean City, Griffiths-Priday, and Pacific Beach state parks. **Razor clamming** is one of the most popular activities on the secluded beaches of this area. To try your hand at clamming, you'll need a license, a shovel, and a tide table. With all three in hand, head out to the beach at low tide and start looking for clam holes. When you spot one, dig fast. Good luck! Also, before heading out to the beach, find out if clamming season is open by calling the Westport-Grayland Chamber of Commerce (© **800/345-6223**).

The 18 miles (29km) of coastline between Westport and Tokeland is called the South Beach or the Cranberry Coast, and along this stretch of beach, there are plenty of places to access the sand and surf. Four state parks provide the best facilities and easiest access. **Twin Harbors State Park** is 2 miles (3km) south of Westport and is the largest of the four, with more than 3 miles (5km) of beach. **Grayland Beach State Park** is just south of the town of Grayland and has less than a mile of beach. Both of these parks have nature trails, picnic areas, and campgrounds. Just outside the marina area of Westport is **Westhaven State Park,** and just south of town is **Westport Light State Park,** where you'll find the popular Dune Trail, a paved 1-mile-long (1.5km) path that parallels the beach. These latter two parks are day-use areas only.

In the South Beach area, charter fishing, clamming, and whale-watching are the big attractions, and most of the activity centers on the marina at Westport. Boats head out daily in summer in search of salmon, tuna, and bottom fish. If you'd like to try your luck at reeling in a big one, try **Bran Lee Charters** (© **800/562-0163** or 360/268-9177; www.branleecharters.com), **Neptune Charters** (© **800/422-0425** or 360/268-0124), or **Deep Sea Charters** (© **800/562-0151** or 360/268-9300; www.oceansportfishing.com). Rates range from about $60 to $110 for a day of fishing. In the fall, salmon fishing is also popular right off the docks in the Westport Marina.

Each year between February and May, gray whales migrating to the calving grounds off Baja California, Mexico, pass by the Washington coast. The whales sometimes come so close to the mouth of Grays Harbor that they can be seen from the observation tower at the marina in Westport. However, for a closer look, you might want to head out on a **whale-watching** boat trip. Contact one of the charter boat companies mentioned above if you're interested. Rates are between $20 and $25 for adults and between $12.50 and $17.50 for children.

Crabbing is another favorite area activity. To give crabbing a try, you'll need a crab ring (they can be bought for $20–$40 or rented for around $6 per day at the Westport Marina) and some bacon or chicken necks for bait. Find a spot on Westport's 1,000-foot-long pier, toss your trap over the side, and sit back and wait for the crabs to come to you—it's that easy. Razor clamming is also popular on the beaches along this stretch of coast.

All along the South Beach area between Grayland and Tokeland, you'll see **cranberry bogs** beside the highway. The cranberry harvest begins around Labor Day and continues on through October. To harvest the tart berries, the bogs are flooded, which causes the ripe berries to float on the surface of the water, where they can be easily scooped up mechanically.

Each year in late April and early May, Bowerman Basin in **Grays Harbor National Wildlife Refuge** ★ (© **360/532-6237**) becomes a staging ground for tens of thousands of Arctic-bound shorebirds. This is one of the largest gatherings of such birds on the West Coast and is also one of the state's biggest annual events for bird-watchers. If you're a birder, you won't want to miss this impressive gathering. The wildlife refuge is adjacent to the Aberdeen/Hoquiam Airport on the west side of Hoquiam.

Between early May and September, the **Westport Ocean Shores Passenger Ferry,** Ocean Shores Marina & RV Park, 1098 Discovery Ave. SE (© **360/289-0414**), connects Westport Marina with Ocean Shores. The ferry operates daily between mid-June and Labor Day and weekends (only) other times. The crossing takes between 20 and 40 minutes, and the fare is $8 for a round-trip ticket.

WHERE TO STAY
OCEAN SHORES & THE NORTH BEACH AREA

If you can't get a room at any of the hotels listed below, contact **Ocean Shores Reservations** (© **800/562-8612** or 360/289-2430; www.oceanshores reservation.com), which handles reservations at many area hotels, motels, resorts, and condominiums.

Iron Springs Ocean Beach Resort ⭐ _Kids_   It's hard to imagine a more picture-perfect little cove than the one on which this rustic resort is set. Steep wooded hills surround the tiny cove, and at the mouth, a sandy beach begins. This is an isolated and little-developed stretch of coast, so even in summer you won't be bothered by crowds. The cottages here are scattered through the woods on a bluff overlooking the ocean and vary quite a bit in design, decor, and size. Although they definitely show their age, they're all modestly comfortable and have fireplaces and complete kitchens. There is also a playground here.

P.O. Box 207, Copalis Beach, WA 98535. © **360/276-4230**. Fax 360/276-4365. www.ironspringsresort.com. 28 units. $76–$116 cottage or apt for 2, $94–$156 cottage or apt for 4. 3-night minimum stay in summer. AE, DISC, MC, V. Pets accepted ($10 per night). **Amenities:** Indoor pool. *In room:* Kitchen, fridge, coffeemaker.

Ocean Crest Resort ⭐⭐ _Kids_   Perched high on a forested bluff and straddling a forested ravine, this hotel seems poised to go plummeting into the ocean below. You simply won't find a more spectacular location anywhere on the Washington coast. The accommodations vary from small studios with no view to two-bedroom apartments with full kitchens and fireplaces. However, our vote for best rooms goes to the large third-floor oceanview studios. These have cathedral ceilings, fireplaces, and balconies. The hotel's restaurant has one of the best views at the resort, and the adjacent lounge is a great spot for a sunset drink. In addition to other amenities, the resort also has a playground. A wooden staircase winds down through the ravine to the beach.

Sunset Beach, Moclips, WA 98562. © **800/684-8439** or 360/276-4465. Fax 360/276-4149. 45 units. $55–$150 double. Lower midweek rates Oct–Feb. AE, DISC, MC, V. Pets $50 deposit, $15/night per pet. **Amenities:** Restaurant (steak and seafood); lounge; indoor pool; health club; Jacuzzi; sauna; massage; coin-op laundry. *In room:* TV, coffeemaker, iron.

Quinault Beach Resort and Casino ⭐⭐ _Kids_   By far the most luxurious resort anywhere on the Washington coast, this large casino resort is located a bit north of the rest of the Ocean Shores developments and thus feels a bit more secluded. With its modern Northwest lodge styling, it also has a far more contemporary feel than other area resorts. However, despite the attractive design and the miles of ocean beaches just outside, it is still the in-house casino that seems to be this resort's main attraction. Don't worry, though—even if you aren't a fan of slot machines, you can actually stay here and almost not even notice the casino. All the rooms here have gas fireplaces, and the rooms are designed so that the fireplace separates the bed from the seating area. Large bathrooms have double sinks.

78 Wash. 115 (P.O. Box 2107), Ocean Shores, WA 98569. © **888/461-2214** or 360/289-9466. Fax 360/ 289-5833. www.quinaultbchresort.com. 150 units. $94–$189 double; $275–$525 suite. AE, DISC, MC, V. **Amenities:** 2 restaurants (Northwest, American); 2 lounges; indoor pool; exercise room; full-service spa; Jacuzzi; children's programs; game room; room service; massage; casino. *In room:* A/C, TV, dataport, refrigerator, coffeemaker, hair dryer, iron.

IN HOQUIAM

Hoquiam's Castle ⭐⭐ _Value_   This stately Victorian mansion, built in 1897 by a local timber baron, is an amazing assemblage of turrets and gables, balconies and bay windows. Rooms here have names inspired by the castlelike setting

(King's, Queen's, Princess's, Knight's, Maid's), and all are furnished in luxurious Victorian style. There are antiques throughout the inn and the quality of construction of this 10,000-square-foot mansion is evident in the wood floors and paneling, crystal chandeliers, and stained-glass windows. Guests can enjoy the view of the city from the turret, play the piano in the parlor, and sip tea on the front porch or sherry in the second-floor lounge. The inn even has its own ballroom.

515 Chenault Ave., Hoquiam, WA 98550. © 877/542-2785 or 360/533-2005. www.hoquiamscastle.com. 5 units. $80–$140 double. Rates include full breakfast. AE, MC, V. *In room:* Hair dryer, iron.

IN THE SOUTH BEACH AREA

Tokeland Hotel ★ *Finds*   Located on the north shore of Willapa Bay, the Tokeland Hotel has been welcoming guests since 1889 and, with its remote setting and simple interior decor, feels like a genuine step back in time. Lawns surround the wood-frame inn, and beyond these lies the water. The first floor is taken up by a large open lobby and dining room, off which is a small library with a fireplace. The rooms are arranged on either side of a long hall as they were at the turn of the 20th century and have painted wood floors. Antique furnishings lend an air of authenticity to the inn, and the shared bathrooms all have claw-foot tubs. The inn's moderately priced dining room is the most popular restaurant for miles around and is particularly noteworthy for its Sunday dinner, which includes a delicious cranberry pot roast (open daily 7:30am–8pm; winter hours vary). Past guests have included Robert Plant, Lindsay Wagner, and Stephen King.

100 Hotel Rd., Tokeland, WA 98590. © 360/267-7006. Fax 360/267-7006. 18 units, all with shared bathroom. $75 double. DISC, MC, V. Pets accepted. **Amenities:** Restaurant (American); bike rentals. *In room:* No phone.

CAMPGROUNDS

On Wash. 109 north of Ocean Shores are two state park campgrounds. **Pacific Beach State Park** (64 campsites) is a small, exposed, and crowded patch of sand with little to recommend it other than good razor clamming nearby. More appealing is **Ocean City State Park** ★ (178 campsites), which at least has trees for protection against the wind. This is a good choice if you plan to bicycle along this stretch of coast. To make a campsite reservation at either of these parks, contact **Washington State Parks** (© 888/226-7688; www.parks.wa.gov/reserve.asp).

WHERE TO DINE
IN THE OCEAN SHORES & NORTH BEACH AREA

The best restaurant in this region is the dining room at the Ocean Crest Resort (see above for details).

IN ABERDEEN

Billy's ★ AMERICAN   Named for an infamous local thug, Billy's evokes Aberdeen's rowdier days as a lawless, Wild West timber town. Although this is a perfectly respectable restaurant these days, there's a bar down the length of the room, a pressed-tin ceiling, and enough old paintings and prints to give this bar and grill just the right dance-hall atmosphere. The menu features everything from burgers to fresh oysters to T-bone steaks.

322 E. Heron St., Aberdeen. © 360/533-7144. Main courses $6–$14. AE, DC, DISC, MC, V. Mon–Fri 7am–11pm; Sat 8am–11pm; Sun 8am–9pm.

Mallard's Bistro & Grill ★★ *Finds* CONTINENTAL   Located in downtown Aberdeen and owned by a Danish chef who cooked all over Europe before eventually locating here, this cozy little restaurant is one of the most unexpectedly enjoyable restaurants in the state. In a town filled with burger joints and cheap Chinese restaurants, Mallards dares to serve such creative fare as a delicious salmon with pinot noir sauce and Asian-inspired oysters. The menu sticks mostly to traditional Continental fare, including coquille St. Jacques, and there are lots of good seafood preparations. The setting, with its many images of mallard ducks all around the dining room, is casual and homey.

118 E. Wishkah St. ✆ 360/532-0731. Reservations recommended. Main courses $12–$24. MC, V. Tues–Fri 11:30am–1:30pm and 5–8pm; Sat 5–8:30pm.

IN THE SOUTH BEACH AREA

Your best bet for a memorable meal in the South Beach area is the dining room at the historic Tokeland Hotel (see above for details).

DRIVING ON TO LONG BEACH

Though it's only about 5 miles (8km) across the mouth of Willapa Bay to the northern tip of the Long Beach Peninsula, it's about 85 miles (137km) around to the town of Long Beach by road. Along the way you skirt the shores of Willapa Bay. There aren't too many towns on this bay, which is why this is one of the least polluted estuaries in the country and is a great place to raise oysters. Punctuating the miles of unspoiled scenery are oyster docks and processing plants.

As you pass through the town of Raymond, keep an eye out for the 200 steel-plate sculptures that comprise the **Raymond Wildlife-Heritage Sculpture Corridor.** The majority of these sculptures are silhouettes that can be seen along U.S. 101 in the most unexpected places. Included are sculptures of Native Americans, modern sea kayakers, bicyclists, and dozens of wild animals. Also here in Raymond, you'll find the **Willapa Seaport Museum** ✦, 310 Alder St. (✆ 360/942-5666), a fascinating little museum dedicated to all things nautical. The museum is open Thursday through Sunday from 10am to 4pm; admission is by donation. This museum is adjacent to Waterfront Park, which has some interesting interpretive displays and is on a 5-mile-long (8km) paved walking/biking trail.

By some accounts, one out of every six oysters consumed in the United States comes from Willapa Bay, and it is in the town of **South Bend** that oystering reaches its zenith. South Bend claims to be the oyster capital of the world and holds its annual **Oyster Stampede** festival each year on Memorial Day weekend. If you just have to have some oysters while you're in town, have a meal at The Boondocks (see below) or drop by **Eastpoint Seafood** (✆ 888/317-8459 or 360/875-5419), which is on U.S. 101 at the north end of South Bend.

South Bend's other claim to fame is its **county courthouse.** Though South Bend is the county seat today, back in 1893 it took a possibly rigged vote and armed force to wrest the title of county seat from Oysterville, across the bay on the Long Beach Peninsula. Construction of the new courthouse began 18 years later, and upon completion, the imposing structure was dubbed a "gilded palace of extravagance." The majestic courthouse, seeming quite out of place in such a quiet backwater, stands on a hill overlooking the town. The copper dome is lined inside with stained glass, and murals decorate the interior walls. It's definitely worth a look.

2 The Long Beach Peninsula

110 miles (177km) NW of Portland, 180 miles (290km) SW of Seattle, 80 miles (129km) W of Longview/Kelso

With 28 uninterrupted miles (45km) of sand, the Long Beach Peninsula, a long narrow strip of low forest and sand dunes, claims to be the world's longest beach (although in recent years this statement has been qualified to "longest beach open to vehicles"). No matter, you get the picture—Long Beach has a long beach. For more than a century, all those miles of sand have been attracting vacationers, primarily from the Portland area and parts of southwestern Washington, and today the Long Beach Peninsula is Washington's most developed stretch of beach. There are dozens of resorts, motels, rental cabins, vacation homes, and campgrounds up and down the peninsula.

Each of the peninsula's towns has its own distinct personality. In Seaview, there are restored Victorian homes. In Long Beach, go-cart tracks and family amusements hold sway. Klipsan Beach and Ocean Park are quiet retirement communities, while Nahcotta is still an active oystering port, albeit in a very attractive setting. Last is the tiny community of Oysterville, which is a National Historic District of restored homes and hands-down the prettiest community on the peninsula.

While kite flying, horseback riding, and beachcombing are the most popular beach activities here, digging for razor clams ranks right up there, too. Razor clams (and the area's oysters) also show up on plenty of area restaurant menus. Bivalves aren't the only seafoods that attract folks to the south coast, either. In Ilwaco, south of Long Beach, there's a fleet of charter fishing boats that can take you out in search of salmon, tuna, or bottom fish.

Long Beach is one of the few beaches on the West Coast that allows vehicular traffic, so if you're of a mind to go for a drive on the beach, feel free. Just remember that the beach is a state highway and a 25-mph speed limit is enforced. There are beach access roads up and down the peninsula, and once you're on the beach, be sure you stay above the clam beds (sand nearest to the low-tide area) and below the dry sand.

ESSENTIALS

GETTING THERE   The Long Beach Peninsula begins just off U.S. 101 in southwest Washington. U.S. 101 leads north to Aberdeen and south to Astoria, Oregon. Wash. 4 leads to Long Beach from Longview.

GETTING AROUND   Pacific Transit System (© 360/642-9418) operates public buses that serve the area from Astoria in the south to Aberdeen in the north.

VISITOR INFORMATION   Contact the **Long Beach Peninsula Visitors Bureau,** P.O. Box 562, Long Beach, WA 98631 (© **800/451-2542** or 360/642-2400; www.funbeach.com), which operates a visitor center at the intersection of U.S. 101 and Pacific Avenue in Seaview.

FESTIVALS   Annual events on the Long Beach Peninsula include the **Ragtime Rhodie Dixieland Jazz Festival** in May, the **Northwest Garlic Festival** on the third weekend in June, the **Sand-Sations** sand-sculptures tournament in late July, the **International Kite Festival** in mid-August, the **Cranberrian Fair** in early October, and the **Water Music Festival** (chamber music) in late October.

SEEING THE SIGHTS

Nine miles (14km) east of Ilwaco on Wash. 103 near the Astoria-Megler Bridge, a 4½-mile-long (7km) span that connects Washington with Oregon, is **Fort Columbia State Park (© 360/642-3078)**, a former military base that guarded the mouth of the Columbia River from 1896 until the end of World War II. The park's wooded bluff has some picnic tables and 5 miles (8km) of hiking trails. The views from here are breathtaking. Today the 1903-vintage buildings have been restored and house an interpretive center with displays on the history of the fort and of the local Chinook Indian tribe. The interpretive center is open daily from 10am to 5pm between late May and late September. The old commanding officer's home is also open (daily 11am–4pm between late May and late Sept). There are also a couple of vacation rental homes here. For reservations, contact Washington State Parks (© **888/226-7688;** www.parks.wa. gov/reserve.asp).

To learn more about the history of the area, stop by the **Ilwaco Heritage Museum,** 115 SE Lake St., Ilwaco (© **360/642-3446**). This modern museum houses displays on the history of southwest Washington with exhibits on Native American culture, exploration and development of the region, and a model of the Columbia River estuary. The museum is open Monday through Saturday from 9am to 5pm and Sunday from noon to 4pm (Oct–Apr Mon–Sat 10am–4pm). Admission is $3 for adults, $2.50 for seniors, $2 for youths 12 to 17, and $1 for children 6 to 11, free for children 6 and under.

Also in Ilwaco is the historic **Colbert House,** which is operated by the Washington State Parks and Recreation Commission. You'll find this restored home at the corner of Quaker and Spruce streets. It's open Friday through Sunday from noon to 4pm between Memorial Day and Labor Day.

Anchoring the south end of the peninsula is forested **Fort Canby State Park** ★★ (© **360/642-3078**), at the mouth of the Columbia River. The park is a former military installation used to guard the river mouth, and many of the bunkers and batteries are still visible. Also within the boundaries of the park are the North Head and Cape Disappointment lighthouses. The former is the windiest lighthouse on the West Coast and has sustained winds as high as 160 miles per hour. The latter lighthouse was built in 1856 and is the oldest lighthouse on the West Coast. The park is also home to the **Lewis and Clark Interpretive Center** ★★ (© **360/642-3029**), which chronicles the 1805–06 journey of the two explorers; it's open daily from 10am to 5pm and admission is by suggested $2 donation. Cape Disappointment, here in the park, was the end of the westward trail for Lewis and Clark. Also within the park are several picnic areas, hiking trails, a campground, and **Waikiki Beach,** the prettiest little beach between here and Moclips. This tiny cove backed by steep cliffs is named for several Hawaiian sailors who lost their lives near here. The park is open from dawn to dusk, and admission is free.

In the past 300 years more than 2,000 vessels and 700 lives have been lost in the treacherous waters at the mouth of the Columbia River, and consequently, the U.S. Coast Guard has its **National Motor Life Boat School** here. Lifeboat drills can be sometimes be observed from observation platforms on the North Jetty. This jetty, completed in 1917, was built to improve the channel across the Columbia Bar. A side effect of the 2-mile-long (3km) jetty was the creation of a much wider beach to the north. This widening of the beach accounts for the town of Long Beach's current distance from the waves.

If you're a kite flyer, or even if you're not, you may want to stop by the **World Kite Museum & Hall of Fame** ★, 112 Third Street NW, Long Beach (© **360/ 642-4020;** www.worldkitemuseum.com), where you can see displays on kites of the world. June through August, it's open daily from 11am to 5pm in summer, Friday through Monday in September and October, and Saturday and Sunday only November through May; admission is $1.50 for adults, $1 for seniors and children.

Up toward the north end of the peninsula, you'll find the historic village of **Oysterville** ★★, an old oystering community that is a National Historic District and is by far the quaintest little village on the peninsula. Old homes with spacious lawns cling to the edge of the marsh. In the days of the California gold rush, Oysterville was shipping tons of oysters to San Francisco, where people were willing to pay as much as $50 a plate for fresh oysters. Today Oysterville is a sleepy little community of restored homes. In the town's white clapboard church, there are occasional music performances. Here in Oysterville, you'll also find **Oysterville Sea Farms** (© **800/CRANBERRY** or 360/665-6585; www. oysterville.net), which has a seafood and cranberry products shop on the waterfront at the north end of the village.

Willapa Bay, which is one of the cleanest estuaries on the West Coast, is still known for its **oysters.** Up and down the peninsula there are oyster farms and processing plants. If you're interested in learning more about the history of the area's oystering industry, drop by the **Willapa Bay Interpretive Center** (© **360/ 665-4547**) on the breakwater beside The Ark Restaurant in Nahcotta. The interpretive center is open Friday through Sunday from 10am to 3pm between Memorial Day and mid-October, and admission is free. The peninsula is also a major producer of cranberries, and if you take a drive down almost any side road north of Long Beach, you'll pass acres of **cranberry bogs.** If you're curious to learn how cranberries are grown, stop in at the **Pacific Coast Cranberry Museum** ★, 2907 Pioneer Rd., Long Beach (© 360/642-5553). The museum, which is on a demonstration cranberry farm, features exhibits on all the stages of cranberry growing both past and present. The museum is open from April to December 15: daily from 10am to 5pm. Admission is free.

Fans of the bizarre won't want to miss **Marsh's Free Museum** ★, 409 S. Pacific Ave., Long Beach (© **360/642-2188;** www.marshsfreemuseum.com), a beachy gift shop filled with all manner of antique arcade games, oddities a la Ripley's Believe It or Not! and, best of all, Jake the alligator man, who has been made famous by tabloids that rank this half-man, half-alligator creature right up there with aliens, Bigfoot, and the latest Elvis sighting.

AREA ACTIVITIES: KITE FLYING, BIRD-WATCHING & CLAMMING

Active vacations are the norm here on the Long Beach Peninsula, and there are plenty of activities to keep you busy. However, one activity you won't be doing much of is swimming in the ocean. Although it gets warm enough in the summer to lie on the beach, the waters here never warm up very much. Add to this the unpredictable currents, riptides, undertows, and heavy surf and you have an ocean that's just not safe for swimming.

Instead of swimming, the beach's number-one activity is **kite flying.** Strong winds blow year-round across the Long Beach Peninsula, and with its 28 miles (45km) of beach, you won't have to worry about kite-eating trees. You'll find several kite shops in Long Beach. Another very popular Long Beach activity is beachcombing. The most sought-after treasures are hand-blown glass fishing floats used by Japanese fishermen.

Beach access is available up and down the peninsula, but the best beaches are at the peninsula's various state parks. The beaches of **Fort Canby State Park,** at the south end of the peninsula, are the most dramatic, while those at **Leadbetter Point State Park,** at the north end of the peninsula, are among the most secluded. Just north of Ocean Park there is beach access at the small **Pacific**

Pines State Park, and south of Ocean Park, there is additional beach access at the west section of Loomis Lake State Park. This latter park is named for a popular fishing lake that is in the park's east section.

If you've ever dreamed of riding a horse down the beach, you can make your dream come true here in Long Beach. On South Tenth Street just in from the beach, you'll find both Skipper's Equestrian Center (© 360/642-3676) and Back Country Wilderness Outfitters (© 360/642-2576). A 1-hour ride will cost you $15.

Walking the dunes is a favorite Long Beach pastime. Between 17th Street South and 16th Street North, there is a 2-mile-long (3km) paved path called the Dunes Trail that parallels the beach. The trail winds through the grassy dunes that separate the town of Long Beach from the stretch of sand for which the town is named. For a half mile of its length, the Dunes Trail parallels an elevated boardwalk that provides view of the beach and ocean over the tops of the dunes.

If you'd just like to get away from the crowds and find a piece of isolated shoreline to call your own, head to Leadbetter Point at the peninsula's northern tip. Here you'll find both Leadbetter Point State Park Natural Area and a portion of the Willapa National Wildlife Refuge (© 360/484-3482). This area is well known for its variety of birds. More than 100 species have been seen here, including the snowy plover, which nests at the point. Because the plovers nest on the sand, a portion of the point is closed to all visitors April through September. During these months you can still hike the trails, use the beach, and explore the marshes.

At Ilwaco, you'll find charter boats that will take you out fishing for salmon, halibut, sturgeon, or bottom fish. Try Pacific Salmon Charters (© 800/831-2695 or 360/642-3466; www.pacificsalmoncharters.com) or Coho Charters (© 800/339-2646 or 360/642-3333; www.cohocharters.com).

Long Island, located in the middle of Willapa Bay and accessible only by private boat, is part of the Willapa National Wildlife Refuge (© 360/484-3482), which has its headquarters about 9 miles (14km) up U.S. 101 from Seaview. The island is known for its grove of huge old red cedars and is popular with sea kayakers. There are a few campsites and some hiking trails.

WHERE TO STAY

If you're heading down this way with the whole family and need an entire vacation home, contact Pacific Realty Property Management, 102 NE Bolstad St., Long Beach, WA 98631 (© 888/879-5479 or 360/642-4549; www.pacreal.com/vacation). Alternatively, you can contact the Long Beach Peninsula's Visitors Bureau (see above), which maintains a list of most of the vacation homes in the area.

Among the most interesting accommodations options in the area are the two former lighthouse-keepers homes at the North Head Lighthouse in Fort Canby State Park. These vacation homes can be rented through Fort Canby State Park (© 800/360-4240 or 360/642-3078) and rent for $215 per night with a 2- to 3-night minimum depending on the season. The two houses are in a clearing in the woods about 100 yards from the old lighthouse, and hiking trails lead from the grounds down to the beach and through the park. There are also two more restored historic homes available at nearby Fort Columbia State Park. One rents for $135 per night and sleeps four people and the other rents for $350 per night and sleeps 12 people. Call the number above for reservations.

Boreas Bed & Breakfast Inn ★★ Although this inn is housed in a reno-vated 1920s beach house, you would never guess it from the contemporary styling both outside and within. The inn is only a few blocks from downtown Long Beach and is separated from the ocean by only the grassy dunes between you and the beach. The upstairs rooms have the best views, but, with their spa-ciousness and private decks, the two downstairs rooms are also very comfortable. One of these downstairs rooms was formerly a sunroom and has two walls of windows. This room also has a whirlpool tub in the bathroom. On the grounds, there is an enclosed gazebo housing a whirlpool spa.

607 N. Ocean Blvd. (P.O. Box 1344), Long Beach, WA 98631. © **888/642-8069** or 360/642-8069. Fax 360/ 642-5353. www.boreasinn.com. 5 units. $130–$140 double. Rates include full breakfast. AE, DISC, MC, V. **Amenities:** Access to nearby health club; Jacuzzi; concierge; massage. In room: Hair dryer.

The Inn at Ilwaco ★ *Finds* Built on a wooded hilltop on the outskirts of tiny Ilwaco at the south end of the Long Beach Peninsula, this inn is a former Pres-byterian church. Though the church itself now serves primarily as a wedding facility and group rental spaces, an attached building, which once served as Sun-day school and minister's home, now houses the inn's guest rooms and a large and comfortable parlor. The setting includes plenty of nautical decor. Ilwaco makes a good base for exploring both the Long Beach Peninsula and Astoria.

120 Williams St. NE (P.O. Box 922), Ilwaco, WA 98624. © **888/244-2523** or 360/642-8686. Fax 360/642-8642. www.longbeachlodging.com. 9 units. $99–$149 double. Rates include full breakfast. MC, V. In room: No phone.

Moby Dick Hotel ★ *Finds* Though it looks a bit like a big yellow bunker from the outside, the Moby Dick is actually a comfortable bed-and-breakfast inn. Built as a hotel back in 1930 (the year before the train stopped running), the hotel quickly fell on hard times. Today it's a casual place, eclectically furnished in a 1930s style that captures the spirit of small historic hotels. The location, up at the north end of the peninsula, is removed from the beach strip of Seaview and Long Beach, and is convenient to Leadbetter Park and its wild dunes and beaches. You'll also be within walking distance of the Ark Restaurant (see below). Low rates, friendly atmosphere, and a tranquil setting make this a great choice. There is a sauna for taking off the chill, and in the summer, dinners are available in the dining room. Breakfasts often included fresh oysters from the inn's oyster beds.

Sandridge Rd. and Bay Ave., Nahcotta, WA 98637. © **360/665-4543.** Fax 360/665-6887. www.nwplace. com/mobydick.html. 8 units, 1 with private bathroom. $85–$110 double. Rates include full breakfast. AE, DISC, MC, V. Pets accepted with $10 fee per night. **Amenities:** Seasonal dining room (Northwest); sauna. In room: No phone.

Shelburne Country Inn ★★ Despite the in-town location, this inn's tone perfectly captures that of a country inn. Step though the front door and you enter rooms filled with a pale light that is filtered by walls of stained-glass win-dows salvaged from an English church. In the main lobby, dark fir-paneled walls, a big oak table, and a fire crackling on the hearth all extend a classic coun-try welcome. Most guest rooms are on the second floor, but, on the ground floor, there are a couple of suites that overlook the gardens and have their own decks. All the guest rooms are filled with antiques and, even if sometimes a bit cramped, all feel very luxurious and old fashioned. The inn's Shoalwater Restau-rant is one of the state's finest restaurants (see below). The Shelburne also oper-ates the China Beach Retreat, which is on the waterfront in nearby Ilwaco (rooms are $199 double and the one suite is $239).

4415 Pacific Hwy. (P.O. Box 250), Seaview, WA 98644. © 800/INN-1896 or 360/642-2442. Fax 360/642-8904. www.theshelburneinn.com. 15 units. $119–$159 double; $189 suite. Rates include full breakfast. AE, MC, V. **Amenities:** Restaurant (Northwest); lounge. In room: Hair dryer.

Sunset View Resort ⚐ (Kids) About midway up the peninsula, you'll find this attractive motel set back in the woods a bit, on the far side of a little bridge. Tall fir trees and attractive gardens surround the resort, and out back, dunes stretch for 100 yards to the beach. Although the furnishings are a bit dated, many of the rooms come equipped with kitchens, which makes this a good choice for families. Some rooms also have fireplaces and balconies (ask for a second-floor room; these have the best views). Although there isn't a pool here, you'll find plenty of other recreational amenities, including those listed below and a sauna, a whirlpool, volleyball and basketball courts, horseshoes, a playground, and a picnic area.

P.O. Box 399, Ocean Park, WA 98640. © 800/272-9199 or 360/665-4494. Fax 360/665-6528. www. washingtoncoast.net. 52 units. May–Sept $65–$111 double. Seasonal discounts Sept–May. AE, DISC, MC, V. Pets accepted ($15). **Amenities:** Tennis court; access to nearby health club; Jacuzzi; sauna; coin-op laundry. In room: TV.

CAMPGROUNDS

The only campground in this area worth recommending is **Fort Canby State Park** (227 campsites), which is at the southern end of the Long Beach Peninsula at the mouth of the Columbia River. This park has campsites on a small lake, as well as some at the foot of North Head. Some of the sites in the latter area are tucked in amid massive boulders. For reservations contact **Washington State Parks** (© 888/226-7688; www.parks.wa.gov/reserve.asp).

WHERE TO DINE

You'll know the moment you see the pies at **My Mom's Pie,** 4316 Pacific Ave. (© 360/642-2342), that they're the real McCoy—flaky and simply oozing fruit filling. For smoked salmon and oysters, fresh fish and crab, and fresh clam chowder, stop in at **Ocean Park Crab & Seafood Market,** 25312 Vernon St., Ocean Park (© 360/665-3474).

The Ark Restaurant & Bakery ⚐⚐ NORTHWEST Located at the north end of the Long Beach Peninsula, the Ark is a gustatory sanctuary in the wilderness. Set at the foot of a working dock and surrounded by oyster canneries and huge piles of oyster shells, the restaurant has its own oyster beds, as well as its own herb and edible-flower garden. You can be sure that whatever you order here will be absolutely fresh, and that's exactly what has kept the Ark afloat since 1981. Of course, oysters are the top dinner choice, and the Ark's oyster platter comes with 16 extra-small oysters. If that's not enough oysters for you, you can order another half dozen for an additional $5. Even if you aren't an oyster fan, you'll find plenty of delicious food on the menu here, and if you have a sweet tooth, be sure to save room for one of the Ark's excellent desserts.

Sandridge Rd., Nahcotta. © 360/665-4133. www.arkrestaurant.com. Reservations highly recommended. Main courses $8.50–$9.25 at lunch, $12–$26.50 at dinner. AE, DISC, MC, V. Summer Tues–Sat 5–9pm, Sun 11am–3pm and 5–9pm; spring and fall closed Mon–Wed; winter closed Mon–Thurs.

42nd Street Cafe ⚐⚐ AMERICAN/NORTHWEST Cheri Walker, chef at this nondescript little restaurant, used to be the chef at the acclaimed Shoalwater Restaurant just up the street, but when she struck out on her own, she decided to create a much more casual place. Still, the food here is some of the best on the peninsula, and it's available three meals a day. At dinner the menu ranges from classic comfort foods such as pot roast and country fried chicken to great pastas (try fettuccine with local clams) and steaks (perhaps with a side of oysters). Remember, this is oyster and razor clam country, so you'll do well to order the blackened oysters with Cajun mayonnaise or the pan-fried razor clams with parsley-caper mayonnaise. At lunch, you might find house-made ravioli or an oyster po'boy. Soups can be a highlight of a meal here, so don't overlook them.

42nd St. and Pacific Hwy., Seaview. (C) 360/642-2323. Reservations recommended. Main dishes $4.25–$7 at lunch, $10–$19 at dinner. MC, V. Wed–Sun 8am–2pm and Mon, Wed–Sun 4:30–8:30pm (closed Tues in winter); summer Tues–Sun 7am–2pm and Mon–Sun 4:30–9:30pm

Sanctuary Restaurant ★★ *Finds* NORTHWEST/SCANDINAVIAN A 1906 church in the community of Chinook, between Long Beach and the Astoria-Megler Bridge, now serves as one of southwest Washington's most memorable dining experiences. The church has changed very little since its days as a house of worship, and people still pack the pews, which are used for bench seating at the tables (should you happen to get a table on the altar, you may wind up in the minister's thronelike chair). The menu includes such staples as pan-fried oysters, but the traditional (Swedish meatballs) and more imaginative Scandinavian dishes are the real attraction here. The fish specialties shouldn't be missed, nor should the *krumkaka* (crumb cake) dessert.

794 U.S. 101 (at Hazel St.) (C) 360/777-8380. www.seattleintheround.com/sanctuary. Reservations recommended. Main courses $12–$21. AE, MC, V. Summer Wed–Sat 5–9pm, Sun 5–8pm; other months, call for hours.

The Shoalwater Restaurant/Heron and Beaver Pub ★★ NORTHWEST The Shoalwater is one of the best restaurants in Washington and should not be missed on a visit to this corner of the state. Stained-glass windows salvaged from an English church suffuse the elegant dining room with a soft light, while furnishings evoke Victorian times. The menu changes frequently, but you can be sure you'll find plenty of excellent oyster and clam dishes (made with local shellfish) at almost any time of year. Since this is cranberry country, you might want to start your meal with an appetizer of paté with cranberry chutney and roasted garlic crème fraîche. Here at the Shelburne Country Inn, you'll also find the casual Heron and Beaver Pub, which serves lighter fare at lower prices, and is open for both lunch and dinner.

In the Shelburne Inn, Wash. 103 and 45th St., Seaview. (C) **360/642-4142.** www.shoalwater.com. Reservations highly recommended. Main courses $13–$24; pub entrees $5.50–$13. AE, DC, DISC, MC, V. Restaurant daily 5:30–9pm. Pub daily 11:30am–3pm and 5:30–9pm.

UP THE COLUMBIA RIVER

Between the Long Beach Peninsula and I-5 at Longview lies one of the state's most enjoyable and little known scenic drives. Wash. 4 passes through several small historic riverfront communities, and between Cathlamet and Longview it runs right alongside the Columbia River, often at the base of steep hillsides or basalt cliffs. The quiet backwaters along this stretch of the river seem little changed by the passing of time.

Heading east from Long Beach on U.S. 101, you first skirt the south end of Willapa Bay, which is the site of the Willapa National Wildlife Refuge. Each year in late April and early May, this area becomes a rest stop for thousands of birds heading north to summer breeding grounds in the Arctic. Roughly 20 miles (32km) east of the junction of U.S. 101 and Wash. 4, you'll come to the **Grays River covered bridge,** which was erected in 1905 and is one of only two covered bridges in Washington. The bridge is a short distance off the highway.

Another 15 miles (24km) east, you'll come to the tiny community of **Skamokawa** (pronounced Skuh-*mah*-kuh-way), which is one of the only remaining Columbia River fishing villages dating from the early 20th century, when salmon canneries abounded along the Columbia River. Here you can visit the **River Life Interpretive Center** (© **360/795-3007**), which is housed in Redmen Hall, a restored 1894 schoolhouse. The center is right on Wash. 4 and is open Wednesday through Saturday from noon to 4pm and Sunday from 1 to 4pm. Just east of Skamokawa lies the Julia Butler Hansen National Wildlife Refuge, which protects the rare Columbia River white-tailed deer, and to the west is the Lewis and Clark National Wildlife Refuge. If you're interested in exploring the waterways of these refuges, contact the **Skamokawa Paddle Center,** 1391 W. State Rte. 4, Skamokawa, WA 98647 (© **888/920-2777** or 360/795-8300; www.skamokawapaddle.com), which offers a wide variety of 1- and 2-day trips. Prices range from $90 to $223 per person. Classes and canoe/kayak rentals are also available.

East of the refuge, you come to Cathlamet, which was settled in 1846 and is the largest town on this stretch of road. Here you can visit the **Wahkiakum Historical Society Museum,** 65 River St., Cathlamet (© **360/795-3954**), learn about the early pioneer history of the region, and see old fishing exhibits. June through September, the museum is open Tuesday through Sunday from 11am to 4pm; October, it's open Tuesday through Sunday from 1 to 4pm; and November through May, it's open Thursday through Sunday from 1 to 4pm. Admission is by donation. Cathlamet is connected by bridge to **Puget Island,** which was settled by Scandinavian fishermen in the late 1800s. Today the island is covered with farms and is a popular spot with bicyclists. The flat, uncrowded roads and river views make for an ideal day's bicycle tour. However, you'll have to bring your own bike as there are no bike rental shops on the island. The last ferry on the Columbia River connects the island to Oregon.

East of Cathlamet begins the most picturesque portion of this drive, with the cliffs of Little Cape Horn marking the start of this scenic stretch of road. Due to its strong winds, the Little Cape Horn area is popular with windsurfers.

WHERE TO STAY

Skamokawa Inn ★ *(Finds)* Located in the tiny historic fishing community of Skamokawa, this inn caters primarily to people coming to town to do a little sea-kayak touring with the affiliated Skamokawa Paddle Center. The inn's rooms, which are in a restored historic building, are modern, comfortable, and cheerful. Two have their own small balconies and all have river views. If you have the family or some friends along, consider the apartment, which is in an adjacent house. The inn is located right on the water, with its own dock. On the ground floor, there's a general store that has a casual dining room as well as a store. Canoes, kayaks, and mountain bikes can all be rented here.

1391 W. State Rte. 4, Skamokawa, WA 98647. © **888/920-2777** or 360/795-8300. Fax 360/795-8304. www.skamokawapaddle.com. 9 units. $90 double; $135–$245 apt or suite. Rates include continental breakfast. MC, V. **Amenities:** Restaurant (American); watersports rentals; bike rentals. *In room:* TV.

3 Vancouver & Vicinity

6 miles (9.5km) N of downtown Portland, 120 miles (193km) SE of Long Beach, 40 miles (64km) S of Longview

Because Vancouver, Washington, is part of the Portland metropolitan area, and because it bears the same name as both a large island and a city in Canada, it is often overlooked by visitors to the Northwest. However, the city has several historic sites and other attractions that make it worth a stop.

It was here, at the Hudson's Bay Company's (HBC) Fort Vancouver, that much of the Northwest's important early pioneer history unfolded. The HBC, a British company, came to the Northwest in search of furs and for most of the first half of the 19th century was the only authority in this remote region. Fur trappers, mountain men, missionaries, explorers, and settlers all made Fort Vancouver their first stop in Oregon.

ESSENTIALS

GETTING THERE   Vancouver is located on I-5 just north across the Columbia River from Portland, Oregon. I-205 bypasses the city to the east, while Wash. 14 heads east up the Columbia Gorge.

With the Portland International Airport just across the river, Vancouver is also well connected to the rest of the world via numerous airlines. The city is also served by Amtrak trains.

VISITOR INFORMATION   For more information on this area, contact the **Southwest Washington Visitor & Convention Bureau,** 101 E. Eighth St, Vancouver, WA 98660 (*©* **877/600-0800** or 360/750-1553; www.vancouverusa. com), which operates a Visitor's Center on Officer's Row at the O.O. Howard House, 750 Anderson St.

VANCOUVER'S HISTORICAL ATTRACTIONS

The city of Vancouver, Washington, was one of the first settlements in the Northwest and consequently has a long pioneer and military history. After the British in the guise of the Hudson's Bay Company (HBC) gave up Fort Vancouver, it became the site of the Vancouver Barracks U.S. military post, and stately homes were built for the officers of the post. The buildings of Officers' Row and their attractive, tree-shaded surroundings are now preserved as the **Vancouver National Historic Reserve** ★★. Within the reserve, which is located just east of I-5 (take the East Mill Plain Blvd. exit just north of the I-5 Interstate Bridge), you'll find not only Officers' Row, Fort Vancouver, and the Pearson Air Museum, but also the **Columbia River Waterfront Trail.** At the west end of this paved riverside trail, in a small park through a walkway under the railroad tracks, you'll find the **oldest apple tree** in the Northwest. It was planted in 1826.

Howard House ★   Start a visit to Officers' Row at this restored Victorian mansion that was once an NCO club for the military post and now serves as the information center for the national historic reserve. After learning a bit about the history of this area, you can stroll the grounds admiring the well-kept homes.

750 Anderson St. *©* **360/992-1820.** www.nps.gov/fova. Free admission. Mar–Oct daily 9am–5pm; Nov–Feb daily 9am–4pm. Closed Thanksgiving and Dec 24–Dec 25.

Fort Vancouver National Historic Site ★★   It was here at Fort Vancouver, a trading post operated by the Hudson's Bay Company, that much of the Northwest's important early pioneer history unfolded. The HBC, a British company, came to the Northwest in search of furs and, for most of the first half of the 19th century, was the only authority in this remote region. Fur trappers, mountain men, missionaries, explorers, and settlers all made Fort Vancouver their first stop in the Oregon country, which at that time also encompassed present-day Washington. Today Fort Vancouver houses several reconstructed buildings that are furnished as they might have been in the middle of the 19th century. In summer, there are living-history programs on Saturday and Sunday at 3pm.

1501 E. Evergreen Blvd. ⓒ **360/696-7655**. www.nps.gov/fova. Admission $2 in summer; free in winter. Mar–Oct daily 9am–5pm (Nov–Feb until 4pm).

Pearson Air Museum ⭐ A very different piece of history is preserved at this small air museum on the far side of Fort Vancouver from Officers' Row. This airfield was established in 1905 and is the oldest operating airfield in the United States. Dozens of vintage aircraft, including several World War I–era biplanes and the plane that made the first transpacific flight, are on display in a large hangar.

1115 E. Fifth St. ⓒ **360/694-7026**. www.pearsonairmuseum.org. Admission $5 adults, $4 seniors, $3 children ages 13–18, $2 children ages 6–12, free for children under 6. Tues–Sun 10am–5pm.

EXPLORING OUTSIDE OF TOWN

In the town of Washougal, 16 miles (26km) east of Vancouver on Wash. 14, you can visit the **Pendleton Woolen Mills and Outlet Shop,** 217th St., Washougal (ⓒ **800/568-2480** or 360/835-2131), and see how their famous wool blankets and classic wool fashions are made. The store is open Monday through Friday from 8am to 5pm, Saturday from 9am to 5pm, and Sunday from 1 to 5pm, with free mill tours offered Monday through Friday at 9, 10, and 11am, and 1:30pm.

North of Vancouver 23 miles (37km) in the town of Woodland are the **Hulda Klager Lilac Gardens,** 115 S. Pekin Rd., Woodland (ⓒ **360/225-8996**). Between late April and Mother's Day each year, these gardens burst into color and the fragrance of lilacs hangs in the air. The gardens are open daily from dawn to dusk. Admission is by donation.

Ten miles (16km) east of Woodland off NE Cedar Creek Road, you'll find the **Cedar Creek Grist Mill,** Grist Mill Road (ⓒ **360/225-5832**), the only remaining 19th-century grist mill in Washington. Built in 1876, the mill was restored over a 10-year period, and in 1989, once again became functional. When the mill is open, volunteers demonstrate how wheat is ground into flour. Hours of operation are Saturday from 1 to 4pm and Sunday from 2 to 4pm. Admission is by donation. Adjacent to the mill is one of Washington's only two historic covered bridges.

WHERE TO STAY

The Heathman Lodge ⭐⭐ Value Mountain lodge meets urban chic at this suburban Vancouver hotel adjacent to the Vancouver Mall, and though it's a 20-minute drive to downtown Portland, the hotel is well placed for exploring both the Columbia Gorge and Mount St. Helens. With its log, stone, and cedar-shingle construction, this hotel conjures up the Northwest's historic mountain lodges. As at Timberline Lodge, this hotel is filled with artwork and embellished with rugged Northwest-inspired craftwork, including totem poles, Eskimo kayak frames, and Pendleton blankets. Guest rooms feature a mix of rustic pine and peeled-hickory furniture as well as rawhide lampshades and Pendleton-inspired bedspreads.

7801 NE Greenwood Dr., Vancouver, WA 98662. ⓒ **888/475-3100** or 360/254-3100. Fax 360/254-6100. www.heathmanlodge.com. 143 units. $89–$139 double; $159–$550 suite. AE, DC, DISC, MC, V. Free parking. **Amenities:** Restaurant (Northwest); lounge; indoor pool; exercise room; Jacuzzi; sauna; concierge; business center; room service; guest laundry; laundry service; dry cleaning. *In room:* A/C, TV, dataport, fridge, microwave, coffeemaker, hair dryer, iron.

WHERE TO DINE

Hudson's, the dining room at Heathman Lodge (see above for details), is one of the city's best restaurants and is open for three meals a day. When it's time for a pint of craft ale, the place to head in Vancouver is **McMenamins on the Columbia,** 1801 SE Columbia River Dr. (© **360/699-1521**), a brewpub with a view.

Beaches Restaurant & Bar ★ *(Kids)* INTERNATIONAL   Sure it's a long way to the beach, but why let that stop you from having a good time? That seems to be the attitude of this waterfront restaurant. The gardens are full of sand and a party atmosphere prevails most of the time (there are early and late happy hours). The menu is long and includes everything from burgers to barbecue chicken pizza to a catfish tortilla wrap. With big walls of glass overlooking the Columbia, sunset dinners are very popular. Despite the large size, service is usually good. To reach the restaurant from I-5, take Wash. 14 east and then take exit 1.

1919 SE Columbia River Dr. © **360/699-1592.** Reservations recommended. Main courses $5–$12 at lunch, $7–$23 at dinner. AE, DC, DISC, MC, V. Mon 11am–9pm; Tues–Fri 11am–10pm; Sat 11:30am–10pm; Sun 11:30am–9pm.

The Grant House Restaurant ★★ NEW AMERICAN   Housed in Officers' Row's historic Grant House (which is named for one-time resident Ulysses S. Grant), this restaurant has the feel of a New England country inn and is an absolute must if you are in Vancouver to explore its many historical buildings. The menu includes both updated comfort foods, such as a tasty apple-and-honey-butter meatloaf, and more creative dishes such as pork loin chop with apricot-mustard sauce and rib-eye steak with crawfish bordelaise. The kalamata and goat cheese ravioli is another winner. Sunday brunch, which includes blintzes and crab cakes, is a good bet, so you might want to schedule your explorations around this meal.

1101 Officers' Row. © **360/696-1727.** Reservations recommended. Main courses $7.50–$9 at lunch, $13–$18 at dinner. AE, DISC, MC, V. Mon–Fri 11am–2pm and 5–9pm; Sat 5–9pm; Sun 10am–2pm.

9

The Cascades

Cloaked in places by dark forests of old-growth trees and stripped bare by logging clear-cuts in others, the Washington Cascades are a patchwork quilt of narrow valleys, rolling foothills, snowcapped volcanic peaks, and rugged mountain ranges. Lakes of the deepest blue are cradled beneath emerald forests. Glaciers carve their way inexorably from peaks that experience some of the heaviest snowfalls in the nation. (It's possible to drive or hike a short distance to the edge of several of these glaciers and listen to their cracking and rumbling as gravity pulls at their centuries-old ice.) And the appropriately named Cascades send countless waterfalls cascading from the heights.

From the Canadian border south more than 150 miles (242km) to Olympia, along the shores of Puget Sound, lies the most densely populated region of the state, yet for the millions of people who live here, gazing upon mountain wilderness merely requires a look eastward on a clear day. Dominating the eastern skyline of northern Puget Sound are volcanic Mount Baker and the North Cascades. In the southern regions of the sound, Mount Rainier, another dormant volcano, looms grandly on the horizon. It's the easy accessibility of these mountains that helps make the cities of Puget Sound so livable. With two national parks, a national volcanic monument, a half dozen major ski areas, one of the largest networks of cross-country ski trails in the country, hundreds of lakes (including the third-deepest lake in the United States), a Bavarian village, and a false-fronted Wild West frontier town, these mountains offer a diversity of recreational and sightseeing activities. Whatever the season, in good weather and bad, active Washingtonians head for the hills whenever they get the chance. Summer and winter are, however, the most popular seasons in these mountains. In summer people come for the wildflowers and to go hiking, and in winter, they come for the skiing and snowboarding.

1 Mount Baker ✶✶ & the North Cascades Scenic Highway ✶✶✶

Diablo Lake: 66 miles (106km) E of Burlington (I-5), 65 miles (105km) W of Winthrop
Mount Baker Ski Area: 62 miles (100km) E of Bellingham

Wolves and grizzly bears still call this wilderness home, and names such as Mount Fury, Mount Terror, and Forbidden Peak are testament to the rugged and remote nature of this terrain. Much of the region is preserved within the two units of North Cascades National Park, one of the least visited national parks in the country. This lack of visitors is easy to understand when you realize there is but one gravel road within the boundaries of the park, and this road originates in the community of Stehekin on the north shore of Lake Chelan. Stehekin can

The Washington Cascades

only be reached by hiking trail, floatplane, or boat, which severely limits the number of vehicles that use this road. However, passing between the two units of the national park is the North Cascades Scenic Highway, which does provide access to viewpoints and trails that lead into the national park. While there is very little road access in this area, there are plenty of trails, and day hikers and backpackers can head off on hundreds of miles of trails through wilderness areas, national forest, national park, and national recreation areas.

Though numerous attempts were made over the years to build a road through the craggy, glacier-sculpted North Cascade mountains, it was not until 1972 that Wash. 20 finally connected the Skagit Valley communities on the west side of the North Cascades with Winthrop on the east side of the mountains. Today the road is known as the North Cascades Scenic Highway, and it's one of the most breathtakingly beautiful stretches of road anywhere in the United States. Unfortunately, because of heavy winter snows and avalanches, the road is only open from April to November (depending on the weather). The scenic highway begins east of Sedro-Woolley, and along its length you'll find more than a dozen campgrounds.

Lying just outside the northwestern corner of North Cascades National Park is 10,778-foot Mount Baker, which on a clear day dominates the skyline to the east of Bellingham and the San Juan Islands. This is the northernmost of Washington's Cascade Range volcanoes, and, as such, rises high above the surrounding North Cascade peaks, which are geologically unrelated to Mount Baker. Because it is open to the winter storms that sweep up the Strait of Juan de Fuca from the Pacific Ocean, Mount Baker usually receives more snow than any other Cascades peak, and in the winter of 1998 and 1999, a world record 1,140 inches fell at the Mount Baker Ski Area.

While it is the North Cascades Scenic Highway, with its mountain vistas and excellent hiking, that attracts most people to this area, the slopes of Mount Baker are almost equally rewarding. In summer, hikers can explore alpine meadows, and in winter, skiers and snowboarders can sample some of the most legendary snows in the country.

ESSENTIALS

GETTING THERE To reach Mount Baker ski area (and, in summer, Heather Meadows and Artist Point), head east from Bellingham on Wash. 542 (the Mount Baker Hwy.). The North Cascades Scenic Highway is Wash. 20, which leaves I-5 at Burlington.

VISITOR INFORMATION For information on the Mount Baker area, contact the **Glacier Public Service Center,** Mount Baker Highway, Glacier (© **360/599-2714**), which is open from mid-May to mid-October and is jointly operated by the National Forest Service and the National Park Service. For information on the North Cascades National Park Complex, Mount Baker National Recreation Area, and Mount Baker–Snoqualmie National Forest, contact the jointly operated **Forest/Park Service Information Office,** 810 Wash. 20, Sedro-Woolley, WA 98284 (© **360/856-5700;** www.nps.gov/noca or www.fs.fed.us/r6/mbs).

VISITING THE MOUNT BAKER AREA

Wash. 542, known as the Mount Baker Highway, is a dead-end road that climbs to 5,140 feet in elevation at a ridge between 10,778-foot Mount Baker and 9,038-foot Mount Shuksan. The road ends at the aptly named **Artist Point** ★★★, an area of rugged beauty nearly unequaled in the state. Rising directly above Artist Point is flat-topped Table Mountain, up which there is a short but precipitous trail. Below Artist Point (3 miles/5km by road) lie **Heather Meadows** and Picture Lake, in which the reflection of Mount Shuksan can be seen when the waters are still. Each year in July and August the meadows of this area burst into bloom and attract crowds of weekend hikers who tramp the many miles of trails that radiate out from here. Between mid-July and September, the **Heather Meadows Visitor Center** has trail maps for the area and information on this region's unusual geology.

Two of the most rewarding hikes in the Mount Baker area actually originate not in the Heather Meadows/Artist Point area but off side roads 1 mile (1.5km) east of the town of Glacier. These are the **Heliotrope Ridge Trail** ★★ (off Forest Service Rd. 39) and the **Skyline Divide Trail** ★★★ (off Forest Service Rd. 37). Both of these trails climb up through meadows with excellent views of Mount Baker, and, from the Heliotrope Ridge Trail, there are also impressive glacier views. Also near Glacier, at milepost 41, is a short trail that leads to 100-foot Nooksack Falls.

In order to park at Heather Meadows, Artist Point, and other trail heads in the area, you'll need a Northwest Forest Pass. These permits cost $5 per day ($30 for an annual pass) and can be purchased at ranger stations and national forest visitor centers.

While Kodak-moment meadows of colorful wildflowers are a big attraction throughout the summer, Mount Baker is better known as one of the nation's top snowboarding areas. Each winter, Mount Baker receives an average of more than 500 inches of snow, and in the winter of 1998 and 1999 set a world record with 1,140 inches of snow. All this snow, combined with lots of extreme terrain, produces awesome skiing and snowboarding conditions. Consequently, **Mount Baker Ski Area** ★★ (© 360/671-0211; www.mtbakerskiarea.com), located at Heather Meadows, is well known throughout the region for always being the first ski area to open and the last to close each year. Daily lift tickets range from $24 to $34. Ski and snowboard rentals are available at the ski area, and snowboards can also be rented in the town of Glacier at **Mt. Baker Snowboard Shop,** 9996 Forest St. (© **360/599-2008**). Cross-country skiers will find a few kilometers of groomed trails at Mount Baker ski area, as well as many more miles at the **Salmon Ridge Sno-Park** farther down the mountain. Telemark skiers and backcountry snowboarders will find lots of great terrain adjacent to Mount Baker ski area.

En route to or from Mount Baker, you can sample local wines at **Mount Baker Vineyards,** 4298 Mt. Baker Hwy., Deming (© **360/592-2300;** www. mountbakervineyards.com); and stock up on gourmet picnic foods at the unexpectedly hip **Everybody's Store,** Highway 9, Van Zandt (© **360/592-2297;** www.everybodys.com).

THE NORTH CASCADES SCENIC HIGHWAY

Wash. 20, the North Cascades Scenic Highway, is a bit slow in sharing its beauties. Though it runs along the Skagit River on the west side of the Cascades, it is not until you get to the Ross Lake area that the scenery becomes truly grand. However, there are several distractions along the way before you reach the most scenic stretch of the highway.

North of Concrete, which was named for the cement it once produced, lie Lake Shannon and Baker Lake, the latter being a popular summer camping and boating destination. From the road leading to **Baker Lake,** you can also access the **Mount Baker National Recreation Area,** which lies on the south side of

Natural History Seminars

Want to track radio-collared mountain caribou? Learn about Lummi Indian basketry? Delve into the mysteries of mycology? You can do any of these things if you sign up for the right class through the North Cascades Institute. Offering more than 80 natural history field seminars each year, the **North Cascades Institute,** 810 State Rte. 20, Sedro-Woolley, WA 98284 (② **360/856-5700,** ext. 209; www.ncascades.org), is a nonprofit educational organization that offers a wide range of courses each year. While these seminars, many of which involve camping out, focus on the North Cascades region, there are programs throughout the state.

Mount Baker. Several trails here lead through the beautiful alpine meadows on the south side of the mountain. The Railroad Grade–Paul Scott Trail is particularly breathtaking.

Between Concrete and Marblemount, the highway parallels the Skagit River, and from December to February each year, hundreds of bald eagles descend on this stretch of the river to feed on dying salmon. Highway turnouts at the prime eagle-watching sites along this stretch of road provide opportunities to observe the eagles. To learn more about the eagles, stop by Rockport's **Eagle Interpretive Center,** Alfred St. (② 360/853-7009 or 360/853-7614; www.skagiteagle. org), which is located 1 block south of Wash. 20 in the Rockport Fire Hall. The center is staffed Saturday and Sunday during eagle-watching season. This center can also provide information on the annual Upper Skagit Bald Eagle Festival, which takes place each year in late January or early February. The best way to do your eagle watching is from a raft floating slowly down the river (no white water here). Companies offering **eagle-watching float trips** include **Chinook Expeditions** (② 800/241-3451; www.chinookexpeditions. com) and **Alpine Adventures** (② 800/723-8386 or 206/323-1220; www.alpine adventures. com). An all-day trip costs about $75.

Right in the middle of the eagle-viewing area, you'll come to the town of Rockport. On its west side is **Rockport State Park,** where you can take a hike through a stand of old-growth Douglas firs, some of which are more than 300 years old. Three miles (5km) east of Rockport, keep an eye out for **Cascadian Farm Roadside Stand,** 55749 Hwy. 20 (② 360/853-8173), which is open May through October and sells organic berries during the summer months.

However, hikers in search of mountain vistas and wildflower-filled meadows should hold out for **Rainy Pass** ✦✦ (and hope that the pass is not living up to its name). Here you'll find an easy paved trail to **Rainy Lake,** which can be combined with the strenuous, but astoundingly soul-satisfying, **Maple Pass Loop.** The view from Maple Pass is one of the finest in the Northwest. The Pacific Crest Trail also crosses the highway at Rainy Pass. If you head north along the Pacific Crest Trail, you will climb to Cutthroat Pass, with more superb views. A few miles farther east, you'll find the trail head for the short, but steep, hike to picturesque **Blue Lake.**

Roughly 20 miles (32km) before reaching the Wild West town of Winthrop, you come to the most breathtaking stretch of the North Cascades Scenic Highway. Here, at **Washington Pass** ✦✦✦ (5,447 ft. in elevation), the granite peak of Liberty Bell Mountain rises 2,200 feet above. Across the valley are the jagged Early Winter Spires, a full 200 feet taller than Liberty Bell Mountain. Below the pass the road has been blasted out of a steep cliff face in one huge switchback. At the pass, the Washington Pass Overlook, with its short walking trail, provides an opportunity to enjoy these last awesome vistas of the North Cascades. With its in-your-face view of craggy peaks, this is the North Cascade Scenic Highway's big payoff and this sight alone makes the drive over the mountains worthwhile.

In Marblemount, the next town you come to, you'll find the **Wilderness Information Center** of the Ross Lake National Recreation Area (© **360/873-4500,** ext. 39), which provides backcountry permits and information.

In the town of Newhalem, a picturesque Seattle City Light company town at the foot of the Gorge Dam, you'll find the **North Cascades Visitor Center** (© **206/386-4495,** ext. 11), the main visitor center for the North Cascades National Park Complex, which includes North Cascades National Park, Ross Lake National Recreation Area, and Lake Chelan National Recreation Area. The visitor center is filled with interesting exhibits on this remote national park. There are several short hikes in the area, and in the autumn, you can see spawning salmon at the base of the hydro-power plant on the edge of town. There is also an attractively landscaped garden (reached by a swinging footbridge) surrounding this powerhouse. Continuing east from Newhalem, the road passes through a deep, narrow gorge, where you can glimpse **Gorge Creek Falls** before reaching **Gorge Dam,** the first and smallest of the dams along this stretch of the Skagit River.

Beyond the Gorge Dam, you soon come to Diablo, another Seattle City Light company town, which stands at the base of Diablo Dam. Diablo is the starting point for one of the most fascinating excursions in this corner of the state—the 4-hour **boat tour of Diablo Lake.** The tours start with a trip up an incline railway to the top of 389-foot-tall Diablo Dam. From there you board a boat for the 5-mile cruise to Ross Lake Dam, where you get a tour of the powerhouse. At the end of all this, you get a chicken or vegetarian spaghetti dinner. Between mid-June and August, tours are offered Thursday through Monday, and in September, they're offered on Saturday and Sunday only. The Ross Deluxe Meal Tour costs $35 for adults, $30 for seniors, $25 for children 6 to 11. There are also 1½-hour tours of **Diablo Dam.** These tours cost only $5 per person, but do not include the boat ride or dinner. For information, or to make a reservation (highly recommended), call **Seattle City Light** (© **206/684-3030;** www.ci. seattle.wa.us/light/tours/).

Continuing on past Diablo, you cross the Thunder Arm of Diablo Lake and climb up to the spectacular **Diablo Lake Overlook** ✹✹. When the sun shines, the glacier-fed lake displays an astounding turquoise color due to the suspended particles of silt in the water. High above the lake you can see glaciated Colonial and Pyramid peaks.

At the **Ross Lake Overlook,** several miles farther east, the dammed waters of this huge reservoir come into view. The lake, and in fact this entire stretch of highway from east of Marblemount to east of Ross Lake, is designated the **Ross Lake National Recreation Area.** The lake itself extends 24 miles (39km) north, with its northern shore lying 1½ miles (2.5km) inside Canada. The only access to the lake from the United States is by trail or water, and with its many shoreline backcountry campsites and East Bank Trail it is a popular backpacker destination. Sea kayakers also frequent these remote waters. See "Where to Stay," below, for information on the Ross Lake Resort, which offers both a water taxi service and shuttle that will haul your kayak or canoe around Ross Dam. Trails lead down to the lake both at the dam (before the Ross Lake Overlook) and east of the overlook (access to the East Bank Trail).

WHERE TO STAY
IN THE MOUNT BAKER AREA

The best accommodations at the foot of Mount Baker are to be had through **Mt. Baker Lodging,** 7425 Mt. Baker Hwy. (P.O. Box 2002), Maple Falls, WA (© 800/709-7669 or 360/599-2453; www.mtbakerlodging.com), which rents out around 30 cabins. Rates range from $115 to $245 per night.

The Inn at Mt. Baker ★★   Located high on a hill at the end of a steep, 3,000-foot-long gravel driveway (don't worry, the inn really is up there), this B&B is by far the best place to stay along the Mt. Baker Highway. A head-on, jaw-dropping view of Mount Baker, is the inn's focal point and all five of the guest rooms have mountain views, as does the Jacuzzi out on the patio. The inn is a large modern home, and all the rooms are spacious and have superb beds and oversize soaking tubs. Perhaps the only drawback here is that the hill leading up to the inn was fairly recently clear cut.

8174 Mt. Baker Hwy. (P.O. Box 5150), Glacier, WA 98244. © 877/567-5526 or 360/599-1359. Fax 360/599-3000. www.theinnatmtbaker.com. 5 units. $100–$110 double. Rates include full breakfast. AE, MC, V. **Amenities:** Jacuzzi; massage. *In room:* No phone.

ALONG THE NORTH CASCADES SCENIC HIGHWAY

Ross Lake Resort ★ *Finds*   Although this is primarily a fishing resort, the fact that all the rooms are in floating cabins makes it unusual enough that even nonanglers might enjoy a stay here. Although most of the cabins are small and rustic, there are two large cabins with vaulted ceilings and modern amenities. If you're looking to get away from it all, this place comes pretty close—there's not even a road to the resort. To reach the resort, you must first drive to Diablo Dam on Wash. 20, then take a tugboat to the end of the lake where a truck carries you around the Ross Dam to the lodge. Alternatively, you can hike in on a 2-mile (3km) trail from milepost 134 on Wash. 20. There's no grocery store or restaurant here, so be sure to bring enough food for your stay. What do you do once you get here? Rent a boat and go fishing, rent a kayak or canoe, do some hiking, or simply sit and relax.

Rockport, WA 98283. © 206/386-4437. www.rosslakeresort.com. 15 units. $68–$181 cabin for 2. MC, V. **Amenities:** Watersports rentals. *In room:* Kitchen, fridge, coffeemaker.

Skagit River Resort ★   The first thing you notice when you arrive at this casual cabin resort is the rabbits. They're everywhere—hundreds of them in all shapes and sizes, contentedly munching the lawns or just sitting quietly. Although the bunnies are one of the main attractions here, it's the theme cabins that keep people coming back. Western, nautical, Victorian, Native American, Adirondack, and hacienda are among the choices of interior decor in these cabins. There are other cabins that are equally comfortable, but the theme cabins are what make this place just a bit different. These cabins are especially popular in winter when folks flock to the area to watch the bald eagles that congregate on the Skagit River. There is also a bed-and-breakfast lodge here.

58468 Clark Cabin Rd., Rockport, WA 98283. © 800/273-2606 or 360/873-2250. Fax 360/873-4077. www.northcascades.com. 33 units. $47–$129 double. AE, DISC, MC, V. Pets accepted with $10 fee per night. **Amenities:** Restaurant (American); exercise room; bike rentals; babysitting; coin-op laundry. *In room:* TV, dataport, kitchen, fridge, coffeemaker.

CAMPGROUNDS

In the Mount Baker Area

There are several campgrounds in the forests along the banks of the Nooksack River along the Mount Baker Highway. **Silver Fir Campground** ✿ (20 campsites) 13 miles (21km) east of Glacier is the closest campground to the Heather Meadows area, and the **Douglas Fir Campground** ✿ (30 campsites) 2 miles (3km) east of Glacier is the next best choice in the area. Reservations can be made at both of these campgrounds by calling the **National Recreation Reservation Service** (☎ 800/280-CAMP; www.reserveusa.com). The most developed campground in the area is at **Silver Lake County Park** (☎ 360/599-2776), which is north of Maple Falls and has 120 campsites.

Along the North Cascades Scenic Highway

Heading over the North Cascades Highway from the west side, you'll find a very nice campground, with walk-in sites, at **Rockport State Park** ✿ (58 campsites) just west of Rockport. This campground is set amid large old-growth trees. Outside the town of Newhalem are **Goodell Creek** (21 campsites) and **Newhalem Creek** ✿ (111 campsites), which is the site of the North Cascades Visitor Center. The next campground east is at **Colonial Creek** ✿ (162 campsites) on the bank of Diablo Lake. This campground has some very nice sites right on the water.

East of Marblemount, there are a couple of small campgrounds on the Cascade River Road, which leads to the trail head for the popular hike to Cascade Pass. **Marble Creek** (24 campsites) is 8 miles (13km) east of Marblemount, and **Mineral Park** (8 campsites) is 15 miles (24km) east of Marblemount. Reservations at state park campgrounds can be made by calling **Washington State Parks Reservations** (☎ 888/226-7688; www.parks.wa.gov). Some National Forest campgrounds also accept reservations. For more information call the **National Recreation Reservation Service** (☎ 800/280-CAMP; www.reserve usa.com).

WHERE TO DINE

IN THE MOUNT BAKER AREA

For microbrews and pizza, try the **North Fork,** 6186 Mt. Baker Hwy., Deming (☎ 360/599-BEER).

Milano's Market & Deli ✿ (Value) ITALIAN   This casual deli and Italian eatery has long been a favorite of snowboarders and skiers coming down off the mountain after a day on the slopes. Fresh pasta dishes are the specialty here, and the menu includes four different types of ravioli (smoked salmon, porcini mushroom, cheese, and meat). The desserts, including tiramisu, cappuccino chocolate torte, and polenta cake, are all big hits with the hungry downhill crowd.

9990 Mt. Baker Hwy., Glacier. ☎ 360/599-2863. Main courses $4.75–$12. MC, V. Mon–Fri 10am–8:30pm; Sat–Sun 7am–9pm.

Seven Loaves Restaurant & Bakery ✿ INTERNATIONAL   Located just west of the tiny town of Glacier, the Seven Loaves Restaurant serves a fairly simple menu that's broad enough to satisfy every kind of diner from vegan to steak lover. Selections include vegetarian and seafood dishes, free-range meats including buffalo, and organic produce from local farms.

9393 Mt. Baker Hwy., Glacier. ☎ 360/599-2290. Main courses $2.50–$16. AE, DISC, MC, V. Summer Thurs 3–9pm, Fri–Sun 11am–9pm; ski season Thurs–Sun 3–9pm. Closed May and most of Oct–Thanksgiving.

ALONG THE NORTH CASCADES SCENIC HIGHWAY

In addition to the restaurant listed here, you can get decent, simple meals at the Eatery Restaurant at the Skagit River Resort, which is also in Marblemount.

Buffalo Run Restaurant ★ *Finds* AMERICAN   From the outside this looks like any other roadside diner, but once you see the menu, it's obvious this place is unique. The restaurant's owners have a buffalo ranch and feature buffalo meat on the menu. There are buffalo burgers, buffalo chili, and buffalo T-bones. You'll also find elk, venison, and ostrich on the menu. Of course there's a buffalo head (and skin) on the wall. You'll find the restaurant right in Marblemount.

60084 Hwy. 20 (milepost 106), Marblemount. ℂ 360/873-2461. www.buffalorunrestaurant.com. Main courses $4.50–$40. AE, DISC, MC, V. Daily 8am–9pm. Closed Nov–Apr.

2 Winthrop & the Methow Valley ★★

193 miles (311km; summer) or 243 miles (391km; winter) E of Seattle, 53 miles (85km) N of Chelan

Driving into Winthrop, you may think you've stumbled into a movie set. A covered wooden sidewalk lines the town's main street, which includes a saloon and a blacksmith's shop. If it's a Saturday in summer, you might even see a shootout (staged). But where are the cameras? No, this isn't a Hollywood set—it's the real Winthrop.

Well, not *exactly* the real Winthrop. Back in 1972, when the North Cascades Scenic Highway opened, Winthrop needed a way to stop a few of the cars that started crossing the mountains on the new highway. Someone suggested that they cash in on their Wild West heritage and put up some old-fashioned cowtown false fronts (based on old photos of the town). This rewriting of history worked and now Winthrop gets plenty of cars to stop. In fact it has become a destination in its own right, known for its cross-country skiing in winter and mountain biking, hiking, and horseback riding in summer.

Winthrop and the Methow River valley in which it is located really do have a Wild West history. Until 1883, there were no white settlers in this picturesque valley. The only inhabitants were Native Americans who annually migrated into the valley to harvest camas bulbs and fish for salmon. The Native Americans felt it was just too cold to live in the Methow Valley, but when the first white settlers showed up, they refused to listen to the Native Americans' weather reports and built their drafty log cabins anyway. Gold was discovered in the late 1800s and fueled a short-lived boom, but it was agriculture in the form of apples that kept the valley alive until the advent of tourism in the 1970s.

Why an Old West theme town? Possibly because Owen Wister, author of *The Virginian,* a Western novel that became a popular television series, was inspired to write his novel after coming to Winthrop to visit his former Harvard University roommate who ran a trading post here. You won't find any trading posts here anymore, but you will find two of the finest mountain lodges in the state.

ESSENTIALS

GETTING THERE   In summer you can take Wash. 20, the North Cascades Scenic Highway, from I-5 at Burlington. However, in winter this road is closed and it's necessary to cross from north of Seattle on U.S. 2 to Wenatchee and then drive north on U.S. 97 to Wash. 153 at Pateros. If you're coming from north-central or eastern Washington, head east on Wash. 20 at Okanogan.

VISITOR INFORMATION For more information on the Methow Valley, contact the **Winthrop Chamber of Commerce,** 204 Hwy. 20, Winthrop, WA 98862 (© **888/4-METHOW** or 509/996-2125; www. winthropwashington. com), which has its office on Winthrop's main intersection.

FESTIVALS Each year in mid-July the **Winthrop Rhythm & Blues Festival** (www.winthropbluesfestival.com) brings a variety of national and regional R&B acts to town for a 3-day music binge.

SPORTS & OUTDOOR ACTIVITIES

If you're here for the outdoors, then sooner or later you're going to need the **Mazama Store,** 50 Lost River Rd. (© **509/996-2855**), which is a general store for the multisport crowd. Not only are outdoor gear and clothing for sale, but there are gourmet groceries, Washington wines and microbrews, an espresso bar, and a deli.

FISHING Fly-fishing is particularly popular in the Methow Valley, and the valley's fly-fishing headquarters is **Mazama Troutfitters,** 50 Lost River Rd. (© **509/996-3674**), which rents all manner of gear, can give you tips on where the fish are biting, and also offers a guide service and classes.

HIKING Hikers will find miles of trails, including the **Pacific Crest Trail,** within a few miles of Winthrop, although the best hiking trails are farther west off the North Cascades Scenic Highway. For information, contact the **Okanogan/Wenatchee National Forest,** Methow Valley Ranger District, 502 Glover St.(P.O. Box 188), Twisp, WA 98856 (© **509/997-2131**).

If you want to head for the hills for a few days but don't want to carry a pack, consider a llama trek. These can be arranged through **Deli Llama Wilderness Adventures,** 17045 Llama Lane, Bow, WA 98232 (© **360/757-4212;** www.deli llama.com); or **Pasayten Llama Packing,** P.O. Box 852, Twisp, WA 98856 (© **509/996-2326;** www.mtllama.com).

HORSEBACK RIDING If you've come to Winthrop because you're a cowboy at heart, you'll probably be interested in doing some horseback riding. **Early Winters Outfitting** (© **800/737-8750** or 509/996-2659; www.earlywinters outfitting.com) in Mazama offers rides ranging from an hour ($18) to overnight ($125) or longer. **North Cascade Outfitters** (© **888/291-4097** or 509/997-1015) in Twisp also offers a variety of rides.

HOT-AIR BALLOONING If you'd like to see the Methow Valley from the air, you can arrange a hot-air balloon flight through **Morning Glory Balloon Tours** (© **509/997-1700**), which charges $165 per person for a 1-hour flight with a champagne picnic at the end of the flight.

MOUNTAIN BIKING With its many miles of gravel and dirt roads and both national forest and MVSTA trails that are open to bikes in the snow-free months, the Methow Valley ranks as the best mountain-biking area in the entire state. Mountain-bike rentals and trail recommendations are available from **Winthrop Mountain Sports,** 257 Riverside Dr. (© **800/719-3826** or 509/ 996-2886; www.winthropmountainsports.com), which is located in downtown Winthrop.

ROCK CLIMBING The best rock climbing in the state surrounds the Methow Valley, and if you'd like to hire a guide to lead you (or are interested in taking some climbing lessons), contact **North Cascades Mountain Guides** in Mazama (© **509/996-3194;** www.ncmountainguides.com), which charges $150 per person per day (2 person minimum) for a day of guided climbing.

WHITE-WATER RAFTING   May through August is white-water rafting season on the Methow River. If you're interested, contact **Osprey River Adventures** (© **800/997-4116** or 509/997-4116; www.methow.com/osprey). Trips are about $70 per person.

WINTER SPORTS ★★★   With its sunshine and powdery winter snows, the Methow Valley is legendary in the Northwest for its cross-country skiing. The **Methow Valley Sport Trails Association** (© **509/996-3287;** www.mvsta.com) maintains approximately 125 miles (200km) of groomed ski trails, which makes this the second most extensive groomed trail system in the country. Trail passes are $15 for 1 day, $11 for a half day, or $35 for 3 days. Children ages 13 to 17 pay half price, and children 12 and under ski free. Snowshoe passes are also available ($3 per day). The greatest concentration of trails for all skill levels are in the vicinity of Sun Mountain Lodge, while the trails around Mazama offer plenty of easy miles for distance skiing. The Rendezvous area trails are long and strenuous, but include huts that can be rented for overnight stays. For information on renting one of these huts, contact **Rendezvous Huts** (© **800/257-2452,** 800/422-3048, or 509/996-2148; www.methow.com/huts). Rental rates start at $25 per person.

You can pick up trail maps and rent equipment at **Sun Mountain Ski** (© **800/572-0493** or 509/996-2211), located at Sun Mountain Lodge; **Winthrop Mountain Sports,** 257 Riverside Dr. (© **800/719-3826** or 509/996-2886; www. winthropmountainsports.com), in downtown Winthrop; Mazama Country Inn (© **509/996-2681**); or **Jack's Hut at Freestone Inn,** 17798 Wash. 20 (© **509/996-2752** or 509/996-3906, ext. 303). All of these either offer a variety of lessons or can point you in the right direction for instruction.

If you happen to be out here with downhill skis or maybe want to do a little telemark skiing, try the small ski hill at **Loup Loup Ski Bowl** (© **509/826-2720;** www.skitheloup.com), 20 minutes east of Twisp on Wash. 20. It's open Wednesday and Friday through Sunday, and daily lift passes are $23 to $28. Although this ski area is small, it does have a quad chairlift. Experienced downhill skiers in search of virgin powder can, if they can afford it, do some heli-skiing with **North Cascade Heli-Skiing** (© **800/494-HELI** or 509/996-3272; www.heli-ski.com). A day of skiing that includes five runs and 10,000 vertical feet of slopes will cost $675 per person. However, most people coming here for heli-skiing opt for a 3-day package that includes room, board, and skiing for $2,240 to $2,380 per person (based on double occupancy). Overnight yurt tours are also available.

If you're interested in taking a backcountry skiing course, contact **North Cascades Mountain Guides** in Mazama (© **509/996-3194;** www.ncmountain guides.com), which offers courses for $125 per person per day (two-person minimum).

You can go dog sledding with **Malamute Express** (© **509/997-6402;** www. malamute-express.com), which offers trips for $200 for one person and $350 for two people.

OTHER AREA ATTRACTIONS

Though Winthrop is primarily a base for skiers, hikers, and mountain bikers, it also has a few interesting shops. If you're interested in the town's history, visit the **Shafer Historical Museum,** Castle Avenue (© **509/996-2712**), which consists of a collection of historic buildings from around the area. It's open Memorial day to Labor Day, Thursday through Monday from 10am to 5pm. Admission is by donation. To find the museum, go up Bridge Street from the junction of Wash. 20 and Riverside Drive and turn right on Castle Avenue.

WHERE TO STAY

If you're interested in renting a cabin or vacation house, contact **Methow Valley Central Reservations** (✆ **800/422-3048** or 509/996-2148; www.methow.com/lodging/).

IN TWISP

Methow Valley Inn 🟊 If you're searching for a classic B&B experience in the Methow Valley, this is it. Built in 1912, this beautifully restored old home is just a block off Twisp's main street and is across from the Methow Brewing Co. pub. The interior is bright and simple, with a tasteful country decor. Breakfast is served in a large sunroom, and, in addition, there are a comfy living room and a study where you can watch movies and munch popcorn. In summer, colorful gardens surround the inn.

234 Second St. (P.O. Box 668), Twisp, WA 98856. ✆ **509/997-2253**. www.methowvalleyinn.com. 7 units, 4 with private bathroom. $89–$99 double with shared bathroom, $99–$109 double with private bathroom. Rates include full breakfast. MC, V. **Amenities:** Concierge; activities desk; massage. *In room:* No phone.

IN WINTHROP

Hotel Rio Vista 🟊 As with all the other buildings in downtown Winthrop, the Rio Vista looks as if it had been built for a Hollywood Western movie set. Behind the false front you'll find modern rooms with pine furnishings and an understated country decor. Step out onto your balcony and you'll have a view of the confluence of the Chewuch and Methow rivers and are likely to see deer, bald eagles, and many other species of birds. A hot tub overlooks the river. The Rio Vista also rents out a loft cabin up the valley near Mazama.

285 Riverside Ave. (P.O. Box 815), Winthrop, WA 98862. ✆ **800/398-0911** or 509/996-3535. www.hotelrio vista.com. 17 units. $50–$100 double. Special off-season and midweek rates. MC, V. **Amenities:** Jacuzzi; massage; babysitting. *In room:* A/C, TV, fridge, coffeemaker.

River Run Inn 🟊 Located only a few hundred yards from downtown Winthrop, this motel on the bank of the Methow River feels as if it is miles from town. The motel rooms all have balconies overlooking the river, with the mountains visible across the valley. Rustic peeled-log furniture made by a local craftsman gives the large motel rooms a Western feel. Aside from the riverside location, the best reason to stay here is the small indoor swimming pool and hot tub. The River Run Inn also rents out both a cabin and a large house and, at press time had plans to build two more cabins.

27 Rader Rd., Winthrop, WA 98862. ✆ **800/757-2709** or 509/996-2173. Fax 509/996-2173. www.riverrun inn.com. 12 units. $70–$105 motel double; $150–$185 cabin; $300–$425 house. MC, V. Pets accepted in motel units only with $10 fee. **Amenities:** Indoor pool; Jacuzzi. *In room:* A/C, TV, coffeemaker.

Sun Mountain Lodge 🟊🟊🟊 *Kids* If you're looking for resort luxuries and proximity to hiking, cross-country skiing, and mountain-biking trails, Sun Mountain Lodge should be your first choice in the region. Perched on a mountaintop with grand views of the Methow Valley and the North Cascades, this luxurious lodge captures the spirit of the West in both its breathtaking setting and its rustic design. In the lobby, flagstone floors and stone fireplaces lend a classically Western style. Most guest rooms feature rustic Western furnishings and views of the mountains. The rooms in the Gardiner wing have balconies and slightly better views than those in the main lodge. If seclusion is what you're after, opt for one of the Patterson Lake cabins. The lodge's main dining room serves superb Northwest cuisine amid views that will take your breath away (see "Where to Dine," below, for details). The lounge has the same great view. In addition to amenities listed below, the resort also is right on the valley's ski trail system and has a ski shop, ski and snowshoe rentals, a ski school, horseback and sleigh rides, an ice-skating pond, lawn games, and a playground.

P.O. Box 1000, Winthrop, WA 98862. © 800/572-0493 or 509/996-2211. Fax 509/996-3133. www.sun mountainlodge.com. 115 units. Summer $165–$310 double, $165–$360 cabins; other months $120–$270 double, $120–$300 cabins. AE, DC, MC, V. **Amenities:** 2 restaurants (Northwest, American); lounge; 2 outdoor pools; 4 unlit outdoor tennis courts; exercise room; full-service spa; 2 Jacuzzis; watersports rentals; bike rentals; children's programs; concierge; activities desk; room service; massage; babysitting. *In room:* A/C, coffeemaker, hair dryer, iron.

WolfRidge Resort ⭐ *Kids*   Set on 60 acres at the edge of a pasture on both the Methow River and the cross-country ski trails, this lodge, with its modern log buildings, is a great choice in winter or summer. The town houses and suites, which have full kitchens, are big enough for families, and the smaller rooms are fine for couples. The pools, game room, and a playground together make this a good spot for a family vacation. However, the wide-open ranch feel and proximity to the ski trails also make this a good bet for active couples.

412-B Wolf Creek Rd., Winthrop, WA 98862. © 800/237-2388 or 509/996-2828. Fax 509/996-2804. www. wolfridgeresort.com. 18 units. $74–$89 double; $118 suite; $169 town house; $174 cabin. MC, V. Pets accepted with $10 fee per night. Call for directions. **Amenities:** Indoor and outdoor pools; Jacuzzi; game room. *In room:* TV, fridge, coffeemaker.

IN MAZAMA

Freestone Inn ⭐⭐⭐   Located at the upper end of the Methow Valley outside the community of Mazama, the Freestone Inn is second only to Sun Mountain Lodge in its luxury and many amenities. The inn's main building, which sits on the shore of a small lake and has a superb view of the mountains, is a huge log lodge complete with massive stone fireplace and a cathedral ceiling. Guest rooms are thoughtfully designed with gas fireplaces and double whirlpool tubs that open to the bedroom so you can lie in the tub and still see the fireplace. All in all these are some of the most memorable rooms in the state. For more privacy, opt for one of the cabins. Families may want to rent one of the large lakeside lodges. The restaurant is one of the finest in the valley (see "Where to Dine," below, for details). In addition to amenities listed below, the inn also has cross-country ski rentals and lessons (ski trails are adjacent), sleigh rides, and a fly-fishing and swimming lake (ice-skating in winter). At press time, there were plans to add a pool.

17798 Wash. 20, Mazama, WA 98833. © 800/639-3809 or 509/996-3906. Fax 509/996-3907. www.free stoneinn.com. 38 units. Summer $140–$260 double, $135–$270 cabin, $275–$450 lodge; winter $120–$235 double, $125–$245 cabin, $250–$405 lodge. Lower rates in spring and fall. AE, DC, DISC, MC, V. **Amenities:** Restaurant (Northwest); lounge; 2 Jacuzzis; watersports rentals; bike rentals; limited children's programs; activities desk; limited room service; massage; babysitting. *In room:* A/C, TV, dataport, fridge, coffeemaker, hair dryer, iron.

The Mazama Country Inn ⭐   Set on the flat valley floor but surrounded by rugged towering peaks and tall pine trees, this modern mountain lodge is secluded and peaceful and offers an escape from the crowds in Winthrop. If you're out here to get some exercise, be it hiking, mountain biking, cross-country skiing, or horseback riding, the Mazama Country Inn makes an excellent base of operations. After a hard day of having fun, you can come back and soak in the hot tub and have dinner in the rustic dining room with its massive free-standing fireplace and high ceiling. The guest rooms are medium-sized and simply furnished, but modern and clean. The inn also rents out 10 cabins ranging in size from one to five bedrooms, with a 2-night minimum ($125–$275 per night double). In addition to amenities listed below, the inn also offers cross-country ski rentals, guided horseback rides, and even has a squash court.

42 Lost River Rd. (HCR 74, Box B9), Mazama, WA 98833. © 800/843-7951 or 509/996-2681. Fax 509/996-2646. www.mazamacountryinn.com. 14 units. Summer $80–$125 double; winter $150–$215 double. Winter rates include all meals. MC, V. Pets accepted in 3 cabins. **Amenities:** Restaurant (American); tennis court; exercise room; Jacuzzi; sauna; bike rentals; massage; coin-op laundry. *In room:* Hair dryer.

CAMPGROUNDS

Lone Fir ⚲ (27 sites) is the first real campground below Washington Pass. Continuing eastward on Wash. 20, you come to **Klipchuck** (46 campsites) and **Early Winters** (13 campsites) campgrounds. There are also several campgrounds west of Early Winters on the Harts Pass Road. **Harts Pass** ⚲ (5 campsites) and **Meadows** ⚲ (14 campsites), a little bit farther on this rough road, are both at high elevations and provide access to the Pacific Crest Trail.

In the Winthrop area, **Pearrygin State Park** ⚲ (83 campsites) is a good choice if you are in need of a hot shower. There are also more than half a dozen Forest Service campgrounds north of here on the Chewuch River and Eightmile Creek. Of these, **Falls Creek** (7 campsites), beside a 75-foot waterfall, and **Buck Lake** (9 campsites) are two of the best. There are also several campgrounds up the Twisp River Road from Twisp. For reservations at **Pearrygin State Park,** contact **Washington State Parks Reservations** (© 888/226-7688; www.parks.wa.gov). For information on all other campgrounds, contact the **Methow Valley Ranger District,** 502 Glover St.(P.O. Box 188), Twisp, WA 98856 (© 509/997-2131; www.fs.fed.us/r6/okanogan). For national forest campground reservations, contact the **National Recreation Reservation Service** (© 800/280-CAMP; www.reserveusa.com).

WHERE TO DINE
IN THE WINTHROP & TWISP AREAS

Down valley from Winthrop, in the town of Twisp, you'll find great baked goodies at **Cinnamon Twisp Bakery** ⚲, 116 N. Glover St. (© 509/997-5030). Here in Twisp, you'll also find, **Sage Cup Café** ⚲, 104 Glover St. (© 509/997-2342), which is located inside the Confluence Gallery and serves good sandwiches.

Duck Brand Cantina ⚲ MEXICAN/INTERNATIONAL   Located right in Winthrop in a funky old building up a flight of rickety stairs, the Duck Brand is a casual restaurant with a big, multilevel deck that's a great spot for a meal on a warm summer day. In cold or rainy weather, you can grab a table in the small dining room and order a plate of fajitas or ribs and a microbrew to wash it all down. Breakfasts here are hearty, and the Duck Brand's muffins and cinnamon rolls make great trail-side snacks.

248 Riverside Ave. (Wash. 20). © 509/996-2192. Reservations recommended in summer. Main courses $4–$18. AE, DC, MC, V. Summer daily 7am–10pm; winter daily 7am–9:30pm.

Sun Mountain Lodge ⚲⚲ NORTHWEST   Although most popular with guests at this mountaintop resort, the dining room here at Sun Mountain Lodge offers both the best meals and the best views in the Winthrop area. Consequently, whether you're staying here or not, your visit to the valley won't be complete without a meal here, preferably one when the sun is shining so you can enjoy the view. The menu changes regularly, but you might start with rabbit sausage or a wild mushroom tart with cambazola sauce and a port reduction. After this you could move on to applewood-smoked pork chops, black-truffle gnocchi, or pink peppercorn seared salmon. Lunches, though much less expensive than dinners, are almost as creative, and you might find venison chili or a crab cake salad on the menu.

Patterson Lake Rd. © 509/996-4707. Reservations recommended. Main courses $9–$15 at lunch, $22–$29 at dinner. AE, DC, MC, V. Mon–Thurs 7:30–11am, 11:30am–2pm, and 5:30–8:30pm; Fri 7:30–11am, 11:30am–2pm, and 5:30–9:30pm; Sat 7:30am–noon and 5:30–9:30pm; Sun 7:30am–noon and 5:30–8:30pm.

Winthrop Brewing Company ★ *Finds* AMERICAN   Located in a tiny, wedge-shaped old schoolhouse in downtown Winthrop, this local watering hole is Winthrop's favorite gathering spot. The walls are covered with the owner's cigarette lighter collection, as well as old rifles and beer coasters from around the world. There's a deck out back overlooking the river and in summer, a beer garden. On Thursday and Friday nights there's usually some kind of live music going on. The menu is typical pub fare—pizza, burgers, fish and chips, steaks, sandwiches, chicken, fish, and ribs.

155 Riverside Ave. © 509/996-3183. Main courses $6–$18. DISC, MC, V. Daily 11:30am–9pm (pub stays open later); winter Tues–Fri 3–8pm.

IN MAZAMA

For gourmet groceries, decent deli food, and espresso drinks drop by the **Mazama Store,** 50 Lost River Rd. (© **509/996-2855**).

Freestone Inn Dining Room ★★ NORTHWEST   The Freestone Inn is one of the two luxury lodges in the valley and its restaurant is, not surprisingly, one of the two best restaurants in the valley. Located pretty much in the lobby of the lodge, the dining room benefits from all the rustic styling of the cathedral-ceilinged space, while the menu is decidedly modern in focus. A recent menu included among the appetizers a tasty caramelized leek, onion, and goat cheese tart and an unusual salad made with smoked Gorgonzola, roasted pears, and Boston bibb lettuce. Main courses likewise include plenty of hearty, yet innovative dishes, such as pork loin scented with toasted cumin, pancetta-wrapped sea scallops, and pan-fried trout with herb-almond basmati rice and lemon-caper butter.

17798 Wash. 20. © **509/996-3906.** Reservations recommended. Main courses $17–$24. AE, DC, DISC, MC, V. Daily 8–10:30am and 5–9:30pm (shorter hours in winter).

3 Lake Chelan ★

166 miles (267km) E of Seattle, 37 miles (60km) N of Wenatchee, 59 miles (95km) S of Winthrop

Formed when a glacier-carved valley flooded, Lake Chelan is 1,500 feet deep, 55 miles (89km) long, and less than 2 miles (3km) wide in most places. This land-locked fjord is the third-deepest lake in the United States (reaching 400 ft. below sea level) and is the longest natural lake in Washington. Only the southern 25 miles (40km) of the lake are accessible by road, yet at the northern end, the community of Stehekin (reachable only by boat, plane, or on foot) has managed to survive for more than 100 years despite not being connected to the outside world by road. Plenty of summer sunshine, clear water, and blue skies have made the lake one of the top destinations in eastern Washington, and today the town of Chelan has the feel of a beach town despite the rugged mountain views all around. At the southern end of the lake, apple orchards cover the foothills, while at the northern end, forests and rugged slopes that are home to mountain goats and black bears come right down to the water's edge. While the southern end of the lake is the domain of ski boats and personal water craft, the northern, remote end is as idyllic a locale as you could ever wish to find and feels as if it is completely cut off from the outside world.

ESSENTIALS

GETTING THERE   Chelan is on U.S. 97, the main north-south highway in central Washington. From Seattle, take U.S. 2 to Wenatchee and then head north.

GETTING AROUND   The Link bus system (© **509/662-1155**) services the Lake Chelan, Wenatchee, and Leavenworth areas.

VISITOR INFORMATION   For more information on this area, contact the **Lake Chelan Chamber of Commerce,** 102 E. Johnson St. (P.O. Box 216), Chelan, WA 98816 (© **800/4-CHELAN** or 509/682-3503; www.lakechelan. com).

EXPLORING CHELAN & LOWER LAKE CHELAN

Downtown Chelan's **Riverwalk Park,** which stretches along both shores of the lake, has a 1-mile (1.5km) paved path and is a pleasant spot for a walk. Lake Chelan history is on display at the **Chelan Museum,** corner of Woodin and Emerson streets (© **509/682-5644**), open April through September Monday through Saturday from 10am to 4pm; other months, Friday and Saturday from 10am to 4pm. Admission is $2 for adults and $1 students and seniors.

UP THE LAKE TO STEHEKIN ★★

If you have time for only one activity while in the Lake Chelan area, it should be an all-day boat ride up the lake to Stehekin, a community accessible only by boat, floatplane, or hiking trail, and located within the Lake Chelan National Recreation Area part of the North Cascades National Park Complex. This remote community has been a vacation destination for more than 100 years and is set amid rugged, glacier-clad mountains at the far north end of Lake Chelan.

The **Lake Chelan Boat Company** (© **509/682-4584;** www.ladyofthelake. com), which has its dock 1 mile (1.5km) west of downtown Chelan on South Shore Road (U.S. 97A), operates three passenger ferries—*Lady of the Lake II, Lady Express,* and *Lady Cat*—between Chelan and Stehekin. The trip encompasses some of the most spectacular scenery in the Northwest as you travel from gentle rolling foothills to deep within the rugged North Cascades mountains. Wildlife, including deer, mountain goats, and even bears, are frequently seen from the boats.

The *Lady of the Lake II* takes 9½ hours for the round-trip (including a 90-min. layover) and charges $25 per person, while the *Lady Express* takes about 6 hours (including a 60-min. layover) and charges $44. The *Lady Cat,* the fastest of the three boats, makes the round-trip in only 4 hours (including a 90-min. layover) but costs $89. Children ages 2 to 11 pay half fare, and free for children under age 2. Unless you plan to stay overnight, you won't have more than 90 minutes to look around Stehekin unless you book a combination ticket that allows you to go up on one of the boats, spend 3¾ to 7¼ hours in Stehekin, and return on a boat other than the one you went up on. These combination tickets are only available in summer.

If you want to get to Stehekin in a hurry, you can make the trip by floatplane on **Chelan Airways** (© **509/682-5555;** www.chelanairways.com), which leaves from the dock next to the ferries. The fare is $120 round-trip. This company also offers flight-seeing trips for between $80 and $150.

A variety of day trips are also operated in conjunction with the two passenger ferries of the **Lake Chelan Boat Company** (© **509/682-4584;** www.ladyofthe lake.com). Tours include the popular bus ride to 312-foot Rainbow Falls ($7 adults, $4 children 6–11, free for children under 6), and a narrated bus trip up the valley to High Bridge and then a picnic lunch ($20 adults, $10 children 6–11, $5 children under 6). Other hiking and biking tours are also available.

Although a road (paved for the first 4 miles/6.5km) once led 23 miles (37km) up the Stehekin Valley to Cottonwood Campground, a flood in 1995 damaged much of the road toward the upper end of the valley. As of 2001, the road was only open as far as Glory Mountain (20 miles/32km up valley). Transportation up the Stehekin Valley Road is provided by two different buses. The National Park Service's shuttle operates between mid-May and mid-October and, depending on how far up the valley you go, costs between $6 and $12 ($3–$6 children 12 and under). Reservations for this bus should be made at least 2 days ahead of time (preferably much farther in advance) by calling the **Golden West Visitor Center** (© **360/856-5700,** ext. 340, then 14). Between late May and the end of September, another bus runs four times a day between Stehekin Landing and High Bridge. No reservations are required for this bus, and the cost is $6. If you just want to ride as far as the Stehekin Pastry Company, the fare is only $1.

A wide range of recreational activities can also be arranged in Stehekin through the **Courtney Log Office** (© **509/682-4677**), which is located 150 yards up the road from the boat landing. These include all of the following activities. Horseback rides are offered through **Cascade Corrals** (© **509/682-7742**) at Stehekin Valley Ranch. A 2½-hour ride costs $38. White-water rafting trips on the Stehekin River are operated by Stehekin Valley Ranch and cost $45 per person. Mountain bikes can be rented from **Discovery Bikes** (© **509/682-3014**), which is located at the Courtney Log Office; bike tours that include breakfast are also available.

Along the length of the Stehekin Valley, there are many miles of excellent hiking trails ranging from easy strolls along the river to strenuous climbs high into the mountain wilderness that surrounds the valley. Many of the valley's trail heads can be accessed from the bus that runs up the valley, which makes this an excellent place for doing a variety of day hikes over several days. There are also many longer trails originating here in Stehekin, which makes this a popular starting point for backpacking trips. For information on hiking trails and to pick up permits for overnight backpacking trips, stop by the **Golden West Visitor Center,** which is operated by the National Park Service and is located near the boat landing. It's open daily between mid-March and mid-October. Fly-fishing on the Stehekin River is also very popular and usually very productive. In winter there is good snowshoeing at Stehekin, and snowshoes can be rented from **North Cascades Stehekin Lodge** (© **509/682-4494**).

SPORTS & OUTDOOR ACTIVITIES

FISHING   Fishing is one of the top recreational activities at Lake Chelan, and in this deep lake's clear waters you'll find chinook and kokanee salmon, lake trout (mackinaw trout), rainbow trout, smallmouth bass, and freshwater lingcod. Although there is bank fishing for stocked rainbows in the lower lake, most other fishing requires a boat. Up in Stehekin there is good fly-fishing for native cutthroat and rainbow trout.

GOLF   Right on the edge of town, golfers will find the municipal **Lake Chelan Golf Course,** 1501 Golf Course Dr. (© **800/246-5361** or 509/682-5361). However, anyone out this way with golf clubs is probably headed to **Desert Canyon Resort,** 1201 Desert Canyon Blvd., Orondo (© **800/258-4173** or 509/784-1111), which is located 17 miles (27km) south of Chelan and has been voted the best public course in Washington.

HANG GLIDING & PARAGLIDING   In recent years, Chelan has become one of the nation's hang gliding and paragliding meccas. Strong winds and thermals allow flyers to sail for a hundred miles or more from the Chelan Sky Park atop Chelan Butte, which is located on the outskirts of town. The top of Chelan Butte is now the Chelan Sky Park. Paragliding lessons are available here through **Chelan Paragliding School** (© **425/432-8900**).

HIKING   Beyond the ends of the roads at the south end of Lake Chelan lie thousands of acres of unspoiled forests and many miles of hiking trails. Access to the trails is from trail heads at road ends or from flag stops along the route of the *Lady of the Lake II.* However, the best trails begin in the Stehekin area. For more information on hiking and biking opportunities, contact the **Chelan Ranger Station,** 428 W. Woodin Ave., Chelan, WA 98816 (© **509/682-2576**).

WATERSPORTS   Opportunities for aquatic activities abound on Lake Chelan. Good places to swim include **Lakeside Park** on the South Shore Road, **Don Morse Memorial Park** on the edge of downtown Chelan, and **Manson Bay Park** in Manson. **Lake Chelan State Park** and **25-Mile Creek State Park,** both on South Shore Road, offer swimming, picnicking, and camping.

You can rent a personal watercraft (around $35 per hr. or $150 per day), a variety of powerboats (about $55 per hr.), and canoes and paddleboats ($10 per hr.) from **Chelan Boat Rentals,** 1210 W. Woodin Ave. (© **509/682-4444**). Boats and personal watercraft are also available from **Shoreline Watercraft Rentals** (© **800/682-1561** or 509/682-1515) and **RSI Sports** (© **800/786-2637** or 509/669-4779).

If you've got the kids along, you'll find it impossible not to spend some time at **Slidewaters,** 102 Waterslide Dr. (© **509/682-5751;** www.slidewaters.com), which has 10 water slides, an inner-tube river ride, a 60-person hot tub, and a swimming pool. Admission is $13 for adults, $10 for children ages 3 to 7. You'll find this water park just outside town off the South Shore Road.

If you want to check out the water from above, call **Chelan Parasailing,** 158 Wapato Way (© **509/687-7245**), which charges around $40 for a parasail ride.

WINTER SPORTS   The Lake Chelan area also offers both cross-country and downhill skiing opportunities at **Echo Valley Ski Area** (© **509/687-3167** or 509/682-4002), a small ski area 7 miles (11km) northwest of Chelan. With only one poma lift and three rope tows, this isn't much of a downhill area. A lift ticket is $15 for the day. Cross-country skiers, on the other hand, will find miles of groomed trails, many of which have great views, at Echo Ridge, which is a short distance past the downhill area. Trail passes are $5 per day. Ski rentals are available at Echo Valley from **Lakeland Ski** (© **509/687-3204**).

WHERE TO STAY
IN CHELAN

Best Western Lakeside Lodge ★ *Kids*   With lake views from every room, indoor and outdoor pools, a whirlpool, and a public park (with beach) adjacent, this comfortable motel on the south shore of the lake is a good choice, especially for families. The guest accommodations range from standard motel rooms to spacious suites with full kitchens. Some of the rooms also have VCRs, and all have balconies or patios. If you're up for a splurge, request one of the large suites, preferably one on the top floor (these have high ceilings).

2312 W. Woodin Ave., Chelan, WA 98816. © 800/468-2781 or 509/682-4396. Fax 509/682-3278. 67 units. Early June to early Sept $149–$199 double, $169–$249 suite; early Sept to early June $69–$139 double, $95–$169 suite. AE, DC, DISC, MC, V. **Amenities:** Indoor and outdoor swimming pools; 2 Jacuzzis; coin-op laundry. *In room:* A/C, TV, refrigerator, coffeemaker.

Campbell's Resort on Lake Chelan ★★
The Campbell Hotel first opened in 1901 and has remained Chelan's most popular lodging ever since. Located on the banks of the lake right in downtown Chelan, Campbell's is now a small convention hotel with a 1,200-foot beach, acres of lawns, and boat docks. Over the past few years, Campbell's has updated most of its rooms, and though the main building's deluxe rooms (which feature furnishings and styling the equal of any Seattle luxury hotel) are still the best rooms, many of the other rooms are looking good these days, too. Fortunately, every room here has a lake view, and many, including several of the cottages, have a kitchen or kitchenette. The dining room is located in the original 1901 hotel, and offers the most elegant dining in town. There's a pub upstairs from the restaurant and, in summer, a beach bar.

104 W. Woodin Ave., Chelan, WA 98816. © 800/553-8225 or 509/682-2561. Fax 509/682-2177. www.campbellsresort.com. 170 units. Early June to early Sept $142–$244 double, $222–$360 suite, $190–$262 2-bedroom family unit. Lower rates off-season. AE, DISC, MC, V. **Amenities:** 2 restaurants (American); lounge; 2 outdoor swimming pools; 2 Jacuzzis; business center; guest laundry service. *In room:* A/C, TV, dataport, coffeemaker, hair dryer.

IN STEHEKIN

If you're heading up to Stehekin and plan to do your own cooking during your stay, bring your own food. Only limited groceries are available here.

North Cascades Stehekin Lodge ★
Located right at Stehekin Landing, the North Cascades Lodge is shaded by tall conifers and overlooks the lake. The variety of accommodations ranges from basic rooms with no lake view to spacious apartments. The studio apartments, which have kitchens, are the best deal and all have lake views. Between May and mid-October, the lodge's restaurant serves three meals a day; the rest of the year, three meals are served on weekends and lunch is available on weekdays. Snowshoe rentals are available.

P.O. Box 457, Chelan, WA 98816. © 509/682-4494. Fax 509/682-5872. www.stehekin.com. 28 units. Memorial Day weekend to Oct 15 $90–$133 double; Oct 16 to Memorial Day weekend $69–$117 double. DISC, MC, V. **Amenities:** Restaurant (American); watersports rentals; bike rentals; children's programs; activities desk; coin-op laundry. *In room:* No phone.

Silver Bay Inn & Resort ★★
Situated on the banks of both the lake and the Stehekin River, Silver Bay rents out two cabins and a house. The views are superb, and should you stay in the Lake View House, a spacious Northwest contemporary home on the banks of both the river and the lake, you'll find antiques, a big sunroom, and a deck with a view of the river. This house also has a separate room with a river view (this is the least expensive accommodation here). Be sure to bring your own food to cook. Bicycles and canoes are available to guests free of charge, and allow guests to explore the lake and the Stehekin environs.

10 Silver Bay Rd. (Box 85), Stehekin, WA 98852. © 800/555-7781 or 509/682-2212. www.silverbayinn.com. 4 units. $135–$245 double or cabin for 2. Additional person $20 extra. Lower rates off-season. Minimum stay 2 nights (5 nights for cabins in summer). MC, V. **Amenities:** Jacuzzi; watersports equipment; bikes. *In room:* Kitchen, no phone.

Stehekin Valley Ranch ★ *Kids*   If you're a camper at heart, then the tent cabins at the Stehekin Valley Ranch should be just fine. With canvas roofs, screen windows, and no electricity or plumbing, these "cabins" are little more than permanent tents. Bathroom facilities are in the nearby main building. For slightly more comfortable accommodations, opt for one of the permanent cabins. Activities available at additional cost include horseback riding, river rafting, and mountain biking.

P.O. Box 36, Stehekin, WA 98852. © 800/536-0745 or 509/682-4677. www.courtneycountry.com. 12 units. $60–$85 per adult, $55–$75 per child 7–12, $40–$60 per child 4–6, $10–$20 per child 3 and under. Cabins $10 more per person than tents. Rates include all meals and transportation in lower valley. $5 off if you bring sleeping bag or sheets. MC, V by phone only for reservations. **Amenities:** Restaurant (American); activities desk. *In room:* No phone.

CAMPGROUNDS

On Lake Chelan, there are two state park campgrounds at the southern end of the lake—**Lake Chelan State Park** (144 campsites) and **Twenty-Five Mile Creek State Park** (71 campsites)—both of which tend to be very crowded and noisy. At the north end of the lake, along the Stehekin Valley Road, there are nine campgrounds, most of which are served by the shuttle bus from Stehekin. **Purple Point** ★ (7 campsites) is right in Stehekin and is the most convenient to the boat landing.

For reservations at the two state parks, contact **Washington State Parks Reservations** (© 888/226-7688; www.parks.wa.gov). For information on campgrounds in the Stehekin Valley, contact the **Golden West Visitor Center** (© 360/856-5700, ext. 340, then 14; www.nps.gov/noca). For national forest campground reservations, contact the **National Recreation Reservation Service** (© 800/280-CAMP; www.reserveusa.com).

WHERE TO DINE
IN CHELAN

If you're looking for a good cup of coffee, try **Latte Da Coffee Stop Cafe,** 303 E. Wapato Ave. (© 509/682-4196), which is housed in an old house on the edge of downtown Chelan. For a touch of old-time Western hospitality, have a meal at **Banjo Creek Farms** (© 509/687-0708; www.banjocreekfarms.com), which does Western barbecues, complete with such appetizers as rattlesnake and Rocky Mountain oysters. Meals ($27 adults, $25 seniors, $18 children 9–16, $10 children 4–8) include a wagon ride, a chance to wander around the barnyard, and live music. Reservations are required. Banjo Creek also offers a variety of other activities throughout the year.

Campbell House Restaurant ★ AMERICAN   Housed in the original 1901 Campbell Hotel, this is Chelan's only upscale restaurant, and as such stays pretty busy in the summer months. While the menu is not overly creative, you'll find more imaginative offerings here than anywhere else in town. The steaks and prime rib are your best bets here. If you prefer burgers to scallops flamed with brandy, then you'll be better off upstairs at the casual pub, which serves inexpensive steaks and other decent pub fare to go with its Northwest microbrews and single-malt Scotches.

104 W. Woodin Ave. © 509/682-4250. Main courses $10–$27. AE, DISC, MC, V. Mon–Thurs 6:45–8:30pm; Fri–Sat 6:45–9pm; Sun 6:45am–1pm and 5:30–8pm. Pub daily 11:30am–10pm. Reduced hours in winter.

Deepwater Brewing & Public House ★ AMERICAN   Located just outside of Chelan on the road to the town of Manson, this big brewpub offers food that's definitely a step above that served at most pubs. On top of that, there are great views of the lake. In summer, the lake-view deck is the place to eat, but big windows let in plenty of views also. The menu includes lots of steaks, plenty of pasta dishes, and a handful of burgers (the fire burger is our favorite). There are usually six of their own brews on tap. Be sure to start your meal with the brandy-fired mushrooms.

225 Manson Hwy. ℂ **509/682-2720.** www.deepwaterbrewing.com. Main courses $7–$24. AE, MC, V. Sun–Thurs 11am–10pm; Fri–Sat 11am–11pm (winter Wed–Sat 4–9pm).

IN STEHEKIN

The dining options in Stehekin are slim, and if you plan to stay in a cabin or camp out, be sure to bring all the food you'll need. Otherwise, simple meals are available at **North Cascades Stehekin Lodge** (ℂ **509/682-4494**), which is located right at the ferry landing in Stehekin. Note that during the winter, the restaurant here is open for three meals a day only on weekends; weekdays, only lunch is available. When you just have to have something sweet, you're in luck; the **Stehekin Pastry Company** (ℂ **509/682-4677**), which is located 2 miles (3km) up valley from the boat landing, serves pastries and ice cream, as well as pizza and espresso.

4 Wenatchee: Apple Capital of the World

20 miles (32km) E of Leavenworth, 37 miles (60km) S of Chelan, 75 miles (121km) N of Ellensburg

Apples are the single largest agricultural industry in Washington—in fact, more than 50% of the fresh apples sold in the United States come from Washington. The combination of warm, sunny days and abundant irrigation water from both the Columbia and Wenatchee rivers have made Wenatchee the center of this apple-growing region. While Wenatchee, which lies at the base of the eastern Cascade slopes on the bank of the Columbia River, isn't exactly a tourist desti-nation in its own right, anyone exploring this region of the state passes through the city sooner or later. Skiers, on the other hand, are familiar with the city as the closest town to the slopes of Mission Ridge ski area.

ESSENTIALS

GETTING THERE   Wenatchee is at the junction of U.S. 2, which connects to I-5 by way of Stevens Pass, and U.S. 97, the main north-south route along the east side of the Cascades. Wash. 28 connects the city to the eastern part of the state.

Wenatchee's **Pangborn Memorial Airport** is served by **Horizon Air.** Amtrak trains stop in Wenatchee en route between Spokane and Seattle.

VISITOR INFORMATION   For more information on the Wenatchee area, contact the **Wenatchee Valley Convention & Visitors Bureau,** 116 N. Wenatchee Ave, Wenatchee, WA 98801 (ℂ **800/57-APPLE** or 509/663-3723; www.wenatcheevalley.org).

GETTING AROUND   The Link bus system (ℂ **509/662-1155;** www.link transit.com) services Wenatchee, Lake Chelan, and Leavenworth areas.

FESTIVALS   The city celebrates its apples each year with the **Washington State Apple Blossom Festival,** which includes more than a week of festivities in late April and early May.

EXPLORING WASHINGTON'S APPLE CAPITAL

At the **Washington Apple Commission Visitors Center,** 2900 Euclid Ave. (ℂ **509/662-3090**), on the northern outskirts of town just off U.S. 97, you can learn all about apples and how they're grown and stored. May through December, it's open Monday through Friday from 8am to 5pm, Saturday from 9am to 5pm, and Sunday from 10am to 4pm; January to April, hours are Monday through Friday from 8am to 5pm. Admission is free.

More apple-industry displays are part of the focus of the **Wenatchee Valley Museum & Cultural Center,** 127 S. Mission St. (© **509/664-3340**), but there are also interesting exhibits on local Native American cultures and the first transpacific flight. Model-railroading buffs will enjoy the HO-scale (3.5mm:1 ft.) Great Northern Railroad. The museum also hosts concerts, lectures, and traveling exhibitions, and a 1919 Wurlitzer organ is often played during concerts and as accompaniment to classic silent films. The museum is open Monday through Saturday from 10 to 4pm. Admission is $3 for adults, $1 for children 6 to 12, and $5 for families.

Though it's only a dozen or so miles from the lush forests of the Cascades, Wenatchee is on the edge of central Washington's arid shrub steppe region. To bring a bit of the mountains' greenery into this high desert, Herman Ohme and his family spent 60 years creating **Ohme Gardens** ★★, 3327 Ohme Rd. (© **509/662-5785;** www.ohmegardens.com), a lush alpine garden covering 9 cliff-top acres north of Wenatchee. The gardens wind along the top of a rocky outcropping that overlooks the Wenatchee Valley, Columbia River, and Cascade peaks. Rock gardens, meadows, fern grottos, and waterfalls give the gardens a very naturalistic feel similar to that of a Japanese garden. The gardens are open from April 15 to October 15, daily from 9am to 6pm (until 7pm in summer). Admission is $6 for adults, $3 for children 7 to 17.

North of Wenatchee on the north side of the town of Entiat, watch for the **Columbia Breaks Fire Interpretive Center** (© **509/663-2062;** www.wildfire center.org), which has two old fire lookouts and the ½-mile Trail of Fire and Forest interpretive trail. This trail explains the role of fires in western forests.

Only a few miles outside town is **Mission Ridge** ski area ★★ (© **509/663-3200** for snow report, or 509/663-6543; www.missionridge.com), which is known for its powder snow (a rarity in the Cascades) and its sunny weather. Lift ticket prices for adults are $37.

CASHMERE: AN EARLY AMERICAN TOWN

West of Wenatchee a few miles, you'll find the town of **Cashmere,** which has adopted an Early American theme. The town's main attraction is the **Aplets & Cotlets Candy Factory and Country Store,** 117 Mission Ave. (© **509/782-2191;** www.libertyorchards.com), where you can tour the kitchens that produce these unusual fruit-and-nut confections. Between April and December, the factory and store are open Monday through Friday from 8am to 5:30pm and Saturday and Sunday from 10am to 4pm; between January and March, they're open Monday through Friday from 8:30am to 4:30pm.

Also worth a visit in Cashmere is the **Chelan County Museum and Historical Pioneer Village,** 600 Cotlets Way (© **509/782-3230**). Nearly 20 old log buildings have been assembled here and are filled with period antiques. Inside the main museum building you'll find exhibits on the early Native American cultures of the region, pioneer history, and natural history. The museum is open from March 1 to October 31, Tuesday through Sunday from 9:30am to 5pm. Admission is $4 for adults, $3 for students and seniors, or $6 for families.

WHERE TO STAY

WestCoast Wenatchee Center Hotel ★★   With Wenatchee's convention center across a sky bridge from the lobby, the WestCoast Wenatchee caters almost exclusively to convention business, but it's also the city's most comfortable hotel. A moderately priced and casual rooftop dining room and lounge provide the best view in town. Room service is also available. Facilities include an indoor/outdoor pool, whirlpool, and exercise room.

201 N. Wenatchee Ave., Wenatchee, WA 98801. ℭ 800/325-4000 or 509/662-1234. Fax 509/662-0782. www.westcoasthotels.com/wenatchee. 147 units. $69–$99 double; $185 suite. AE, DC, DISC, MC, V. **Amenities:** Restaurant (American); lounge; indoor/outdoor pool; exercise room; 2 Jacuzzis; room service (Sun–Thurs 6:30am–2pm and 5–9pm; Fri–Sat 7:30am–2pm and 5–11pm); guest laundry service. *In room:* A/C, TV, dataport, coffeemaker, hair dryer, iron.

WHERE TO DINE

If it's a hot day, you can get a creamy malted milk shake or root beer float at **Bellmore's Owl Drug,** 39 S. Wenatchee Ave. (ℭ **509/662-7133**), an old-fashioned soda fountain in downtown Wenatchee.

The John Horan House ★★ AMERICAN   Though it's in a rather unlikely spot surrounded by industrial complexes, the Horan House, where the wealthy of Wenatchee dine, is well worth searching out. Secluded in its own little apple orchard, the 1899 Victorian farmhouse is a world apart. The menu runs the gamut from traditional preparations such as filet mignon with béarnaise sauce to specials such as Columbia River steelhead with roasted red pepper cream sauce. A menu of small plates allows diners with smaller appetites and wallets to enjoy this restaurant also.

2 Horan Rd. ℭ **509/663-0018.** www.johnhoranhouse.com. Reservations recommended. Main courses $12–$40. DISC, MC, V. Mon–Sat 5–10pm. Cross the Wenatchee River bridge from downtown, take the first right, the next right, and then, at the end of the road, turn right a third time; at the end of this road, turn left onto the restaurant driveway.

McGlinn's Public House ★ AMERICAN   Located inside one of downtown Wenatchee's few historic buildings, this casual pub turns out good wood-oven pizzas, as well as burgers and a handful of more creative dishes. Although they don't brew their own beers here, they have lots of good regional microbrews. If you're really hungry, be sure to try the wood-fired jojos (potato wedges). There's live jazz every Wednesday night.

111 Orondo Ave. ℭ **509/663-9073.** Main courses $6–$14. AE, DISC, MC, V. Sun–Thurs 11am–11pm; Fri–Sat 11am–midnight.

5 Leavenworth: Washington's Own Bavarian Village ★★★

108 miles (174km) E of Everett, 22 miles (35km) W of Wenatchee, 58 miles (93km) SW of Chelan

You're out for a Sunday drive through the mountains, just enjoying the views, maybe doing a bit of hiking or cross-country skiing, when you come around a bend and find yourself in the Bavarian Alps. Folks in lederhosen and dirndls are dancing in the streets, a polka band is playing the old oompah-pah, and all the buildings look like alpine chalets. Have you just entered the Twilight Zone? No, it's just Leavenworth, Washington's Bavarian village.

Many an unsuspecting traveler has had just this experience, but if you're reading this, you'll be prepared for the sight of a Bavarian village transported to the middle of the Washington Cascades. Whether you think it's the most romantic town in the state, a great place to go shopping, the perfect base for hiking and skiing, or just another example of überkitsch, there's no denying that Leavenworth makes an impression.

ESSENTIALS

GETTING THERE   From I-5, take U.S. 2 from Everett, or, if you're coming from the south, take I-405 to Bothell and then head northeast to Monroe, where you pick up U.S. 2 heading east. From U.S. 97 in the central part of the state, head west on U.S. 2.

VISITOR INFORMATION   For more information on this area, contact the **Leavenworth Chamber of Commerce & Visitor Center,** P.O. Box 327, Leavenworth, WA 98826 (© **509/548-5807;** www.leavenworth.org), or, when you're in town, drop by the Visitor Center, 220 Ninth St., which is inside the Obertal Mall.

GETTING AROUND   The Link bus system (© **509/662-1155;** www.link transit.com) services the Leavenworth, Wenatchee, and Lake Chelan areas.

FESTIVALS   During the annual **Maifest** (mid-May) and **Washington State Autumn Leaf Festival** (late Sept), Leavenworth rolls out the barrel and takes to the streets and parks with polka bands, Bavarian dancing, and plenty of crafts vendors. In June, more music hits town with the **Leavenworth International Accordion Celebration.** In mid-September, the **Wenatchee River Salmon Festival** celebrates the annual return of salmon to the river, and in October there's **Oktoberfest.** In December, the whole town gets lit up in one of the most impressive **Christmas Lighting Festivals** in the Northwest.

EXPLORING LEAVENWORTH

Leavenworth's main attraction is the town itself. Back in the early 1960s, this was just another mountain town struggling to get by on a limited economy. Sure the valley was beautiful, but beauty wasn't enough to bring in the bucks. A few years after a motel with alpine architecture opened in town, Leavenworth decided to give itself a complete makeover. Today nearly every commercial building in town, from the gas station to the Safeway, looks as if it had been built by Bavarian gnomes. What may come as a surprise is that they did a good job! Stroll around town and you'll convince yourself that you've just had the world's cheapest trip to the Alps. People here even speak German.

Any time of year the town's most popular tourist activity seems to be shopping for genuine Bavarian souvenirs in the many gift shops—you'll find cuckoo clocks, Hummel figurines, imported lace, and nutcrackers. In fact, if nutcrackers are your passion, don't miss the **Leavenworth Nutcracker Museum,** 735 Front St. (© **509/548-4708;** www.nussknackerhaus.com), which has more than 4,000 nutcrackers of all shapes and sizes. The museum is open May through October from 2 to 5pm daily and November through April on weekends only. Admission is $2.50 for adults and $1 ages 6 to 17.

Classical music fans should be sure to see what's happening at the **Icicle Creek Music Center** ★ (© **877/265-6026** or 509/548-6347; www.icicle.org), which is located at the Sleeping Lady resort and has programs throughout the year. There are also many musical performances and festivals in the small Front Street Park in downtown Leavenworth, where a large gazebo serves as a band-stand. If you're looking for something to do on a Friday night, drop by the **Community Coffeehouse,** Chumstick Grange Hall, 621 Front St. (© **509/ 548-5779**), which has live acoustic music ranging from Celtic to contemporary to classic.

Just east of Leavenworth begin the apple and pear orchards of the Wenatchee Valley. In summer and fall, you can taste the fruits of the valley at farm stands along U.S. 2. **Smallwood's Harvest** (© **509/548-4196**) and **Prey's Fruit Barn** (© **509/548-5771**) are the biggest and best farm stands along this stretch of road.

OUTDOOR ACTIVITIES: FROM HORSEBACK RIDES TO DOGSLEDDING

If your interests tend toward hiking rather than Hummel figurines, you'll still find plenty to do around Leavenworth. Leavenworth is on the valley floor at the confluence of the Wenatchee River and Icicle Creek, and rising all around are the steep, forested mountainsides of the Stuart Range and Entiat Mountains. Spring through fall, there are rafting, hiking, mountain biking, and horseback riding, and, in winter, there are downhill and cross-country skiing and snowmobiling.

North of town 25 miles (40km), you'll find **Lake Wenatchee,** a year-round recreation area with hiking and cross-country ski trails, horseback riding, canoe rentals, windsurfing, swimming, fishing, mountain biking, camping, and snowmobiling. **Lake Wenatchee State Park** (© **509/763-3101**) is the center of recreational activity here.

If you need to rent some gear, contact **Leavenworth Outfitters Outdoor Center,** 21312 Wash. 207 (© **800/347-7934** or 509/763-3733; www.thrill makers.com), which rents mountain bikes, cross-country skis, kayaks, and canoes.

FISHING Icicle Creek, which runs through Leavenworth, has a short summer salmon season for fish headed upstream to the Leavenworth Fish Hatchery. Lake Wenatchee, at 5 miles (8km) in length, is the biggest lake in the area and holds kokanee, as well as Dolly Varden and rainbows. To fish for kokanee, you'll need a boat. Several of the rivers and streams in the Leavenworth area are open to fly-fishing only. If you want to take a fly-fishing class while you're in the area, contact **English Flyfishing School of Leavenworth** (© **509/548-5218**).

GOLF Golfers can play 18 holes at the **Leavenworth Golf Club** (© **509/ 548-7267**), which charges $26 to $29 for a round of golf and is located on the outskirts of town, or north of Leavenworth near Lake Wenatchee at **Kahler Glen Golf Course,** 20890 Kahler Dr. (© **509/763-3785**), which charges $24 to $36 for 18 holes. If you want to practice your putting, check out the **Enzian Falls Championship Putting Course** (© **509/548-5269**), which is located across from the Enzian Motor Inn and is a beautiful bent-grass 18-hole putting course (not to be confused with your usual tacky miniature golf course).

HIKING Right in town, you'll find a pleasant paved walking path in **Waterfront Park.** Out at the **fish hatchery** on Icicle Road, there is also a mile-long interpretive trail with information on the hatchery. In winter, both of these areas have cross-country ski trails. In Tumwater Canyon, the narrow gorge that serves as something of a gateway to Leavenworth as you approach from the west, there's an easy hiking trail along the banks of the Wenatchee River.

Just outside Leavenworth, in the **Alpine Lakes Wilderness** ★★★, lies some of the most beautiful mountain scenery in the state, and the trails that lead into this wilderness are among the most popular. So popular, in fact, that backpackers must reserve camping permits months in advance to overnight in such heavily visited areas as the Enchantment Lakes basin. Most of the trails in the area are best suited for overnight trips because they climb steeply and steadily for many miles before reaching the more scenic areas. For information on hiking trails in Wenatchee National Forest, contact the **Leavenworth Ranger Station,** 600 Sherbourne St., Leavenworth, WA (© **509/548-6977**). To apply for a backpacking permit (reservations are accepted starting in late Feb), call the ranger station or visit their website at www.fs.fed.us/r6/wenatchee. Permits go fast, so apply early.

HORSEBACK RIDING   If you'd like to go horseback riding, contact **Eagle Creek Ranch** (© **800/221-7433** or 509/548-7798; www.eaglecreek.ws), which offers everything from 1½-hour-long rides ($25) to day trips ($80) and wagon rides ($15 adults, $7.50 children); or **Icicle Outfitters & Guides** (© **800/497-3912** or 509/763-3647; www.icicleoutfitters.com), which offers a similar variety of rides and has stables both at Lake Wenatchee State Park and in Leavenworth on Icicle Road near the fish hatchery. A 1½-hour ride will cost you $36.

MOUNTAIN BIKING   From easy rides on meandering dirt roads to grueling climbs to mountaintops with spectacular views, the Leavenworth area has some of the best mountain biking routes in the state. Mountain bikes can be rented at **Der Sportsmann,** 837 Front St. (© **509/548-5623**), and **Leavenworth Mountain Sports,** 940 Wash. 2 (© **509/548-7864**), which is right next door to the Chevron station. Expect to pay $20 to $40 per day for a mountain bike. Ask at either of these shops for ride recommendations. You can also get a guide to area mountain biking from the Leavenworth Visitor Center.

ROCK CLIMBING   Two miles (3km) west of Cashmere on U.S. 2, you'll find **Peshastin Pinnacles State Park,** Washington's only state park created exclusively for rock climbing. The **Snow Creek Wall,** which is located about a mile up the trail to the Enchantment Lakes area, is another great climbing spot. The trail head is located about 4 miles (6.5km) up Icicle Creek Road. Over on the west side of Stevens Pass, the **Index Town Walls** outside the tiny community of Index are the area's other great climbing site. For climbing gear and advice, stop by **Leavenworth Mountain Sports,** 940 Wash. 2 (© **509/548-7874**).

WHITE-WATER RAFTING   The Wenatchee River flows right through Leavenworth and just downstream from town becomes one of the best white-water rafting rivers in the state. Rafting season runs from April to July. If you're interested, contact **All Rivers Adventure** (© **800/743-5628** or 509/782-2254; www.allrivers.com), **Osprey Rafting Co.** (© **800/743-6269;** www.shootthe rapids.com), or **River Riders** (© **800/448-RAFT** or 206/448-RAFT). A half-day trip on the Wenatchee costs about $50 per person, and a full day $65 to $70.

WINTER SPORTS   Some of the best downhill skiing and snowboarding in the state is available 40 miles (64km) west of Leavenworth at **Stevens Pass** ★★ (© **206/812-4510** for general information, or 206/634-1645 for snow conditions; www.stevenspass.com). Lift tickets range in price from $27 to $43. There are plenty of intermediate and advanced runs here, but not much in the way of beginner runs. Looking for steep, deep, untracked snow? Head out for some snowcat skiing with **Leavenworth Snowcat Skiing** (© **866/500-1514** or 509/ 548-1514; www.leavenworthsnowcatskiing.com), which charges $210 for a day of skiing that might include 3-mile-long (5km) runs and up to 20,000 vertical feet of skiing each day.

Cross-country skiers can find plenty of groomed trails in the area. **Stevens Pass Nordic Center** (© **360/812-4510**) has mostly intermediate and expert level trails. These trails are open Friday through Sunday and on holidays, and a trail pass costs $12 for adults. The **Leavenworth Winter Sports Club** (© **509/ 548-5477;** www.skileavenworth.com) maintains 15 miles (24km) of groomed trails (including 3 miles/5km of lighted trails for night skiing) at several locations around Leavenworth. A trail pass runs $8 per day. This ski club also operates the beginner-level **Leavenworth Ski Hill,** a mile outside of town. Although small, this ski area has a ski jump.

Skis can be rented at **Der Sportsmann,** 837 Front St. (© 800/548-4145 or 509/548-5623; www.dersportsmann.com), which charges $14 to $22 per day for cross-country skis and $25 for snowboards. Snowshoes ($12 per day) can also be rented.

Dog sledding isn't just an Alaskan sport, and if you'd like to find out what it's like, you've got a couple of options in the Leavenworth area. **Enchanted Mountain Tours** (© 800/521-1694 or 360/856-9168) offers dog sledding tours. A half-day excursion costs about $135 for one or $240 for two. Dogsled rides are also offered by **Alaska Dreamin' Sled Dog Company** (© 509/763-8017), which has rides as short as 20 to 30 minutes ($30 adults, $20 children 6–12, free for children 5 and under with a paying adult).

If you'd rather experience the snow from a horse-drawn sleigh, you can do that, too. Sleigh rides are offered by **Red-Tail Canyon Farm,** 11780 Freund Canyon Rd., Leavenworth (© 800/678-4512 or 509/548-4512; www.redtail canyonfarm.com); and **Eagle Creek Ranch,** Eagle Creek Road (© 800/221-RIDE or 509/548-7798; www.eaglecreek.ws/). Rides cost $15 adults, and $7.50 for children.

WHERE TO STAY
EXPENSIVE
Mountain Home Lodge ★★   Set 2½ miles (4km) up a very steep, narrow road that is only paved in its lower stretch, this mountain lodge is surrounded by a 20-acre meadow and has a spectacular view of the craggy Stuart Range. In winter, the road up here is not plowed and guests are brought to the lodge by Snowcat. At that time of year, 40 miles (64km) of cross-country ski trails are the main attraction (cross-country skis and snowshoes are available), but there are also guided snowmobile tours. In summer, hiking and mountain biking are the big draws. Guest rooms vary in size and each is individually decorated with themes that reflect the area's activities (Mountain Trout, The Harvest, The Ranch, The Mountain View). However, The Hide Away, atop the lodge, is the best room in the house (excluding the suite). If you're looking to get away from it all, this is the place! During the summer, when rates include only breakfast, gourmet lunches ($15) and dinners ($35) are available.

8201 Mountain Home Rd. (P.O. Box 687), Leavenworth, WA 98826. © 800/414-2378 or 509/548-7077. Fax 509/548-5008. www.mthome.com. 12 units. Summer $110–$160 double, $200 suite, $275 cabin; winter $270–$310 double, $360 suite, $455 cabin. Summer rates include full breakfast; winter rates include 3 meals daily. 2-night minimum weekends, holidays, and winter season. DISC, MC, V. **Amenities:** Restaurant (American); indoor pool; lit outdoor tennis court; Jacuzzi; bike rentals; concierge; room service; massage. *In room:* A/C, no phone.

Sleeping Lady ★★★   Although primarily a conference resort, Sleeping Lady (the name comes from a nearby mountain) is one of the most luxurious and best-designed mountain retreats in the state. Set on the outskirts of Leavenworth amid ponderosa pines and granite boulders, the small resort looks much like the summer camp it once was, with red-roofed green cabins tucked amid the pines. Guest rooms and a cabin, all of which are done in a rustic contemporary style, abound in natural wood and have high ceilings with exposed beams. The grounds, including a meadow on the bank of Icicle Creek, a rocky knoll, a pond, and outdoor artwork, are beautifully landscaped and a delight to wander. Meals here feature produce from the resort's large organic vegetable garden, and throughout the year, classical music performances and plays are staged. The boulder-lined swimming pool here is one of the most memorable pools in the state.

7375 Icicle Rd., Leavenworth, WA 98826. ⓒ 800/574-2123 or 509/548-6344. Fax 509/548-6312. www. sleepinglady.com. 59 units. $250–$280 double; $325 cabin. Rates include 3 meals. AE, DISC, MC, V. **Amenities:** 2 restaurants (Northwest, deli); lounge; outdoor pool; exercise room; Jacuzzi; sauna; bike rentals; business center; massage; coin-op laundry; dry cleaning. *In room:* Dataport, coffeemaker.

MODERATE

Abendblume Inn ★★ *Value*   This alpine chalet is a luxurious and romantic B&B overlooking Leavenworth and the valley. An eye for detail is apparent throughout the inn, from the hand-carved front door to the wrought-iron stair railing. In winter, guests frequently gather around the fireplace in the living room. Although there are a couple of smaller rooms, the large rooms with balconies overlooking the valley are the best. In these you'll find fireplaces, VCRs, and wonderfully luxurious beds and linens, but it's the bathrooms that are the real attractions. Our favorite has a triangular tub for two, plush terry-cloth robes and towels, two sinks, and heated marble floors. Nowhere in Leavenworth is there a more romantic room. Buffet breakfasts include enough variety to keep everyone happy. Guests also have use of both indoor and outdoor spas.

12570 Ranger Rd. (P.O. Box 981), Leavenworth, WA 98826. ⓒ 800/669-7634 or 509/548-4059. Fax 509/548-4059. www.abendblume.com. 7 units. $85–$165 double. Rates include full breakfast. AE, DISC, MC, V. **Amenities:** Jacuzzi; concierge; bikes; massage. *In room:* A/C, TV/VCR, hair dryer, iron.

Blackbird Lodge ★   Located right in downtown Leavenworth overlooking the Icicle River, this hotel offers the convenience of being within walking distance of all the town's shops and restaurants but with the feel of a country inn. Though the exterior is Bavarian chalet, this inn adopts something of a mountain lodge decor in its lobby, which has a slate floor and dark, woodsy decor. This mountain-lodge styling alone sets the Blackbird apart from other moderately priced lodgings in town. The guest rooms are large, but otherwise are fairly standard motel-style rooms. However, the suites are large and very attractive; some have fireplaces or whirlpool tubs or both. The lodge also rents out an adjacent renovated cottage.

305 Eighth St., Leavenworth, WA 98826. ⓒ 800/446-0240 or 509/548-5800. Fax 509/548-7134. www.black birdlodge.com. 21 units. June 15–Jan 20 $99–$189 double. Lower midweek rates Jan 21–June 14. Rates include full breakfast. AE, DISC, MC, V. Pets accepted in cottage with $8 fee per night. **Amenities:** Jacuzzi; limited room service. *In room:* A/C, TV.

Enzian Inn ★   Located on the highway just outside downtown Leavenworth, the Enzian, which is something of an upgraded motel, offers both convenience and amenities. Of course, it has an alpine exterior, complete with half-timbering, steep roofs, and turrets, and inside you'll find an attractive lobby with a high ceiling and a stone fireplace. To continue the Bavarian theme, the guest rooms are decorated with reproduction antique furniture imported from Austria. If you feel like splurging, the tower suite is richly appointed with burgundy carpets, a heavy carved-wood canopy bed, and a double whirlpool tub in the sitting room. Other amenities include a racquetball court and complimentary use of cross-country ski equipment.

590 U.S. 2, Leavenworth, WA 98826. ⓒ 800/223-8511 or 509/548-5269. www.enzianinn.com. 104 units. $95–$160 double; $175–$195 suite. Rates include full breakfast. AE, DISC, MC, V. **Amenities:** 2 pools (1 indoor, 1 outdoor); 18-hole championship putting golf course; 2 Jacuzzis; babysitting. *In room:* A/C, TV/VCR, dataport, coffeemaker, hair dryer, iron.

Haus Lorelei ⭐ Although it is located only a few blocks from downtown Leavenworth, this 1903 home feels like a secluded mountain estate. From the setting atop a bluff overlooking the Wenatchee River you have a splendid view of the mountains and can hear the river tumbling over the rocks below. Rocks also play an integral part in this home's construction. The stone foundation wall has a decidedly European feel, and the massive river-rock fireplace took 3 years to build and cost more than the house itself. The guest rooms on the main floor are romantic retreats designed for couples, while the larger rooms on the second floor are set up to accommodate families.

347 Division St., Leavenworth, WA 98826. © **800/514-8868** or 509/548-5726. Fax 509/548-6548. www. hauslorelei.com. 8 units. $95–$129 double. Rates include full breakfast. No credit cards. **Amenities:** Unlit outdoor tennis court; access to nearby health club; Jacuzzi; massage. *In room:* No phone.

Run of the River Bed & Breakfast ⭐⭐ Rustic yet contemporary, this log house on 2 acres outside of town is one of the Northwest's most tranquil B&Bs. You can almost feel the weight fall from your shoulders as you drive through the alpine rock garden that lines the driveway. Step through the front door and you enter a house full of bare wood, hand-hewn log furniture, and exposed stones (in both the fireplaces and entry floor). This extensive use of natural materials gives the inn a timeless mountain-lodge atmosphere that's complemented by contemporary architecture. This inn is also one of the most luxurious in the state. After extensive renovation in 2001, all the accommodations are now large suites, some of which have lofts that are great spaces for a bit of quiet reading. However, for a quiet moment the porch swings just can't be beat. Bicyclists will love all the old bikes used in the decor and landscaping here.

9308 E. Leavenworth Rd. (P.O. Box 285), Leavenworth, WA 98826. © **800/288-6491** or 509/548-7171. www. runoftheriver.com. 6 units. $205–$245 double. 2- to 3-night minimum May–Oct and Dec 1–20. DISC, MC, V. **Amenities:** Complimentary bikes; massage. *In room:* TV/VCR, refrigerator.

INEXPENSIVE

Inexpensive rooms in Leavenworth are also available at Lorraine's Edel House (see "Where to Dine," below).

Hotel Pension Anna ⭐ *Finds* Though the guest rooms in the Pension Anna's main building are attractively appointed with pine furniture, including a four-poster bed in the honeymoon suite, the annex building contains the inn's two most outstanding rooms. This annex is a renovated church built in 1913 (and later moved to this site), and the Old Chapel Suite is a grand space that includes part of the old choir loft (now a sleeping loft) and the old baptismal font. Ceilings 20 feet high give the room an expansive feel, and in the bedroom you'll find an ornately carved headboard framed by draperies that reach to the ceiling. Though considerably smaller, the Parish Nook Room has an ornate king-size bed, marble-top bedside stands, and the original arched windows. Only slightly more expensive than a regular room, the Parish Nook is the inn's best deal.

926 Commercial St., Leavenworth, WA 98826. © **800/509-ANNA** or 509/548-6273. www.pensionanna. com. 15 units. $89–$119 double; $169–$209 suite. Rates include full breakfast. AE, DISC, MC, V. *In room:* A/C.

CAMPGROUNDS

Tumwater (84 campsites) is the biggest campground in the Leavenworth area, yet is always full on summer weekends. Up Icicle Road on the west side of Leavenworth, there are seven campgrounds.

The Lake Wenatchee area is one of the most popular summer camping destinations in the state and there are lots of choices in the area. If you want creature comforts (hot showers) stay at **Lake Wenatchee State Park** ⭐ (197 campsites), which is at the south end of the lake. This campground has a sandy beach and a great view up the lake. Farther up the south shore of the lake, the Forest Service's **Glacier View Campground** (23 campsites) provides a similar lakeside atmosphere with walk-in campsites. Right outside the entrance to the state park, you'll find the **Nason Creek Campground** (73 campsites), which has some nice sites right on this large creek. Northwest of Lake Wenatchee, there are several campgrounds along both the White River and the Little Wenatchee River.

For reservations at Lake Wenatchee State Park, contact **Washington State Parks Reservations** (© 888/226-7688; www.parks.wa.gov). For information on all other campgrounds, contact the **Lake Wenatchee Ranger Station,** 22976 Wash. 207, Leavenworth, WA 98826 (© 509/763-3103; www.fs.fed.us/r6/ wenatchee); or the **Leavenworth Ranger Station,** 600 Sherbourne St., Leavenworth, WA 98826 (© 509/548-6977; www.fs.fed.us/r6/wenatchee). For national forest campground reservations, contact the **National Recreation Reservation Service** (© 800/280-CAMP; www.reserveusa.com).

WHERE TO DINE

For delectable baked goods, drop by the **Homefires Bakery,** 13013 Bayne Rd. (© 509/548-7362), which is housed in an old log cabin off Icicle Road near the fish hatchery. And what would a Bavarian town be without its own brewpub? For local craft brews, drop by the **Leavenworth Brewery,** 636 Front St. (© 509/ 548-4545).

Andreas Keller ★ Kids GERMAN Down in a cellar (*Keller*) opposite the gazebo on Front Street, you'll find one of Leavenworth's true German experiences. From the waitresses shouting across the restaurant in German to the accordionist who plays on the weekends, everything about this place is Bavarian. Take a seat and you'll be surrounded by *Gemütlichkeit.* Rotisseried chicken and wursts are the staples here, washed down with Bavarian beer. Be sure to get something with the wine kraut; it's delicious (so is the German potato salad). Casual and fun enough that even the kids will enjoy a meal here.

829 Front St. © 509/548-6000. www.andreaskellerrestaurant.com. Reservations recommended. Main courses $7–$9 at lunch, $7–$17 at dinner. MC, V. Sun–Thurs 11am–8:30pm; Fri 11am–9pm; Sat 11am–10pm (may close earlier in off-season).

Cafe Mozart Restaurant ★★ GERMAN/CONTINENTAL Located upstairs from the ever-popular Andreas Keller, this restaurant serves upscale German food in a refined atmosphere. The Camembert Amadeus, served with a lingonberry sauce, and the smoked trout with horseradish sauce both make interesting starts to a meal here. Follow this up with Bavarian onion steak or Munich-style sauerbraten for a gourmet German meal. Of course, Mozart is played on the stereo, and on Friday and Saturday nights, there is live harp music.

829 Front St. © 509/548-0600. www.cafemozartrestaurant.com. Reservations recommended. Main courses $7.50–$13 at lunch, $12–$30 at dinner. AE, MC, V. Daily 11am–4pm and 4:30–9pm.

Lorraines's Edel House ★★ INTERNATIONAL This restaurant, a simple little house above the Wenatchee River in the center of town, is Leavenworth's premier non-Bavarian restaurant with most of the menu offerings drawing on Asian and Mediterranean influences. There are always several pasta dishes, as well as such substantial entrees as soy-ginger roast duck with an orange glaze or grilled salmon. You might even find some "new" German dishes on the menu (sort of German meets Northwest). The restaurant also has a room and a cottage for rent at reasonable rates ($45–$105).

320 Ninth St. ✆ **800/487-3335** or 509/548-4412. http://lorrainesedelhaus.com. Reservations recommended. Main courses $12–$24. DISC, MC, V. Daily 5–9pm.

Restaurant Osterreich ★★ AUSTRIAN/CONTINENTAL   Located in the Tyrolean Ritz Hotel and down a flight of stairs from street level, this restaurant may be difficult to find, but is well worth searching out. While lots of restaurants in Leavenworth do German food, the Osterreich turns meat-and-potato meals into memorable events. While the regular menu leans toward the goulash and sauerkraut spectrum, the daily specials menu is much more interesting and might include wild boar tenderloin or pan-seared venison medallions.

633A Front St. ✆ **509/548-4031.** www.leavenworthdining.com. Reservations recommended. Main courses $18.25–$28.50. AE, DISC, MC, V. Wed–Sun 5–9pm. Closed Nov 1–Nov 20.

6 The Snoqualmie Pass Route ★★

Snoqualmie Pass: 50 miles (81km) E of Seattle, 53 miles (85km) W of Ellensburg

While Seattle has become a sprawling city of congested highways and high housing prices, there is a reason so many put up with such drawbacks. Less than an hour east of the city lie mountains so vast and rugged that you could hike for a week without ever crossing a road. In winter, The Summit at Snoqualmie Pass ski area is so close to the city that people head up after work for a bit of night skiing.

Between the city and this wilderness lies the Snoqualmie Valley, the Seattle region's last bit of bucolic countryside. Here you'll find small towns, pastures full of spotted cows, U-pick farms, and even a few unexpected attractions, including an impressive waterfall and, in summer, a medieval fair. While driving the back roads of the Snoqualmie Valley, keep an eye out for historic markers that include old photos and details about the valley's past.

ESSENTIALS
GETTING THERE   Snoqualmie Pass is on I-90 between Seattle and Ellensburg.

VISITOR INFORMATION   For more information on the area, contact the **Snoqualmie Pass Visitor Center** (✆ **425/434-6111**), which is located just off I-90 at Snoqualmie Pass and is operated by the National Forest Service. Information is also available through the **Cle Elum/Roslyn Chamber of Commerce,** 401 W. First St. (P.O. Box 43), Cle Elum, WA 98922 (✆ **509/674-5958;** www. cleelumroslyn.org).

EXPLORING THE SNOQUALMIE VALLEY
Snoqualmie Falls ★★, the valley's biggest attraction, plummet 270 feet into a pool of deep blue water. The falls are surrounded by a park owned by Puget Power, which operates a hydroelectric plant inside the rock wall behind the falls. The plant, built in 1898, was the world's first underground electric-generating facility. Within the park you'll find two overlooks near the lip of the falls and a half-mile-long trail leading down to the base of the falls. The river below the falls is popular both for fishing and for white-water kayaking. These falls will be familiar to anyone who remembers the opening sequence of David Lynch's *Twin Peaks,* which was filmed in this area. To reach the falls, take I-90 east from Seattle for 35 to 45 minutes and get off at exit 27. If you're hungry for lunch, try the restaurant at Salish Lodge, the hotel at the top of the falls.

Snoqualmie Falls are located just outside the town of **Snoqualmie,** which is where you'll find the restored 1890 railroad depot that houses the **Northwest**

Railway Museum, Wash. 202 (℗ **425/888-3030**). The museum, which is an absolute must for anyone with a child who is familiar with Thomas the Tank Engine, operates the **Snoqualmie Valley Railroad** on weekends May through October. The 40-minute railway excursions, using steam or diesel trains, run between here and the town of **North Bend.** Fares are $7 for adults, $6 for seniors, and $5 for children ages 3 to 12. Be sure to call ahead for a current schedule. The museum, which is free, displays railroad memorabilia and also has a large display of rolling stock. A big hit with kids!

Between Fall City and the town of **Carnation,** you'll pass several U-pick farms, where you can pick your own berries during the summer or pumpkins in the fall.

The Snoqualmie Valley is also the site of **Camlann Medieval Village,** 10320 Kelly Rd. NE (℗ **425/788-8624;** www.camlann.com), which is located north of Carnation off Wash. 203. On weekends between mid-July and late August, this reproduction of a medieval village is home to knights and squires, minstrels, and assorted other costumed merrymakers. There are crafts stalls, food booths, and, the highlight each day, jousting matches. Medieval clothing is available for rent if you forgot to pack yours. Throughout the year, there is a wide variety of banquets and seasonal festivals, and the village's Bors Hede restaurant is open Tuesday through Sunday for traditional dinners. Fair admission is $9 for adults, $5 for seniors and children age 12 and under. Admission to both the fair and a banquet is $39.

Thirty miles (48km) to the east of Snoqualmie Pass, you'll find the remote town of **Roslyn,** which was just a quietly decaying old coal-mining town until television turned it into Cicely, Alaska, for the hit TV show *Northern Exposure.* Although Cicely is but a fading memory now, visitors still wander up and down the town's 2-block-long main street soaking up the mining-town atmosphere. To learn more about the town's history, drop by the **Roslyn Museum,** 203 Pennsylvania Ave. (℗ **509/649-2776**), the town's main street. About the only other activity in town is wandering through the town's 25 cemeteries, which are up the hill from the museum. These cemeteries contain the graves of miners who lived and died in Roslyn.

SPORTS & OUTDOOR ACTIVITIES

HIKING   Outside of North Bend rises **Mount Si,** one of the most frequently climbed mountains in the state. This mountain, carved by glaciers long ago, rises abruptly from the floor of the valley outside North Bend and presents a dramatic face to the valley. If you are the least bit athletic, it is hard to resist the temptation to hike to the summit, where awesome views are the payoff. Be forewarned, however, that it's a strenuous 8-mile (13km) round-trip hike, and you'll need to carry lots of water. To reach the trail head, drive east of downtown North Bend on North Bend Way, turn left on Mount Si Road, turn right after crossing the Snoqualmie River, and continue another 2 miles (3.5km).

Farther east on I-90, at Snoqualmie Pass and before you reach it, there are several trail heads. Some trails lead to mountain summits, others to glacier-carved lakes, and still others past waterfalls deep in the forest. Due to their proximity to Seattle, these trails can be very crowded, and you'll need a Northwest Forest Pass in order to park at national forest trail heads. Passes are available at the ranger station in North Bend. A Northwest Forest Pass is not necessary for parking at the Mount Si trail head, which is on state land. For more information, contact the **North Bend Ranger District** (℗ **425/888-1421;** www.fs.fed.us/r6/mbs).

HORSEBACK RIDING   If you're interested in spending a few hours or a few days in the saddle, contact **High Country Outfitters** (© **888/235-0111** or 509/674-4903; www.highcountry-outfitters.com), which charges about $90 for a day ride and $160 a day for overnight rides.

MOUNTAIN BIKING   Iron Horse State Park/John Wayne Pioneer Trail, a railroad right-of-way that has been converted to a gravel path stretching more than 110 miles, provides one of the most unusual mountain-biking routes in the Northwest. The trail passes under Snoqualmie Pass by way of the 2½-mile-long (4km) Snoqualmie Tunnel, which is usually open to bicycles from May through October. To ride the tunnel you'll need good lights, warm clothes, and rain gear (water constantly drips from the ceiling of the tunnel). To access the trail from the west side, take exit 38 off I-90. From the east side, take exit 62 off I-90.

SKIING   While much of the terrain is not very interesting and the snow can be frustratingly unreliable due to winter rains, **The Summit at Snoqualmie Pass** ★★ (© **425/434-7669,** or 206/236-1600 for snow conditions; www.summit-at-snoqualmie.com) is the closest ski area to Seattle and consequently sees a lot of business both on weekends and for after-work night skiing. There are 22 lifts and 65 ski runs here, and the past couple of years have seen more than $10 million worth of improvements. Rentals and lessons are available. Adult lift ticket prices range from $24 for night skiing to $38 for a weekend all-day pass. Call for hours of operation.

At Snoqualmie Pass, there are many miles of both groomed and ungroomed cross-country ski trails. **Summit Nordic Center** (© **425/434-7669,** ext. 4531, or 425/434-6708) offers rentals, instruction, and many miles of groomed trails, some of which are lighted for night skiing. Trail fees run $8 to $12.

There are also several sno-parks along I-90 at Snoqualmie Pass. Some of these have groomed trails while others have trails that are marked but not groomed. **Sno-Park permits,** which are required for parking at these areas, are available at ski shops. If you plan to ski on groomed trails, you'll have to pay an additional fee for your Sno-Park permit.

In winter, **Bee Line Tours** (© **800/959-8387** or 206/632-5162; www.beelinetours.com) provides bus service from Seattle area hotels to the Summit at Snoqualmie ski area. Round-trip fare is $35.

WHERE TO STAY
ON THE WEST SIDE

Salish Lodge & Spa ★★★   Set at the top of 270-foot Snoqualmie Falls and only 35 minutes east of Seattle on I-90, Salish Lodge is a popular weekend getaway spot for folks from Seattle. With its country lodge atmosphere, the Salish aims for casual comfort and hits the mark, though the emphasis is clearly on luxury. Guest rooms, which are designed for romantic weekend getaways, all have fireplaces and whirlpool tubs, feather beds, and down comforters. To make this an even more attractive getaway, there's a full-service spa. The lodge's country breakfast is a legendary feast that may just keep you full right through to dinner. By the way, if you were a fan of *Twin Peaks,* you'll immediately recognize this hotel.

6501 Railroad Ave. SE (P.O. Box 1109), Snoqualmie Falls, WA 98065. © **800/826-6124,** 800/2-SALISH, or 425/888-2556. www.salishlodge.com. 91 units. $199–$389 double; $499–$999 suite. Resort fee additional $12.50. AE, DC, MC, V. Valet parking $5. **Amenities:** Restaurant (Northwest); lounge with view of the falls; exercise room; full-service spa with Jacuzzis and saunas; complimentary mountain bikes; activities desk; room service (daily 7am–10pm); massage; laundry service; dry cleaning. *In room:* A/C, TV, dataport, minibar, coffeemaker, hair dryer, iron.

ON THE EAST SIDE

Hidden Valley Guest Ranch ★★   If you're looking to get away from it all but don't have the time or inclination to head to the wilds of Montana, this 700-acre guest ranch is as good a substitute as you'll find in Washington. The setting, on a grassy ridge above Swauk Creek, is the absolute epitome of a mountain ranch setting, and the cabins are suitably rustic yet have comfortably modern amenities. The Appletree Cabin is the best. While horseback riding ($35 for 1½ hr.) is the favorite activity most of the year, when the snow falls, this is a great place to do some cross-country skiing or snowshoeing. The ranch is 15 minutes east of Cle Elum off Wash. 970, which connects to U.S. 97 (the route over Blewett Pass to Leavenworth and Wenatchee).

3942 Hidden Valley Rd., Cle Elum, WA 98922. © **800/5-COWBOY** or 509/857-2322. Fax 509/857-2130. www.hvranch.com. 13 units. May 1–Oct 15 $220 double; Oct 16–Apr 30 $120 double. Rates include all meals. 2-night minimum in summer. MC, V. **Amenities:** Restaurant (American); outdoor pool; outdoor lit tennis court; Jacuzzi; game room; massage. *In room:* Coffeemaker.

Iron Horse Inn ★   Railroad buffs won't want to miss an opportunity to stay at this restored Chicago, Milwaukee, St. Paul and Pacific Railroad bunkhouse. The inn is filled with railroading memorabilia and each of the guest rooms is named for a railroad worker who once lived here. The rooms vary in size and are simply furnished with antiques. However, the most popular rooms here are the two cabooses on short lengths of track beside the inn. These are large enough to sleep four or five people.

526 Marie Ave. (P.O. Box 629), South Cle Elum, WA 98943. © **800/22-TWAIN** or 509/674-5939. Fax 509/674-1708. www.ironhorseinnbb.com. 10 units, 6 with private bathroom. $70–$80 double with shared bathroom, $85–$135 double with private bathroom; $135 suite; $125 caboose. Rates include full breakfast. MC, V. **Amenities:** Jacuzzi. *In room:* No phone.

CAMPGROUNDS

Along the I-90 corridor, there are only a couple of campground choices on the west side of Snoqualmie Pass. **Tinkham Campground** (48 campsites) at exit 42 off I-90 is the closest Forest Service campground to Seattle. It is set on the bank of the South Fork Snoqualmie River. **Denny Creek Campground** (33 campsites) is so close to the freeway that campers are lulled to sleep by the roaring of trucks.

   Kachess Campground (120 campsites), near the north end of Kachess Lake, is the biggest campground in the area. Powerboating and fishing are the most popular activities here, but there are also some nearby trail heads providing access to the Alpine Lakes Wilderness. The Cle Elum Lake area offers the I-90 corridor's greatest concentration of campgrounds including **Wish Poosh** (39 campsites), **Cle Elum River** (23 campsites), **Red Mountain** (10 campsites), and **Salmon la Sac** ★ (99 campsites), which is this area's biggest and busiest campground.

   For information on campgrounds in this area, contact the **Snoqualmie Pass Visitor Center** (© **425/434-6111**), which is located just off I-90 at the pass. For national forest campground reservations, contact the **National Recreation Reservation Service** (© **800/280-CAMP**; www.reserveusa.com).

WHERE TO DINE
IN THE SNOQUALMIE VALLEY

The dining room at the **Salish Lodge** (see above) is by far the best restaurant on the west side of Snoqualmie Pass.

DINING & NIGHTLIFE IN ROSLYN

For fresh-baked bread and pastries, check out **Roslyn Bakery,** 30 N. First St., Roslyn (✆ **509/649-2521**). If you're heading to the hills and want to pack some great jerky, stop by **Carek's Market** ✰, 510 S. A St., Roslyn (✆ **509/649-2930**). Good pizzas can be had at **Village Pizza,** 105 Pennsylvania Ave., Roslyn (✆ **509/649-2992**). For nightlife, don't miss **The Brick Bar & Grill** ✰, 1 Pennsylvania Ave., Roslyn (✆ **509/649-2643**), which claims to be the oldest operating saloon in Washington and has a unique flowing-water spittoon under the bar. This place is an absolute classic. If it's good microbrews that you crave, wander up the street to the **Roslyn Brewery,** 208 Pennsylvania Ave. (✆ **509/ 649-2232**), which is a much more modern place.

Roslyn Cafe ✰ AMERICAN   Made famous back in the days of *Northern Exposure,* this casual little cafe is a favorite of both locals and tourists. The menu features such standards as steaks, meatloaf, and corned beef and cabbage, though it's the breakfasts that most people rave about.

201 Pennsylvania Ave. ✆ 509/649-2763. Main courses $6–$11. MC, V. Summer Sun–Thurs 7am–6:30pm, Fri–Sat 7am–8:30pm; other months shorter hours.

7 Mount Rainier National Park ✰✰✰ & Environs

Paradise: 110 miles (177km) SE of Seattle, 70 miles (113km) SE of Tacoma, 150 miles (242km) NE of Portland, 85 miles (137km) NW of Yakima

At 14,410 feet high, Mount Rainier is the tallest mountain in Washington, and to the sun-starved residents of Seattle and south Puget Sound, the dormant volcano is a giant weather gauge. When the skies clear over Puget Sound, the phrase "The Mountain is out" is often heard around the region. And when the Mountain is out, all eyes turn to admire its broad slopes.

Those slopes remain snow-covered throughout the year due to the region's infamous moisture-laden air, which has made Mount Rainier one of the snowiest spots in the country. In 1972, the mountain set a record when 93½ feet of snow fell in 1 year (and that record held until Washington's Mount Baker received 95 ft. in the winter of 1998–99). Such record snowfalls have created numerous glaciers on the mountain's flanks, and one of these, the Carbon Glacier, is the lowest-elevation glacier in the continental United States.

Snow and glaciers notwithstanding, Rainier has a heart of fire. Steam vents at the mountain's summit are evidence that, though this volcanic peak has been dormant for more than 150 years, it could erupt again at any time. However, scientists believe that Rainier's volcanic activity occurs in 3,000-year cycles— and luckily we have another 500 years to go before there's another big eruption.

Known to Native Americans as Tahoma, Mount Rainier received its current name in 1792 when British explorer Capt. George Vancouver named the mountain for a friend (who never even visited the region). The first ascent to the mountain's summit was made in 1870 by Gen. Hazard Stevens and Philemon Van Trump, and it was 14 years later that James Longmire built the first hotel on the mountain's flanks. In 1899, Mount Rainier became the fifth national park.

ESSENTIALS

GETTING THERE   If you're coming from Seattle and your destination is Paradise (the park's most popular area), head for the southwest (Nisqually) park entrance. Take I-5 south to exit 127 and then head east on Wash. 512. Take the Wash. 7 exit and head south toward Elbe. At Elbe, continue east on Wash. 706.

If you're coming from Seattle and are heading for the northeast (White River) park entrance en route to Sunrise or Crystal Mountain, take I-90 to I-405 south. At Renton, take Wash. 169 south to Enumclaw, where you pick up Wash. 410 heading east.

Note that in winter only the road from the Nisqually entrance to Paradise is kept open.

From Portland, head north on I-5 to exit 68 and then take U.S. 12 east to the town of Morton. From Morton, head north on Wash. 7 to Elbe and then turn east on Wash. 706, which will bring you to the Nisqually (southwest) park entrance.

From May 1 to late September, **Grayline of Seattle** (© 800/426-7505) operates one bus daily between Seattle and Mount Rainier; the round-trip fare is $54 for adults and $27 for children. Between May and October, the **Rainier Shuttle** (© 360/569-2331; www.rainiershuttle.com) operates between Seattle-Tacoma International Airport and Mount Rainier National Park ($46 plus each way between the airport and Paradise; $37 each way from the airport to the town of Ashford). This company also operates a shuttle between the town of Ashford and Paradise ($12). Keep in mind that going into the park, you'll also have to pay a $5 admission.

VISITOR INFORMATION　For more park information, contact **Mount Rainier National Park,** Tahoma Woods, Star Route, Ashford, WA 98304 (© **360/569-2211;** www.nps.gov/mora).

PARK ADMISSION　The park entrance fee is $10 per vehicle and $5 per person for pedestrians or cyclists. Another option, if you plan to visit several national parks in a single year, is the National Parks Pass or the Golden Eagle Passport, an annual pass good at all national parks and recreation areas. The pass costs $50 (plus $15 for the Golden Eagle upgrade) and is available at all national park visitor centers. If you're over 62, you can get a Golden Age Passport for $10, and if you have a disability, you can get a free Golden Access Passport.

SEEING THE HIGHLIGHTS

Just past the main southwest entrance (Nisqually), you'll come to **Longmire,** site of the National Park Inn, Longmire Museum (exhibits on the park's natural and human history; open daily year-round), a hiker information center that issues backcountry permits, and a ski-touring center where you can rent cross-country skis in winter.

The road then climbs to **Paradise** (elevation 5,400 ft.), the aptly named mountainside aerie that affords a breathtaking close-up view of the mountain. Paradise is the park's most popular destination, so expect crowds. During July and August the meadows here are ablaze with wildflowers. The circular **Henry M. Jackson Memorial Visitor Center** (© **360/569-2211,** ext. 2328) provides 360° panoramic views. The visitor center is open daily from early May to mid-October and on weekends and holidays from mid-October to early May. A 1¼-mile (2km) walk from the visitor center will bring you to a spot from which you can look down on the Nisqually Glacier. Many miles of other trails lead out from Paradise, looping through meadows and up onto snowfields above timberline. It's not unusual to find plenty of snow at Paradise as late as July. In 1972, the area set a world's record for snowfall in one year: 93.5 feet. This record held until the 1998 and 1999 winter season during which La Niña climatic conditions dumped 95 feet of snow on Mount Baker, which lies to the north of Mount Rainier.

In summer you can continue beyond Paradise to the **Ohanapecosh Visitor Center** (© **360/569-2211,** ext. 2352), which is open weekends from late May to mid-June and daily from mid-June to early October. Not far from this visitor center, you can walk through the **Grove of the Patriarchs** (see "Hiking & Backpacking," below, for details). Continuing around the mountain, you'll reach the turnoff for Sunrise.

Continuing counterclockwise around the mountain, you'll come to Cayuse Pass. A short detour from this pass will bring you to the picturesque **Chinook Pass** area, where there is a good 4½-mile (7km) day hike loop trail that begins at Tipsoo Lake and circles Naches Peak.

Continuing around the mountain, you'll come to the turnoff for the park's **White River entrance.** This road leads to some of the park's best day hikes, and a spur road leads to the White River Campground. At 6,400 feet, **Sunrise** is the highest spot in the park accessible by car. A beautiful old log lodge serves as the **Sunrise Visitor Center** (© **360/569-2211,** ext. 2357), which is open daily from July through mid-September. From here you get a superb view of Mount Rainier, seemingly at arm's length, and **Emmons Glacier,** which is the largest glacier in the 48 contiguous states. From Sunrise, you can also see Mount Baker to the north and Mount Adams to the south. Some of the park's most scenic trails begin at Sunrise, providing lots of options for day hikes.

If you want to see a bit of dense forest or hike without crowds, head for the park's **Carbon River entrance** in the northwest corner. This is the least visited region of the park because it only offers views to those willing to hike several miles uphill. About 3 miles (5km) up the trail, you'll come face to face with the Carbon River Glacier, which is the lowest-elevation glacier in the contiguous 48 states. At its lower end this glacier plows through dense rain forest, an ominous and unforgettable sight. Continuing up this trail another 2 miles (3km) (following the glacier for much of the way) will bring you to beautiful wild-flower meadows and close-up views of the northwest flank of Mount Rainier. The road into this area is in very bad shape and has washed out twice in recent years. Currently high-clearance vehicles are recommended, but you can some-times make it through in a regular passenger vehicle if you drive slowly.

OUTDOOR ACTIVITIES IN & NEAR THE NATIONAL PARK

If, after a long day of taking advantage of the outdoor activities available in the park, you'd like to soak in a hot tub or get a massage, contact the little wood-land spa called **Wellspring** (© **360/569-2514;** www.wellspringspa.com). You'll find Wellspring in Ashford not far from the Nisqually park entrance. An hour in the hot tub costs $10 per person, while an hour massage costs $60. Alterna-tively, you can soak in a hot tub and get a massage at nearby **Stormking** (© **360/569-2964;** www.stormkingspa.com). Both of these places also have cabins available for overnight guests.

HIKING & BACKPACKING   Hikers have more than 240 miles (386km) of trails to explore within the park, though the vast majority of park visitors do their hiking at only two places—Paradise and Sunrise. However, despite the crowds, these two alpine areas do offer the most scenic day hiking opportunities.

At **Paradise** 🐾🐾, the 5-mile (8km) **Skyline Trail** 🐾🐾🐾 is the highest trail at Paradise and climbs through beautiful meadows above the tree line. Unfortu-nately, the meadows here, which are among the park's most beautiful, have been heavily damaged by hikers' boots over the past 100 years, and now there are signs everywhere telling hikers to stay on the trails. Along the route of this trail there are views of Mount Adams, Mount St. Helens, and the Nisqually Glacier. The **Lakes Trail,** of similar length, heads downhill to the Reflection Lakes, which have picture-perfect views of the mountain reflected in their waters. However, be forewarned that these lakes lie right alongside the road through the park, and are very popular with people who park by the roadside and get out of their cars for a brief stroll by the lakes.

At **Sunrise** 🐾🐾🐾 there are also numerous trails of varying lengths. Among these, the 5-mile (8km) **Burroughs Mountain Trail** and the 5½-mile (9km) **Mount Fremont Trail** are both very rewarding—the latter even offers a chance to see mountain goats. The **Summerland Trail,** which starts 3 miles (5km) from the White River park entrance (the road to Sunrise), is another very popular day hike. This trail starts in forest and climbs 2,000 feet up into meadows with a great view of the mountain.

If you'd rather avoid most of the crowds, try the 2½-mile (4km) round-trip trail to **Snow Lake,** which is set at the foot of Unicorn Peak. This trail involves only a few hundred feet of elevation gain. You'll find the trail head between Paradise and Ohanapecosh. For a longer day hike, try the 11-mile (18km) round-trip hike to **Indian Henry's Hunting Ground,** which involves more than 2,000 feet of elevation gain. This trail starts from the Kautz Creek turnout east of Longmire. In 1947, a huge mudflow swept down Kautz Creek and buried the road here under 30 feet of mud. Up in the northwest corner of the park, the 6-mile (9.5km) round-trip trail from Mowich Lake to **Spray Park** is another breathtaking route that starts in the forest and climbs a little more than 2,000 feet into beautiful alpine meadows.

The park's single most memorable low-elevation hike is the **Grove of the Patriarchs Trail** 😊😊. This 1½-mile (2.5km) round-trip trail is fairly flat (good for kids) and leads through a forest of huge old trees to a grove of 1,000-year-old red cedars on an island in the Ohanapecosh River. The trail head for this hike is near the Steven Canyon park entrance (southeast entrance).

Another interesting and easy low-elevation walk is the **Trail of the Shadows,** a ¾-mile (1km) loop trail in Longmire. This trail, which circles a wet meadow, leads past bubbling mineral springs.

There are also naturalist-led programs and walks throughout the spring, summer, and fall, and on winter weekends there are guided snowshoe walks. Check the park newspaper for schedules.

The 95-mile-long (153km) **Wonderland Trail** 😊😊, which circles the mountain, is the quintessential Mount Rainier backpacking trip. This trail takes 10 days to 2 weeks to complete and offers up spectacular scenery. However, there are also many shorter overnight hikes. Before heading out on any overnight backpacking trip, you'll need to pick up a permit at the Longmire Hiker Information Center, the Paradise Ranger Station, the White River Hiker Information Center, or, seasonally, the Wilkeson Ranger Station on the road to the Carbon River entrance to the park. During the summer, reservations can be made up to 2 months in advance for backcountry campsites. Backcountry reservations cost $20 per party.

HORSEBACK RIDING   If you'd like to do some horseback riding, you've got a couple of choices in the area. In Elbe, you'll find **EZ Times Outfitters,** 18703 Wash. 706 (© **360/569-2449**), which leads rides into the Elbe State Forest. During the summer, horseback riding is also available at **Crystal Mountain ski area** 😊😊 (© **360/663-2265**). East of White Pass on U.S. 12, you'll find **Indian Creek Corral** (© **509/672-2400**) near the shore of Rimrock Lake. Expect to pay $20 to $25 for a 1-hour ride and around $30 for a 2-hour ride.

MOUNTAIN BIKING   Within the national park all trails are closed to mountain bikes, but cyclists are allowed to ride the West Side Road, a gravel road that has long been closed to cars due to mud slides that have repeatedly washed out one short stretch of the road. Off this road are several little-used hiking trails if you want to combine a ride with a hike. Outside the park, at Crystal Mountain ski area (off Wash. 410 north of the park), you'll find lift-accessed mountain-bike trails in the summer.

MOUNTAINEERING   Climbers will know of Mount Rainier's reputation as a training ground for making attempts on higher peaks, such as Mount Everest. If you're interested in taking a mountain-climbing class, contact **Rainier Mountaineering,** P.O. Box Q, Ashford, WA 98304 (© **360/569-2227;** www.rmi guides.com), which operates inside Mount Rainier National Park and offers 1-day classes for $154, 3-day summit climbs for $728, and a 5-day mountaineering seminar for $1,094.

WHITE-WATER RAFTING   The Tieton River, which flows down the eastern slopes of the Cascades to the east of the national park, is one of the state's most popular rafting rivers. However, the rafting season lasts for only about 3 weeks during the annual September drawdown of water from Rimrock Reservoir. Rafting companies offering trips on this river include **Alpine Adventures** (© **800/723-8386** or 206/323-1220; www.alpineadventures.com) and **River Riders** (© **800/448-RAFT** or 206/448-RAFT; www.riverrider.com). Expect to pay $60 to $80.

WINTER SPORTS   In winter, there's good cross-country skiing at Paradise, and at Longmire, you'll find a ski touring and rental shop at the National Park Inn (© 360/569-2411). Skis rent for around $15 per day. Daily between Christmas and New Year's and on winter weekends, there are 2-hour **guided snowshoe walks** at Paradise, with snowshoes provided ($1 suggested donation). Snowshoes ($12 per day) can also be rented in Longmire, should you want to explore on your own. Snowboarding is popular throughout the year, though there is no lift to get you up the slope, and it's about a 1½-hour climb to the best snowboarding area.

Outside the park, near the town of Packwood, you can ski cross-country from hut to hut on a 75-mile (121km) trail system. For more information, contact the **Mount Tahoma Trails Association,** P.O. Box 206, Ashford, WA 98304 (© **360/569-2451;** www.skimtta.com). Unfortunately, many of these trails are at such low elevations that snow cover is unreliable, and the official season for these trails does not begin until the end of December. You'll find their information center at the west end of Ashford behind the fire station.

Just outside the northeast corner of the park, off Wash. 410, you'll find **Crystal Mountain Resort** (© **360/663-2265** for general information, or 888/ SKI-6199 for snow conditions; www.skicrystal.com), which most Washingtonians agree is the state's best all-around ski area due to the variety of terrain. Lift ticket prices range from $20 for night skiing to $43 for a weekend all-day pass. Call for hours of operation. Experienced backcountry skiers will also find some challenging cross-country skiing here at Crystal Mountain.

You'll also find downhill and cross-country skiing less than 20 miles (32km) from the southeast corner of the park on U.S. 12 at the small **White Pass Ski Area** ★ (© **509/672-3100;** www.skiwhitepass.com). Rental equipment is available. Lift rates range from $17 for an adult half-day midweek ticket to $36 for a full-day weekend ticket. Nordic track passes are $8.

OTHER ACTIVITIES & ATTRACTIONS OUTSIDE THE PARK

Between Memorial Day and the end of September, the **Mt. Rainier Scenic Railroad** (© **888/STEAM-11** or 360/569-2588; www.mrsr.com) operates vintage steam locomotives and both enclosed and open passenger cars along a 14-mile (23km) stretch of track between Elbe and Mineral Lake, just west of the park's Nisqually entrance. The trips last 1½ hours and cost $11.50 for adults, $10.50 for seniors, $8.50 for children 4 to 12, and free for children under 3.

WHERE TO STAY
INSIDE THE PARK

National Park Inn ★   Located in Longmire, in the southwest corner of the park, this rustic lodge opened in 1920. Because the setting here is not as spectacular as that of the Paradise Inn, this lodge is not nearly as popular, and consequently room reservations are easier to come by. The inn's front veranda does, however, have a view of the mountain, and it is here that guests often gather at sunset on clear days. Because this lodge stays open in the winter, it is popular with cross-country skiers and snowshoers. Guest rooms vary in size and have rustic furnishings. The inn's restaurant manages to have something for everyone. There's also a lounge with a river-rock fireplace that's perfect for winter-night relaxing. A gift shop and cross-country ski/snowshoe rental shop are adjacent to the inn.

Mount Rainier National Park, Ashford, WA 98304. © **360/569-2275.** www.guestservices.com/rainier. 25 units, 7 with shared bathroom. $75 double with shared bathroom, $104–$150 double with private bathroom. AE, DC, DISC, MC, V. Free parking. **Amenities:** Restaurant (American); lounge. *In room:* No phone.

Paradise Inn 🖈🖈 *Value* Built in 1917 high on the flanks of Mount Rainier in an area aptly known as Paradise, this rustic lodge should be your first choice of accommodations in the park (book early). Cedar-shake siding, huge exposed beams, cathedral ceilings, and a gigantic stone fireplace make this the quintessential mountain retreat. Offering breathtaking views of the mountain, the inn is also the starting point for miles of trails that in summer wander through flower-filled meadows. Guest rooms, which vary in size, all have carpets, drapes, and rustic hickory furniture. The Sunday brunch in the inn's large dining room is legendary. A snack bar and lounge are dining options.

Mount Rainier National Park, Ashford, WA 98304. © **360/569-2275.** www.guestservices.com/rainier. 117 units, 33 with shared bathroom. $76 double with shared bathroom, $114–$150 double with private bathroom; $155 suite. AE, DC, DISC, MC, V. Closed early Oct to mid-May. Free parking. **Amenities:** 2 restaurants (American, snack bar); lounge. *In room:* No phone.

OUTSIDE THE SOUTHWEST (NISQUALLY) ENTRANCE

Alexander's Country Inn 🖈🖈 Located just outside the park's Nisqually entrance, this large B&B first opened as an inn back in 1912. Today, as then, it is one of the preferred places to stay in the area, offering not only comfortable rooms but some of the best food for many miles around. The first floor is taken up by the dining room, and on the second floor, you'll find a big lounge where you can sit by the fire on a cold night. By far the best room in the house is the tower suite, which is in a turret and has plenty of windows looking out on the woods (there's also a second, smaller turret suite). After a hard day of playing on the mountain, there's no better place to relax than in the hot tub overlooking the inn's trout pond. The inn also rents two three-bedroom houses.

37515 State Rd. 706 E., Ashford, WA 98304. © **800/654-7615** or 360/569-2300. Fax 360/569-2323. www. alexanderscountryinn.com. 14 units. May–Oct $110 double, $140 suite, $225 house; Nov–Apr $89 double, $110 suite, $175 house. Rates include full breakfast. MC, V. **Amenities:** Restaurant (American); Jacuzzi. *In room:* No phone.

The Hobo Inn *Kids* If you're a railroad buff, you won't want to pass up this opportunity to spend the night in a remodeled caboose. Each of the eight cabooses is a little bit different (one even has its own private hot tub). Though the oldest of the cars dates from 1916, they have all been outfitted with comfortable beds and bathrooms. Some have bay windows while others have cupolas. For the total railroad experience, you can have a drink in the Side-Track Room, dine in the adjacent Mount Rainier Dining Co. dining car restaurant, and go for a ride on the Mount Rainier Scenic Railroad.

P.O. Box 10, Elbe, WA 98330. © **360/569-2500.** 8 units. May–Dec $70–$85 double; Jan–Apr $50–$65 double. AE, DISC, MC, V.

Stormking 🖈 *Finds* With two modern cabins and a three-room bed-and-breakfast inn, Stormking offers a bit of variety for a Mount Rainier vacation. Our favorite cabin is set on the far side of a footbridge over a tiny pond and has a slate-floored entry hall, parquet floors, a woodstove, a stereo system with plenty of relaxing music, and a high ceiling. In the big bathroom, which has a flagstone floor and is filled with plants, you'll find a double shower amid the greenery. There's also a hot tub on the back deck. The second cabin also has its own hot tub, and there is one for B&B guests as well.

P.O. Box 126, Ashford, WA 98304. ✆ 360/569-2964. www.stormkingspa.com. 5 units. $70–$110 B&B double; $125–$155 cabin. Winter cabin rates include continental breakfast. MC, V. Pets accepted in B&B with $20 fee per night. **Amenities:** Spa; Jacuzzi; massage. *In room:* No phone.

Wellspring ★★ (Value)   This little retreat definitely isn't for everyone (although even Al Gore has stayed here), but it is certainly the most unique accommodation in the area. Private hot tubs and wood-fired saunas will take the chill off even the coldest night, and massages are also available to soothe aching muscles. Accommodations are an eclectic and fanciful mix. In the modern log cabins, which are tucked up against the edge of the forest, you'll find feather beds, woodstoves, and vaulted ceilings. In The Nest, there's a queen-size bed suspended from the ceiling by ropes and situated under a skylight. In the Three Bears Cottage, you'll find rustic log furniture and a full kitchen. In the Tatoosh Room, you'll find a large stone fireplace, a whirlpool tub, and a waterfall shower. The newest rooms are three tent cabins, and there's even a tiny treehouse room! Hot tubs and saunas are an additional $5 to $10 per person per hour.

54922 Kernahan Rd., Ashford, WA 98304. ✆ 360/569-2514. www.wellspringspa.com. 11 units. $85–$150 double. Rates for most rooms include continental breakfast. MC, V. **Amenities:** 2 Jacuzzis; 2 saunas; massage. *In room:* Fridge, coffeemaker.

Whittaker's Bunkhouse ★   Though it definitely is nothing fancy, this lodge, a former mill-workers' bunkhouse built in 1912, is the lodging of choice for climbers headed to or from the summit of Mount Rainier. The Bunkhouse is owned by Lou Whittaker, one of Mount Rainier's most famous climbers (and owner of Rainier Mountaineering), and in the lodge's espresso shop, you'll find lots of climbing photos and certificates Whittaker received for climbing Mount Everest. The guest rooms are small and Spartan, but they do have private bathrooms.

30205 SR 706 E. (P.O. Box E), Ashford, WA 98304. ✆ 360/569-2439. Fax 360/569-2436. www.welcometo ashford.com. 20 units. $75 double; $25 dorm. AE, MC, V. **Amenities:** Jacuzzi. *In room:* No phone.

OUTSIDE THE NORTHEAST (WHITE RIVER) ENTRANCE

Alta Crystal Resort at Mt. Rainier ★   This is the closest lodging to the northeast (White River) park entrance and the Sunrise area, and although this condominium resort with its wooded grounds is most popular in winter when skiers flock to Crystal Mountain's slopes (just minutes away), there's also plenty to do in summer. After spending the day hiking nearby trails, you can go for a swim or soak your body in a hot tub in the woods. Accommodations are in one-bedroom and loft chalets. The former sleep up to four people and the latter have bed space for up to six people. All of the condos have fireplaces.

68317 Wash. 410 E., Greenwater, WA 98022. ✆ 800/277-6475 or 360/663-2500. Fax 360/663-0728. www. altacrystalresort.com. 24 units. $139–$239 chalet for 1–6 people. AE, MC, V. **Amenities:** Outdoor pool; Jacuzzi; bike rentals. *In room:* TV/VCR, dataport, kitchen, fridge, coffeemaker, hair dryer.

CAMPGROUNDS

There are six main campgrounds within Mount Rainier National Park, and because all the park's campgrounds stay full on summer weekends, you should be sure to either have a reservation (required for Ohanapecosh and Cougar Rock from late June to Labor Day) or arrive early in the day. Reservations can be made through the **National Park Reservation Service** (© **800/365-CAMP;** http:// reservations.nps.gov). Campsite fees range from $9 to $15 per campsite per night. No electrical or water hookups are available. Only the Sunshine Point Campground and, depending on snow level and road conditions, the Ipsut Creek Campground, stay open all year. The rest are open summer through early fall, with the White River Campground usually closing first.

Ohanapecosh (188 campsites), located in the southeast corner of the park, is the largest but is a long way from the alpine meadows that are what most visitors want to see. The closest campground to Paradise is **Cougar Rock** (173 campsites). **White River** ✿ (112 campsites) is close to Sunrise, which is one of the most spectacular spots in the park. **Sunshine Point** (18 campsites) is near the Nisqually entrance. Up in the northwest corner of the park, there is **Ipsut Creek** (31 campsites), although due to frequent winter flood damage, the road to this campground isn't always open.

In addition to drive-in campgrounds and the many backcountry camps, there are two walk-in campgrounds that often have spaces available, even on weekends. **Mowich Lake** ✿ (30 campsites) is in the northwest corner of the park not far from Ipsut Creek Campground, and the sites are only 50 yards from the parking lot. If you're prepared for a longer walk in, consider **Sunrise** ✿ (8 campsites), which is officially a backcountry campsite but is only about a mile from the Sunrise parking lot (a backcountry camping permit is required).

When the park campgrounds are full, try **La Wis Wis** (90 campsites), a national forest campground on U.S. 12 and the Cowlitz River near the Ohanapecosh entrance. There are also numerous unremarkable National Forest Service campgrounds along U.S. 12 east of White Pass and along Wash. 410 east of the park.

For information on campgrounds in the national park, contact **Mount Rainier National Park,** Tahoma Woods, Star Route, Ashford, WA 98304 (© **360/569-2211;** www.nps.gov/mora). For information on national forest campgrounds east of the park, contact the **Naches Ranger District,** 10061 U.S. 12, Naches, WA 98937 (© **509/653-2205;** www.fs.fed.us/r6/wenatchee); and for those west of the park, contact the **Cowlitz Valley Ranger District,** 10024 U.S. 12 (P.O. Box 670), Randle, WA 98377 (© **360/497-1100;** www.fs.fed.us/ r6/gpnf). For national forest campground reservations, contact the **National Recreation Reservation Service** (© **800/280-CAMP;** www.reserveusa.com).

WHERE TO DINE

In the park there are dining rooms at Paradise Inn, open from mid-May to early October, and the National Park Inn, open year-round. As the only formal dining options within the park, these restaurants tend to stay busy. For quick meals, there are snack bars at the Henry M. Jackson Memorial Visitor Center, at Paradise Inn, and at Sunrise Lodge. In Ashford you'll find the **Copper Creek Restaurant,** 35707 SR 706 E., Ashford (© **360/569-2326**), which does good berry pies.

Alexander's ✿ AMERICAN Alexander's, which is also a popular B&B, is the best place to dine outside the Nisqually entrance to the park. Fresh trout from the inn's pond is the dinner of choice here, but you'll also find beef stew, pork ribs, and pasta on the menu. Whatever you order, just be sure to save room for the wild blackberry pie.

37515 SR 706 E., Ashford. © **800/654-7615** or 360/569-2300. www.alexanderscountryinn.com. Reservations recommended. Main courses $14–$24. MC, V. Mid-May to Oct daily 8am–9pm; Nov to mid-May Fri 3–8pm, Sat 8am–8pm, Sun 8am–7pm.

Mt. Rainier Railroad Dining Co. ⭐ *Kids* AMERICAN   You can't miss this unusual restaurant in Elbe—just watch for all the cabooses of the adjacent Hobo Inn. Meals are basic, with steaks and fried seafoods the staples of the dinner menu, but the surroundings make this place worth a stop. You'll be dining in an old railroad dining car. Your car won't go anywhere, but you'll still get a sense of being on a rail journey.

Wash. 7, Elbe. © **360/569-2505.** Main courses $8–$19. AE, DISC, MC, V. Summer daily 8am–9pm; shorter hours in other seasons.

8 Mount St. Helens National Volcanic Monument ⭐⭐⭐

Coldwater Ridge Visitor Center: 90 miles (145km) N of Portland, 168 miles (271km) S of Seattle

Named in 1792 by Capt. George Vancouver for his friend Baron St. Helens, Mount St. Helens was once considered the most perfect of the Cascade peaks, a snow-covered cone rising above lush forests. However, on May 18, 1980, all that changed when Mount St. Helens erupted with a violent explosion previously unknown in modern times.

The eruption blew out the side of the volcano and removed the top 1,300 feet of the peak, causing the largest landslide in recorded history. This blast is estimated to have traveled at up to 650 miles per hour, with air temperatures of up to 800°F. The eruption also sent more than 540 million tons of ash nearly 16 miles (26km) into the atmosphere. This massive volume of ash rained down on an area of 22,000 square miles (35,420km²) and could be measured as far away as Denver.

Today the volcano and 110,000 acres of both devastated and undisturbed forests have been preserved as Mount St. Helens National Volcanic Monument. Several visitor centers provide information on the eruption and the subsequent changes that have taken place here.

ESSENTIALS

GETTING THERE   Mount St. Helens National Volcanic Monument is accessed by three different routes. The one with all the major information centers is Wash. 504, the Spirit Lake Highway, which heads east from I-5 at Castle Rock. The southern section of the monument is reached via Wash. 503 from I-5 at Woodland. The east side of the monument is reached via U.S. 12 from I-5 at exit 68.

VISITOR INFORMATION   For more information on the national monument, contact **Mount St. Helens National Volcanic Monument,** 42218 NE Yale Bridge Rd., Amboy, WA 98601 (© **360/247-3900;** www.fs.fed.us/gpnf/mshnvm).

ADMISSION   Admission to one monument visitor center (or Ape Cave) is $3 ($1 children 5–15) and to two or more visitor centers (and Ape Cave), is $6 ($2 children 5–15). If you just want to park at one of the monument's trail heads and go for a hike, all you need is a valid Northwest Forest Pass, which costs $5 per day. If it's winter, you'll need a sno-park permit ($8 per day). Also, keep in mind that Golden Eagle, Golden Age, and Golden Access passes will also get you into the monument visitor centers (but not the Mount St. Helens Visitor Center at Silver Lake, which is operated by Washington state).

EXPLORING THE NATIONAL MONUMENT
MOUNT ST. HELENS WEST

The best place to start an exploration of the monument is at the **Mount St. Helens Visitor Center** ⭐ (© **360/274-2100**), which is located at Silver Lake, 5 miles (8km) east of Castle Rock on Wash. 504. The visitor center houses extensive exhibits on the eruption and its effects on the region. This center is open daily from 9am to 4pm. Before even reaching this center, you can stop and watch a 25-minute, 70mm film about the eruption at the **Mount St. Helens Cinedome Theater** (© **360/274-8000**), which is located at exit 49 off I-5 (tickets $6 adults, $5 seniors and children).

Continuing east from the visitor center, you'll come to the **Hoffstadt Bluffs Visitor Center** (© **360/274-7750**) at milepost 27 (open daily 9am–7pm in summer; shorter hr. in winter), which has a snack bar and is the takeoff site for 20-minute helicopter flights over Mount St. Helens ($99 with a three-person minimum). A few miles farther, just past milepost 33, you'll arrive at the **Forest Learning Center** (© **360/414-3439**), which is open mid-May through September daily 10am to 6pm, October daily 10am to 5pm. This is primarily a promotional center for the timber industry, but it does show a short but fascinating video about the eruption. The video theater is designed to resemble an ash-covered landscape. There are also displays on how forests destroyed by the blast have been replanted. Outside either of these centers, you can usually see, far below on the floor of the Toutle River valley, numerous elk.

The **Coldwater Ridge Visitor Center** ⭐⭐ (© **360/274-2131**), which is at milepost 47 on Wash. 504, only 8 miles (13km) from the crater, is the second of the national monument's official visitor centers. This center features interpretive displays on the events leading up to the eruption and the subsequent slow regeneration of life around the volcano. You'll also find a picnic area, interpretive trail, restaurant, and boat launch at Coldwater Lake. Hours are from late April to late September daily from 10am to 6pm, and late September to late April daily from 10am to 5pm.

Of all the many visitor centers, none offers a more awe-inspiring view than that from the **Johnston Ridge Observatory** ⭐⭐ (© **360/274-2140**), which is located 10 miles (16km) past the Coldwater Ridge Visitor Center. Built into the mountainside and designed to blend into the landscape, this observatory houses the equipment that is still used to monitor activity within Mount St. Helens. The observatory is open May through October daily from 10am to 6pm. If you're up for a bit of hiking, the single best trail on this side of the monument is the Boundary Ridge Trail, which heads east from the Johnston Ridge Observatory, with a jaw-dropping view of the blast zone the entire way. This trail leads for many miles across the monument, so you can hike as much or as little as you want. There is a good turnaround point about 1 mile (1.5km) out from the observatory.

MOUNT ST. HELENS EAST

For a different perspective on the devastation wrought by Mount St. Helens's eruption, drive around to the mountain's east side and the road up to Windy Ridge. Although it takes a couple of hours longer to get to this side of the mountain, you will be rewarded by equaling amazing views, better hiking opportunities, and smaller crowds. To reach the east side of the mountain, take U.S. 12 east from exit 68 off I-5. In Randle, head south on Local Route 25. The **Woods Creek Information Station,** on Route 25 just before the junction with Route 26, has information on this part of the monument. South of Woods Creek,

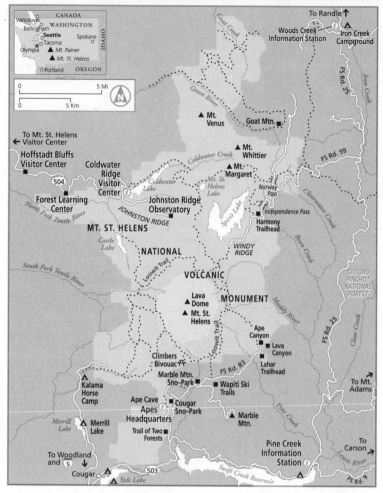

watch for Route 99, the road to the **Windy Ridge Viewpoint.** This road crosses many miles of blown-down trees, and though the sight of the thousands of trees that were felled by a single blast is quite bleak, it reminds one of the awesome power of nature. More than 2 decades after the eruption, life is slowly returning to this devastated forest. At the **Windy Ridge Viewpoint,** visitors get one of the best close-up views of the crater. A staircase of 439 stairs climbs 220 feet up the hill above the parking area for even better views. Below Windy Ridge lies Spirit Lake, which was once one of the most popular summer vacation spots in the Washington Cascades. Today the lake is desolate and lifeless. The 1-mile-long (1.5km) Harmony Trail leads down to the shore of Spirit Lake and is a very worthwhile hike. Just keep in mind that it is a 600-foot climb back up to the trail head parking lot.

MOUNT ST. HELENS SOUTH
The south side of the monument was the least affected by the eruption, and consequently does not offer the dramatic scenes of devastation to be seen on the east

Bigfoot: Lost Primate or Tabloid Hoax?

The legend of Bigfoot is firmly entrenched in the Northwest, and though there aren't too many people around who have seen one of its footprints, the reports have been steady enough over the years to keep the belief alive.

Variously described over the years as being anywhere from under 5 feet tall to over 8 feet tall, most Bigfoots share the common traits of being hairy and very shy of humans. In a few instances they have displayed aggressive behavior, but for the most part they have simply seemed curious about human activities. More frequent than actual sightings have been discoveries of Bigfoot tracks, and it was just such tracks, found north of the Klamath River in California, that prompted a reporter for the *Humboldt Times* newspaper to coin the term Bigfoot in 1958. This beast's other common name, Sasquatch, is derived from a Native American name used in the Fraser River valley of British Columbia.

Though Bigfoot reports have come from all over the country (and all over the world for that matter), the region from Northern California to southern British Columbia has produced by far the most incidents. Since the first settlers began arriving in this region, there have been hundreds of reports of giant footprints and handprints, as well as actual sightings of these large apelike creatures.

Among the most famous reports are that of "Jacko," a wild man captured in British Columbia in 1884. However, after the first newspaper report of this curious beast, there were no more reports. The single most famous sighting was that of two Sasquatch hunters who, in 1967, spotted Bigfoot and managed to film it on their movie camera.

If you'd like to do a bit of searching for Sasquatch, you should pick up a copy of the *Field Guide to Sasquatch* by David George Gordon (Sasquatch Books, 1992). This little book details the history of Bigfoot in the Northwest and cites various sightings over the years. It even gives tips on how to recognize Sasquatch footprints and what to do if you should have a Bigfoot encounter. Also well worth reading is Robert Michael Pyle's *Where Bigfoot Walks: Crossing the Dark Divide* (Houghton Mifflin, 1997), which documents Pyle's explorations of the Bigfoot legend in Washington's southern Cascades.

and west sides of the monument. However, this area offers some good hiking and a couple of very interesting volcanic features. The first of these features you'll come to is the **Ape Cave,** a lava tube that was formed 1,900 years ago when lava poured from the volcano. When the lava finally stopped flowing, it left a 2-mile-long (3km) cave that is the longest continuous lava tube in the Western Hemisphere. At the Ape's Headquarters, you can join a regular ranger-led exploration of the cave or rent a lantern for exploring the cave on your own. This center is open daily from late May to early September.

Of the trails on this side of the monument, the **Lava Canyon Trail** is the most fascinating. It follows a canyon that was unearthed by a mudflow that swept down this side of the mountain after the eruption.

On Wash. 503, the road leading to the south side of the monument, you'll find, in the town of Ariel, the **Lelooska Foundation** ⭐⭐, 165 Merwin Village Rd. (© **360/231-4454** or 360/225-9522; www.lelooska.com). Something of a Native American cultural center, this combination museum and art gallery features Native American arts and crafts from around the country, though the emphasis is on the work of northwest artists. This is one of the finest Native American galleries in the state. Additionally, one Saturday evening each month in the spring and fall, there are performances of traditional Northwest Coast Native American masked dances, which are accompanied by traditional story-telling. The performances are held in a reproduction of a traditional cedar long-house. Tickets are $8.50 for adults and $7 for children 12 and under.

CLIMBING THE MOUNTAIN

If you are an experienced hiker in good physical condition, you may want to consider climbing to the top of Mount St. Helens. It is an 8- to 10-hour, 10-mile (16km) hike and can require an ice ax. Permits are required year-round, and between April 1 and October 31 there is a fee of $15 per person for these permits. Because this is a very popular climb (summer weekends book up months in advance), it is advisable to make a reservation (© **360/247-3961**); reservations are accepted beginning February 1. However, if you don't have a reservation, you can try your luck by stopping by **Jack's Restaurant and Store** on Wash. 503, 5 miles (8km) west of the town of Cougar. Each evening at 6pm (arrive 15 min. early to get your name into the lottery), this store has a lottery of climbing permits for the next day. Between November 1 and March 31, when permits are free and reservations aren't necessary, you can expect lots of snow. The trail head is on the south side of the monument. A $5 Northwest Forest Pass (which can also be obtained at Jack's) is required for parking at the trail head.

A FEW UNIQUE WAYS TO SEE THE NATIONAL MONUMENT

If you'd like a bird's-eye view of the volcano, you can take a **helicopter flight** from the Hoffstadt Bluffs Visitor Center (© **360/274-7750**), $99 per person. Alternatively, you can go up in a small plane with **C&C Aviation** (© **800/516-6969** or 503/760-6969; www.ccavn.com), which flies out of the Evergreen Airport in Vancouver, Washington ($77 per person; two-person minimum). **Mount St. Helens Tours** (© **360/274-6542;** www.ecoparkresort.com) offers van tours ($60 per person; three-person minimum) that are narrated by survivors of the big blast.

To turn your visit into an educational experience, sign up for a seminar with the **Mount St. Helens Institute,** P.O. Box 820762, Vancouver, WA 98682 (© **360/891-5095;** www.mountsthelensinstitute.org).

WHERE TO STAY

There aren't too many noteworthy accommodations in this neck of the woods due in part to the fact that so many people visiting Mount St. Helens do so as a day trip from Portland. However, you will find a couple of basic motels at the Castle Rock exit off I-5 (the exit for the Spirit Lake Hwy.). These include the **Timberland Inn & Suites,** 1271 Mt. St. Helens Way NE (© **360/274-6002**), and the **Mt. St. Helens Motel,** 1340 Mt. St. Helens Way NE (© **360/274-7721**).

Blue Heron Inn Bed & Breakfast ⭐⭐ Although this modern inn on the road to the Coldwater and Johnston Ridge visitor centers calls itself a bed-and-breakfast, it also serves dinner, which makes it an excellent choice if you're searching for comfort and convenience in this area. Set on 5 acres of land across the highway from Silver Lake and Sequest State Park, the inn has an excellent view of Mount St. Helens. Lots of decks provide plenty of places for relaxing and soaking up the view, and during cooler weather, you can sit by the fire in the parlor. This inn is by far the best bet for accommodations in the area and is close to the Mount St. Helens Visitor Center.

2846 Spirit Lake Hwy., Castle Rock, WA 98611. ℭ 800/959-4049 or 360/274-9595. www.blueheroninn.com. 7 units. $185–$235 double (Nov–Apr 2nd night is half price). Rates include full dinner and breakfast. DISC, MC, V. *In room:* A/C, TV, hair dryer.

Mount St. Helens Adventures Tours Eco-Park and Tent & Breakfast ⭐ *(Kids)*   This company's tented camp located inside the blast zone (though outside the monument) is by far the most unusual accommodation in the vicinity of Mount St. Helens. The large safari-style tents are set up on the shore of a small lake amid the devastation wrought when the volcano blew its top. The camp is down a former logging road on private property and guests are transported there by van. The Eco-Park, on the other hand, is right on Wash. 504 (at the above address) and can be reached by personal vehicle. This lodging consists of modern cabins and tent cabins. Logger dinner shows ($15.95) are also staged here at the Eco-Park during the summer.

14000 Spirit Lake Hwy. (P.O. Box 149), Toutle, WA 98649. ℭ 360/274-6542. Fax 360/274-5731. www.eco parkresort.com. 5 tents at Tent & Breakfast, 6 cabins at Eco-Park. Tent & Breakfast $285 double (rates include dinner, breakfast, and transportation); Eco-Park cabins $60–$70 double. MC, V. Pets accepted in cabins ($10). **Amenities:** Restaurant (American); activities desk. *In room:* No phone.

CAMPGROUNDS

West of the monument, **Sequest State Park** (88 campsites), set amid impressive old-growth trees on Wash. 504 about 5 miles (8km) off I-5, is the closest public campground to Coldwater Ridge. This campground is set on Silver Lake adjacent to the Mount St. Helens Visitor Center. For reservations, contact **Washington State Parks Reservations** (ℭ 888/226-7688; www.parks.wa.gov).

East of the monument, **Iron Creek** ⭐ (98 campsites), a Forest Service campground, is the closest to Windy Ridge. This campground is set amid old-growth trees on the bank of the Cispus River.

South of the monument, there are a couple of conveniently located campgrounds on Yale Lake—**Cougar** (60 campsites) and **Beaver Bay** (78 campsites)—and, at the east end of Swift Reservoir, **Swift** (93 campsites). For more tranquillity, try little **Merrill Lake** (7 campsites), which is operated by the Washington Department of Natural Resources. Although a bit out of the way for exploring the monument, the **Lower Falls Recreation Area** ⭐⭐ (42 campsites) on the Lewis River is a beautiful spot set beside the waterfalls for which it is named. For information on national forest campgrounds in the area, contact the **Cowlitz Valley Ranger District,** 10024 U.S. 12 (P.O. Box 670), Randle, WA 98377 (ℭ 360/497-1100; www.fs.fed.us/r6/gpnf). For national forest campground reservations, contact the **National Recreation Reservation Service** (ℭ 800/280-CAMP; www.reserveusa.com).

WHERE TO DINE

There aren't a whole lot of dining options in the vicinity of the monument, but not to be missed are the berry cobblers served at the **19 Mile House,** 9440 Spirit Lake Hwy., Toutle (ℭ 360/274-8779), which is 19 miles (31km) up the Spirit Lake Highway (Wash. 504) and is open from April or May until October.

They've got good burgers here, too. Other options include the **Mount St. Helens Restaurant** at the Hoffstadt Bluffs Visitor Center (Spirit Lake Hwy. milepost 27) and the restaurant at the Coldwater Ridge Visitor Center (Spirit Lake Hwy. milepost 43).

9 The Columbia Gorge & the Mount Adams Area

Stevenson: 45 miles (72km) E of Vancouver, 25 miles (40km) W of White Salmon

The Columbia Gorge, which begins a few miles east of Vancouver, Washington, and extends eastward for nearly 70 miles (113km), cuts through the Cascade Range and connects the rain-soaked west-side forests with the sagebrush scrublands of eastern Washington. This change in climate is caused by moist air condensing into snow and rain as it passes over the crest of the Cascades. Most of the air's moisture falls on the western slopes, so that the eastern slopes and the land stretching for hundreds of miles beyond lie in what's called a rain shadow. Perhaps nowhere else on earth can you witness this rain-shadow effect so clearly. Between the two extremes lies a community of plants that's unique to the Columbia Gorge. Springtime in the gorge sees colorful displays of wildflowers, many of which occur naturally only here in the Columbia Gorge.

The Columbia River is older than the hills. It's older than the mountains, too. And it's this great age that accounts for the river's dramatic gorge through the Cascades. The mountains have actually risen up *around* the river. Although the river's geologic history dates back 40 million years or so, it was a series of recent events, geologically speaking, that gave the Columbia Gorge its very distinctive appearance. About 15,000 years ago, toward the end of the last Ice Age, in what is now Montana, huge glacial ice dams burst and sent floodwaters racing down the Columbia. As the floodwaters swept through the Columbia Gorge, they were as much as 1,200 feet high. Ice and rock carried by the floodwaters helped the river scour out the sides of the once gently sloping valley, leaving behind the steep-walled gorge that we know today. The waterfalls that elicit so many oohs and aahs are the most dramatic evidence of these great floods. As early as 1915 a scenic highway was built through the gorge and in 1986 much of the area was designated the **Columbia Gorge National Scenic Area** to preserve its spectacular and unique natural beauty.

While the Oregon side of the Columbia Gorge has the spectacular waterfalls and tends to get all the publicity, it is actually from the Washington side, along **Wash. 14 (Columbia River Scenic Highway)**, that you get the best views. From this highway the views take in both the southern wall of the Columbia Gorge and the snowcapped summit of Mount Hood. It is also on the Washington side of the Gorge, in Stevenson, that you'll find the informative Columbia Gorge Interpretive Center.

Roughly 45 miles (72km) north of White Salmon rises Mount Adams, which, at 12,276 feet in elevation, is the second highest peak in Washington. However, because it is so inaccessible from Puget Sound and can't be seen from most of Portland (the nearest metropolitan area), it remains one of the least visited major peaks in the state. Though few get to this massive peak, those who do often make the strenuous, though nontechnical, climb to the mountain's summit.

ESSENTIALS

GETTING THERE   Wash. 14 parallels the Columbia River from Vancouver through the Columbia Gorge and into eastern Washington. Mount Adams lies to the north of the Gorge and is accessed via Wash. 141 from White Salmon.

VISITOR INFORMATION   For more information on the Columbia Gorge, contact the **Columbia River Gorge National Scenic Area,** 902 Wasco Ave., Suite 200, Hood River, OR 97031 (℃ **541/386-2333;** www.fs.fed.us/r6/ columbia). There's also a **Forest Service Information Center** in the lobby of **Skamania Lodge,** 1131 SW Skamania Lodge Dr. (℃ **509/427-2528**), in Stevenson, Washington. Information is also available from the **Skamania County Chamber of Commerce,** P.O. Box 1037, Stevenson, WA 98648 (℃ **800/989-9178** or 509/427-8911; www.skamania.org). For detailed information on the Oregon side of the Columbia Gorge, see *Frommer's Oregon.*

AN INTRODUCTION TO THE GORGE

Columbia Gorge Interpretive Center ★★   This museum in Stevenson, Washington, is the best introduction to the Columbia Gorge; the museum focuses on the Gorge's early Native American inhabitants and the development of the area by white settlers. Exhibits contain historical photographs by Edward Curtis and other photos that illustrate the story of portage companies and paddle-wheelers that once operated along this stretch of the Columbia River. Period quotations and explanations of Gorge history put the museum's many artifacts in their proper context. A relic you can't miss is a 37-foot-high replica of a 19th-century fish wheel, which gives an understanding of how salmon runs have been threatened in the past and the present. Displays also frankly discuss other problems that the coming of civilization brought to this area. A slide program tells the history of the formation of the Gorge, and when the volcanoes erupt, the floor in the theater actually shakes from the intensity of the low-volume sound track. When it's not cloudy, the center has an awesome view of the south side of the Gorge.

990 SW Rock Creek Dr., Stevenson. ℃ 509/427-8211. www.columbiagorge.org. Admission $6 adults, $5 seniors and students, $4 children 6–12, free for children 5 and under. Daily 10am–5pm. Closed Thanksgiving, Dec 25, and Jan 1.

EXPLORING THE GORGE

Heading east from Vancouver, Wash. 14 passes through the industrial towns of Camas and Washougal before finally breaking free of the Portland/Vancouver metropolitan area. For much of the way, the highway stays close to the river, but at Cape Horn, an area where basalt cliffs rise straight out of the water, the highway climbs high above the river, providing one of the best views along this stretch of the highway. Several pull-offs let you stop and enjoy the views.

Roughly 35 miles (56km) east of Vancouver, you come to **Beacon Rock,** an 800-foot-tall monolith that has a 1-mile (1.5km) trail to its summit. The trail, which for much of the way consists of metal stairways and catwalks, was built between 1915 and 1918 by Henry Biddle, who saved Beacon Rock from being blasted into rubble for a jetty at the mouth of the Columbia River. Continuing east, you'll come to Stevenson, which is the site of the above-mentioned Columbia Gorge Interpretive Center.

Beyond Stevenson, you come to the town of Carson, where you can avail yourself of the therapeutic waters of the **Carson Hot Springs Resort** (℃ **800/ 607-3678** or 509/427-8292), located just north of town. It's open daily from 7:30am to 7:30pm; charges are $12 for a soak that includes a postsoak wrap and $55 for an hour's massage. The resort has been in business since 1897 and looks every bit its age. However, it's just this old-fashioned appeal that keeps people coming back year after year to soak in the hot mineral springs (separate men's and women's soaking tubs) and get massaged. Some very basic hotel rooms

($35–$45) and cabins ($45–$60) are also available. If you're looking for natural hot springs, the folks here can give you directions to some that are nearby.

If you're up for a strenuous but rewarding hike, the 3-mile (5km) trail to the summit of 2,948-foot **Dog Mountain** provides ample views up and down the Gorge. In spring, the wildflower displays in the meadows on Dog Mountain's slopes are some of the finest in the Gorge. You'll find the trail head on Wash. 14, 12 miles (19km) east of the Bridge of the Gods, a bridge that now spans the river at a site where a huge landslide once blocked the Columbia, creating a natural "bridge" across the river.

For a less strenuous, though no less scenic hike, drive 5 miles (8km) east of Bingen and turn left onto Rowland Lake Road. In just over a mile, you'll come to the gravel roadside parking area for the **Catherine Creek** area. On the south side of the road, there is a 1¼-mile (2km) paved path that leads to several view-points. On the north side, there is an unpaved trail that leads up through the Catherine Creek canyon and connects to trails that climb up into the hills. Keep an eye out for poison oak.

THE MOUNT ADAMS AREA

While Mount Adams's summit is popular with mountain climbers, at lower elevations there are also excellent trails for hikers and backpackers. The favorite summer spot for a hike is **Bird Creek Meadows** on the Yakama Indian Reservation north of the town of Trout Lake. These meadows are ablaze with wild-flowers in July. Eight miles west of Trout Lake, you can explore several **ice caves.** The caves were formed by lava flows centuries ago. For more information on hiking on Mount Adams, contact the **Gifford Pinchot National Forest,** Mt. Adams Ranger District, 2455 Wash. 141, Trout Lake, WA 98650 (© **509/ 395-3400;** www.fs.fed.us/r6/gpnf/).

THE EAST END OF THE GORGE

Between The Dalles Dam and the town of Goldendale (north of Wash. 14 on U.S. 97), there are a few unusual attractions that are well worth a visit if you are exploring down at this eastern end of the Gorge. In addition to the attractions listed here, you'll also find three wineries. **Maryhill Winery,** 9774 Hwy. 14, Maryhill (© **877/627-9445;** www.maryhillwinery.com), has the best view of any winery in the Northwest and also produces some very good wines. **Cascade Cliffs Vineyard & Winery,** milepost 88.6, Hwy. 14, Wishram (© **509/767-1100**), is set at the foot of 400-foot-tall basalt cliffs and produces, among other wines, Nebbiolo and Barbera. **Marshal's Winery,** 150 Oak Creek Rd., Dallesport (© **509/767-4633**), which is located 2 miles (3km) up a gravel road, is a tiny family-run winery that produces some of Washington's smoothest Cabernet Sauvignons and Merlots, as well as some unusual sweet wines.

Horsethief Lake State Park ★ *Finds*   Located between The Dalles Dam and Wishram on Wash. 14, Horsethief Lake is a popular fishing area and camp-ground. However, long before the area was designated a state park, this was a gathering ground for Native Americans. The park lies not far from the famous Celilo Falls, which were, before being inundated by the waters behind The Dalles Dam, the most prolific salmon-fishing area in the Northwest. Each year for thousands of years Native Americans would gather here from all over the Northwest. These Native Americans left signs of their annual visits, in the form of petroglyphs, on rocks that are now protected within this park. Petroglyphs abound here, the most famous of which is Tsagaglalal ("she who watches"), which is a large face that gazes down on the Columbia River. Due to past vandalism, the only way to see this and other park petroglyphs is on ranger-led walks held on Friday and Saturday mornings at 10am. Reservations for these walks should be made at least 2 to 3 weeks in advance.

Wash. 14. 𝒞 509/767-1159. Free admission. Apr–Oct daily 6:30am–dusk. Closed Nov–Mar.

Maryhill Museum of Art/Stonehenge Monument ★★ *Finds* Between 1914 and 1926, atop a remote windswept bluff overlooking the Columbia River, eccentric entrepreneur Sam Hill built a grand mansion he called Maryhill. Though he never lived in the mansion, he did turn it into a museum that today is one of the finest, most eclectic, and least visited of the state's major museums. There is an acclaimed collection of sculptures and drawings by Auguste Rodin. An extensive collection of Native American artifacts includes the finest display of baskets in the state. Furniture, jewelry, and other items that once belonged to Hill's friend Queen Marie of Romania, are also on display, as are a collection of miniature French fashion mannequins from just after World War II. Note that the Rodins and fashion mannequins are sometimes loaned out to other museums. The lush grounds surrounding the museum have sculptures, picnic tables, and plenty of shade trees, making this an ideal spot for a picnic lunch (there's also a cafe inside the museum). A few miles east of Maryhill, stands Hill's concrete reproduction of Stonehenge, which he had built as a memorial to local men who died in World War I.

35 Maryhill Museum Dr. (Wash. 14). 𝒞 509/773-3733. www.maryhillmuseum.org. Admission $7 adults, $6 seniors, $2 children 6–12. Mar 15–Nov 15 daily 9am–5pm. Closed Nov 16–Mar 14.

Goldendale Observatory State Park Interpretive Center ★ If you happen to be an amateur astronomer, you won't want to miss a visit to the Goldendale Observatory. The central 24½-inch reflector is one of the largest public telescopes in the country—large enough for scientific research—but instead, it's dedicated to sharing the stars with the general public. The observatory is out in this remote part of the state because this region's dry weather and distance from city lights almost guarantees that every night will be a good night for stargazing.

1602 Observatory Dr., Goldendale. 𝒞 509/773-3141. Admission by donation. Apr–Sept Wed–Sun 2–5pm and 8pm–midnight; Oct–Mar Sat 1–5pm and 7–9pm, Sun 1–5pm.

SPORTS & OUTDOOR ACTIVITIES

The Columbia Gorge is one of the nation's top boardsailing spots, and if you're here to ride the wind, or just want to watch others as they race back and forth across the river, head to the **fish hatchery,** west of the mouth of the White Salmon River, or **Swell City,** a park about 3 miles (5km) west of the Hood River Bridge. **Bob's Beach,** in downtown Stevenson, is another popular spot.

When there isn't enough wind for sailing, there's still the option to go **rafting** on the White Salmon River. Companies offering raft trips on this river include **Zoller's Outdoor Odysseys** (𝒞 800/366-2004; www.zooraft.com), **AAA Rafting** (𝒞 800/866-RAFT or 509/493-2511), and **Renegade River Rafters** (𝒞 509/427-RAFT). The river-rafting season runs March through October, and a half-day trip will cost around $60 per person.

If you're interested in a bit of horseback riding, contact **Northwestern Lake Riding Stable** (𝒞 509/493-4965; www.nwstables.com), which is at Northwestern Lake off Wash. 141 north of White Salmon. A 1-hour ride is $20.

WHERE TO STAY
IN STEVENSON

Dolce Skamania Lodge ★★★   Boasting the most spectacular vistas of any hotel in the Gorge, Skamania Lodge is also the only golf resort in the area. Although golf is the preferred sport here, the hotel is well situated whether you brought your sailboard, hiking boots, or mountain bike. The interior decor is classically rustic with lots of rock and natural wood, and throughout the hotel there are Northwest Indian artworks and artifacts on display. Huge windows in the lobby take in a superb view of the Gorge. Of course, the river-view guest rooms are more expensive than the forest-view rooms (which overlook more parking lot than forest), but these rooms are well worth the extra cost. There are also rooms with fireplaces available. The lodge was planning to add 59 new rooms at press time, so you might want to request one of these new rooms.

P.O. Box 189, Stevenson, WA 98648. ✆ **800/221-7117** or 509/427-7700. www.dolce.com/skamania. 253 units. $169–$199 double; $239–$385 suite (lower rates in winter). AE, DC, DISC, MC, V. **Amenities:** Restaurant (Northwest); lounge; indoor pool; 18-hole golf course; 2 unlit outdoor tennis courts; exercise room; Jacuzzi; sauna; bike rentals; children's programs; activities desk; business center; room service (daily 6–10am); massage; babysitting; laundry service. In room: A/C, TV, dataport, minibar, coffeemaker, hair dryer, iron.

IN LYLE

Lyle Hotel ★ (Finds)   Located at the east end of the Gorge in the tiny town of Lyle, this old-fashioned hotel first opened for business in 1905. Today the rooms, though small and lacking private bathrooms, have a cozy, traditional feel, with quilts on the old wood or brass beds. Large windows let in lots of light. Best of all, there is an excellent restaurant on the ground floor, which makes this your best base for exploring the eastern end of the Gorge.

Seventh St. and Lyle Ave. (P.O. Box 114), Lyle, WA 98635. ✆ **509/365-5953.** Fax 509/365-2668. www.lyle hotel.com. 10 units, all with shared bathrooms. $59 double. Rates include continental breakfast Mon–Sat. AE, MC, V. **Amenities:** Restaurant (International); lounge. In room: No phone.

IN GLENWOOD

Flying L Ranch ★   With its meadows and ponderosa pines, this 160-acre ranch in a wide valley at the foot of Mount Adams is the ideal base for exploring this area. In summer, you can head up to the alpine meadows on the slopes of the mountain, and in winter, there are cross-country ski trails on the ranch and also nearby. While the two cabins, tucked under the pine trees, offer lots of room and privacy, the rooms in the old 1940s lodge have a classic ranch feel. Other rooms are in a separate guesthouse with a rooftop observation deck. The hot tub has a view of the mountain.

25 Flying L Lane, Glenwood, WA 98619. ✆ **888/682-3267** or 509/364-3488. Fax 509/364-3634. www.mt adams.com. 14 units, 11 with private bathroom. $70 double with shared bathroom, $85–$110 double with private bathroom; $120–$140 cabin. Rates include full breakfast. AE, MC, V. **Amenities:** Jacuzzi; bikes. In room: No phone.

IN HOOD RIVER, OREGON

Columbia Gorge Hotel ★★   Located just west of the town of River off I-84 and opened shortly after the Columbia River Scenic Highway was completed in 1915, this little oasis of luxury offers the same genteel atmosphere that was once enjoyed by the likes of Rudolph Valentino and Clark Gable. With its yellow-stucco walls and red-tile roofs, this hotel would be right at home in Beverly Hills, and the hotel gardens could hold their own in Victoria, British Columbia. However, despite the attractive furnishings and gardens, it is almost impossible to notice anything but the view from the windows. The hotel is perched more

than 200 feet above the river on a steep cliff. Guest rooms are all a little different, with a mixture of antiques and classic furnishings. There are canopy beds,
brass beds, and even some hand-carved wooden beds. Unfortunately, many of
the rooms are rather cramped, as are the bathrooms, most of which have older
fixtures. However, some rooms have soaking tubs and fireplaces.

4000 Westcliff Dr., Hood River, OR 97031. © 800/345-1921 or 541/386-5566. Fax 541/387-5414. www.
columbiagorgehotel.com. 39 units. $169–$279 double. Rates include multicourse breakfast. AE, DC, DISC,
MC, V. Pets accepted with $25 fee per night. **Amenities:** Restaurant (Northwest/Continental); lounge;
concierge; room service (daily 7–11am); massage. *In room:* A/C, TV, dataport, hair dryer, iron, safe.

WHERE TO DINE
IN STEVENSON

The dining room of **Dolce Skamania Lodge** (see above for details) is by far the
best restaurant on the Washington side of the Gorge. There are also quite a few
good restaurants across the river in Hood River, Oregon, including the following:

Sixth Street Bistro ★★ AMERICAN/INTERNATIONAL   Located just a
block off Oak Street toward the river, the Sixth Street Bistro has an intimate
little dining room and patio on the lower floor and a lounge with a balcony on
the second floor. Both have their own entrance, but they share the same menu
so there's a choice of ambience. There are numerous international touches, such
as chicken satay, pad Thai, and hummus, and also plenty of juicy burgers and
interesting pasta dishes, including house-made ravioli that changes daily. You'll
also find seasonal specials and plenty of vegetarian dishes as well.

509 Cascade Ave. © **541/386-5737.** Reservations recommended. Main courses $9–$20. MC, V. Daily
11:30am–10pm.

Stonehedge Inn ★★ CONTINENTAL   Built as a summer vacation home
in 1898, the Stonehedge Inn is located in the woods west of downtown Hood
River and is down a long gravel driveway off Cascade Drive. When you finally
find the restaurant, you'll feel as though you've arrived at a remote Maine woods
lodge. Inside the old home, there's a small lounge with a bar taken from an old
tavern, and several dining rooms, all of which have a genuinely old-time feel.
Although the entree menu sticks to traditional Continental dishes such as steak
Diane, rack of lamb, and chicken cordon bleu, you'll find some more creative
offerings, such as grilled goat cheese with roasted garlic or seared ahi tuna.
Whatever you order, be sure to save room for the unusual bread pudding.
New owners have been upgrading the restaurant and have added a huge patio
dining area.

3405 Cascade Dr. © **541/386-3940.** Reservations recommended. Main courses $10–$27. AE, DISC, MC, V.
Daily 5–8 or 9pm.

10

Eastern Washington

For many people who live on the wet west side of the Cascades, life in Washington would be nearly impossible if it were not for the sunny east side of the mountains. Eastern Washington lies in the rain shadow of the Cascades, and many parts of the region receive less than 10 inches of rain per year. The lack of rain is also accompanied by plenty of sunshine—an average of 300 days per year. Statistics like these prove irresistible to folks from Puget Sound, who often head over to eastern Washington to dry out.

Though there's little rainfall, rivers such as the Columbia, which meanders through much of this region, have provided, with the assistance of dams such as the huge Grand Coulee Dam, sufficient irrigation water to make the region a major agricultural area. Apples, pears, cherries, wine grapes (and wine), wheat, and potatoes have become the staple crops of a land that once grew little more than sagebrush and bunchgrass. The Columbia River was also responsible thousands of years ago for creating the region's most fascinating geological wonders—a dry waterfall that was once four times larger than Niagara Falls and abandoned riverbeds known as coulees.

Down in the southeastern corner of the state, near the college and wheat-farming town of Walla Walla, the desert gives way to the Blue Mountains. It was near here that the region's first white settlers, Marcus and Narcissa Whitman, set up a mission in order to convert Native Americans to Christianity. They were later massacred by Cayuse Indians angered by the Whitmans' inability to cure a measles epidemic. In recent years, Walla Walla has become Washington's fastest-growing winery region. To the north of Walla Walla lie the Palouse Hills, a scenic region of rolling hills that are blanketed with the most productive wheat farms in the United States.

Though Yakima attracts sunseekers from the western part of the state, it is Spokane, at the far eastern end of the state only a few miles from Idaho, that is the region's largest city. With its proximity to forests and mountains and its setting on the banks of the Spokane River, it appeals to those who value outdoor activities. The city's far easterly location, however, makes it seem less a part of the Northwest and more a part of the Rocky Mountain states.

1 Ellensburg: A Glimpse of the Wild West

110 miles (177km) SE of Seattle, 36 miles (58km) N of Yakima, 75 miles (121km) S of Wenatchee

Ellensburg, which lies on the edge of cattle- and sheep-ranching country just east of the last Cascade foothills, is a town with a split personality. On the one hand, it is a small college town, site of Central Washington University. However, it is also a classic cow town best known as the site of the Ellensburg Rodeo, one of the West's top rodeos. A downtown full of historic commercial buildings further adds to the character of this town, and proximity to the mountains and ski area at Snoqualmie Pass make it a good base for summer hiking or winter skiing. Although the town isn't really a destination per se, its proximity to Seattle and its sunny climate make it a quick escape from the Puget Sound rains.

Most of the buildings in the town's downtown historic district, one of the most attractive in the state, date from 1889, the year in which most of the town's commercial buildings were destroyed in a fire on the Fourth of July. Had it not been for this fire, the town would likely have become the state capital (due to its central location). But with only one commercial building remaining, how could the government set up business in Ellensburg? Instead of becoming the capital, the town became the site of the state college that is now Central Washington University.

While the Ellensburg Rodeo is responsible for perpetuating this town's Wild West image, the Clymer Museum, devoted to the works of John Clymer, who illustrated more than 80 *Saturday Evening Post* magazine covers, does its share as well. Adding one last unusual ingredient to the eclectic milieu of Ellensburg is the Chimpanzee and Human Communication Institute, where chimps have been taught to use American Sign Language.

ESSENTIALS

GETTING THERE   Ellensburg is on I-90. Just east of town, I-82 leads southeast to Yakima and the Tri-Cities area (Wash. 821 provides a scenic route south to Yakima). U.S. 97 leads north over Blewett Pass to Leavenworth and Wenatchee.

VISITOR INFORMATION   Contact the **Ellensburg Chamber of Commerce,** 609 N. Main St., Ellensburg, WA 98926 (© **888/925-2204** or 509/925-3138; www.ellensburg-chamber.com or http://ellensburg.ws).

FESTIVALS   The third weekend of May each year sees the annual Western Art Association's **National Western Art Show & Auction** (© **509/962-2934**), which features works by some of the nation's finest Western artists. The annual Ellensburg Rodeo, held each year on Labor Day weekend, is the town's biggest event and is one of the top 10 rodeos in the United States. For more information, contact the **Ellensburg Rodeo and Kittitas County Fair,** 712 S. Main St. (© **800/637-2444** or 509/962-7831; http://ellensburgrodeo.com). On the last weekend in July, the city stages its annual **Jazz in the Valley** (© **509/925-4443** or 509/925-2002) festival, a 3-day binge of jazz and blues.

EXPLORING THE TOWN

Ellensburg's most unusual attraction can be experienced at the university's **Chimpanzee and Human Communication Institute,** Nicholson Boulevard and D Street (© **509/963-2244;** www.cwu.edu/~cwuchci), a research facility that stages what it calls **"Chimposiums."** At these programs, visitors learn about the primate communication project and get to observe several chimpanzees that have learned to use American Sign Language (ASL). Among these chimps is the famous Washoe, which was the first chimpanzee to learn ASL. The programs, held on Saturday and Sunday, cost $10 for adults and $7.50 for students; reservations are recommended.

The Western art of Ellensburg native John Clymer is displayed at the **Clymer Museum of Art,** 416 N. Pearl St. (© **509/962-6416;** www.clymermuseum. com). A member of the prestigious Cowboy Artists of America, Clymer is best known for producing more than 80 *Saturday Evening Post* covers. The museum is open Monday through Thursday from 10am to 5pm, Friday from 10am to

Eastern Washington

The Gorge at George

Although it is roughly 150 miles (242km) from Seattle to the community of George, Washington, the town each summer attracts tens of thousands of music fans who drive from Seattle and all over the Northwest to attend concerts (primarily rock) at a natural amphitheater overlooking the Columbia River. **The Gorge Amphitheatre,** 754 Silica Rd. NW, George (© **206/464-2000,** ext. 7469; www.hob.com/venues/concerts/gorge), is in a spectacular setting that's surrounded by basalt cliffs.

8pm, and Saturday and Sunday from noon to 5pm; admission by donation. In this same block you'll find Ellensburg's oldest art gallery. **Gallery One,** 408½ N. Pearl St. (© **509/925-2670**), features works by regional, national, and international artists. More art can be seen at the **Sarah Spurgeon Art Gallery,** Randall Hall (© **509/963-2665**), on the campus of Central Washington University. This gallery is open Monday through Friday from 8:30am to 4:30pm and Saturday and Sunday from noon to 3pm; admission is free. For a look at some unique local art, cruise by **Dick & Jane's Spot,** 101 N. Pearl Street. The house and yard here are decorated with hundreds of colorful objects, including thousands of little reflective disks. However, the town's most famous work of art is the *Ellensburg Bull,* a cement statue that sits on a bench in a plaza in the downtown historic district.

Downtown you'll also find the **Kittitas County Museum,** 114 E. Third St. (© **509/925-3778**), which has an interesting collection of Native American artifacts, as well as a large rock and mineral collection that focuses on petrified wood. May through September, the museum is open Monday through Saturday from 10am to 4pm (other months, it's open Tues–Sat noon–4pm). Admission is by donation.

If you want to shop for some of the region's rare Ellensburg blue agate, stop by the **Ellensburg Agate Shop,** 201 S. Main St. (© **509/925-4998**). *Be forewarned:* This pale blue semiprecious stone can be quite pricey.

Some 4½ miles (7.5km) southeast of town you'll find **Olmstead Place State Park** (© **509/925-1943**), a heritage site that preserves a pioneer homestead of the 1870s. Northwest of Ellensburg at exit 101 off I-90, in the town of Thorp, is the **Thorp Mill** (© **509/964-9640;** www.thorp.org), an 1880s gristmill that now houses a museum; it's open Wednesday through Sunday from 1 to 4pm from Memorial Day weekend to the end of September.

Anyone wanting to cool off on a hot summer day should make for the waters of the nearby Yakima River, which offers lots of easy floating. **Rill Adventures,** 10471 Thorp Hwy. North (© **888/281-1561** or 509/964-2520), rents rafts, with prices ranging from $60 to $90 per day. The section of this river south of town, through Yakima Canyon, is a popular stretch of river with tubers and canoeists, and is a favorite of fly anglers as well.

WHERE TO STAY

The Inn at Goose Creek ✪   Located just off I-90 on the south side of Ellensburg, this inn is sort of a cross between a highway off-ramp motel and a bed-and-breakfast inn. Though it's in a nondescript building surrounded by gas stations and fast-food restaurants, it keeps all this at bay with the over-the-top modern country decor in the lobby. All of the 10 suites here are also decorated to the max and each has a different theme (Ellensburg Rodeo, Victorian, Sports Fan, Christmas). There are down comforters on all the beds, and all the rooms have whirlpool tubs.

1720 Canyon Rd., Ellensburg, WA 98926. (℃ **800/533-0822** or 509/962-8030. Fax 509/962-8031. www.inn atgoosecreek.com. 10 units. Apr–Oct $99–$115 double; Nov–Mar $89–$109 double. Rates include continental breakfast. AE, MC, V. *In room:* A/C, TV, dataport, fridge, coffeemaker, hair dryer, iron.

WHERE TO DINE

If you're in need of some espresso, pull up a saddle at the Cowboy Espresso Bar inside **Jaguar's,** 423 N. Pearl St. (℃ **509/962-6081**), a Western-clothing store. Alternatively, you can drive up to the window at **D & M Coffee,** 408 S. Main St. (℃ **509/962-6333**), which is located in a 1920s gas station, or step inside **D&M Coffee,** Third and Pine streets (℃ **509/962-9333**), which is in a building that was once a gas station. If you're looking for a place to hang out and have a beer or glass of wine, check out **Pearl's on Pearl,** 311 N. Pearl St. (℃ **509/ 962-8899**), a smoke-free bar that has live jazz, blues, and rock and attracts Ellensburg professionals and professors.

Valley Café ✿ *Finds* INTERNATIONAL   Behind the shining black glass facade of this easily overlooked vintage cafe, you'll find a classic 1930s diner straight out of an Edward Hopper painting. Take a seat in one of the wooden booths and you'll swear you've stepped back in time. The menu, however, is quite contemporary and features such dishes as herb-rubbed lamb chops, chicken with spicy peanut sauce, and cioppino. At lunch, meals are just as likely to range the globe. Lots of local wines are available.

105 W. Third St. (℃ **509/925-3050**. Main courses $9–$21.50. AE, DISC, DC, MC, V. Sun–Thurs 11am–9pm; Fri–Sat 11am–9 or 10pm (closes earlier in winter).

The Yellow Church Cafe ✿ AMERICAN   Though primarily an inexpensive college lunch place, this restaurant is well worth checking out for its setting in a renovated little yellow church that was built back in 1923. Saturday and Sunday breakfasts are among the most popular meals here, and the baked goods are hot items. Pastas and salads are good, and the dinner menu includes inexpensive steaks and prawn dishes that are usually good bets. However, throughout the week there are always interesting specials listed on the blackboard. If you can't find a table on the main floor, check up in the choir loft.

111 S. Pearl St. (℃ **509/933-2233**. www.yellowchurchcafe.com. Main courses $4.50–$8 at lunch, $9–$14 at dinner. AE, MC, V. Mon–Fri 11am–8pm; Sat–Sun 7am–8pm.

2 Yakima & the Wine Country

150 miles (242km) SE of Seattle, 92 miles (148km) NW of Richland, 195 miles (314km) SW of Spokane

Considering the fact that Washington is notorious for its rainfall, it may seem hard to believe that eastern Washington's Yakima Valley receives only about 8 inches of rain per year. Located only 3 hours from Seattle, Yakima is in another world—the sunny side of the Cascades. Despite the lack of rainfall, the area has become one of Washington's main apple-growing regions. Hops, used in making beer, are another important crop in the Yakima Valley, but it is grapes and the wines produced from those grapes that have been bringing the valley international attention in recent years. On a visit to Yakima, you can sample the area's bounties at fruit stands, wineries, and microbreweries.

The city of Yakima lies at the western end of the Yakima Valley winery region, while at the eastern end is the Tri-Cities area, which is comprised of the cities of Richland, Kennewick, and Pasco. Although the Tri-Cities area has its share of wineries, it is best known as the site of the Hanford Site, the huge military reservation where the first nuclear bomb was developed. Today Hanford is notorious for its many nuclear contamination sites, which luckily are well removed from any towns or vineyards, so there's no need to worry about glow-in-the-dark wine.

All the land around Yakima was once the homeland of the Yakama people. The first white settlers, Catholic missionaries, arrived in 1847 and set up their mission south of present-day Yakima, and by the 1850s growing hostilities between settlers and Native Americans had led to the establishment of Fort Simcoe, 38 miles (61km) west of Yakima. In 1880, when residents of Yakima City refused to sell land to the Northern Pacific Railroad, the railroad built North Yakima 4 miles (6.5km) away and proceeded to move 50 buildings from Yakima City to the new town site, which grew into the Yakima of today.

Despite the many wineries up and down the Yakima Valley, the region has never really caught on as a wine-touring destination and there are very few B&Bs or memorable restaurants in the region. This is due to several factors. First, the wineries begin more than 20 miles (32km) away from Yakima, and so the city of Yakima isn't exactly an ideal base for exploring this wine country. Also, the small towns scattered along the length of the Yakima Valley are basically farm towns and are certainly not what you would call quaint. In fact Sunnyside has stockyards, the stench of which permeates the town. Vineyards are just part of the picture here, and you'll have to drive through a lot of unattractive scenery to reach the wineries. However, despite these caveats, a visit to the Yakima Valley can be worthwhile if you are looking to familiarize yourself with Washington wine.

ESSENTIALS

GETTING THERE   Yakima is on I-82 at the junction with U.S. 12, which connects to I-5 south of Centralia. U.S. 97 connects to I-84 east of The Dalles, Oregon.

The Yakima Municipal Airport, on the southern outskirts of town, is served by Horizon Airlines.

VISITOR INFORMATION   Contact the **Yakima Valley Visitors & Convention Bureau,** 10 N. Eighth St., Yakima, WA 98901 (© **800/221-0751** or 509/575-3010; www.visityakima.com). For information on Toppenish, contact the **Toppenish Chamber of Commerce,** P.O. Box 28, Toppenish, WA 98948 (© **509/865-3262**).

GETTING AROUND   If you need a taxi, contact **Cascade Cab** (© **509/ 453-3113**).

FESTIVALS   **Red Wine and Chocolate,** held each year over the Presidents' Day weekend, marks the start of the wine-tasting season at Yakima Valley wineries. The annual **Spring Barrel Tasting** in late April is Yakima's biggest wine festival. During this festival, the previous year's vintages are tasted before being bottled. **Thanksgiving in Wine Country** is another big wine-tasting weekend. Each year over the Fourth of July weekend the **Toppenish Pow Wow**

& **Rodeo** brings crowds of people to Toppenish to watch broncobusters and Native American dances. The fourth full weekend in September sees the skies over Prosser fill with hot-air balloons in the **Great Prosser Balloon Rally.**

WINE-COUNTRY TOURING

Located on the same latitude as France's main wine regions, the **Yakima Valley** is Washington's premier wine region. The valley sees sunshine on about 300 days of the year, which, combined with the rich volcanic soil, provides near perfect grape-growing conditions. The only thing missing here is rain. Central Washington is virtually a desert, but irrigation long ago overcame this minor inconvenience and today the area produces award-winning chardonnay, Riesling, chenin blanc, sauvignon blanc, semillon, Gewürztraminer, cabernet sauvignon, merlot, Lemberger, and muscat wines. Because of the clear weather here at harvest, and because freezing weather often arrives when there are still grapes on the vines, many wineries in the valley produce limited amounts of sweet and delicious ice wine, which is made from frozen berries. Quite a few wineries here are also now producing port.

The Yakima Valley wine country stretches roughly from Zillah (about 20 miles/32km east of Yakima) to the Tri-Cities area (Richland, Pasco, and Kennewick), although the Tri-Cities area is officially in a Columbia Valley appellation. You can get a guide and map of the wine country from the Yakima Valley Visitors & Convention Bureau or the **Yakima Valley Winery Association,** P.O. Box 39, Grandview, WA 98930 (© **800/258-7270;** www.yakimavalleywine. com). This map covers the area from Zillah to Benton City's Red Hills region. For a map of Tri-Cities area wineries, contact the **Columbia Valley Winery Association** (© **866/360-6611** or 509/585-0903; www.columbiavalleywine. com). However, even without a map, signs throughout the valley point the way to various vineyards and wineries, and you can just follow Yakima Valley Highway/Wine Country Road (U.S. 12) between Zillah and Prosser, dropping in at whichever wineries strike your fancy. There are more than 30 wineries in the valley, and you could easily spend a week here visiting them all. However, most people spend no more than a weekend in the area. We suggest picking no more than four or five to visit during a day of wine tasting. It's also advisable to have a designated driver.

THE ZILLAH AREA

While in Zillah, don't miss the opportunity to see the **Teapot Dome gas station,** a national historic building built in 1922 in the shape of a giant teapot to call attention to a scandal in the administration of President Warren G. Harding. You'll find the teapot on the south side of I-82. Also, if you want to pick up some fresh Yakima Valley fruit or indulge in fresh peach sundae (in season, of course), drop by **Donald Fruit & Mercantile,** 2560 Donald-Wapato Rd., Wapato (© **509/877-3115**), which first opened in 1911 and is reached by driving north from exit 44 off I-82.

Bonair Winery ★   This small family-run winery just outside Zillah produces a number of semisweet wines (including a couple of different meads) and even some red wines for under $10 ($9.99 to be exact). They also do a variety of dry wines, including decent chardonnay. Good values and a good sense of humor make this winery a must if you are *not* a wine snob.

500 S. Bonair Rd. © **509/829-6027.** www.bonairwine.com. Mon–Thurs 10am–5pm; Fri–Sun 10am–4:30pm. Take exit 50 off I-82, go north to Highland Dr., and then turn right on Bonair Rd.

Claar Cellars   Although the Claar Cellars winery is north of the Tri-Cities area, it recently opened a tasting room here in Zillah so as to reach more of the people touring the wine country. Claar Cellars produces only wines from estate-grown grapes (the vineyards were planted in 1980). The Riesling and late-harvest Rieslings here can be quite good.

1001 Vintage Valley Pkwy. (C) **509/829-6810**. www.claarcellars.com. Daily 10am–5pm (winter 11am–4pm). Take exit 52 off I-82.

Eaton Hill Winery ⭐   Housed in the old Rinehold Cannery building, this just might be the most laid-back wine-tasting room in the valley. This winery focuses on Cabernet Sauvignon and chardonnay, and generally has a wide selection of vintages available.

530 Gurley Rd. (C) **509/854-2220**. Fri–Wed 10am–5pm (winter Sat–Sun noon–4pm). Take exit 58 off I-82; go west on Yakima Valley Hwy., then right on Gurley Rd.

Horizon's Edge Winery   This small winery's strong points are its muscat dessert wine and its port, and it also produces respectable (if light) pinot noir.

4530 E. Zillah Dr. (C) **509/829-6401**. Thurs–Mon 11am–5pm (winter by appointment). Take exit 54 off I-82 and go 3 miles (5km) east on E. Zillah Dr.

Hyatt Vineyards ⭐   With its wide lawns, valley views, and immaculately tended gardens, it's obvious that this winery does a brisk wedding business and is a good spot for a picnic. Although they do a wide range of red wines, the main reason to drop by is to try their black muscat dessert wines.

2020 Gilbert Rd. (C) **509/829-6333**. www.hyattvineyards.com. Daily 11am–5pm (11am–4:30pm in winter). Closed Jan, limited days Feb. Take exit 50 off I-82, go north to Highland Dr., turn left on Bonair Rd., and turn right on Gilbert Rd.

Portteus Vineyards ⭐⭐   With excellent views across the valley, this winery produces some of the best red wines in the Yakima Valley. Bold, full-bodied wines are the hallmark here. While most of the wines here are in the $20 to $25 range, the very drinkable Rattlesnake Red weighs in at under $15.

5201 Highland Dr. (C) **509/829-6970**. Daily noon–5pm (Dec 1–Feb 15 call for hr.). Take exit 50 off I-82, go north, and then follow Highland east as far as it goes.

Tefft Cellars ⭐   Tefft produces primarily easy drinking, moderately priced wines, including a good red table wine, Cabernet Sauvignon, and Merlot. They also do an unusual cabernet port. The winery also has a B&B. Lots of good values are to be had here.

1320 Independence Rd. (C) **888/303-7651** or 509/837-7651. www.tefftcellars.com. Daily 10am–5pm (Dec–Feb 14 by appointment). Take exit 63 off I-82; go north on Outlook Rd. and west on Independence Rd.

SUNNYSIDE

If you need some cheese to go with your wine, drop by Sunnyside's **Darigold Dairy Fair Cheese Factory,** 400 Alexander Rd. ((C) **509/837-4321**), which is a half mile south of exit 67 off I-82. A sort of circus atmosphere prevails, and ice cream and sandwiches are available, as well as plenty of cheese. The cheese factory is open Monday through Saturday from 10am to 8pm and Sunday from 10am to 6pm.

Washington Hills Cellars ⭐   Just off the interstate in Sunnyside, you'll find, in a former Carnation building, one of the most versatile of the Yakima Valley wineries. Washington Hills produces wines under three different labels (and in three different price ranges). Most tend to be soft, ready-to-drink wines.

111 E. Lincoln Ave. 📞 **509/839-9463**. Daily 9am–5pm. Take exit 67 off I-82, north on Midvale Rd. to Lincoln Ave.

PROSSER

Here in Prosser, at exit 80 off I-82, you can also stop in at **Chukar Cherry Company,** 320 Wine Country Rd. (📞 **509/786-2055**), and sample dried cherries and lots of other dried fruits and candies.

Chinook Wines ⭐ Dry wines, both red and white, are the focus at this Prosser winery, which is a husband-and-wife operation. The reds are big and bold and tend to be fairly pricey. There's a pretty garden that's perfect for an afternoon picnic.

Wine Country Rd. at Wittkopf Loop. 📞 **509/786-2725**. May–Oct Sat–Sun noon–5pm. Take exit 82 off I-82 and go east on Wine Country Rd. (away from Prosser).

Columbia Crest ⭐ Located roughly 25 miles (40km) south of Prosser on more than 2,000 acres of vineyards overlooking the Columbia River, Columbia Crest is one of the largest wineries in the state. Although it's out of the way, the winery is worth visiting for its dramatic setting and château-like facility.

Wash. 221, Paterson. 📞 **888/309-WINE** or 509/875-2061. www.columbia-crest.com. Daily 10am–4:30pm. Take Wash. 221 south from Prosser.

The Hogue Cellars ⭐⭐ Located in an industrial park just off the freeway, Hogue is one of Washington's largest wineries. In the tasting room, you'll have an opportunity to sample wines from three different Hogue labels that represent three different levels of wine. Keep an eye out for their Champoux Vineyard Cabernet Sauvignon and vineyard-designate and reserve chardonnays.

2800 Lee Rd. 📞 **509/786-4557**. www.hogue-cellars.com. Daily 10am–5pm. Take exit 82 off I-82 and go east on Wine Country Rd. (away from Prosser).

Kestrel Vintners This is one of the newer wineries in the area and has set as its goal producing premium Cabernet Sauvignon, Merlot, and chardonnay. You'll find the tasting room in an industrial park outside Prosser.

2890 Lee Rd. 📞 **888/343-CORK**. Mon–Sat 10am–5pm; Sun 11am–5pm. Take exit 82 off I-82, go east on Wine Country Rd., and turn left on Bennitz Rd. and then right on Lee Rd.

Pontin del Roza This small family-owned winery has been producing wines since 1984 and does a wide variety of whites and reds.

35502 N. Hinzerling Rd. 📞 **509/786-4449**. Daily 10am–5pm. Take exit 80 off I-82 and go north, then go east on Johnson Rd. and north on Hinzerling Rd.

Thurston Wolfe Winery ⭐ This small, family winery, located in an industrial park outside of Prosser, focuses its attentions on producing exclusively red wines—zinfandel, Grenache, Lemberger, and Syrah. They also do a port.

2880 Lee Rd., Suite C. 📞 **509/786-3313**. Fri–Sun 11am–5pm. Closed Dec–Mar. Take exit 82 off I-82, go east on Wine Country Rd. and continue 100 yd. past Hogue Cellars.

Willow Crest Winery ⭐⭐ Set high in the hills north of Prosser, this is one of the Yakima Valley's smallest wineries and does a very limited variety of wines. However, since winemaker David Minick likes to experiment, you'll often find some rather unusual wines here, such as a Syrah port and a Syrah sparkling wine. Well worth the drive.

135701 Snipes Rd. 📞 **509/786-7999**. Sat–Sun 10am–5pm. Closed mid-Dec to Presidents' Day weekend. Take exit 80 off I-82; go north on Gap Rd., then right on Snipes Rd.

Yakima River Winery Founded in 1978, and located across the river from downtown Prosser, is another of the old family-owned wineries in the valley. This winery specializes in barrel-aged red wines, but also does a port.

143302 N. River Rd. ✆ 509/786-2805. www.yakimavalleywinery.com. Daily 9am–5pm. Take exit 80 off I-82, go south toward Prosser, and turn right on N. River Rd.

BENTON CITY

Blackwood Canyon ★★ Dedicated to an old-world style of winemaking, this winery produces the most distinctive wines in the valley (and some of the most expensive; mostly in the $30–$100 range). The high tasting fee is due in large part to the fact that the wines here are expensive and tastings usually feature wines as many as 10 years old.

53258 N. Sunset Rd., Benton City. ✆ 509/588-6249. $20 tasting fee. Mon–Sat 10am–6pm; Sun noon–6pm. Take exit 96 off I-82, go east on Wash. 224, and then turn left on Sunset Rd.

Kiona Vineyards ★ Located down a gravel road in the Red Hills region of the valley, this large winery produces a wide variety of easy-to-drink wines at moderate prices.

44612 N. Sunset Rd. ✆ 509/588-6716. Daily noon–5pm. Take exit 96 off I-82, go east on Wash. 224, and then turn left on Sunset Rd.

Oakwood Cellars The view of Rattlesnake Mountain makes this boutique winery a good choice for a picnic on a day of tasting wines in the Benton City area. Oakwood Cellars produces a wide range of both red and white wines.

40504 N. De Moss Rd. ✆ 509/588-5332. Sat–Sun noon–5pm (winter by appointment). Take exit 96 off I-82; go east on Wash. 224, then left on De Moss Rd.

Seth Ryan Winery The Red Hills region around Benton City is home to several of the Yakima Valley's top boutique wineries, including Seth Ryan. The winery produces six varietals, plus a blush wine called Rapture and a Bordeaux-style Meritage blend. Prices for whites are quite reasonable.

353006 Sunset Rd. ✆ 509/588-6780. www.sethryan.com. Sat–Sun 11am–6pm (winter noon–5pm). Take exit 96 off I-82, go east on Wash. 224, and turn left on Sunset Rd.

Terra Blanca Vintners ★ This is one of the region's newest wineries and produces its wines under two distinct labels that represent different qualities (and prices) of wine. The pricier whites are good bets; the reds have a lot of tannins. Terra Blanca also produces a wide range of dessert wines.

34715 N. De Moss Rd. ✆ 509/588-6082. www.terrablanca.com. Daily 11am–6pm (Dec 25–Feb 14 by appointment). Take exit 96 off I-82; go east on Wash. 224, then left on De Moss Rd.

THE TRI-CITIES AREA

Barnard Griffin ★ Lots of good white wines, including semillon, fumé blanc, and chardonnay, can usually be had here, and the winery also does a good job with its dessert wines.

878 Tulip Lane, Richland. ✆ 509/627-0266. Daily 10am–6pm. Take exit 3 off I-182 and turn left on Columbia Dr.

Bookwalter Winery ★★ Producing everything from light, drinkable picnic wines to complex, full-bodied Cabernet Sauvignon and Merlot, this winery on the west side of Richland is one of the valley's more reliable wineries. No matter what your tastes, you're likely to find something here that you'll like.

894 Tulip Lane, Richland. ✆ 509/627-5000. www.bookwalterwines.com. Mon–Sat 10am–6pm; Sun 10am–5pm. Take exit 3 off I-182 and turn left on Columbia Dr.

Gordon Brothers Cellars ★   This winery tasting room is located on the edge of the suburbs, and though the setting is none too impressive, the wines are generally quite good. Prices are generally in the $10 to $20 range.

5960 Burden Blvd., Pasco. © 509/547-6331. www.gordonwines.com. Daily 10am–6pm. Take exit 9 off I-182; go north on Rd. 68 and then east on Burden Blvd.

TOPPENISH & ITS MURALS

Before or after visiting wineries around Zillah, you might want to drive into the town of **Toppenish.** Toppenish was just a quiet little cow town until someone got the great idea of enlivening a few town walls with historical murals. Today, there are more than 60 **murals** depicting aspects of Toppenish history. You'll see these murals on walls all over town, and if you stop in at almost any store in town you can pick up a map to the murals. Though some murals have taken as much as a month to paint, each year on the first Saturday in June, crowds descend on the town to watch a new mural created in just 1 day. One of the best ways to see the murals is on a horse-drawn trolley tour with **Toppenish Mural Tours** (© **509/697-8995**). Tours last 1½ hours and cost $10 for adults, $8 for seniors, and $5 for children.

Toppenish is within the boundaries of the Yakama Indian Reservation, which operates the **Cultural Heritage Center** on U.S. 97 (© **509/865-2800**), just outside town. This large building, designed to resemble the traditional Yakama winter lodge, contains a museum, library, gift shop, and restaurant serving salmon, buffalo, fry bread, and a traditional Yakama salmon soup called luk-a-meen. Exhibits in the museum present the history and culture of the Yakama people. The Yakama are well known for their beadwork and you'll find pieces for sale in the gift shop. The center is open daily from 8am to 5pm; admission is $4 for adults, $2 for seniors and students, $1 for children ages 7 to 10, 75¢ for children 6 and under.

Several other attractions in town provide glimpses into the town's and the region's history. The most entertaining of these is the **Yakima Valley Rail & Steam Museum,** 10 S. Asotin Ave. (© **509/865-1911**), which has its museum in the town's 1911 railway depot and also operates, on weekends, 18-mile (29km) scenic railway excursions on the Toppenish, Simcoe & Western Railroad. Excursions are $8 for adults and $5 for children. The Yakima Valley is one of the world's top hops-growing regions, and it is here that you will find the **American Hop Museum,** 22 S. B St. (© **509/865-HOPS**), where you can learn all about this crucial beer ingredient. The museum is open May through September daily from 11am to 4pm; admission by donation.

Fort Simcoe, 27 miles (43km) west of Toppenish in the Cascade foothills, was established in 1856 because of conflicts between Indians and settlers. Today, the fort is preserved as **Fort Simcoe State Park Heritage Site** (© **509/874-2372**) and is the site of surprisingly elegant quarters that were used for only a few years before becoming the Indian Agency headquarters and school. The park's buildings are open April through September daily from 8am to 5pm. However, the grounds are open daily.

ATTRACTIONS & ACTIVITIES IN THE YAKIMA AREA

Local history is chronicled at the **Yakima Valley Museum** ★★, 2105 Tieton Dr. (© **509/248-0747**; http://yakimavalleymuseum.org), where a collection of restored horse-drawn vehicles is on display. There are also displays on the Yakama tribe and on former Supreme Court justice and environmentalist William O. Douglas, who was a Yakima resident. Perhaps the museum's most

Of Apples & Birdies

Golfers take note. Here in Yakima, you'll find a golf course with the world's only green on an apple-shaped island. The **Apple Tree Golf Course,** 8804 Occidental Ave. (© **509/966-5877;** www.appletreegolf. com), on the west side of town is rated among the best golf courses in the state but is most noteworthy for its unusual apple island. Greens fees are $22 to $53.

enjoyable exhibit is a functioning replica of a 1930s soda fountain. The museum is open Monday through Friday from 10am to 5pm and Saturday and Sunday from noon to 5pm; admission is $3 for adults, $1.50 for seniors and students. The museum also operates the **Gilbert House,** an 1898 Victorian farmhouse, at 2109 W. Yakima Ave. This historic home is open April through December on Friday and the first Sunday of each month from 1 to 4pm; admission is $2.50.

If you're interested in learning more about the other fruits of this region (apples, pears, cherries), drop by the **Washington's Fruit Place Visitor Center,** 105 S. 18th St., Suite 103 (© **509/576-3090**), which is located east of downtown off Yakima Avenue. Hours vary with the seasons, so call ahead.

Extending for 10 miles (16km) between Union Gap and Selah Gap, the **Yakima Greenway** follows the banks of the **Yakima River,** with 10 miles (16km) of paved pathways within the greenway. The easiest place to access the path is at Sherman Park on Nob Hill Boulevard. In summer, **kayaking, rafting, and tubing** are popular on this section of the river, and the **bird-watching** is good year-round.

If you'd like to see another scenic stretch of the river, head north to Selah and then take Wash. 821 north through the **Yakima River Canyon.** The river has been around for longer than the surrounding hills, which have risen concurrent with the river slicing through them.

ATTRACTIONS & ACTIVITIES IN THE TRI-CITIES AREA

If you're interested in learning more about the history (including the nuclear history), science, and technology of this region, pay a visit to the **Columbia River Exhibition of History, Science & Technology,** 95 Lee Blvd., Richland (© **509/943-9000;** www.crehst.org), which is located adjacent to the attractive Howard Amon Park in downtown Richland. Be sure to ask to watch the video on the great floods that scoured this landscape during the last ice age. The museum is open Monday through Saturday from 10am to 5pm and Sunday from noon to 5pm.

Up river from the Tri-Cities area are both the Hanford Site (where the plutonium for the first nuclear bombs was made) and the Hanford Reach National Monument, which was designated in 2000 by President Clinton. The Hanford Reach is the last free-flowing stretch of the Columbia River in the United States. Although there are some remote areas of the monument that are accessible by vehicle, the best way to see this new national monument is on the jet boat tours offered by **Columbia River Journeys** (© **888/486-9119** or 509/734-9941; www.columbiariverjourneys.com). The 4-hour tours cost $42 for adults and $32 for children. Along the way you'll see not only a the wild shores of the Columbia River but also the nuclear reactors of the Hanford Site.

WHERE TO STAY

For a list of bed-and-breakfast inns in the wine country, contact the **Yakima Valley Winery Association,** P.O. Box 39, Grandview, WA 98930 (© **800/ 258-7270;** www.yakimavalleywine.com).

IN YAKIMA

Birchfield Manor ★★   Located 2½ miles (4km) east of Yakima, Birchfield Manor is surrounded by pastures and is well known for its elegant dinners. Both upstairs from the dining room in the 1910 Victorian farmhouse and in a new building constructed to resemble a vintage home, you'll find antiques-filled guest rooms, most of which have good views out over the countryside. Several of these rooms have fireplaces, whirlpool tubs, and decks to take in the view. Breakfasts here are nearly as legendary as the dinners and are a great start for a day of wine-country touring. Note that the rooms in the new building have TVs and phones.

2018 Birchfield Rd., Yakima, WA 98901. © **800/375-3420** or 509/452-1960. Fax 509/452-2334. www.birchfieldmanor.com. 11 units. $99–$199 double. Rates include full breakfast. AE, DC, DISC, MC, V. **Amenities:** Restaurant (Continental); outdoor pool; room service. *In room:* A/C, coffeemaker, hair dryer, iron, no phone.

Oxford Inn ★   Located east of I-82 on the banks of the Yakima River, this is Yakima's most pleasant and popular budget accommodation. As such it regularly books up on weekends. The rooms are spacious, and many have balconies overlooking the river. Most also have refrigerators. Walkers and joggers will be pleased to find a 10-mile (16km) riverside walking/biking path running past the motel. Right next door you'll find the affiliated Oxford Suites, which offers larger rooms and complimentary buffet breakfasts.

1603 Terrace Heights Dr., Yakima, WA 98901. © **800/521-3050** or 509/457-4444. Fax 509/453-7593. www.oxfordsuites.com. 96 units. $59–$79 double. Rates include continental breakfast. AE, DC, DISC, MC, V. Pets accepted with $15 fee. **Amenities:** Outdoor pool; exercise room; Jacuzzi; coin-op laundry. *In room:* A/C, TV, fridge, coffeemaker.

BETWEEN ZILLAH & BENTON CITY

Outlook Inn Bed & Breakfast ★   Located on the grounds of Tefft Cellars winery and surrounded by vineyards, this inn offers about as thorough an immersion in wine-country touring as you can have in the Yakima Valley. Guest rooms are simply furnished, and the back deck has a great view of Mount Adams and Mount Rainier. Best of all, the winery's tasting room is right outside the front door. The only drawback is the distance to the nearest good restaurant.

1320 Independence Rd., Outlook, WA 98938. © **888/303-7651** or 509/837-7651. Fax 509/839-7337. www.tefftcellars.com. 3 units, 1 with private bathroom. $50–$75 double. MC, V. *In room:* A/C, TV.

IN THE TRI-CITIES AREA

Tri-Cities/Richland Hampton Inn ★★ *(Kids)*   Located right on the banks of the Columbia River adjacent to Richland's Howard Amon Park, this newer hotel claims the best location of any hotel in the Tri-Cities area. Not only do you have the walking paths and green lawns of the park right next door, but there are good restaurants within a short walk. Rooms are well-designed and comfortable and many have balconies overlooking the river. With the indoor pool, complimentary breakfast, and park next door, this is a good bet for families.

486 Bradley Blvd., Richland, WA 99352. © **800/HAMPTON** or 509/943-4400. Fax 509/943-1797. www.hampton-inn.com. 130 units. $79–$99 double; $225 suite. Rates include continental breakfast. AE, DC, DISC, MC, V. **Amenities:** Indoor swimming pool; exercise room; Jacuzzi; courtesy shuttle van; business center; coin-op laundry. *In room:* A/C, TV, dataport, fridge, coffeemaker, hair dryer, free local calls.

WHERE TO DINE
IN YAKIMA

For good coffee, your best bet is **Seattle's Best Coffee,** 402 E. Yakima Ave. (© **509/453-9366**). If you're looking for a convivial place to hoist a pint of microbrew ale, **Grant's Pub** ★★, 32 N. Front St. (© **509/575-2922**), housed in Yakima's restored train station, is the place. This is the oldest brewpub in the country.

Birchfield Manor Country Inn ★★ CONTINENTAL   Birchfield Manor, a grand old farmhouse on the eastern outskirts of Yakima, doubles as both Yakima's best B&B and its best restaurant. The dining room looks as if a wealthy family had cleared out the regular furniture and brought in a few extra tables for a holiday dinner. The menu changes with the season and includes a choice of five or six entrees, and while the house specialty is salmon in puff pastry with a chardonnay sauce, other offerings can be very tempting as well. The filet mignon with cabernet sauce and steak Diane with a brandy cream sauce are two other standout dishes here. The dinner includes fresh-baked bread, an appetizer, and salad.

2018 Birchfield Rd. © 509/452-1960. www.birchfieldmanor.com. Reservations required. 3-course dinner $33–$48. AE, DC, DISC, MC, V. Seatings Thurs–Fri 7pm; Sat 6 and 8:45pm.

Deli de Pasta ★ ITALIAN   It's small and inconspicuous, but Deli de Pasta has long been one of Yakima's best and most popular restaurants. All the pastas and sauces are made fresh on the premises and the menu lets you mix and match the two. You can combine black-pepper penne with a creamy lemon sauce or herb linguine with pesto or rotelli with marinara sauce or whatever. However, it's the smoked-salmon ravioli with a basil-cream sauce that is our personal favorite and that has been the restaurant's biggest hit. A good wine list includes lots of local wines.

7 N. Front St. © 509/453-0571. Reservations recommended. Complete meals $12–$24. AE, MC, V. Mon–Thurs 5–8:30pm; Fri–Sat 5–9:30pm.

Gasperetti's ★★ NORTHERN ITALIAN/NORTHWEST   Though this restaurant is very nondescript from the outside, the owners have done much to create a feeling of elegance inside. The menu changes every other week and, though primarily Italian in flavor, often includes inspiration from seasonal Northwest ingredients. The rack of lamb, a regular on the menu, often comes with a delicious soy-cilantro vinaigrette. A fine selection of local wines complements the menu offerings. The extensive dessert list is, in itself, worth the visit, with Belgian white chocolate cheesecake a real standout. This restaurant is a favorite of Yakima's wealthier residents and has a very formal atmosphere.

1013 N. First St. © 509/248-0628. Reservations recommended. Main courses $9.50–$28.50. AE, DISC, MC, V. Tues–Fri 11:30am–2:30pm and 5–9pm; Sat 5–9pm.

IN ZILLAH & TOPPENISH

Heritage Inn Restaurant ★ *Finds* AMERICAN/NATIVE AMERICAN   Located on the grounds of the Yakama Nation Cultural Heritage Center, this casual restaurant is noteworthy for its Native American dishes, including a traditional Yakama salmon stew and fry bread. In fact, even the salad bar comes with fry bread. There are also buffalo burgers, buffalo steaks, and buffalo stew. For dessert, don't pass up the huckleberry pie.

Yakama Nation Cultural Heritage Center, 280 Buster Rd., Toppenish. © 509/865-2551. Main courses $3.50–$8 at lunch; $7–$19 at dinner. MC, V. Mon–Thurs 7:30am–8pm; Fri–Sat 8am–9pm; Sun 8am–2pm.

IN SUNNYSIDE

Snipes Mountain Microbrewery & Restaurant ✦ PUB FARE   While it might at first seem treasonous to dine at a brewpub in the heart of wine country, keep in mind that the Yakima Valley is also one of the nation's main hops-growing regions. While most of the food here is fairly basic (burgers, sandwiches, pizza), you can also get seafood satay and hazelnut-crusted rack of lamb. The beers are decent, and local wines are also available. Basically, this is one of the only decent places to eat between Yakima and the Tri-Cities area.

905 Yakima Valley Hwy. ℂ 509/837-2739. Main courses $6–$22. AE, DISC, MC, V. Sun–Thurs 10am–10pm; Fri–Sat 11am–11pm.

IN GRANDVIEW

Dykstra House Restaurant ✦ ITALIAN/CONTINENTAL   This eclectic eatery, housed in a historic building that dates from 1914, is primarily a lunch spot, but on Friday and Saturday nights dinners are also served. Friday is Italian night and usually features familiar standards. Saturday night is a bit more eclectic, and there might be salmon in puff pastry, chicken Mediterranean, or pork loin. Lunches are equally unpredictable—you never know what might show up on the menu, which makes a meal here all the more fun. There's a good selection of local wines to accompany meals.

114 Birch Ave. ℂ 509/882-2082. Reservations required for dinner. Main courses $12–$17. AE, DC, DISC, MC, V. Tues–Thurs 9:30am–4:30pm; Fri 9:30am–4:30pm and 6–9pm; Sat 11am–2pm and 6–9pm.

IN THE TRI-CITIES AREA

For breakfast, a snack, or a cup of coffee, drop by **Taste,** 701 George Washington Way, Richland (ℂ **509/946-4142**), in downtown Richland. If you're just in the mood for some pub food and a microbrew, head to **Atomic Ale Brewpub & Eatery,** 1015 Lee Blvd., Richland (ℂ **509/946-5465**), which is just a block off Richland's George Washington Way in downtown Richland.

Aioli's ✦✦ *Finds* MEDITERRANEAN   Half a block from Richland's riverfront Howard Amon Park, you'll find one of the most enjoyable little restaurants in central Washington. With only a handful of tables and a tiny wine bar, Aioli's is a cozy place with a suitably Mediterranean decor that is surprisingly chic. By far the best deal here, and a must if you are in the mood for a full meal, is to get the $11.50 tapas platter, which includes four selections from the day's tapas specials list. Keep an eye out for the chicken made with cumin, coriander, and cinnamon. Plenty of wines by the glass and by the bottle make this restaurant a must if you're in the area on a wine-tasting trip.

94 Lee Blvd., Richland. ℂ 509/942-1914. Tapas $1.75–$7; main courses $7.25–$16.50. AE, DC, MC, V. Mon 11am–3pm; Tues–Thurs 11am–9pm; Fri–Sat 11am–10pm.

Sundance Grill ✦✦ CONTINENTAL/NORTHWEST   The Sundance Grill, currently located in a rather nondescript strip mall, is one of the Tri-Cities' most contemporary restaurants, and it's the closest you'll come in this area to a dash of urban chic. The menu mixes traditional with contemporary. You might start your meal with a bowl of steamed clams or crab cakes accompanied by aioli or Thai dipping sauce and then move on to broiled or seared salmon topped with rock shrimp and a sherry cream sauce or perhaps prime rib with apple-horseradish sauce. Before ordering a big meal, you might want to first take a look at the dessert tray. This restaurant has plans to move to a new location on the Columbia River in Richland, so be sure to call ahead first.

413 N. Kellogg St., Kennewick. ℂ 509/783-6505. Reservations recommended. Main courses $6–$13 at lunch, $15–$32 at dinner. AE, DISC, MC, V. Mon–Sat 11am–4pm and 5–9:30pm.

3 Walla Walla

50 miles (81km) E of Richland/Pasco/Kennewick, 155 miles (250km) S of Spokane, 39 miles (63km) NE of Pendleton

Although Walla Walla is perhaps best known as the home of the Walla Walla sweet onion, in recent years the town has become the epicenter of a burgeoning wine industry. New wineries have been popping up as fast as champagne corks on New Year's eve, making this town the single best locale in the state for a few days of wine touring. The explosion of wineries has also brought on something of a downtown renaissance that includes a restored historic hotel, new restaurants, and a few wine bars.

Before there was wine, it was onions that made Walla Walla famous (well maybe not exactly famous). The Walla Walla onion is a big sweet variety, similar to the Vidalia onion of Georgia, and owes its sweetness not to sugar but to a high water content and a low sulfur content. These onions, which can weigh as much as 2 pounds, are legendary around the Northwest as the very best onions for putting on burgers at summer barbecues. Between June and August each year, produce stands all over the valley sell big bags of these sweet onions. There's even a Walla Walla Sweet Onion Festival here in early July.

This is also a college town with three schools of higher learning: Walla Walla College, Whitman College, and Walla Walla Community College. Due in large part to these colleges, the town wears a rather cultured air. The town's residential streets, lined with stately old homes and large shade trees, add yet another layer to Walla Walla's character. A stroll or drive through the town's old neighborhoods conjures up times past when the pace of life was slower.

Walla Walla is also one of the oldest communities in the Northwest and was the site of both an early mission and one of the region's first forts. Before white settlers arrived, the area was home to several Indian tribes, and it is from these tribes that the town's name, which means "many waters" or "small, rapid streams" has come.

ESSENTIALS

GETTING THERE Walla Walla is on U.S. 12, 45 miles (72km) east of I-82/I-182 in the Tri-Cities area. From I-82 west of Richland, take I-182 to Pasco and continue south and then west on U.S. 12. From Pendleton, Oregon, and I-84, take Ore. 11 north. From Spokane, take U.S. 195 south to Colfax, continuing south on Wash. 26 and then Wash. 127. In Dodge, you pick up U.S. 12 and continue south to Walla Walla.

Walla Walla Regional Airport is served by Horizon Airlines.

VISITOR INFORMATION Contact the **Walla Walla Area Chamber of Commerce,** 29 E. Sumach St., Walla Walla, WA 99362 (© **877/WWVISIT;** www.wallawalla.org).

GETTING AROUND Rental cars are available in Walla Walla through Hertz and Budget.

FESTIVALS In early May there's the Walla Walla Balloon Stampede, and in mid-July there's the Walla Walla Sweet Onion Blues Fest. Area wine festivals include the Spring Barrel Tasting over the first two weekends in May and the Holiday Barrel Tasting on the first weekend in December.

EXPLORING THE TOWN

The **Whitman Mission National Historic Site** (© 509/522-6360; www.nps. gov/whmi), 7 miles (11km) west of Walla Walla just off U.S. 12, is dedicated to a tragic page in Northwest history. Missionaries Marcus and Narcissa Whitman were some of the very first settlers to travel overland to the Northwest and arrived in this area in 1836. Although the Whitmans had come here to convert the local Native Americans, Marcus Whitman was also a doctor and often treated the local Cayuse people. During the mid-1840s a wagon train brought a measles epidemic to the area, and the Cayuse, who had no resistance to the disease, began dying. Though Whitman was able to save his own family, most of the Cayuse who contracted the disease died from it. Legend has it that the Cayuse had a tradition of killing medicine men who could not cure an illness, and on November 29, 1847, several Cayuse attacked and killed the Whitmans and 11 other residents of the mission. The massacre at the Whitman mission prompted a war on the Cayuse and a demand for territorial status for what was at that time the Oregon country. In 1848, in response to pleas brought about by the Whitman massacre, Oregon (which at that time included present-day Washington state) became the first territory west of the Rocky Mountains.

Today nothing remains of the mission, but a trail leads through the mission site and the locations of buildings are outlined with concrete. An interpretive center provides historical background on the mission and includes numerous artifacts from the days when the Whitmans worked with the Cayuse. The site is open daily (except Thanksgiving, Christmas, and New Year's Day) until dusk; the museum is open from 8am to 6pm in summer and from 8am to 4:30pm in other months. Admission is $2 per person or $4 per family.

In town, you'll find the **Fort Walla Walla Museum Complex,** 755 Myra Rd. (© **509/525-7703;** www.fortwallawallamusuem.org). The museum is a collection of pioneer-era buildings, including log cabins, a one-room schoolhouse, an old railway station, and several other buildings. It's open April through October, Tuesday through Sunday from 10am to 5pm. Admission is $5 for adults, $4 for seniors and students, and $1 for children ages 6 to 12, free for children under 6. In addition to the displays on pioneer life, there's a large collection of horse-era farming equipment, including an old combine being pulled by 33 life-size fiberglass mules.

WINE TOURING

Although Washington's main winery region lies to the west of the Tri-Cities area, the Walla Walla area has seen a proliferation of wineries recently and has become the state's hottest new wine region. The climate and soils are perfect for growing wine grapes, and the emphasis is now on Syrah grapes. In fact, because Walla Walla is such an attractive town, this is a far more appealing wine-touring region than the Yakima Valley. In addition to the area wineries listed below, which are open to the public on a regular basis, there are some that are generally only open by appointment or on a couple of weekends a year.

IN WALLA WALLA

Canoe Ridge Vineyard ★   Taking its name from a nearby vineyard region, this winery is housed in an old streetcar engine house on the outskirts of Walla Walla. The emphasis is on Cabernet Sauvignon and Merlot, which tend to be very tannic, but for our money, the white wines are better and are also better values (the chardonnays are particularly good values).

1102 W. Cherry St., Walla Walla. © **509/527-0885.** www.canoeridgevineyard.com. Summer daily 11am–5pm; winter daily 11am–4pm. From U.S. 12, go south on W. Pine St. and then right on 13th Ave.

Cayuse Vineyards ★★ Located just down the street from the Waterbrook tasting room. French winemaker Christophe Baron produces Rhone- and Bordeaux-style wines, with the focus on deliciously smooth and oaky Syrah and Viognier.

17 E. Main St. ☎ **509/526-0686**. www.cayusevineyards.com. Hours vary throughout the year, call ahead. From U.S. 12, take Second Ave. to Main St.

Glen Fiona With its tasting room in Walla Walla's historic railroad depot (which also houses Jacobi's restaurant), Glen Fiona is one of Walla Walla's top red-wine producers. This small winery produces only Syrahs, which tend to be big, bold wines.

416 N. Second Ave. ☎ **509/522-2566**. www.glenfiona.com. Sat 11am–4pm.

Patrick M. Paul Vineyards In business since 1988, this is one of the smaller wineries in the area and produces only about 500 cases of wine per year. Yet even with such a small production, they manage to do Cabernet Sauvignon, cabernet franc, Merlot, and chardonnay.

1554 School Ave. ☎ **509/526-0676**. Sat–Sun 1–4pm. From U.S. 12, take Wilbur Ave. south to Alder St., turn left, and continue to School Ave.

Seven Hills Winery ★ Housed in the same renovated woodworking-mill building that also houses the Whitehouse-Crawford Restaurant, this winery produces some excellent red wines, including Merlot and Syrah. Most wines are in the $22 to $32 range.

212 N. Third Ave. ☎ **877/777-7870** or 509/529-7198. www.sevenhillswinery.com. Tues–Sat 11am–5pm (call for reduced hours in winter).

Waterbrook Winery ★ Although Waterbrook Winery itself is located in nearby Lowden, the winery's tasting room is in downtown Walla Walla. The focus here is on Cabernet Sauvignon and Merlot in the $20 to $25 range. Whites include chardonnay, sauvignon blanc, and the less familiar Viognier, all of which can be both quite drinkable and very reasonably priced. There are some good values to be had here.

31 E. Main St. ☎ **509/522-1262**. www.waterbrook.com. Daily 10:30am–4:30pm.

WEST OF WALLA WALLA

Three Rivers Winery This large new winery may be the wave of the future for the Walla Walla wine business. Housed in a large new building in the middle of the Walla Walla farm country, Three Rivers produces a wide range of wines from robust Syrahs and Sangioveses to late-harvest Gewürztraminer.

5641 W. Hwy. 12 ☎ **509/526-9463**. www.threeriverswinery.com. Daily 10am–5pm. Located 8 miles (13km) west of Walla Walla on U.S. 12.

Woodward Canyon Winery ★★ This winery is well known in the Northwest for its full-bodied red wines and vineyard-designate chardonnays and is considered one of Washington's best wineries. The tasting room is in a renovated old farmhouse adjacent to the winery.

11920 W. Hwy. 12, Lowden. ☎ **509/525-4129**. www.woodwardcanyon.com. Spring and summer Mon–Sat 10am–5pm, Sun noon–5pm; fall and winter Mon–Sat 10am–4pm, Sun noon–4pm. On U.S. 12, 12 miles (19km) west of Walla Walla.

L'Ecole No. 41 ★ Housed in a former elementary school and using children's art on its labels, this is one of the oldest wineries in this region. This winery started with semillon and Merlot, and the semillon is still one of their best wines, though the chardonnays and Cabernet Merlots are good also. Mostly in the $15 to $25 range.

41 Lowden School Rd., Lowden. © **509/525-0940.** www.lecole.com. Daily 11am–4pm (call for winter hr.). On U.S. 12, 12 miles (19km) west of Walla Walla.

EAST OF WALLA WALLA

At the Walla Walla Airport, you'll find several small wineries most of which are open primarily by appointment. These include **Reininger,** 720 C St. (© **509/522-1924;** www.reiningerwinery.com), **Russell Creek,** C Street and Aeronica Avenue (© **509/386-4401;** www.russellcreek-winery.com), **Tamarack Cellars,** 700 C St. (© **509/526-3533;** www.tamarackcellars.com), and **Buty,** 675 E St. (© **509/527-0901;** www.butywinery.com).

Trey Marie Winery   Located adjacent to the Walla Walla airport, this winery produces an exceptional red blend called Trutina, the composition of which varies from year to year. This winery is affiliated with Dunham Cellars, with which it shares the winery.

150 E. Boeing Rd. © **509/529-1371.** www.treymarie.com. Daily 11am–4pm. Take the airport exit off U.S. 12 east of downtown.

Walla Walla Vintners ★   This small winery does only red wines and in the past has produced some excellent Cabernet Sauvignon and Merlot.

225 Vineyard Lane. © **509/525-4724.** www.wallawallavintners.com. Sat 10:30am–4:30pm. Located east of town off Mill Creek Rd.

SPORTS & OUTDOOR ACTIVITIES

Though the land immediately surrounding Walla Walla is rolling farm country, less than 20 miles (32km) to the east the **Blue Mountains** rise to more than 6,000 feet. Hiking, mountain biking, fishing, and hunting are all popular in these little-visited mountains. For more information, contact the **Walla Walla Ranger District,** 1415 W. Rose St., Walla Walla, WA 99362 (© **509/522-6290;** www.fs.fed.us/r6/uma/).

WHERE TO STAY

Green Gables Inn ★   Located on a quiet, shady street, this large 1909 home, with its three large front gables, is only a block from the Whitman College campus, which makes it a good choice if you are here on college business or to visit your kids. Two sitting rooms downstairs are furnished with antiques and have fireplaces at each end that make it quite cozy on a chilly evening. Guest room names are from the book *Anne of Green Gables.* Dryad's Bubble is filled with Maxfield Parrish prints and has a claw-foot tub, while in the master suite, you'll find a fireplace, whirlpool tub, deck, and mahogany furniture. The carriage house easily sleeps four and has 1½ bathrooms and a kitchen.

922 Bonsella St., Walla Walla, WA 99362. © **888/525-5501** or 509/525-5501. www.greengablesinn.com. 5 units, 1 carriage house. $105–$135 double; $135 carriage house for 2, $35 each additional guest. Rates include full breakfast. AE, DISC, MC, V. *In room:* A/C, TV/VCR, fridge, hair dryer.

Marcus Whitman Hotel ★★   Originally opened in 1928, this historic high-rise hotel in downtown Walla Walla recently underwent a complete restoration and reopened to the public in February 2001. The Marcus Whitman today makes an excellent base for a Walla Walla wine tour. Not only is there an excellent restaurant and wine bar on the premises, but several others are within a few blocks of the hotel. Guest rooms were designed with a classic elegance to match that of the lobby, which if filled with dark wood paneling, ornate plasterwork, and lots of original details. Most of the guest rooms are in a modern addition, so if you absolutely must stay in the original tower, you'll have to spring for one of the luxurious suites. Other than the suites, the best rooms are the king executives, which are spacious and well designed.

6 W. Rose ST. (P.O. Box 607), Walla Walla, WA 99362. © **866/826-9422** or 509/525-2200. Fax 509/529-9282. www.marcuswhitmanhotel.com. 91 units. $89–$139 double; $149–$279 suite. AE, DC, DISC, MC, V. **Amenities:** Restaurant (Northwest); lounge; exercise room; concierge; business center; room service; laundry service; dry cleaning. *In room:* A/C, TV, dataport, coffeemaker, hair dryer, iron.

Mill Creek Inn ★★ *(Finds* Set on a classically picturesque farm a few miles outside of town, this inn is surrounded by green lawns and big shade trees. The main house's wide veranda, hammocks under the trees, and colorful perennial gardens all add up to the quintessential farm getaway everyone imagines when they think of running away to their own green acres. Guest rooms are in a collection of converted outbuildings, including an old summer kitchen, a bunkhouse, and even the old chicken coop (which now has vaulted ceilings and its own kitchen). An on-site winery makes this an ideal place to use as a base for a wine tour of the Walla Walla area.

2014 Mill Creek Rd., Walla Walla, WA 99362. © **509/522-1234.** www.millcreekbb.com. 5 units. $135–$164 double. Rates include full breakfast. 2-night minimum for cottages. AE, MC, V. Pets accepted with $15 fee per night. *In room:* No phone.

WHERE TO DINE

For breakfast, lunch, or snacks, **Merchants Ltd.,** 21 E. Main St. (© **509/ 525-0900**), has long been Walla Walla's favorite downtown establishment. Basically a huge, glorified deli, it even has live music some evenings. When it's coffee time, try **Coffee Perk,** 4 S. First Ave. (© **509/526-0636**), a favorite downtown espresso place. If it's pub food and microbrews you're after, then head to **Mill Creek Brew Pub,** 11 S. Palouse St. (© **509/522-2440**).

Grapefields ★★ FRENCH Riding the Walla Walla wine wave, this casual bistro, wine bar, and wine shop is the ideal spot in town for a light meal. The menu, though simple, is thoroughly Gallic, with lots of small dishes that are perfect for accompanying a glass of wine. Be sure to get an order of the olive cake, a sort of sponge cake embedded with olives and served with aioli. If you're looking for something to accompany a robust red wine, order the charcuterie plate of mixed cured meats or maybe the paté. The daily specials menu sometimes strays from French (coconut curry soup) and there's also a daily pizza special. Oh, by the way, the wine list here has lots of wines from outside the immediate vicinity, in case you want to expand your horizons.

4 E. Main St. © 509/522-3993. Main courses $7–$9. MC, V. Tues–Thurs 11am–9pm; Fri–Sat 11am–10pm; Sun noon–6pm.

Paisano ★ *(Value* ITALIAN At this casual Italian restaurant in downtown Walla Wall, a welcome small-town sophistication prevails. The menu includes well-prepared Italian classics and a pizza of the day, but you'll also find less familiar fare, including a flavorful veal da Vinci, which is made with shiitake mushrooms, Marsala wine, and sun-dried tomatoes. We like to start a meal here with the pesto Napoléon. If the pesto ravioli shows up on the specials menu, order it. It's creamy yet not too rich. There's a sidewalk cafe area complete with a low fence topped with flower boxes. The wine list features plenty of local wines.

26 E. Main St. © 509/527-3511. Reservations recommended. Main courses $13–$19. MC, V. Mon–Sat 11am–2pm and 5–8:30pm.

Whitehouse-Crawford ★★ NORTHWEST   Housed in what was once a woodworking mill, this stylish restaurant has brought a touch of urban sophistication to remote Walla Walla. The menu is as creative as you'll find anywhere east or west of the Cascades and changes daily. However, you can count on reliable preparations of grilled beef tenderloin as well as smoked pork tenderloin. Anything with the brick-oven flatbread is another good bet, as are, of course, any dishes with Walla Walla sweet onions. Of course, because this is wine country, there are plenty of excellent wines available, many of which can be ordered by the glass. If you don't have the deep pockets necessary to eat in the main dining room, you can dine in the wine bar, and wherever you choose to sit, you'll likely get a glimpse into the adjacent Seven Hills Winery, which shares the building with the restaurant.

55 W. Cherry St. ⓒ 509/525-2222. Reservations highly recommended. Main courses $12–$32. AE, DISC, MC, V. Wed–Sun 5–9pm.

4 The Palouse: A Slice of Small-Town Rural Washington

Dayton: 33 miles (53km) NE of Walla Walla, 62 miles (100km) E of Tri-Cities, 129 miles (208km) SW of Spokane

Between Walla Walla and Spokane lie the rolling Palouse Hills, which are among the most productive wheat lands in the nation. Before the settlement of the region by whites, the Native American peoples had discovered that the Palouse, as it's known, offered ideal grazing land for horses. Horses had reached the Northwest sometime after the Spanish conquered the southern regions of North America, and by the time Lewis and Clark passed through the Palouse, the region's Native Americans had become well known for their horses, which they had bred for stamina and sure-footedness. On the site of present-day Dayton, there was even a Native American horse-racing track. Today these native-bred horses are known as Appaloosas for the Palouse Hills from which they came.

Although the Lewis and Clark expedition passed through this area in 1806, it was not until the 1850s that the first pioneers began settling in the area. By the 1880s, the region was booming as a major wheat- and barley-growing region. Throughout the Palouse, small towns that have long been out of the mainstream of Northwest development are nestled along creek banks below rolling hills. Several of these towns are classic examples of small-town America, with attractive Victorian homes lining their shady streets. Between the towns, the region's roads wind up hill and down, through a zebra-striped landscape. This distinctive striping is due to the farming practice of alternating sections of wheat with land left untilled to reduce erosion on the steep hills.

ESSENTIALS

GETTING THERE   U.S. 12, which runs from Walla Walla to Clarkston, is the main route through the southern part of the Palouse. From Lewiston, Idaho, across the Snake River from Clarkston, U.S. 195 runs north through the heart of the Palouse to Spokane.

VISITOR INFORMATION   For more information on the Dayton area, contact the **Dayton Chamber of Commerce,** 166 E. Main St. (P.O. Box 22), Dayton, WA 99328 (ⓒ **800/882-6299** or 509/382-4825; www.historicdayton. com). For more information on the Pullman area, contact the **Pullman Chamber of Commerce,** 415 N. Grand Ave., Pullman, WA 99163 (ⓒ **800/ 365-6948** or 509/334-3565; www.pullman-wa.com).

EXPLORING THE PALOUSE

Among the many little towns along the route from Walla Walla to Spokane, **Dayton** is by far the prettiest. Its old-fashioned small-town American feel is as genuine as it gets. Dayton was once one of the most important towns in this region and is still the county seat of Columbia County. Its 1887 **Columbia County Courthouse** is the oldest county courthouse still in use as such in the state of Washington. It's open Monday through Friday from 8:30am to 4:30pm. Here you'll also find the **Dayton Depot,** Commercial Street (© 509/ 382-2026), the oldest railway depot in the state (built 1881), which is open for tours Tuesday through Saturday from 11am to 4pm (sometimes also Sun in summer). Admission is $2. All in all, Dayton has 90 buildings on the National Historic Register. On the second Sunday in October each year there is a historic homes tour. In nearby Waitsburg, where there are more Victorian homes, you can also tour the 1883 **Bruce Memorial Museum** (© 509/337-6582), which is open Friday and Saturday from 1 to 4pm and is filled with Victorian-era furnishings.

About 44 miles (71km) northwest of Dayton, you'll find **Palouse Falls State Park.** The spectacular falls here cascade 198 feet into a rock-walled canyon. South of town 21 miles (34km), you'll find **Ski Bluewood** (© 509/382-4725; www.bluewood.com), a small ski area in the Blue Mountains.

Pullman is the largest town in the region and is the home of Washington State University. The university's **Museum of Art,** Fine Arts Center, Stadium Way (© 509/335-1910), is worth a visit. It's open Monday and Wednesday through Friday from 10am to 4pm, Tuesday from 10am to 9pm, and Saturday and Sunday from 1 to 5pm; admission is free. Also on the WSU campus, you'll find the **Museum of Anthropology,** College Hall, Room 110 (© 509/ 335-3441), which has exhibits on human evolution. The museum is open Monday through Thursday from 9am to 4pm, Friday from 9am to 3pm (closed June 16–Aug 15); admission is free.

In **Colfax** you can take a look at the **Codger Pole,** the largest chain-saw sculpture in the world. The pole depicts the members of two football teams that got together in 1988 to replay their 1938 game. You'll find the Codger Pole on John Crawford Boulevard just off Main Street. Some 18 miles (29km) north of Colfax, **Kamiak Butte County Park** provides the ideal vantage point for surveying the vast Palouse. Nearby is **Steptoe Butte State Park,** which also offers good views of the surrounding landscape.

A trip to the Palouse can also include an exploration of Hell's Canyon, which was carved by the Snake River and is the deepest gorge in North America. **Beamer's Hells Canyon Tours** (© 800/522-6966 or 509/758-4800; www.hells canyontours.com), which operates out of Clarkston, Washington, offers a variety of day and overnight jet boat trips up the Snake River. Prices range from $49 for a half-day tour to $98 for full-day tour. Overnight trips are $230.

WHERE TO STAY

The Purple House ⭐ Well, it isn't quite purple, more a tasteful plum, but this 1882 Queen Anne Victorian home certainly does stand out from the other houses in the neighborhood. With its backyard pool and antiques-filled rooms, it is the most distinctive accommodation in the Palouse. German hostess Christine Williscroft takes great pride in her cooking and is sometimes willing to prepare dinners as well as breakfast. The inn is located a block off Dayton's main street.

415 E. Clay St., Dayton, WA 99328. © **800/486-2574** or 509/382-3159. 4 units, 2 with private bathroom. $85–$125 double. Rates include full breakfast. MC, V. Pets accepted with $20 fee per night. **Amenities:** Outdoor pool. *In room:* A/C.

The Weinhard Hotel ★   Constructed in 1889 to house a saloon operated by Jacob Weinhard, the nephew of Portland, Oregon, brewer Henry Weinhard, this brick building is now a comfortable and generally inexpensive Victorian inn. In the large lobby, you'll find a grand piano and, off in one corner, board games and magazines. Guest rooms have high ceilings with overhead fans and in each room there is at least one piece of antique furniture. The best room in the house has a whirlpool tub in the bathroom. Up on the roof, you'll find a terrace garden where you can enjoy a cup of espresso.

235 E. Main St., Dayton, WA 99328. © **509/382-4032.** Fax 509/382-2640. www.weinhard.com. 15 units. $70–$125 double. Rates include continental breakfast. AE, MC, V. Attended pets accepted with $20 fee per night. **Amenities:** Restaurant (American); concierge. *In room:* A/C, TV/VCR, dataport.

WHERE TO DINE
IN DAYTON

Patit Creek Restaurant ★★ FRENCH   This restaurant, located in a little green cottage beside the road on the north side of Dayton, is worth the trip to this small Palouse town. Don't let the proximity to the highway worry you; stained-glass windows hide the passing traffic from diners and allow guests to focus on their food. Though lunches include everything from a smoked turkey sandwich to top sirloin steak bordelaise (and all at reasonable prices), dinners are on a very different level. You might start a meal with chèvre-stuffed dates or a delicious smoked salmon cheesecake. The entree menu includes such dishes as filet mignon *poivre verte* with green peppercorns, cognac, and cream; and sautéed duck breast with red wine, currant, and port demi-glace.

725 Dayton Ave. © **509/382-2625.** Reservations recommended. Main courses $10–$13 at lunch, $18.50–$27.50 at dinner. MC, V. Wed–Fri 11:30am–1:30 or 2pm and 4:30–8 or 9pm; Sat 4:30–8 or 9pm.

5 Spokane

284 miles (457km) E of Seattle, 195 miles (314km) NE of Yakima, 155 miles (250km) N of Walla Walla

Until the 1974 World's Fair focused the eyes of the nation on Spokane and its renovated waterfront and downtown area, this city was little more than a forgotten railroad town deep in the inland Northwest. Today, however, Spokane is the second-largest city in Washington, the largest city between Seattle and Minneapolis, and a center for both commercial and cultural pursuits. Although Spokane isn't really a tourist destination, its proximity to Lake Coeur d'Alene and several Idaho ski areas makes it something of a jumping-off point for explorations of the northern Idaho Rocky Mountains.

For thousands of years Native Americans lived along the Spokane River, and it was at Spokane Falls that the Spokan-ee tribe congregated each year to catch salmon. When the first explorers and fur traders arrived in 1807, it was near these falls that they chose to establish a trading post where they could barter with the Native Americans for beaver pelts. Spokan House (the original spelling had no letter *e*), established in 1810 downriver from Spokane Falls, became the first settlement in the area, but it was not until 1872 that a settlement was established at the falls themselves. When the Northern Pacific Railroad arrived in 1881, the town of Spokan Falls became the most important town in the region. However, in the summer of 1889 the city's downtown commercial district was destroyed by fire. Within 2 years the city had fully recovered from the fire and also changed the spelling of its name.

Today, the Spokane River is still this city's greatest asset. Along the river you'll find numerous parks and a paved hiking/biking trail. The falls themselves are an impressive sight, despite being hemmed in by industrial buildings, and only a few miles from downtown, the Spokane River still looks wild and untamed.

ESSENTIALS

GETTING THERE   Spokane is on I-90, Washington's east-west interstate. U.S. 2 is an alternative route from western Washington. U.S. 395 is the main route from Canada south to Spokane. U.S. 195 connects to Lewiston, Idaho.

Spokane International Airport (© **509/455-6455;** www.spoknaeairports. net) is located 10 miles (16km) west of downtown and is served by Air Canada, Alaska Airlines, America West, Big Sky Airlines, Delta, Horizon, Northwest, Southwest, and United.

Amtrak passenger trains provide service to Spokane. The station is at 221 W. First Ave.

VISITOR INFORMATION   Contact the **Spokane Area Convention & Visitors Bureau,** 801 W. Riverside Ave., Suite 301, Spokane, WA 99201 (© **509/ 624-1341**); or the **Spokane Area Visitor Information Center,** 201 W. Main Ave., Spokane, WA 99201 (© **888/248-3230** or 509/747-3230; www.spokaneareacvb.org or www.spokane.net).

GETTING AROUND   **Rental cars** are available from Alamo, Avis, Dollar, Hertz, National, and Thrifty. If you need a taxi, contact **Spokane Cab** (© **509/ 535-2535**). Public bus service is provided by the **Spokane Transit Authority** (© **509/328-7433;** www.spokanetransit.com); the fare is 75¢.

FESTIVALS   Spokane's nickname is the Lilac City, and the city's biggest annual event is the **Lilac Festival,** which is held each year in mid-May. On the first Sunday in May, the city holds its annual **Lilac Bloomsday Run,** one of the largest timed races in the world (more than 50,000 runners participate).

WHAT TO SEE & DO

Spokane has made it very easy for visitors to get a sense of what the city is all about by mapping out a Spokane City Drive that takes in all the city's highlights. The well-marked route meanders through Spokane and passes by all the city attractions listed below. The drive also takes in some great vistas from the hills to the south of the city.

RIVERFRONT PARK

Created for the 1974 World's Fair Expo and set on an island in the middle of the Spokane River, 100-acre **Riverfront Park** ♣ (© **509/456-4-FUN;** www. spokaneriverfrontpark.com) is the city's pride and joy. The land on which the park stands was once a maze of railroad tracks and depots, and the polluted river was nearly inaccessible to the public. The creation of the park helped rejuvenate downtown Spokane, and today crowds flock here to enjoy everything from

Factoid

In 1910, Spokane became the first city in the country to celebrate Father's Day.

Crosbyana Room **5**
Jundt Art Center & Museum **4**
Northwest Museum of Arts & Culture **2**
Riverfront Park **3**
Riverside State Park **1**
Manito Park **6**

summertime concerts to ice-skating in the winter. Activities for both adults and children abound. The restored 1909 **Looff Carrousel** ★★, with its hand-carved horses, is one of the most beautiful in the country. More contemporary entertainment is offered at the **IMAX Theatre** (© **509/625-6686**), where 70mm films are shown on screens five stories high. A family fun center includes kiddie rides, miniature golf, and arcade games. Throughout the summer there are many special events.

Serving as a spectacular backdrop for the park is the Spokane River, which here cascades over Spokane Falls. The best view of the falls is from the Gondola Skyride that swings out over the falls; rides cost $4.75. The gondola operates spring through fall.

MANITO PARK

Manito Park ★★ (© **509/625-6622**), Spokane's other major green space, is a far more traditional place than Riverfront Park and is located south of downtown beginning at the corner of Division Street and 18th Avenue. Here at Manito, which is located among rocks and pine forest, you'll find several of the most beautiful public gardens in the Northwest. Foremost of these is the classically proportioned Duncan Garden, a formal garden patterned after those of 17th-century Europe. Adjacent to this garden is the Gaiser Conservatory, which brims with exotic tropical plants. The perennial garden and rose garden are at their exuberant peaks in June and should not be missed. The lilac garden is also well worth a visit during the May flowering season. There is also the Nishinomiya Japanese Garden, a strolling pond garden that is a tranquil spot for contemplation. This garden is open from April 1 to November 1 from 8am to a half-hour before dusk. Within this expansive park, you'll also find a picnic area, duck pond, and playground.

MORE ATTRACTIONS

Northwest Museum of Arts & Culture ★★　Before its $28-million renovation and expansion, this museum was the Cheney Cowles Museum, a small regional museum. Now, in this new incarnation, this is one of the finest museums in the Northwest. From the dramatic architecture and landscaping to the eclectic collections and exhibits, this museum makes a big impression. One of the most unusual exhibits is a celebration of small town life that will run through June 2004. In this exhibit life in America's small towns is put on display as a historical and artistic museum piece. There's also an extensive Plateau Indians exhibit. Other galleries are used to mount temporary art exhibits. With its well-balanced blend of history, art, and culture, this museum is now one of the best reasons to visit Spokane.

2316 W. First Ave. ✆ **509/456-3931**. Admission $7 adults, $5 seniors and students, free for children 5 and under; open by donation first Fri of each month. Tues, Thurs, and Sat–Sun 11am–5pm; Wed and Fri 11am–8pm.

Crosbyana Room ★　Bing Crosby got his start here in Spokane, where he spent most of his youth. When young Bing's aspirations soared beyond the bounds of Spokane and he made his name in Los Angeles, the members of his band who chose to stay safely at home must have long regretted their decision. All of Crosby's gold records, his Oscar, and plenty of other memorabilia (including a Bing-endorsed mousetrap and a Bing Crosby Ice Cream box) are on view. You can also take a look at Crosby's boyhood home, which is now home to the Gonzaga Alumni Association, 508 E. Sharp St. Inside you'll find more Bing memorabilia. This building is open Monday through Friday from 8am to 4:30pm.

Crosby Student Center, Gonzaga University, 502 E. Boone Ave. ✆ **509/328-4097**. Free admission. Sept–May Mon–Fri 7:30am–midnight, Sat–Sun 11am–midnight; June–Aug Mon–Fri 8:30am–4pm. Closed holidays.

WINE TOURING

While the Spokane area is far too cold to produce much in the way of wine grapes, there are a handful of wineries in the area that produce wines from Yakima and Columbia Valley grapes.

Caterina ★★　Located downtown in the historic Broadview Dairy Building, Caterina is one of the most consistent wineries in the state. Prices are moderate ($10–$20) and the Merlots are among the best in the state. Good chardonnay also.

905 N. Washington St. ✆ **509/328-5069**. www.caterina.com. Daily noon–5pm. Take exit 281 off I-90, go north on Division St. and then left on N. River Dr.

Arbor Crest Wine Cellars ★★　Located northeast of downtown Spokane in the historic Cliff House atop a 450-foot-high bluff overlooking the Spokane River, this winery boasts the most spectacular setting of any winery in the state. Reds tend to be very light, though drinkable, with the exception of their full-bodied Dionysus blend. Decent chardonnay as well.

4705 N. Fruithill Rd. ✆ **509/927-9463**. www.arborcrest.com. Daily noon–5pm. Take exit 287 off I-90, go north on Argonne Rd., turn right on Upriver Dr. and then left on Fruithill Rd.

Latah Creek Wine Cellars Housed in a Spanish mission–style building amid industrial complexes that back I-90, this winery seems more interested in its extensive gift shop offerings than its wines. Although it's known for its Merlot, we've found the reds to have very odd flavors. A May wine is a specialty here.

13030 E. Indiana Ave. ℂ **509/926-0164.** www.latahcreek.com. Daily 9am–5pm. Take exit 289, go north on Pines Rd. and then turn right on Indiana Ave.

Knipprath Cellars ⭐ Housed in an old school building in a residential neighborhood on Spokane's east side, this small winery is most noteworthy for its port wines, one of which is flavored with chocolate and is absolutely delicious.

5634 E. Commerce Ave. ℂ **509/534-5121.** www.knipprath-cellars.com. Thurs–Sun noon–5pm. Take exit 287, go north on Argonne Rd., turn left on Trent Ave., then turn right on Fancher Rd.

Wyvern Winery Located amid the pines west of Spokane, Worden Winery has its tasting room in a large log house that looks as if it should be selling buffalo jerky rather than chardonnay and Riesling. Expect good reserve chardonnays and decent light-bodied red wines at reasonable prices.

7271 W. 45th Ave. ℂ **509/455-7835.** Daily noon–5pm. Take exit 276 off I-90 and follow signs.

SPORTS & OUTDOOR ACTIVITIES

Walkers, joggers, and cyclists will want to get in some exercise on the **Spokane River Centennial Trail.** The paved trail starts at Nine Mile Falls west of the city and parallels the river for 37 miles (60km) to the Idaho state line, where it connects to the Idaho Centennial Trail for a final leg into Coeur d'Alene (for a total of 65 miles/105km of pathway). Bicycle rentals are available at Riverfront Park.

Riverside State Park ⭐⭐ (ℂ **509/456-3964**), which lies along the banks of the meandering Spokane River on the west edge of the city, has 32 miles (52km) of hiking trails, picnic areas, campgrounds, and access to the Spokane River Centennial Trail. Despite its proximity to the city, the park has a surprisingly wild feel, and the river, as it flows through the park, is one of the prettiest stretches of river in the state. The Bowl and Pitcher Overlook, near the park headquarters, provides a vista of huge basalt boulders on the banks of the river. Adjacent to the park is the Spokane House Interpretive Site, which tells the story of the early fur trade in this area and is open from Memorial Day to Labor Day, Thursday through Monday from 10am to 6pm. To find the park, drive north from downtown on Maple Street, turn left on Northwest Boulevard, left on Menach Drive, and right on Downriver Drive.

For a great view of the region, head northwest 30 miles (48km) to **Mount Spokane State Park** (ℂ **509/238-4258**), where you can drive to the top of the mountain. Hiking trails wander for miles through the forest here.

SKIING Within an hour of Spokane are two small downhill ski areas—**Mt. Spokane Ski & Snowboard Park** (ℂ **509/238-2200** for general information, or 509/443-1397 for the snow line; www.mtspokane.com), 30 miles (48km) northwest of the city; and **49 Degrees North Ski Area,** 50 miles (81km) north on U.S. 395 (ℂ **509/935-6649;** www.ski49n.com). However, it is the ski areas farther afield, in Idaho and Montana, that garner all the attention in this region. Within 2 to 4 hours of Spokane are Red Mountain, Schweitzer, Lookout Pass, Silver Mountain Resort, and The Big Mountain. Cross-country skiers will find 15½ miles (25km) of great groomed trails at **Mount Spokane State Park** (ℂ **509/238-4258**).

SHOPPING

Three renovated downtown buildings provide some interesting shopping opportunities here in Spokane. The **Flour Mill,** 621 W. Mallon Ave. (just across Riverfront Park from downtown), is housed in an old mill that was built beside Spokane Falls and has, in addition to its many interesting shops and restaurants, displays on the mill and Spokane history. **Steam Plant Square,** 159 S. Lincoln St., is the most recent recycling of a downtown industrial building. In this case, the steam plant that once produced heat for all of downtown Spokane has been turned into a fashionable space that preserved as much of the original workings as possible. Old boilers and pipes when juxtaposed against the modern restaurant and shopping facilities here give the entire space the feel of some strange post-apocalyptic sci-fi setting. The **Bennet Block** on the corner of Main Avenue and Stevens Street, also houses specialty shops and restaurants.

WHERE TO STAY

Angelica's Bed and Breakfast ⭐ Located in an elegant tree-shaded neighborhood on a hillside above downtown Spokane, this 1907 Craftsman brick home was designed by celebrated Spokane architect Kirtland Cutter and is filled with elegant period touches including hardwood floors, a tiled fireplace, diamond-pane leaded glass windows, an original frieze on the dining room wall, and lots of built-in cabinetry. It is these many architectural details that make this home so distinctive. Guest rooms are very tastefully furnished. In one room you'll find a wicker bed and in another there is a four-poster, but all of the beds come with down comforters. A small second-story sun porch and a long veranda provide spaces for enjoying the pleasant surroundings of the neighborhood.

1321 W. Ninth Ave., Spokane, WA 99204. ℂ **800/987-0053** or 509/624-5598. Fax 509/624-5598. www. angelicasbb.com. 4 units. $90–$110 double. Rates include full breakfast. AE, MC, V. *In room:* A/C, TV, dataport, hair dryer, iron.

The Fotheringham House ⭐⭐ Located in the historic Browne's Addition neighborhood, this pretty Queen Anne Victorian home, built in 1891 by the first mayor of Spokane, is right across the street from Patsy Clark's Mansion, Spokane's most elegant restaurant. The inn is set behind a white picket fence and is surrounded by a colorful perennial garden. Inside you'll find an abundance of ornate woodwork and antique furniture. Most of the furnishings are period antiques, and in the large shared bathroom you'll find the original claw-foot bathtub.

2128 W. Second Ave., Spokane, WA 99204. ℂ **509/838-1891.** Fax 509/838-1807. www.fotheringham.net. 4 units, 1 with private bathroom. $95–$115 double. Rates include full breakfast. AE, MC, V. *In room:* A/C, hair dryer, no phone.

Hotel Lusso ⭐⭐ This is hands-down the most luxurious hotel in Spokane, so if you like luxury and pampering, this is the place to stay. Affecting a sort of contemporary Italianate styling, this boutique hotel has a very posh European feel. Because the hotel was created from two existing buildings, the rooms here are all a little bit different. Some of the standard rooms can be a bit small, but upgrades are possible in $20 increments. We'd suggest opting to upgrade one or two levels. Most of the rooms have 12- to 14-foot ceilings that make even the smallest rooms feel big. For a splurge, there are the penthouse suites, which have deluxe bathrooms with double whirlpool tubs surrounded by walls of glass. The hotel's Fugazzi restaurant is one of Spokane's hippest and best restaurants. There's also a separate lounge and a complimentary reception each afternoon.

1 N. Post St., Spokane, WA 99201. ℂ **509/747-9750.** Fax 509/747-9751. www.hotellusso.com. 60 units. $155–$175 double; $195–$295 suite. Rates include continental breakfast. AE, DC, DISC, MC, V. **Amenities:**

Restaurant (Northwest), lounge; access to nearby health club; concierge; courtesy airport and downtown shuttle service; room service; massage; dry cleaning. *In room:* A/C, TV, dataport, minibar, hair dryer, iron.

The Kempis Hotel Suites ★★   Housed in a renovated 1906 apartment building, this luxury all-suite hotel abounds in historic character and is filled with antique furnishings. The lobby, with its tile floor and pair of open, polished-wood stairways, has a very European feel, while the guest suites feel like the apartments of wealthy 19th-century city dwellers. Although this small hotel has been impeccably restored, lots of original touches—old light fixtures, built-in cabinets, squeaky wood floors—remind guests that this is indeed a historic building. The suites feel like apartments rather than hotel rooms and are furnished with antiques. All have full kitchens and most also have claw-foot tubs. The hotel's Winged Lion restaurant is one of Spokane's finest restaurants. There is also an adjacent lounge that feels like a 19th-century living room.

326 W. Sixth Ave., Spokane, WA 99204. © **888/236-4321** or 509/747-4321. Fax 509/747-4301. www. thekempis.com. 15 units. $119–$179 double. Rates include continental breakfast. AE, DC, DISC, MC, V. **Amenities:** Restaurant (Northwest); lounge; exercise room; concierge; business center; room service; coin-op laundry; dry cleaning. *In room:* A/C, TV/VCR, dataport, kitchen, coffeemaker, hair dryer, iron.

WestCoast Grand at the Park ★★ *Kids*   Although this is primarily a convention hotel, its location adjacent to downtown Spokane's Riverfront Park makes this the most conveniently located hotel in the city if your plans are to spend some time exploring downtown. In addition to the fun that can be had in Riverfront Park, the hotel also offers a resortlike lagoon-style pool complete with water slide, which makes this a great place for a families. A wide variety of rooms accommodate all types of travelers. Anyone wishing a bit more luxury than the standard rooms afford may want to opt for the executive rooms, which come with balconies overlooking the pool or the river.

303 W. North River Dr., Spokane, WA 99201. © **800/325-4000** or 509/326-8000. Fax 509/325-7329. www. westcoasthotels.com/gap. 402 units. $89–$159 double; $235–$950 suite. AE, DC, DISC, MC, V. Pets accepted. **Amenities:** Restaurant (Continental, American); lounge; 2 swimming pools (1 indoor, 1 outdoor); exercise room; Jacuzzi; sauna; concierge; room service (daily 5:30am–11pm); laundry service; dry cleaning. *In room:* A/C, TV, dataport, coffeemaker, hair dryer, iron.

WHERE TO DINE

For espresso and muffins, we like **Cabin Coffee,** 141 S. Cannon St. (© **509/747-3088**), which is located just a few blocks from the new Northwest Museum of Arts & Culture. For a unique coffee experience, search out Steam Plant Square, at the corner of Lincoln Street and First Avenue. Here you'll find **Have Beans Espresso/The Coffee Boiler,** 159 S. Lincoln St. (© **509/344-0304**), which is located *inside* an old boiler that once produced the steam to heat downtown Spokane. **The Milk Bottle,** 802 W. Garland Ave. (© **509/325-1772**), located a few miles north of downtown, is another unique Spokane establishment. In this case it's an old-time ice cream parlor fronted by a three-story cement milk bottle.

The Elk ★ *Value* INTERNATIONAL   The Elk has been around since the early 1900s when it was the Elk Drug Company, supplying medicines and soda fountain treats to neighborhood residents. Today it has been restored and turned into a chic little pub serving the best of Northwest microbrews along with such unusual pub fare as grilled lamb sandwiches, seared ahi sandwiches, and Anasazibean burgers. The excellent and unusual chicken Caesar soft tacos are our favorite light lunch in Spokane. During the warmer months, try to get a table out front on the sidewalk patio. This is one of Spokane's best bets for cheap eats.

1931 W. Pacific Ave. ☎ **509/363-1973**. Main courses $6.25–$9.25. MC, V. Sun–Thurs 11am–10pm; Fri–Sat 11am–11pm.

Fugazzi ★★ INTERNATIONAL With its blend of contemporary styling and earthy materials (brick walls and wood floor), this restaurant feels both hip and cozy, historical yet stylish. It also happens to serve some of the best food in town. Using the freshest seasonal ingredients, Fugazzi assembles menus that cater to the city's adventuresome palates. How about spicy pecan-crusted calamari to start things out? If you're here with several people or have a big appetite, the various appetizer sampler platters are always good choices. The menu often has a decided slant toward seafood, which is usually well prepared, and Asian flavors also show up a lot.

1 N. Post St. ☎ 509/624-1133. Reservations recommended. Main courses $8–$12 at lunch, $17–$30 at dinner. AE, DISC, MC, V. Mon–Thurs 11:30am–2:30pm and 5–9pm; Fri–Sat 11:30am–2:30pm and 5–10pm.

Milford's Fish House and Oyster Bar ★★ SEAFOOD On the opposite side of the Spokane River from downtown, you'll find the city's best seafood restaurant. With its pressed-tin ceiling and walls covered with old ads, Milford's manages to look as if it's been around since the time of the Great Fire of 1889, and in fact many of the fixtures here were salvaged from various old buildings around town. Sidle up to the bar and peruse the day's oyster menu, then take a seat in one of the back rooms. Although there are people who disagree, we think the oysters are the ticket here. Start with some on the half shell and then move on to baked or pan-fried oysters. The menu changes regularly, but plenty of local favorites, including alder-planked salmon and halibut filets show up frequently.

719 N. Monroe St. ☎ 509/326-7251. Reservations recommended. Main courses $17–$27. MC, V. Sun–Mon 4–9pm; Tues–Sat 5–10pm.

Patsy Clark's Mansion ★★ INTERNATIONAL Built in 1895 to be the grandest mansion in Spokane, Patsy Clark's is still just that. There are 26 rooms, each with a different style, nine fireplaces, and Tiffany stained-glass windows and lamps. The menu changes frequently, but two mainstays that first-timers shouldn't miss are the grilled New York steak with Jack Daniel's whisky sauce and the Chilean sea bass with dill-havarti soufflé. Patsy Clark's tends to attract a very well-heeled clientele, so we suggest dressing for dinner or lunch.

2208 W. Second Ave. ☎ 509/838-8300. Reservations recommended. Main courses $9–$14 at lunch, $24–$36 at dinner. MC, V. Mon–Thurs 11:30am–1:45pm and 5–9pm; Fri 11:30am–1:45pm and 5–10pm; Sat 5–10pm; Sun 10am–1:30pm (brunch) and 5–8pm.

Steam Plant Grill ★ *Finds* INTERNATIONAL Housed in a renovated former steam-generating plant that is now a historic landmark, the Steam Plant Grill is the most unusual restaurant in Spokane. Although utterly contemporary in design, the restaurant is surrounded by the girders, pipes, and boilers that once served to pump steam heat to the buildings of downtown Spokane. The food isn't all that memorable, but it is decent and there's plenty of variety. Burgers, sandwiches, and wraps comprise most of the menu, but there are also more substantial entrees such as grilled salmon and steaks. The restaurant also serves the microbrews of the Coeur d'Alene Brewing Company.

159 S. Lincoln St. ☎ 509/777-3900. Reservations recommended. Main courses $6.25–$17. AE, DISC, MC, V. Sun–Thurs 11:30am–9pm; Fri–Sat 11:30am–11pm.

SPOKANE AFTER DARK

As one of the largest cities in Washington, Spokane has a lively cultural and nightlife scene. To find out what's going on around Spokane, pick up a copy of

The Inlander, a free weekly arts-and-entertainment newspaper. You'll find copies in restaurants, record stores, and bookstores. Particularly noteworthy are the concerts held throughout the year at the **Cathedral of St. John the Evangelist,** 127 E. 12th Ave. (© **509/838-4277**), a Gothic cathedral with a 5,000-pipe organ. If you've just had a hard afternoon of having fun at Riverside Park and you need a cold ale to cool you off, head to the nearby **Ram Restaurant & Big Horn Brewery,** 908 N. Howard St. (© **509/326-3745**), across the street from the Arena.

6 The Grand Coulee Dam Area

85 miles (137km) W of Spokane, 92 miles (148km) NE of Wenatchee

Grand Coulee, formerly a wide, dry valley, is a geologic anomaly left over from the last Ice Age. At that time, a glacier dammed an upstream tributary of the Columbia River and formed a huge lake in what is today Montana. When this prehistoric lake burst through its ice dam, massive floods poured down from the Rocky Mountains. So great was the volume of water that the Columbia River overflowed its normal channel and, as these flood waters flowed southward, they carved deep valleys into the basalt landscape of central Washington. As the floodwaters reached the Cascade Range, they were forced together into one great torrent that was so powerful it scoured out the Columbia Gorge, carving cliffs and leaving us with today's beautiful waterfalls. With the end of the Ice Age, however, the Columbia returned to its original channel and the temporary flood channels were left high and dry. Early French explorers called these dry channels *coulées,* and the largest of them all was Grand Coulee, which is 50 miles (81km) long, between 2 miles (3km) and 5 miles (8km) wide, and 1,000 feet deep.

Located at the northern end of the Grand Coulee, Grand Coulee Dam has long been considered one of the greatest engineering marvels of the 20th century. Constructed during the Great Depression, it was the largest man-made structure on earth at the time of its completion in 1941 and is still the largest concrete dam in North America. The dam is 5,223 feet wide (almost a mile), and impounds the waters of the Columbia River, forming 130-mile-long (209km) Roosevelt Lake. Despite the name, the Grand Coulee Dam did not, however, fill the Grand Coulee with water. That did not happen until the 1950s when Dry Falls Dam was built at the south end of the coulee and waters from Roosevelt Lake were used to fill the Grand Coulee and form 31-mile-long (50km) Banks Lake. The waters of both Roosevelt Lake and Banks Lake have been used to irrigate the arid lands of eastern Washington, turning this region into productive farmlands. The Grand Coulee Dam is also a major producer of hydroelectric power.

ESSENTIALS

GETTING THERE   The towns of Grand Coulee, Coulee Dam, and Electric City are at the junction of Wash. 155, which runs south to Coulee City and north to Omak, and Wash. 174, which runs west to Wash. 17 and east to U.S. 2.

VISITOR INFORMATION   Contact the **Grand Coulee Dam Area Chamber of Commerce,** P.O. Box 760, Grand Coulee, WA 99133-0760 (© **800/268-5332;** www.grandcouleedam.org).

WHAT TO SEE & DO

You can learn the history of the dam by stopping in at the **Grand Coulee Dam Visitor Arrival Center** (© **509/633-9265**), which is open daily. This center is also where you can arrange for a free guided tour of the dam (tours are held on the hr. throughout the summer and, between Oct and Memorial Day weekend, at 10am, noon, and 2 and 4pm). However, in the wake of the September 11, 2001, terrorist attacks, tours were suspended, so be sure to call first to confirm that tours are once again being offered. Every night between the end of May and the end of September, the **world's largest laser-light show** is projected onto the face of the dam. The accompanying narration is broadcast over the radio at 90.1 FM and tells the history of Grand Coulee and the dam. There is also a self-guided walking tour through historic Coulee Dam, the government town built to house workers during the construction of the dam.

Lake Roosevelt, with its 660 miles (1,063km) of shoreline, provides ample opportunities for watersports and fishing and comprises the **Lake Roosevelt National Recreation Area,** 1008 Crest Dr., Coulee Dam, WA 99116 (© **509/ 738-6266** or 509/725-2715; www.nps.gov/laro). Along the shores of the lake are 17 car campgrounds and an equal number of boat-in campgrounds. About 22 miles (35km) north of Davenport, at the confluence of the Spokane and Columbia rivers, stands **Fort Spokane,** which was built in 1880. Four of the original buildings are still standing. An 1892 brick guardhouse here now serves as a visitor center, though the recreation area's main visitor center is the Grand Coulee Dam Visitor Arrival Center right at the dam.

Much of the land bordering Roosevelt Lake lies within the Colville Indian Reservation. In the town of Coulee Dam, you can visit the **Colville Confeder-ated Tribes Museum,** 512 Mead Way (© **509/633-0751**), a small museum with interesting displays of baskets and tribal regalia, as well as historical pho-tos. The museum is open April through December, Monday through Saturday from 10am to 6pm. Admission is by donation. The Colville tribes also operate the adjacent **Coulee Dam Casino,** 515 Birch St. (© **800/556-7492**).

Some 30 miles (48km) down the Grand Coulee, just south of Coulee City on Wash. 17, you can have a look at a natural wonder that's as impressive as the dam. **Dry Falls** are the remains of a massive waterfall created by the same flood of water that scoured out the Grand Coulee. At their peak flow, the waters cas-cading 400 feet over these falls stretched 3½ miles (5.5km) wide (in comparison, Niagara Falls are only 1 mile/1.5km wide and 165 ft. tall). **The Dry Falls Visi-tor Center** (© **509/632-5214** or 509/633-9192) is located at the Dry Falls Overlook on Wash. 17. If you're interested in going to the base of the falls, con-tinue south 2 miles (3km) to **Sun Lakes State Park,** which has a road leading back to the falls. Within this park you'll also find a campground and lakes for swimming, boating, and fishing.

For a glimpse of another unusual waterfall, head 10 miles (16km) south of Coulee City on Pinto Ridge Road. Here you'll find **Summer Falls State Park,** which is the site of Summer Falls, an impressive man-made waterfall formed by the runoff water from the Grand Coulee's Banks Lake. The 165-foot-tall falls pour over a basalt cliff and into Billy Clapp Lake.

Ten miles (16km) south of Sun Lakes State Park, you'll find **Lake Lenore Caves.** These caves were created by the same floodwaters that carved Dry Falls. In this case, the waters tore off chunks of basalt as they flowed past the cliffs above today's Lake Lenore. The caves were later used by wandering bands of pre-historic Indians. There are seven caves accessible along an established trail.

Continuing south will bring you to **Soap Lake,** an alkaline lake named for the soapsuds that gather on its shores. For centuries the lake has attracted peo-ple who believe the waters have medicinal properties. Once a busy health spa,

Soap Lake today is a quiet little town. However, it does have a couple of good lodges where you can soak in the lake's waters. A public town beach also provides access to the lake.

About 25 miles (40km) south of Soap Lake lies **Moses Lake**, which is popular with water-skiers. South of Moses Lake lies the Potholes Reservoir and Columbia National Wildlife Refuge. This area is a stark contrast of desert and water, with lots of basalt outcroppings adding drama to the landscape. To explore this region, drive south from Moses Lake on Wash. 17, west on Wash. 262, south on K2 SE Road (which becomes Morgan Lake Rd.), west on Wash. 26.

WHERE TO STAY
IN COULEE DAM

Columbia River Inn ⭐ Located right across the street from Grand Coulee Dam Visitor Center, this remodeled motel is convenient for viewing the laser light show (just cross the street to the park). Guest rooms have attractive pine furnishings and small balconies with partial dam views, and some have their own whirlpool tubs.

10 Lincoln St., Coulee Dam, WA 99116. ℂ **800/633-6421** or 509/633-2100. Fax 509/633-2633. www.columbiariverinn.com. 36 units. $75–$95 double; $95–$190 suite. AE, DISC, MC, V. **Amenities:** Outdoor pool; coin-op laundry. *In room:* A/C, TV, dataport, coffeemaker.

Four Winds Guest House ⭐ Located in the picture-perfect company town that was built to house engineers and laborers working on the dam, this inn is in a former engineers dorm where Pres. Franklin D. Roosevelt once held a meeting during his visit to the dam site. The guest rooms are simply furnished.

301 Lincoln St., Coulee Dam, WA 99116. ℂ **800/786-3146** or 509/633-3146. Fax 509/633-2454. http://four windsguesthouseb-b.uswestdex.com. 10 units, 1 with private bathroom. $65 double with shared bathroom; $85 double with private bathroom. Rates include continental breakfast. AE, DISC, MC, V. **Amenities:** Access to nearby health club. *In room:* No phone.

IN SOAP LAKE

The Notaras Lodge ⭐⭐ A modern log building only steps from the lake offers the most interesting lodgings in Soap Lake. Each room at the lodge is decorated differently and many commemorate local and national celebrities. Unusual woodworking, log beds, Native American artifacts, and Western trappings are all part of the fantasy world at the Notaras Lodge. Eight rooms have whirlpool tubs, and all the rooms have lake water piped into them so you can soak in the therapeutic waters.

P.O. Box 987, Soap Lake, WA 98851. ℂ **509/246-0462.** www.notaraslodge.com. 14 units. $65–$125 double. DISC, MC, V. Pets accepted with $50 deposit and $10 fee. **Amenities:** Restaurant (American); lounge; massage. *In room:* A/C, TV, fridge.

Appendix:
Washington in Depth

While this state in the upper-left-hand corner of the country shares a name with the nation's capital, there the similarities end. This Washington is infinitely more varied than that other Washington, despite not having the long history, politics, or monumental buildings. Not only are there vast green forests of conifers, the shimmering waters of Puget Sound, snow-clad volcanic peaks, and Seattle's countless espresso bars, but there are also vineyards and arid shrub-steppe landscapes, orca whales and Roosevelt elk, Microsoft and Amazon.com. Want to know a bit more? Read on, and you'll gain a little perspective on this fascinating state.

1 The Natural Environment

The state of Washington encompasses a vast area that contains within its boundaries an amazing diversity of natural environments—not only lush forests, but glacier-covered peaks, alpine meadows, grasslands, and sagebrush-covered hills. Together these diverse environments support a surprisingly wide variety of natural life that has evolved to fill the many niches created by Northwest geography.

Washington's Pacific Ocean coastline stretches for roughly 150 miles (242km), from the Columbia River to the tip of the Olympic Peninsula, and inland waters including Puget Sound, the Strait of Juan de Fuca, and the myriad of channels through the San Juan Islands add hundreds of more miles of coastline. This extensive shoreline provides habitat for numerous species of marine mammals, as well as large populations of seabirds such as cormorants, tufted puffins, and pigeon guillemots. Of the marine mammals that frequent Washington waters, the largest and most impressive are the more than 20,000 Pacific gray whales that pass by the state each year between December and April as they make their annual migration south to their breeding grounds off Baja California. These whales can often be seen from shore at various points along the coast, and numerous whale-watching tours operate out of Grays Harbor. More frequently spotted, however, are harbor seals and Steller's and California sea lions, which are often seen lounging on rocks, especially in the San Juan Islands. Off the remote beaches of the Olympic Peninsula, there's even a small population of sea otters, and river otters can sometimes be spotted in the San Juan Islands and Puget Sound.

Washington's Pacific coastline is roughly divided into a wild and rugged northern coast, at the base of the Olympic Mountains, and a more developed southern coast characterized by long sandy beaches backed by low dunes. Rain, however, is this coastline's single most defining character, especially along the northern shoreline. As moist winds from the Pacific Ocean rise up and over the Olympic Mountains, the winds drop their moisture as rain and snow. In the northwest corner of Washington state, on the western slopes of the Olympic Mountains, rain is measured not by the inch but by the foot; and annual rainfall can exceed 12 feet! This tremendous amount of rain has produced the country's only temperate rain forests and some of the largest trees on earth. Although the Sitka spruce is the most characteristic tree of these rain forests, it is the

Douglas fir, common throughout the Northwest and second only to the coast redwood of Northern California in overall size, that's the most impressive, sometimes reaching 300 feet in height. Other common trees of the rain forest include western hemlocks, Alaska cedars, western red cedars, and big-leaf maples. These latter trees are often draped with thick mats of moss.

More than a century of intensive logging has, however, left the region's forests of centuries-old trees shrunken to remnant groves scattered in often remote and inaccessible areas. How much exactly is still left is a matter of hot debate between the timber industry and environmentalists, and the battle to save the remaining old-growth forests continues, with both sides claiming victories and losses with each passing year. Among this region's most celebrated and controversial wild residents is the northern spotted owl, which, because of its large requirements for undisturbed old-growth forest and its listing as a federally threatened species, brought logging of old-growth forests to a virtual halt in the early 1990s. Today, concern is also focused on the marbled murrelet, a small bird that feeds on the open ocean but nests in old-growth forests.

The Olympic Mountains, which rise to 7,965 feet at the top of Mount Olympus, are a rugged range capped with alpine meadows, glaciers, and ice fields. Although black-tailed deer are the most common large mammals of these mountains, there is also a population of mountain goats in Olympic National Park. However, these goats are not native to this area and, because of the damage they cause the fragile high-elevation meadows, attempts have been made to remove them. The Roosevelt elk, the largest commonly encountered land mammal in the state, can be found here and throughout the western regions of the state. It was to protect these animals that the land now known as Olympic National Park was originally set aside.

To the east of the Olympic Peninsula lie the lowlands of the Puget Sound region. Because of the mild climate of this area, this is the most densely populated region of the state. Puget Sound is a maze of waterways that were formed by glacial activity during the last Ice Age, when the polar ice sheets that stretched southward into the region carved out long narrow valleys that were later flooded as the glaciers retreated.

Just north of Puget Sound, in the waters surrounding the San Juan Islands, live some of the Northwest's most celebrated residents—orca whales, which are also known as killer whales. Once maligned as the wolves of the sea, these largest members of the porpoise family have become a symbol of the region. During the summer, numerous tour companies in the San Juan Islands offer whale-watching tours. Bald eagles also flock to the Puget Sound area. Although they can be seen throughout the year around Puget Sound and in the San Juan Islands, they gather in largest numbers each winter on the Skagit River, north of Seattle.

To the east of Puget Sound rise the mountains of the 700-mile-long (1,127km) Cascade Range, which stretches from Northern California to southern British Columbia. The most prominent features of the Cascades are its volcanic peaks: Mount Baker, Glacier Peak, Mount Rainier, Mount St. Helens, and Mount Adams. The eruption of Mount St. Helens on May 18, 1980, vividly reminded Washingtonians that this is still a volcanically active region, and geologists warn that, based on past eruption cycles, Mount Rainier might be next.

The same rainfall that gives the Olympic Peninsula its rain forests leaves the Cascades with frequent heavy snows and dozens of glaciers, among which are the largest glacier, the lowest elevation glacier, and the only advancing glacier in the 48 contiguous states. In 1972, Mount Rainier set a world record when

93½ feet of snow fell in one winter. However, that record was broken during the winter of 1998–99, when 1,140 inches (95 ft.) of snow fell on Mount Baker.

Among the wild residents of the Cascades are mountain goats that can sometimes be seen in the North Cascades, along the shores of Lake Chelan, and in Mount Rainier National Park. Picas and marmots are some of the high country's smaller but more visible and audible residents. The former is a mouse-sized relative of the rabbit, while the latter is the largest member of the squirrel family. Both live in high meadows and rocky slopes and both can be recognized by their distinctive whistles. The pica's is small and squeaky, while the marmot's is high, loud, and shrill. In the remote northern section of North Cascades National Park there are even wolves and grizzly bears, though these large predators are almost never encountered by humans. Cougars also roam the forests throughout the Northwest and are as elusive as the grizzly and the wolf.

East of the Cascades, less than 200 miles (322km) from the rain-forest valleys of the Olympic Peninsula, so little rain falls that only sagebrush, grasses, and a few other hardy plants can survive. This arid landscape, known as the Columbia Plateau, is a vast, dry, shrub-steppe region that stretches eastward to the Rockies, a side range of which actually reaches into the northeast corner of the state. The Columbia Plateau was formed 10 million to 15 million years ago by sheets of lava flowing over the land and covering more than 100,000 square miles (161,000km²). Through this desolate landscape flows the Columbia River, which, together with its tributary the Snake, forms the second-largest river drainage in the United States.

During the last Ice Age, roughly 12,000 to 15,000 years ago, a glacier blocked the flow of the Columbia, forming a huge lake behind its ice dam. This vast prehistoric lake repeatedly burst its ice dam, sending massive and devastating walls of water flooding down the Columbia. These floodwaters were sometimes 1,000 feet high and carried with them ice and rocks, which scoured out the Columbia Gorge in much the same way that glaciers scoured out California's Yosemite Valley. In both places the results were similar—tall, narrow waterfalls. These same floodwaters also scoured the landscape of eastern Washington, leaving in their wake abandoned river channels known as coulees and channeled scablands. The most famous of these coulees is Grand Coulee, site of one of the largest dams on earth.

This and the dozens of other dams on the Columbia and Snake rivers have become the focus of one of the region's current environmental battles. Though many of these dams have fish ladders to allow salmon to return upriver to spawn, salmon populations have been steadily dwindling for more than a century. Overfishing for salmon canneries in the late 19th century struck the first major blow to salmon populations, and the large dams, mostly built during the middle part of the 20th century, created further barriers both to returning adults and to young salmon headed downstream to the Pacific. Among the obstacles faced by these young salmon are slower river flow in the reservoirs behind the dams, turbines that kill fish by the thousands, and irrigation canals that often confuse salmon into swimming out of the river and into farm fields. Compounding the problem has been the use of fish hatcheries to supplement wild salmon populations (hatchery fish tend to be less vigorous than wild salmon). A salmon recovery plan adopted to save threatened runs of native salmon has yet to be fully implemented, as farmers, electricity producers, shipping companies, and major users of hydroelectric power continue to fight its requirements. With new listings of salmon runs under the Endangered Species Act, more restrictions on development near salmon streams have begun to be instituted throughout the Puget Sound region. Out in the southeastern corner of the state, however, the battle rages over removal of dams on the Snake River. Even the seeming wild and untamed Olympic Peninsula has been the focus of a heated debate over the removal of two small dams on the Elwha River.

2 Washington Today

While Washington is a large and diverse state, encompassing not only rain forests and shrub-steppe but also volcanoes and glaciers, the vast majority of the population lives between the Cascades and Puget Sound in places where it is only necessary to lift one's eyes to understand why Washington is such a popular vacation destination. From Olympia to Bellingham, a quick glance toward the horizon (on a sunny day, that is) will present a mesmerizing view over the shimmering waters of Puget Sound to the snow-covered peaks of the Olympic Mountains, the massive mound of Mount Rainier, the glacier-clad slopes of Mount Baker, or the forested shores of the San Juan Islands. With horizons like these, it's easy to see why people would want to live here.

If, when you lift your eyes, it happens to be summer and the sun happens to be shining and you happen to be in Seattle at the time, you will likely find that Seattle can be irresistibly seductive. Not only is there the bustle of the city to entertain you, but the San Juan Islands, Mount St. Helens National Volcanic Monument, and the state's three national parks—Mount Rainier, North Cascades, and Olympic—are all relatively close at hand. However, if you're averse to crowds, consider visiting in the spring or fall when you might luck into a sunny week and won't have to deal with high hotel rates and long lines for ferries. Feeling really adventurous? Try a wintertime visit and see for yourself how much it rains here. Not only will you find great bargains on hotel room rates in Seattle, but you might even be mistaken for a local.

Washingtonians for the most part don't let the weather stand between them and the outdoors. The temptation is too great to head for the hills, the river, the beach, the sound, or the islands. Consequently, life in Washington's cities tends to revolve as much around parks, gardens, waterfronts, and other outdoor spaces as it does around such traditional urban pastimes as shopping, the performing arts, and dining. And when such green spaces as Seattle's Discovery and Green Lake parks, Tacoma's Point Defiance Park, and Spokane's Riverfront and Minto parks aren't wild enough to satisfy the craving for an outdoor experience, most of the state's population can be in a national park, national forest, or state park within an hour or two. Parks, both small and large, are where people find tranquillity, where summer festivals are held, and where locals take their visiting friends and relatives.

The region's outdoors aesthetic does not, however, preclude a strong support of the arts. The Seattle Opera is one of the finest companies in the country (well known for its stagings of Wagner's *Ring* series), as is the Seattle Symphony, which, performs in Benaroya Hall, adjacent to the Seattle Art Museum. Seattle is also a center for live theater, especially small, fringe theater productions. Tacoma, Olympia, and Spokane all have large, modern, and active performing arts centers as well. Just as bad weather doesn't stop Washingtonians from enjoying the outdoors, good weather is no barrier to the performing arts. During the summer months, numerous festivals around the state take music, theater, and dance outdoors. These festivals feature everything from chamber music to polka bands to alternative rock.

Neither are the visual arts overlooked. Currently in the works are a new International Glass Museum in Tacoma (which should be open to the public by the time you read this) and a new home for the Tacoma Art Museum. In December 2001, Spokane opened its impressive new Northwest Museum of Arts and Culture. In Seattle, the performing arts and the visual arts have been melded together in the form of Microsoft cofounder Paul Allen's Experience Music Project. This museum of rock 'n' roll music was inspired by Allen's obsession with Jimi Hendrix, who was a Seattle native. The design of the museum, by avant-garde architect Frank Gehry, has added yet another bizarre piece of architecture to the city that gave the world the Space Needle.

In the year 2000, and also by the hand of Allen, Seattle's venerable and much-disparaged Kingdome came crashing down in a cloud of dust as demolition experts imploded the massive cement structure in order to make way for a new football stadium for the Seattle Seahawks football team, which happens to be owned by Allen. That new stadium, which now stands side by side with the Seattle Mariners' Safeco Field, is scheduled for completion in time for the 2002 football season. Allen has also been behind the redevelopment of much of the land that once surrounded the Kingdome, including a renovation of the old Union Station.

However, recent years have not been all sunshine and grande espressos here in Latte Land. The World Trade Organization riots in 1999 focused the world's attention on Seattle, casting the city in a less-than-flattering light. In 2001, riots broke out again, this time during the city's annual Fat Tuesday celebrations (similar to Mardi Gras). The city was then rocked by a powerful earthquake that left many historic Pioneer Square buildings severely damaged. With the crash of the dot.com economy, Seattle has been particularly hard hit, but so far Microsoft and most of Seattle's largest tech companies have managed to weather the storm. At press time, it was still uncertain what effect layoffs at Boeing would have on the state's economy. In the wake of the terrorist attacks of September 11, 2001, the airplane manufacturer announced large layoffs.

However, despite economic ups and downs, Washingtonians continue to share a common interest in the outdoors, and it is this interest that dominates the character of the region. Nowhere else in the country is such a diverse natural beauty so close at hand, even for those who live in the cities. And if winters are long, gray, and rainy, well, you just put on a colorful rain jacket, fill the travel mug with a double tall raspberry latte, and head for the hills, mountains, rivers, or coast regardless.

3 Washington History 101

EARLY HISTORY From the bays and rivers of Puget Sound to the rolling grasslands of southeastern Washington's Palouse region, what is today the state of Washington has been populated by numerous Native American tribes for thousands of years. Exactly how long humans have resided in what is now Washington is still open to debate. Human remains more than 12,000 years old have been found at a mastodon kill site on the

Dateline

- 15,000 to 12,000 B.C. Massive floods, as much as 1,000 feet deep, rage down the Columbia River and carve the Columbia Gorge.
- 10,000 B.C. Earliest known human inhabitation of the Northwest.
- 1774 Spanish explorer Juan Perez sails to 54° north latitude; Bruno de Heceta and Francisco de la Bodega y Quadra chart the Northwest coast.

continues

Olympic Peninsula (the tusks of this ancient pachyderm can be seen in Sequim's Museum & Arts Center). The bones of the controversial Kennewick Man, discovered in 1996 on the banks of the Columbia River in eastern Washington, have been dated at more than 9,000 years of age.

It is estimated that before the arrival of Euro-Americans in this region, there were 125 distinct Northwest tribes speaking 50 languages. However, between the 1780s, when white explorers and traders began frequenting the Northwest coast, and the 1830s, when the first settlers began arriving, the Native American population of the Northwest was reduced to perhaps a tenth of its historic numbers. It was not war that wiped out these people, but diseases such as smallpox, measles, malaria, and influenza. Native Americans had no resistance to these diseases and entire tribes were soon decimated by fast-spreading epidemics.

Throughout the Puget Sound region, there were numerous small tribes that subsisted primarily on salmon, halibut, shellfish, and whales. While seafood was a mainstay of the native diet, cedar trees were the most important building material. Cedar was used by these tribes to build both longhouses and large canoes. Even clothing was made from the bark of cedar trees. The natural abundance of the region allowed many of these tribes to develop complex cultures, though it was farther north, in present-day British Columbia and Alaska, that wealth was displayed in the shape of huge totem poles.

It was the Columbia River tribes, however, that became the richest of the Washington tribes through their control of Celilo Falls, which was historically the richest salmon fishing location in the Northwest. These massive falls on the Columbia River east of present-day The Dalles, Oregon,

1785 James Hanna becomes the first fur trader to ship pelts from the Northwest to China.

1805–06 Expedition led by Meriwether Lewis and William Clark crosses the continent and spends the winter at the mouth of the Columbia River.

1810 Spokan House is established as a fur-trading post near present-day Spokane.

1819 Spain cedes all lands above 42° north latitude.

1824 Russia gives up claims to land south of Alaska; Fort Vancouver is founded by Hudson's Bay Company.

1833 The Hudson's Bay Company's Fort Nisqually becomes the first non-native settlement on Puget Sound.

1845 Pioneers from Missouri establish New Market, the first town in Washington, at present-day Tumwater.

1846 The 49th parallel is established as the boundary between American and British territories in the Northwest.

1847 Marcus and Narcissa Whitman and several other residents of their mission are massacred by Cayuse Indians.

1852 Seattle is founded.

1853 Washington becomes a U.S. territory.

1859 U.S. and Britain come to the brink of war over a pig killed on San Juan Island.

1883 Northern Pacific Railroad connects Puget Sound with St. Paul, Minnesota.

1889 Washington gains statehood.

1897 Klondike gold rush begins, bringing prosperity to Seattle.

1916 William Boeing launches his first airplane from the waters of Seattle's Lake Union.

1928 Washington's domed capitol building, the tallest domed state capitol in the nation, is completed.

1940s Boeing airplane plants turn out thousands of B-17s and B-29s.

1943 In eastern Washington, U.S. government builds top-secret plutonium-manufacturing plant that produces the nuclear material for the bomb dropped on Nagasaki; Japanese

continues

witnessed the annual passage of millions of salmon, which were speared and dip-netted by Native Americans who then smoked the fish to preserve it for the winter. Some Native Americans still fish for Columbia River salmon as they once did, perched on precarious wooden platforms and with dip net in hand. However, Celilo Falls are gone, inundated beneath the reservoir created by The Dalles Dam, which was completed in 1957. You can learn more about the history of Columbia River tribes at the Columbia Gorge Interpretive Center in Stevenson, Washington. You can also see a superb collection of Native American baskets at the Columbia Gorge's Maryhill Museum of Art, which is east of The Dalles.

Today, there are numerous reservations across the state, and at several of these, including the Yakama, Makah, Suquamish, and Colville reservations, you can learn about these respective tribes at museums and cultural centers. You can also do a bit of gambling at quite a few Indian casinos all across the state.

Americans are relocated to internment camps.

- 1962 Seattle's Century 21 world's fair gives the city its most identifiable structure: the Space Needle.
- 1971 Starbucks coffee is founded in Seattle.
- 1980 Mount St. Helens erupts violently on May 18.
- 1997 Boeing merges with competitor McDonnell Douglas.
- 1999 Safeco Field, the Seattle Mariners' retractable roof baseball stadium, opens. Rioting erupts at Seattle meeting of the World Trade Organization (WTO).
- 2000 Kingdome is demolished to make way for a new football stadium. Experience Music Project opens at Seattle Center.
- 2001 Riots break out during annual Fat Tuesday celebration. Earthquake damages numerous historic buildings in Pioneer Square area. While the Euro-American history of Washington extends back only to the late 18th century and settlers did not begin arriving until the middle of the 19th century, this region has been home to Native American cultures for thousands of years.

THE AGE OF EXPLORATION   Though a Spanish ship reached what is now southern Oregon in 1542, the Spanish had no interest in the gray and rainy coast. Nor did famed British buccaneer Sir Francis Drake, who in 1579 sailed his ship the *Golden Hind* as far north as the mouth of Oregon's Rogue River. Drake called off his explorations in the face of what he described as "thicke and stinking fogges."

Though the Spanish laid claim to all of North America's west coast, they had little interest in the lands north of Mexico. However, when the Spanish found out that Russian fur traders were establishing themselves in Alaska and along the North Pacific coast, Spain took a new interest in the Northwest. Several Spanish expeditions sailed north from Mexico to reassert the Spanish claim to the region. In 1775, Spanish explorers Bruno de Heceta and Francisco de la Bodega y Quadra charted much of the Northwest coast, and though they found the mouth of the Columbia River, they did not enter it.

Within a few years, the Spanish found their claims to the region also being challenged by English traders. Capt. James Cook, on a voyage of discovery that began in 1776, spent time at Nootka Sound on Vancouver Island, where the native peoples were eager to trade furs. Though Cook was killed in Hawaii later in the same voyage, his crew discovered en route back to England that the Chinese would pay astronomical prices for Northwest furs, especially sea otter pelts.

By 1785, the fur trade between the Northwest and China was well underway, with the British now asserting a claim to the Pacific Northwest. The Spanish and

English teetered on the brink of war, but a compromise was worked out and the Spanish agreed to allow continued English trade in the area.

The negotiations of this settlement took place in 1792 at Nootka Sound (in present-day British Columbia), with Capt. George Vancouver serving as English envoy. Before reaching Nootka Sound, Vancouver spent time exploring and mapping much of the Northwest. Though he passed the Columbia River off as unimportant, he sailed up the Strait of Juan de Fuca and discovered a large inland sea that he named Puget Sound, after one of his lieutenants. Vancouver's negotiations at Nootka failed to establish a firm British claim to the land, but with sea otter populations decimated by several intense years of trading, interest in the Northwest was waning in both England and Spain.

Now a new player entered the Northwest arena of trade and exploration in the person of American trader Robert Gray. Risking a passage through treacherous sandbars, Gray sailed his ship, *Columbia Rediviva,* into the mouth of the long-speculated-upon Great River of the West, which he named the Columbia River after his ship. This discovery established the first American claim to the region. When news of Gray's discovery reached the United States and England, both countries began speculating on a northern water route across North America. Such a route, if it existed, would facilitate trade with the Northwest.

In 1793, Scotsman Alexander MacKenzie made the first overland trip across North America north of New Spain. Crossing British Canada on foot, MacKenzie arrived somewhere north of Vancouver Island. After reading MacKenzie's account of his journey, Thomas Jefferson decided that the United States needed to find a better route overland to the Northwest. To this end he commissioned Meriwether Lewis and William Clark to lead an expedition up the Missouri River in hopes of finding a single easy portage that would lead to the Columbia River. Beginning in 1804, the members of the Lewis and Clark expedition paddled up the Missouri, crossed the Rocky Mountains on foot, and then paddled down the Columbia River to its mouth. A French-Canadian trapper and his Native American wife, Sacagawea, were enlisted as interpreters, and it was the presence of Sacagawea that helped the expedition gain acceptance among Western tribes. After spending the very dismal, wet winter of 1805–06 at the mouth of the Columbia, the expedition headed back east. Discoveries made by the expedition added greatly to the scientific and geographical knowledge of the continent. In Fort Canby State Park, at the mouth of the Columbia River, you'll find the Lewis and Clark Interpretive Center.

In 1819, the Spanish relinquished all claims north of the present California-Oregon state line, and the Russians gave up their claims to all lands south of Alaska. This left only the British and Americans dickering for control of the Northwest.

SETTLEMENT   Only 6 years after Lewis and Clark spent the winter at the mouth of the Columbia, employees of John Jacob Astor's Pacific Fur Company managed to establish themselves at the mouth of the Columbia River on the Oregon side at a site they called Fort Astoria. However, during the War of 1812, they handed over the fort to the British. In the wake of this war, the British still dominated the region, but American trade was tolerated. No firm decision was arrived at concerning possession of the Northwest.

With the decline of the sea otter population, British fur traders turned to the beaver and headed inland up the Columbia River. For the next 30 years or so, fur-trading companies would be the sole authority in the Northwest. Fur-trading posts (including Spokan House, which was established in 1810 near present-day Spokane) were established throughout the region, though most were on the eastern edge of the territory in the foothills of the Rocky Mountains. The powerful Hudson's Bay Company (HBC) eventually became the single fur-trading company in the Northwest.

In 1824, the HBC established its Northwest headquarters at Fort Vancouver, 100 miles (161km) up the Columbia near the mouth of the Willamette River. Between 1824 and 1846, when the 49th parallel was established as the boundary between British and American northwestern lands, Fort Vancouver was the most important settlement in the region. Today, a replica of the fort has been built and is part of the Vancouver National Historic Reserve.

By the 1830s, the future of the Northwest had arrived in the form of American missionaries. The first was Jason Lee, who established his mission in the Willamette Valley near present-day Salem, Oregon. Two years later, in 1836, Marcus and Narcissa Whitman, along with Henry and Eliza Spaulding, made the overland trek to Fort Vancouver, then backtracked into what is now eastern Washington and Idaho, to establish two missions. This journey soon inspired other settlers to make the difficult overland crossing.

In 1840, a slow trickle of American settlers began making the 2,000-mile (3,220km) journey across the continent. Their destination was the Oregon country, which had been promoted as a veritable Eden with wide expanses of land just waiting to be claimed. In 1843, Marcus Whitman, after traveling east to plead with his superiors not to shut down his mission, headed back west, leading 900 settlers along the Oregon Trail. Before these settlers arrived, the small population of retired trappers, missionaries, and HBC employees who were living at Fort Vancouver and in nearby Oregon City had formed a provisional government in anticipation of the land-claim problems that would arise with the influx of settlers to the region.

In 1844, Oregon City became the first incorporated town west of the Rocky Mountains. This outpost in the wilderness, a gateway to the fertile lands of the Willamette Valley, was the destination of the wagon trains that began traveling the Oregon Trail, and which each year brought more and more settlers to the region. As the land in the Willamette Valley was claimed, settlers began fanning out to different regions of the Northwest so that during the late 1840s and early 1850s many new towns, including Seattle and Portland, were founded.

Many wagon trains stopped at the Whitman mission near present-day Walla Walla, and it was one of these groups of pioneers that brought the measles to the region. Native Americans of the Cayuse tribe, many of whom lived at the Whitman mission, had no resistance to the disease, and soon their population was decimated. Whitman, who was looked upon as a doctor, was unable to stop the spread of the disease. In retribution for his inability to cure the Native Americans at the mission, several Cayuse attacked the remote outpost and killed the Whitmans and several other whites who were staying there. At Walla Walla's Whitman Mission National Historic Site you can learn more about this sad chapter in Northwest history.

It was the Whitman massacre and the subsequent demand for territorial status and U.S. military protection that brought about the establishment of the first U.S. territory west of the Rockies. Though the line between American and British land in the Northwest had been established at the 49th parallel (the current Canadian-American border) in 1846, it was not until 1848, in the wake of the Whitman massacre, that Oregon was finally given U.S. territorial status.

Washington, however, would have to wait another 5 years, until 1853, to officially become a territory.

The establishment of the 49th parallel as the boundary between U.S. and British territories extended only as far as the main channel between the mainland and Vancouver Island, which was firmly in the hands of the British. However, because there was disagreement over where the main channel was, American and British troops jointly occupied San Juan Island. When, in 1859, a British pig rooting in an American soldier's potato patch was shot and killed, the two nations came to the brink of war. It took international arbitration to settle the disagreement, which was finally resolved by turning San Juan Island over to U.S. control. Both the American Camp and the English Camp are preserved as part of the San Juan National Historic Park.

In 1881, the first transcontinental railroad reached Spokane, in eastern Washington, and finally linked the Northwest with the eastern United States. In 1883, Tacoma became the end of the line for the Northern Pacific Railroad tracks that originated in St. Paul, Minnesota. With the arrival of the railroads, Washington took a great leap forward in its development. No longer a remote wilderness, the region began to attract industry, and in 1889 Washington gained statehood.

One curious footnote to the state's early railroad history was the boom and bust of Port Townsend. This seaport town on the Olympic Peninsula was convinced that it would become the end of the line for the railroad and experienced a wave of real estate speculation in anticipation of the railroad's arrival. Victorian mansions were built and sturdy brick commercial buildings were constructed along the town's waterfront. The railroad never arrived, and Port Townsend never became the metropolis it had hoped it would become. Today, the town is one of the most perfectly preserved Victorian communities in the West.

INDUSTRIALIZATION & THE 20TH CENTURY From the very beginning of Euro-American settlement in the Northwest, the region based its growth on an extractive economy. The early fur traders completely wiped out Washington's sea otter population (which has since been reestablished, with otters from Alaska, off the Olympic Peninsula). Lumber and salmon, the two natural resources that Washington had in the greatest concentrations, were both exploited relentlessly, and the history of the timber and salmon-fishing industries ran parallel to one another for more than a century. At the close of the 20th century, both industries had arrived at similar situations—severely depleted wild resources and government intervention to preserve the remaining old-growth forests and wild salmon populations.

Resource extraction in the Northwest took off in 1848, when gold was discovered in California. Washington benefited immensely from the sudden demand for lumber, and even oysters were shipped from the Washington waters to the tables of San Francisco restaurants. In fact, so many oysters were shipped south from Willapa Bay that the entire native oyster population was wiped out, and seed oysters had to be imported from Japan to reestablish the oyster beds. Today, Willapa Bay is still one of the nation's largest producers of oysters.

It would, however, take a second gold rush, this time the 1897 gold rush in Alaska and the Klondike, to bring real prosperity to the state. With the vast majority of miners passing through Seattle on both their northward and southward journeys, the merchants of the city enjoyed a thriving business. Seattle merchants supplied hopeful northbound miners with the tools of the trade and also helped miners divest themselves of their hard-earned money when they returned from the gold fields. You can learn about this latter gold rush at Seattle's Klondike Gold Rush National Historic Park.

However, trees were still the foundation of the state's economy. Nurtured on steady rains, such trees as Douglas fir, Sitka spruce, western red cedar, and hemlock grew tall and straight, sometimes as tall as 300 feet. The first sawmill in the Northwest began operation near present-day Vancouver, Washington, in 1828. In the early years of logging in the region, sawmills and logging companies would level a forest and then move on to greener forests. By the turn of the 20th century the government had gained more control over public forests in an attempt to slow the destruction of the region's forestlands, and sawmill owners were buying up huge tracts of land. At the outbreak of World War I, more than 20% of the forest-land in the Northwest was owned by three companies—Weyerhaeuser, the Northern Pacific Railroad, and the Southern Pacific Railroad—and more than 50% of the workforce labored in the timber industry.

The timber industry has always been extremely susceptible to fluctuations in the economy and experienced a roller-coaster ride of boom and bust throughout the 20th century. Boom times in the 1970s brought on record-breaking production that came to a screeching halt in the 1980s and 1990s, first with a nationwide recession, and then with the listing of the northern spotted owl as a threatened species. In the 19th century, in the early years of the Northwest timber industry, there was a belief that the forests of the region were endless. However, by the latter half of the 20th century, big lumber companies had realized that the forests were dwindling. Tree farms had been planted, but the large old trees continued to be cut. By the 1980s, environmentalists, shocked by vast clear-cuts on public lands, began trying to save the last old-growth trees. Today, the battle between the timber industry and environmentalists continues.

Just as trees in the Northwest were huge and plentiful, so too were the salmon. These fish, which spend their adult lives in the open ocean before returning to fresh water to spawn, were the mainstay of the diet for Northwest Indians for thousands of years before the first whites arrived in the region. However, within 10 years of the opening of the first salmon cannery in the Northwest, the fish population was severely depleted. In 1877, the first fish hatchery was developed to replenish dwindling runs of salmon, and that same year Washington canceled the salmon-fishing season. Salmon canning reached a peak on the Columbia River in 1895 and on Puget Sound in 1913. Later in the 20th century, salmon runs would be further reduced by the construction of numerous dams on the Columbia and Snake rivers. Today, the salmon populations of the Northwest are so diminished that entire runs of salmon have been listed as threatened or endangered.

In 1916, William Boeing launched a small seaplane from the waters of Seattle's Lake Union and laid down the foundation for what would become the Seattle area's single largest employer: Boeing. The company became a major employer in Seattle when it began manufacturing B-17s and B-29s for the war effort and today continues to be one of the largest employers in the state. The city's fortunes have been so closely linked to the aircraft manufacturer that in the past any cutback in production at Boeing has had a devastating ripple effect on the local economy. However, with the global ascendancy in recent years of Bill Gates's software giant Microsoft (based just outside Seattle), and the even more recent growth of Seattle-based Amazon.com, the Seattle economy has begun to diversify.

Index